Applerouth Tutoring Services, LLC
P.O. Box 49348
Atlanta, GA 30359
E-mail: info@applerouth.com

Author: Jed Applerouth, PhD
Chief Editor and Layout Design: Richard Vigneault
Contributing Editors: Desirina Boskovich, Emma Templeton
Contributing Writers: Desirina Boskovich, Marshall Findlay, Linda Dreilinger
Interior Ad Design: Justine Rubin
Interior Illustrations: Azekeal McNees, Jeffrey Poole, Alexander Rubin, Brandon Sadler, Christopher Rodriguez

March 2015

Manufactured in the United States of America.

ISBN 978-0-9823330-7-5

Special Thanks

A supersized thanks to our project coordinator, lead editor, writer, and head designer, Richard Vigneault. Richard's dedication, creativity, and many talents made this book possible.

Thanks to our content creators:

Reading and English wizard, Desirina Boskovich, for providing the bulk of our Reading and English passages and practice problems, as well as providing editing support.

Linda Dreilinger for her rocking Reading and English content and her layout support.

Math maestro, Marshall Findlay, who expertly crafted hundreds of Math problems for the book!

Our Math team: Drew Robinson, Bronwyn Dowling and Bill Markowitz

Our Science team: Jenn Gaulding and Michiel Shortt

Our title wizard and pedagogical consultant: Jon Weininger

Thanks to our design and graphics team:

Our lead illustrator: Azekeal McNees

Our illustration team: Xandy Rubin, Jeff Poole, Brandon Montgomery and Chris Rodriguez

Our design team: Matt Michelson, Delminquoe Cunningham, Tom Wood, Jessica Chris and Justine Rubin

Thanks to our editing team:

Emma Templeton, Desirina Boskovich,
Marshall Findlay, John Cadenhead,
Marc Erickson, and Phil Silverman

Table of Contents

Rhetorical Skills

Math 188

The Basics

Geometry

Algebra

Arithmetic

Trigonometry

Math Outro

Reading 546

Introduction to the ACT

Letter from Jed

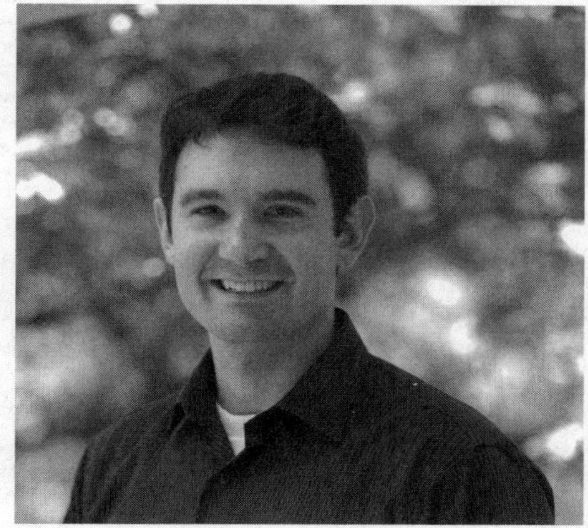

Every year over a million students partake in the time-honored ritual of taking the ACT. If you are reading this book, then your time has come to join the ranks and see just how high you can raise your score.

The ACT, like any other test, can be studied and mastered. Succeeding on the ACT does not require the waving of a magic wand. It requires a combination of effort and the proper tools. We've worked for years to create the ultimate ACT preparation tool. And now it's in your hands.

We kept several principles in mind when we designed this book:

1) Keep things simple and clear.
2) Break things into smaller steps and build on them.
3) Keep things visually interesting.
4) Use humor whenever possible: it's okay to laugh while learning.

This book is comprehensive. We've analyzed every aspect of the ACT to bring you the strategies included in this book. And most importantly: this book works. We've been using preliminary versions of this book with our students for several years and have watched them achieve impressive gains. On average, our privately tutored students increase their ACT scores by 3 to 4 points. Some of our students have achieved score increases of more than 10 points. We've helped high-scoring students hit the golden 36, and we've helped students bring section scores from the teens into the 30's. Our approach has worked for students at **every** score level.

We hope you enjoy the book; use it well, and hit the scores you need to get into the schools of your dreams. If you are looking for additional information or resources to help you along the way, please check us out online at www.applerouth.com.

Thanks and good luck!

Jed Applerouth

ACT FAQs

What is the ACT?

The ACT is one of the leading college admission assessments in America. The ACT was created in 1959 by the mastermind behind the Iowa Tests of Basic Skills, E.F. Lindquist. Lindquist designed the ACT to focus more on actual academic achievement than did the SAT, which was designed to assess innate aptitude. As a result, the two tests are markedly different.

How does the ACT differ from the SAT?

The ACT has a **science section**; the SAT does not. The ACT **does not test vocab**. The ACT goes into slightly **more advanced math** than does the SAT, but the ACT **math is not as "tricky."** The ACT has **four long sections** that always come in the same order: English, Math, Reading and Science. The SAT has 10 shorter sections, which don't always come in the same order. The **essay is optional** on the ACT and takes place at the end of the test. The essay is mandatory on the SAT and is always the first section of the test. Finally, the ACT is a **shorter** test, but it puts more **emphasis on speed**: get ready to break out your timer!

How does the ACT essay work and how does it impact your score?

Unlike the SAT, which bakes the essay into its Writing section, the ACT gives you the option to take the essay at the conclusion of the four standard sections. Every student who takes the ACT should **complete the essay at least one time**, as many colleges will require it for admissions. Most colleges will not view the essay with the same degree of importance as they view the English section, but they still want to see that you can write an essay in a timely fashion. Your ACT essay, combined with your responses on the admissions essays, will give colleges a more complete picture of your personal writing ability. Colleges will generally consider your English score and your essay score separately. Colleges **rarely** refer to the composite "Writing score" which is a combination of your English section subscore (1-36) and your essay score (2-12).

What do colleges really think about the ACT?

There is a misconception that the ACT is somehow a "softer" test than the SAT. This is nonsense. Admissions directors are just as happy taking a great ACT score as a great SAT score.

What do students think about the ACT?

Many of our students strongly prefer the ACT to the SAT. They love picking up easy points on the science section and chucking their vocab cards in the trash. They like the familiar language and presentation of the content, coupled with the lack of SAT trickiness. In short, they feel more at home on the ACT, and this translates to a higher score! More students than ever are choosing the ACT as the path to college, and the ACT is poised to overtake the SAT as the most popular college assessment in the country.

How important is my ACT score?

For most students, their ACT score is profoundly important to the college admissions process. After considering your GPA and academic schedule strength, most colleges look to your ACT score next. Other aspects of your application—recommendations, admissions essays and activities—are subordinate to your score on the ACT. Strong scores open the door to better colleges and universities, and create the chance to win valuable scholarships.

Why do colleges put so much weight on the ACT?

Colleges want to ensure that the students they pick for their incoming classes will be able to succeed academically. To make better picks, admissions officers first look to high school GPA: the single best predictor of success in college. But a 3.2 cumulative GPA at one school means something completely different from a 3.2 at another school, even one right down the street. Colleges need another efficient measure that is standardized, the same for all students; that's where the ACT fits in. It turns out students with stronger ACT scores tend to achieve stronger grades in college. A strong ACT score increases the confidence of admissions officers that you have what it takes to succeed in college.

What does the ACT test?

The ACT tests one thing: your ability to take the ACT. It is not an intelligence test, and it certainly does not test any innate aptitude. Given enough time, energy and dedication to the process of preparing for this test, a student can see a dramatic increase in his or her test score.

What do the scores actually mean?

The section scores have to do with statistics. You achieve a raw score based on the number of questions you get right. This raw score is placed on a curve, a statistical distribution, based on the number of students who achieved the same raw score. The curve ranges from the lowest score of 1 to the highest score of 36, with a median score of approximately 20.5. The curve is a bit skewed, as less than 1% of the population scores between 1 and 11. If you score an 11 on a section, you are effectively at the base of the curve. If you score a 12, you have out-scored roughly 3% of students. If you score a 20, you've out-scored 48% of students. A score of 26 puts you at the 84th percentile, 32 at the 98th percentile and 36 at the 100th percentile.

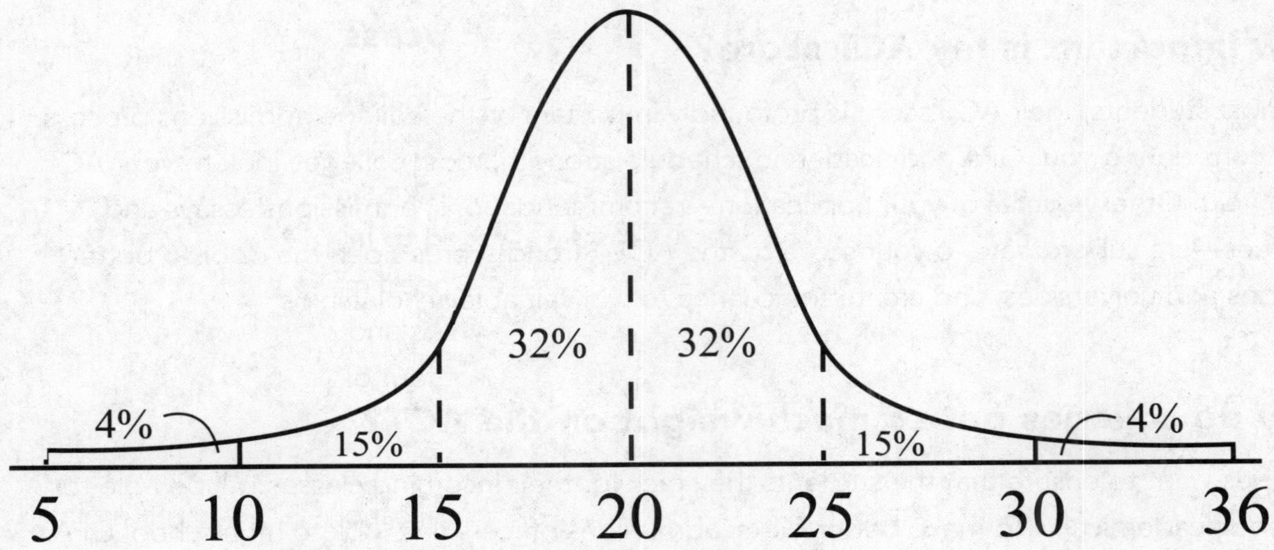

What score do I need to get into a particular college?

More competitive schools require more competitive scores. To find out the average score for incoming students for a particular school, visit the school's web site or contact its admissions office. The College Board's website, www.collegeboard.com, has a great tool which allows you to enter the name of a school, click on "Applying" on the left, go to the "SAT & ACT Scores" tab and see the breakdown of ACT scores for admitted freshmen. In order to submit a highly competitive application, you should aim for an ACT score in the top 25% for each school to which you are applying.

Additionally, you can create an account at **www.applerouth.com** to build your very own **personalized college tracker**. Click "Add College" and enter the names of colleges in which you are interested. Check back as you improve your score to see where you fall in each school's desired ACT score range.

How much can I improve my ACT score?

Most students have the potential to dramatically improve their ACT scores. On average our privately tutored students pick up **over 3 points**, and some achieve much greater gains, attaining increases of over 10 points. What differentiates the most successful students from those who are less successful is their level of dedication, motivation, and the amount of time they invest in the process. If you invest 100 hours toward achieving a higher score, your chance of picking up 7 points is much greater than if you invest 20 hours. The more time you invest, the more homework you complete, and the more practice tests you complete under timed conditions, the better you will tend to do on the ACT.

How much time do I need to spend on this process?

This completely depends on your introductory score and your ultimate goal. If you need to pick up a mere point, you may need only a handful of hours of preparation. If you are shooting for an increase of 4 or 5 points, your investment will need to be much more substantial. On average, if you are shooting **for a gain of 3 points or greater, you will need to invest 50-60 hours** in this process. Some students need much less preparation, and some need more. However, everyone must put in the time to drill problems and complete timed sections and tests. Each practice test takes roughly three hours, and you will want to complete at least four of them to get ready for the official test.

Considering how important your ACT score is to your college application, 50-60 hours is really a modest investment. Remember, for most college admissions offices, ACT score is second in importance only to your GPA. However, at some larger state schools, ACT and GPA receive almost equal weight. It takes roughly 4000 hours of class time to generate a high school GPA and only 60 hours to attain a competitive ACT score. Dedicating time to your ACT score is the single most efficient way to improve your odds of gaining admission to a competitive college.

How often should I take the ACT?

Generally three times should be adequate to achieve your optimal score, but there is no penalty for taking the ACT as many times as you need to achieve the score you seek. An increasing number of schools will "superscore" your tests and create a composite ACT score, combining the highest section scores from different administrations to create your "Super" score.

Because ACTs vary in difficulty from one administration to the next, it's in your best interest to take this test multiple times until you reach your target score. Just as there are easier and harder tests, students have good and bad days. Even when you are fully prepared, certain factors beyond your control can influence your score: were the passages easy or hard for you? How effectively did you guess? Did you make careless errors? There is some luck involved, and the more frequently you take the ACT, the more you minimize the "luck" component.

The more you take this test, the more comfortable and confident you become. You eventually move into a zone where you know what to expect and achieve a level of mastery of the testing process. As students move from their first to their second ACT, they tend to achieve their biggest score increases. Students generally see smaller gains through their third ACT.

Should I set goals for each test I take?

Absolutely! Always keep your ultimate goal in mind, and view each test as a stepping stone towards this goal. Set distinct section goals for each test you plan to take. Say, for example, your introductory score is a 26 English, 27 Math, 25 Reading and 24 Science, giving you a composite score of 25, and you want to pick up 3 points. Set short term goals for each test you plan to take, and write them down. "In October my goal is 27 E, 27 M, 26 R, 25 S. In December my goal is 28 E, 28 M, 27 R, 26 S. My goal for June is 29 E, 29 M, 28 R, 27 S." Setting and attaining short term goals has a positive impact on your sense of confidence and your level of motivation. Use these short term goals to help you attain your ultimate goal.

When should I take the ACT?

Fall and winter of junior year are ideal times to take the first ACT. The December or February ACT is a natural first test. For students who are enrolled in Algebra II as juniors, we generally recommend February as the first official ACT; this gives them a semester to hone their Algebra II skills. The majority of our students, having finished Algebra II as sophomores, are ready to jump in at the beginning of junior year.

Keep your schedule in mind! If you have a major time commitment in the fall, wait until the winter to start your prep.

It is quite common to prep intensely and take two ACTs back to back. Once you've knocked out a test or two, it's fine to take breaks and come back for one later in the year.
Many of our students see their greatest gains on the June ACT. This has to do with our students'

growing familiarity and comfort with the test as well as their freedom from academic and extracurricular obligations. Once school is out, students can really focus on the June ACT.

Ideally students will take the ACT two to three times their **junior year.** ACTs administered during the fall of their senior year are available as back-ups. The September, October, and December tests of senior year will all count for regular admissions. The October test is generally the last ACT that will count for Early Decision / Early Action.

How do I register for the ACT?

Log in to www.actstudent.org. Click "Sign up/Log in" and create an account. Follow the instructions. Make sure to sign up early to secure a spot at a preferred location. The good locations can fill up quickly.

What do I need to take to the ACT?

- A few No. 2 pencils (no mechanical pencils)
- Your registration information, printed from the computer
- Your driver's license or other form of photo ID
- A digital watch or one with a second hand
- Your graphing calculator and extra batteries
- Snacks and water
- Layers of clothing, in the event you are in a cold or hot room

When can I expect my scores to be available?

ACT Inc. has been consistently posting the scores online 17 calendar days after an official ACT. Your scores should be available to view at www.actstudent.org. If you took the ACT plus Writing, you will need to wait a few additional weeks for your essay and full score report.

How do I report my ACT scores to schools?

When you sign up for an ACT administration, you can select up to four schools to receive your ACT scores free of charge. You can send your scores to additional schools for $10 per school, per test. After the test, you can log in to www.actstudent.org, click on the link- Send Your Scores- and follow the directions.

Do I have to send all of my ACT scores?

ACT Inc. allows you to send particular scores and withhold others. If a college superscores the ACT, it is in your best interest to send all tests which contain a personal best on any section. Keep in mind, some colleges **require** that you send all of your scores. That will be made clear during the application process.

What is extended time? Do I need it? Can I get it?

Some students with diagnosed disabilities are allowed to take the ACT with accommodations such as extended time. Only a licensed psychologist can make the diagnosis of whether a student needs extended time to compensate for an attentional or learning disability. In most cases, before ACT Inc. will consider granting extended time or any other accommodation, your high school must acknowledge your disability and grant you the accommodation for it.

Do I need additional ACT prep materials to supplement this book?

Most of our students purchase the supplemental flash cards we have created to help reinforce the key math and grammar concepts tested on the ACT. You can find these online at www. applerouth.com/materials. Most of our students also buy *The Real ACT Prep Guide* in addition to this book. The 5 practice tests are perfect for mock tests, and the timed sections will allow you to work on your pacing and time-management skills.

The Structure of the ACT

The ACT consists of 4 timed sections: English, Math, Reading, and Science. A fifth section, the Essay section, is optional. The order of the sections on the ACT is the same every test:

1 English

The English section consists of **five passages** designed to test your grammatical and rhetorical skills. You have **45 minutes** to answer a total of **75 multiple choice questions.**

2 Math

The Math section consists of sixty, progressively harder questions testing your knowledge of Arithmetic, Algebra, Geometry, and Trigonometry. You have **60 minutes** to answer **60 multiple choice questions**.

3 Reading

The Reading section consists of **four passages** designed to test your reading comprehension skills. You will be given one passage each from the four areas of Prose/Fiction, Social Sciences, Humanities, and Natural Sciences. You have **35 minutes** to answer **40 multiple choice questions**.

4 Science

The Science section consists of seven passages detailing scientific studies. This section is designed to test your ability to quickly gather data from tables and graphs; it is NOT primarily a test of your science knowledge. You have **35 minutes** to answer a total of **40 multiple choice questions**.

If you sign up for the ACT plus Writing, you will be given 30 minutes at the end of the test to write an essay that demonstrates both critical thinking and writing ability.

Pacing and Practice

Time is your most precious resource on the ACT. It is the key to a high score. No matter what section poses a timing challenge for you, there are some universal good habits that will help you stay on pace.

Be sure to bring your own watch, in case the clock is placed behind you or if there is no clock in the testing room.

1 Keep your Eye on the Clock

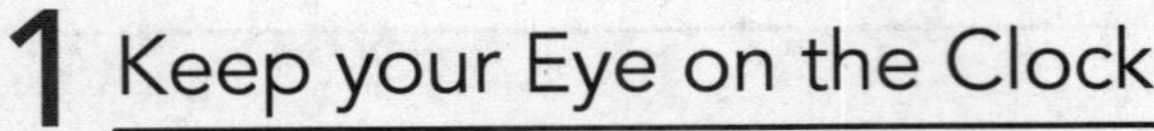

To skillfully manage your pacing, you must develop a habit of regularly **checking in with the clock**. You don't want to go 15 minutes without looking at the clock, then realize, "WOW, I am way behind schedule!"

A far more effective strategy is to **check in with the clock every few questions** to ensure that you are pacing well and smartly allocating your time. This will help you cut down on "OMG!!!!" moments.

2 Actively Read

When you skillfully read the questions and **underline key content** with your pencil, you are able to answer the questions more quickly. Passively reading followed by re-reading is a major time-sink.

3 Stay on Task

Every question type has a step-by-step strategy, which we will outline for you. **Get started on the first step right away**. Stick with the steps. Don't stray from the path.

As a general rule, if you are spending more than a minute on a single question (with the exception of some of the hardest math problems), you need to speed things up!

4 Don't Spin your Wheels

Once you have skillfully narrowed down your answer choices, it's time to **pick one and move on**. There's no time for wheel spinning or second guessing! In the immortal words of Jay-Z, we're "on to the next one."

Now that you know the four good timing habits, to push your timing even further, you need to shift from the "macro" to the "micro" level. It's time to focus on **timing intervals**, the number of seconds you spend on each question.

Learn your Intervals

If you divide the amount of time allotted for a complete section by the number of questions in a section, you arrive at the average time allowed per question.

Section	Minutes	Questions	Seconds per Question
English	45	75	**36**
Math	60	60	**60**
Reading	35	40	**52.5** (including reading time)
Science	35	40	**52.5** (including reading time)

It's important that you learn to manage these intervals and identify your areas of timing strength and weakness.

Keep in mind that questions on the Math section get **progressively harder.** In terms of difficulty and time requirements, questions 1 and 60 are worlds apart! A good strategy is to allocate 30 seconds per question on the first twenty math questions, 1 minute per question for the next 20 math questions and then $1\frac{1}{2}$ minutes per question for the last 20.

Timing Drills: The Art of Getting Faster

The best way to increase your speed on the ACT is to conduct **timing drills**. Once you've identified the section that is giving you the biggest timing challenge, it's time to drill.

1 Determine your natural pacing

Get a timer (most smartphones or watches will do fine) and find a quiet room. Start the timer and complete a full section, without breaks, to determine your natural speed.

Let's say you do a timed Reading section, and it takes you 40 minutes, rather than 35, to answer all the questions. So you are **five minutes over the limit**. Let's find out where you're spending that extra time.

2 Determine where the time is going

Try another Reading section, but this time work with the clock and record how long it takes you to do **each problem.** Then analyze the results.

Problem	Seconds	Correct
1	45	√
2	74	X
3	37	√
4	56	√
5	138	X

Where are you spending your time? Are you **spinning your wheels** and spending 2-3 minutes on certain problems? Are you getting these time-intensive problems right?

> It's common for students to miss the problems on which they spend the **most** time!

If you see this happen in your own drills, you can feel confident that guessing and moving on when you come to a challenging question **will not hurt your score!**

Improving your speed is not about thinking faster or being smarter, it's just about getting comfortable with a faster pace.

3 Set new timing targets

Establish new timing "ceilings" for each question: the time at which you will force yourself to guess and move on. If you were previously averaging 70 seconds/question, set a new limit of 60 seconds/question.

Conduct a timing drill at this accelerated pace. How did you do? Were you able to increase your pace without sacrificing accuracy? If you were too aggressive too quickly, bring it back a step. Try 65 seconds/questions, and keep on drilling!

The Importance of Practice Tests

No ACT prep program would be complete without **timed practice tests.** Timed tests allow you to practice your time management skills while also testing your knowledge of each subject. They also help you build mental endurance, self-regulation strategies, and self-motivation techniques.

In this book are **2 complete ACT practice tests**. These are fabulous tools to help you prepare for the actual ACT. Take one timed test early in your study schedule to help identify areas that need improvement, and use the second test to monitor your progress closer to the test.

In addition to the practice tests, you will find complete passages in the English, Reading, and Science chapters. If you take your first practice test and identify a particular section that poses a timing challenge, use these sections for timing drills. Remember, it takes practice to get used to a new pace. So bust out that stopwatch, smart phone, or sundial and get to it!

How To Use This Book

This book is divided into to the key sections of the ACT: English, Math, Reading, Science, and Essay. Each chapter contains strategies, illustrated explanations, and practice sections.

As you make your way through the book you will notice little call-outs in the margins. These are our **Tutor Tips**, which highlight material that you will want to remember and provide you with additional strategies and tricks.

It's a good idea to flip through a chapter that you've already read and review the Tutor Tips.

Active Learning (AKA mind your E's and S's)

Practice is the key to raising your ACT score. This book is not designed to be a boring lecture on the history of the ACT. That kind of passive learning is not very fun, is *certainly* not **fabulous**, and frankly does very little to raise your score. This book is instead designed to guide you, much as a private tutor would, in the kind of **smart practice** that will prepare you for test day.

Every section has dozens, if not hundreds, of example problems, each marked with an **"E" symbol**. Every example is followed by a solution "bubble" marked with an **"S" symbol**. Most of the ACT secrets and strategies taught in this book are found in these solution bubbles! Give every example your best shot, and read the solutions for tips to prepare you for the next example.

The Short Lists

The sections of this book that teach content rather than strategy will be followed by what we call a **Short List**. This list summarizes the most important information from the preceding section. It would be wise to review these Short Lists before you take your exam.

Mantras

At the end of every chapter of this study guide, you will find a series of **mantras**. Mantras are helpful, easy-to-remember statements that remind you of your strategies. Repeat these to yourself when you are stuck in traffic, on your way to study hall, or in the shower. **Know them; love them; use them**.

The Practice Problems

This book has over 700 different practice problems—not including examples and practice tests—that are modeled off of real ACT problems. After completing each set of practice problems, be sure to check your answers.

Ways To Study

There is no single, "right" way to prepare for the ACT. You should consider your own unique strengths and weaknesses when deciding on the study plan that will work best for you. Let's look at two approaches to ACT prep:

1 The Comprehensive Review

Each week complete a series of lessons and practice problems from each of the four sections: English, Math, Reading, and Science. In week 1, you may tackle Properties of Numbers in Math, Get to the Point in Science, and Punctuation in English. This balanced approach will keep you moving forward on all fronts as you prepare to take on all the sections of the ACT.

2 Isolate and Focus

Take a practice test. Determine your individual areas of weakness. Use the book to focus on the areas where you are weakest. If your Reading score is low, put your energy there. If you are grappling with Geometry, go there first. You can use your mock tests as feedback to guide your preparation.

Don't Cram: Spread out your ACT Review over Time

Memory researchers have found that packing all of your review into long sessions is not nearly as effective as spacing your study over multiple, shorter sessions. Each time you review a concept, you strengthen and "reinforce" it, etching the material deeper and deeper into your brain, so it will be there when you need it on test day!

Review the Next Day

As soon as you learn a new concept in this book, review it within **24 hours** to help **lock it into your memory**. Researchers have found that this practice dramatically increases your ability to recall what you have learned on test day!

ACT Study Schedules

To optimize your studying, you can create your own plan of attack and schedule your preparation over time.

If creating your own study schedule is daunting, don't worry! We've taken care of that. The following pages contain suggested practice based on your intended length of study. Feel free to mix and match to find the perfect study guide for you!

One Day Study Plan

If you pick up this book, look at a calendar, and realize that the ACT you have registered for is tomorrow, don't freak out. Relax. Deep breath. Don't try to study everything; focus on the following sections to get the most bang out of your limited study time.

One Week Study Plan

One week may be enough time to review if you already have a strong foundation. If this your first test, however, you will only be able to skim the major content areas.

One Month Study Plan

If you have carved out one month to study for your ACT, you should plan on studying 6 to 7 hours a week (not in one sitting). You'll remember more if you break your study time up into 2-hour or 3-hour sessions.

Week 1

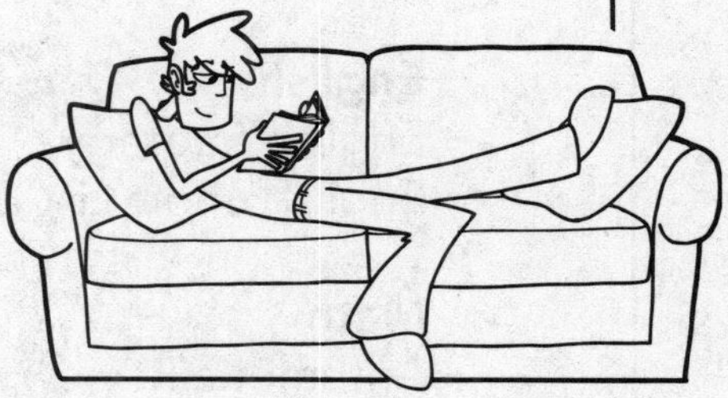

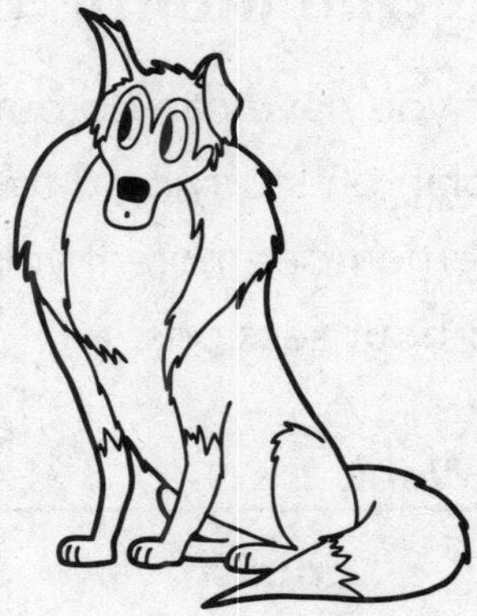

Week 4

Check your practice test during the week before the ACT. Review sections that need improvement!

Four weeks may not be enough time to get your best score on the ACT. If you have **6-8 weeks** to prepare, you can add more practice problems and get in your fifty to sixty hours of prep.

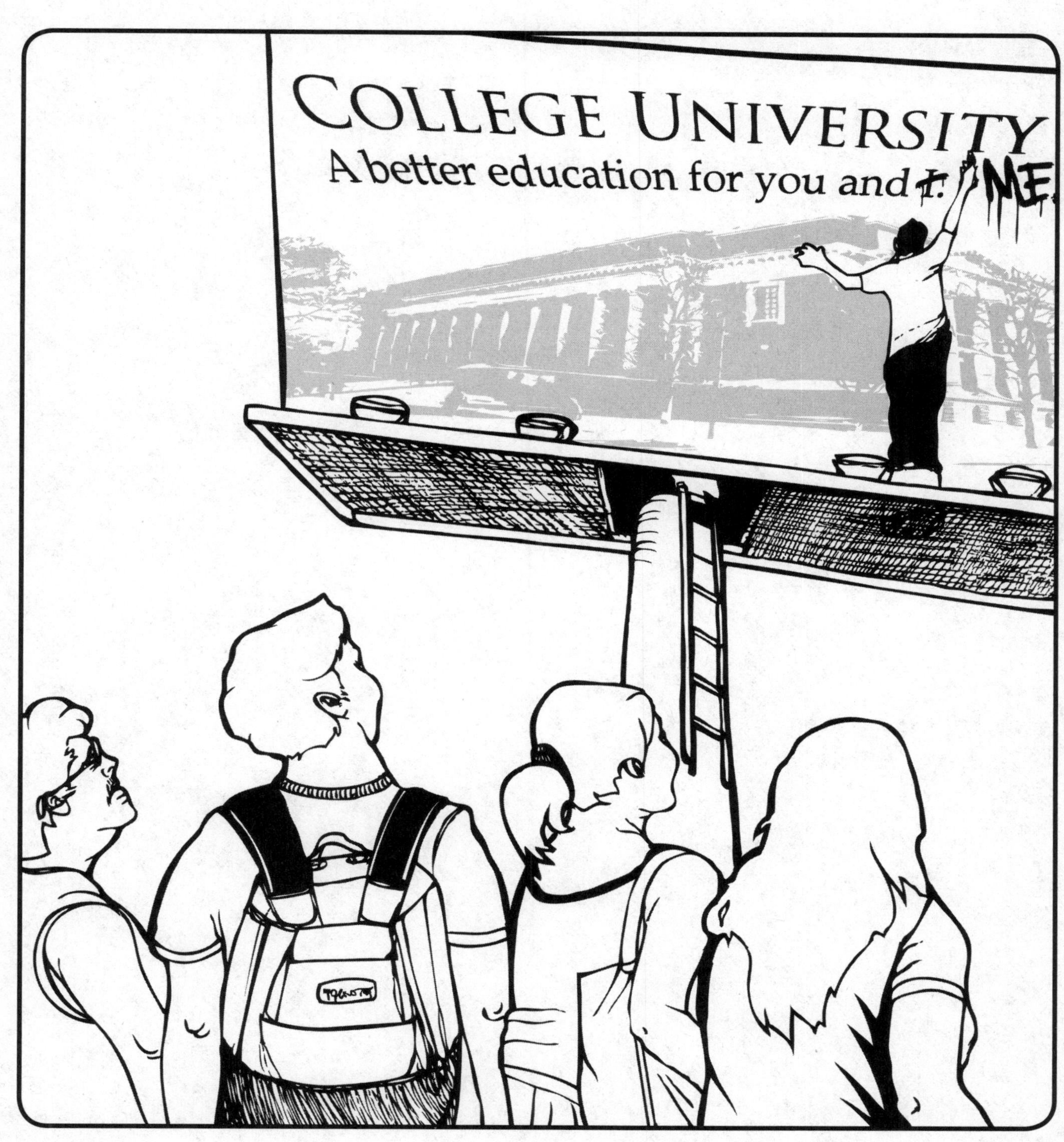

English

English

In the English section, you will play the role of editor-in-chief, correcting grammar errors and improving the flow of five less-than-perfect passages.

Structure

You will have **45 minutes** to answer **75 multiple choice questions**, divided evenly among **five passages**.

These passages tend to be easy reads: no AP Literature or Ye Olde English dictionary required. A passage could just as easily discuss the thrills and hazards of whitewater rafting as the life and times of Benjamin Franklin.

What's Tested

To nail the English section, you will need to learn a set of 23 discrete rules. These rules cover the two main types of questions on the ACT English section:

1 Grammar Questions

These questions test your mastery of the classic rules of Standard Written English, including punctuation rules, subject/verb agreement, and proper pronoun usage.

2 Rhetorical Skills Questions

These questions test your ability to comprehend the flow and function of a passage. Your job is to make sure the author of the passage stays on topic and makes logical transitions.

The percentages below indicate the percentage of ACT English questions that test each concept. Throughout this chapter, you will find five full English passages testing only the content you have learned up to that point.

Grammar/Mechanics Rules

Punctuation....................15%
Illogical Connectors....................8%
Redundancy....................7%
Improper Verb Tense....................6%
Fragments....................4%
Practice Passage One

Possession....................4%
Brevity....................3%
Pronouns....................3%
Run-ons....................3%
Subject/Verb Agreement....................3%
Practice Passage Two

Awkward....................3%
Prepositions....................2%
Vocabulary in Context....................2%
Misplaced Modifiers....................2%
Adjective/Adverb....................1%
Parallelism....................1%
Casual Language....................1%
Unclear Antecedents....................1%
Practice Passage Three

Rhetorical Skills

Adding/Deleting Information....................8%
Effective Wording....................8%
Practice Passage Four

Least/NOT....................6%
Order/Placement....................4%
Overall Function....................3%
Practice Passage Five

Grammar Strategy

About 40 of the 75 questions in the English section test your knowledge of grammar rules. Follow this step-by-step guide to conquer these questions.

Grammar/Mechanics Strategy

1. Read the sentence and **listen for a mistake**.
2. If there is an error you can identify, **give your own correction.** If your correction shows up in the answer choices, choose it! If you didn't spot an error or your correction didn't show up in the choices, move to Step 3.
3. Quickly **scan the answer choices** to determine what grammar concept is being tested.
4. **Test each answer choice** in the context of the passage. Eliminate wrong answers.
5. **Plug in** the remaining choices**. Choose** the one that sounds best.

Let's see this strategy in action!

E1 In 1980, physicist Luis Alvarez and his son, geologist Walter Alvarez announced a startling discovery.

A. NO CHANGE
B. son, geologist Walter Alvarez,
C. son geologist, Walter Alvarez,
D. son geologist Walter Alvarez,

1 **Listen** for a mistake

In 1980, physicist Luis Alvarez and his <u>son, geologist Walter Alvarez</u> announced a startling discovery.

A. NO CHANGE
B. son, geologist Walter Alvarez,
C. son geologist, Walter Alvarez,
D. son geologist Walter Alvarez,

Sounds a little funky...
I'm not sure why!

2 Give your **own correction**

In 1980, physicist Luis Alvarez and his <u>son, geologist Walter Alvarez</u> announced a startling discovery.

A. NO CHANGE
B. son, geologist Walter Alvarez,
C. son geologist, Walter Alvarez,
D. son geologist Walter Alvarez,

I don't know how to fix this one. On to the answers!

3 **Scan** the answer choices

A. NO CHANGE
B. son, geologist Walter Alvarez,
C. son geologist, Walter Alvarez,
D. son geologist Walter Alvarez,

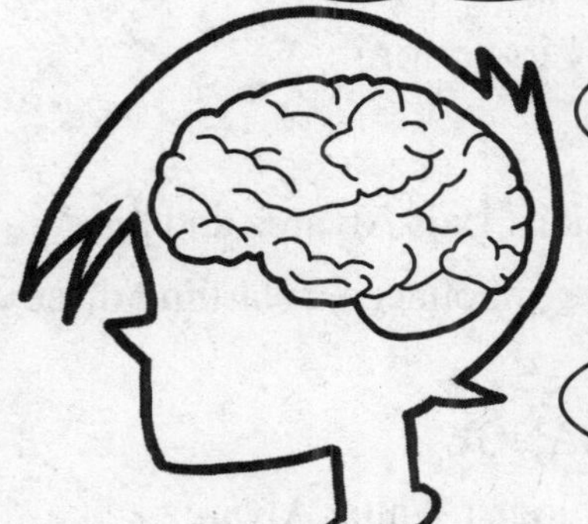

Hm... commas are moving around...

...must be a comma problem...

...exaggerate the pause!

Test each answer choice

A

In 1980, physicist Luis Alvarez and his **<u>son, geologist Walter Alvarez</u>** announced a startling discovery.

A. NO CHANGE
B. son, geologist Walter Alvarez,
C. son geologist, Walter Alvarez,
D. son geologist Walter Alvarez,

… Luis Alvarez and his son,
(PAUSE) geologist Walter Alvarez announced

Only Walter Alvarez announced??
No way. They both announced it! Nix A!

B

In 1980, physicist Luis Alvarez and his **<u>son, geologist Walter Alvarez,</u>** announced a startling discovery.

~~A. NO CHANGE~~
B. son, geologist Walter Alvarez,
C. son geologist, Walter Alvarez,
D. son geologist Walter Alvarez,

… Luis Alverez and his son, (PAUSE)
geologist Walter Alvarez , (PAUSE) announced

The pauses sound comfortable.
*And they **both** announced it!*
That solves the problem in A. Keep B!

C

In 1980, physicist Luis Alvarez and his **son geologist, Walter Alvarez,** announced a startling discovery.

~~A. NO CHANGE~~
√ B. son, geologist Walter Alvarez,
C. son geologist, Walter Alvarez,
D. son geologist Walter Alvarez,

… Luis Alvarez and his son geologist, (PAUSE) Walter Alvarez, (PAUSE) announced

X

"His son geologist..." This sounds jumbled. I need that pause to keep ideas separated. Eliminate C!

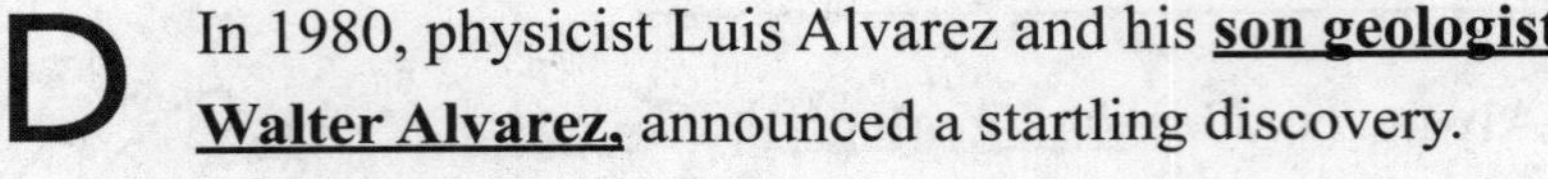

D

In 1980, physicist Luis Alvarez and his **son geologist Walter Alvarez,** announced a startling discovery.

~~A. NO CHANGE~~
√ B. son, geologist Walter Alvarez,
~~C. son geologist, Walter Alvarez,~~
D. son geologist Walter Alvarez,

… Luis Alverez and his son geologist Walter Alvarez, (PAUSE) announced

"Son geologist" again! Get that junk outta here! We chucked that turkey in C. Nixing D!

5 **Plug in** the remaining choices

In 1980, physicist Luis Alvarez and his **<u>son, geologist Walter Alvarez,</u>** announced a startling discovery.

~~A. NO CHANGE~~
√ B. son, geologist Walter Alvarez,
~~C. son geologist, Walter Alvarez,~~
~~D. son geologist Walter Alvarez,~~

Only one choice left!
B still sounds good!

***B** is our answer!*

15%
of English questions on the ACT

Punctuation

Don't punk out on punctuation! It is the most frequently tested concept on the English section. You need to get tight with your commas, semicolons, and colons.

Comma Errors

The most frequently tested grammar error on the ACT is the comma error. The ACT writers are comma junkies. They love commas like cats love catnip, squirrels love nuts, and Kanye West loves himself.

More often than not, your task will be to **cut out unnecessary commas** and let the sentence flow. Otherwise, your sentence, may look, something like, this ob-noxious, uncommonly comma-rich example, of a choppy, fragment-ed, sentence.

Don't be afraid of reading sentences under your breath when testing comma placement!

Your Secret Weapon

To nail ACT questions testing comma errors, you must learn to trust your **ear**.

You can **hear** commas. Commas live where you naturally break in your speech. If you can **extend a pause** in a sentence, and it still sounds right, you likely have a comma on your hands!

Let's practice. Read the following sentences aloud. Each time you come to a comma, greatly **exaggerate the pause**. When there's no comma, blaze ahead without stopping.

Most students, although, they mean well, overuse, the comma.

Now that's just plain silly. Did you notice your ear getting frustrated at having to constantly stop and start? Too many commas! Try this next one:

Most students although they mean well overuse the comma.

Notice how you started to feel rushed and a bit jumbled by the end of the sentence? There were too many ideas and not enough commas.
Now try the last one:

Most students, STOP although they mean well, STOP overuse the comma.

Perfect! This *feels* right.
Let's practice using our ear to feel out proper comma usage.

E1 Some horses, which I had never paid much attention to began stampeding through Aunt Bessie's kitchen.

S Some horses, which I had never paid much attention to, STOP began stampeding through Aunt Bessie's kitchen.

Those pauses feel more natural! We need that second pause.

Read aloud to let your inner grammarian come to life. Remember to exaggerate that pause to test the comma!

E2 Canada exports, hockey pucks for example, while Trinidad imports Pez™ dispensers.

S Canada exports hockey pucks, STOP for example, STOP while Trinidad imports Pez™ dispensers.

The initial sentence had a strange break:

Canada exports... (pause) ... hockey pucks for example...

That's one funky pause! We can lose that comma.

E3 The next afternoon, using her sandwich, as bait she was able to lure the mouse out of the cupboard, located directly next to the refrigerator.

S The next afternoon, using her sandwich as bait, STOP she was able to lure the mouse out of the cupboard, STOP located directly next to the refrigerator.

The original sentence gets a bit jumbled:

...using her sandwich, as bait she was able...

Wait... is ***she*** the bait? That comma forces a pause that really changes the meaning of the sentence! Lose it.

In school you learned to call these subordinate clauses **appositives.**

The lesson here is **trust your ear.**

Now let's dive deeper into why your ear objects to certain pauses and is drawn to others.

Commas Separate Related Ideas

Your ear likes breaks between different ideas. Commas provide those breaks. Without commas, different ideas run together and get jumbled. Let's look at a sentence we've seen before:

Most students, although they mean well, overuse the comma.

In this sentence, we have two ideas at play:

1. Most students overuse the comma.
2. They (the students) mean well.

Commas allow us to put these two related ideas in the same sentence. Notice that we are sticking the second idea **into** the first idea, and we are using commas to keep things separate.

The fact that commas keep things separate leads us to one of our most fundamental grammar rules on the ACT:

> If you **open** it with a comma, **close** it with a comma!

ACT writers often start a clause with a comma but then forget to close it. It's your job to remember to finish what you started.

Slipping Ideas Out of a Sentence

When you have commas at both the beginning and end of a supporting clause, you can **slip the clause out**, while keeping the primary idea intact.

Let's take a lesson from the Grammar Mechanics. They will demonstrate how commas grease up the edges of a secondary idea for easy removal.

Introducing: **The Grammar Mechanics!**

1 Add the grease

Most students , *although they mean well* , overuse the comma

2 Slip out the clause

Most students *although they mean well* overuse the comma

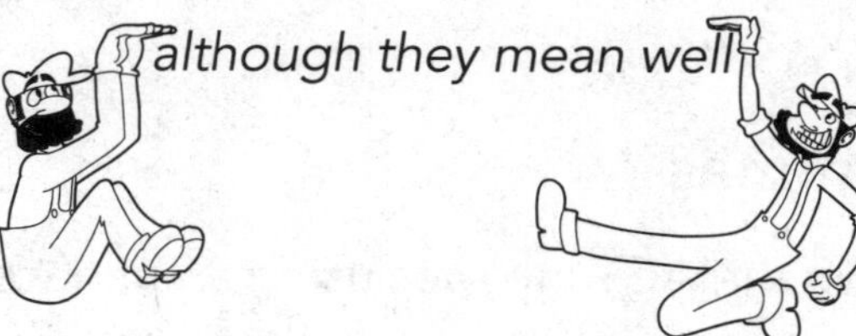
although they mean well

3 Push 'em together

Most students overuse the comma.

The second idea doesn't always have to be placed in the middle. It can also live at the beginning or end of the sentence.

Most students, **although they mean well**, may overuse the comma.

Although they mean well, most students may overuse the comma.

Most students may overuse the comma, **although they mean well**.

In each case, notice that the second idea can be slipped out without impacting the primary idea, thanks to our trusty comma.

E4 My new iPhone 6.0 my dearest friend and most trusty companion just took out a third mortgage on my house despite our previous agreement that it would always check with me before completing any major transactions.

S My new iPhone 6.0, STOP my dearest friend and most trusty companion, STOP just took out a third mortgage on my house, STOP despite our previous agreement that it would always check with me before completing any major transactions.

*It is clear that **my dearest friend and most trusty companion** is a second idea (in this case, an appositive) which needs commas to hold it on both ends. We also need to put on the brakes when **house** meets **despite**; a comma keeps those ideas from colliding.*

Unnecessary commas

A very common trap on the ACT involves using an unnecessary comma when there is no second idea.

E5 Michelangelo portrayed David, during the moments before his battle with Goliath.

S *Do we really need a comma here? Do we have two intersecting ideas? Actually, we only have one unified idea:*

Michelangelo portrayed...

David during the moments before his battle with Goliath.

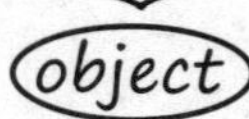

*Michelangelo is not simply portraying **David**. Michelangelo is specifically recreating **David during the moments before his battle with Goliath**. You **cannot** break up this clause with a comma.*

E6 The college professor deliberated, over whether to give the pop quiz to the class.

S *In this sentence is there a second idea? Again, the answer is no. We have only one idea: The professor is **deliberating over whether to give the quiz.** That's a single, unified idea. There is no break, so we have no need for a comma.*

However, for example, in my opinion

Whenever you are working with supporting clauses like **however**, **for example**, and **in my opinion**, you need to use opening and closing commas.

- Visiting my aunt is, ***however***, preferable to sitting at home watching the *Desperate Housewives of Minnesota* marathon.
- One theory, ***for example,*** is that chickens prefer long grain rice to white rice.
- Although he seemed content to wear his dad's loafers, ***in my opinion,*** he should have stuck to his trusted Chuck Taylors.

PULSE CHECK

Identify the error (if present) in each of the following sentences.

1. Flying horses, in her opinion were prettier and more intimidating than turtles that knew karate.

2. What had started as a dare during recess had quickly escalated into the town's first annual Hog Olympics.

3. Walking through the forest of deep regret Humberto the clown-impersonator from Gdańsk frolicked with gentle forest nymphs and drank at the pool of passion-flower forgiveness.

4. Erupting in protest my taste buds which until recently had never been exposed to 3-Mile Island Death Sauce decided to precipitously end our 16-year relationship.

5. Clancy's over-investment in dryer lint futures, forced him to fire his housekeeper when the stock market took a spill.

Answers

1. Flying horses, in her opinion, were prettier and more intimidating than turtles that knew karate.

2. Correct!

3. Walking through the forest of deep regret, Humberto, the clown-impersonator from Gdańsk, frolicked with gentle forest nymphs and drank at the pool of passion-flower forgiveness.

4. Erupting in protest, my taste buds, which until recently had never been exposed to 3-Mile Island Death Sauce, decided to precipitously end our 16-year relationship.

5. Clancy's over-investment in dryer lint futures forced him to fire his housekeeper when the stock market took a spill.

Comma Practice Problems

Select the answer choice that produces the best sentence.

1. Sally came home, from the salon, with freshly manicured nails and a tightly curled perm that brought back all the glory of the eighties.

A. NO CHANGE
B. home from the salon with freshly manicured nails, and a tightly curled perm
C. home from the salon with freshly manicured nails and a tightly curled perm
D. home from the salon, with freshly manicured nails and a tightly curled perm,

2. Some people, however are so allergic to peanuts, that just touching a trace amount of peanut butter can cause an extreme reaction, or even a condition called anaphylactic shock.

F. NO CHANGE
G. people, however, are so allergic to peanuts
H. people however, are so allergic to peanuts,
J. people, however, are so allergic to peanuts;

3. Who can possibly resist, the big, sad eyes of a puppy begging for a treat?

A. NO CHANGE
B. resist, the big sad eyes of a puppy,
C. resist the big, sad eyes of a puppy,
D. resist the big, sad eyes of a puppy

4. Of course I now, know, that, instead of lamb, a Grecian delicacy, I should have served mint jello to the kindergartners.

F. NO CHANGE
G. now, know that
H. now know that
J. now know, that

5. The best coffee is made from beans that are roasted in small batches, then ground, by hand just before brewing a cup for one.

A. NO CHANGE
B. ground by hand, just
C. ground, by hand, just
D. ground by hand. Just

6. When Sam claimed that he would walk a thousand miles just to end up at her door, Joon was flattered, but believed he must be exaggerating.

F. NO CHANGE
G. door Joon was flattered. But
H. door Joon was flattered, but,
J. door, Joon was flattered; but

7. Bacon and <u>eggs gained popularity, as a breakfast food, in the 1920s,</u> when public relations pioneer Edward Bernays set about promoting bacon sales, using physicians' recommendations for a 'hearty breakfast.'

A. NO CHANGE
B. eggs gained popularity as a breakfast food, in the 1920s
C. eggs, gained popularity as a breakfast food in the 1920s,
D. eggs gained popularity as a breakfast food in the 1920s,

8. For as long as he could remember, Johnny had wanted to become a private <u>detective, when he grew up investigating crimes</u> in the fashion of the heroes of film noir.

F. NO CHANGE
G. detective when he grew up, investigating crimes
H. detective when he grew up, investigating crimes,
J. detective; when he grew up investigating crime

The Semicolon

The semicolon separates two independent clauses. Authors use the "semi" instead of a period when they want to show the close connection between two adjoining ideas.

> Semicolons are great; I just cannot get enough of them!

Another way to think about a semicolon is to look at the component pieces. You have a period on top of a comma. The period says: "full stop." The comma says "connection." At its core, the semi-colon is an intimately connected full stop.

A clause is **independent** when it can stand on its own as a complete sentence.

Let's see the semicolon in action:

> It suddenly rained cats and dogs; a Dachsund broke my umbrella.

In this case, our semi is doing its job: separating, yet connecting, two independent clauses. Go Semi!

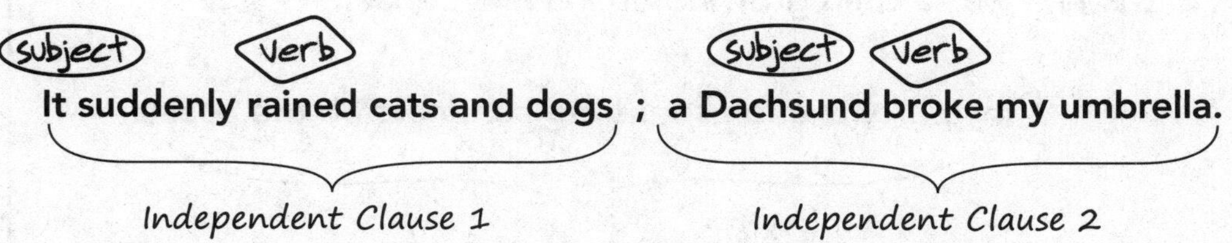

You can always replace a semicolon with a period, but NEVER with a comma!

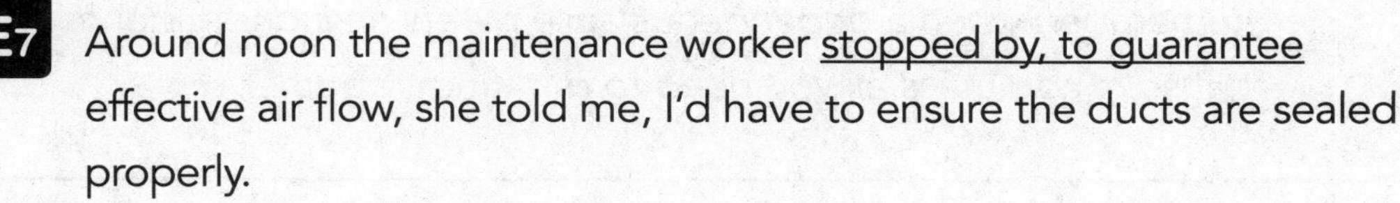

E7 Around noon the maintenance worker <u>stopped by, to guarantee</u> effective air flow, she told me, I'd have to ensure the ducts are sealed properly.

S Around noon the maintenance worker stopped by; to guarantee effective airflow, she told me, I'd have to ensure the ducts are sealed properly.

This one is a bit tricky. Because we have two independent ideas and no conjunction (FANBOYS), we need a semi-colon to make this structure work.

Semicolons and FANBOYS are two ways to avoid run-ons, but make sure you don't accidentally create a fragment!

For
And
Nor
But
Or
Yet
So

E8 When I was a child growing up in New Canaan; my parents and I spent our summers on the coast.

S When I was a child growing up in New Canaan**,** my parents and I spent our summers on the coast.

The ACT writers just stuck a semi between an independent and a dependent clause, but that's a comma's job! You cannot ignore that period at the top of the semi!

Dependent Clause

When I was a child growing up in New Canaan,

my parents and I spent our summers on the coast.

Independent Clause

Remember: when a dependent clause meets an independent clause, a comma is all you need to put them together.

Introducing: the Colon

The colon is an expert at making **introductions**. That is its primary function. When you want to introduce an independent clause, dependent clause, or list with style, use a colon!

Ladies and gentlemen, I present to you:

An Independent Clause

There was only one explanation: Zach Galifianakis lives between two ferns.

A Dependent Clause

Wilhelmina's travels were extensive: trips to every major capital in Europe and Asia.

A List

I have three hobbies: snorkeling, wombat training, and Snooki impersonating.

E9 Shamus, <u>it turns out is:</u> an angler fish that my uncle Angus had raised since his childhood in Melbourne.

S Shamus, <u>it turns out, is</u> an angler fish that my uncle Angus had raised since his childhood in Melbourne.

In this case the colon is actually getting between a verb and its object! The essential idea is that ***Shamus is an angler fish****. The clause* ***"it turns out"*** *is stuck in the middle, so we need commas on both ends. We have no use for a colon in this situation.*

E10 There is only one thing in the entire animal kingdom that is more fearsome than a <u>shark, that is</u> a shark riding a lion that is being carried by a giant eagle.

S There is only one thing in the entire animal kingdom that is more fearsome than a <u>shark:</u> a shark riding a lion that is being carried by a giant eagle.

*We **need** a colon here. The original sentence was a run-on, and the words **"there is only one thing"** set us up for an introduction.*

PULSE CHECK

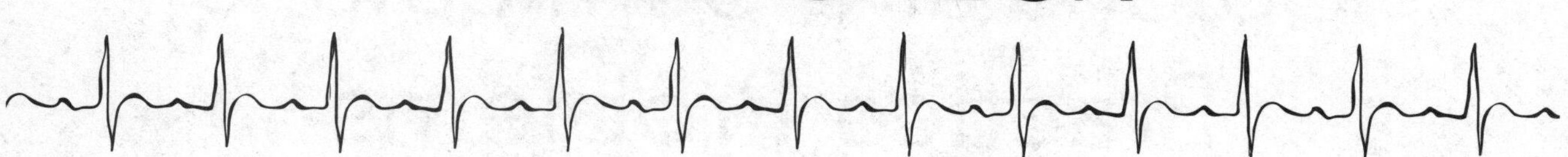

Identify the error (if present) in each of the following sentences.

1. There's just one thing you need to know about bears, don't get between them and honey.

2. It was a beautiful day: for a picnic.

3. Abraham Lincoln is revered by many for the role he played in ending slavery, most people are surprised to learn that he was also a seasoned vampire hunter.

4. The basket overflowed with various kinds of fruit: apples, oranges, bananas, and grapes.

5. The clown impersonator seemed to inspire my little sister Annie, she raided our mom's make-up cabinet, stacked our mattresses, and bounced all night long.

Answers

1. There's just one thing you need to know about bears**:** don't get between them and honey.

2. It was a beautiful day for a picnic.

3. Abraham Lincoln is revered by many for the role he played in ending slavery**;** most people are surprised to learn that he was also a seasoned vampire hunter.

4. Correct!

5. The clown impersonator seemed to inspire my little sister Annie**;** she raided our mom's make-up cabinet, stacked our mattresses, and bounced all night long.

Colons and Semicolons Practice Problems

Select the answer choice that produces the best sentence.

1. The message was waiting on the answering machine; red light blinking insistently.

A. NO CHANGE
B. machine; the red light blinked
C. machine, the red light blinked
D. machine. Red light blinking

2. There's only one way to protect your investment portfolio from market turmoil, it is diversify, diversify, diversify.

F. NO CHANGE
G. turmoil,
H. turmoil;
J. turmoil:

3. A great way to pass the time during winter is planning a garden. Paging through seed catalogs, sketching various layouts.

A. NO CHANGE
B. garden: paging
C. garden; paging
D. garden paging

4. If you're a bookworm? There's probably nothing you like more than curling up with a good book.

F. NO CHANGE
G. bookworm, there's
H. bookworm; there's
J. bookworm. There's

5. The first thing I bought for my new dog Joey was, a big red rubber ball that he loved to chase.

A. NO CHANGE
B. Joey was a
C. Joey was: a
D. Joey: was a

6. They decided to post an ad in the newspaper, offering a free hyena to any good home.

F. NO CHANGE
G. newspaper; offering
H. newspaper. Offering
J. newspaper, offers

7. As I began my journey into the tangled woods, my best friend had some words of advice, beware of poisoned apples, friendly woodsmen, and houses built from candy.

A. NO CHANGE
B. advice: beware
C. advice, to beware
D. advice. Which was beware

8. Annie's Bakery would specialize in custom cakes for all occasions, they offered cakes for everything from birthdays to weddings.

F. NO CHANGE
G. occasions; from
H. occasions, from
J. occasions. From

9. If you've ever had an unfortunate run-in with super glue: then you know the stuff is simply impossible to unstick.

A. NO CHANGE
B. super glue; then
C. super glue. Then
D. super glue, then

10. In the midwest, the weather in April is completely unpredictable from one hour to another; with daily temperatures ranging from balmy to below freezing.

F. NO CHANGE
G. another. With daily temperatures ranging
H. another, daily temperatures range
J. another, with daily temperatures ranging

8%
of English questions on the ACT

Illogical Connectors

When you're combining two independent clauses with a conjunction, make sure you're making a logical connection.

Not all FANBOYS are interchangeable. Pick the one that makes sense!

E1 Because Bjorn covered his principal's car with bacon, eggs, and hashbrowns, he was not suspended.

S **Even though** Bjorn covered his principal's car with bacon, eggs, and hashbrowns, he was not suspended.

Logically, covering the principal's car with various breakfast items will not prevent one's suspension. We need a connector that illustrates the **contrasting** *relationship between the two events.*

E2 For months the public had eagerly anticipated the reunion tour of Led Zeppelin, and popular opinion changed quickly when the band's lead singer was unable to hit the high notes in the first concert of the tour.

S

(+) *positive direction*

For months the public had eagerly anticipated the reunion…

but

popular opinion changed quickly…

(−) *negative direction*

There is change of direction in the logic of this sentence. People were initially excited. Then people were not so excited. The conjuction ***and*** *doesn't fit; we need* ***but*** *to show contrast.*

PULSE CHECK

Identify the error (if present) in each of the following sentences.

1. Most people thought that Auntie Gladys, with her thick cockney accent, was born in London's West End, and she had never even left Kansas!

2. My little brother realized too late that his plastic superhero did not have the power of flight; consequently, we watched the red and blue figure plummet into our mother's beet garden two floors below.

3. Katniss and Elmer's meticulously planned outdoor wedding had to be moved inside at the last minute, and it started to rain.

4. Abjit diligently trained for eight months, but he was able to finish all 26 miles of the Boston Marathon.

5. According to the review of Guillermo's new novel, the plot was muddled and confusing, and the book was redeemed by its insightful character development.

Answers

1. Most people thought that Auntie Gladys, with her thick cockney accent, was born in London's West End *even though* she had never even left Kansas!

2. Correct!

3. Elmer's meticulously planned outdoor wedding had to be moved inside at the last minute *because* it started to rain.

4. Abjit diligently trained for eight months, *so* he was able to finish all 26 miles of the Boston Marathon.

5. According to the review of Guillermo's new novel, the plot was muddled and confusing, *but* the book was redeemed by its insightful character development.

Illogical Connectors Practice Problems

Select the answer choice that produces the best sentence.

1. In the movie Titanic, actress Kate Winslet speaks with a convincing blue-blooded American accent <u>and</u> she was born in Reading, England.
   - **A.** NO CHANGE
   - **B.** so
   - **C.** as
   - **D.** although

2. Breakdancing originated in the South Bronx in the 1970s, <u>and</u> many people assume that it originated in the 1980s.
   - **F.** NO CHANGE
   - **G.** yet
   - **H.** because
   - **J.** for

3. Francois' entire fraternity was looking forward to spring break and their annual camping trip on the arctic tundra. <u>In contrast,</u> the trip was canceled at the last minute, due to inclement weather.
   - **A.** NO CHANGE
   - **B.** Otherwise,
   - **C.** Consequently,
   - **D.** However,

4. When a skunk infiltrated the St. Hildegard's wood pile, Samuel St. Hildegard dearly hoped someone else would be chosen to chase it away. <u>But</u> alas, it was he who drew the shortest straw.
   - **F.** NO CHANGE
   - **G.** So
   - **H.** And
   - **J.** Then

5. After stuffing himself with crab cakes at Yani's Floating Yacht Palace, Jackson had little desire to go swimming with his cousin as he'd promised. <u>Accordingly,</u> he stripped down to his swim trunks and dived in.
   - **A.** NO CHANGE
   - **B.** Nevertheless,
   - **C.** And so being,
   - **D.** Therefore,

6. There was one thing Wilhemina knew for sure about lobsters: stay away from the pincers. <u>Therefore,</u> when a large lobster attempted to share her beach towel, she vacated the area in a hurry.
   - **F.** NO CHANGE
   - **G.** Nonetheless,
   - **H.** Despite this,
   - **J.** And so on,

7. As a childhood star, Roberto was loved for his gap-toothed smile and first-grade witticisms. <u>However,</u> his successful adult career has benefited from his easy grin and juvenile sense of humor.
   - **A.** NO CHANGE
   - **B.** Conversely,
   - **C.** On the other hand,
   - **D.** Likewise,

8. Twin sisters Mela and Milla drew a line down the middle of their bedroom, dividing it perfectly in half. Indeed, they still found themselves mired in disputes over cleaning duties.

F. NO CHANGE
G. In fact,
H. Even so,
J. The implication being,

9. Afflicted by a witch's curse that turned everything he tried to eat into bland, overcooked oatmeal, Santiago dreaded meal times. Meanwhile, his sister Serafina suffered from a similar curse: everything she ate turned into plain yogurt.

A. NO CHANGE
B. Finally,
C. Thus,
D. However,

10. As it neared four o'clock and yawns began to fill the conference room, we all hoped the speaker would get the hint, and he just kept droning on 'til nearly five.

F. NO CHANGE
G. so
H. but
J. while

11. Windbreaker, the golden retriever, loved going on summer vacations with his people, especially since they were always rolling down the windows to air out the car; he loved sticking his nose in the breeze.

A. NO CHANGE
B. notwithstanding the fact that
C. and for example
D. in addition

12. As I reached the fifteenth floor of the Hearst building, the elevator lost power, trapping me inside with the reporter for more than twelve hours. Therefore, the interview was uneventful.

F. NO CHANGE
G. Instead,
H. Furthermore,
J. Otherwise,

13. The Association of Muffin Men meets twice monthly to compare notes on the latest baking techniques. As the case may be, the Federation of Fiddlestick Fashioners only convenes once every few years.

A. NO CHANGE
B. Moreover,
C. In contrast,
D. By the same token,

14. Joan debated which bottle of wine to bring for a hostess gift -- which of the two bottles would have been fine, but she wanted to keep one for a special occasion.

F. NO CHANGE
G. not each
H. neither
J. either

7%
of English questions on the ACT

Redundancy

Redundancy errors involve saying the same thing several times or unnecessarily defining an obvious idea. Cut out ~~and remove~~ the ~~repeated~~ repetition!

Repetition Redundancy

Often, the ACT writers will unnecessarily repeat or rephrase an idea:

I **studied** and **prepared** for the test

Initially this product was **first** offered

I do my **annual** taxes **every year**

It was a **surprisingly astonishing** outcome

Frequently, underprepared students **often** do poorly on exams

The queen offered **renewed** inspiration **all over again**

The **recent** increase in migration over the **last few years**

At **a future date** the winners will **later** receive confirmation

Over many months, as time went by, my puppy was able to

Once is enough!

When you are solving redundancy questions, cross off answer choices that repeat information already given in the sentence.

The results of the soil tests indicated a chemical problem that threatened to postpone and delay the construction of the building.

A. NO CHANGE
B. to a later date
C. by delaying
D. DELETE the underlined portion

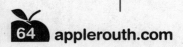

The results of the soil tests indicated a chemical problem that threatened to postpone the construction of the building.

Three of the four choices fail to fix the redundancy in the sentence. We don't need a synonym of ***postpone*** *such as* ***later***, ***delay*** *or* ***delaying***. *The correct answer is the shortest and simplest option:* **D**.

Note the power of DELETE!
In redundancy problems, when DELETE is a choice, it is almost always the correct answer!

The choreographers decided that their work needed to reflect and show the multiple, numerous abilities of the ensemble dance troupe.

F. NO CHANGE
G. reflect and show the multiple
H. mirror and reflect the numerous
J. reflect the numerous

S

The choreographers decided that their work needed to **reflect the numerous** abilities of the ensemble dance troupe.

This question gives us not one, but ***two*** *redundancies! We can eliminate answer choices that fail to fix either one of our redundancies. This actually makes it much easier for us. The only choice that trims the fat on both ends is choice* ***J.***

Definition Redundancy

Frequently the ACT will give you a word and then define it, creating a redundancy.

The **criminal**, who had **broken the law**, was tried in court.
I am looking for my **canine dog**.
I was trapped in a **congested traffic jam**.
She used an **artificial** preservative that was **not natural.**
He traversed the lush, **sloping hill.**

Looking at these examples we can easily see the redundancies. Isn't every dog a canine? Doesn't every hill have a slope? What conflict doesn't need to be resolved? **Simply trim the unnecessary definition**.

E3 Billy walked up onto the grass-covered lawn.

A. NO CHANGE
B. mowed, grass-covered lawn
C. grass-covered, lawn
D. lawn

S Billy walked up onto the **lawn**.

Lawns, by ***definition****, are grass-covered!* ***D is our answer.***

E4 My new job opportunity may or may not offer valuable training and connections to enhance my career development.

F. NO CHANGE
G. might offer
H. could provide important and
J. might indeed provide one with

E4 My new job opportunity **might offer** valuable training and connections to enhance my career development.

In this case, our trickiest answer choice is H. It solves for the ***may or may not*** *redundancy but opens up a* ***brand new redundancy*** *with* ***important*** *and* ***valuable****. Sneaky! And incorrect. Our correct answer is short and sweet:* ***G****.*

PULSE CHECK

Identify the error (if present) in each of the following sentences.

1. I stopped at the bank, a local financial institution, to withdraw some cash for my date.
2. For years, Melinda refused to go to bed; she'd yell and shout and raise her voice while beating her fists on the pillow.
3. The eccentric neighbor turned out to be writing a novel that was a book about a fisherman who catches a magical fish.
4. The dream involved a terrifying figure, who was very frightening, looking in my windows repeatedly.
5. By the time he was 7, Samuel was actually very tall for his age and not short.

Answers

1. I stopped at the *local bank* to withdraw some cash for my date.
2. For years, Melinda refused to go to bed; she'd *yell* while beating her fists on the pillow.
3. The eccentric neighbor turned out to be writing *a novel* about a fisherman who catches a magical fish.
4. The dream involved a *terrifying figure looking* in my windows repeatedly.
5. By the time he was 7, Samuel was actually very *tall* for his age.

Redundancy Practice Problems

Select the answer choice that produces the best sentence.

1. I was seated next to him at a friend's wedding; he seemed pleased that I'd read his book of which he was the author.

   A. NO CHANGE
   B. book by him.
   C. book that he'd written.
   D. book.

2. This little dog is such a good boy, I believe he should get a treat to have.

   F. NO CHANGE
   G. treat that he would enjoy.
   H. treat that would be enjoyable for him.
   J. treat.

3. He wrote a letter in which he explained that he would do everything he could to help.

   A. NO CHANGE
   B. carefully made clear and explained
   C. put into words and explained
   D. communicated a clarifying explanation

4. At first to begin with, Marshall believed that he'd discovered the hamburger of which he'd dreamed for so long.

   F. NO CHANGE
   G. At first, Marshall
   H. At first in the beginning, Marshall
   J. At first, Marshall initially

5. She told the class of students that she was impressed with all their good ideas.

   A. NO CHANGE
   B. class of pupils
   C. class
   D. class of learners

6. Houseplants aren't for everyone, but during the winter a collection of multiple vibrant green plants can create a more cheerful environment.

   F. NO CHANGE
   G. a collection of various assorted
   H. a collection of several different
   J. a collection of

7. Griselda decided she'd had enough; it was time to begin demanding better treatment.

   A. NO CHANGE
   B. demanding and requesting
   C. requiring and insisting upon
   D. insistently requesting her demand for

8. When the casting list was posted, Terry was devastated to discover the information that his name was missing.

   F. NO CHANGE
   G. that
   H. the fact that
   J. the piece of news that

Improper Verb Tense

6% of English questions on the ACT

Verbs shouldn't make you tense. Just remember these tense rules, and you'll start to relax.

Tense Switch

What happens in Vegas stays in Vegas. Likewise, what happened in the past should stay in the past. Don't get creative and mix up your verb tenses. Pick one and stick with it.

E1 The Mayan empire, after enduring for more than six hundred years, is believed to have collapsed when overpopulation, climate change, and drought limit its ability to sustain its population.

S The Mayan empire, after enduring for more than six hundred years, is believed to have collapsed when overpopulation, climate change, and drought **limited** its ability to sustain its population.

Past stays past. ***Mayan empire?*** *Past.* ***Have collapsed?*** *Past. We need to bring* **limit** *to the past.*

Check the tense of other verbs in the sentence!

ING is no good

ING is a common culprit on the ACT. Most of the time, a verb ending in ING indicates an improper verb tense.

E2 The parochial school has decided requiring all students to take a minimum of three semesters of science to better prepare them for college.

ING IS NO GOOD!
Don't be fooled; verbs ending in *-ing* often give away a sentence fragment.

S The parochial school has decided ***to*** *require* all students to take a minimum of three semesters of science to better prepare them for college.

*ING **I**s **N**o **G**ood. The infinitive does the job.*

Being is bad!

When you see the word **being**, you can be fairly sure that it signals an error. Being is not your friend. Being will pull your chair out from under you and not feel bad. Because it is bad!

In 1865 the poet Walt Whitman composed the elegy, *O Captain! My Captain* with his purpose being to honor and eulogize the slain president, Abraham Lincoln.

S In 1865 the poet Walt Whitman composed the elegy, *O Captain! My Captain*, **in order to** honor and eulogize the slain president, Abraham Lincoln.

*When you see **BEING**—it's busted!*

PULSE CHECK

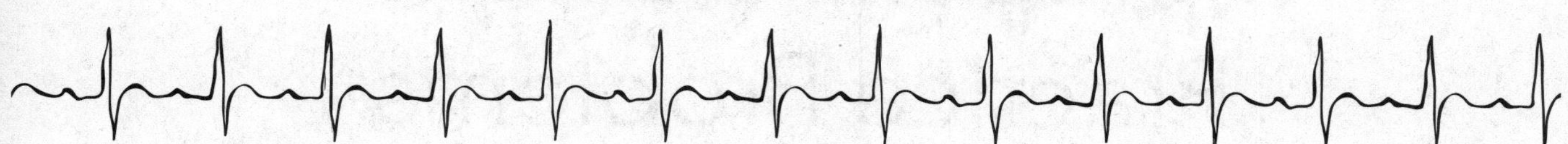

Identify the error (if present) in each of the following sentences.

1. By the time she was 15 years old, LeAnn Rimes is one of the most successful country-western singers in the United States.

2. The world's first astronauts were not only brave beyond compare but are also some of the world's nicest people.

3. Although Jane Austen wrote *Pride and Prejudice* more than a century ago, it is still one of the best-selling and most-loved novels today.

4. Having millions of dollars in its event fund, Perri's Pug Rescue Reservation was able to throw the biggest gala in the history of Coweta County.

5. After studying astrophysics for sixteen consecutive hours, Bart worried he'd forget how to spell his name on the actual exam because his brain turns to ooze.

Answers

1. By the time she was 15 years old, LeAnn Rimes *was* one of the most successful country-western singers in the United States.

2. The world's first astronauts were not only brave beyond compare but *were* also some of the world's nicest people.

3. Correct!

4. *Because it had millions of dollars in its event fund*, Perri's Pug Rescue Reservation was able to throw the biggest gala in the history of Coweta County.

5. After studying astrophysics for sixteen consecutive hours, Bart worried he'd forget how to spell his name on the actual exam because his brain *had turned to ooze*.

Improper Verb Tense Practice Problems

Select the answer choice that produces the best sentence.

1. Ever since he retired last March, Abner was practicing archery every day to qualify for the Olympics.

   A. NO CHANGE
   B. had been practicing
   C. has been practicing
   D. is practicing

2. Over the past four years, Umberto has worked to designing the perfect bathing suit that makes everyone look ten pounds thinner.

   F. NO CHANGE
   G. has been working to design
   H. having been working to design
   J. working to design

3. The Mayan Empire, after thriving for centuries, is believed to have finally ended when the last of its people are absorbed into the Toltec society long before the Spanish arrived in Latin America.

   A. NO CHANGE
   B. having been
   C. have been
   D. were

4. Back in the nineties, life-size reproductions of 1970s disco divas and 1980s glam rockers made entirely out of ice were often the focal point of Esmeralda's elaborate music-themed parties.

   F. NO CHANGE
   G. has often been
   H. were often being
   J. is often

5. When Bobbie Rae hog-tied her calf in less than 30 seconds last summer, she had been the first woman to win first prize at the Effingham County Annual Hog-tying Festival.

   A. NO CHANGE
   B. has been
   C. would be
   D. was

6. Despite local support, the *Neighborhood Gazette* newspaper lost 60 percent of its readership since it debuted, and by last year was losing as many as 350 readers a month.

   F. NO CHANGE
   G. has lost
   H. has been losing
   J. loses

7. After the incident with the mysterious growth of mushrooms, Carl promised to never leave wet towels on the bathroom floor again.

   A. NO CHANGE
   B. never leaving
   C. never having left
   D. not to have left

8. I couldn't wait to take my 27-pound rooster Rufus to the state fair, where I was sure he will win first prize.

F. NO CHANGE
G. he would win
H. he wins
J. he will be winning

9. Heidi raced to deliver her next pizza before it got cold, but after the run-in with the skateboarder, she knew she will be late.

A. NO CHANGE
B. knew she would
C. knows she will
D. knows she would

10. First, you give a mouse a cookie; the next thing you know, he will be rounding you up to work in the cookie mines.

F. NO CHANGE
G. would be
H. was
J. would have been

11. Now that the spring sun is warming the ground, the daffodils were emerging in full force.

A. NO CHANGE
B. were emerged
C. are emerging
D. emerged

12. Remembering the outbreak of sad clowns in the region, PJ made sure to pack his special remedy: No-Frown Around Town Clown Spray.

F. NO CHANGE
G. to be packing
H. he packs
J. to have packed

13. It was time to replace the old building's many broken windows, which had fallen prey to stray baseballs, rambunctious vandals, and falling sticks.

A. NO CHANGE
B. will fall
C. fall
D. having fallen

14. Soon after Hiram Jones filed a patent for his special clown spray, his competitors are hounding him for his many proprietary secrets.

F. NO CHANGE
G. were hounding
H. have been hounding
J. will be hounding

15. It was at the smoothie counter that Cherise finally broke down and tells me about what happened that day at the blueberry farm.

A. NO CHANGE
B. is telling
C. had told
D. told

4% of English questions on the ACT

Fragments

When it comes to spotting fragments, the main question you need to ask yourself is: Where is the verb?

Every sentence needs an **independent** subject and verb. The ACT writers will drop in one of these fragment-makers to ruin a perfectly good sentence:

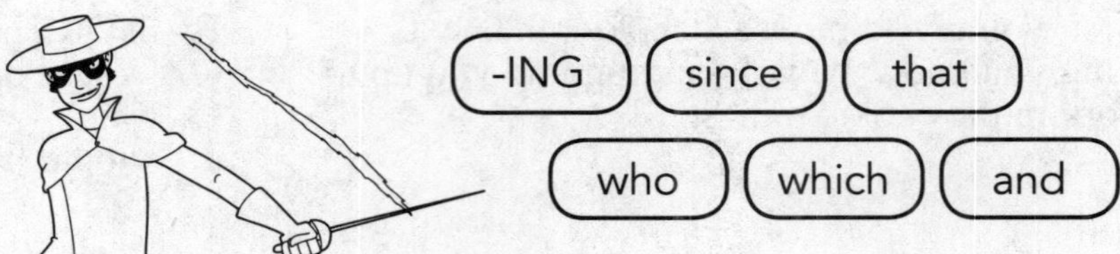

E1 All the demands on the president for resolving international crises, mediating foreign conflicts and addressing global economic issues, leading him to ignore domestic issues and minimized his effectiveness.

Looking closer, you must ask yourself: what's my subject and what's the corresponding verb?

To help find the subject, cross out prepositional phrases like "on the president" and "for resolving international crises." If it's in a prepositional phrase, it can't be the subject!

S All the demands ~~on the president for resolving international crises, mediating foreign conflicts and addressing global economic issues~~, leading him to ignore domestic issues and minimized his effectiveness.

If you cross off all the distracting clauses you are left with:

All the demands ... leading him to ignore domestic issues and minimized his effectiveness.

Now it is much easier to see that this is a fragment. There is no active verb. The problem is the ING. We need an active verb to pair with ***demands.*** *And since* ***minimized*** *is in the past, we need a past tense verb.* ***Led*** *would give us a complete sentence.*

All the demands... **led** him to ignore domestic issues and minimized his effectiveness.

ING

Many ACT fragments are caused by ING.

Since art classes in elementary schools are central to cultivating creativity, art education deserving continuing support.

Since art classes in elementary schools are central to cultivating creativity, art education **deserves** continuing support.

ING is no good! *All you need here is a present tense verb to make it a complete sentence.*

EVERYBODY NOW:
ING IS NO GOOD!
don't be fooled, verbs ending in -ing often give away a sentence fragment.

Being

Being is almost always wrong.

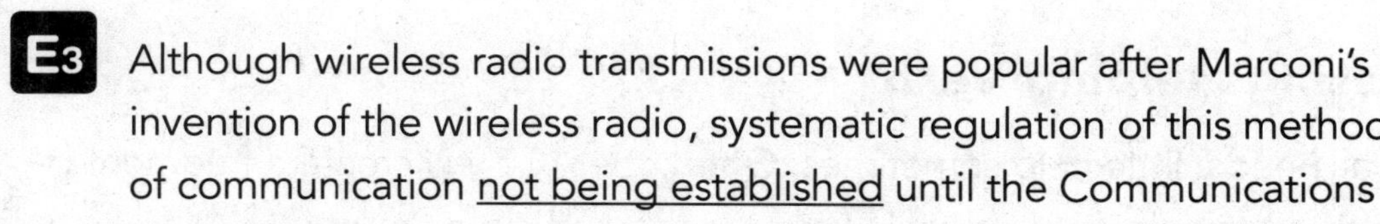

E3 Although wireless radio transmissions were popular after Marconi's invention of the wireless radio, systematic regulation of this method of communication not being established until the Communications Act of 1934.

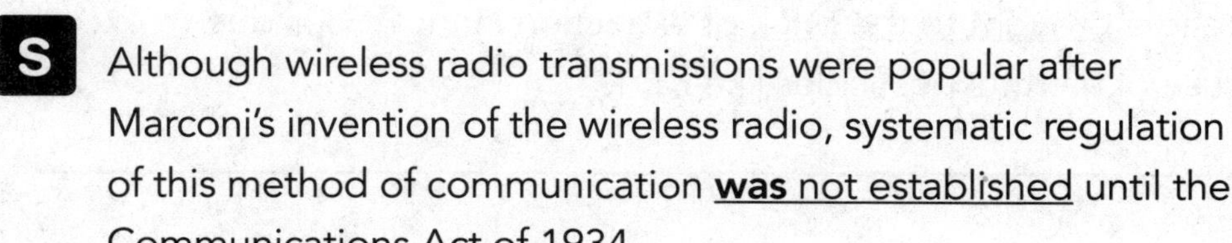

S Although wireless radio transmissions were popular after Marconi's invention of the wireless radio, systematic regulation of this method of communication **was** not established until the Communications Act of 1934.

Here, the past tense verb makes this a complete sentence.

When I see **being** I think BeINGO!

Being... GO! GET OUTTA HERE.

The Wicked Which

We're not in Kansas anymore, Toto! **Which** will quickly turn an independent clause into a dependent one, leaving you with a fragment.

John Cage has said that his music, which was powerfully influenced by the soundscape of modern life, but the works of earlier composers also provided a strong structural foundation for his compositions.

S John Cage has said that his music was powerfully influenced by the soundscape of modern life, but the works of earlier composers also provided a strong structural foundation for his compositions.

*Banish that **which**! It does not belong here.*

The bold words below are examples of helping verbs:

is bringing
was swimming
has frosted
will decimate
have pulverized

Missing Helping Verb

We all need a little help sometimes. Often, the ACT will create a fragment by omitting the helping verb while keeping the participle around.

One of the most majestic birds of prey in North America, the bald eagle brought to the brink of extinction in the 1960s due to excessive use of harmful pesticides like DDT.

One of the most majestic birds of prey in North America, the bald eagle **was** brought to the brink of extinction in the 1960s due to excessive use of harmful pesticides like DDT.

*The helping verb **was** makes this sentence complete.*

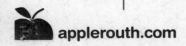

Who

These three little letters can equal one big problem.

E6 Charlie Chaplin, one of the most versatile performers of the 20th century, who acquired fame as an actor, writer, director, producer, composer, and choreographer.

S Charlie Chaplin, one of the most versatile performers of the 20th century, **acquired fame** as an actor, writer, director, producer, composer, and choreographer.

***Who** is unnecessary in this sentence; it just wrecks your perfectly good independent clause.*

The Sneaky Since

The word **since** should be a signal to you that a fragment is looming.

E7 Since some people are convinced that Tarot card reading, a method of divining the future, is a legitimate way to make sound decisions, but others consider it antiquated, superstitious, and ridiculous.

S Some people are convinced that Tarot card reading, a method of divining the future, is a legitimate way to make sound decisions, but others consider it antiquated, superstitious, and ridiculous.

*Once you oust that sneaky **since**, you have a complete sentence.*

That

When you see ***that*** in a sentence, double check to make sure you have a complete sentence with a subject and verb.

Keep your eyes open for these classic fragment-makers:

-ING
BEING
WHICH
WHO
SINCE
THAT
AND

E8 The teacher that planned a trip to the botanical gardens because she thought it would be educational for students to see all the different varieties of local flowering plants.

S The teacher **planned** a trip to the botanical gardens because she thought it would be educational for students to see all the different varieties of local flowering plants.

*T**hat** strikes again! Once you remove **that**, you have a complete sentence.*

And

Last but not least, **and** is not always your friend. Double check to make sure it isn't trying to trip you up.

E9 Because budgetary limitations will compel some municipalities to lay off police officers, and so the state legislature must determine whether to provide additional financial support to those cities.

S Because budgetary limitations will compel some municipalities to lay off police **officers,** the state legislature must determine whether to provide additional financial support to those cities.

Because is locked in. Because this happened, that happened. Not because this happened, and that happened. We need that second clause to be independent!

PULSE CHECK

Identify the error (if present) in each of the following sentences.

1. Revered by millions for his role in ending apartheid in South Africa, and Nelson Mandela was awarded the Nobel Peace Prize in 1993.

2. To protect the gray wolf from extinction in North America, regulations having been created by the Federal Government to keep the wolves' habitats intact.

3. Senior citizens on fixed incomes in the United States face a challenge, being that they must reconcile high prescription medication prices with their limited budgets.

4. Frequently out of town on business, Lebron James, treated like a king every time he returns home.

5. Anton von Leeuwenhoek, often referred to as the "Father of Microbiology," who created more than four hundred different types of microscopes.

Answers

1. Revered by millions for his role in ending apartheid in *South Africa, Nelson Mandela* was awarded the Nobel Peace Prize in 1993.

2. To protect the gray wolf from extinction in North America, regulations *were created* by the Federal Government to keep the wolves' habitats intact.

3. Senior citizens on fixed incomes in the United States face a challenge *because they must reconcile* high prescription medication prices with their limited budgets.

4. Frequently out of town on business, Lebron James *is treated* like a king every time he returns home.

5. Anton von Leeuwenhoek, often referred to as the "Father of Microbiology," *created* more than four hundred different types of microscopes.

Fragments Practice Problems

Select the answer choice that produces the best sentence.

1. Facing a great challenge, <u>Lacey, who is</u> the first woman to attempt to fly across the English Channel without any pilot training.

A. NO CHANGE
B. Lacey is
C. Lacey, being
D. Lacey as

2. My favorite book by Vladimir Nabokov, *The Real Life of Sebastian Knight*, <u>which was</u> his first book written in English.

F. NO CHANGE
G. that was
H. being
J. was

3. Because Eileen had poor vision and even worse balance, <u>and she was</u> always falling over.

A. NO CHANGE
B. and was
C. she was
D. that she was

4. <u>Since</u> many people believe dancing can be an intense and entertaining aerobic work out.

F. NO CHANGE
G. Being that
H. As
J. DELETE the underlined portion

5. David Lynch's cult classic, Twin Peaks, <u>that is so complicated with</u> multiple confusing plot twists and character changes, that most people have trouble following the storyline.

A. NO CHANGE
B. so complicated with
C. is so complicated, with
D. appearing to be so complicated due to

6. After having spent a week in the jungle, where a hot shower was out of the question, and the food was even worse.

F. NO CHANGE
G. I had spent
H. I, having spent
J. Spending

7. American Idol's Adam Lambert replacing the late great frontman Freddie Mercury and accompanying the classic rock band Queen on their reunion tour around the world.

A. NO CHANGE
B. will replace
C. will be replacing
D. having replaced

8. For graphic designers, who pay special attention to the many different types of fonts, and the particular typeface used in a design can be an area of great contention.

F. NO CHANGE
G. so the
H. since the
J. the

9. It being one thing to watch someone on television eat a heaping plate of worms and crickets, and another entirely to do it yourself.

A. NO CHANGE
B. Because it's
C. Being that it's
D. It is

10. After fantasizing many times about what I would say when I was interviewed by Terry Gross on Fresh Air, and now completely tongue-tied.

F. NO CHANGE
G. so that I was now
H. now being
J. I was now

ENGLISH PRACTICE 1

9 Minutes—15 Questions

DIRECTIONS: In the passage that follows, certain words and phrases are underlined and numbered. In the right-hand column, you will find alternatives for the underlined part. In most cases, you are to choose the one that best expresses the idea, makes the statement appropriate for standard written English, or is worded most consistently with the style and tone of the passage as a whole. If you think the original version is best, choose "NO CHANGE." In some cases you will find in the right-hand column a question about the underlined part. You are to choose the best answer to the question.

This passage tests only the grammar concepts that you have learned up to this point.

Practice these concepts in the context of a passage. Since the ACT will give you 45 minutes for 5 passages, this passage should take you about **9 minutes.**

PASSAGE I

Demystifying Dreams

Dreams are strange things. Often more vivid than real <u>life dreams frequently involve extreme emotions</u>[1], ranging from blissful happiness to intense anger or desperate fear. Sometimes the events of our dreams are obviously connected to experiences of the day before; sometimes they seem completely random. Sometimes dreams remain clear and vivid the next day, or even for years; sometimes they <u>were</u>[2] forgotten instantly on waking. If you've ever wondered what causes <u>dreaming you're</u>[3] not alone. This question has long plagued philosophers and scientists <u>for many years</u>[4]. There have been dozens of theories about what happens to the mind during sleep – and why it happens.

1. A. NO CHANGE
   B. life dreams, frequently, involve extreme emotions, ranging
   C. life, dreams, frequently, involve extreme emotions
   D. life, dreams frequently involve extreme emotions

2. F. NO CHANGE
   G. are
   H. had been
   J. might have been

3. A. NO CHANGE
   B. dreaming, you're
   C. dreaming your
   D. dreaming, your

4. F. NO CHANGE
   G. for some time.
   H. who tried to answer it.
   J. DELETE the underlined portion.

But finally, the question remains unresolved.
5

Many ancient cultures viewed dreams as messages from the divine. Dreams were seen as prophecies, giving humans insight into the future,
6
or guidance for living their lives. Others saw dreams as a way to speak with their ancestors, perhaps a way to receive wisdom from those who had passed on.

In the modern era, the famous psychologist Sigmund Freud was one of the first thinkers to give serious attention to dreams. According to Freud, dreams were manifestations of the dreamer's unconscious desires. Revealing
7
thoughts and fantasies which could be held without the dreamer's knowledge. Freud's theory was embraced by many, and the idea of dreams
8
as messages from the unconscious mind is now pervasive in popular culture.

More recently, psychologists have suggested and proposed that dreams help people mentally
9
rehearse responses to stressful situations, preparing them for appropriate reactions in real life. Others believe that dreaming serves no purpose, but is
10
simply the interesting byproduct of the mind's ability to think, plan, and remember – and also shut down and go to sleep.

Neurobiologists— scientists who study the

5. A. NO CHANGE
   B. To this day,
   C. And therefore,
   D. On the other hand,

6. F. NO CHANGE
   G. prophecies; giving humans
   H. prophecies, giving human's
   J. prophecies giving human's

7. A. NO CHANGE
   B. desires; revealing
   C. desires, revealing
   D. desires. And reveal

8. F. NO CHANGE
   G. when
   H. or
   J. but

9. A. NO CHANGE
   B. the proposition
   C. and said
   D. DELETE the underlined portion.

10. F. NO CHANGE
    G. purpose; but is
    H. purpose but, is
    J. purpose, but, is

function of the brain – approach dreaming from a different perspective. They want to understand what actually causes the brain to create these images and experiences. And as if [11] researchers have confirmed that dreams typically occur during REM sleep (so-called because of the rapid eye movements associated with higher brain activity), much else remains unknown. What area of the brain is the area that controls [12] dreaming? What neurological function might dreaming serve? On these questions, the jury is still out.

Wherever they will come [13] from, dreams are powerful things. Dreams have factored into spiritual experiences, scientific discoveries, and creative inspiration. For example, the biologist James Watson first envisioned the structure of DNA in a dream. The popular series *Twilight* was originally based on a dream. About [14] a girl and a vampire sitting in a field. Dreams have even inspired political leaders to go to war and change religions, altering the course of history. Unless, [15] one day, we'll better understand dreams... but hopefully, they will always hold some mystery.

11. A. NO CHANGE
B. when
C. since
D. while

12. F. NO CHANGE
G. is the location that controls
H. controls and regulates
J. controls

13. A. NO CHANGE
B. came
C. come
D. comes

14. F. NO CHANGE
G. Its author dreaming about
H. Its author dreamed about
J. Its author's dream about

15. A. NO CHANGE
B. Nevertheless,
C. Maybe,
D. Moreover,

END OF PRACTICE PASSAGE 1
ANSWERS AVAILABLE ON PAGE 185

Possession

4%
of grammar questions on the ACT

Who owns what? The key to possession is understanding the apostrophe and where it fits.

In most cases, you simply add an **'s** to a noun in order to show ownership. When you have a plural or singular noun ending in **s**, pop in the **'** after the **s.**

The dog's bone.

The dogs' bone.

It's and Its

It's is the contraction of **It** and **is**. *It's great to see you!*
Its shows possession. *The dog loves its bone.*

Who's and Whose

Who's is the contraction of **who** and **is**.
Whose shows possession.

Whose owl is that? Who's that owl?

E1 *The Times* decided to expand <u>its'</u> editorial coverage of world music and dance.

A. NO CHANGE
B. its
C. it's
D. whose

Its' is never a correct answer!

S ***The Times** is a singular entity. It has singular ownership of its coverage. Remember, **Its** shows ownership! **Our answer is B!***

E2 At Los Pollos Hermanos, each of our <u>ingredient's quality</u> is tested by a team of 75 *abuelas* to ensure the authentic taste of Gustavo's original recipe.

F. NO CHANGE
G. ingredients' quality
H. ingredients qualities
J. ingredient quality's

Breaking Bueno
Los Pollos Hermanos uses only the finest herbs and spices: an abundance of fresh ingredients in every bite.

S *The word **each** tells us that we have multiple ingredients. Knowing this, we can immediately eliminate F, which denotes a single ingredient.*

*Now the issue is ownership. **Quality** <u>belongs to</u> **ingredients**, so we **need** an apostrophe: we can eliminate H. Choice J is strange in that the quality is showing ownership, rather than the ingredients: eliminate J. **Our answer is G!***

E3 Linda Lohannesberg, <u>who's</u> stardom I previously celebrated, is now spending her waking hours training orangutans to make salads for White House guests.

A. NO CHANGE
B. whose
C. of who's
D. of whose

S *Remember **whose** shows possession and **who's** is a contraction! **Who is** stardom does not make sense. We need to stick with **whose**. And **of whose** just sounds wonky.*

*Linda L., **whose** stardom I previously celebrated… This works! **B is our answer!***

Possession Practice Problems

Select the answer choice that produces the best sentence.

1. <u>Babies</u> first attempts at speech often generate excited responses from adults, but that's no excuse for my aunt's behavior this weekend.

   A. NO CHANGE
   B. Baby's
   C. Babys
   D. Babies'

2. On <u>Kathmandus</u> busiest commercial avenue, I faceplanted in front of thousands and thousands of people.

   F. NO CHANGE
   G. Kathmandus'
   H. Kathmandu's
   J. Kathmandu its

3. Teachers provide the necessary materials, and students are rewarded for improving <u>his or her</u> study skills.

   A. NO CHANGE
   B. one's
   C. there
   D. their

4. <u>Rumor's</u> have abounded ever since.

   F. NO CHANGE
   G. Rumors
   J. Rumors'
   K. Rumor

5. Fondly, the conquistadors reminisced about <u>their many adventure's</u> back in the old days.

   A. NO CHANGE
   B. there many adventures'
   C. their many adventures
   D. they're many adventures

6. Everyone claims that the old house at the end of the block is haunted, but so far <u>its been reluctant to give up its</u> secrets.

   F. NO CHANGE
   G. it's been reluctant to give up it's
   H. its been reluctant to give up it's
   J. it's been reluctant to give up its

7. *Carrie*, one of <u>Stephen King's most famous novels</u>, is the story of a high school misfit with unusual abilities.

   A. NO CHANGE
   B. Stephen Kings most famous novels
   C. Stephen King's most famous novel's
   D. Stephen King's most famous novels'

Brevity

3%
of English questions on the ACT

Short, sweet, and to the point: that is the ACT's motto. If you come across a sentence that seems too long for its own good, it probably is. Just remember: less is more.

E1 When you see the flashing blue lights approaching in your rear view mirror, this is when you know it's time to change your radio station from Hard Rock to NPR.

S When you see the flashing blue lights approaching in your rear view mirror, **you know** it's time to change your radio station from Hard Rock to NPR.

This is when *is a dead giveaway that there are too many words in the sentence. The same goes for "this is what" and "this is where."*

Grammar cop says: cut to the chase! Be brief, be bright, be gone.

E2 Catnip Bassfender's reception needless to say was less enthusiastic than that of Guillermo Brzenk and his breakdancing woodpecker.

S Catnip Bassfender's **reception was** less enthusiastic than that of Guillermo Brzenk and his breakdancing woodpecker.

Needless to say *is a phrase you never need to say! It adds nothing. Often, your task is to simply cut out unnecessary fluff.*

PULSE CHECK

Identify the error (if present) in each of the following sentences.

1. On February 9, 1964, The Beatles appeared live on The Ed Sullivan Show being the inauguration of both the band and a new type of rock and roll in America.

2. In the early morning of May 20, 1927, Charles Lindbergh left Roosevelt Field in New York in his monoplane, *The Spirit of St. Louis*, with his purpose being to complete the first transatlantic flight.

3. All of Edward's lifelong dreams to become a ballet dancer with the American Ballet Company came to an end last Thursday; this is when he knocked over the other dancers during his final pirouette in Swan Lake.

4. Sharon found it nearly impossible to rent a car in Reykjavik, this being because she does not speak Icelandic.

Answers

1. On February 9, 1964, The Beatles appeared live on The Ed Sullivan Show, *thus inaugurating* both the band and a new type of rock and roll in America.

2. In the early morning of May 20, 1927, Charles Lindbergh left Roosevelt Field in New York in his monoplane, *The Spirit of St. Louis*, *to complete* the first transatlantic flight.

3. All of Edward's lifelong dreams to become a ballet dancer with the American Ballet Company came to an end last Thursday *when* he knocked over the other dancers during his final pirouette in Swan Lake.

4. Sharon found it nearly impossible to rent a car in Reykjavik *because* she does not speak Icelandic.

Brevity Practice Problems

1. Norton is morally opposed to killing anything, insects included, the reason being he has recently converted to Jainism.

   A. NO CHANGE
   B. the reason being that
   C. the reason being because
   D. because

2. Jamarian was reading Edgar Allan Poe's "The Tell-Tale Heart," this is when he heard a loud thump down the hall that nearly scared him to death.

   F. NO CHANGE
   G. at this moment in time
   H. which is the moment when
   J. when

3. Jazlyn installed new energy-efficient insulation in her attic the purpose of which is to lower her heating and cooling bills.

   A. NO CHANGE
   B. the reason is
   C. the purpose being
   D. DELETE the underlined portion.

4. The Harvard University Press recently released a new catalogue of books they have to be made available for sale.

   F. NO CHANGE
   G. that are currently available to be sold.
   H. that are available to be sold.
   J. for sale.

5. Whether you do or whether you don't like the film *Lady and the Tramp*, you have to admit that the spaghetti scene is a romantic classic of modern cinema.

   A. NO CHANGE
   B. Whether or not you
   C. Whether it so happens that you do or don't
   D. Whether it is you who does or doesn't

6. Dottie was waiting by the mail box all day due to the fact that she was expecting a birthday card from her grandniece.

   F. NO CHANGE
   G. the fact being that
   H. because
   J. due to

7. After a grueling day at the shark-jumping park, Addison suggested we stop for a meal of some sushi.

   A. NO CHANGE
   B. for a lunch composed of
   C. to take in some nourishment in the form of
   D. for

3%
of English questions on the ACT

Pronoun Error

A pronoun is a word that takes the place of a noun. Pronouns can either be subjects or objects in a sentence.

Remember, subjects **do** the acting and objects are **acted upon**. Below is a chart in case you get confused:

	Subject	Object
1st Person Singular	I	Me
2nd Person Singular	You	You
3rd Person Singular	He, She, It, Who	Him, Her, It, Whom
1st Person Plural	We	Us
2nd Person Plural	You	You
3rd Person Plural	They	Them

Who is for Humans!

My aunt, **who** loves chasing frisbees...

The dog **that** gave me socks for Christmas...

The Difficult Case of I vs. Me

The ACT knows that sometimes it is hard to decide when to use **I** and when to use **me** in a sentence. Just remember that **I** is the ***subject*** pronoun (does the action), and **me** is the ***object*** pronoun (the action is done to it).

*I do things. Things happen to **me**.*

When the ACT gives you a long list of names including I or me, take out all the other people's names and only leave the ***I/me***—it will make it easier for your ear to guide you!

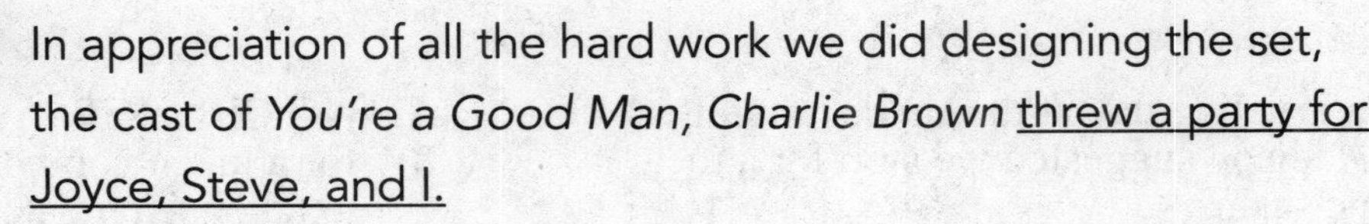

E1 In appreciation of all the hard work we did designing the set, the cast of *You're a Good Man, Charlie Brown* <u>threw a party for Joyce, Steve, and I.</u>

S In appreciation of all the hard work we did designing the set, the cast of *You're a Good Man, Charlie Brown* threw a party for ~~Joyce, Steve, and~~ **me**.

What is the pronoun ***I*** *doing in that sentence? Nothing! The cast is throwing the party. The pronoun needs to be an object:* ***me****. Cross out* ***Joyce*** *and* ***Steve,*** *and let your ear do all the work.*

Pronoun Antecedent Agreement

Be on the lookout for pronouns that do not agree with their antecedents. The antecedent is the word or words the pronoun replaces.

E2 Every member of the football team shaved their head when the team won the game against its biggest rival.

S Every member of the football team shaved **his** head when the team won the game against its biggest rival.

Did every member shave ***their*** *head? Do they share one head?* **Every** *is a singular word, so we can't use the plural pronoun* **their** *to replace it. We need the singular pronoun* **his** *or* ***her.***

This error frequently slips into our everyday conversation. Your ear might not catch these common mistakes.

E3 Because the U.S. Army anticipated only a brief engagement in Falluja, they only had enough supplies for 24 days of combat.

S Because the U.S. Army anticipated only a brief engagement in Falluja, it only had enough supplies for 24 days of combat.

The U.S. Army is a singular entity, a thing, an it. **It** *takes the place of a singular noun.*

E4 It is well known that Google™ <u>treats their employees well.</u>

S It is well known that Google™ <u>treats **its** employees well.</u>

*Again, like an army, a company is a single entity, therefore it treats **its** employees well.*

Sneaky Singular Words

Remember this list of <u>singular</u> words that seem plural:

Anybody, Anyone
Everybody, Everyone
Nobody, No one
Nothing, Everything
Amount, Number
Each, None
Either, Neither
Group, Family
Audience, Team, Club

PULSE CHECK

Identify the error (if present) in each of the following sentences.

1. Over the course of the 40-week academic calendar, roughly three dozen students will take its turn as Most Popular Kid of the Third Grade.

2. Marjorie gained unlikely celebrity for her "Bouncing On Air" initiative, in which she trained adults whom had never learned to properly pogo.

3. The students in Ms. Odewabe's underwater basket weaving class have discovered working together heightens its creativity.

4. According to our calculations, Millie and me have spent more than $427 on our collection of super bouncy balls.

5. Just between you and I, Albie's new girlfriend is a compulsive liar: I saw that self-righteous vegetarian stuffing her face at Fat Matt's Rib Shack on Tuesday.

Answers

1. Over the course of the 40-week academic calendar, roughly three dozen students will take *their* turn as Most Popular Kid of the Third Grade.

2. Marjorie gained unlikely celebrity for her "Bouncing On Air" initiative, in which she trained adults *who* had never learned to properly pogo.

3. The students in Ms. Odewabe's underwater basket weaving class have discovered working together heightens *their* creativity.

4. According to our calculations, *Millie and I* have spent more than $427 on our collection of super bouncy balls.

5. Just *between you and me*, Albie's new girlfriend is a compulsive liar: I saw that self-righteous vegetarian stuffing her face at Fat Matt's Rib Shack on Tuesday.

Pronoun Error Practice Problems

1. Due to continuous budget shortfalls, a new law requires state politicians to pay for his or her own transportation from now on, without the hope of reimbursement.

   A. NO CHANGE
   B. one's
   C. their
   D. oneself's

2. There was a good working relationship between my coach and I because each of us had respect for the other.

   F. NO CHANGE
   G. I and my coach
   H. my coach and myself
   J. my coach and me

3. Polls indicated that the public thought the political candidate that gave out red, white, and blue gum balls reading "Vote for Me" was too immature to be seriously considered for public office.

   A. NO CHANGE
   B. which
   C. who
   D. whom

4. My current employer is a company that specializes in manufacturing and distributing jack-in-the-box toys modeled after celebrities.

   F. NO CHANGE
   G. whose
   H. this
   J. whom

5. Our tour guide for the day was a friendly young woman whom, after showing us around the main academic buildings on campus, showed us some of her own favorite landmarks.

A. NO CHANGE
B. who
C. which
D. OMIT the underlined portion.

6. Glen was gleeful about the 10-foot waves cresting on the beach, creating the perfect conditions for he and his dog to go surfing.

F. NO CHANGE
G. his dog and himself
H. him and his dog
J. his dog and he

7. The bear's winter hideout— a warm, dry cave lined with a bed of leaves— keeps them safe during the snowy months of hibernation.

A. NO CHANGE
B. it
C. one
D. those

8. The three-story glass house was commissioned by the new city officials, those wanted to prove that government transparency would be taken seriously this term.

F. NO CHANGE
G. they
H. who
J. whom

3%
of English questions on the ACT

Run-Ons

A run-on is a series of independent clauses stuck together without the appropriate punctuation or conjunction.

The flying squirrel had not eaten in two days, it was famished.

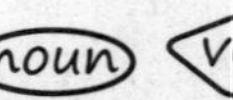

The flying squirrel had not eaten in two days, it was famished.

Independent Clause 1 — *Independent Clause 2*

S *There are **four ways** to fix a comma splice:*

1 Add a period

The flying squirrel had not eaten in two days. It was famished.

2 Add a semicolon

The flying squirrel had not eaten in two days; it was famished.

3 Add a conjunction

The flying squirrel had not eaten in two days, so it was famished.

4 Make one clause dependent

Because the flying squirrel had not eaten in two days, it was famished.

Dependent Clause — *Independent Clause*

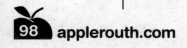

As you can see, we have two independent clauses separated by a comma. A comma cannot do that!

PULSE CHECK

Identify the error (if present) in each of the following sentences.

1. Maura, a veritable recluse, has a terrible sense of style, when she does leave the house, she only wears ancient flannel pajamas.

2. Singing the sweetest notes I've ever heard, the nightingale outside my window woke me up this morning, she does every day.

3. Santiago is originally from North Dakota but, because he is fluent in Spanish, everyone assumes he was born in South America.

4. Wilhelmina is always trying to save money and she paid five dollars for her latest haircut, which is hideous.

5. Studies show that eating a bowl of oatmeal adds a healthy dose of fiber to your diet, it can also significantly lower your cholesterol, decreasing your risk of heart disease.

Answers

1. Maura, a veritable recluse, has a terrible sense *of style; when* she does leave the house, she only wears ancient flannel pajamas.

2. Singing the sweetest notes I've ever heard, the nightingale outside my window woke me up this morning *as she does every day.*

3. Santiago is originally from *North Dakota, but* because he is fluent in Spanish, everyone assumes he was born in South America.

4. Wilhelmina is always trying to save *money. She* paid five dollars for her latest haircut, which is hideous.

5. Studies show that eating a bowl of oatmeal adds a healthy dose of fiber to your *diet, and it* can also significantly lower your cholesterol, decreasing your risk of heart disease.

Run-On Practice Problems

1. As a cake decorator, Trenton Trenilson has enriched the world of baked goods, he uses as his work's inspiration Monet's early oil paintings.

   A. NO CHANGE
   B. his work is inspired by
   C. using as his work's inspiration
   D. his inspiration for his work was

2. Last year, my mother became the first woman in our family to earn a master's degree, she is also the first family member to go on to study for a doctorate degree.

   F. NO CHANGE
   G. as well as
   H. she was also
   J. also, she is

3. It has taken my mother thirty years of creative and persistent effort to finally convince me the universe never intended me to be a platinum blond.

   A NO CHANGE
   B. effort to finally convince me,
   C. effort, she finally convinced me
   D. effort, finally convinces me

4. Conrad sent Jillian nineteen text messages about the stolen sledgehammer, and received no response, he decided she was probably not planning to respond.

   F. NO CHANGE
   G. after receiving no response, he decided
   H. after he received no response, deciding
   J. received no response, after this he

5. Farmer Chad was determined to make hay while the sun shone, unfortunately, his pitchfork broke just as he was getting started.

   A NO CHANGE
   B. was shining, unfortunately,
   C. shone, it was unfortunate that
   D. shone, but unfortunately,

6. A magical ruby hidden deep in the fern forest possesses fantastical powers, many covet it and would do anything to find it.

   F. NO CHANGE
   G. fantastical powers, making many
   H. fantastical powers, that's why
   J. such fantastical powers that many

7. Sagging under the weight of 129 Wild West adventure novels, the bookshelf clearly needed some extra support.

   A. NO CHANGE
   B. it was clear that the bookshelf needed
   C. the bookshelf clearly needing
   D. and the bookshelf clearly needed

8. My addiction to fresh croissants was getting expensive, I decided to invest in some French baking lessons.

   F. NO CHANGE
   G. expensive; I decided
   H. expensive, I then decided
   J. expensive, the decision was made

Subject-Verb Agreement

3%
of English questions on the ACT

If the subject of your sentence is plural, then the verb must also be plural. If the subject is singular, then the verb must be singular. If a verb is underlined, check that subject!

Subject after the verb

Sometimes the ACT writers try to catch you off-guard by slipping a subject in **after the verb.**

E1 Over the misty mountaintops glide the majestic grey eagle.

S Over the misty mountaintops **glides** the majestic grey eagle.

Your ear hears "mountaintops glide," which is a plural noun and a plural verb. But the ***eagle*** *is doing the gliding— that's our subject! Let's flip it to see this clearly:*

The majestic grey eagle **glides** over the misty mountaintops.

Perfect! It's hard to miss when you get the order right.

If the ACT gets cute with subject-verb order, flip it!

E2 Despite the prevalence in Latin American culture of macabre folktales about El Chupacabra, only recently have physical evidence in the form of cave paintings been discovered in the mountains of Peru.

S Despite the prevalence in Latin American culture of macabre folktales about El Chupacabra, only recently **has** physical evidence in the form of cave painting been discovered in the mountains of Peru.

*The key to answering these problems correctly is to identify the subject (**evidence**) and match it with the verb (**has**).*

PULSE CHECK

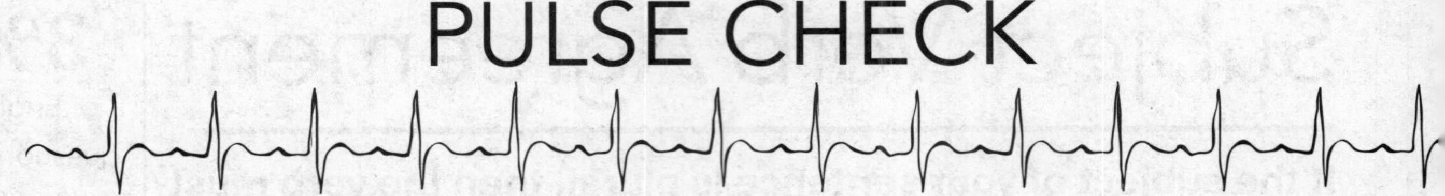

Identify the error (if present) in each of the following sentences.

1. Even though whipped cream and chocolate syrup are great, there are nothing like maraschino cherries on an ice cream sundae!

2. Soaring gracefully over the icy waters of Lake Champlain are a flock of geese, honking like a New York City cab driver in the middle of rush hour.

3. There is two things to remember when sky diving: breathe and don't look down.

4. Frolicking merrily through the peppermint forest of bubble gum trees is a band of cuddly, animated forest friends, all of whom make you desperately wish you had never agreed to babysit your three-year-old niece.

5. Of the myriad explanations Herbie gave to explain how his underwear ended up atop a street light at the end of the cul-de-sac, there were only one that remotely resembled the truth.

Answers

1. Even though whipped cream and chocolate syrup are great, *there is nothing* like maraschino cherries on an ice cream sundae!

2. Soaring gracefully over the icy waters of Lake Champlain *is a flock of geese*, honking like a New York City cab driver in the middle of rush hour.

3. *There are two things* to remember when sky diving: breathe and don't look down.

4. Correct! Band is singular and so is the verb.

5. Of the myriad explanations Herbie gave to explain how his underwear ended up atop a street light at the end of the cul-de-sac, *there was only one* that remotely resembled the truth.

Subject and Verb Separated

The second way that the ACT complicates subject/verb agreement is by separating the subject and the verb in a sentence. **Circle** the subject, **cross out** distractors between the subject and verb, and **check** subject/verb agreement.

E1 <u>The relationship between the clownfish and the sea anemone are</u> truly symbiotic, for both receive protection from predators.

Nouns between your subject and verb can trick you up. Cross them out!

S The relationship between the clownfish and the sea anemone <u>**is**</u> truly symbiotic, for both receive protection from predators.

...relationship ~~between the clownfish and the sea anemone~~

are truly symbiotic, for both receive protection from predators.

*The modifying clause separating the subject and the verb is just getting in the way. Get rid of it! Now we see that **relationship** is our singular subject which requires a singular verb: **is**.*

E2 The library near the town's fast food restaurants <u>have</u> more books than all of the others combined.

S The library near the town's fast food restaurants <u>**has**</u> more books than all of the others combined.

verb

The **library** ~~near the town's fast food restaurants~~ **have** more books than all of the others combined.

*The ACT writers are trying to trick you again! They put a plural word right next to our verb. **Restaurants** is NOT our subject! Library **have**? Nah, man, that ain't right. Library **has**!*

Either/Or...Neither/Nor

If you have two singular subjects joined by **either** or **neither**, you need a singular verb to match.

Neither Sara nor Tracy want to babysit on Saturday.

She

Neither Sara nor Tracy **wants** to babysit on Saturday.

***Sara** is singular and **Tracy** is too! So when they are joined by a **neither/nor**, we have to use a **singular** verb. A great strategy here is simply to replace the entire either/or or neither/nor phrase with the singular pronoun **he**, **she**, or **it**.*

The mistake students make is to say "neither of them want." You can't lump those girls together! It's neither **Tracy wants** nor **Sara wants.**

Tricky Words

Remember our list of words that seem plural but are actually **singular**! When one of these words is the subject, the verb should **always** be singular.

anybody, anyone	group, family, audience, team, club
amount, number	nobody, no one
each	none
everybody, everyone	nothing, everything

The word **both** is always plural! It always implies **two subjects!**

PULSE CHECK

Identify the error (if present) in each of the following sentences.

1. The welcoming reception hosted for us by the purple-skinned aliens reveal interesting details about their preferred forms of entertainment.

2. Whipped up by the wind, the waves rolling in against the rocky beach points to a storm off the coast.

3. If one of those of sad, frowning clowns are walking around this town, I don't know what I'll do.

4. One of the ancient city's favorite attractions, the Cloisters, is known for an austere, stony beauty.

5. It turned out that my delicious bowl of oat and honey clusters have actually been tainted with raisins all along.

Answers

1. The welcoming reception hosted for us by the purple-skinned aliens *reveals* interesting details about their preferred forms of entertainment.

2. Whipped up by the wind, the waves rolling in against the rocky beach *point* to a storm off the coast.

3. If one of those of sad, frowning clowns *is* walking around this town, I don't know what I'll do.

4. Correct!

5. It turned out that my delicious bowl of oat and honey clusters *has* actually been tainted with raisins all along.

Subject/Verb Agreement Practice Problems

1. Although the fishermen of the Red Reef prefers salmon to walleye, experts concur that walleye is the more delicious of the two fish.

   A. NO CHANGE
   B. prefer
   C. preferring
   D. has a greater preference for

2. Recent research by several historians question the long-held belief that Marie Antoinette was the 'great princess' quoted by Jean Jaques Rousseau as saying, "Let them eat cake."

   F. NO CHANGE
   G. questioning
   H. questions
   J. have questioned

3. Nico, the world's most prolific writer of haiku poems, are inspired by his bonsai trees and model train collection.

   A. NO CHANGE
   B. is
   C. being
   D. DELETE the underlined portion.

4. *The Da Vinci Code*, the fourth of Dan Brown's byzantine and suspenseful thrillers, soon were the nation's most popular novel.

   F. NO CHANGE
   G. were recognized as
   H. were seen as
   J. was

5. The President, who recently authorized the Mutant Registration acts, were indicted for racketeering charges early this morning.

   A. NO CHANGE
   B. was
   C. being
   D. having been

6. The old radio, as it plays a succession of the past decade's greatest hits, take us back to the past.

   F. NO CHANGE
   G. takes
   H. are taking
   J. have taken

7. Hot Sandal, the reigning band of the Tri-City's famous regional battle of the bands, is playing tonight at Lucy Lou's Watering Hole.

A. NO CHANGE
B. are playing
C. play
D. are going to be playing

8. My favorite restaurant in town, known for scrumptious burritos and chalupas, are going to be launching a brand new taco.

F. NO CHANGE
G. is going to launch
H. having launched
J. are launching

9. The dusty old books that line the many shelves of the quiet library is filled with useful information on hunting vampires.

A. NO CHANGE
B. are
C. being
D. that is

10. Roger, who loves to remind us that "good fences make good neighbors," mend the fences on a regular basis.

F. NO CHANGE
G. are mending
H. have mended
J. mends

ENGLISH PRACTICE 2

9 Minutes—15 Questions

DIRECTIONS: In the passage that follows, certain words and phrases are underlined and numbered. In the right-hand column, you will find alternatives for the underlined part. In most cases, you are to choose the one that best expresses the idea, makes the statement appropriate for standard written English, or is worded most consistently with the style and tone of the passage as a whole. If you think the original version is best, choose "NO CHANGE." In some cases you will find in the right-hand column a question about the underlined part. You are to choose the best answer to the question.

This passage tests the grammar concepts that you have learned up to this point.

Practice these concepts in the context of a passage. Since the ACT will give you 45 minutes for 5 passages, this passage should take you about **9 minutes.**

PASSAGE II

Steam Engine

A hundred years ago, New York City was powered by steam. Though those days are now gone by, there are, still, many [1] places where the city's steam-powered past can be seen. Pratt Institute, for example, is home to one of the last working steam engines, the oldest of their [2] kind in the Northeast. Up until recently, the plant produced energy to power the campus. Though it is no longer tied into the campus' main power grid, the steam engine remains operational.

Pratt Institute is located on a quiet, wooded street in Brooklyn's [3] Fort Greene neighborhood, the area is [4] home to stately brownstones, well-tended flowerbeds, and young moms with strollers.

1. A. NO CHANGE
B. by, there are still many
C. by there are, still, many
D. by, there are still, many

2. F. NO CHANGE
G. its
H. these
J. those

3. A. NO CHANGE
B. Brooklyns'
C. Brooklyns
D. Brooklyn

4. F. NO CHANGE
G. neighborhood. This area which is
H. neighborhood, this area is
J. neighborhood. The area is

But it's also a short walk to the location where you'll find the [5] Brooklyn Navy Yard and industrial neighborhoods. There, dirty streets and ramshackle apartments hark back to the Brooklyn of yesteryear. So perhaps it's a fitting setting for an old-fashioned steam engine.

5. A. NO CHANGE
   B. location of the
   C. site where you'll find
   D. OMIT the underlined portion.

The room which houses the steam plant is a tinkerer's paradise, [6] filled with exposed brass pipes and antique switchboards. The machinery is painted a bold, fire-engine red. Its keeper, Conrad Milster, has been tending the steam plant since 1958. Now in his seventies, Mr. Milster continues to maintain the engine, he's [7] also eager to share its story with students, neighbors, and anyone who wanders into the plant. This appreciation for the plant isn't limited to just humans, either: a dozen stray cats have also wandered in, making the steam plant one's [8] home.

6. F. NO CHANGE
   G. tinkerers paradise
   H. tinkerers' paradise
   J. paradise for tinkerer's

7. A. NO CHANGE
   B. engine,
   C. engine, he is
   D. engine. He's

8. F. NO CHANGE
   G. its
   H. their
   J. ones'

Every year, once annually, [9] Pratt Institute hosts a steam-powered New Year's Eve celebration where students, staff, and faculty ring in the New Year with a vast collection of whistles acquired by Mr. Milster over the years. Revelers tug ropes attached to levers, releasing steam from the engine into the whistles.

9. A. NO CHANGE
   B. Annually every year,
   C. Every year, annually,
   D. Every year,

In so doing, they create [10] a triumphant din—a cacophony of ear-piercing shrieks and resonant bellows. The resulting cloud of steam reduces visibility to just a couple of feet.

This plant, it [11] has been generating electricity since 1887, is still in impressive condition; the machinery is well-maintained and the aesthetic could accurately be described as [12] unchanged.

Over the decades, the caretakers of this landmark are [13] successful at protecting it from destruction, ensuring that students can enjoy a delightful symbol of their university's history [14].

Furthermore [15], because it is located on a piece of valuable real estate, the plant's future is uncertain. With some luck—and continued support from the community—the old steam engine will be around to help Pratt's community ring in many more new years.

10. **F.** NO CHANGE
G. he or she creates
H. it creates
J. one creates

11. **A.** NO CHANGE
B. the one that
C. the plant
D. which

12. **F.** NO CHANGE
G. is for the most part totally
H. basically could be called
J. is

13. **A.** NO CHANGE
B. have been
C. had been
D. has been

14. **F.** NO CHANGE
G. universities history
H. universitys history
J. universities' history

15. **A.** NO CHANGE
B. Indeed,
C. However,
D. Consequently,

END OF PRACTICE PASSAGE 2
ANSWERS AVAILABLE ON PAGE 185

Awkward Structure

3%
of English questions on the ACT

Sometimes a sentence just sounds wrong. If you're given a choice to get across the same idea in a simpler way, choose it. Get shorter and reorder!

E1 Believing my sister, it is that I know she will pick me up on time.

S **I believe that** my sister will pick me up on time.

Get shorter and reorder! Subject first, then verb, then object. That's how you do the ACT English Shuffle.

E2 Brutus advanced to the final round of the ice skating competition because two consecutive triple Axels were completed without flaws by him.

The phrases in awkward sentences are all jumbled. Find the order that makes the most sense.

S Brutus advanced to the final round of the ice skating competition because **he flawlessly completed two consecutive triple Axels.**

Remember: ***short is sweet.*** *Say what you have to say with as few words as possible without changing the meaning of the sentence.*

PULSE CHECK

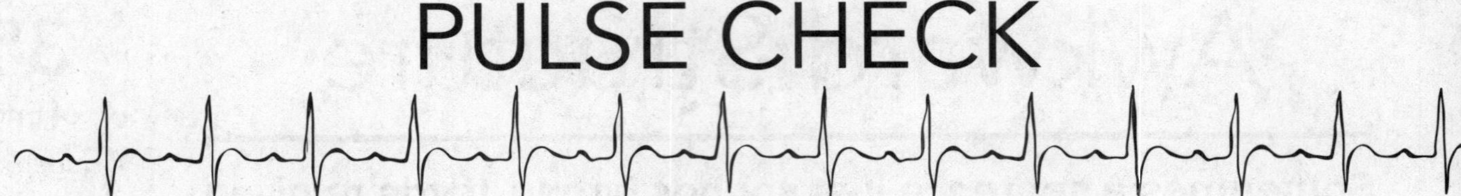

Identify the error (if present) in each of the following sentences.

1. The reason for which Chieu was elected is because of all the students who had run he had the cleverest and brightest posters.

2. Being that Santiago has won the Ballroom Dance Competition at the Elks Lounge for five years running, it is expected that he will be this year's favorite.

3. A strong, howling wind whipped the back porch door open; that is when Noori woke up.

4. Despite not wishing to be a published poet, Emily Dickinson remains one of America's favorite poets writing during the 19th century.

5. Due to there being a lack of interest in the Biology Department's presentation on the mating habits of the Congolese fruit fly, it has been canceled.

Answers

1. *Chieu was elected because, of all the students running,* he had the cleverest and brightest posters.

2. *Having won the Ballroom Dance competition at the Elks Lounge for the past five years, Santiago is expected to be* this year's favorite.

3. *Noori woke up when a strong, howling wind whipped open the back porch door.*

4. *Even though Emily Dickinson did not wish to be published,* she remains one of America's favorite 19th century poets.

5. The Biology Department's presentation on the mating habits of the Congolese fruit fly *has been canceled due to a lack of interest.*

Prepositions

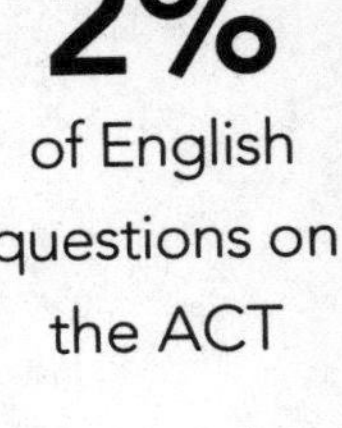

2%
of English questions on the ACT

Some problems involve linking particular words with an appropriate preposition.

VERB!
PREPOSITION!
Ugh, I need a new job.

For example, you **abide by** the law, rather than **to** or **with** the law. Your actions may be **consistent with** your beliefs, rather than consistent **to** them. In most cases, the context of the sentence determines the appropriate preposition.

E1 Akbar is circulating a petition among his neighbors in the hope <u>to achieve</u> his lifelong goal of permanently eradicating plastic lawn flamingos from his community.

Don't be afraid to read the sentence quietly to yourself.

S Akbar is circulating a petition among his neighbors in the hope **<u>of achieving</u>** his lifelong goal of permanently eradicating plastic lawn flamingos from his community.

In this instance, ***of*** *is the proper preposition and* ***-ing*** *is the proper verb form.*

Preposition pairs

In English there are certain prepositions that pair with verbs. You've heard these pairs all your life. Now it's time to pick them out on the ACT.

Zoltan's sunny disposition is inconsistent to the neo-gothic clothing he wears to the mall.

Zoltan's sunny disposition is inconsistent with the neo-gothic clothing he wears to the mall.

*The word **inconsistent** is always paired with the preposition **with**—no exceptions. Following are other common verb/preposition pairs.*

Trust your instincts if you get stuck on this type of question. Chances are you have heard these combinations many times in your life.

Common Prepositional Phrases

verb	preposition
abide	by
accuse	of
agree	to/with/on/upon
apologize	for
apply	to/for
approve	of
argue	with/about/over
arrive	at
believe	in
blame	for
care	about/for

verb	preposition
charge	for/with
compare	with/to
complain	about/of/to
consist	of
contribute	to
count	upon/on
cover	with
decide	upon/on
depend	upon/on
differ	about/from over/with
discriminate	against

verb	preposition
distinguish	from/between
dream	of/about
escape	from
excel	in
excuse	for
forget	about
forgive	for
hide	from
hope	for
insist	upon/on
object	to
participate	in
prevent	from
prohibit	from
protect	against/from

verb	preposition
provide	for/with
recover	from
rely	upon/on
rescue	from
respond	to
stare	at
stop	from
subscribe	to
substitute	for
succeed	in
thank	for
vote	for/on/against
wait	for/on
worry	about

PULSE CHECK

Identify the error (if present) in each of the following sentences.

1. My neighbor Ben Dover will never forgive his parents about their terrible choice in naming him.

2. Southern by birth, Dixie has suffered with terrible teasing about her accent by her fellow classmates in New York.

3. After further investigation, it appears that Samson falsely accused Delilah with chopping off his luscious locks.

4. Three weeks after his parents suspended his allowance, and in desperate need of funds, Rigoberto finally realized he needed a summer job and applied with Ed's World of Twinkies.

5. Despite their families' objections to their union, Jim and Pamela succeeded with getting married in a private ceremony last month.

Answers

1. My neighbor Ben Dover will never forgive his parents *for* their terrible choice in naming him.

2. Southern by birth, Dixie has *suffered from* terrible teasing about her accent by her fellow classmates in New York.

3. After further investigation, it appears that Samson falsely *accused Delilah of* chopping off his luscious locks.

4. Three weeks after his parents suspended his allowance, and in desperate need of funds, Rigoberto finally realized he needed a summer job and *applied to* Ed's World of Twinkies.

5. Despite their families' objections to their union, Jim and Pamela *succeeded in* getting married in a private ceremony last month.

Prepositions Practice Problems

1. My younger brother's opinions on everything differ so greatly with mine that it's hard to believe we're even related.

   A. NO CHANGE
   B. to
   C. from
   D. against

2. Tired of his neighbor's cats invading his property and falling asleep inside his garage, Orlando finally succeeded in keeping them away by gluing a strongly-worded note to an unlucky orange tabby.

   F. NO CHANGE
   G. succeeded with
   H. found success of
   J. was successful about

3. The term "silk-screening" comes from a nineteenth-century technique to which specific parts of a screen of porous fiber, silk, or polyester are blocked off with non-permeable material to create a stencil to be inked into cloth or paper.

   A. NO CHANGE
   B. in which
   C. on which
   D. which regards

4. After a heated argument between the vegetarians and the omnivores at the table, we agreed everyone should have the right for ordering what they choose.

   F. NO CHANGE
   G. right of ordering
   H. right to order
   J. right ordering

5. My worst fears were proved as correct, when we returned from our vacation to find the fridge unplugged and the house filled with the stench of rotten food.

   A. NO CHANGE
   B. were proved in being
   C were proving as
   D. proved to be

6. Hester hid her favorite book of household wizardry spells in the freezer, where she would have easy access of it whenever she ran into any complications in the kitchen.

   F. NO CHANGE
   G. access by
   H. accessibility with
   J. access to

2%
of English
questions on
the ACT

Vocabulary in Context

Vocabulary in Context problems are straightforward. Your task is to plug the answer choices back into the context of the sentence, one at a time, and let your ear find the answer.

Finding the Best Fit

In the event your ear is stuck and no single choice is rising to the top, check if three share a common element. If so, choose the odd man out.

E1 The soldiers successfully finalized their tour of duty and returned home after having served 18 consecutive months in the field.

A. NO CHANGE
B. completed
C. implemented
D. achieved

S *Let's walk through the steps. Plug each answer choice back into the sentence, paraphrasing as needed.*

A. The soldiers **finalized** their tour in 18 months.
Is that how we normally use finalize? People usually talk about finalizing plans or drafts—implying that there are a series of versions, ending in a final one. There are no versions of a tour, which is why this sounds funny. Let's eliminate A.

B. The soldiers **completed** their tour in 18 months.
This actually sounds pretty good. A tour has a beginning and an end. ***Completed*** *captures that. Leave B.*

C. The soldiers **implemented** their tour in 18 months.
People talk about implementing a plan, a solution, or a proposal. A ***tour*** *is quite different. This one is a stretch. Let's squiggle it for now.*

D. The soldiers **achieved** their tour in 18 months.
When you hear achieve, you may think of achieving an outcome or a goal. The tour wasn't an outcome or goal. This one is out.

Between ***completed*** *and* ***implemented****, plugging them back in a second time to be sure,* ***completed*** *is a better fit.* ***B is our answer!***

E2 Dozens of soft lamps <u>elucidated</u> the interior of the newly designed Nexxus Gallery, creating an ambience that enabled viewers to experience a heightened intimacy with each work of art.

F. NO CHANGE
G. enlightened
H. irradiated
J. illuminated

S *Let's plug each answer choice back into the context:*

F. The lamps **elucidated** the interior.
Are you solid on the word elucidate? It does have the root ***luc****, which has to do with light. Let's keep it for now.*

G. The lamps **enlightened** the interior.
Enlightened obviously has the word light in it, but in most cases, enlightened has to do with ***learning*** *and* ***education****. "Enlighten me!" Let's go ahead and eliminate G.*

H. The lamps **irradiated** the interior.
Are we talking about Marie Curie? Radioactive particles? I don't think our intention is to irradiate the gallery. Let's take the bold step of eliminating H.

J. The lamps **illuminated** the interior.
This sounds spot on. Let me enlighten you; lamps illuminate. Let's not eliminate illuminate.

We are left with ***elucidate*** *and* ***illuminate****. We know that* ***illuminate*** *works, but we are unsure about elucidate. Always go with what you know.* ***J is our answer.***

Common Flips

The ACT authors sometimes test similar sounding vocabulary:

Set	vs.	Sat
Then	vs.	Than
Effect	vs.	Affect
Excess	vs.	Access
Their	vs.	They're
Principle	vs.	Principal

E3 The author <u>past over</u> obscurity and from there into legend.

A. NO CHANGE
B. past into
C. passed over
D. passed into

S We are testing ***past*** versus ***passed*** as the verb in our sentence. To begin, ***past*** is not a verb; it is used primarily as a noun, AKA "Stop living in the past!" or as an adjective: "my past relationships have been rocky!"

We are clearly looking for a verb, so we need to stick with ***passed****, leaving us with C or D. Now we must decide the proper preposition. When you pass* ***over*** *something, you usually avoid it. But we know the author was obscure since he went* ***from there*** *into legend. Passed* ***into*** *makes more sense.* ***D is our answer!***

PULSE CHECK

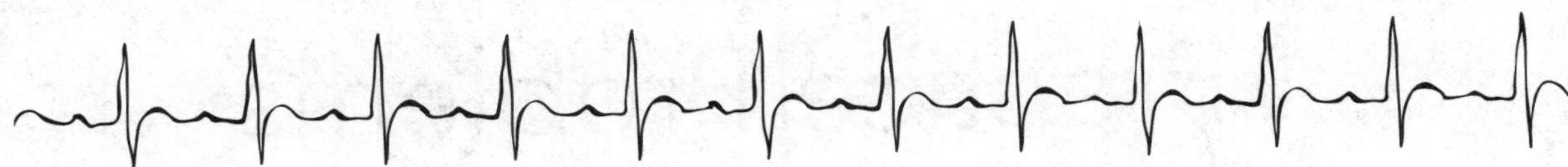

Identify the error (if present) in each of the following sentences.

1. No one could have guessed the affect the new robot would have on the household.
2. When you're going through customs, they'll definitely want to see you're passport.
3. The clowns are there, and their quite angry about the condition of they're clown car.
4. It's simply astonishing, the effect that a pet can have on it's owner.
5. Who's moldy sandwich is sitting in the refrigerator?

Answers

1. No one could have guessed the *effect* the new robot would have on the household.
2. When you're going through customs, they'll definitely want to see *your* passport.
3. The clowns are there, and *they're* quite angry about the condition of *their* clown car.
4. It's simply astonishing, the effect that a pet can have on *its* owner.
5. *Whose* moldy sandwich is sitting in the refrigerator?

Vocabulary in Context Practice Problems

Select the answer choice that produces the best sentence.

1. Stefan couldn't wait for his friends to taste the new teriyaki sauce he'd <u>coined</u>.

   A. NO CHANGE
   B. invented
   C. fabricated
   D. instituted

2. As the full moon draws near, werewolves benefit from <u>aggravated</u> sensory abilities.

   F. NO CHANGE
   G. heightened
   H. raised
   J. lifted

3. During the third Martian war, many young women <u>opposed</u> bravely in the dusty red trenches.

   A. NO CHANGE
   B. campaigned
   C. repressed
   D. fought

4. The angry <u>contest</u> in the grocery store produce section began when two old ladies happened to reach for the same grapefruit at the identical moment.

   F. NO CHANGE
   G. dispute
   H. challenge
   J. difference

5. The tropical flowers at the botanical garden bloomed delightfully in a <u>realistic</u> display.

   F. NO CHANGE
   G. lurid
   H. garish
   J. vivid

Misplaced Modifier

2%
of English questions on the ACT

A clause is always looking for something to modify. It will indiscriminately modify whatever it is touching.

Make sure the modifier is **as close as possible** to the noun/pronoun it is modifying. Otherwise, you end up with some pretty strange sentences.

E1 Ripping through her street, Emily was terrified of the tornado.

modifier *object*

Ripping through her street, Emily was terrified of the tornado.

S Ripping through the street, **the tornado** terrified Emily.

modifier *object*

*Do we really want to say **Emily** is ripping through her street? Probably not. The **tornado** is to blame!*

We need to bring the actual culprit closer to the modifier to clear poor Emily's name.

First, you have to identify the modifier and see if it is acting appropriately.

E2 <u>Timmy found his stray gerbil cleaning his room.</u>

S <u>While cleaning his room, Timmy found his stray gerbil.</u>

*How did Timmy train his gerbil to clean his room? What's his hourly rate? Hm... it is much more likely that **Timmy**, not his gerbil, was cleaning his room. Remember, place your modifier **right next to** the noun doing the action.*

E3 <u>Loved for their small size and chipper dispositions, more and more people are breeding Chiweenies, which are Chihuahua and Daschund mixes.</u>

S <u>More and more people are breeding Chiweenies, Chihuahua and Daschund mixes, loved for their small size and chipper dispositions.</u>

*It has been said that owners begin to look like their pets after they have lived together for many years. Even so, it's doubful the **people** that breed these dogs are loved for **their small size and chipper dispositions**. More likely, the modifier was meant to refer to the little **Chiweenies** themselves.*

E4 When I walked into the kitchen, I saw that Rex was cooking lasagna, not his mom.

S When I walked into the kitchen, **I saw that Rex, not his mom, was cooking lasagna.**

I certainly hope Rex wasn't cooking his mother! Unless there is another Hannibal Lector in the making, Rex was cooking the ***lasagna****.*

E5 Flying out the window, Naomi spotted her errant parrot.

S Naomi spotted her errant parrot flying out the window.

Do we even need to address this? Unless Naomi is from Krypton like Superman, it was the errant parrot that was flying out the window.

E6 Nhuy-i found her lost diamond ring searching under her couch cushions.

S While searching under her couch cushions, Nhuy-i found her lost diamond ring.

Perhaps the diamond ring was looking for loose change. It is more likely that **Nhuy-i** *was the one* ***searching under her couch cushions****.*

PULSE CHECK

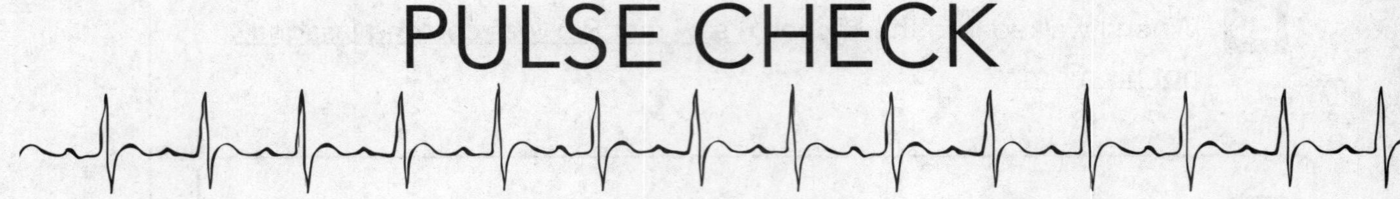

Identify the error (if present) in each of the following sentences.

1. Leaning too closely to her birthday candles, Eunice's hair burst into flames.

2. Last Halloween our dentist passed out toothbrushes dressed as Napoleon Bonaparte instead of candy.

3. Harold tripped over his pet turtle dancing across his room.

4. The spy plane spotted our secret hideout flying through the sky.

5. Running through the woods to escape Sasquatch, the brambles tore Ida's skirt.

Answers

1. *Eunice's hair burst into flames while she was leaning too closely to her birthday candles.*

2. Last Halloween our dentist*, dressed as Napoleon Bonaparte, passed out toothbrushes instead of candy.*

3. *Dancing across his room,* Harold tripped over his pet turtle.

4. *Flying through the sky,* the spy plane spotted our secret hideout.

5. *The brambles tore Ida's skirt as she was running through the woods to escape Sasquatch.*

Misplaced Modifier Practice Problems

1. Prized for their rarity, collectors will pay thousands of dollars for Baccarat perfume bottles designed by Salvador Dali.

A. NO CHANGE
B. Collectors will pay thousands of dollars, prized for their rarity, for Baccarat perfume bottles designed by Salvador Dali.
C. Designed by Salvador Dali, collectors will pay thousands of dollars for Baccarat perfume bottles, prized for their rarity.
D. Collectors will pay thousands of dollars for Baccarat perfume bottles, prized for their rarity and designed by Salvador Dali.

2. Finding his sister's diary fascinating, all the pages were read thoroughly by Horatio.

F. NO CHANGE
G. Horatio thoroughly read all the pages.
H. thoroughly all the pages were read by Horatio.
J. its pages were all read thoroughly by Horatio.

3. We believe we have found Amelia Earhart's crashed Lockheed 10E exploring the Pacific Ocean off the coast of New Britain Island near New Guinea.

A. NO CHANGE
B. While exploring the Pacific Ocean, we believe we have found Amelia Earhart's crashed Lockheed 10E
C. Exploring the Pacific Ocean, Amelia Earhart's crashed Lockheed 10E was, we believe, found
D. Amelia Earhart's crashed Lockheed 10E was found, we believe, exploring the Pacific Ocean

4. Soaked in rum and set aflame, diners were impressed by the exotic bananas foster served at the popular Florida restaurant.

F. NO CHANGE
G. Diners were impressed, soaked in rum and set aflame, by the exotic bananas foster served
H. The exotic bananas foster impressed diners, soaked in rum and set aflame
J. Soaked in rum and set aflame, the exotic bananas foster impressed diners

5. Enjoying the spring day, the laundry was hung out to dry as the maid sang folk songs from her childhood.

A. NO CHANGE
B. the maid hung the laundry out to dry and
C. the maid hanging laundry out to dry and singing
D. the laundry being hung out to dry by the maid who

1%
of English questions on the ACT

Adjectives and Adverbs

The ACT often uses adjectives when an adverb is needed, or an adverb when an adjective is needed.

An adjective describes a noun or a pronoun. An adverb describes a **verb**, an **adjective**, or another **adverb**, and the vast majority of adverbs end in **–ly**.

E1 In 2007, Steve Jobs <u>announced the release of the iPhone, a clever designed mobile phone</u>, that would go on to rock the telecommunications industry and send technophiles running to Apple outlets.

S

...release of the iPhone, <u>a **cleverly** designed mobile phone</u>...

Clever *is not modifying the phone, but how it was* ***designed****.*
It may have been a clever phone, but it was ***cleverly*** *designed.*
We need an adverb to describe the adjective. All about the ***-ly****!!*

E2 Come quick! I think our platypus was just elected Mayor.

Good is an adjective. **Well** is an adverb!!

S Come quickly! I think our platypus was just elected Mayor.

Quick *describes the verb* ***come****, therefore it needs to be an adverb. Just add* ***-ly!***

E3 After years of being ignored, Jorgen was surprised when the cute girl next door commented on how good he played the bassoon.

S After years of being ignored, Jorgen was surprised when the cute girl next door commented on how **well** he played the bassoon.

The cute girl is complimenting how well Jorgen ***played****.*
Since played is a verb, we need an adverb, well, to describe it.

For "-EST" you need three

When comparing two things, -ER does the trick: hard**er**, bett**er**, fast**er**, strong**er**. Only when comparing three or more things can you use -EST: hard**est**, b**est**, fast**est**, strong**est**.

E4 Between my Coach and Chanel purses, I like the Chanel one best.

S Between my Coach and Chanel purses, I like the Chanel one **better**.

We are only comparing two things here, a Coach and a Chanel purse. Since there are only two purses, we have to use -ER.

PULSE CHECK

Identify the error (if present) in each of the following sentences.

1. Before I registered for Dr. Platnic's Advanced Theories of Cultural Rhetoric and Protest seminar, my roommate warned me that it was surprising difficult.
2. Some people have no problem paying exorbitant amounts for designer shoes because these shoes are not only stunning but also beautiful handmade.
3. I was shocked when I went to the organic produce market and found that Chinese eggplants were priced so high.
4. Of my two brothers, Jonas is definitely the strongest.
5. Despite being light seasoned, the tripe Olga made was delicious.

Answers

1. Before I registered for Dr. Platnic's Advanced Theories of Cultural Rhetoric and Protest seminar, my roommate warned me that it was *surprisingly* difficult.
2. Some people have no problem paying exorbitant amounts for designer shoes because these shoes are not only stunning but also *beautifully* handmade.
3. I was shocked when I went to the organic produce market and found that Chinese eggplants were priced so *highly*.
4. Of my two brothers, Jonas is definitely *stronger*.
5. Despite being *lightly* seasoned, the tripe Olga made was delicious.

Adjective/Adverb Practice Problems

1. Terry played swift and vicious on the basketball court, yet he never won a championship.

   A. NO CHANGE
   B. swiftly vicious
   C. viciously swift
   D. swiftly and viciously

2. Despite early predictions of clear skies all day, by noon the snow had begun to fall quite heavily.

   F. NO CHANGE
   G. quite heavy
   H. quietly heavily
   J. quietly heavy

3. When the Flaming Lips finally came on stage, an intensely excited wave of applause rippled through the crowd.

   A. NO CHANGE
   B. intense excitedly
   C. intensely excitedly
   D. intense excitingly

4. With the hamburgers flamingly nice on the grill, it was time to whip up some taters and slaw.

   F. NO CHANGE
   G. flame nicely
   H. flaming nice
   J. flaming nicely

5. The bebop reunion tour got derailed on a train out of Sydney, where unusual and hottest weather caused the tracks to expand, temporarily shutting down the railroad.

   A. NO CHANGE
   B. unusually hot
   C. unusually hotly
   D. unusual hotly

6. The contemporary artist Macchiato's unusual series of still life paintings began when he was hit with a blinding flashingly of insight while waiting at the counter of his local coffee shop.

   F. NO CHANGE
   G. blind flashing
   H. blinding flash
   J. blindingly flash

1%
of English questions on the ACT

Parallelism

Parallelism is just a fancy way of saying that words in lists or comparisons must be similar.

Parallelism in Lists

All items in a list must be the same part of speech whether they are nouns, adjectives, adverbs, or verbs. If your list contains only verbs, each verb must be the same tense.

A talented and versatile artist, Steve Martin has been a comedian, a playwright, and directed several Hollywood films.

Let's have a closer look at this list:

noun noun 

...Steve Martin has been a comedian, a playwright, and directed several Hollywood films.

You do not want to mess with parallel cop! He will bring your ACT score down!

S

noun noun noun

...Steve Martin has been a comedian, a playwright, and a director of several Hollywood films.

Parallel cop won't stand for this egregious infraction of our grammar laws. Let's obey our rules of parallel structure and keep our list parallel. Adjust the sentence so all the words in the list are the same part of speech.

Many of our university's philosophy students are believers in political anarchy, rebel against contemporary conventions, and the power of individual thought.

S Many of our university's philosophy students are believers in political anarchy, rebellion against contemporary conventions, and the power of individual thought.

In the original list, you had a noun ***(believers)****, a verb* ***(rebel)*** *and another noun* ***(power)****. The simplest way to fix this is to change your list so it only contains nouns.*

E3 Horace Vandergelder disagrees with Harry Winston about what is the definition of a fine race horse and how to appraise one.

S Horace Vandergelder disagrees with Harry Winston about how to define and appraise a fine race horse.

In the example, Horace and Harry are disagreeing about the ***definition*** *(noun) and* ***to appraise*** *(verb). Their arguments would be better understood if they discussed the same part of speech—verbs:* ***define*** *and* ***appraise****.*

E4 To be elected President of the United States, a candidate must be a fourteen-year resident of the United States and have been born a citizen of the country.

S To be elected President of the United States, a candidate must be a fourteen-year resident of the United States and a natural-born citizen.

*To make the example parallel, a candidate must be two different nouns (****fourteen-year resident*** *and* ***natural-born citizen****) rather than a noun and a verb.*

PULSE CHECK

Identify the error (if present) in each of the following sentences.

1. Sally was a great nurse, bringing me orange juice and made me a can of soup.

2. By the end of the Great Alien War of 3030, we were happy to return to our toilet paper farms and working in the tire factories.

3. After Rebecca forgot the brochures and Margaret ruined the cookies, the PTA meeting was a complete flop.

4. Theodore's favorite parts of attending a game at the ballpark were eating hotdogs and the wonderful views.

5. The boss instructed us to file our reports, tidy our desks, and cleaning our wastebaskets.

Answers

1. Sally was a great nurse, bringing me orange juice and *making* me a can of soup.

2. By the end of the Great Alien War of 3030, we were happy to return to our toilet paper farms and *tire factories*.

3. Correct!

4. Theodore's favorite parts of attending a game at the ballpark were *the hotdogs* and the wonderful views.

5. The boss instructed us to file our reports, tidy our desks, and *clean our wastebaskets*.

Parallelism Practice Problems

Select the answer choice that produces the best sentence.

1. If he wanted his stint on MTV's "The Real World" to bring him fame and fortune, Fabio realized he would have to be a belligerent debater, an inconsiderate roommate and flirt incessantly with all the girls.

   A. NO CHANGE
   B. and an incessant flirt
   C. and to flirt incessantly
   D. and be flirting incessantly

2. The new, yet alarming, trend of childhood obesity in Nepalese tree frogs seems to be caused by poor nutrition, peer pressure and not exercising.

   F. NO CHANGE
   G. and because of not enough exercise.
   H. lack of exercise.
   J. OMIT the underlined portion.

3. While the other high school juniors mocked Sheldon for his insipid, sentimental poetry, Corrine was intoxicated with his macabre imagery and florid language.

   A. NO CHANGE
   B. macabre imagery and using florid language.
   C. use of macabre imagery and including florid language.
   D. using macabre imagery and his florid language.

4. As a goldfish who lived in a bowl, Otto had three main interests: watching Animal Planet, playing solitaire, and he loved to remodel his plastic castle.

   F. NO CHANGE
   G. to remodel his plastic castle.
   H. the remodeling of his plastic castle.
   J. remodeling his plastic castle.

5. During his decades-long career, Bob Baluga's many roles included everything from performing at carnivals to talk show host.

   A. NO CHANGE
   B. carnival performer
   C. being a carnival performer
   D. carnival performances

1%
of English questions on the ACT

Casual Language

Occasionally the test writers will ask you to fix language that is too informal or casual.

These answer choices will stand out as they break with the formal tone of standard ACT passages. If the writers give you an option of saying something in a formal versus an informal way, the formal way is always correct.

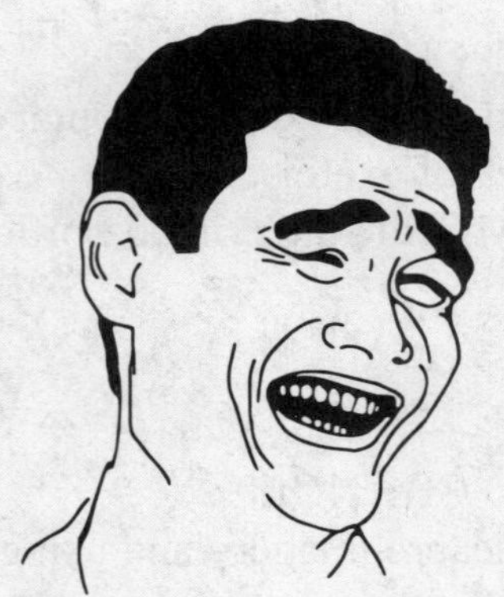

Informal/Casual	Formal
Stick around for a while	Remain constant
Teeny, tiny	Small
Shoot the breeze	Converse
She was way off base	She was incorrect
Let it all hang out	Relax
Blown to smithereens	Demolished
Man, I'm jonesin' for a snack	I am hungry

E1 When he announced his intentions to join the famed and highly exclusive Moscow Ballet, there was a great deal of debate regarding whether a US-born dancer could hack it; following his first performance, however, international critics warmed greatly to Webster's portrayal of the Swan King in Tchaikovsky's *Swan Lake*.

A. NO CHANGE
B. was up to snuff;
C. could succeed in that environment;
D. could hang with the Russians;

S *In this case, we need to look at the level of formality of the passage. It looks fairly straightforward and buttoned up.* ***Up to snuff*****,** ***hang with the Russkies****, and* ***could not hack it****: all of these are examples of informal language. It's always better to stick with the most formal, boring language provided:* ***C is our answer!***

PULSE CHECK

Identify the error (if present) in each of the following sentences.

1. Tucker and Dale were so delighted to have their own hunting cabin that they barely noticed how busted up it was.
2. The new university president was one cool cat, impressing the entire campus with his numerous accolades.
3. From the grinding noises emanating from the organ room, it was evident that the ancient instrument was fixing to break down.
4. The kids couldn't wait for the circus to come to town, bringing with it the promise of a real blast.
5. From sunrise to sunset, they put in some elbow grease to bring in the crops before they were blighted by the harsh winds of winter.

Answers

1. Tucker and Dale were so delighted to have their own hunting cabin that they barely noticed how *dilapidated* it was.
2. The new university president was *accomplished*, impressing the entire campus with his numerous accolades.
3. From the grinding noises emanating from the organ room, it was evident that the ancient instrument was *about to* break down.
4. The kids couldn't wait for the circus to come to town, bringing with it the promise of a *good time*.
5. From sunrise to sunset, they *labored* to bring in the crops before they were blighted by the harsh winds of winter.

1%
of grammar questions on the ACT

Unclear Antecedents

Sometimes a pronoun reference is ambiguous. If it's not clear who "he" or "she" is, be more specific!

E1 Mr. Miyagi and Daniel-san were surprised that his front snap kick, a classic move, proved to be too much for the Cobra Kai's star athlete, Johnny Lawrence.

S Mr. Miyagi and Daniel-san were surprised that Daniel-san's front snap kick, a classic move, proved to be too much for the Cobra Kai's star athlete, Johnny Lawrence.

Whose front kick? Mr. Miyagi's? Or Daniel-san's? Be specific to avoid pronoun confusion!

E2 When Ingrid and Helga visited the Ikea bakery, she noticed her favorite cupcake, KYPKKÄKKEN, was no longer on the menu.

S When Ingrid and Helga visited the Ikea bakery, Helga noticed her favorite cupcake, KYPKKÄKKEN, was no longer on the menu.

The pronoun ***she*** *is too vague. We need to clarify who is noticing the absent dessert.*

PULSE CHECK

Identify the error (if present) in each of the following sentences.

1. Despite her dislike of sand and surf, Mary Ellen and Meredith went to the beach on their vacation.

2. Nathaniel and Marcus, best friends since they were in kindergarten, were disconsolate when his parents decided to move to Cairo, Egypt.

3. She had always dreamed of making it big in Hollywood, like Shirley Temple or Audrey Hepburn, which is why Cordelia and her mother went to every open call audition they could find.

4. Needing an A on his final physics project to pass the course, Otis and Bob worked on it together all night long.

5. Yessenia and Yasmina decided to try speed dating because she refused to go on another blind date.

Answers

---

1. Despite *Mary Ellen's* dislike of sand and surf, *she* and Meredith went to the beach on their vacation.

2. Nathaniel and Marcus, best friends since they were in kindergarten, were disconsolate when *Nathaniel's* parents decided to move to Cairo, Egypt.

3. *Cordelia* had always dreamed of making it big in Hollywood, like Shirley Temple or Audrey Hepburn, which is why *she* and her mother went to every open call audition they could find.

4. *Otis, needing an A on his final physics project to pass the course, worked on it with Bob* all night long.

5. Yessenia and Yasmina decided to try speed dating because *Yasmina* refused to go on another blind date.

ENGLISH PRACTICE 3

9 Minutes—15 Questions

DIRECTIONS: In the passage that follows, certain words and phrases are underlined and numbered. In the right-hand column, you will find alternatives for the underlined part. In most cases, you are to choose the one that best expresses the idea, makes the statement appropriate for standard written English, or is worded most consistently with the style and tone of the passage as a whole. If you think the original version is best, choose "NO CHANGE." In some cases you will find in the right-hand column a question about the underlined part. You are to choose the best answer to the question.

This passage tests only the grammar concepts that you have learned up to this point.

Practice these concepts in the context of a passage. Since the ACT will give you 45 minutes for 5 passages, this passage should take you about **9 minutes.**

PASSAGE III

Eureka Springs

Eureka Springs is the kind of vacation spot that induces[1] you to escape for a week, a month, or an entire summer. Nestled in the hilly country of Carroll County, Arkansas, it's accessible only by narrow, winding roads: an exhausting drive, especially if you're prone to getting car sick. But once your there, it's[2] like stepping into another world. In some ways, the town feels oddly untouched by time. Its historic streets are invitingly walkable, filled with charming boutiques, cozy restaurants, casual bars, and vintage hotels. Shopkeepers are with their customers striking up friendly conversations[3]—especially if you visit during the off-season, as I did this past January.

1. **A.** NO CHANGE
   B. beckons
   C. provokes
   D. incites

2. **F.** NO CHANGE
   G. you're there, its
   H. your their, it's
   J. you're there, it's

3. **A.** NO CHANGE
   B. striking up, friendly, conversations with their customers
   C. friendly with striking up their conversations with customers
   D. friendly, striking up conversations with their customers

An unseasonable warm[4] afternoon was the perfect time to walk around and enjoy the scenery. The weather was perfect, and, there were no troublesome wasps or mosquitoes[5] to ruin the mood!

A quartet of street musicians had gathered on the sidewalk, where they sang and played their banjos and guitars, filling the air with pleasant tunes.[6] My traveling companion and I—along with our little dog—stepped into a fun shop specializing exclusively in condiments, especially hot sauces. Excited in[7] having company, the eccentric proprietor buzzed around the restaurant, chatting happily and served[8] up tasty morsels for us to sample, like a candied jalapeno that was both spicy and sweet. The dog got a cracker. After buying a jar of spicy olives, we bid the shopkeeper an affectionate goodbye, and continued along.

We stopped, as we walked to read the plaques mounted along the sidewalk.[9] The brass plaques tell the story of a resort town with a long history, dating back to the 1880s and 1890s.

4. F. NO CHANGE
   G. An unseasonable and warm
   H. A warmly unseasonable
   J. An unseasonably warm

5. A. NO CHANGE
   B. and there were no troublesome wasps or mosquitoes
   C. and there were no troublesome wasps, or mosquitoes,
   D. and, there were no troublesome wasps, or mosquitoes

6. F. NO CHANGE
   G. giving off good vibrations.
   H. treating all the peeps nearby to a melodic sound.
   J. stimulating our eardrums with a complex arrangement of musical notes.

7. A. NO CHANGE
   B. about
   C. for
   D. to

8. F. NO CHANGE
   G. serving
   H. he served
   J. he serves

9. A. NO CHANGE
   B. As we walked, we stopped to read the plaques mounted along the sidewalk.
   C. As we walked, mounted along the sidewalk, we stopped to read the plaques.
   D. As we walked, we stopped, mounted along the sidewalk to read the plaques.

GO ON TO THE NEXT PAGE.

Filled with natural springs bubble from the hillside, [10]

the town provided [11] a relaxing holiday spot and trendy health spas to wealthy vacationers of the Victorian era. Eureka Spring's many historic homes and buildings are a monument to this Victorian past. Hours we spent [12] wandering around looking at these beautiful homes, decorated with intricate and detailed trim, and painted in gorgeous pastels like yellow, pink, purple, and green.

We did not stay in one of these Victorian bed and breakfasts. Indeed, [13] our chosen lodging was a cabin in a forest, overlooking a lake.

It [14] also has a historic past, being one of half-a-dozen built by the famous WPA (Work Projects Administration) in the 1930s. Sponsored by the government during the days of the Great Depression, many communities benefited, and projects were completed by the WPA. [15] The WPA built to such high standards, many of the buildings they completed are still in perfect condition—like the charming log cabin where I slept, nestled on the boundary between woods and lake.

10. F. NO CHANGE
    G. springs, bubble
    H. springs that bubble
    J. springs, which bubbling

11. A. NO CHANGE
    B. might provide
    C. provides
    D. is providing

12. F. NO CHANGE
    G. We spent hours
    H. When we spent hours
    J. Spending hours

13. A. NO CHANGE
    B. Instead,
    C. In fact,
    D. Indisputably

14. F. NO CHANGE
    G. The Lake
    H. The forest
    J. The cabin

15. A. NO CHANGE
    B. many communities derived great benefit by the WPA's projects.
    C. the WPA completed projects benefiting many communities.
    D. many communities were benefited by projects completed by the WPA.

END OF PRACTICE PASSAGE 3
ANSWERS AVAILABLE ON PAGE 185

Rhetorical Skills

Beyond mechanics, the ACT authors will also assess your rhetorical skills: your ability to comprehend the flow and function of a passage.

The ACT authors test these skills using questions such as: *What is the proper order of sentences or paragraphs? Is this content relevant to this paragraph? Did the author meet his or her goals in crafting the passage?*

Your job is to make sure the passage does two things:

1 Stays on topic

2 Transitions smoothly from one idea to next

To answer Rhetorical Skills questions, you will need to think bigger. Broaden your focus to include surrounding sentences and to understand the flow of the passage.

Let's look at a typical Rhetorical Skills question:

I'd heard that the theme park's attractions were even more popular at night, <u>not just the roller coasters but also the romantic river cruises.</u>

Given that all the choices are true, which one most effectively leads readers to the rest of the essay?

A. NO CHANGE
B. and it is the most popular park in the Northeast.
C. so yesterday I stayed up late to find out for myself.
D. the park having many snack booths open well past midnight.

Question prompts are a dead giveaway that you're dealing with a Rhetorical Skills question.

S

For the first time in the English section we have a prompt giving us a specific task to accomplish. In this case we need to find which choice "effectively leads readers to the rest of the essay."

*We need more context! We cannot pick an answer until we know if we're heading towards a discussion of **attractions** (A), the **popularity** of the park (B), a personal **narrative** (C), or the **food options** (D).*

Until we know where we are going, we cannot point things in the right direction. Without reading for more context, this question is impossible!

E2

I'd heard that the theme park's attractions were even more popular at night, <u>not just the roller coasters but also the romantic river cruises</u>. My first destination was the Haunted Schoolhouse, where I was so scared I nearly jumped out of my sneakers. My next stop was Humberto's Clowning Academy where I learned to juggle small plastic animals while balancing on a pile of dusty mattresses.

Given that all the choices are true which one most effectively leads readers to the rest of the essay?

A. NO CHANGE
B. and it is the most popular park in the Northeast.
C. so yesterday I stayed up late to find out for myself.
D. the park having many snack booths open well past midnight.

S

*Now we have enough information to work with. Is there a mention of **coasters** or **cruises**? Nope, A is out. Did we read anything about **popularity**? Nope, cross off B. Was there a personal narrative? You betcha: **My's** and **I's** all over the place!*
C looks good. And snack booths — not a chance. D is out.

C is our answer!

Rhetorical Skills Strategy

About 30% of the 75 questions in the English section test your Rhetorical Skills. Follow this step-by-step guide to conquer these questions.

Rhetorical Skills Strategy

1. Read the question actively and determine your **task**.
2. Read the passage in **context**, keeping your task in mind.
3. When applicable, come up with your **own answer**.
4. **Eliminate** wrong answers focusing on specific words in each choice.
5. **Plug in** the remaining choices; **choose** the one that sounds best.

Let's see this strategy in action!

It's been several years since I last saw Erik, but we still speak every weekend. He often rants loudly about the barnacles creeping up his boat's hull, and accuses jealous neighbors of encouraging their ascent. <u>I listen to every word he says.</u>

Given that all the choices are true, which one most clearly expresses the author's skepticism about the claims of his old friend?

A. NO CHANGE
B. He knows a lot about marine biology.
C. He can have some pretty wild ideas.
D. He has never been that close with his neighbors.

1 Determine your **task**

Given that all the choices are true, which one most clearly expresses the author's skepticism.

Okay - so we are looking for an answer choice that communicates **skepticism** or **doubt**.

2 Read the passage in **context**

It's been several years since I last saw Erik, but we still speak every weekend. He often rants loudly about the barnacles creeping up his boat's hull, and accuses jealous neighbors of encouraging their ascent. I listen to every word he says.

So... Erik is claiming his neighbors are encouraging barnacles. Interesting...

3 If possible, come up with your **own answer**

Since we are choosing which answer choice has the best wording, we can't come up with our own answer. On to the choices!

Eliminate wrong answers

Given that all the choices are true, which one most clearly <u>expresses the author's skepticism</u> about the claims of his old friend?

A. I listen to every word he says.
B. He knows a lot about marine biology.
C. He can have some pretty wild ideas.
D. He has never been that close with his neighbors.

"I listen to every word he says"
That's not skepticism: that's genuine interest! A is wrong.

B

Given that all the choices are true, which one most clearly <u>expresses the author's skepticism</u> about the claims of his old friend?

~~**A.** I listen to every word he says.~~
B. He knows a lot about marine biology.
C. He can have some pretty wild ideas.
D. He has never been that close with his neighbors.

"He knows a lot"...?
That's way off. I'm looking for words of **doubt**, not praise! B is wrong.

C Given that all the choices are true, which one most clearly <u>expresses the author's skepticism</u> about the claims of his old friend?

~~**A.** I listen to every word he says.~~

~~**B.** He knows a lot about marine biology.~~

C. He can have some pretty wild ideas.

D. He has never been that close with his neighbors.

This sounds great!
"Wild ideas" definitely sounds like skepticism.

D Given that all the choices are true, which one most clearly <u>expresses the author's skepticism</u> about the claims of his old friend?

~~A. I listen to every word he says.~~

~~B. He knows a lot about marine biology.~~

C. He can have some pretty wild ideas.

D. He has never been that close with his neighbors.

"never been that close" ...?

That's just irrelevant!
Clearly wrong answer here.

5 **Plug in** the remaining choices

It's been several years since I last saw Erik, but we still speak every weekend. He often rants loudly about the barnacles creeping up his boat's hull, and accuses jealous neighbors of encouraging their ascent. He can have some pretty wild ideas.

Given that all the choices are true, which one most clearly **expresses the author's skepticism** about the claims of his old friend?

~~**A.** I listen to every word he says.~~
~~**B.** He knows a lot about marine biology.~~
(**C.**) He can have some pretty wild ideas.
~~**D.** He has never been that close with his neighbors.~~

Choice C accomplishes our task of expressing skepticism!

8%

of English questions on the ACT

Adding/Deleting Information

The ACT writers will frequently propose adding a new sentence to the passage, or deleting an existing one. It is your task to determine whether the proposed change would further develop or distract from the point the author is attempting to make.

There are two potential structures for Adding Information questions: *Yes/No + Why* and *Accomplishing a Task*.

Yes/No + Why

For this structure, you must first answer the **Yes/No** question, and from there move on to the rationale.

Frequently the answer choices will look like this.

A. Yes (for a Good Reason)
B. Yes (for a Bad Reason)
C. No (for a Good Reason)
D. No (for a Bad Reason)

Notice that both A and C have good reasons. A student who does not choose **Yes** or **No** first may be tricked by the multiple good sounding reasons.

For the sake of efficiency, always choose **Yes** or **No** first! To make this choice, you will need to determine if the addition:

 Stays on Topic

 Transitions Smoothly between Ideas

When the correct answer is **No**, it is usually because the new information strayed off topic.

When the correct answer is **Yes**, it is usually because the new sentence provides a logical transition or accomplishes a goal of the author.

Once I returned home from my semester abroad, I heard through the grapevine that Dooley's Café, my favorite eatery, was under new management and had undergone many significant changes. [1] The restaurant had added a second counter, which greatly reduced the wait time. Though the quesadillas were gone, the new Bagel-Blast Jell-O Supreme was actually quite tasty. The prices had come down on certain items, including my old standby: Lava-drenched, peanut drizzle flatbread. The owners had also upgraded the seating to include more than just the bean bag chairs of old. Finally, my back wouldn't hurt after lunch!

1. At this point, the writer is considering adding the following statement:

> I expected the changes would all be for the worst, but pleasantly they weren't.

Should the writer make this addition here?

A. Yes, because it gives evidence that, contrary to rumors, the eatery had not changed management.

B. Yes, because it provides a logical transition between the preceding sentence and the rest of the paragraph.

C. No, because it creates a digression and does not logically fit in the essay.

D. No, because it conflicts with the narrator's feelings about the changes to the eatery expressed in the rest of this paragraph.

Solve the **Yes/No**

*First, our sentence needs to **stay on topic** and **maintain the flow** of the paragraph. If we make the addition, the paragraph flows like this:*

- When I came back I learned Dooley's had **changed**...
- The **changes** were surprisingly pleasant...
- There was *less wait time, tasty dishes, and better seating.*

Are we **on topic?**

We lead by talking about change, mention the changes in our added sentence, and then enumerate the changes. We are clearly on topic!

Is there a **good flow**?

The addition helps us transition from the first sentence to the specific examples. This sentence looks like a winner! Cross off answers C and D.

2 Determine the Yes/No **rationale**

*We have two options in the **Yes** category.*

A. *Yes, because it gives evidence that, contrary to rumors, the eatery had not changed management.*

B. *Yes, because it provides a logical transition between the preceding sentence and the rest of the paragraph.*

*Do you see the problem with A? It claims that the eatery had **not** changed management. This **whole paragraph** is about a change in management! A gets the **Yes/No** correct, but gives a bad reason.*

B is the winner!

Washington DC has earned the distinction of being the city in which a driver is most likely to have an auto accident. To help reduce the rate of accidents, legislators banned cell phone usage while driving. Studies showed that drivers were distracted while using cell phones and were just as likely to have an accident as individuals who were driving while intoxicated. [2] The first year following the passing of the legislation, accidents dropped 25 percent.

2. At this point, the writer is considering adding the following true statement:

Some cities restrict texting while driving as an alternative to a complete cell phone ban.

Should the writer make this addition here?

F. Yes, because it provides an explanation of the terms used in the preceding sentence.

G. Yes, because it suggests a method that could have prevented the event described later in this paragraph.

H. No, because it contradicts the point made earlier that the city banned cell phone usage.

J. No, because it creates a digression that may distract the reader from the main focus of this paragraph.

S

1 Solve the **Yes/No**

*Are we on topic? We are focusing exclusively on **Washington DC**. Does info about other cities support our point? Nope! We have a clear distraction here. We need a **No** answer.*

2 Determine the **rationale**

*Next we look to the rationale. H claims that the new sentence contradicts the fact that Washington DC banned cell-phone use. The new sentence doesn't even mention DC. "Contradict" is false. **J is our answer!***

Three out of four times that you are asked to add new content, the answer will be **No!**

Accomplishing a Task

Often the ACT writers will ask you to choose a sentence that, if added, would best accomplish a task. The golden rule for this question type is simple:

Underline your task!

The correct answer will have **specific words** that help accomplish your task. Underlining that task will make it easier to check back when you are measuring up the answer choices.

Let's look at some common tasks:

- Give another supporting example
- Reflect the point made earlier in the paragraph
- Introduce the next paragraph
- Provide evidence to support a point

Stick to the task! Often, wrong answer choices will provide wonderful information but utterly fail to accomplish the task at hand. Don't be fooled!

If you **underline your task** and match it with **specific words** in the answer choices, this question type will be a breeze.

There was much speculation regarding Hughes' whereabouts: perhaps he had left the country and was living incognito, or perhaps he was hiding in one of his many properties scattered throughout the nation. [3]

3. Which of the following true statements, if added here, would best develop the point being made in the preceding sentence?

A. His airline designs led to widespread innovation in the fledgling airline industry.

B. Many have questioned his political motives and speculated about his involvement with national elections.

C. Still another theory is that Hughes had gone into protective custody and was living in a bunker underneath Sandusky, Ohio.

D. Many missing persons turn up of their own accord after years of absence.

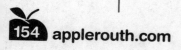

S *First, let's find and underline our task:*

Which choice would best <u>develop the point</u> being made in the <u>preceding sentence</u>?

*All we care about is the point from the previous sentence, which is that folks were **speculating** about the **location of Hughes**.*

Let's go through our choices.

A. ***Airline industry?*** *... Survey says... nope!*
B. ***Speculation*** *I like, but **political motives** is off-task. Lose B.*
C. ***Theory*** *is related to **speculation** and **Sandusky** is a location where we might find **Hughes**. Me gusta!*
D. *Interesting point, but no mention of Hughes. This one is out!*

*Some of these options are interesting and even on topic. However, only one choice accomplishes our task: **C is our answer**.*

Responding to what I thought were the sounds of a bar fight in the kitchen, I entered to find my dad standing hunched over in front of the refrigerator—a closed glass jar of Pandora's Volcanic Salsa clenched tightly between his hands.

From the redness of his face and knuckles, I guessed that he had been working on the lid for a good ten minutes. When he saw me, he stood up straight and visibly attempted to disguise his frustration. After he had explained in detail the chemical reaction that must have rendered the seal unbreakable by human hands, I held out mine for a shot at the jar. [4]

4. Which of the following sentences, if added at this point, would most directly convey to the reader the impression that the narrator's father did not believe she would be able to open the jar?

F. I figured he could use a chance to rest his own tired knuckles.

G. I read about a secret way to open stubborn jars, and was eager to try it out.

H. I could tell he was thankful for my assistance.

J. With a sigh and a skeptical expression, he handed it over.

S *Again, our first step is to* ***underline our task.***

Which choice would most directly <u>convey the impression that the narrator's father did not believe she would be able to open the jar</u>?

Since this task doesn't involve any other sentences from the passage, we can actually answer the question by focusing on the answer choices.

F. *Nothing about the father's belief here, just his knuckles. Cross it out.*

G. *This one doesn't even mention the father at all. Lose it.*

H. *Finally we're talking about the father! But* ***thankful****? Does that convey* ***disbelief****? Right focus, wrong idea.*

J. *Aha! This one is about the father, and* ***skeptical*** *is a synonym for* ***disbelieving****.*

J is our answer!

Adding Information Recap

Remember: whenever you're asked to add information, you need to

1 Stay **on topic**

2 **Transition smoothly** between ideas

For **Yes/No** questions, first pick **Yes** or **No**, then focus on the rationale.

For **Accomplishing a Task** questions, <u>underline the task</u> and *stick to it.*

Deleting Information

The ACT writers will frequently ask you what the passage would primarily lose if particular information were deleted. For example, take this sentence:

> My cousin David has red hair, constantly plays bagpipes, and lives in a cave; obviously, we don't hang out too frequently.

What would we lose if we deleted the phrase **constantly plays bagpipes and lives in a cave?** The deletion would leave us with:

> My cousin David has red hair; obviously, we don't hang out too frequently.

Unless I harbor some secret resentment toward redheads, we lost key information about why I don't hang out with David! We need that phrase!

Last month a new tenant took over the apartment above my own. I met him in the mail room. His name was Heisenberg. He had eyes like the Indian Ocean and a pony tail that would not quit. He seemed like a really nice guy. We talked about German philosophy and exchanged strudel recipes. Over the next few weeks I noticed that he was just as nice as he seemed and he worked odd hours. He also installed a new hardwood floor in his apartment— and boy did he love to dance! [5]

Sunday afternoon my chandelier was shaking to SouljaBoy. Monday evening my picture frames were pulsating to the Texas-Two-Step.

5. If the writer were to delete the phrase "— and boy did he love to dance!", ending the sentence with the word "apartment," the essay would primarily lose a detail that:

   A. is ironic but essential for understanding the narrator's interest in Heisenberg.

   B. reinforces the idea that Heisenberg had moved in upstairs.

   C. contradicts the idea that neighbors are friendly and thoughtful.

   D. is humorous and foreshadows what will follow in the next paragraph.

S *We need to figure out what the phrase "**and boy did he love to dance**" brings to the table. Let's remove the phrase and read nearby sentences for context:*

> ...Over the next few weeks I noticed that he was just as nice as he seemed and he worked odd hours. He also installed a new hardwood floor in his apartment. Sunday afternoon my chandelier was shaking to SouljaBoy. Monday evening my picture frames were pulsating to the Texas-Two-Step.

*Without that phrase, it's not completely clear why his **chandelier** was shaking or picture frames were pulsating. Let's narrow down our answer choices:*

A. is ironic but essential for understanding the narrator's interest...
__Essential__ is too strong. The narrator could still be interested in exchanging more strudel recipes, or pony tail grooming tips.

B. reinforces the idea that Heisenberg had moved in upstairs.
*How does Heisenberg's dance interest **reinforce** that he lives upstairs? This takes a logical leap or two. Nix B.*

C. contradicts the idea that neighbors are friendly and thoughtful.
Again, it takes a logical leap to say a dance interest makes someone unfriendly! Bad answer.

(D.) is humorous and foreshadows what will follow in the next paragraph.
*Does his love of dancing **foreshadow** the next paragraph? Absolutely. The next paragraph is all about the impact of his dancing. We have a winner!*

The works of Christo and Jeanne Claude involve wrapping enormous objects in fabric and creating architectural landscapes that evoke the imagination. One of their most celebrated art projects involved wrapping the sharp exterior of the German parliament building, the Reichstag, in metallic, billowing fabric. [6] More than a hundred mountain climbers and assistants accomplished the enormous task of wrapping the building. For nearly two weeks the center of Germany's government became an art piece that drew in tens of thousands of curious visitors.

6. If the writer were to delete the words *sharp*, *metallic,* and *billowing* from the preceding sentence, the paragraph would lose descriptive details that primarily

F. support the writer's case that the art project was worthwhile.

G. describe the artistic process used to create the project.

H. reveal the visitors' emotional responses to the project.

J. help depict the appearance of the art project.

S *Let's delete the words in question and see what happens.*

> One of their most celebrated art projects involved wrapping the exterior of the German parliament building, the Reichstag, in fabric. More than a hundred mountain climbers and assistants accomplished the enormous task of wrapping the building.

We still know the basics of the project, but we lose a bunch of descriptive adjectives that help us visualize the project. Let's narrow down our answer choices:

F. The author never made a **case** for the project's **worth** in the first place! Hard to lose what was never there.

G **Process** is **how** something happens, not what it **looks** like.

H. **Emotional**? None of our words deal with emotion.

(J.) Don't overthink it! Adjectives describe **appearance**. J it is!

8%
of English questions on the ACT

Effective Wording

Often, the ACT writers will ask you to choose a wording that best accomplishes a specific task.

You solve Effective Wording questions the same way you solved *Accomplish a Task* questions from the Adding Information section.

1. **Underline** your task
2. Match your task to **specific words** in the answers

Stick to your task and all will be right in the world.

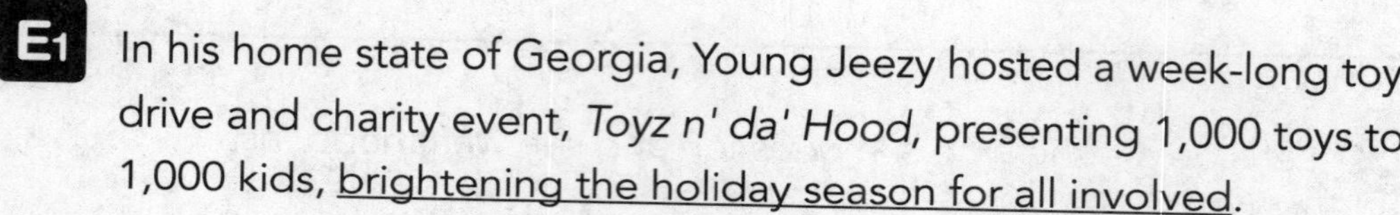

E1 In his home state of Georgia, Young Jeezy hosted a week-long toy drive and charity event, *Toyz n' da' Hood*, presenting 1,000 toys to 1,000 kids, brightening the holiday season for all involved.

Given that all the choices are true, which one provides the reader with the most specific and detailed information about Young Jeezy?

A. NO CHANGE
B. mostly children who came from disadvantaged homes.
C. giving the media a feel-good holiday story.
D. fulfilling one of his life-long dreams of giving back to his community.

Keep in mind that the correct answer might be to keep the sentence as is!

S *Before we do anything else, we must **underline our task**!*

Given that all the choices are true, which one provides the reader with the most specific and detailed information about Young Jeezy?

*So all we care about is getting **more information about Jeezy.***

*If we compare specific words in our answer choices to our task, this question is simple: Choices A, B, and C mention Jeezy a whopping zero times! Only D brings on the Jeezy. **Our answer is D!***

E2 George Washington was rumored to have worn wooden teeth. The truth is much more interesting indeed! Rumors followed Washington wherever he went, due to his elevated place in society. His makeshift dentures contained a cornucopia of interesting objects including a walrus tusk, a cow's tooth, metal, and springs.

Given that all of the choices are true, which one provides the best transition from the opening sentence of this paragraph to its final sentence?

F. NO CHANGE
G. Dental hygiene was a principal concern for men during the colonial period.
H. His mouth was filled with more material than a small junkyard.
J. He neglected his own mouth but brushed his horse's teeth daily.

S *Our task is to provide the <u>best transition</u> from the <u>opening sentence to the final sentence</u>. Let's look at those sentences:*

Opening: **Washington** was rumored to have worn **wooden teeth**.
Closing: His **dentures** contained all kinds of **funky things**.

*So we clearly need a choice that has something to do with **rumors about Washington's teeth**.*

Let's check the answers:

F. This one mentions Washington, but ***not teeth***! Cross it off.
G. This choice covers teeth, but ***where's Washington***? Lose it.
H. Here we have ***Washington*** <u>and</u> his ***mouth*** mentioned! Keep it!
J. This one ***breaks the flow*** by talking about a horse. Nix it.

The best answer is H!

Effective Wording Recap

Remember: whenever you're asked to pick the most effective wording:

1. **Underline** your task
2. Match your task to **specific words** in the choices

ENGLISH PRACTICE 4

9 Minutes—15 Questions

This passage tests only the grammar concepts that you have learned up to this point. Practice these concepts in the context of a full passage.

Since the ACT will give you 45 minutes for 5 passages, this passage should take you about **9 minutes.**

PASSAGE IV

Chili Cook-Off

Food lovers never forget there[1] first chili cook-off. I certainly won't—because that's where I met my wife. But we didn't get off to the most greatest start.[2] In fact, I almost poisoned her. [3]

[1] Originally, my buddy Sam had to talk me into participating. [2] I'd never cooked chili for a crowd before. [3] But cooking up a pot of chili for a Sunday cookout was one thing; busting out my old recipe for a table full of judges was another thing altogether. [4] "Come on," Sam insisted. "It's for a good cause." I couldn't argue. The money from the ticket sales were being[4] donated to a local soup kitchen, helping folks who were down on their luck get a good meal themselves. [5]

1. A. NO CHANGE
   B. they're
   C. there are
   D. their

2. F. NO CHANGE
   G. one of the most great starts.
   H. the most great start.
   J. the greatest start.

3. If the preceding sentence were deleted, the essay would primarily lose:
   A. foreshadowing of an event to come.
   B. a transition to the second paragraph.
   C. a statement of the story's theme.
   D. a key fact in the narrative.

4. F. NO CHANGE
   G. would be
   H. were to be
   J. are being

5. Upon reviewing this paragraph and realizing that some information has been left out, the writer composes the following sentence:

   Sure, my chili got rave reviews from friends.

   This sentence should most logically be placed after Sentence:
   A. 1.
   B. 2.
   C. 3.
   D. 4.

I didn't want to get shown up in front of a bunch of chili experts; my usual recipe wouldn't fly. I decided to do some research: I pored over cookbooks, polled family and friends, and even searched the internet. Nevertheless, [6] I found the perfect secret ingredient.

On Friday, I called in sick to work and spent the day cooking. I soaked and boiled the beans, seeded and chopped the chillies, I was also steaming and peeling [7] the tomatoes. Then I added a generous amount of my secret ingredient. As we drove to the cook-off, the aroma of fresh chili filling the car, Sam portrayed [8] his ulterior motive.

One of the judges was a girl he liked. [9]

6. **F.** NO CHANGE
G. As always,
H. Originally,
J. Finally,

7. **A.** NO CHANGE
B. and steamed and peeled
C. I also steamed and peeled
D. steaming and peeling

8. **F.** NO CHANGE
G. revealed
H. exhibited
J. illustrated

9. At this point, the writer is considering adding the following sentence:

> Though they'd only chatted a few times, he hoped to impress her with my chili.

Should the writer make this addition here?

A. Yes, because it offers an important description of Sam's character.
B. Yes, because it provides information about Sam's motivation.
C. No, because it restates information that has already been provided.
D. No, because it complicates the narrative with unnecessary detail.

She turned out to be the girl-next-door type, with a friendly smile and a nice face. I liked her right away. But would she like my chili? As we ladled up bowls for the judges, Sam explained that I'd spearheaded the preparation—and that I'd added an ingredient so secret, even he didn't know what it was.

The judges dug in, grunting with appreciation. But Sam's crush didn't seem to be enjoying herself.

In fact, her spoon was suddenly dropped and she started to cough. Then, she turned white and her eyes started to water. Sam and I ran over, followed by the other judges.

"Mango," she gasped.

"How did you know?" I asked, stunned.

"Very... allergic," she managed. "Purse. Now." She pointed toward her bag, in hoping to indicate where she kept her bottle of antihistamines. She quickly washed down a couple of pills with a glass of water. After a couple minutes, she seemed to recover.

10. Given that all the choices are true, which one provides information that is new and specific?

F. NO CHANGE.
G. an approachable manner.
H. a pleasant appearance.
J. a smattering of freckles.

11. Given that all the choices are true, which one provides the most insight into the judges' opinion of the chili?

A. NO CHANGE.
B. eating quickly.
C. blowing away steam.
D. speculating on the secret ingredient.

12. **F.** NO CHANGE
G. her spoon having suddenly been dropped, she
H. her spoon suddenly being dropped, she
J. she suddenly dropped her spoon and

13. **A.** NO CHANGE
B. hoping to indicate
C. in hopes for indicating
D. to hope to indicate

GO ON TO THE NEXT PAGE.

I was mortified by the whole ordeal. "Let me take you home," I said. "Really. It's the least I can do." She agreed. As I drove, I asked her questions about her life. I learned that she was training to be a nurse, that she volunteered with the soup kitchen, and that she was a big fan of chili of all kinds. Although [14] she'd never encountered a recipe with mango in it before. When we reached her house, she invited me in for a cup of coffee... and the rest is history.

My chili didn't win the competition. It didn't even get third prize. But I won something much better that night—the heart of the woman who [15] would become my wife.

14. **F.** NO CHANGE
G. kinds, although
H. kinds; although
J. kinds. Though

15. **A.** NO CHANGE
B. she who
C. of whom
D. whom

END OF PRACTICE PASSAGE 4
ANSWERS AVAILABLE ON PAGE 186

LEAST and NOT

6% of English questions on the ACT

You will often be asked to spot the answer choice that is the LEAST acceptable or that is NOT acceptable.

If you see LEAST or NOT, you are looking for the choice that does not fit in.

Three of these things belong together
One of these is not the same
Spot the one that's not like the others
Now it's time to play our game!

A B C D

Did you notice which one was different? It was the horse!!!! Of course.

Most of the time, you do not even have to read the sentence to find the right answer: simply pick the choice that sticks out. For practice, let's try one without looking at an underlined portion at all.

80 percent of LEAST/NOT questions follow this pattern.

Which of the following alternatives to the underlined portion would be LEAST acceptable?

A. Therefore
B. However
C. By contrast
D. On the contrary

S *We don't even need an underlined portion to answer this! **However**, **by contrast**, and **on the contrary** are all transition words that indicate a contrast. **Therefore** sticks out like a sore thumb! **A is our answer.***

Let's get some practice spotting the odd man out. In each of the following lists of words, circle the one that is LEAST like the others.

1. design, come up with, develop, bring forth
2. sent, delivered, transported, evacuated
3. relished, tasted, reveled in, delighted in
4. although, in that, since, as
5. scaled down, reduced size, teeny tiny, small scale
6. communicating, conversing, talking, saying
7. on occasion, once in a while, now and then, time or again
8. after my, when my, my, once my

Answers:
1. bring forth **2.** evacuated **3.** tasted **4.** although **5.** teeny tiny **6.** saying **7.** time or again **8.** my

How'd you do? Spotting the sore thumb is a skill that will serve you well!

Let's try a few that are more challenging and require a bit of context to solve.

E2 The horse whisperer, San Joaqin Balboa, was a contortionist and a criminal lawyer.

Which of the following alternatives to the underlined portion would NOT be acceptable?

F. contortionist. Balboa was also
G. contortionist, he was also
H. contortionist; he was also
J. contortionist. In addition, Balboa was

S *Our odd man out is determined by punctuation. We have three properly punctuated sentences and one comma splice!*
G is the answer!

E3 The students who graduated from the Taco Grande Culinary Institute (TGCI) made their living selling Gordita franchises to itinerant monks.

Which of the following alternatives to the underlined portion would NOT be acceptable?

A. earned their living by
B. made their living from
C. made their living in
D. earned their living

S *Our odd man out is determined by idiomatic phrases. We have three proper idioms and one improper: You do not make your living* ***in*** *something.* ***C is the answer!***

4%
of English questions on the ACT

Order / Placement

Order/Placement questions ask you to move a sentence or a paragraph to its proper place in a passage.

To answer Order/Placement questions, you will need to pay close attention to the logical connections between paragraphs and sentences. Events have to proceed logically; you cannot make an omelet before you buy the eggs! Similarly, you must introduce a pronoun before you use it; you cannot say "**his** car was fast" before you identify who "**he**" is.

Logical Tags

No sentence is an island. Every sentence is linked to the preceding and following sentences by related words which we call "**tags**."

Let's take a look at two simple sentences:

1 I trust my dog.

2 He wouldn't steal.

There is a **link** between these two sentences.

1 I trust **my dog.**

2 **He** wouldn't steal.

I trust **my dog.** **He** wouldn't steal.

He and **my dog** are **tags** that give the sentences their proper order. Focusing on tags is key to solving Order/Placement puzzles! When you are working with Order/Placement questions, think of the entire paragraph as a series of linked puzzle pieces. Let's see that in action:

> I awoke profoundly **hungry**. So I perused the **fridge**, but all I could find was marshmallow cream. I heaped that **marshmallowy goodness** onto a roll and took a bite. Finally I had found a **meal** that suited my refined palate.

One sentence flows logically to the next, thanks to all the tags!
If you move the sentences around, the logical order is disturbed:

> Finally I had found a **meal** that suited my refined palate. I heaped that **marshmallowy goodness** onto a roll and took a bite. I awoke profoundly **hungry**. So I perused the **fridge**, but all I could find was marshmallow cream.

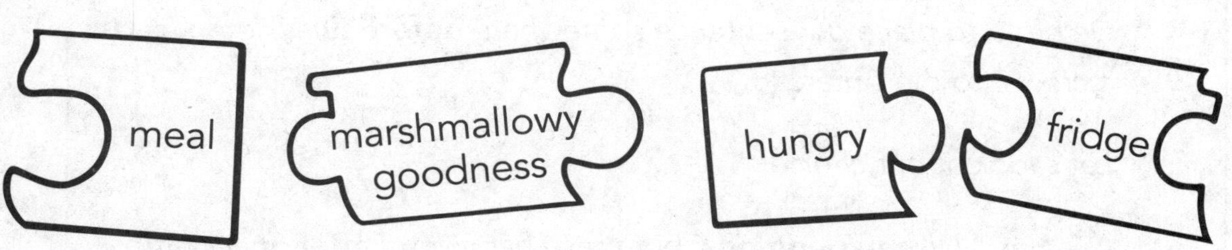

If you come across a confusing paragraph like this on the ACT, an Order/Placement question can't be far off!

You can see that order matters! Tags are the key to figuring out that order.

E1 [1] Born in Dublin in 1874, Ernest Shackleton displayed an early passion for exploration and adventure. [2] As a child he was a voracious reader, which only fueled his far-flung imagination and spirit. [3] Before long he was renting skiffs and voyaging deep into the icy waters of the North Atlantic. [4] By 1909 he led the first expedition to pinpoint the approximate location of the South Magnetic Pole, deep in the heart of the Antarctic. [5] He went on to lead one of the most daring expeditions in history, and today he is celebrated as a model of leadership. [6] These trips increased his confidence and contributed to his growing celebrity, leading to his first commission of an Antarctic bound vessel.

For the sake of the logic and coherence of the preceding paragraph, Sentence 6 should be placed:

A. where it is now.
B. after Sentence 2.
C. after Sentence 3.
D. after Sentence 4.

S *First, let's look at the **tags** in the sentence we're asked to place.*

*The sentence seems to assume that we know what **"these trips"** refers to, so we need to place Sentence 6 **after** a sentence that discusses **trips**. We also see **"leading to his first commission,"** so we need to place our sentence somewhere* **before** *Shackleton leads a crew into the Antarctic.*

Let's look at our choices:

A. *Hm... I like **expeditions**, but these happened **after** Shackleton had his "first commission." The chronology is off here. Lose A.*
B. *Sentence 2 talks about reading, not taking trips. No tag!*
C. *Sentence 3 talks about **early voyages**, which could be our tag for **"these trips!"** This might be a winner.*
D. *Sentence 4 mentions one expedition, but "these trips" is plural!*

*Tags take us home! **C is our answer**.*

Word Order

Some Order/Placement questions deal with the logical order of words within a single sentence.

 I was still waiting on my mother, who had driven to pick up some macaroni and cheese <u>to the store</u> when I complained about having nothing good to eat.

The best placement for the underlined portion would be:

F. where it is now.
G. after the word *mother* (and before the comma).
H. after the word *driven*.
J. after the word *eat* (and before the period).

S *To figure out where "to the store" lives, plug in and try out each answer choice. Let your ear guide you home!*

F. pick up mac-n-cheese to the store
We normally pick things up ***at*** *the store, or maybe* ***from*** *the store. Nix this one.*

G. I was waiting on my mother to the store.
We usually wait on people to ***do*** *something.* ***The store*** *isn't a verb. Cross off B.*

H. who had driven to the store to pick up...
We drive to the store all the time! This one sounds good.

J. I complained about having nothing good to eat to the store.
Unless the store is listening to our complaints, this one is nonsense. Nix it.

Our ear only likes one of these: ***H is our answer.***

Order/Placement Recap

1 **Focus on TAGS** **2** **Listen to your EAR**

3%

of English questions on the ACT

Function of a Passage

You will occasionally be asked to decide whether a passage's author accomplished his or her intention, purpose, or goal.

Function of a Passage questions always follow a **Yes/No + Why** format. This means we can use our tried and true strategy for this structure:

1 Solve the **Yes/No**

2 Focus on the **Rationale**

Let's look at how these questions are worded, ignoring the passage for now:

> Suppose the writer had decided to write an essay about the <u>manner in which Monarch butterflies navigate during their winter migration</u>. Would this essay successfully fulfill the writer's goal?

So our first step is to determine whether the essay achieves the stated goal: to write an essay about the manner in which Monarch butterflies **navigate**.

To answer this question, we can ask a number of supporting questions:

- Does a high percentage of the essay focus on navigation?
- Does every paragraph mention navigation, or just one out of six?
- Is navigation introduced early in the essay?
- Does the conclusion circle back to navigation?

The more "yes" answers you have to these questions, the more likely it is that the essay achieves its stated goal. Let's read the passage to get some answers.

The Monarch butterfly is perhaps the best known of all North American butterflies. The fluttering of its tawny-orange, black-tipped wings can be seen from kitchen windows across the country. Up close, the female Monarch can be identified from the thick veins of black running across its 9-centimeter wingspan. The slightly larger males are distinguished by white spots on the underside of their wings. These spots are actually scales, known as the androcronium, which release pheromones during the breeding season to attract potential mates.

Adult Monarchs are not picky when it comes to food. They will feed on the nectar of just about any plant in your backyard—including wild carrot, lilac, alfalfa, and their very own "butterfly weed." Male Monarchs will even resort to an aptly-named process called "mud-puddling," wherein the butterfly absorbs moisture and minerals by lying in damp soil or wet gravel.

This process is behind the Monarch's attraction to humans on hot, sweaty days, and is also the reason butterflies are sometimes found lying in oil stains on driveways in the summer. [1]

1. Suppose the writer had decided to write an essay about the manner in which Monarch butterflies navigate during their winter migration. Would this essay successfully fulfill the writer's goal?

A. Yes, because the essay explains the manner in which the butterflies travel during their winter journey.

B. Yes, because the essay details the breeding habits of Monarch butterflies, which gives the reader an understanding of how the butterfly survives and thrives in the wild.

C. No, because the essay does not explain the structure of Monarch butterflies' wings, so the reader has no basis for understanding migration habits.

D. No, because the essay limits itself to describing the physical appearance and eating habits of Monarch butterflies.

S 1 Solve the **Yes/No**

*Let's get some answers! Does most of the essay talk about navigation? Hm... Do we even **see** the word "navigate" anywhere? Synonyms of "navigate"? It doesn't look like it.*
*We have a **No** answer on our hands! Eliminate choices A and B.*

2 Focus on the **Rationale**

So we are looking for a good explanation for why the passage does not fulfill the goal of discussing navigation patterns. We already have our own answer to this: the passage never mentions migration!

Choice D gets it: the essay only describes the appearance and eating habits of butterflies. Nothing about migration.

D is our answer!

Function of a Passage Recap

1. Underline the **goal**
2. Scan the passage for **synonyms**
3. Determine the **Yes/No** response
4. Eliminate the incorrect **rationale**

ENGLISH PRACTICE 5

9 Minutes—15 Questions

This passage tests only the grammar concepts that you have learned up to this point. Practice these concepts in the context of a full passage.

Since the ACT will give you 45 minutes for 5 passages, this passage should take you about **9 minutes.**

PASSAGE V

> The following paragraphs may or may not be in the most logical order. Each paragraph is numbered in brackets, and question 14 will ask you to choose where Paragraph 3 should most logically be placed.

Time Travel

[1]

For nearly as long as humans have had a concept of "the past" and "the future," we've imagined what it might be like to travel in time. These fantasies have long appeared in literature, even in ancient myths. For example, a Hindu tale describes a king who journeys to heaven. To (1) meet the creator, but when he returns to Earth, eons have passed and society has changed completely. Similarly, the Japanese have an ancient legend about a fisherman who visits the Dragon God in a watery kingdom, only to discover upon his return under the sea (2) that three centuries have passed. These types of tales might well be considered the ancestors of contemporary science fiction.

1. **A.** NO CHANGE
   B. king who journeys to heaven to
   C. king, who journeys to heaven, to
   D. king who journeys to heaven, to

2. The best placement for the underlined portion would be:
   F. where it is now.
   G. after the word fisherman.
   H. after the word kingdom.
   J. after the word passed.

[2]

In 1895, H. G. Wells published his influential novel *The Time Machine*, and in doing so created an entirely new genre. [3]

During this new era of fast-paced technological progress, many <u>previously unimaginable</u> [4] things now seemed possible. At the same time, the field of theoretical physics took a major leap, with Einstein's breakthroughs in special and general relativity. While many early time travel tales depicted the protagonist being transported <u>by</u> [5] magic, now science fiction authors explored time travel tales powered by technology.

[3]

Another well-known time travel paradox is the predestination <u>paradox. In this scenario,</u> [6] the time traveler's actions in the past create the circumstances that lead to the traveler's presence there in the first place. For example, the traveler intends to stop

3. The writer wants to add a sentence here that would evoke the society's fascination with time travel. Given all are true, which of the following would most effectively accomplish this?

A. The book was a bestseller for years on end.
B. Time travel seized the public's imagination.
C. H. G. Wells was just the first of many storytellers to come.
D. Less than a decade later, the first "flying machine" took to the air.

4. **F.** NO CHANGE
G. previous unimaginably
H. previously unimaginably
J. previous unimaginable

5. Which of the following alternatives to the underlined portion would be LEAST acceptable?

A. with
B. through
C. via
D. amid

6. Which of the following alternatives to the underlined portion would NOT be acceptable?

F. paradox, a scenario in which
G. paradox; in this scenario,
H. paradox, in which
J. paradox, in this scenario,

a war from occurring, but his or her actions actually launch[7] the war!

7. Which of the following alternatives to the underlined portion would be LEAST acceptable?

A. set off
B. start
C. begin
D. hurl

This one[8] is also referred to as "a causal loop."

8. F. NO CHANGE
G. And this
H. This paradox
J. This is the one that

[4]

But whether or not time travel is physically possible, it does seem to create some contradictions. One of the most well-known and famous ones of these[9] is called "The Grandfather Paradox." The thought experiment goes something like this: What if you were able to travel back in time and stop your grandfather from ever meeting your grandmother, thus ensuring that you were never born? If you were never born, you could never travel back in time. But if a person like[10] you never traveled back in time, you would still be alive, and you could travel back in time… where you would stop your grandfather from meeting your grandmother! [11]

9. A. NO CHANGE
B. well-known, famous ones of these
C. well-known and famous
D. famous

10. F. NO CHANGE
G. someone such as
H. someone like
J. OMIT the underlined portion

11. Which of the following sentences, if added here, would best reflect the point made in this paragraph?

A. The paradox creates a contradictory loop where each action erases itself.
B. But who would want to do such a thing?
C. The idea of time travel offers many such thought experiments.
D. This paradox can be extended to other situations, too.

[5]

Some people believe that because of the paradoxes involved, time travel must be <u>impossible, others hold</u> [12] that there must be some way to resolve the paradox.

<u>Regardless,</u> [13] fascinating thought experiments such as these definitely make great fuel for science fiction stories and films, from *Back to the Future* to *The Butterfly Effect.* Whether or not time travel will ever be possible, it sure does make for a good story! [14]

12. **F.** NO CHANGE
G. impossible, while others hold
H. impossible. Others holding
J. impossible, others holding

13. Which of the following alternatives to the underlined portion would NOT be acceptable?

A. Nonetheless,
B. In any case,
C. Without regard to,
D. Nevertheless,

14. For the sake of the logic and coherence of this essay, Paragraph 3 should be placed:

F. where it is now.
G. after Paragraph 1.
H. after Paragraph 4.
J. after Paragraph 5.

Question 15 asks about the preceding passage as a whole

15. Suppose the writer had intended to write a brief essay discussing the role of time travel in literature.Would this essay successfully fulfill the writer's goal?

A. Yes, because it focuses exclusively on the evolution of the time travel genre in science fiction.
B. Yes, because it describes how Einstein's research could make time travel possible.
C. No, because the essay focuses on society's interest in time travel and its paradoxes.
D. No, because the essay focuses on scientific evidence for and against the possibility of time travel.

END OF PRACTICE PASSAGE 5
ANSWERS AVAILABLE ON PAGE 186

The English Short List

Exaggerate the pause!

1 Punctuation

Listen for missing/unnecessary **commas**.
Semicolons are intimately connected full-stops.
Colons **introduce** things: explanations and lists.

2 Redundancy

When in doubt, **cut it out!**

Once is enough!

3 Improper Verb Tense

What happened in the past **stays in the past!**
Check **other verbs** in the sentence for proper tense.

4 Subject/Verb Agreement

What's the subject?
Cross out **prepositional phrases** in the way.

Where's the verb?

5 Fragments

Beware the wicked **which**!
-ING is no good!

6 Pronoun Error

I do things; things happen to **me**.

7 Possession

Apostrophes show possession;
It's is an exception.

8 Run-ons

Four ways to fix a run-on:

1) add a **period**
2) add a **semicolon**
3) add a **conjunction**
3) make one clause **dependent**

9 Adjectives & Adverbs

Adjectives modify nouns.
Adverbs modify **verbs** and **adjectives.**

Adverbs carry the -ly

10 Misplaced Modifiers

Modifiers touch the noun they modify.

*Keep your friends close, and your **modifiers closer!***

11 Rhetorical Skills

Stay on topic and **keep the flow!**
Remove all **distractions**, and don't add any!
Circle your task and stick to it!
When ordering sentences, look for **logical tags.**

*When dealing with a LEAST or a NOT, look for the **odd one out!***

English Mantras

Short is sweet.

Trust your ear!

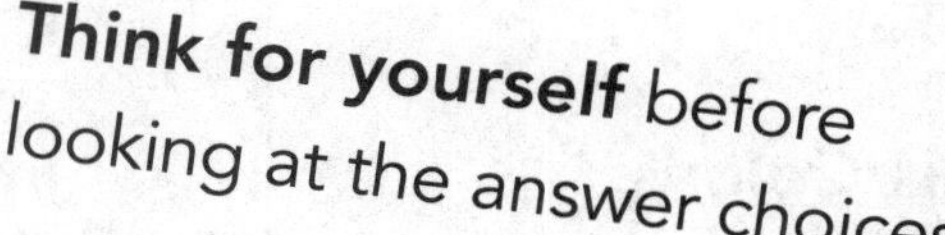

Think for yourself before looking at the answer choices

Stay on topic
Keep the flow

Let the answer choices guide you to the error.

Always read in context!
Read the full sentence when plugging-in.

Actively read the questions.
Get your **pencil moving**!

English Answers

Commas

1. C
2. G
3. D
4. H
5. B
6. F
7. D
8. G

Semis/Colons

1. B
2. J
3. B
4. G
5. B
6. F
7. B
8. H
9. D
10. J

Illogical Connectors

1. D
2. G
3. D
4. F
5. B
6. F
7. D
8. H
9. A
10. H
11. A
12. J
13. C
14. J

Redundancy

1. D
2. J
3. A
4. G
5. C
6. J
7. A
8. G

Improper Verb Tense

1. C
2. G
3. D
4. F
5. D
6. G
7. A
8. G
9. B
10. F
11. C
12. F
13. A
14. G
15. D

Fragments

1. B
2. J
3. C
4. J
5. C
6. G
7. C
8. J
9. D
10. J

Possession

1. D
2. H
3. D
4. G
5. C
6. J
7. A

Brevity

1. D
2. J
3. D
4. J
5. B
6. H
7. D

Pronoun Error

1. C
2. J
3. C
4. F
5. B
6. H
7. B
8. H

Run-Ons

1. C
2. G
3. A
4. G
5. D
6. J
7. A
8. G

Subject Verb Agreement

1. B
2. H
3. B
4. J
5. B
6. G
7. A
8. G
9. B
10. J

Prepositions

1. C
2. F
3. B
4. H
5. D
6. J

Vocabulary in Context

1. B
2. G
3. D
4. G
5. J

Misplaced Modifiers

1. D
2. G
3. B
4. J
5. B

Adjective/Adverb

1. D
2. F
3. A
4. J
5. B
6. H

Parallelism

1. B
2. H
3. A
4. J
5. B

Practice Passage 1

1. D
2. G
3. B
4. J
5. B
6. F
7. C
8. F
9. D
10. F
11. D
12. J
13. C
14. H
15. C

Practice Passage 2

1. B
2. G
3. A
4. J
5. D
6. F
7. D
8. H
9. D
10. F
11. D
12. J
13. B
14. F
15. C

Practice Passage 3

1. B
2. J
3. D
4. J
5. B
6. F
7. B
8. G
9. B
10. H
11. A
12. G
13. B
14. J
15. C

Practice Passage 4

1. D
2. J
3. A
4. G
5. B
6. J
7. B
8. G
9. B
10. J
11. A
12. D
13. G
14. G
15. A

Practice Passage 5

1. B
2. H
3. B
4. F
5. D
6. J
7. D
8. H
9. D
10. J
11. A
12. G
13. C
14. H
15. C

$V = \frac{1}{2} \frac{4\pi r^3}{3}$
$V = \pi r^2 h$
A
B
C
H
W
H_2
W_2
l_1
l_2
30°
90°
110°
145°
x | f(x)
2 | −1
4 | −1/2
8 | −1/4
16 | −1/8
D= r · t
X
Y
c^2
b^2
a^2
3
$C = 2\pi r$
$A = \pi r^2$

MATH

Secret to Math

WRITE EVERYTHING DOWN

Seriously.

Many struggling students need to **write** more, not know more.

The biggest difference between students who get an average score on Math and students who get an exceptional score is the quality of their written work.

No magic beans or brain surgery required. If you fix your work, you will unleash the potential that's been there all along.

The solution bubbles after each example will model perfect work. Check your work against ours to improve!

Math Problem Type Breakdown

Geometry 35%

Perimeter, Area, and Volume	9%
Triangles	5%
Angles	4%
Equation of a Line	3%
Circles	3%
Coordinate Systems	3%
Proportional Shapes	2%
Equation of a Circle	1%
Number Lines	1%
Slope	1%
Diagonals and Symmetry	1%
Reflections	1%
Shifting Graphs	1%

Algebra 35%

Complex Word Problems	7%
Basic Algebra	6%
Polynomials	4%
Charts, Tables, and Graphs	3%
Mean, Median, and Mode	3%
D=RT	2%
Functions	2%
Min/Max	2%
Graphing Information	2%
Logarithm	1%
Composite Functions	1%
Wacked-Out Functions	1%
Direct/Inverse Proportions	1%

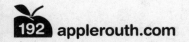

Math Problem Type Breakdown

Arithmetic	**25%**
Exponents	4%
Inequalities	3%
Fractions	3%
Percent	2%
Absolute Value	2%
Sequences	2%
Ratios	2%
Probability	2%
Combinations and Permutations	1%
Matrix	1%
Scientific Notation	1%
Logic Tests	1%
Square Roots	1%

Trigonometry	**6%**
SohCahToa	3%
Trig Identities	1%
Working with Formulas	1%
Unit Circle	1%
Graphing Sin/Cos	<1%

Practice Problem Difficulties

After every section, you will find practice problems to test your newfound skills. Each problem is marked with 1 to 3 stars, indicating the difficulty of that problem.

★ *Low-level problems (#'s 1-20 on the ACT)*

★★ *Mid-level problems (#'s 21-40 on the ACT)*

★★★ *High-level problems (#'s 41-60 on the ACT)*

Art of Translation

Wordy problems are very common on the ACT. These problems depend almost entirely on correct translation. If you can correctly turn the words into math, the math is pretty easy.

Here is a quick rundown of common terms and their math equivalents:

Word	Math Meaning
What, how much, a number	Some variable (x)
Is, was, equals	=
Sum, increase, more than, greater than	Add (+)
Subtract, less than, exceeds	Subtract (–)
Difference	Subtract (–)
Of, times	Multiply (×)
Product	Multiply (×)
Divisible by, divided by, out of, per	Divide (÷)
Percent (%)	Multiply by $\frac{1}{100}$

Remember the secret to math: **write everything down!**

With these problems, the best thing to do is mark out the words as you translate them into math.

E1 The product of two positive integers is 30 and their difference is one. What is the sum of the two numbers?

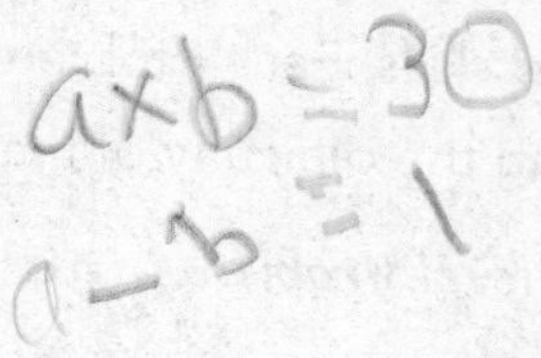

S 1 Circle what you're solving for

The product of two positive integers is 30 and their difference is one. **What is the sum** of the two numbers?

2 Translate piece-by-piece, marking out as you go

~~The product of two positive integers~~	~~is 30~~
$a \times b$	**= 30**

$a \times b = 30$

and ~~their difference~~	~~is one.~~
$a - b$	**= 1**

$a - b = 1$

~~What is~~	~~the sum of the two numbers?~~
? =	**$a + b$**

$a + b = ?$

From here we have a choice of two approaches. We can solve this problem algebraically or work around the algebra. Let's consider both approaches, starting with the shortcut.

3 Option 1: Shortcut

We need two factors of 30 that are one unit apart.

$a \times b = 30$
$a - b = 1$

*Let's find our factors of **30**:*

1×30
2×15
3×10
5×6 *bingo!*

BINGO!

5 and 6 it is! Now we just need the sum:

$5 + 6 = 11$ *That's our answer!*

4 Option 2: Substitution

If we didn't see the shortcut, we can tackle the algebra directly, using some good old fashioned ***substitution****. We'll use one equation to get a* ***replacement for a****.*

$$a - b = 1$$
$$\boxed{a = 1 + b}$$

Now we substitute a's replacement into the other equation.

$$(a) \times b = 30$$
$$(1 + b) \times b = 30$$
$$b + b^2 = 30$$
$$b^2 + b - 30 = 0$$
$$(b + 6)(b - 5) = 0$$
$$b = -6 \quad \boxed{b = 5}$$

We need a positive integer.

Substitute 5 for b in the ***original equation****.*

$$a - b = 1$$
$$a - 5 = 1$$
$$\boxed{a = 6}$$

Now add our a and b.

$$a + b = 5 + 6 = \textcircled{11}$$

This route is definitely longer, but tougher problems might not have a shortcut. For those problems, careful substitution is your best friend!

E2 If a given number is divided by x and the result is 6 times the original number, what is the value of x?

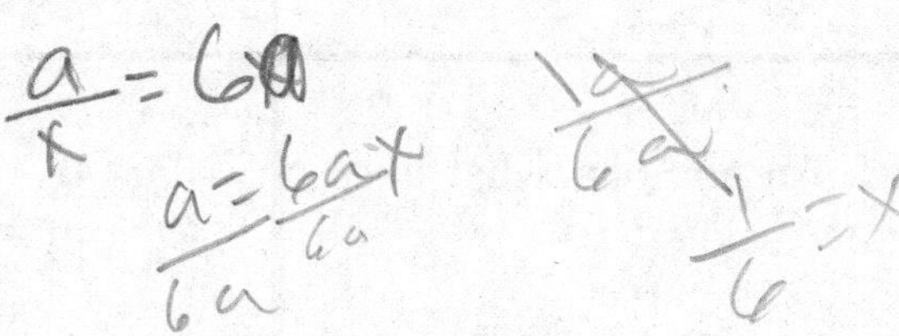

S **1** Circle what you're solving for

If a given number is divided by x and the result is 6 times the original number, **what is the value of x ?**

2 Translate piece-by-piece, marking out as you go

~~If a given number is divided by x~~	~~the result is~~	~~6 times the original number~~
$\frac{a}{x}$	=	**6a**

So we have our formula: $\frac{a}{x} = 6a$

We are solving for x, so let's isolate x:

$$a = 6ax$$

$$\frac{a}{6a} = x$$

$$\frac{1}{6} = x$$

Always double-check what you circled to make sure that you are solving the correct problem.

Art of Translation Practice Problems

1. If six is three-fourths of a number, what is the number?

A. -6
B. 4
C. 2
D. 8
E. 10

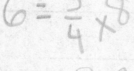

★

2. If half of a number is equal to 5 more than twice the number, what is the number?

F. $-\frac{10}{3}$
G. $-\frac{3}{10}$
H. 0
J. $\frac{3}{10}$
K. $\frac{10}{3}$

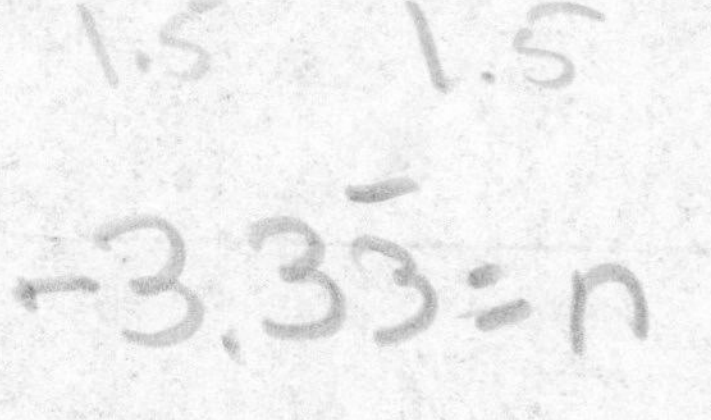

★

3. If 7 more than three times a number is equal to 25, what is half the number?

A. 2
B. 3
C. 4
D. 6
E. $3\frac{1}{2}$

★

4. a is the sum of $2b$ and 3 more than b. If $b = 4$, then a is

F. 8
G. 9
H. 15
J. 18
K. 19

★

5. A painter charges \$35 per hour for each hour he works on a house plus a one-time fee of \$45. If he charges \$220 after painting a house, how many hours did he work?

A. $4\frac{1}{3}$

B. 5

C. $5\frac{1}{2}$

D. $6\frac{1}{3}$

E. 7

★★

6. If the sum of one-half of a certain number and one-third of the same number is 30, what is the number?

F. 20
G. 25
H. 30
J. 36
K. 40

★

7. If 6 more than a certain number is tripled the result is 66. What is the number?

A. 11
B. 16
C. 22
D. 33
E. 60

★★

8. If s is t less than four times u, what is t in terms of s and u ?

F. $4u + s$

G. $4u - s$

H. $\frac{1}{4}u + s$

J. $\frac{1}{4}u - s$

K. $\frac{u+s}{4}$

★★

Working Backwards

There are times when you attempt to solve a problem on the ACT, and you get stuck. When you cannot make any progress tackling a problem head-on, a smart approach is to work backwards from the answer choices.

E1 John has x pieces of candy in his pocket. He gives half of the candies to Kerri, and one-third of the remaining candies to Lori. If he is left with 10 candies in his pocket, what is the value of x ?

A. 60
B. 50
C. 40
D. 30
E. 20

S *We could solve this using algebra, but we can also solve this by working backwards. We only have 5 choices; we know one of these has to be the answer. If we plug each answer choice into the problem, we can determine which one works.*

Notice that the answer choices are in order from largest to smallest. It's a good strategy to start in the middle with choice **C or H.**

C. *So John has* **40** *pieces and gives half (20) to Kerri, leaving him with 20 pieces himself. He then goes and gives away one third:*

$$\frac{1}{3}(20) \approx 7 \longrightarrow 20 - 7 = \boxed{13} \text{ Too high!}$$

So if he starts with **40** *pieces, John ends up with* **13**, *not* **10**. *We need a smaller starting number; A and B are out. Let's try D.*

D. *If John has* **30** *pieces and gives half (15) to Kerri, then he will be left with 15 pieces himself. He then gives away the third:*

$$\frac{1}{3}(15) = 5 \longrightarrow 15 - 5 = (10) \text{ Yeah!}$$

That was much easier than using algebra, and possibly even faster! In 2 steps we have our answer: choice (**D**)*!*

Notice the power of working backwards! As soon as you decide that **C** is too big or small, you've narrowed it down to only two choices!

E2 If $|8 - 3x| \geq 40$, which of the following could equal x?

F. −10
G. −2
H. 0
J. 9
K. 16

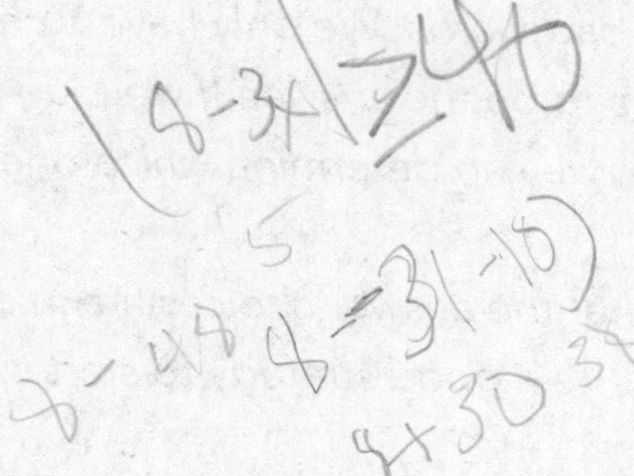

Always circle what you're solving for!

S *Again — let's start from the middle, at* **H.**

x = ?

H. $|8 - 3(0)| \geq 40$

$|8| \geq 40$ *Nope! We need a larger number!*

J. $|8 - 3(9)| \geq 40$

$|8 - 27| \geq 40$

$|-19| \geq 40$ *Nope! Try again.*

(K.) $|8 - 3(16)| \geq 40,$

$|8 - 48| \geq 40$

$|-40| \geq 40$ *Yes! That's our answer!*

Working Backwards Practice Problems

1. A kindergarten class wants to buy a $64 aquarium for the classroom. If the teacher and students agree to split the cost such that the teacher pays three times as much as the students, how much, in dollars, should the teacher pay?

A. 16
B. 32
C. 40
D. 48
E. 56

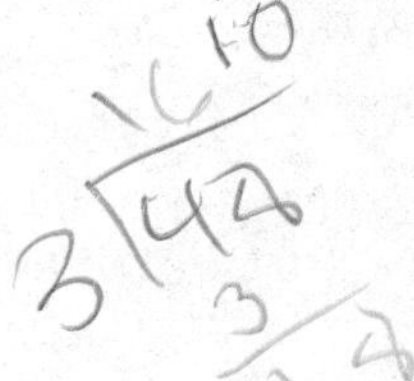

★

2. John is 6 years older than Mark. 6 years ago John was twice as old as Mark. How old is John today?

F. 6
G. 9
H. 12
J. 18
K. 24

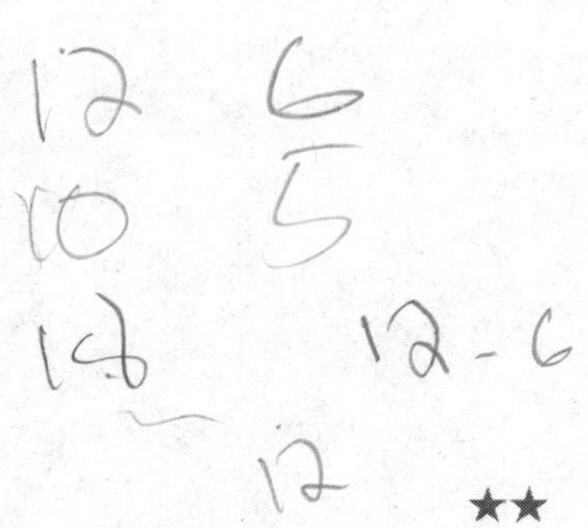

★★

3. A drawer, filled with only red and blue socks, contains 20 socks. If John adds one blue and one red sock to the drawer, the ratio of red to blue socks in the drawer will increase. What is the greatest number of red socks that could originally have been in the drawer?

A. 5
B. 9
C. 10
D. 11
E. 19

★★

4. Jamal has a bag of marbles. He gives exactly $\frac{1}{3}$ of his marbles to Isaac, and has $\frac{2}{3}$ of his original number of marbles remaining. If Jamal is able to repeat this action at least 3 more times without breaking any marbles into pieces, how many marbles could he have started with?

F. 12
G. 18
H. 24
J. 57
K. 81

★★

5. Scott has exactly twice as many trading cards as Todd. Ryan has exactly four times as many trading cards as Scott. If the three of them have fewer than 100 trading cards combined, what is the maximum number of trading cards Todd could have?

A. 6
B. 9
C. 10
D. 12
E. 18

★★

6. A Spanish teacher wants to have a party for her students, and she needs to buy candy to put in the piñata. She buys $100 worth of 2 types of candy. One type of candy costs $0.10 a piece and another type costs $0.25 a piece. If she bought 550 pieces of candy in total, how many pieces of the more expensive candy did she buy?

F. 200
G. 240
H. 280
J. 300
K. 380

★★

7. Two identical 6-inch deep water buckets drain at uniform rates of 1inch per hour. If bucket one begins draining at 12 p.m., and bucket two begins draining at 2 p.m., at what time will bucket two have exactly five times as much water as bucket one?

A. 4:00 p.m.
B. 4:30 p.m.
C. 5:00 p.m.
D. 5:30 p.m.
E. 6:00 p.m.

★★★

Properties of Numbers

In order to tackle ACT math questions, you must learn some basic number properties and definitions.

Before we jump into the problem types, let's learn the language of ACT math.

Definitions and Important Concepts

Positive Integers: Whole numbers greater than zero: 1, 2, 3, 4, 5, ...

Negative Integers: Whole numbers less than zero: – 1, – 2, – 3, – 4, ...

Even Integers: Integers with units digit: 0, 2, 4, 6, or 8.

Odd Integers: Integers with units digit: 1, 3, 5, 7, or 9.

Zero: An integer that is neither positive nor negative.

Irrational Number: Infinite decimals (3.14159...) or imperfect roots ($\sqrt{5}$).

Imaginary Number: The number "i" is equal to the **square root of –1.**

Undefined: Anything **divided by zero** is undefined, bad, impossible.

Rational numbers are all numbers that are not irrational.

Real numbers are all numbers that are not imaginary.

Let's see how the ACT can test this vocab directly.

E1 If n is an odd integer, which of the following must be an odd integer?

A. $n - 1$
B. $n + 1$
C. $2n$
D. $3n + 1$
E. $4n + 1$

If the problem says "must be," you can usually pick a number, plug-in, and eliminate wrong answers.

S *Easy as pie. Just plug in a number! The problem says that* **n** *must be odd, so let's try* **3**.

A. **3** – 1 = 2 *Two is even, so this one is out.*

B. **3** + 1 = 4 *This one is out, too.*

C. 2(**3**) = 6 *Nope.*

D. 3(**3**) + 1 = 10 *Not so much.*

(E.) 4(**3**) + 1 = 13 *Now we're talking!*

The Mighty Decimal Point

The digits of a number have different names according to their distance from the decimal point.

E2 Given the number: **5,947.382**

List the:

_____ Thousandths digit

_____ Tens digit

_____ Ones/Units digit

_____ Tenths digit

_____ Hundredths digit

_____ Hundreds digit

_____ Thousands digit

S

2 Thousandths digit

4 Tens digit

7 Ones/Units digit

3 Tenths digit

8 Hundredths digit

9 Hundreds digit

5 Thousands digit

E3 How many three-digit integers have the hundreds digit equal to 2 and the units digit equal to 5?

F. 9
G. 10
H. 20
J. 190
K. 200

S *The simplest thing to do here is to list the numbers that satisfy the requirements:*

2 for the **hundreds**
? for the **tens**
5 for the **units**

2_5	
205	255
215	265
225	275
235	285
245	295

We have **10** *numbers in our set, so our answer is* ***G.***

Prime Numbers

Prime numbers are positive integers greater than **1** that are divisible by only **1** and themselves.

E4 List the first 10 prime numbers.

S *2, 3, 5, 7, 11, 13, 17, 19, 23, 29*

E5 What is the sum of the smallest prime number greater than 10 and the smallest prime number greater than 30?

A. 42
B. 44
C. 46
D. 48
E. 50

S *The smallest prime number greater than 10 is 11.*
The smallest prime number greater than 30 is 31.

11 + 31 = (42), ***A.***

Inclusive Problems

Inclusive simply means ***count both end points***. If you're asked to find the number of integers "between 300 and 200 inclusive," you might immediately think, "300 – 200 = 100, so there are 100," but there are actually **101** because you have to count both of the end points.

To find the number of terms between two points, simply subtract the end points and add one.

0 to 9 is 10 integers!

Try it with 10 and 20 to prove it to yourself:

10, 11, 12, 13, 14, 15, 16, 17, 18, 19, 20

Count 'em: not 10 integers, but 11!

E6 How many integers in the set of all integers from 100 to 300, inclusive, are multiples of 10?

F. 20
G. 21
H. 22
J. 100
K. 200

S *You can solve this multiple ways. You could do the math:*

$$300 - 100 = 200; \frac{200}{10} = 20; 20 + 1 = \textcircled{21}, \text{ G.}$$

Or you could count the multiples of 10 in smaller groups:

$$\frac{100\text{-}190}{10} + \frac{200\text{-}290}{10} + \frac{300}{1} = \textcircled{21}, \text{ G.}$$

Factors and Multiples

Prime factors are prime numbers that divide into a number. A **factor tree** is an easy way to find prime factors.

E7 What is the greatest prime factor of 52?

S *To create a factor tree, start by dividing by the smallest positive integer (greater than 1) that will go evenly into 52. Because 52 is an even number, start with 2.*

*Then, continue to divide by the **smallest prime number** possible until you have a prime number at the bottom of each branch.*

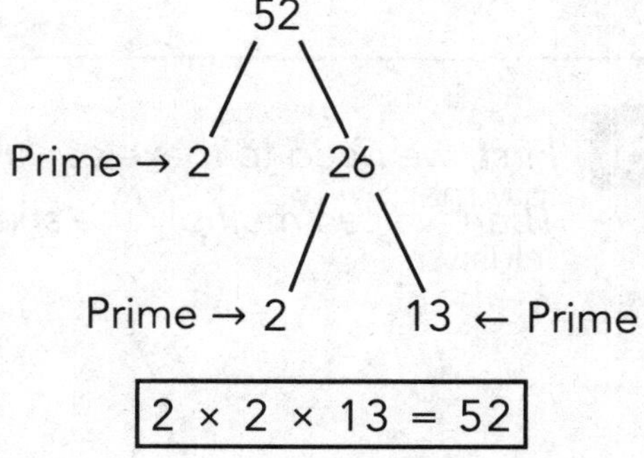

*We're asked for the **greatest prime factor**, so our answer is* (13).

Least Common Multiple

The Least Common Multiple (LCM) of two integers is the smallest number that both integers will divide into evenly.

E8 What is the least common multiple of 9 and 15?

S *All you have to do with LCM problems is list multiples until you find a match:*

	×1	×2	×3	×4	×5
9:	9	18	27	36	(45)
15:	15	30	(45)		

Voilà! We have our Least Common Multiple: **(45)**

Greatest Common Factor

The "GCF" is the largest integer that will divide into a set of numbers.

E9 What is the greatest common factor of 18 and 12?

Don't confuse GCF with the BFG, the Big Friendly Giant.

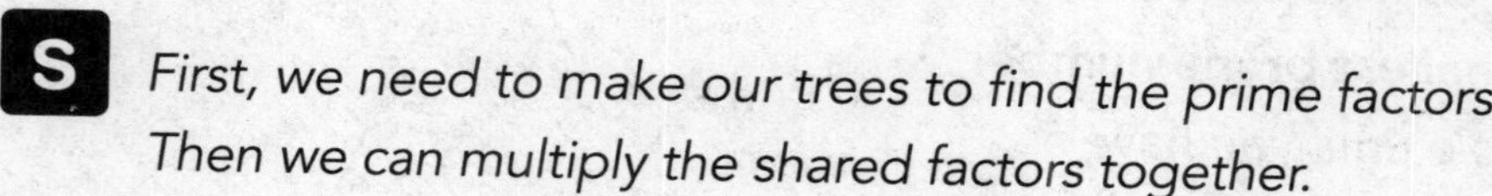

S *First, we need to make our trees to find the prime factors. Then we can multiply the shared factors together.*

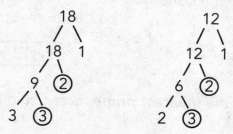

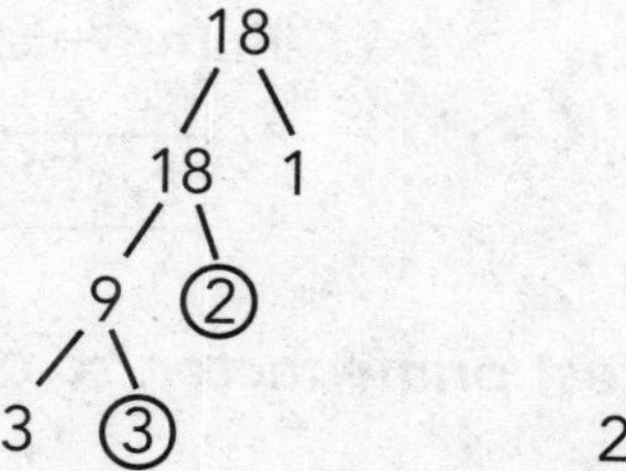

12 → 12, 1; 12 → 6, (2); 6 → 2, (3)

Our GCF is : $2 \times 3 =$ (6)

Properties of Numbers Practice Problems

1. If the number 4.06 is rounded to the nearest tenth and then tripled, what is the resulting number?

A. 4.1
B. 4.2
C. 8.2
D. 12.2
E. 12.3

★

2. A number was rounded to 23.7. Which of the following could have been the number before it was rounded?

F. 23.000
G. 23.604
H. 23.709
J. 23.760
K. 24.000

★

3. Which of the following sets represents all positive factors of 12 ?

A. 1, 12
B. 2, 4, 6
C. 2, 3, 4, 6
D. 12, 24, 36
E. 1, 2, 3, 4, 6, 12

★

4. What is the least common multiple of 30, 18, and 12 ?

F. 20
G. 60
H. 132
J. 180
K. 6,480

★★

5. If m and n are positive integers, and $(m + n)(m)$ is even, which of the following must be true?

A. If m is odd, then n is odd.
B. If m is odd, then n is even.
C. If m is even, then n is even.
D. If m is even, then n is odd.
E. m must be even.

★★★

6. What is the least positive integer that is divisible by the numbers 1 through 6, inclusive?

F. 21
G. 30
H. 40
J. 60
K. 120

★

7. For all positive integers *x*, which of the following is the greatest common factor of $216x$ and $120x$?

A. 6
B. 24
C. x
D. $6x$
E. $24x$

★★

8. What is the least common multiple of 90, 80, and 70 ?

F. 80
G. 120
H. 240
J. 5,040
K. 504,000

★★

9. Which of the following is not a factor of $5^3 - 5^2$?

A. 2
B. 3
C. 4
D. 5
E. 10

★

10. The sum of the prime numbers between 0 and 10 is how much less than the sum of prime numbers between 10 and 15 ?

F. 6
G. 7
H. 9
J. 11
K. 13

★★

11. Let S be the set of all integers between one and twenty, and let x be a prime number in set S such that $2 \leq x < 10$. Then, x could be equal to how many different integers?

A. 3
B. 4
C. 5
D. 6
E. 8

★★

12. For how many integer values of x is $50 > 2x - 7 > 30$ true?

F. 8
G. 9
H. 10
J. 11
K. 20

13. Which of the following complex numbers is a sum of $\sqrt{-8}$ and $\sqrt{-32}$?

A. $-2\sqrt{2}$
B. $-4\sqrt{2}$
C. $2i\sqrt{2}$
D. $4i\sqrt{2}$
E. $6i\sqrt{2}$

14. From the set of odd integers between 8 and 18, how many distinct pairs of different numbers have a sum of 26 ?

F. 1
G. 2
H. 3
J. 4
K. 5

★★

15. Set M contains the first 50 positive integers. A new set N is formed by multiplying all the integers in set M by 3 and subtracting 5 from each integer. What is the difference between the greatest number in set N and the greatest number in set M ?

A. 50
B. 65
C. 85
D. 95
E. 145

16. If x, y, and z are consecutive integers, and $x < y < z$, which of the following could be the units digit of y if the units digit of the product of x and z is 4 ?

F. 3
G. 4
H. 5
J. 6
K. 7

★★★

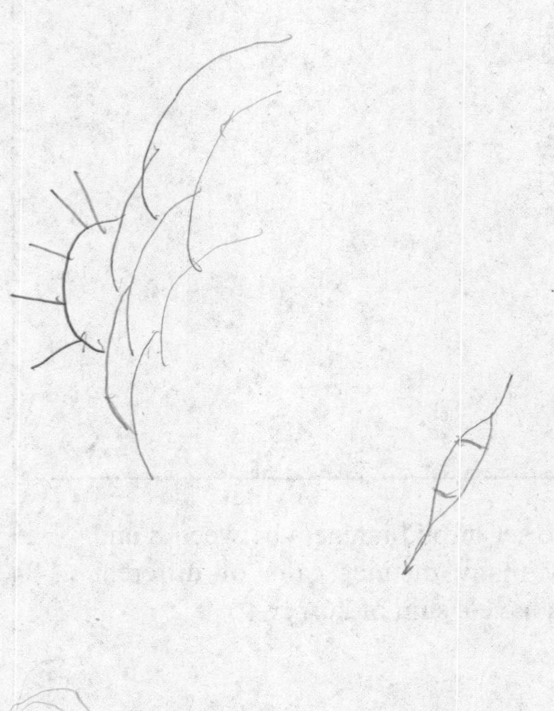

Picking Numbers

2%
of all math questions on the ACT

Algebra questions often ask for an answer in terms of one or more variables. If all answer choices contain the same variables, you can tackle the problem in two ways:

Strategy 1: Algebra

Solve the problem head-on using **algebra**. This method often takes more time and exposes you to a greater risk of careless errors.

Strategy 2: Picking Numbers

Solve the problem by **picking numbers**. This strategy gets rid of the algebra; all you have to do is add, subtract, multiply, and divide. Also, this method is often faster than the algebraic method.

Let's try strategy 2, Picking Numbers:

E1 The sum of two positive consecutive integers is x. In terms of x, what is the value of the smaller of these two integers?

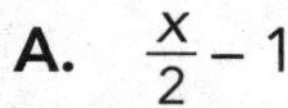

A. $\frac{x}{2} - 1$

B. $\frac{x-1}{2}$

C. $\frac{x}{2}$

D. $\frac{x}{2} + 2$

E. $\frac{x}{2} + 1$

Remember, when you see the same variable in each answer choice, it's picking numbers time!

S 1 Write **what we know** about our numbers

Our numbers are:

1. **Positive** – *no negatives allowed!*
2. **Consecutive** – *2 and 3; 17 and 18; 98 and 99, etc.*
3. **Integers** – *no fractions or decimals allowed!*

*We also know that our numbers **add up to x**.*

2 **Pick** Numbers

As long as we follow the rules, we can pick almost anything!
*Let's keep it simple and make our smaller integer **2**.*
*This would make our larger, consecutive integer **3**.*

Smaller integer + Larger integer = x

$2 + 3 = x$

$\boxed{5 = x}$

Put a box around the variables that you have picked.

Circle what you are solving for.

3 **Plug in** and solve

Now we can simply plug our x-value into the answer choices.

$\boxed{x = 5}$ **target:** (2)

A. $\frac{x}{2} - 1 \longrightarrow \frac{5}{2} - 1 = 2.5 - 1 = 1.5$ *Nope, not 2!*

B. $\frac{x-1}{2} \longrightarrow \frac{5-1}{2} = \frac{4}{2} = \mathbf{2}$ *That's our target!*

C. $\frac{x}{2} \longrightarrow \frac{5}{2} = 2.5$ *Nope!*

D. $\frac{x}{2} + 2 \longrightarrow \frac{5}{2} + 2 = 2.5 + 2 = 4.5$ *Nope!*

E. $\frac{x}{2} + 1 \longrightarrow \frac{5}{2} + 1 = 2.5 + 1 = 3.5$ *Nope!*

*There's only one choice that hits our target of **2**. Our answer is* (B).

Guidelines for Picking Numbers:

1 **Do NOT pick 0 or 1**. These numbers do strange things to equations and functions that no other numbers do. They can cause confusion, so it's best to steer clear of them.

2 If you are solving an equation like $x + y = z$, it's better to pick numbers for the two variables on the same side and **SOLVE for the loner**. So pick $x = 2$ and $y = 3$, then solve for $z = 5$ and go from there!

3 Pick numbers that **follow the rules** of the problem. For example: in a problem using the equation $x + y = z$, you couldn't pick 2 for x, 3 for y, and 6 for z: $2 + 3 \neq 6$.

Pick numbers that do NOT appear in the problem. This will minimize confusion.

4 If you pick numbers and two answer choices give you the correct answer, you must pick different numbers and **repeat the process** with the answer choices that worked the first time (this doesn't happen very often).

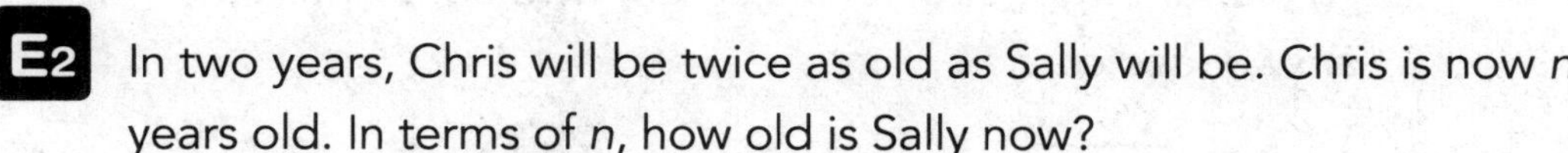

E2 In two years, Chris will be twice as old as Sally will be. Chris is now n years old. In terms of n, how old is Sally now?

F. $\frac{n}{2}$

G. $\frac{n}{2} - 2$

H. $\frac{n}{2} - 1$

J. $n - 2$

K. $2n - 1$

Remember, when you see variables in the answers, pick numbers!

Don't forget to circle your target!

S 1 Write what we know about our numbers

*There are **two periods of time**: now and 2 years from now. Chris is n years old now. Our **target** is how old Sally is now.*

	Now	2 years from now
Chris	***n***	
Sally	**target**	

2 Pick Numbers

*Let's say that 2 years from now, Chris will be **10 years old**. That means 2 years from now, Sally will be half his age, or **5 years old**. We can **subtract 2** to find their ages now:*

	Now	2 years from now
Chris	**8**	10
Sally	**3**	5

3 Plug in and Solve

*To hit our target of **3**, let's plug our n-value, **8**, into the answer choices.*

n = 8 **target:** 

F. $\frac{n}{2} \longrightarrow \frac{\mathbf{8}}{2} = 4$ *nope*

G. $\frac{n}{2} - 2 \longrightarrow \frac{\mathbf{8}}{2} - 2 = 4 - 2 = 2$ *nope*

H. $\frac{n}{2} - 1 \longrightarrow \frac{\mathbf{8}}{2} - 1 = 4 - 1 = (3)$ *Aww yea!*

J. $n - 2 \longrightarrow \mathbf{8} - 2 = 6$ *nope*

K. $2n - 1 \longrightarrow 2(\mathbf{8}) - 1 = 16 - 1 = 15$ *nope*

The only answer that works is (H).

E3 The sum of 5 consecutive even integers is s. In terms of s, what is the largest of these 5 integers?

A. $\frac{s}{5}$

B. $\frac{s-4}{5}$

C. $\frac{s+4}{5}$

D. $\frac{s-20}{5}$

E. $\frac{s+20}{5}$

S

1 Write what we know about our numbers

Our numbers are ***consecutive****,* ***even****, and* ***integers****.*
They add up to ***s****, and our target is the* ***largest*** *integer.*

2 Pick Numbers

Let's pick an easy number to start us off: **2**.
So our consecutive even integers are: 2, 4, 6, 8, and (10).

$$2 + 4 + 6 + 8 + 10 = \boxed{30 = s}$$

3 Plug in and solve

$\boxed{s = 30}$ **target:** 

A. $\frac{s}{5} \longrightarrow \frac{30}{5} = 6$ *Nope, not 10!*

B. $\frac{s-4}{5} \longrightarrow \frac{30-4}{5} = \frac{26}{5} = 5.2$ *Nope.*

C. $\frac{s+4}{5} \longrightarrow \frac{30+4}{5} = \frac{34}{5} = 6.8$ *Nope.*

D. $\frac{s-20}{5} \longrightarrow \frac{30-20}{5} = \frac{10}{5} = 2$ *Nope.*

E. $\frac{s+20}{5} \longrightarrow \frac{30+20}{5} = \frac{50}{5} = (10)$ *Bullseye!*

A common mistake is to choose 2, 3, 4, 5 and 6.

Remember, we need consecutive **EVEN** integers!

Picking Numbers Practice Problems

1. If a, b, and c are nonzero numbers such that $a = bc$, which of the following must be equivalent to ac?

   A. $\frac{b}{a}$

   B. b^2c

   C. bc

   D. $\frac{a^2}{b}$

   E. $\frac{a}{c}$

★

2. If $x = 3z$ and $y = 9z$, what is x in terms of y?

   F. $3y$

   G. $6y$

   H. y

   J. $\frac{y}{6}$

   K. $\frac{y}{3}$

★

3. Train A travels 75 mph less than twice the speed of Train B. If the speed of Train A is k mph, which of the following expressions represents the speed of Train B, in miles per hour?

   A. $\frac{k + 75}{2}$

   B. $\frac{k - 75}{2}$

   C. $k + 75$

   D. $2k + 75$

   E. $2k - 75$

★★

4. The side of a square is d inches longer than the side of a second square. The perimeter of the first square is how much longer, in inches, than the perimeter of the second square?

   F. $\frac{4}{d}$

   G. $\frac{d}{4}$

   H. d

   J. $4d$

   K. d^2

★★

5. Which of the following equations expresses z in terms of x for all real numbers x, y, and z such that $x^3 = y$ and $y^2 = z$?

A. x^6

B. x^5

C. x^3

D. x

E. $\frac{x}{2}$

★★

---

6. Which of the following statements about odd and/or even numbers is always true?

F. The sum of any 2 odd numbers is odd.
G. The sum of any 2 even integers is odd.
H. The quotient of any 2 even numbers is odd.
J. The quotient of any 2 even numbers is even.
K. The product of any 2 odd numbers is odd.

★★

7. If a and b are real numbers such that $a < -1$ and $b > 1$, then which of the following inequalities must be true?

A. $\frac{a}{b} > 1$

B. $|a|^2 < b$

C. $\frac{a}{2} - 3 < \frac{b}{2} - 3$

D. $a^2 > b^2$

E. $a^{-2} < b^{-2}$

★★★

4%
of all math questions on the ACT

Angles

For almost every geometry question on the ACT, you will need to know the basic rules of angles.

1 There are **180°** on each side of a **straight line**.

In line *m*, $\angle 1 + \angle 2 + \angle 3 = 180°$.

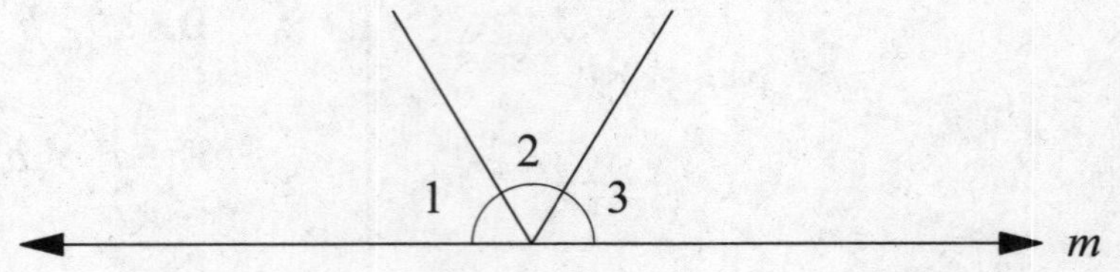

2 There are **180°** in any **triangle**.

In triangle *EFG*, $\angle e + \angle f + \angle g = 180°$.

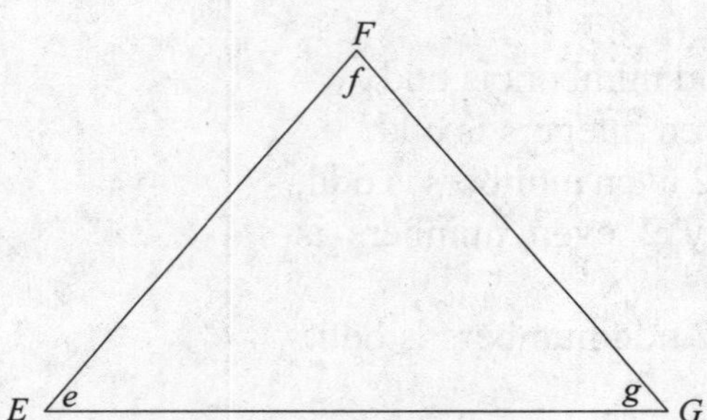

3 There are **360°** in any **quadrilateral**.

In quadrilateral ABCD, $\angle a + \angle b + \angle c + \angle d = 360°$.

4 Vertical angles are **equal**

Vertical angles occur whenever two lines cross to form opposing angles.

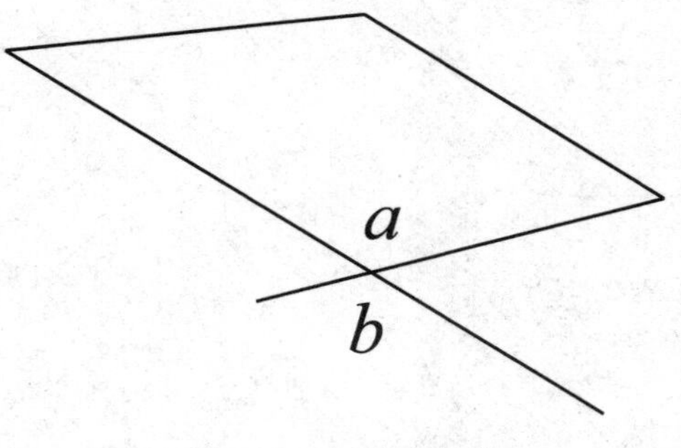

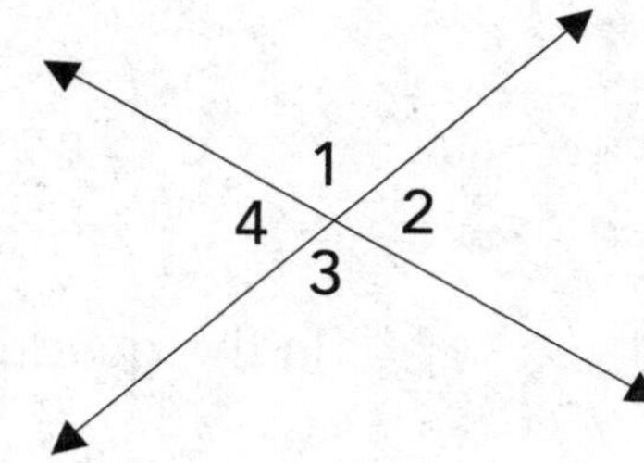

$\angle a = \angle b$

$\angle 1 = \angle 3$ and $\angle 2 = \angle 4$

Now let's put these basic angles rules to the test!

E1

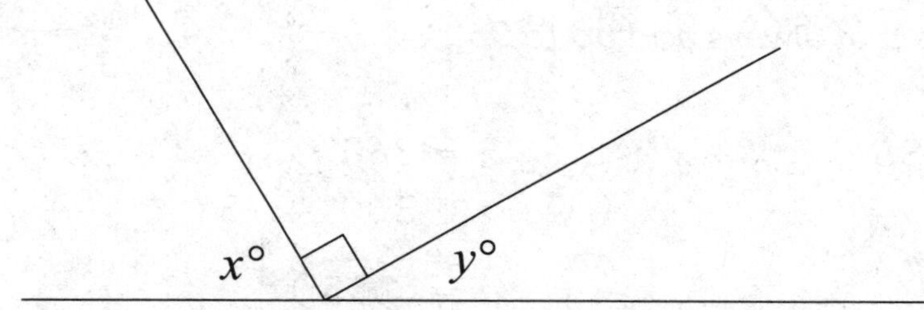

What is the value of x + y in the figure above?

S *Since a line always has 180° on either side, x + y = 180 – 90 =* **90°**

E2

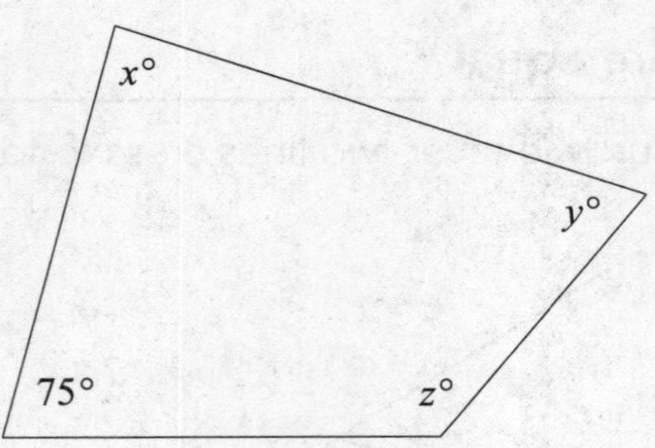

In the quadrilateral above, $x + y + z = ?$

S *All quadrilaterals (four-sided figures) have four angles that always add up to 360°.*

$x + y + z = ?$

So: $x + y + z + 75 = 360°$

$x + y + z = 360° - 75°$

$x + y + z = \boxed{285°}$

Breaking up Shapes

Good news! There's no need to worry about unusual shapes; if you can remember that triangles have 180° and quadrilaterals have 360°, all you have to do is **split complex shapes** into **triangles** and **rectangles**.

E3

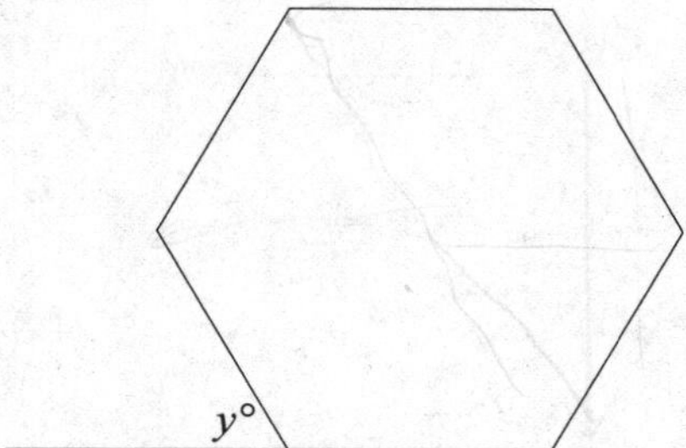

If all interior angles of the polygon above are congruent, what is the value of y ?

A. 60
B. 72
C. 75
D. 105
E. 120

For all you math machines:

We can use the formula for the sum of the interior angles of a polygon with n sides.
$(n - 2) \times 180$

S *We know there are 180° on one side of a line, so we just need to find the measure of* <u>*the interior angle*</u> *on the same line as y.*

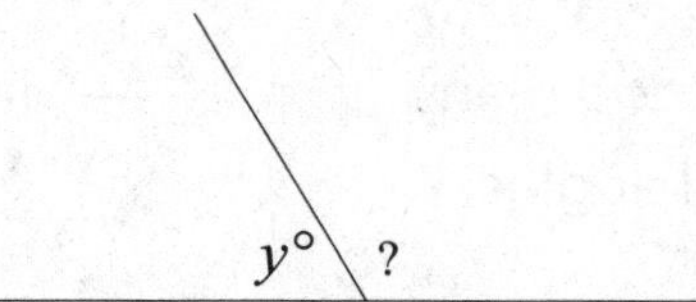

To do this, we can break the shape into triangles and rectangles:

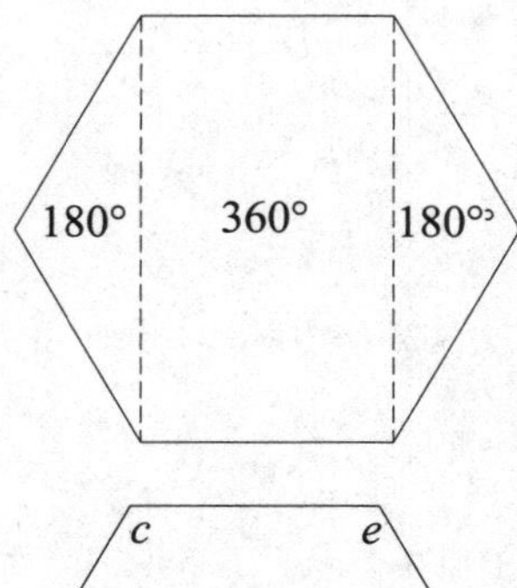

The sum of the interior angles:
180° + 360° + 180° = 720°

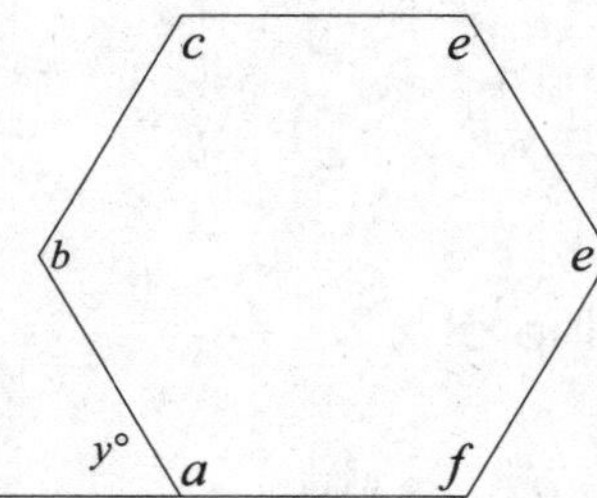

We know that all interior angles of the polygon are ***congruent****:*

a = b = c = d = e = f

We also know that:

a + b + c + d + e + f = 720°

So, $\frac{720}{6} = 120°$

The measure of each interior angle is **120°**.

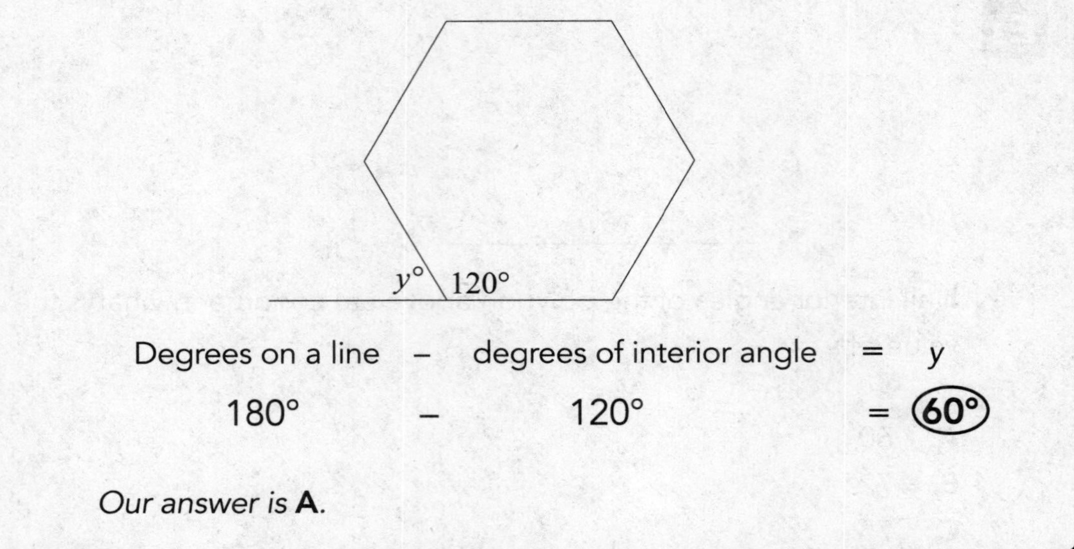

Degrees on a line − degrees of interior angle = y

$180° - 120° = 60°$

Our answer is **A**.

One note about breaking up polygons: the lines you draw **cannot cross.** When your lines intersect they create central angles that are not part of the original shape.

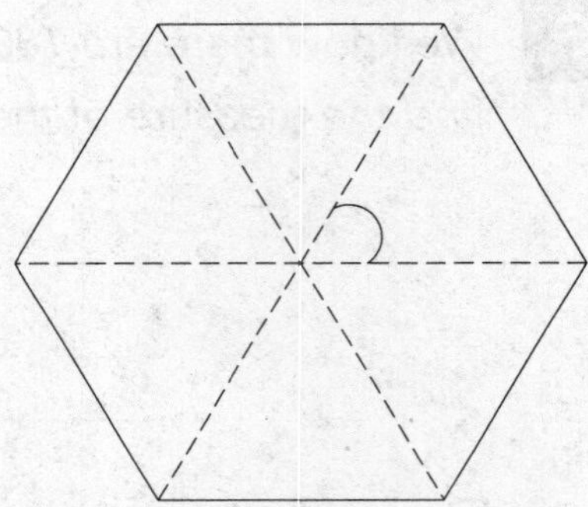

This would give us six triangles.
$6(180°) = 1080°$, which is 360° too many because of those pesky central angles.

E4

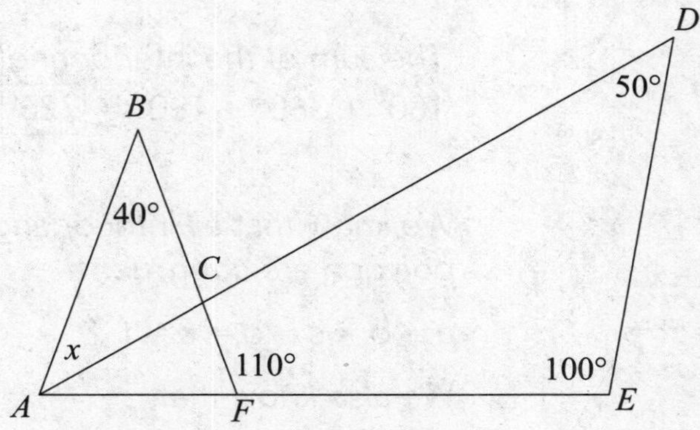

In the figure above, what is the value of x?

S *We've got to see all of the shapes here. The shapes that include angles we know are* ***quadrilateral*** *CDEF and* ***triangle*** *ABC.*

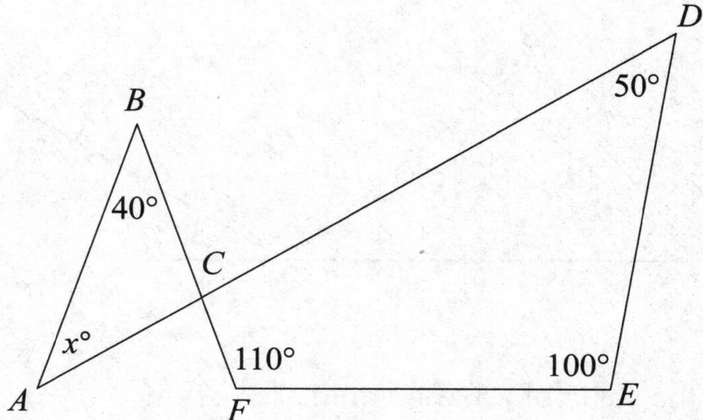

The angles in any quadrilateral add up to 360°. The missing angle in quadrilateral CDEF is

$360° - 50° - 100° - 110° = \boxed{100°}$

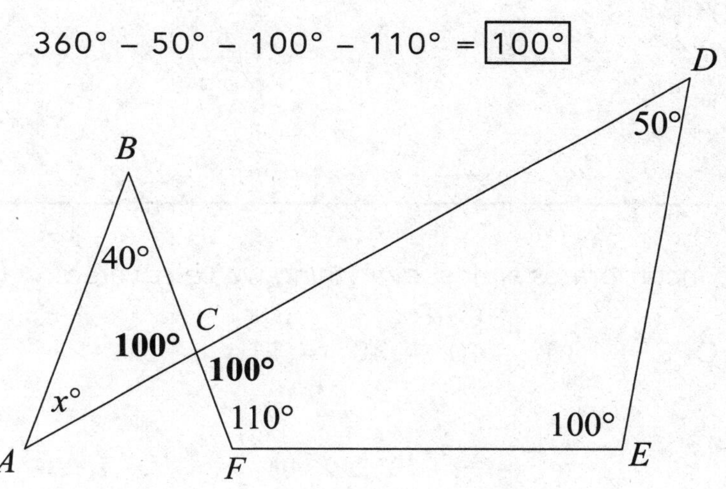

Remember, vertical angles are congruent, so the third angle in triangle ABC is 100°.

The angles in any triangle add up to 180°.

$x = 180° - 40° - 100° = \textcircled{40°}$

E5

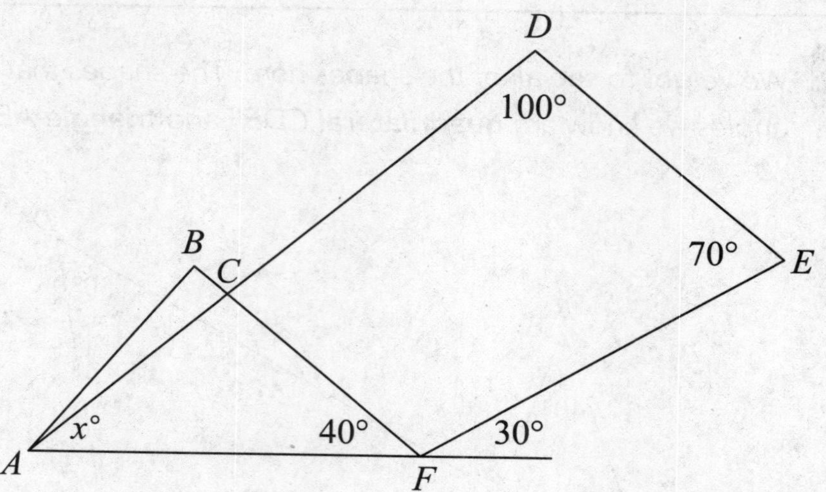

What is the value of x in the figure above?

A. 40°
B. 75°
C. 80°
D. 100°
E. 110°

This one incorporates almost everything we've covered.

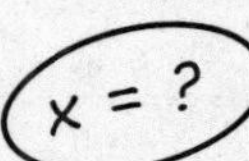

$\angle CFE = 180° - 40° - 30° = 110°$

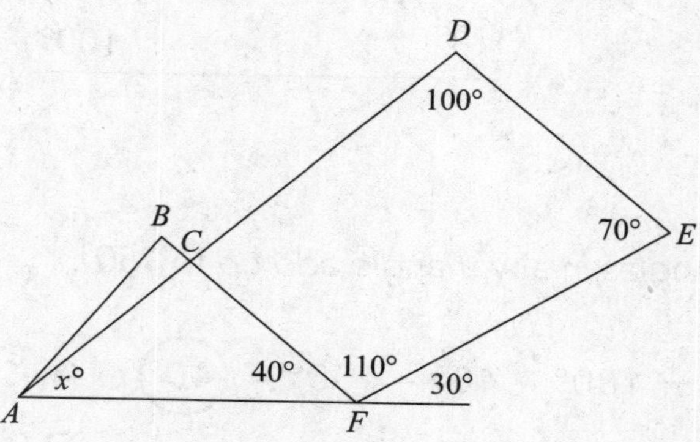

All quadrilaterals have 360°.

To find ∠DCF, the missing angle in quadrilateral CDEF:

$360° - 70° - 100° - 110° = \boxed{80°}$

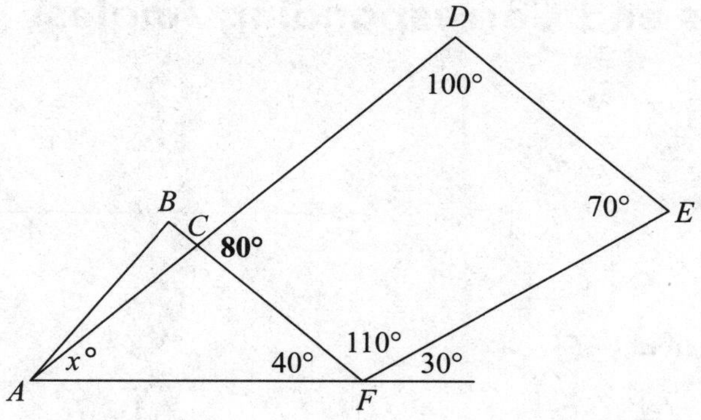

Now we need to find ∠ACF, the missing angle in triangle ACF. We know that ∠ACF and ∠DCF form a line, so they must add up to 180°:

$\angle ACF + 80° = 180°$
$\angle ACF = 180° - 80° = 100°$

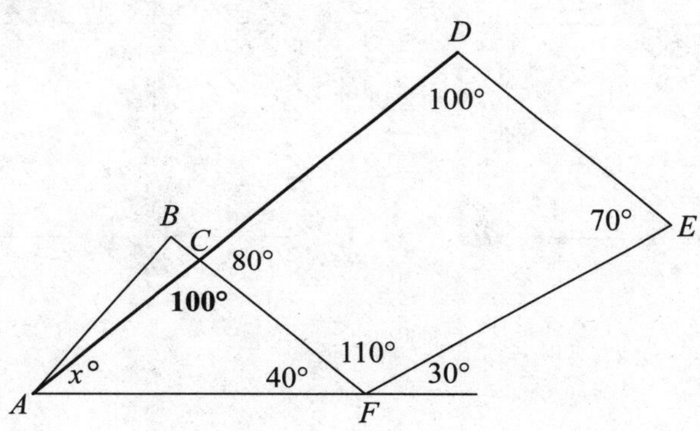

There are 180° in any triangle, so

$x = 180° - 40° - 100° = \boxed{40°}$

Our answer is **A**.

The symbol || means parallel.

Parallel Lines and Corresponding Angles

The rules are easy:
When line $l \parallel m$

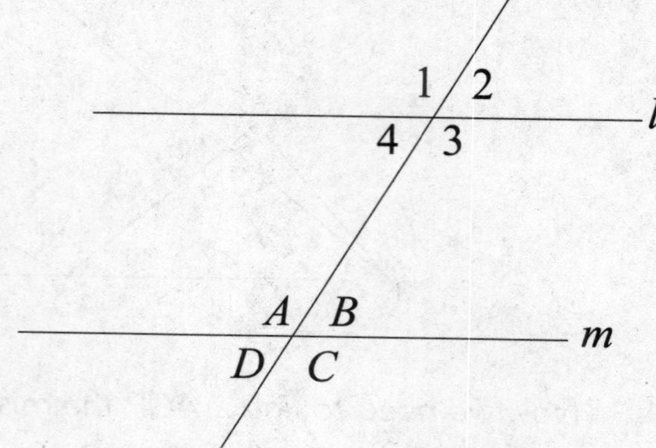

$\angle 1 = \angle 3 = \angle A = \angle C$

$\angle 2 = \angle 4 = \angle B = \angle D$

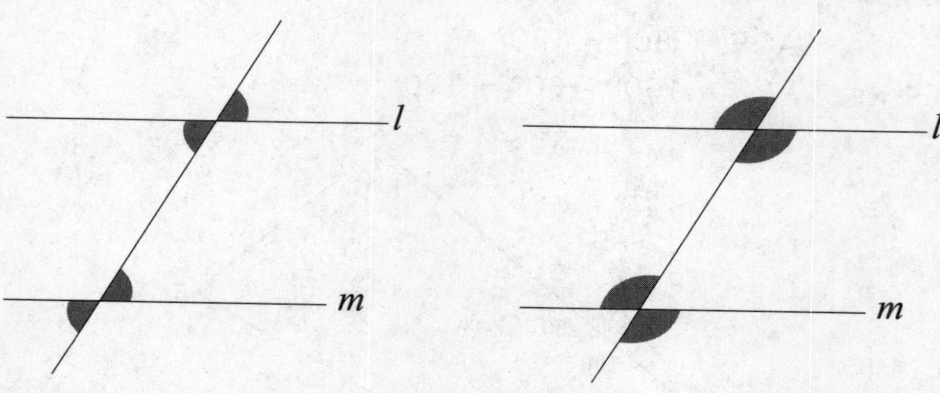

E6

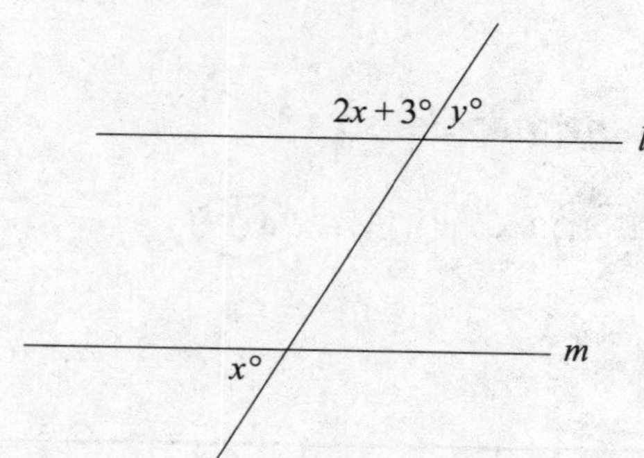

In the figure above, $l \parallel m$. What is the value of y ?

A. 40
B. 59
C. 72
D. 177
E. 180

S *We know that **BIG = BIG**, so all BIG angles = (2x + 3)°.*

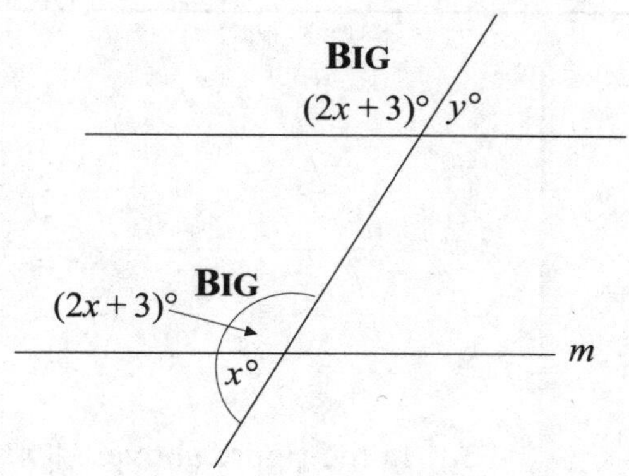

There are 180° on one side of a line, so

$$(2x + 3) + x = 180$$
$$3x + 3 = 180$$
$$3x = 177$$
$$x = \boxed{59}$$

Since x was a small angle, we know that all small angles = 59.

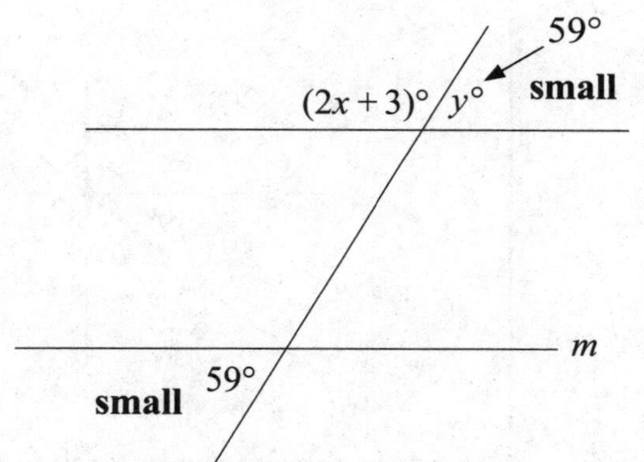

*And since y is a small angle, y = **59**!*

Summary of Angles

1. Angles in a **triangle** add up to **180°**
2. Angles in a **quadrilateral** add up to **360°**
3. Angles on one side of a **line** add up to **180°**
4. **Vertical angles** are equal
5. When working with parallel lines, **BIG = BIG** and **small = small**

Angles Practice Problems

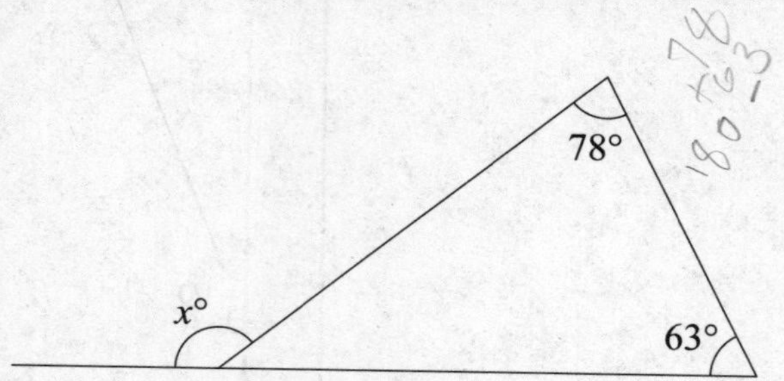

1. Given the figure above, what is the value of x ?

A. 102
B. 117
C. 141
D. 180
E. Cannot be determined from the information given

★

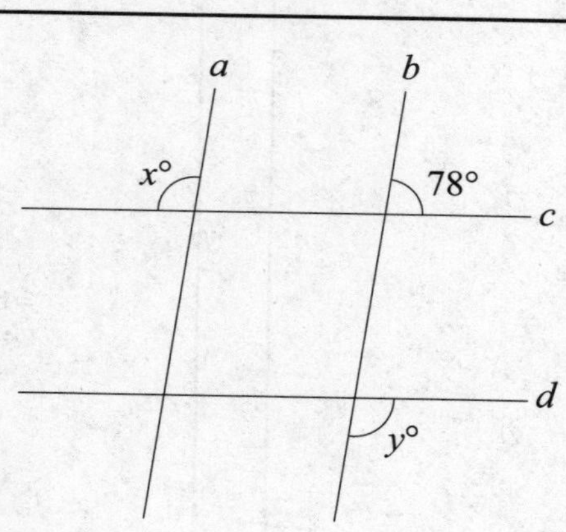

2. In the figure above, parallel lines a and b intersect parallel lines c and d. What is the sum of x and y, if it can be determined?

F. 204
G. 180
H. 140
J. 98
K. Cannot be determined from the information given

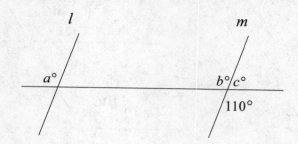

★★

3. In the figure above, $l \parallel m$. What is the value of $a + b + c$?

A. 180
B. 240
C. 260
D. 290
E. 300

★

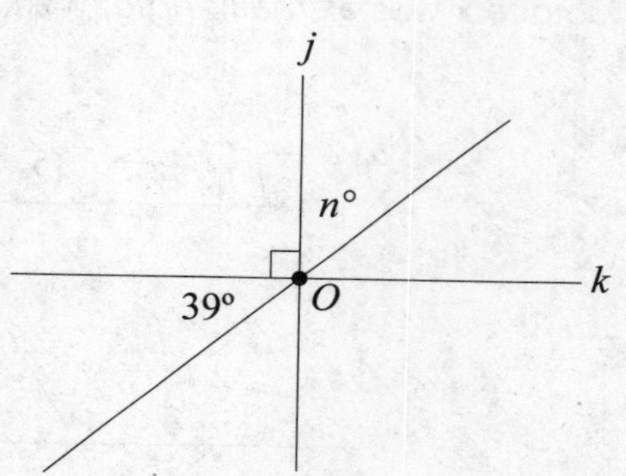

4. In the figure above, line j is perpendicular to line k, and the two intersect at O. What is the value of n ?

F. 39
G. 47
H. 51
J. 53
K. 61

★

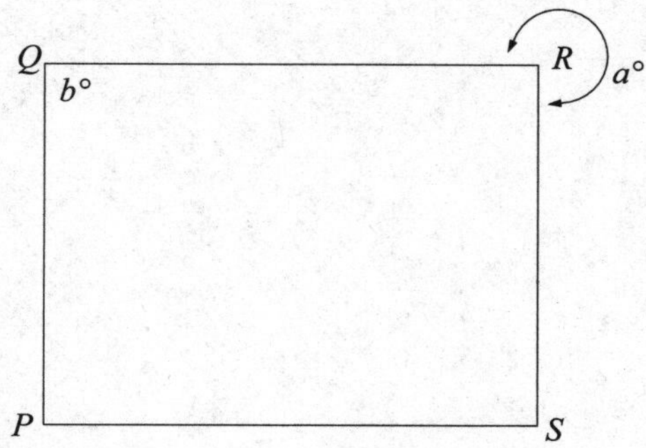

5. In the figure above, $PQRS$ is a parallelogram. If $a = 271$, what is the value of b ?

A. 85
B. 89
C. 90
D. 91
E. 95

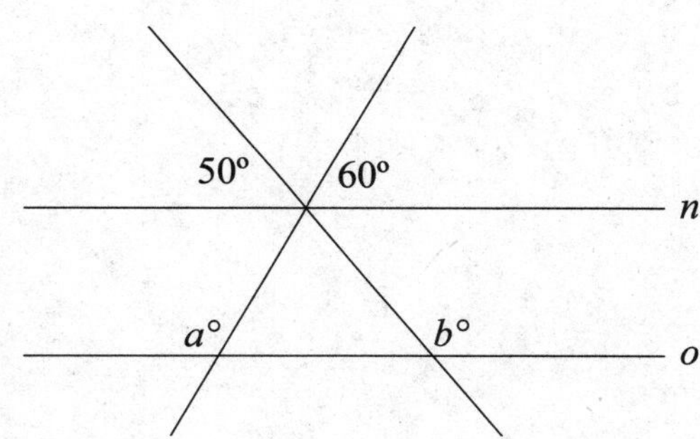

6. In the figure above, line n is parallel to line o. What is the value of $a + b$?

F. 110
G. 180
H. 210
J. 230
K. 250

★★

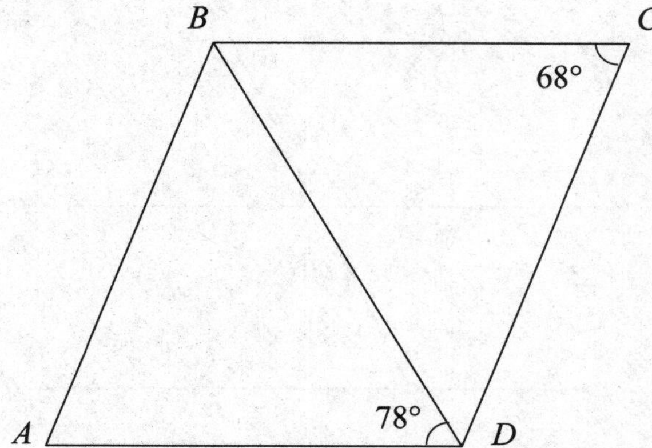

7. In the parallelogram $ABCD$ above, the measure of $\angle BCD$ is 68° and the measure of $\angle ADB$ is 78°. What is the measure of $\angle BDC$?

A. 15
B. 34
C. 37
D. 53
E. 59

★★★

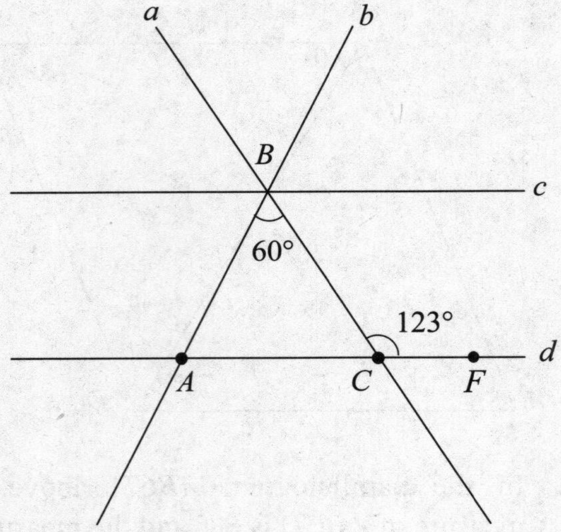

8. In the figure above, lines c and d are parallel and lines a and b intersect at point B on line c. Line a intersects line d at point C and line b intersects line d at point A. If point F is on line d, $\angle ABC$ is 60°, and $\angle BCF$ is 123°, how many angles formed by lines a, b, c, and d have a measure of 57° ?

F. 4
G. 6
H. 8
J. 9
K. 10

★★★

Triangles

5% of all math questions on the ACT

There are some triangle basics you need to remember:

1. The three angles of a triangle add up to 180°.
2. The longest side is always opposite the largest angle.
3. The area is $\frac{1}{2}$ base × height.

Isosceles Triangle

Isosceles Triangles have two equal sides. The key is to remember that if two sides are equal, then the angles opposite them are equal (and if two angles of a triangle are equal, you know the two sides opposite them are also equal).

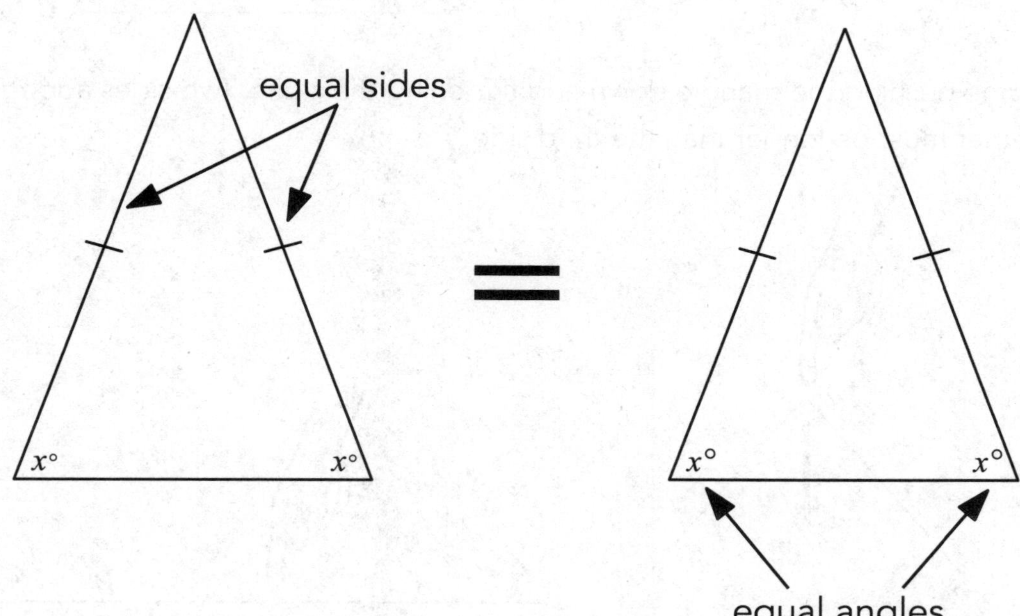

Equilateral Triangle

Equilateral Triangles have 3 equal sides and 3 equal angles. Each angle measures 60°.

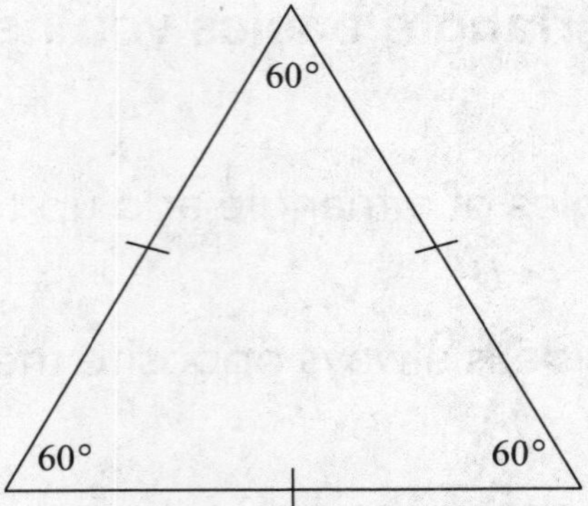

Side Lengths

If you add the lengths of two of the sides of any triangle together, the result is always bigger than the length of the third side:

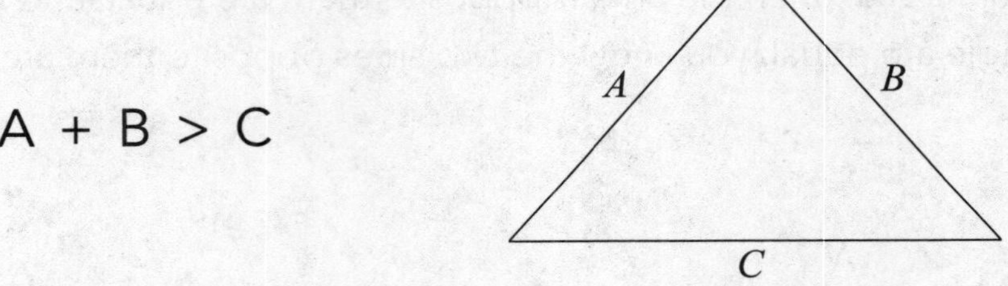

Imagine pushing the triangle down and flattening the sides. Two sides added together must be longer than the third side.

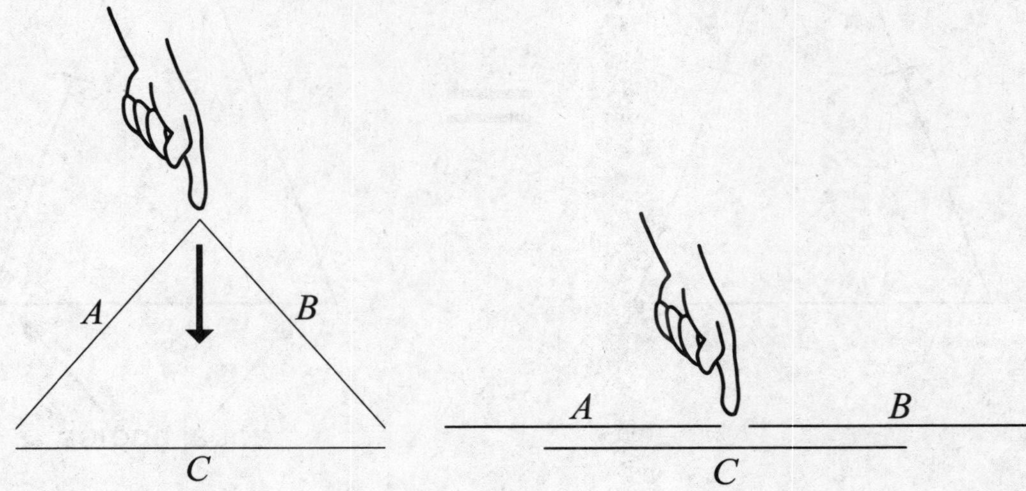

E1

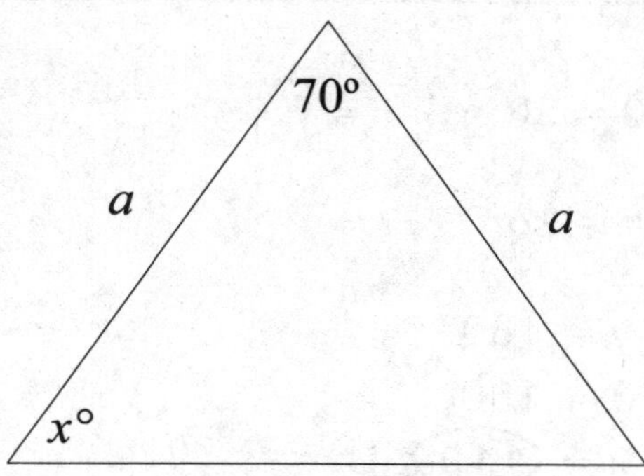

What is the value of x in the triangle above?

S *Because two sides have length* **a**, *we know this is an* ***isosceles*** *triangle, which means the triangle also has two equal angles.*

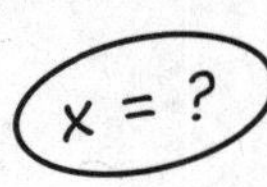

Isosceles triangle: two equal sides, two equal angles.

$$x + x + 70 = 180$$
$$2x = 110$$
$$x = \frac{110}{2}$$
$$x = 55$$

Use your calculator to double check: 55° + 55° + 70° = 180°.

E2

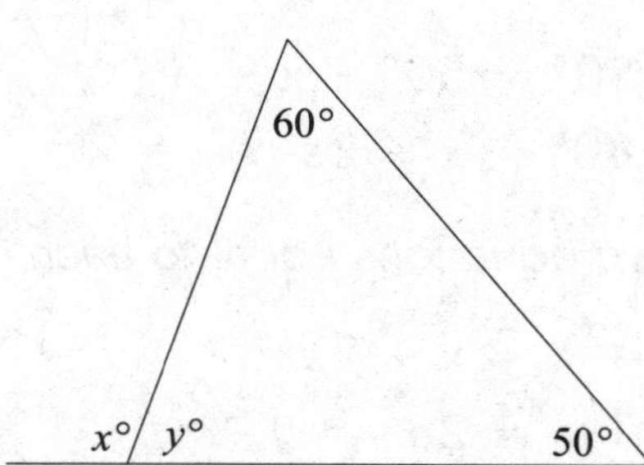

In the figure above, what is the value of x?

A. 30
B. 50
C. 60
D. 110
E. 120

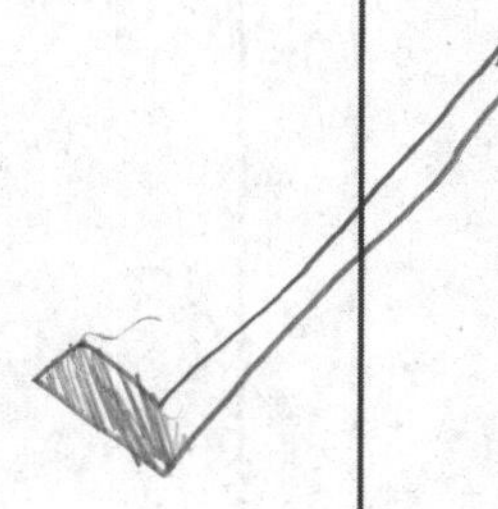

Shortcut
An external angle of a triangle = the sum of the two internal angles it doesn't touch, x = 60 + 50 in this case.

S

$$180 - 60 - 50 = 70 = y$$

x and y form a line, so:

$$x + y = 180°$$
$$x + 70 = 180$$
$$x = 110$$, **D.**

E3

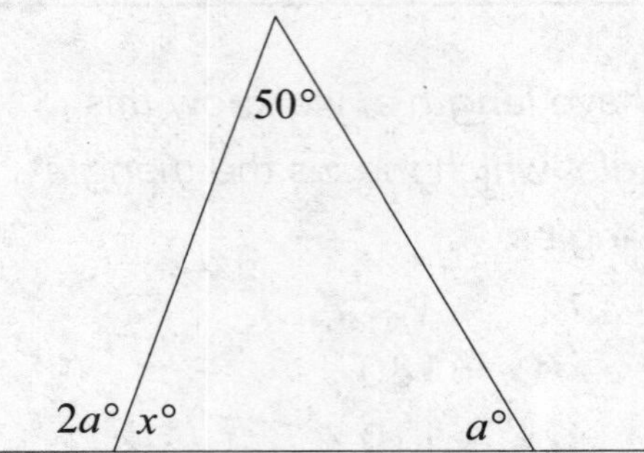

What is the value of x in the figure above?

Remember, when you have two equations that are equal to the same thing, you can set them equal to each other!

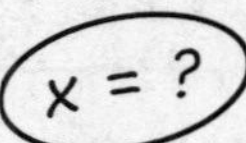

S *We know there are **180°** in triangles and straight lines.*

Triangle: $180° = 50° + x + a$

Line: $180° = x + 2a$

We can set these two equations equal to each other.

$$50° + x + a = x + 2a$$
$$50° + a = 2a$$
$$\boxed{50°} = a$$

*Now we can plug **50** in for **a** in one of our original equations!*

$$180° = 50° + x + 50°$$
$$180° = x + 100°$$
$$80° = x$$

E4

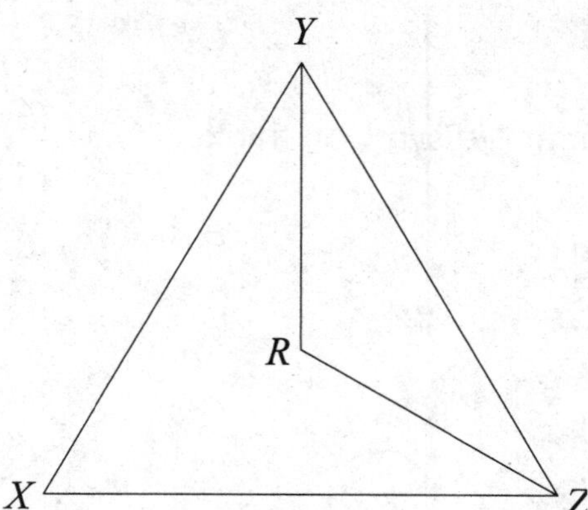

In equilateral triangle *XYZ* above, $\overline{RZ}$ and $\overline{RY}$ are the angle bisectors of $\angle XZY$ and $\angle XYZ$, respectively. What is the measure of $\angle YRZ$?

A. 30°
B. 60°
C. 70°
D. 90°
E. 120°

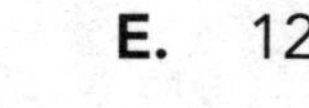

An angle **bisector** is a line that divides an angle in half.

S *XYZ is equilateral, so all three angles are* **60°**.

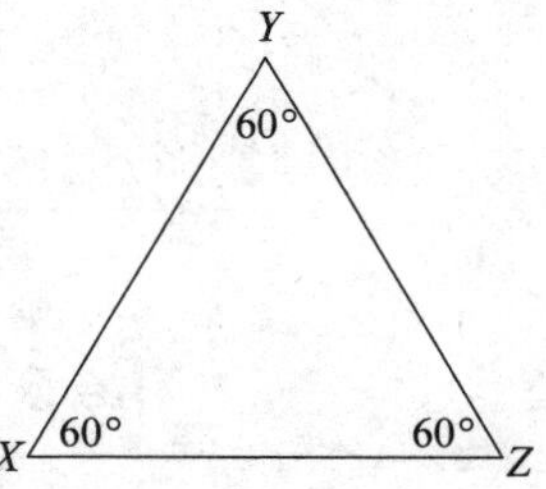

$\overline{RZ}$ and $\overline{RY}$ are angle bisectors, which means they cut $\angle XZY$ and $\angle XYZ$ in half. So $\angle RZY$ and $\angle RYZ$ are both **30°**.

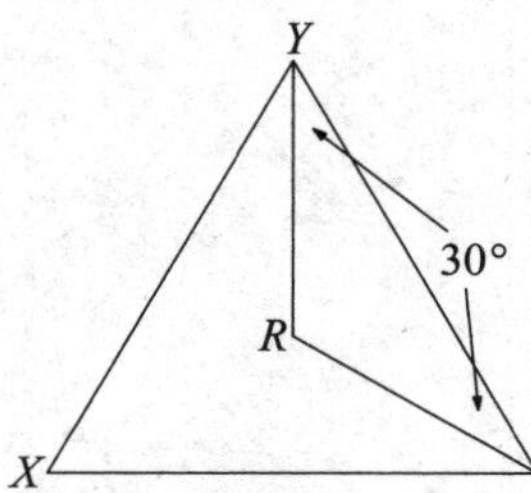

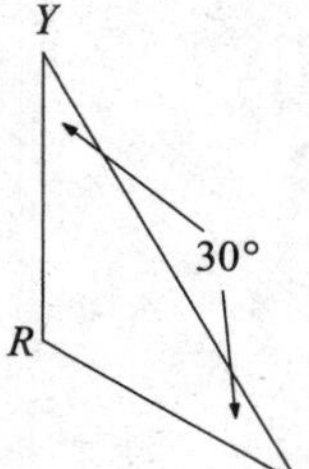

Like all triangles, ΔRYZ has 180°.

$\angle YRZ = 180 - 30 - 30 =$ **120°**, **E.**

Right Triangles

When you see the right angle symbol, think Pythagorean Theorem!

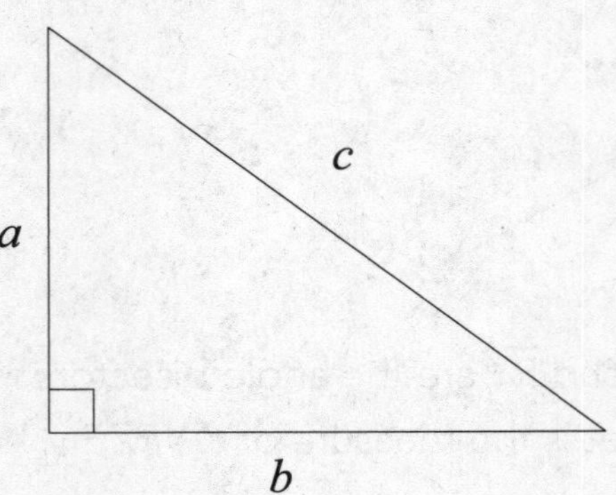

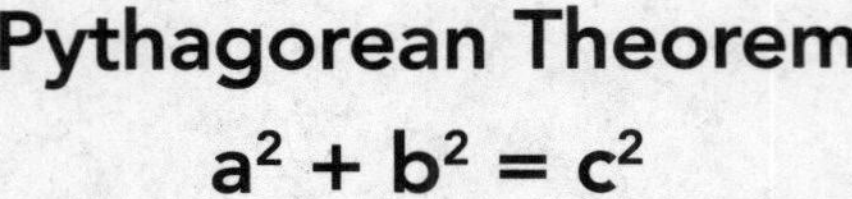

Pythagorean Theorem

$$a^2 + b^2 = c^2$$

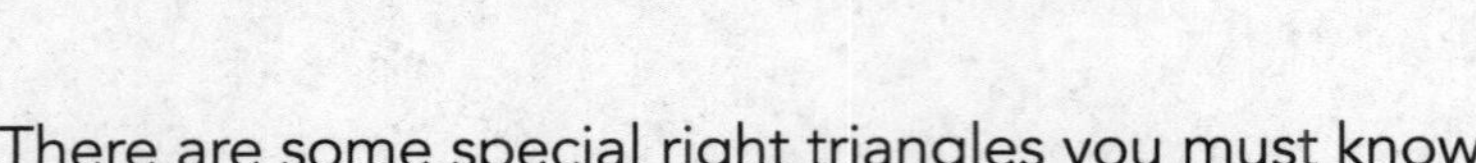

There are some special right triangles you must know.

Look out for multiples of these special right triangles (e.g. 6:8:10 or 10:24:26).

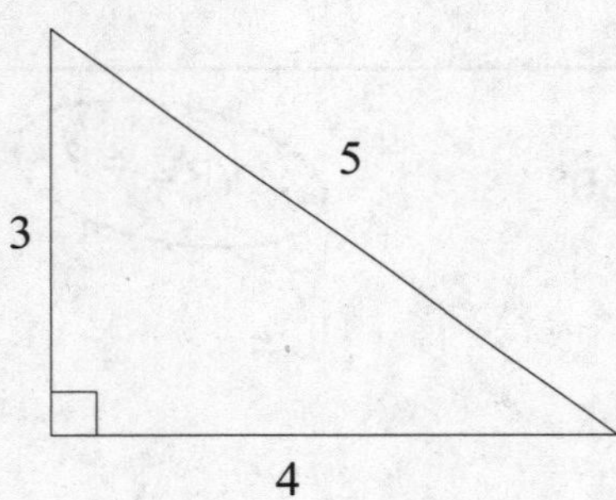

The 3 – 4 – 5 Triangle

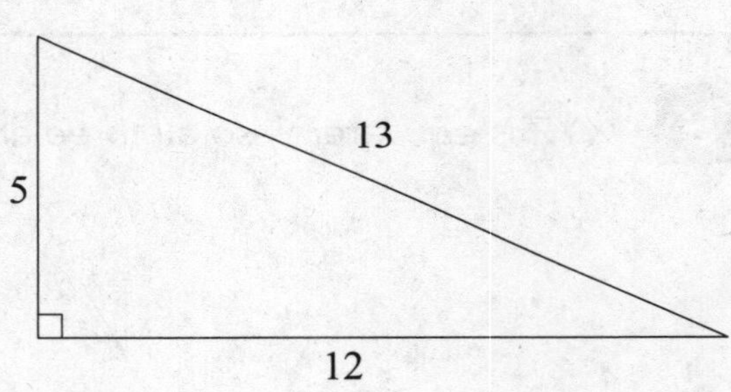

The 5 – 12 – 13 Triangle

There are also special right triangles known by their angle measurements:

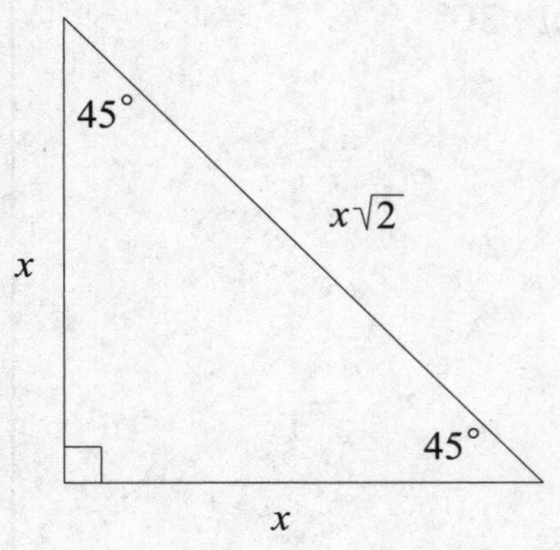

45°– 45°– 90° Triangle

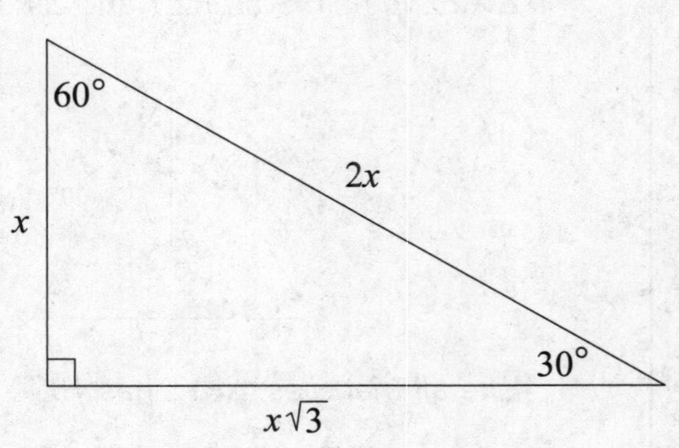

30°– 60°– 90° Triangle

For these special triangles, if we know one side is 2, we can fill in the rest:

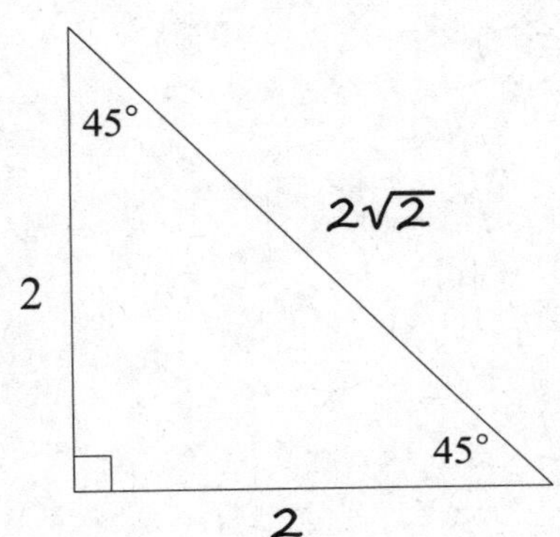

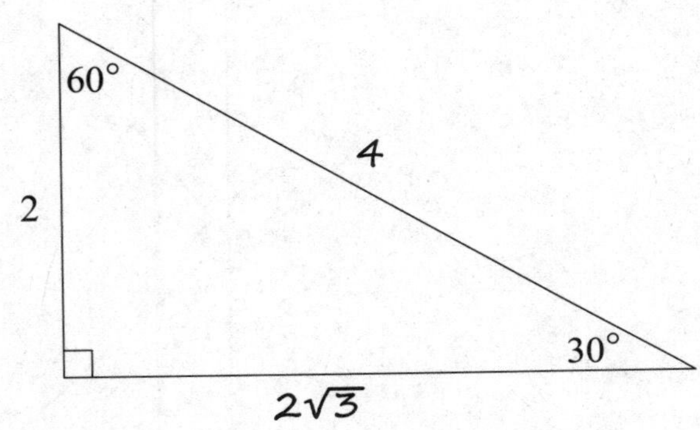

E5 What is the perimeter of a right triangle whose legs have lengths 12 and 16?

A. 12
B. 16
C. 20
D. 48
E. 428

S *First, let's draw the triangle.*
Then we can find the perimeter:

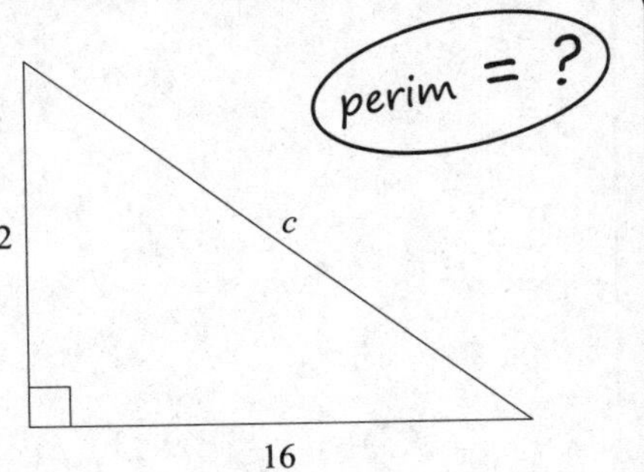

Perimeter = 12 + 16 + c

One side is missing!
Luckily, we have a right triangle,
so we can break out the Pythagorean Theorem:

$$a^2 + b^2 = c^2$$
$$12^2 + 16^2 = c^2$$
$$144 + 256 = c^2$$
$$400 = c^2$$
$$\sqrt{400} = \sqrt{c^2}$$
$$20 = c$$

Perimeter = 12 + 16 + 20 = (48), **D.**

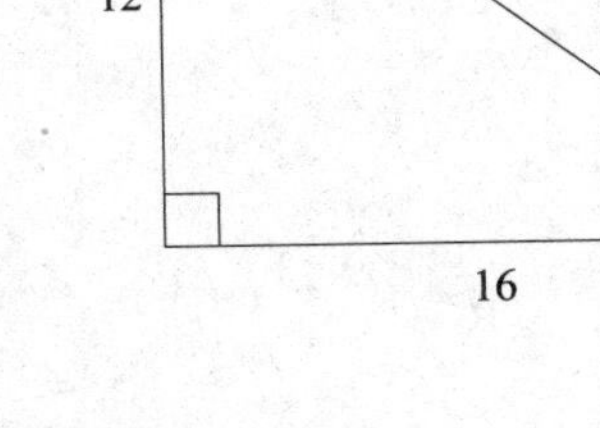

If you see that this is just a multiple of the 3-4-5 right triangle, you can multiply each side by 4, and you have c = 5(4) = 20.

E6

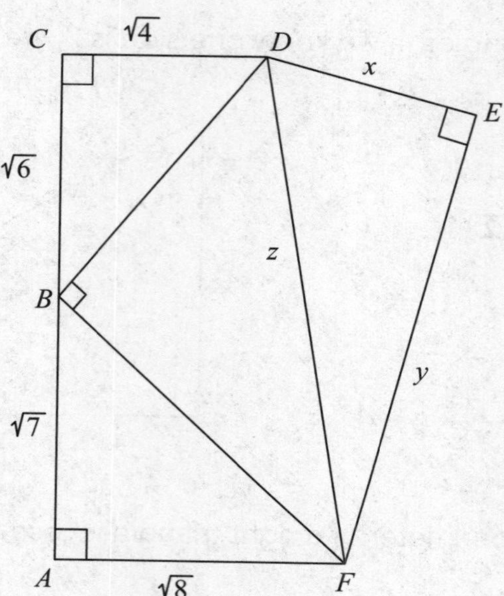

In the figure above, what is the value of $x^2 + y^2$?

S *Let's pick a starting point.*
Pythagoras tells us that $x^2 + y^2 = z^2$. *So we need to find* z^2.

$x^2 + y^2 = ?$

1

$$(\sqrt{6})^2 + (\sqrt{4})^2 = \overline{BD}^2$$
$$6 + 4 = \overline{BD}^2$$
$$10 = \overline{BD}^2$$
$$\sqrt{10} = \overline{BD}$$

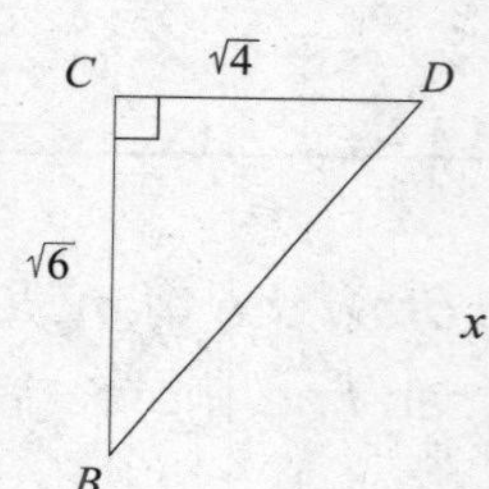

2

$$(\sqrt{7})^2 + (\sqrt{8})^2 = \overline{BF}^2$$
$$7 + 8 = \overline{BF}^2$$
$$15 = \overline{BF}^2$$
$$\sqrt{15} = \overline{BF}$$

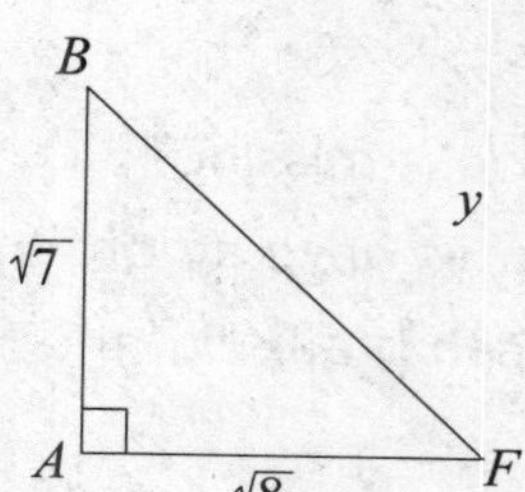

3

$$\overline{BD}^2 + \overline{BF}^2 = z^2$$
$$(\sqrt{10})^2 + (\sqrt{15})^2 = z^2$$
$$10 + 15 = z^2$$
$$\textcircled{25} = z^2 = x^2 + y^2$$

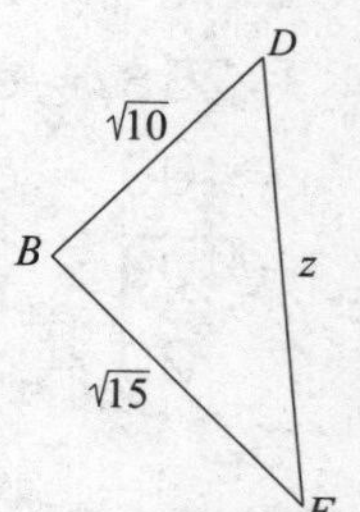

Note that you don't need to solve for either x or y. You don't even need to solve for z. All you **need** is z^2 and you are done.

Triangles Practice Problems

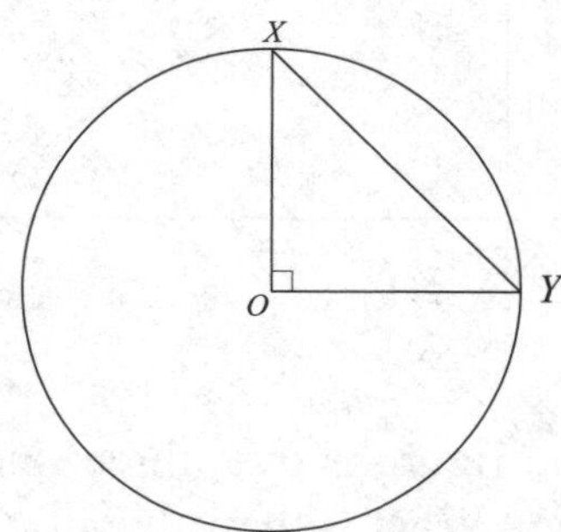

1. Point O is the center of the circle above, and the radius of the circle is 6. What is the length of $\overline{XY}$?

A. 3
B. $3\sqrt{3}$
C. 6
D. $6\sqrt{2}$
E. $6\sqrt{3}$

★★

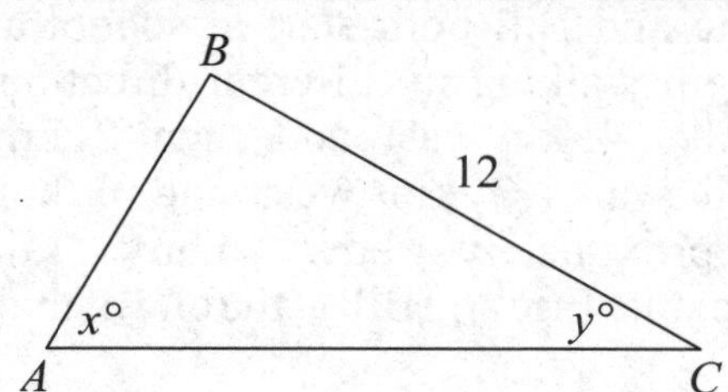

2. In the triangle above, $x = 60$ and $y = 30$. Which of the following statements must be true concerning the figure above?

I. $AC > 12$
II. $AB > 12$
III. $AC > AB$

F. I only
G. II only
H. III only
J. I and III only
K. I, II and III

★

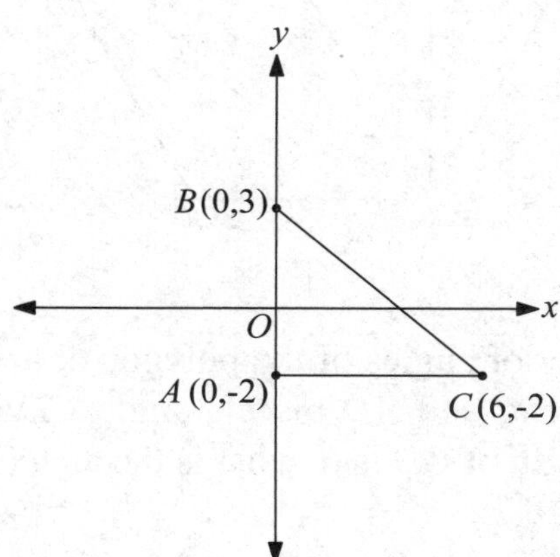

3. What is the area of $\Delta\ ABC$ in the figure above?

A. 12
B. 15
C. 24
D. 28
E. 30

★

4. A shepherd creates a pen for his sheep that is 24 feet wide and 32 feet long. How many feet long is the diagonal from one corner to its opposite corner?

F. 28
G. 40
H. 56
J. 448
K. 1600

★★

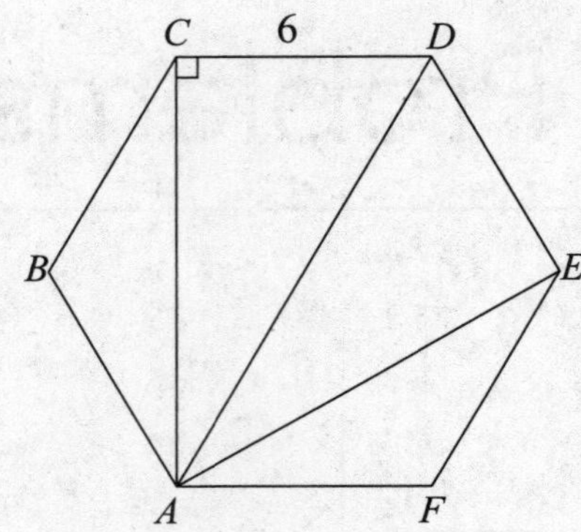

5. All interior angles of the polygon above are congruent, and $\overline{AD}$ bisects angle CDE. If the length of $\overline{CD}$ is 6, what is the area of ΔACD ?

A. $36\sqrt{3}$
B. $36\sqrt{2}$
C. 36
D. $18\sqrt{3}$
E. $18\sqrt{2}$

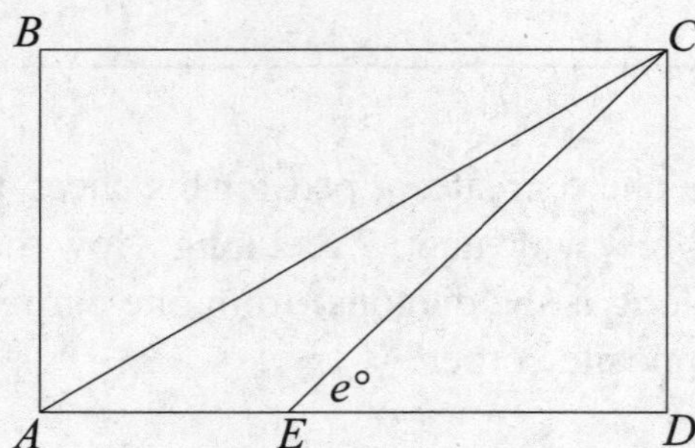

6. In the figure above, $ABCD$ is a rectangle and $CD = ED$. What is the value of e ?

F. 30
G. 45
H. 60
J. 75
K. 90

★★

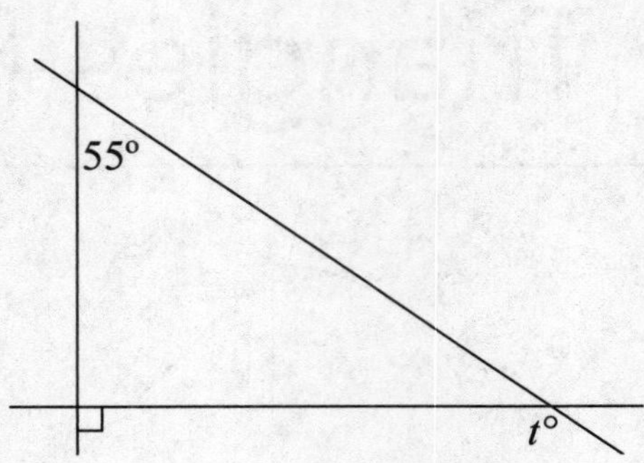

7. In the figure above, three lines intersect as shown. What is the value of t ?

A. 125
B. 135
C. 145
D. 155
E. 165

★

8. Eric and Bill both start at school and then begin walking in different directions. Eric walks 4 km east and then 2 km north. Bill walks 3 km west and 6 km south. Approximately how many kilometers separate Eric and Bill at the end of their walk ?

F. 7.0
G. 9.2
H. 10.6
J. 12.4
K. 15.0

★★

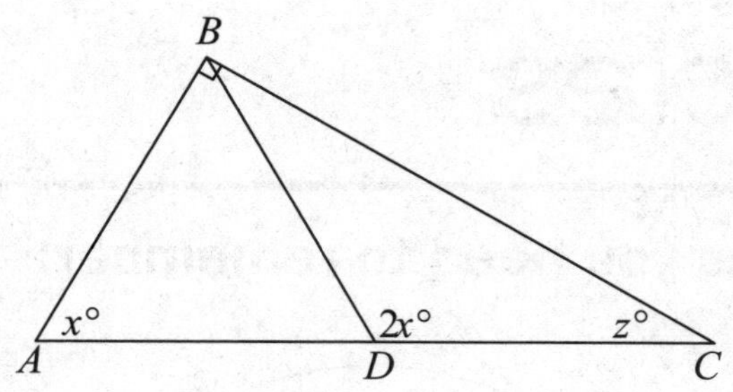

9. In the figure above, Δ *ABD* is equilateral. What is the value of z ?

A. 30
B. 45
C. 75
D. 90
E. 120

10. What is the distance, in coordinate units, between (4, 3) and (10, 7) in the standard (x, y) coordinate plane?

F. $\sqrt{10}$
G. $\sqrt{20}$
H. $\sqrt{52}$
J. 5
K. 7

★★

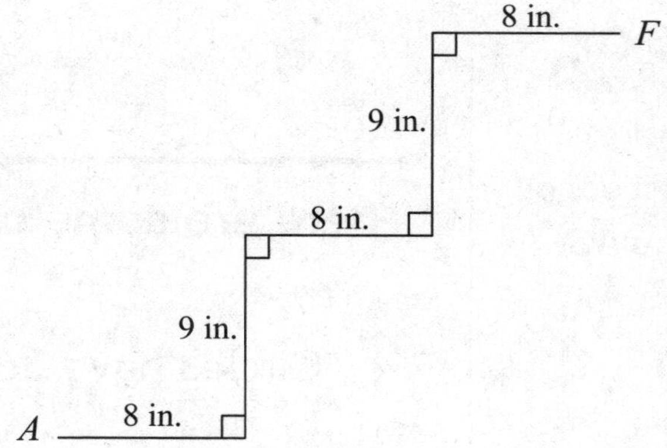

11. The figure above shows a staircase with the height and depth of each stair as indicated. If the stairs are to be replaced with a ramp from A to F, what will be the length, in inches, of the ramp?

A. 17
B. 30
C. 36
D. 42
E. 51

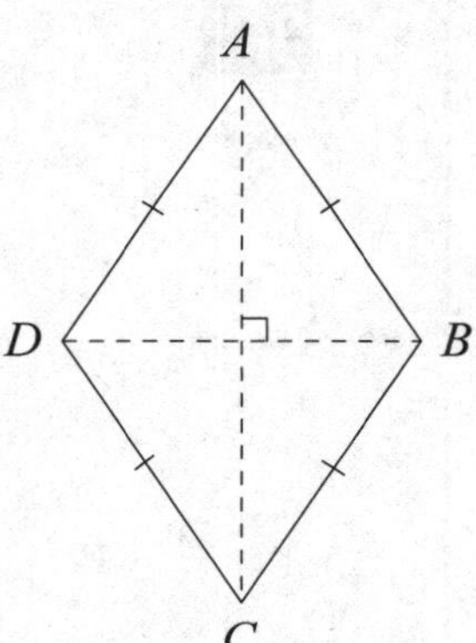

12. If $\overline{AC}$ = 18 centimeters and $\overline{BD}$ = 14 centimeters in the rhombus *ABCD* shown below, what is its area, in centimeters ?

F. 16
G. 32
H. 63
J. 126
K. 252

3%
of all math questions on the ACT

Circles

There are some circle basics you need to remember:

1. Circles have 360°
2. Diameter = d
3. Radius (r) = $\frac{d}{2}$
4. Area = πr^2
5. Circumference = $2\pi r$ or πd

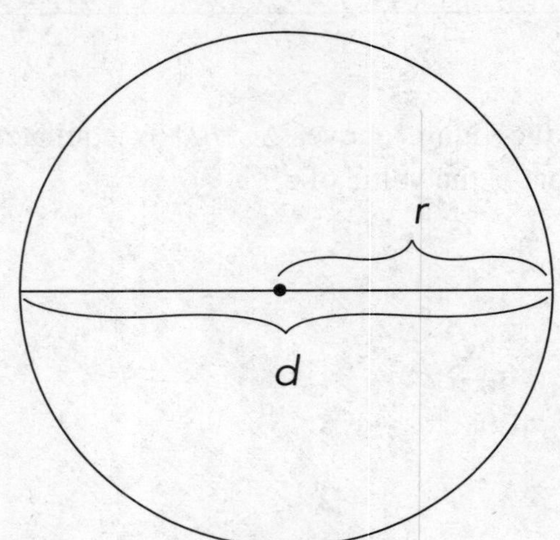

E1

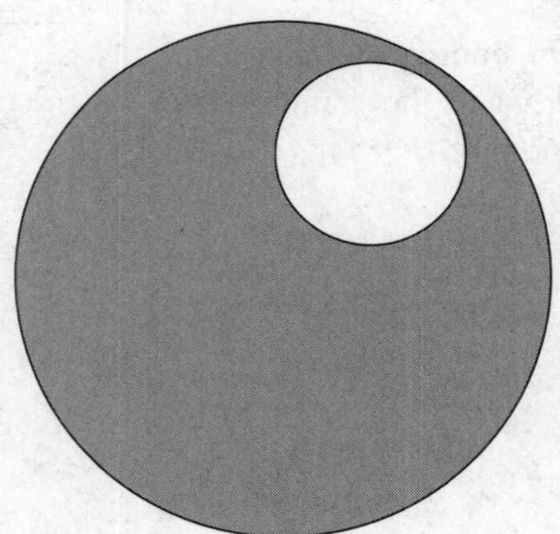

In the figure above, a smaller circle with radius 3 is inside a larger circle with radius x. What is the area of the shaded region in terms of x?

A. $x - 3$
B. $x^2 - 3\pi$
C. $\pi x^2 - 9$
D. $\pi(x^2 - 3)$
E. $\pi(x^2 - 9)$

S *Let's work with the circles one at a time.* *shaded area= ?*

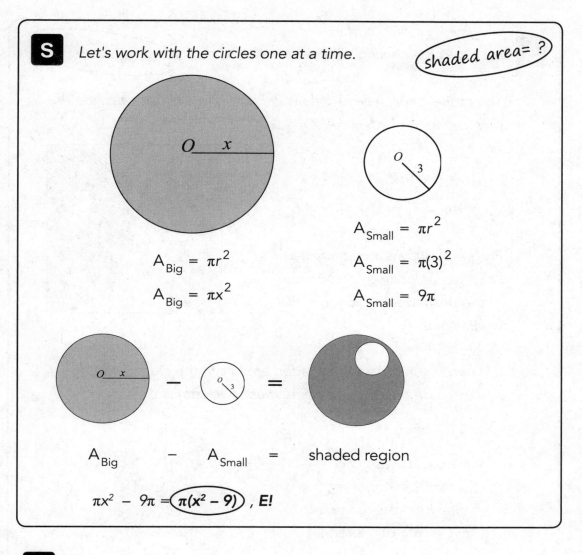

O x

O 3

$A_{Small} = \pi r^2$

$A_{Big} = \pi r^2$ $A_{Small} = \pi(3)^2$

$A_{Big} = \pi x^2$ $A_{Small} = 9\pi$

O x − O 3 =

A_{Big} − A_{Small} = shaded region

$\pi x^2 - 9\pi = \boldsymbol{\pi(x^2 - 9)}$, ***E!***

Pick a number for x and plug it in to check your answer.

E2

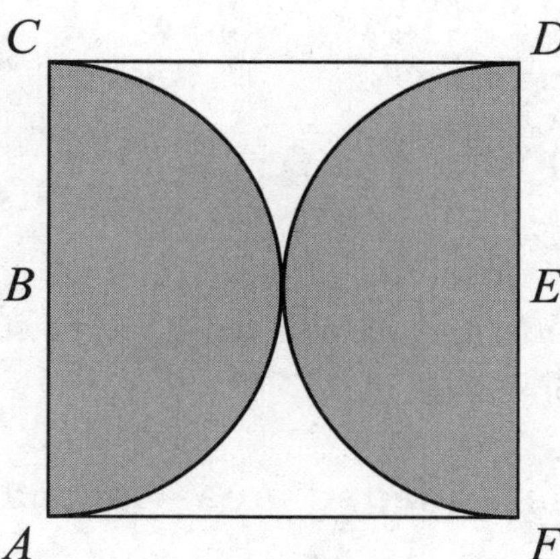

In square $ACDF$, arcs $\overset{\frown}{AC}$ and $\overset{\frown}{DF}$ are semicircles with centers at B and E, respectively. If the radius of each semicircle is 2, what is the area of the unshaded region?

S *Let's start by labeling what we know.*

unshaded area= ?

The radius of each semicircle is 2. From that, we can calculate the side and area of sqaure ACDF:

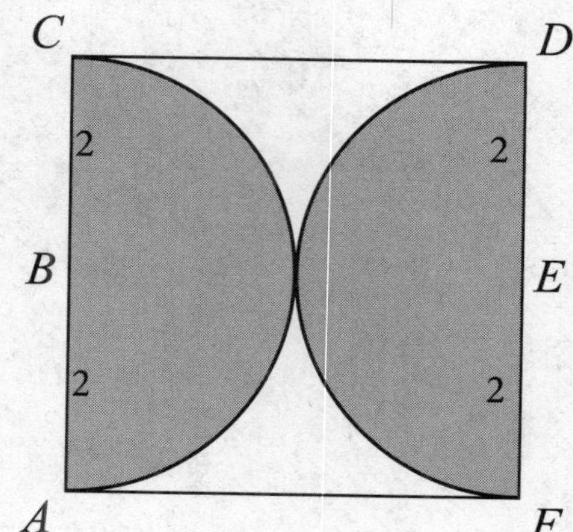

side = 2 + 2 = **4**.

Area = $\text{side}^2 = 4^2 =$ **16**.

*Progress! But we aren't finished yet. We are looking for the area of the **unshaded** region, not the whole square.*

*We need to **subtract** the shaded area from the area of square ACDF. To do this, let's combine these two semicircles:*

If we put these two semicircles together, they form one complete circle with diameter 4.

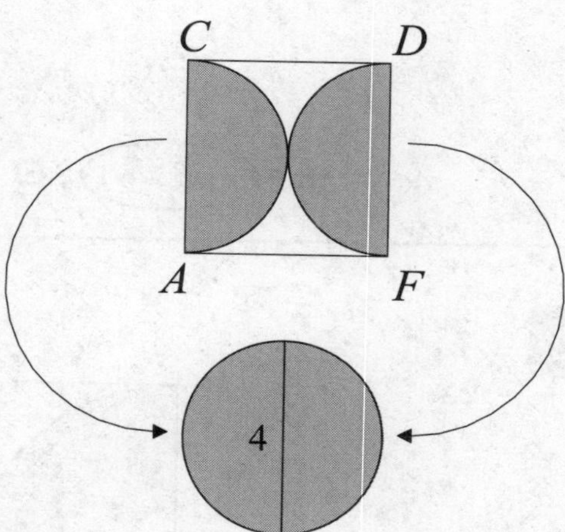

*Our **shaded circle**'s area is:*

$A = \pi(2)^2$

$A = 4\pi$

Remember: Area of a circle = πr^2. Be careful not to use the diameter here.

*Now, to get to our final answer, we need to **subtract** the shaded area from the total area.*

Total area – shaded area = unshaded area

16 – **4π** = unshaded area

16 – 4π = unshaded area

E3

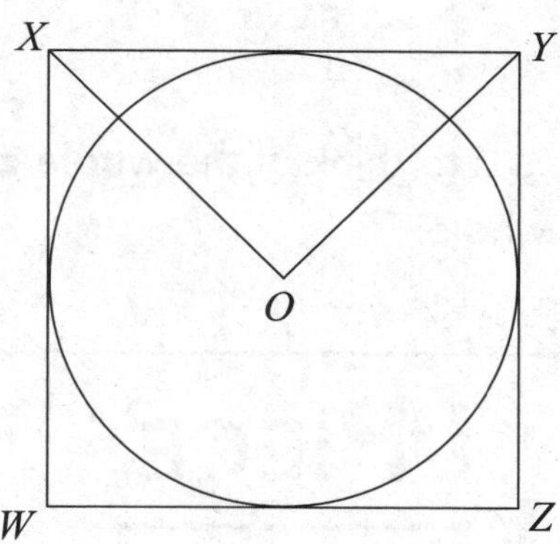

In the figure above, a circle with center *O* is inscribed in square *WXYZ*. If the radius of the circle is 4, what is the area of $\triangle OXY$?

"Inscribed in" simply means one shape is drawn within another shape.

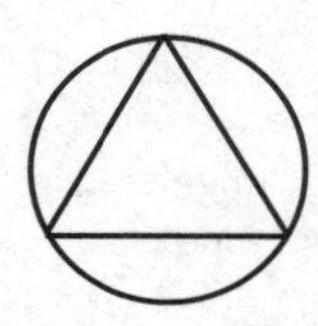

Usually one of the shapes is a circle.

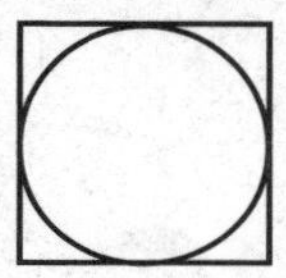

S *We're asked to find the area of a triangle:* $A = \frac{1}{2}bh$. *We're going to need a* ***base*** *and a* ***height****.*

Area$_{\triangle OXY}$ = ?

1 *If we draw the height, we also draw a radius. And since we know every radius of this circle is equal to 4, we know our* **height = 4**.

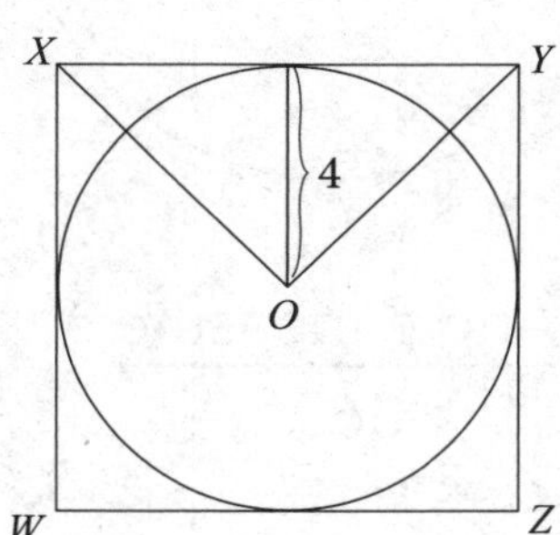

2 *To find the base, we need to draw some extra radii. By adding two radii together, we can find the side length of square WXYZ:* 4 + 4 = **8** *And that's the base of our triangle!*

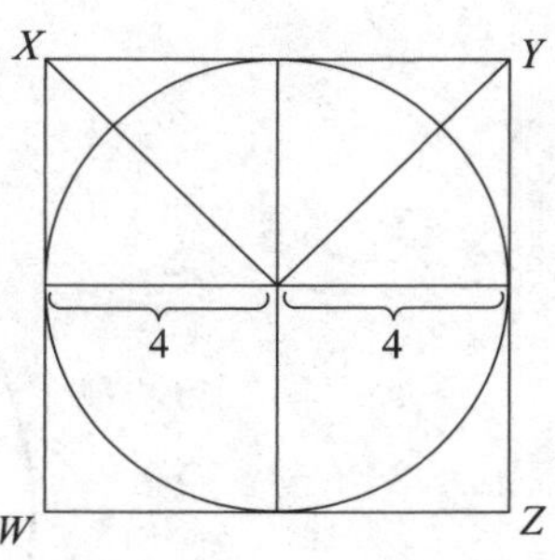

3 *Now we simply plug and chug:*

Area = ½ b(h)

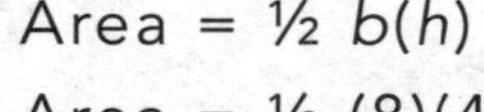

Area = ½ (8)(4)

Area = (16)

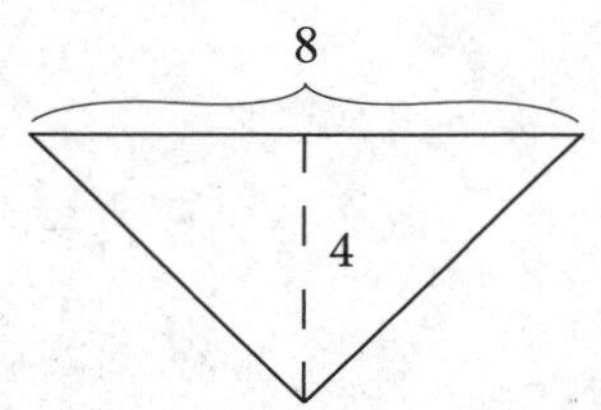

Visual Check
The area of square *WXYZ* is 64, and 16 is ¼ of 64. Triangle *OXY* looks to be about ¼ the area of the square!

Arcs and Wedges

The key for arcs and wedges is to think of the **whole circle** first, and then compare the pieces to the whole.

Remember that the circumference is $2\pi r$, and area is πr^2. So, if you have the radius, you can solve for anything.

Circle problems often boil down to setting up these comparisons and cross multiplying to find a missing piece.

$$\frac{\text{PIECE}}{\text{WHOLE}}$$

An **interior angle** is a piece of the whole 360°.

An **arc** is a piece of the whole circumference.

A **wedge** is a piece of the whole circle area.

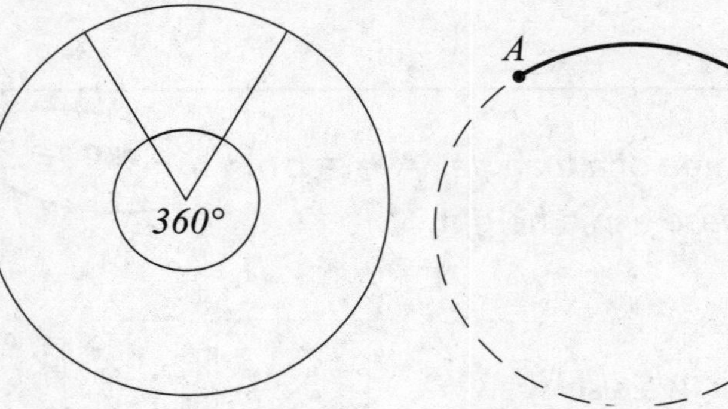

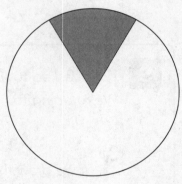

$$\frac{\text{Angle measure}}{360^\circ} = \frac{\text{Arc length}}{\text{Circumference}} = \frac{\text{Wedge area}}{\text{Circle area}}$$

E4

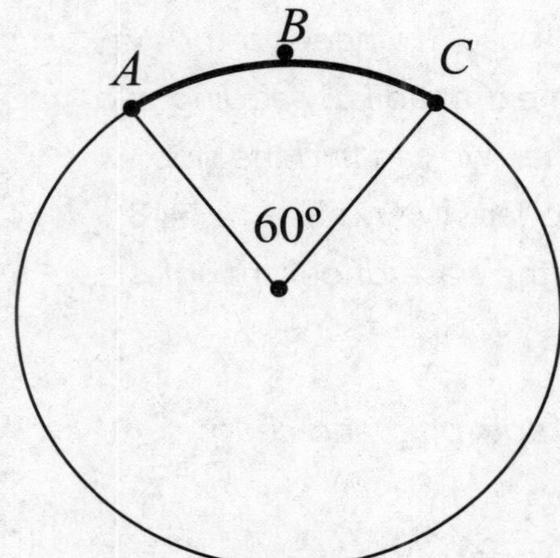

If the area of the circle above is 36π, what is the length of the arc $\overset{\frown}{ABC}$?

S *To find a **piece**, we have to find the **whole**. And an arc is a **piece** of the **circumference**.*

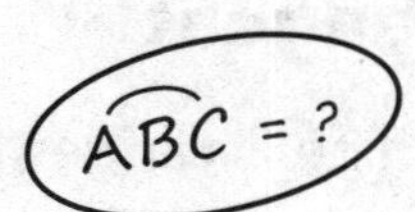

$$C = 2\pi r$$ We need a radius!

1 Find the **radius**

*We can use the area (**36π**) to find **r**.*

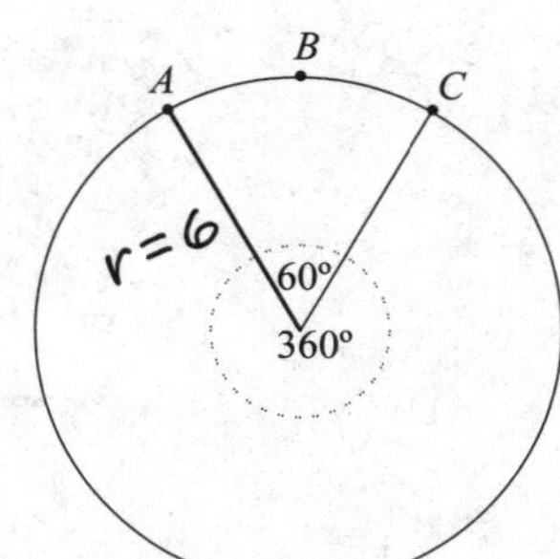

$$A = \pi r^2$$
$$36\pi = \pi r^2$$
$$36 = r^2$$
$$\mathbf{6} = r$$

2 Find the **circumference** ← The whole!

*We can use the radius to find **C**.*

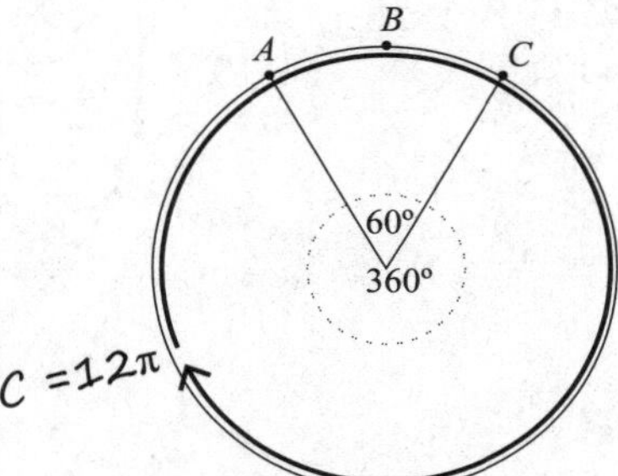

$$C = 2\pi r$$
$$C = 2\pi(6)$$
$$C = \boxed{12\pi}$$

3 Make the **comparison**

*We can use the interior angle (**60°**) for a comparison.*

$$\frac{\text{Arc length}}{\text{Circumference}} = \frac{\text{Interior Angle}}{\text{Whole Circle}} = \frac{\textbf{PIECE}}{\textbf{WHOLE}}$$

ABC / 12π = 60° / 360°

$$\frac{\overset{\frown}{ABC}}{12\pi} = \frac{60°}{360°}$$

$$\frac{\overset{\frown}{ABC}}{12\pi} = \frac{1}{6}$$ ← Our arc is equal to $\frac{1}{6}$ of the circumference

$$\overset{\frown}{ABC} = (12\pi)\frac{1}{6} = \boxed{2\pi}$$

Tangent

A line is **tangent** to a circle when it intersects the circle at **exactly 1 point**. The intersection of a circle's radius and a line tangent to the circle creates a right angle. Watch out, Pythagoras is just around the corner.

A circle inscribed in a shape is tangent to the sides of that shape.

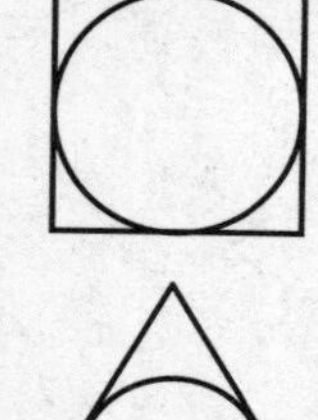

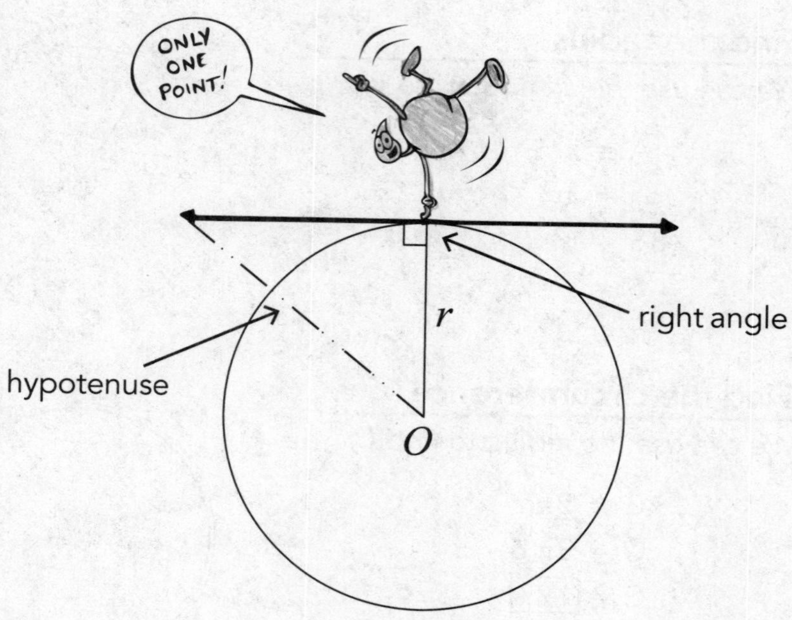

Circles Recap

1. Circles have 360°
2. Area = πr^2
3. Circumference = $2\pi r$
4. Tangent Line + Radius = Right angle
5. $\frac{\text{PIECE}}{\text{WHOLE}} = \frac{\text{Int. Angle}}{360°} = \frac{\text{Arc}}{\text{Circ.}} = \frac{\text{Wedge Area}}{\text{Whole Area}}$

Circles Practice Problems

1. If the circumference of a circle is 8, what is the radius of the circle?

A. 8π

B. $\frac{8}{\pi}$

C. 4π

D. $\frac{4}{\pi}$

E. 2π

★

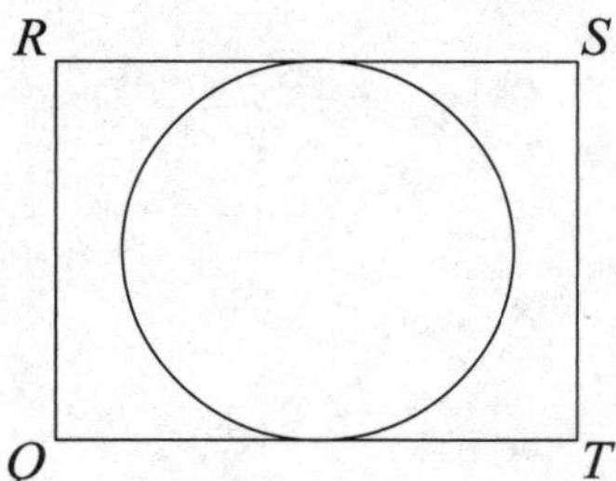
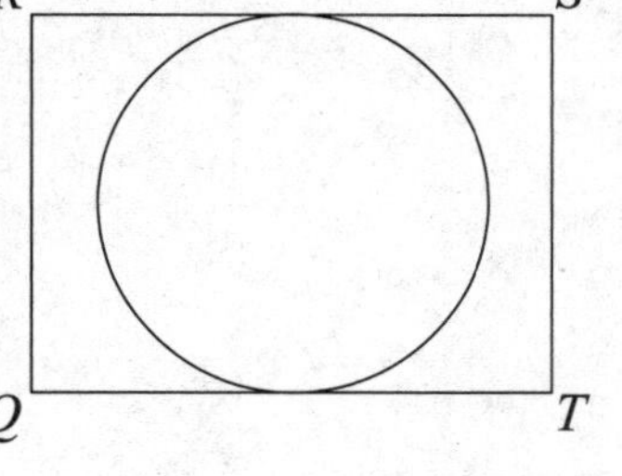

2. In the figure above, the circle is tangent to sides $\overline{QT}$ and $\overline{RS}$ of the 12-by-16 rectangle, $QRST$. What is the circumference of the circle?

F. 8π
G. 12π
H. 16π
J. 24π
K. 36π

★

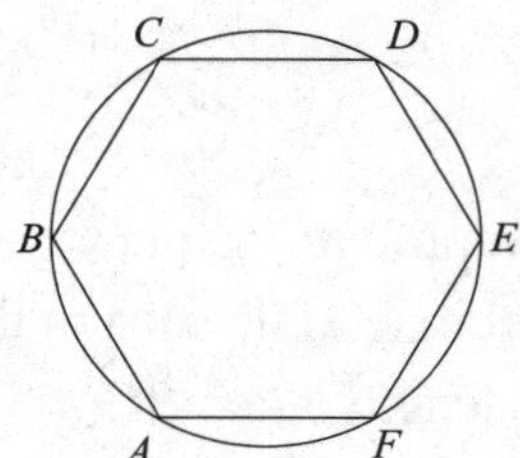

3. In the figure above, regular hexagon $ABCDEF$ is inscribed in the circle. What is the degree measure of arc $\overset{\frown}{ABE}$?

A. 360
B. 270
C. 240
D. 180
E. 120

★★

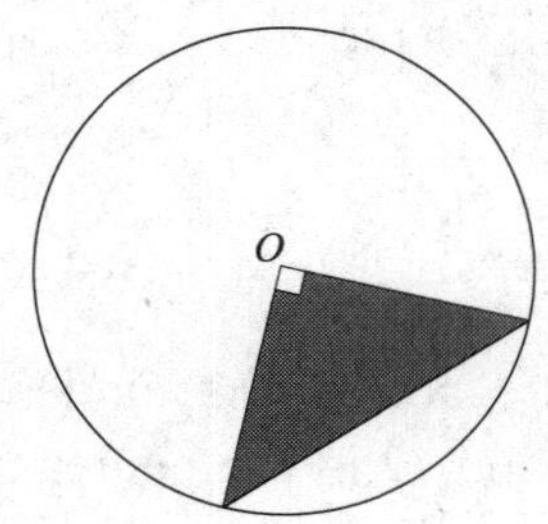

4. In the figure above, O is the center of the circle with radius 10. What is the area of the shaded portion of the circle?

F. 25
G. 50
H. 25π
J. 50π
K. 100

★

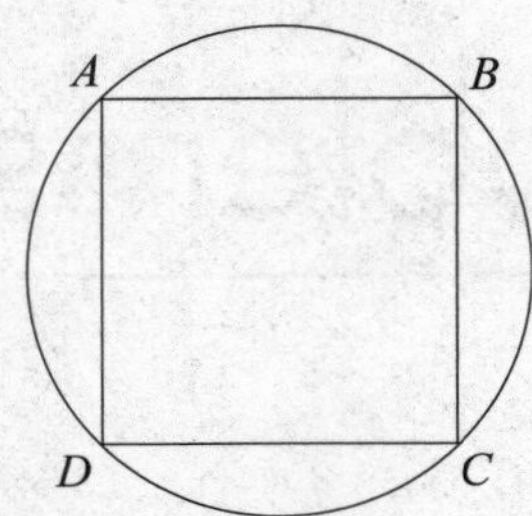

5. In the figure above, square $ABCD$ is inscribed in the circle. If the area of the circle is 64π, what is the length of arc $\overset{\frown}{BC}$?

A. 2π
B. 4π
C. 8π
D. 16π
E. 32π

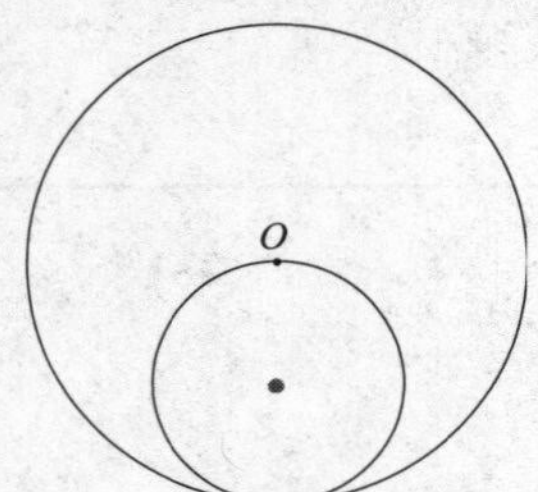

6. In the figure above, the circles are tangent as shown, and O is the center of the larger circle. If the radius of the larger circle is 12, what is the area of the smaller circle?

F. 6π
G. 9π
H. 12π
J. 16π
K. 36π

★★

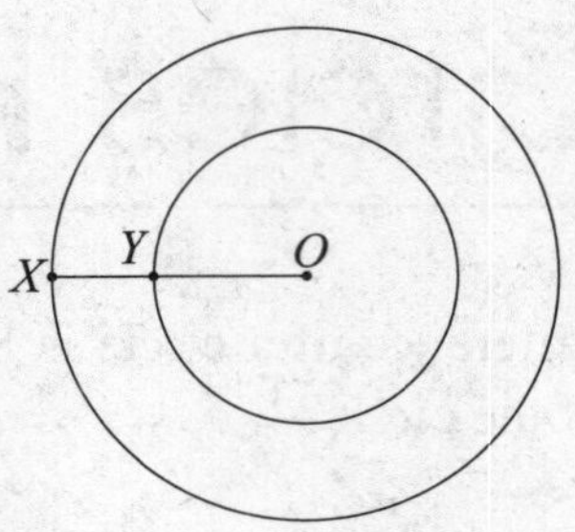

7. In the figure above, O is the center of both circles. If $\overline{YO} = 3$ and $\overline{XY} = 2$, what is the ratio of the area of the smaller circle to the area of the larger circle?

A. 2:5
B. 3:5
C. 2:3
D. 9:25
E. 4:9

★★

8. A bicycle wheel made 500 revolutions while travelling 9000π inches in a straight line along a trail. What is the diameter, in inches, of the wheel?

F. 9
G. 9π
H. 18
J. 18π
K. 27

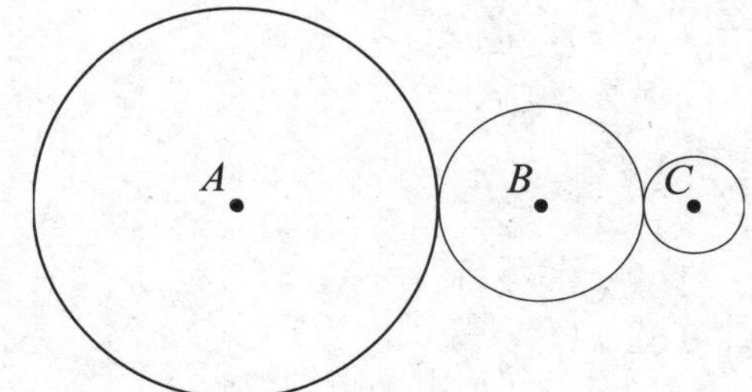

9. In the figure above, the three circles are tangent as shown. The diameter of the circle with center A is twice the diameter of the circle with center B, and the diameter of the circle with center B is twice the diameter of circle with center C. What is the ratio of the area of the smallest circle to the area of largest circle?

A. 1:4
B. 1:8
C. 1:12
D. 1:16
E. 1:64

★★

10. Jim takes a seat on a Ferris wheel that rotates at a constant rate of 1 revolution every 5 minutes. What is the degree measure of the arc Jim travels in his first 3 minutes on the ride?

F. 30
G. 60
H. 108
J. 216
K. 360

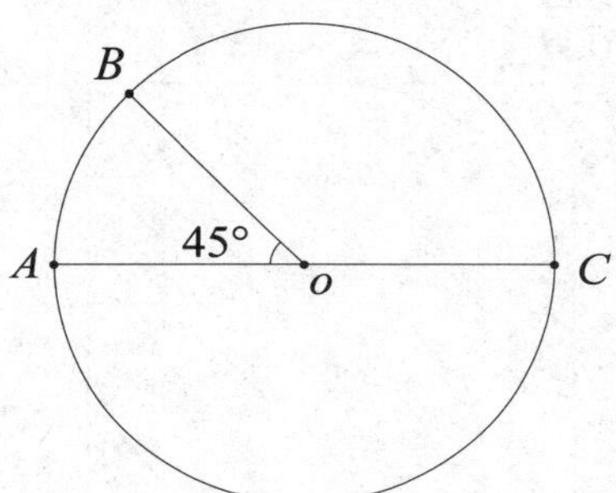

11. Points A and C are the endpoints of the diameter of a circle with center at O, as shown above. Point B is a point on the circle, and $\angle AOB$ measures 45°. The arc formed by $\angle AOB$ is what percent of arc $\widehat{ABC}$?

A. 50%
B. 33.5%
C. 25%
D. 20%
E. 14.5%

★★

12. Five spheres, each of radius 2, are placed together so that each sphere is tangent to at least one other sphere. If A is the center of one of the spheres and B is the center of another of the spheres, what is the greatest possible length of $\overline{AB}$?

F. 7
G. 8
H. 9.5
J. 11
K. 16

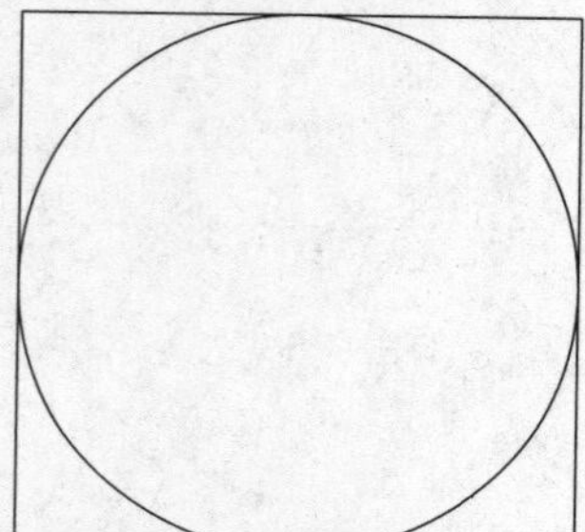

13. In the figure above, a circle with a radius of r is inscribed inside a square. In terms of r, what is the distance from the center of the circle to one of the corners of the square?

A. $\frac{r}{2}$

B. r

C. $\frac{r\sqrt{2}}{2}$

D. $r\sqrt{2}$

E. Cannot be determined by the information given

★★★

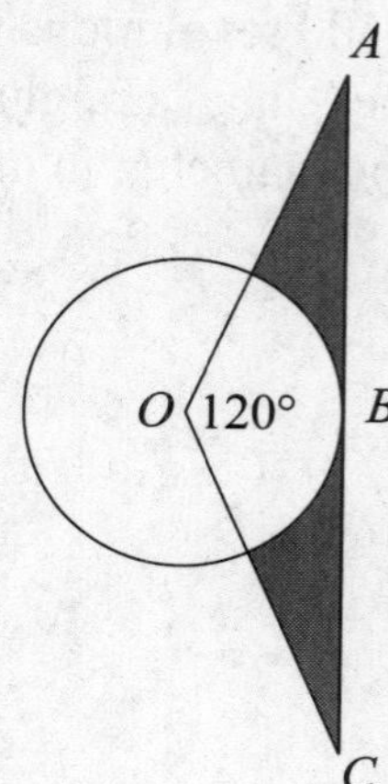

14. In the figure above, the center of the circle is O, and $\overline{AC}$ is tangent to the circle at B. If B is the midpoint of $\overline{AC}$ and the area of the circle is 81π, what is the total area of the shaded region?

F. $27\pi - 18\sqrt{3}$
G. $81\sqrt{3} - 27\pi$
H. $81\sqrt{3}$
J. $162\sqrt{3} - 27\pi$
K. $162\sqrt{3}$

★★★

Perimeter, Area, and Volume

9%
of all math questions on the ACT

Perimeter

Perimeter is the distance around the **outside** edge of a shape.

The perimeter of this square is:

$4 + 4 + 4 + 4 = \mathbf{16}$

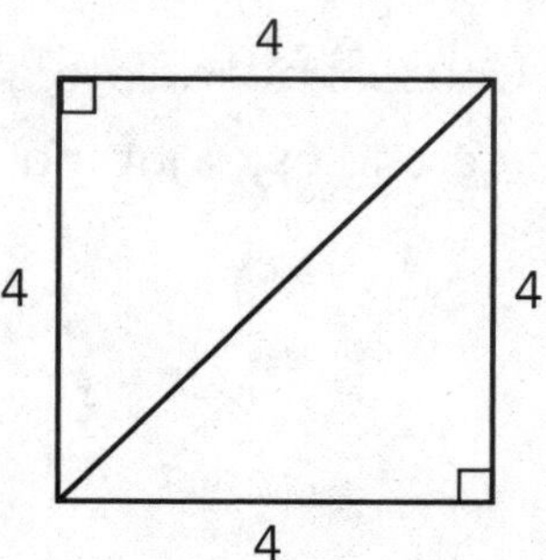

E1

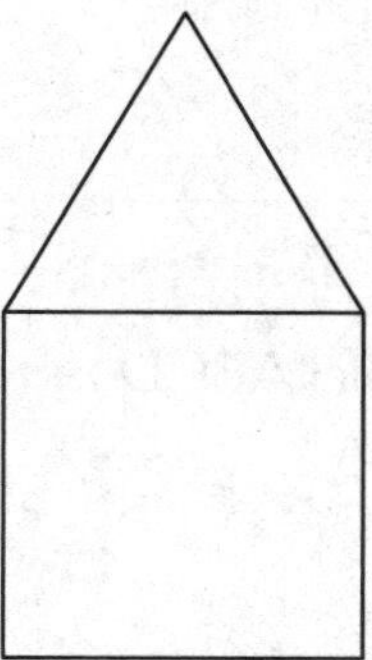

In the figure above, the triangle is equilateral and the area of the square is 25. What is the perimeter of the triangle?

Make sure not to count any internal lines as part of the perimeter. Even if the diagonal of a square is shown, it is not part of the perimeter.

S

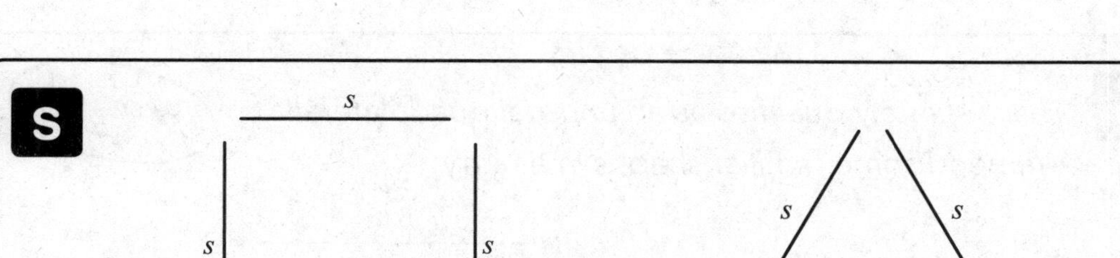

Area □ $= s^2$

$25 = s^2$

$\sqrt{25} = \sqrt{s^2}$

$5 = s$

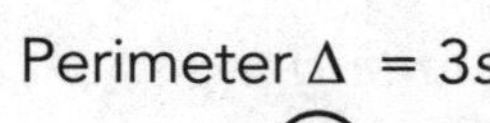

Perimeter $\Delta = 3s$

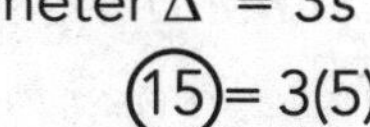

(15) $= 3(5)$

Area

Here are some tricks to remember when solving for the area of a 2-D shape.

1. Area of a triangle = $\frac{1}{2}$ base × height
2. Area of a rectangle = length × width
3. Unusual quadrilaterals: Break unfamiliar shapes into shapes you know: rectangles, right triangles, circles and semicircles.

E2

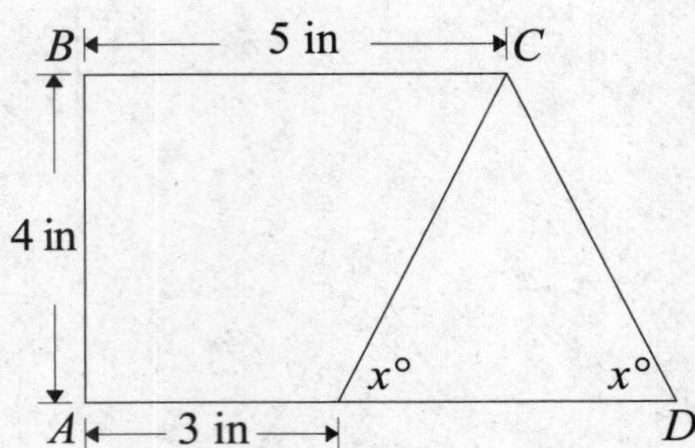

What is the area of trapezoid ABCD in the figure above?

A. 18 square inches
B. 24 square inches
C. 28 square inches
D. 32 square inches
E. 60 square inches

S *This definitely qualifies as an unusual quadrilateral! We need some familiar shapes in a hurry.*

Area$_{ABCD}$ = ?

Drop a line straight down from C to $\overline{AD}$, creating a rectangle and cutting the triangle in half into ***two right triangles****.*

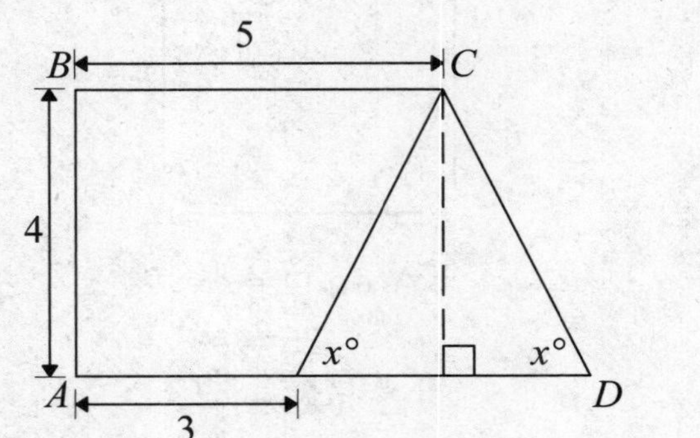

*The base of the triangle on the left is **2** because $5 - 3 = 2$. The base of the triangle on the right is also **2** because we cut the original triangle in half when we drew our line. Now we're set!*

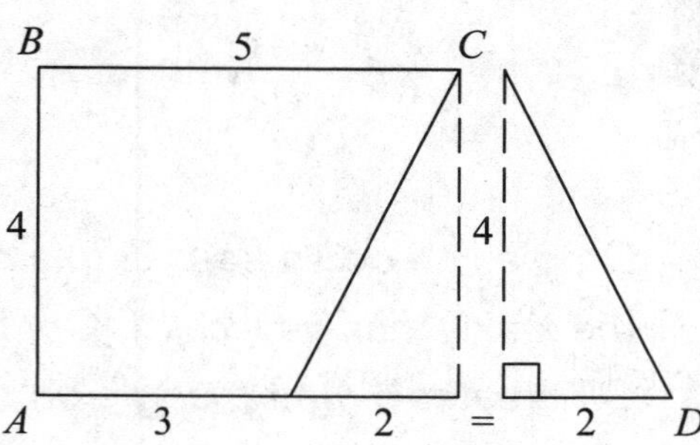

1 The area of the new rectangle is

$(5)(4) = \boxed{20}$

2 The area of the newly formed triangle is

$\frac{1}{2}(2)(4) = \boxed{4}$

3 The total area of ABCD is

20 + 4 = **24 square inches**, **B.**

E3

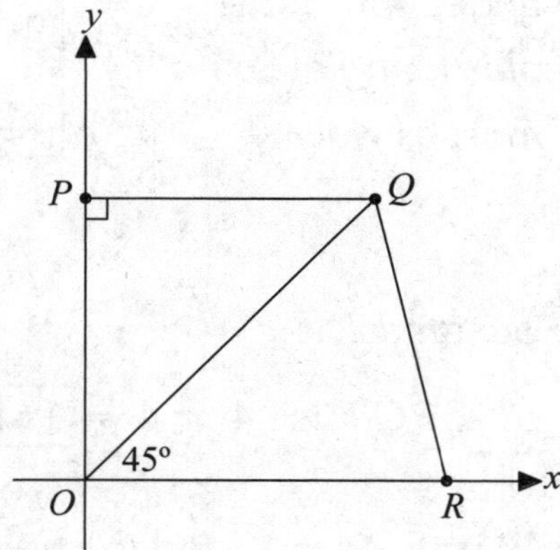

In the xy-plane above, the length of $\overline{OR}$ is 5, and the coordinates of point P are (0, 4). What is the area of quadrilateral OPQR ?

F. 9
G. 12
H. 18
J. 20
K. 22

S

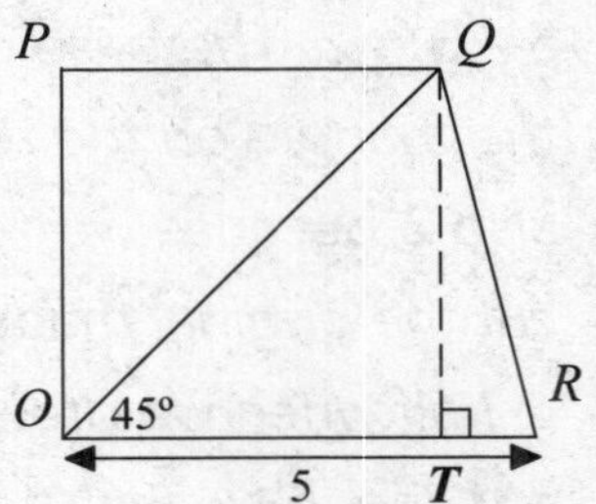

Drop a line down from Q to a point on the x-axis that we'll call T. Our new line, $\overline{QT}$ creates a right triangle on the right, and a rectangle on the left.

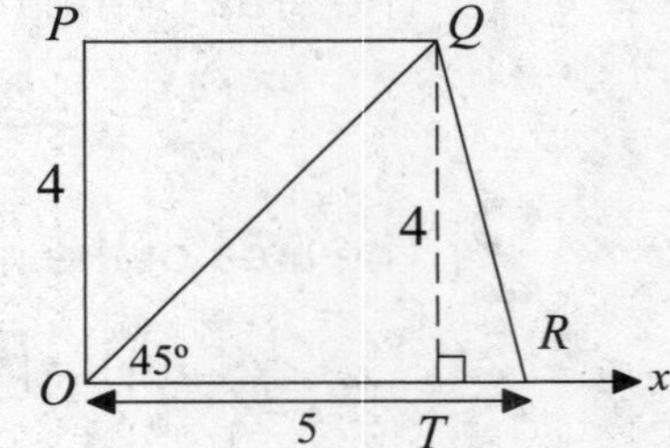

From the coordinates of point P, we learn that $\overline{OP}$ = ***4****. Because $\overline{PQ}$ is perpendicular to the y-axis, $\overline{QT}$ must* ***also*** *equal 4.*

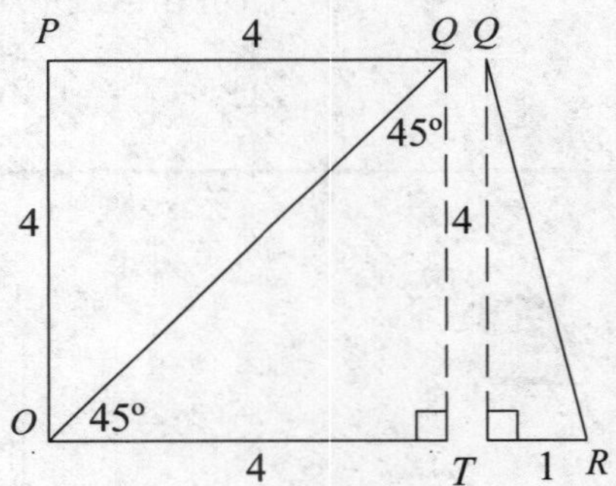

Looking at ΔOQT we notice that we have a 45° and a 90° angle. We can subtract these angles from 180° to give us our third angle: 45°. POW! We have an ***isoscoles*** *triangle! So if $\overline{QT}$ equals 4, $\overline{OT}$ must as well.*

Now we can find our areas!

The area of OPQT is 4 × 4 = **16**

The ***base*** *of ΔQTR is* 5 – 4 = **1**, *and the* ***height*** *is 4.*

The area of ΔQTR is $\frac{1}{2}$ (1)(4) = **2**

Now we add the two areas together: 16 + 2 = **18**

H *is our answer!*

Volume

Volume is the space occupied by a three dimensional shape. A simple example is the space inside a box. You can think of the volume as the area of the shape on the end multiplied by the height.

Volume = **area** of shape on end × **height**

Boxes

A **box** is simply multiple **rectangles** stacked on top of one another.

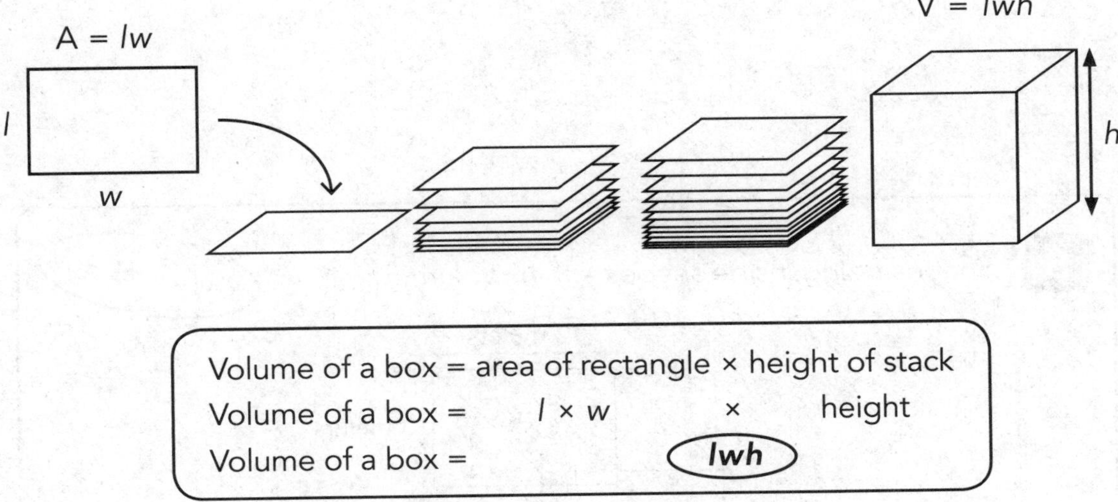

A **cube** is a special type of box where the length, width, and height are all **equal**. The volume of a cube is therefore simply one side **cubed**.

$V = s \times s \times s$
$V = s^3$

Cylinders

A **cylinder** is simply multiple **circles** stacked on top of one another.

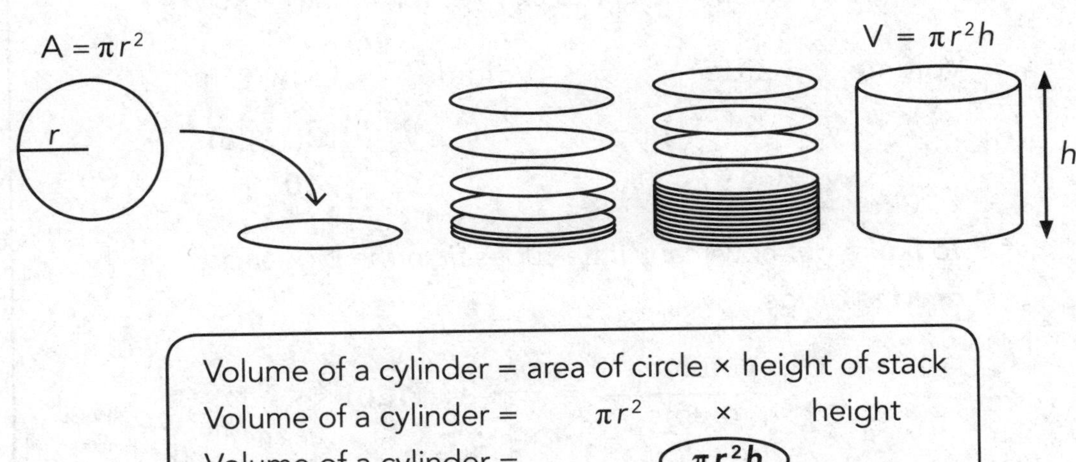

A = πr²
r
V = πr²h
h
Volume of a cylinder = area of circle × height of stack
Volume of a cylinder = πr² × height
Volume of a cylinder = πr²h

E4

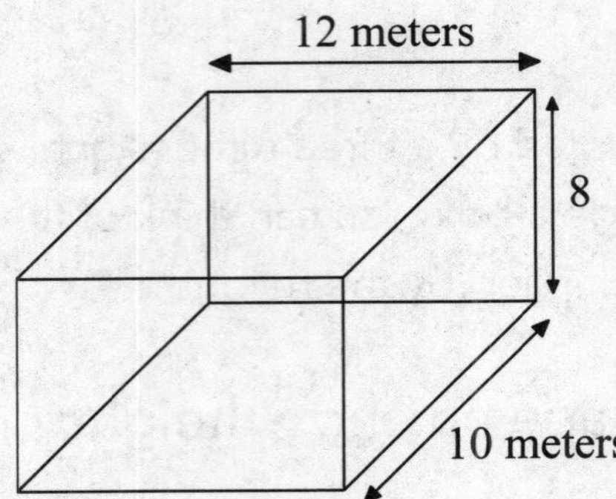

What is the maximum number of cubes with side length 2 meters that will fit into the rectangular box shown above?

S *Shapes fitting inside shapes – think volume!*

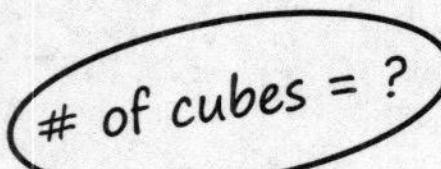

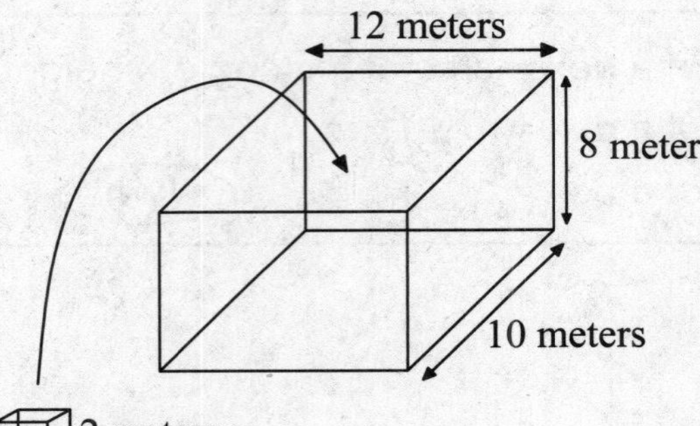

So how many of the little cubes can we fit into the big box?

$\text{Volume}_{\text{Little}} = \text{side}^3$

$V_L = 2^3$

$V_L = \mathbf{8}$

$\text{Volume}_{\text{Big}} = l \times w \times h$

$V_B = 10(12)(8)$

$V_B = \mathbf{960}$

To figure out how many little cubes fit in the bigger box, we need to divide.

$$\frac{\text{Volume}_{\text{Big}}}{\text{Volume}_{\text{Little}}} = \frac{960}{8} = \boxed{120}$$

We can fit 120 small cubes into the figure.

Surface Area

To find the surface area of any three-dimensional shape, find the area of each side individually, and then add them all together.

To find the surface area of a **cube**, all you need to do is find the area of one side, which is a square, and multiply by 6 (the number of sides on a cube).

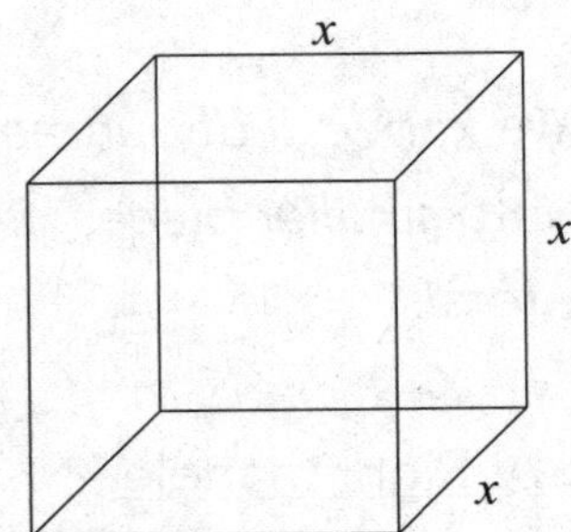

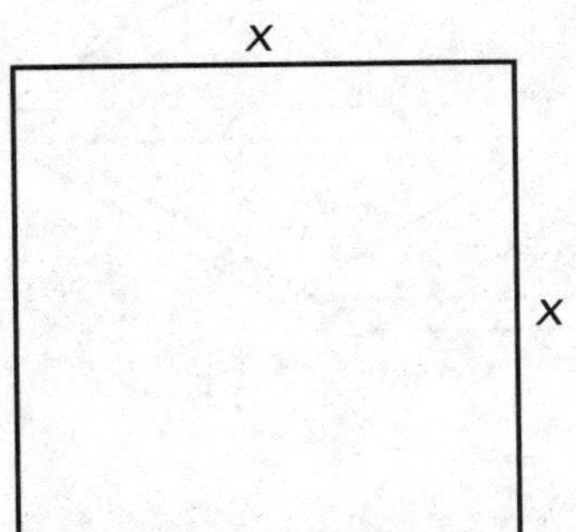

The area of one side of a cube is x^2.
Surface area = $6x^2$. (Add the areas of all of the sides to get the surface area.)

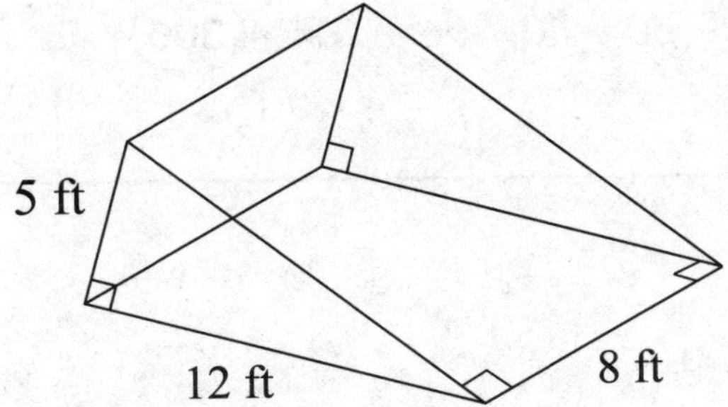

What is the surface area, in square feet, of the solid wedge shown above?

A. 104
B. 200
C. 204
D. 270
E. 300

S *We are missing the hypotenuse of side A below, so first we need to use Pythag's theorem or handily remember that 5-12-**13** is a special right triangle!*

surface area = ?

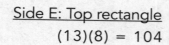

Once we know all of our measurements, we can break the whole shape into smaller pieces, then add their individual areas together for the total:

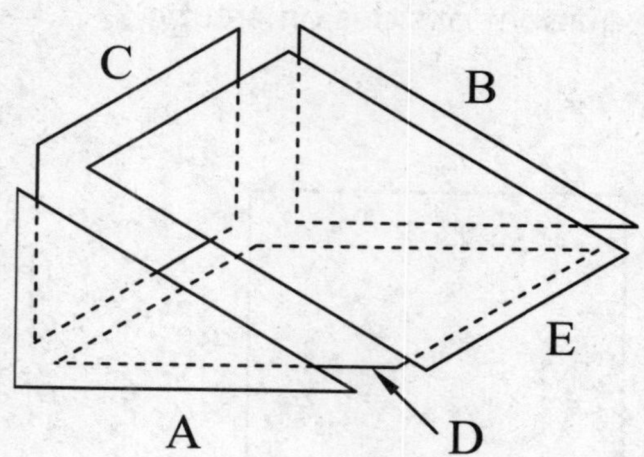

Side A: Right triangle

$\frac{1}{2}(12)(5) = 30$

Side B: Right triangle

$\frac{1}{2}(12)(5) = 30$

Side C: Back rectangle

$(5)(8) = 40$

Side D: Bottom rectangle

$(12)(8) = 96$

Side E: Top rectangle

$(13)(8) = 104$

Total is $30 + 30 + 40 + 96 + 104 =$ **300**, **E**

Perimeter, Area, and Volume Practice Problems

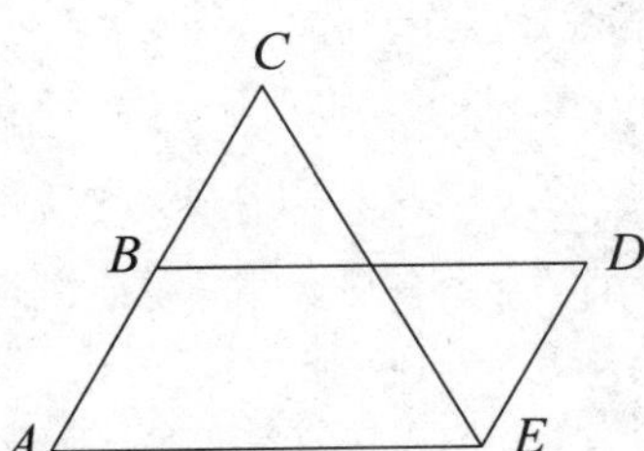

1. In the figure above, $\triangle ACE$ is an equilateral triangle and *ABDE* is a parallelogram. If *B* is the midpoint of $\overline{AC}$ and the perimeter of ΔACE is 12, what is the perimeter of parallelogram *ABDE* ?

A. 6
B. 8
C. 12
D. 16
E. 18

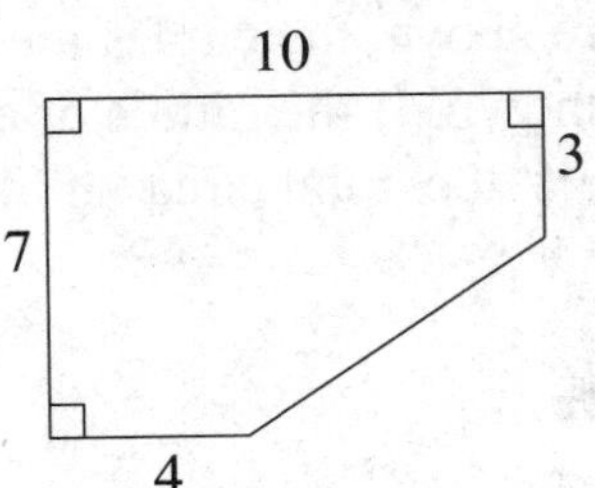

2. What is the area of the five-sided figure above ?

F. 32
G. 46
H. 58
J. 70
K. 84

★

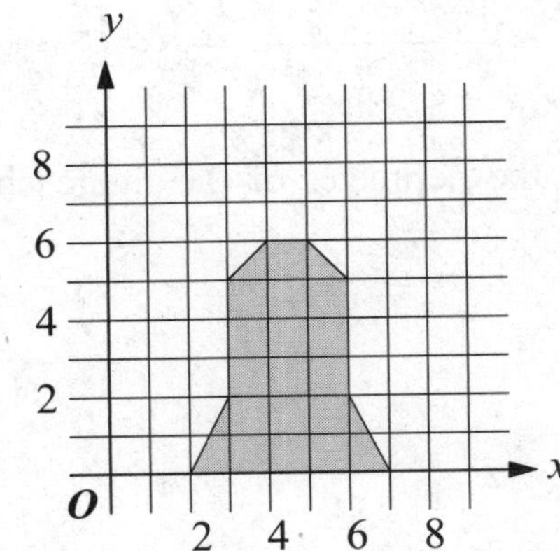

3. What is the area of the shaded region in the figure above ?

A. 16
B. 17
C. 18
D. 19
E. 20

★

4. If there is no waste, how many square feet of linoleum are needed to cover a floor that is 6 yards by 9 yards ? (1 yard = 3 feet)

F. 18
G. 27
H. 54
J. 162
K. 486

★

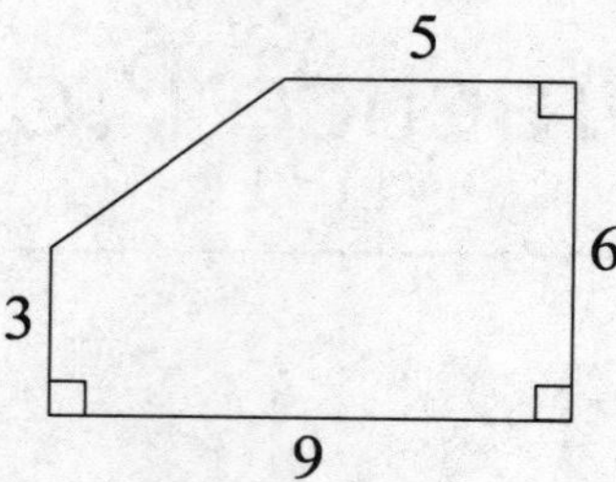

5. What is the perimeter of the figure above?

A. 54
B. 30
C. 28
D. 25
E. 23

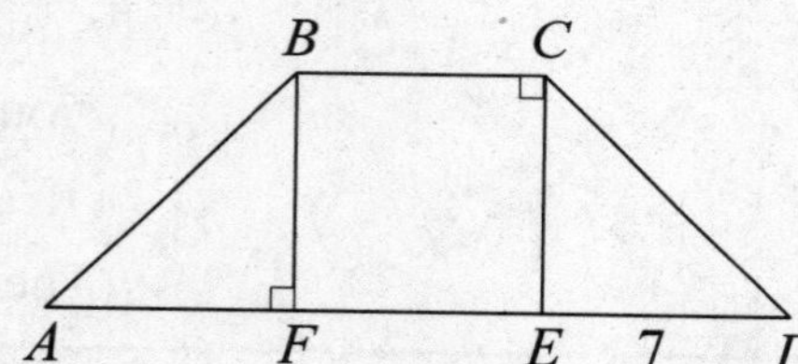

6. In the figure above, $\overline{AF} = \overline{FE} = \overline{ED}$, and the area of the trapezoid $ABCD$ is 98 square inches. What is the perimeter of the trapezoid?

F. $14 + 7\sqrt{2}$
G. 28
H. $28 + 7\sqrt{2}$
J. $28 + 14\sqrt{2}$
K. 42

★★

7. The perimeter of a certain rectangle is 5 times its width. What is the ratio of the length of the rectangle to the width of the rectangle?

A. 1:2
B. 1:5
C. 2:3
D. 2:5
E. 3:2

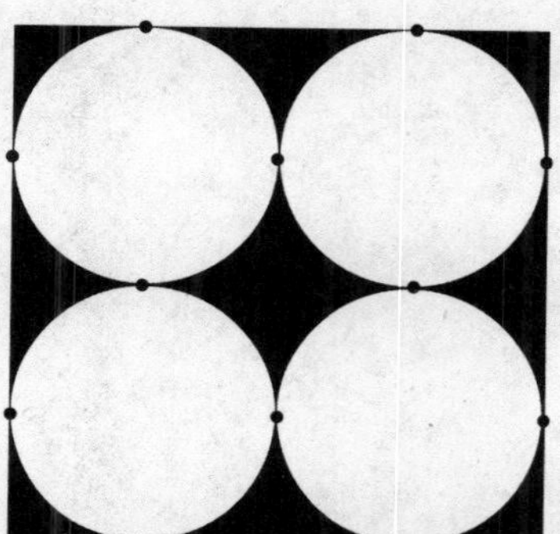

8. In the square above, the circles are tangent at the points shown. If the radius of each circle is 2, what is the total area of the shaded regions?

F. $16 - 4\pi$
G. $16 - 16\pi$
H. $64 - 4\pi$
J. $64 - 8\pi$
K. $64 - 16\pi$

★★

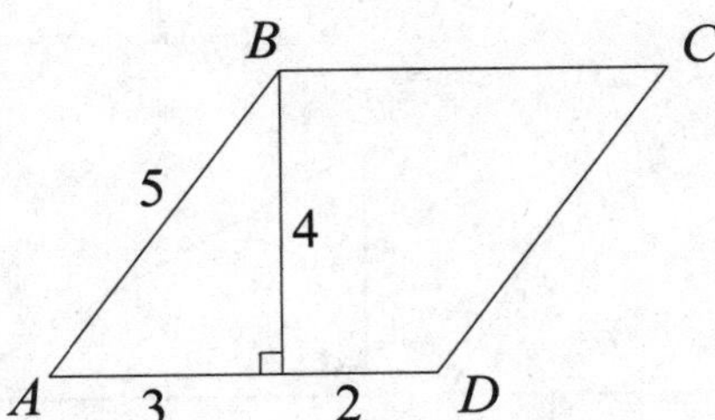

9. Parallelogram $ABCD$ is shown above with dimensions in centimeters. What is the area, in square centimeters, of the parallelogram?

A. 14
B. 20
C. 23
D. 24
E. 25

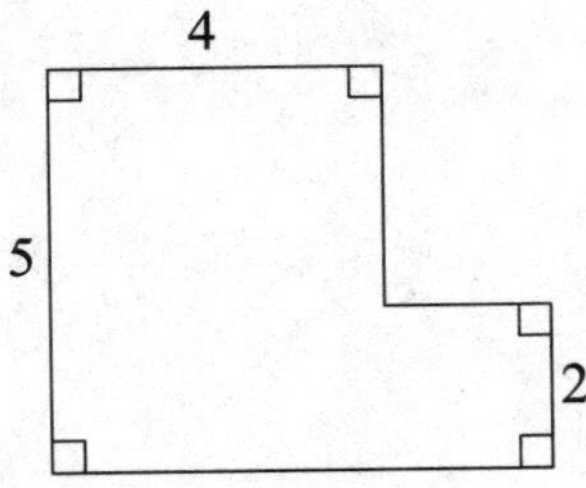

10. The area of the figure above is 24. What is the perimeter of the figure?

F. 17
G. 20
H. 22
J. 24
K. It cannot be determined from the information provided.

★★

11. If the height of a triangle is increased by 20% and the base of the same triangle is decreased by 20%, what is the effect on the area of the triangle?

A. The area is increased by 40%.
B. The area is increased by 20%.
C. The area is unchanged.
D. The area is decreased by 10%.
E. The area is decreased by 4%.

12. Ahmad fills a spherical beach ball, which has a diameter of 6 inches, with air until it is full. How many such beach balls could he fill using the amount of air in a spherical beach ball with diameter 18 inches? (The volume of a sphere with radius r is given by $\frac{4}{3}\pi r^3$.)

F. 1.5
G. 3
H. 9
J. 27
K. 23

★★★

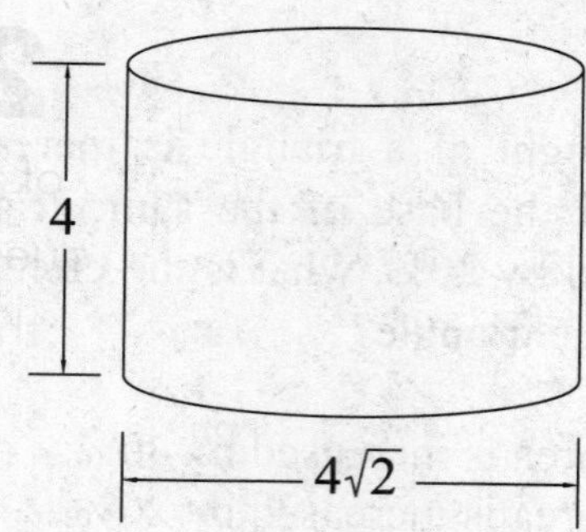

13. What is volume of the largest rectangular box that will fit completely in the right circular cylinder shown above?

A. $12\sqrt{2}$
B. 16
C. $16\sqrt{2}$
D. 64
E. $64\sqrt{2}$

★★★

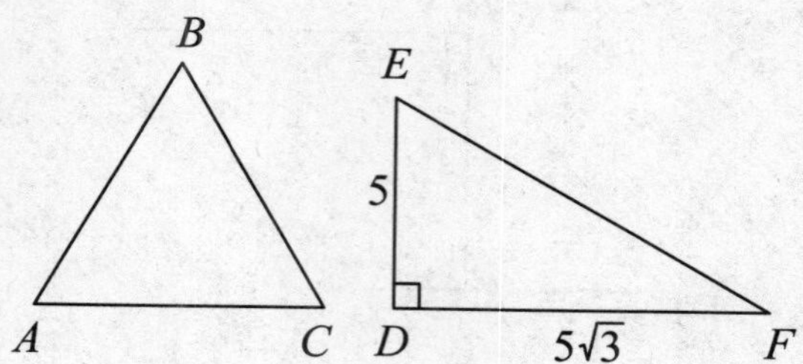

14. For the triangles above, the area of ΔABC is twice of the area of ΔDEF. If ΔABC is equilateral, what is the perimeter of ΔABC?

F. 15
G. $15\sqrt{2}$
H. $15\sqrt{3}$
J. $25\sqrt{3}$
K. 30

★★★

Proportional Shapes

2% of all math questions on the ACT

Proportional shapes are all about ratios. Shapes that are proportional have a fixed relationship.

Similar triangles

Similar triangles are the most common proportional shapes on the ACT. These are triangles that have the **same angle measures**; any time you see them, think **ratios**!

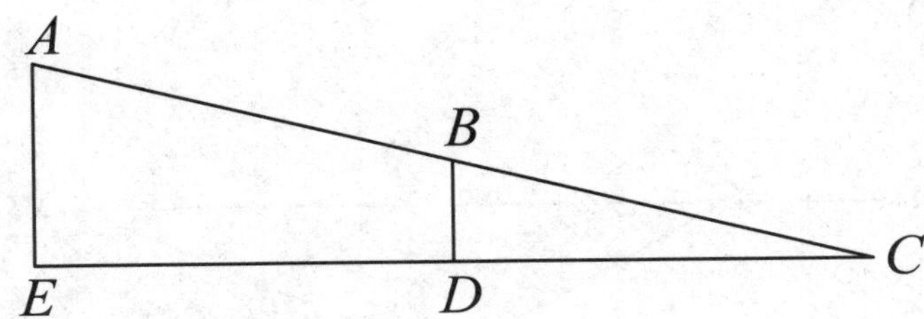

In the triangle above, $\overline{AE} \parallel \overline{BD}$. If $\overline{EC} = 40$, $\overline{AE} = 10$, and $\overline{ED} = 20$, what is the value of $\overline{BD}$?

ALWAYS label first.

$\overline{BD} = ?$

*This is a proportional shape: a **locked ratio**.*

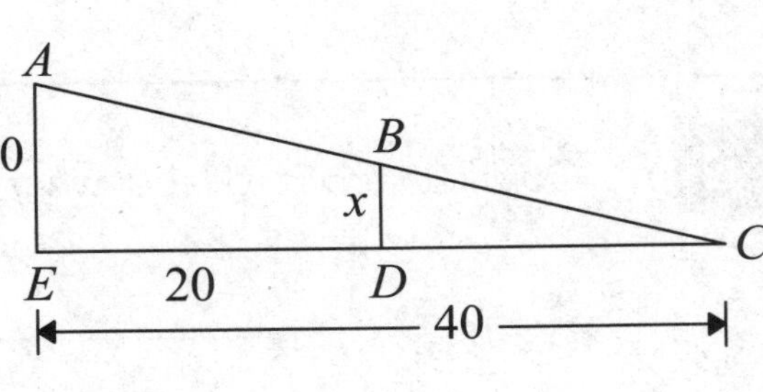

1 *Find the ratio for △AEC:*

$$\frac{\text{Length}}{\text{Height}} = \frac{40}{10} = \boxed{\frac{4}{1}}$$

This is our locked ratio for both shapes.

2 *Find $\overline{DC}$*

$\overline{EC} - \overline{ED} = \overline{DC}$

$40 - 20 = \overline{DC}$

$20 = \overline{DC}$

3 *Apply the **locked ratio** to △BDC:*

$\frac{\text{Length}}{\text{Height}} = \frac{20}{x} = \frac{4}{1}$

$4x = 20$

$x = \boxed{5}$

E2

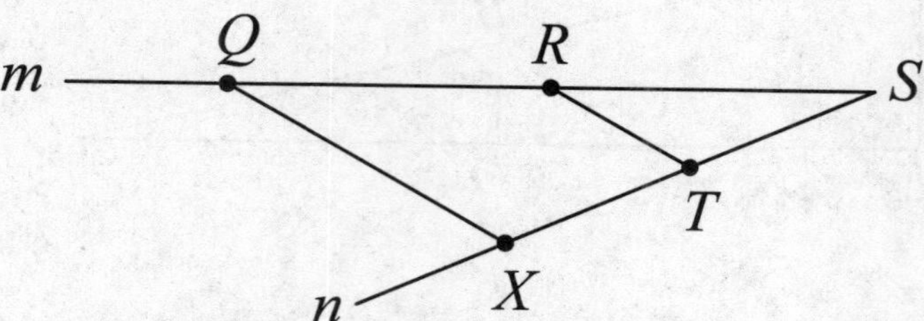

In the figure above, Q, R, and S lie on line m, and X, T, and S lie on line n. R is the midpoint of $\overline{QS}$ and T is the midpoint of $\overline{XS}$. If $\overline{QS} = 8$, $\overline{TS} = 3$, and $\overline{RT} = 2$, what is the perimeter of quadrilateral $QRTX$?

S *Our first step is to label what we know:*

perimeter$_{QRTX}$ = ?

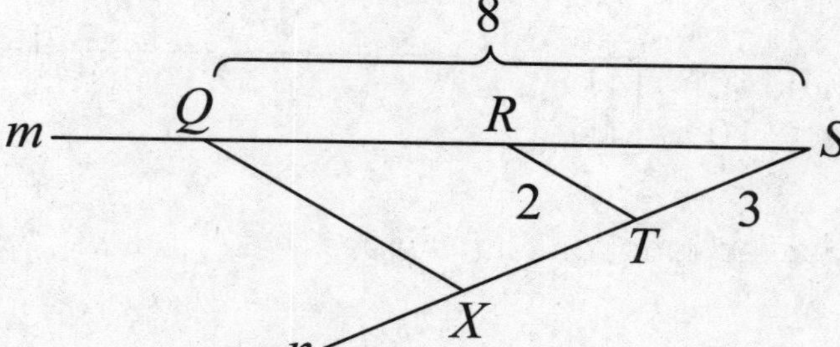

If $\overline{TS} = 3$, then $\overline{XT} = 3$ because T is the midpoint of $\overline{XS}$. And if $\overline{QS} = 8$, then $\overline{QR} = 4$ and $\overline{RS} = 4$ because R is the midpoint of $\overline{QS}$.

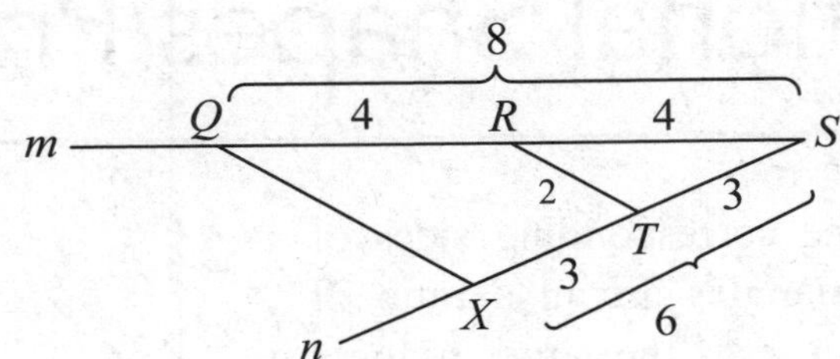

Now we can clearly see the relationship between the larger shape and the smaller proportional shape.

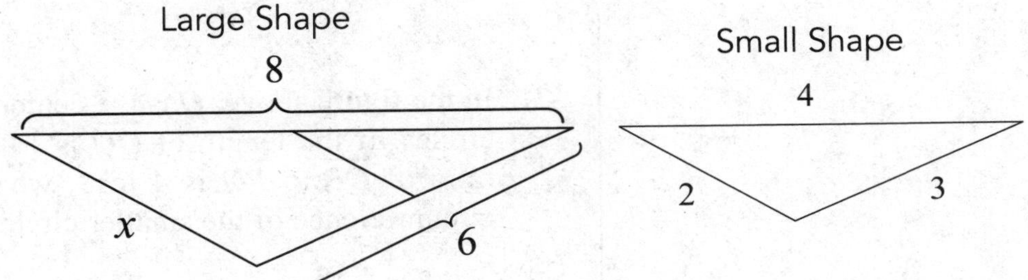

Let's look at our ratios:

$$\frac{\text{Large}}{\text{Small}} = \frac{8}{4} = \frac{6}{3} = \frac{x}{2}$$

Using our ***locked ratio****, we can solve for x.*

$$\frac{6}{3} = \frac{x}{2}$$

$$3x = 12$$

$$x = \boxed{4}$$

Our final step is to add up all the sides of quadrilateral QRTX.

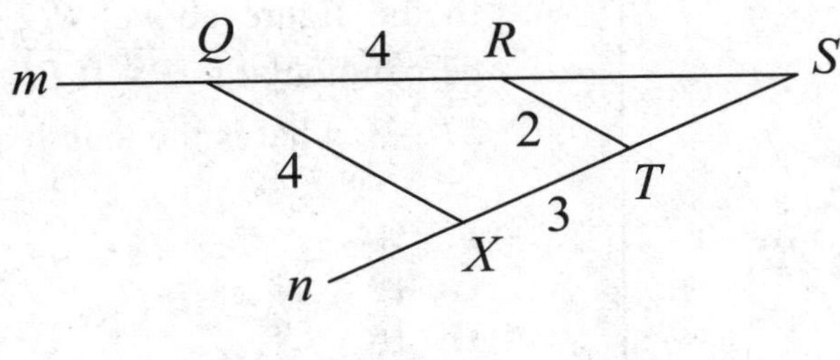

$4 + 4 + 3 + 2 = 13$ (circled)

Proportional Shapes Practice Problems

1. The lengths of the corresponding sides of 2 similar right triangles are in a ratio of 3:8. The hypotenuse of the larger triangle is 48 centimeters long. How long is the hypotenuse of the smaller triangle, in centimeters?

A. 11
B. 18
C. 24
D. 26
E. 32

★

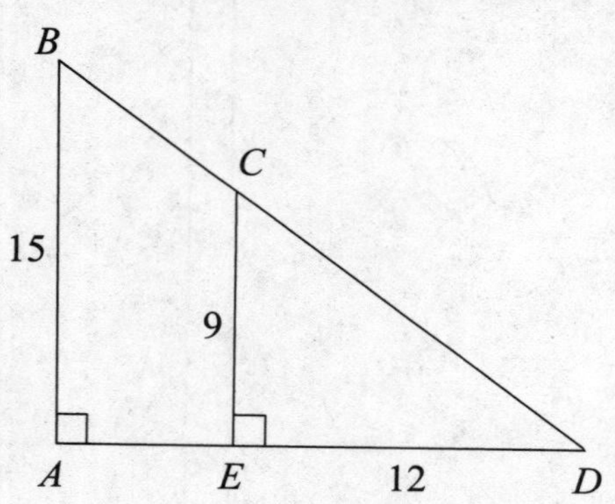

2. In the figure above, $\overline{AB}$ and $\overline{CE}$ are parallel, and $\overline{AD}$ is perpendicular to $\overline{BA}$ and $\overline{CE}$. The length of $\overline{AB}$ is 15 inches, the length of $\overline{CE}$ is 9 inches, and the length of $\overline{ED}$ is 12 inches. What is the length of $\overline{BD}$?

F. 15
G. 18
H. 20
J. 24
K. 25

★★

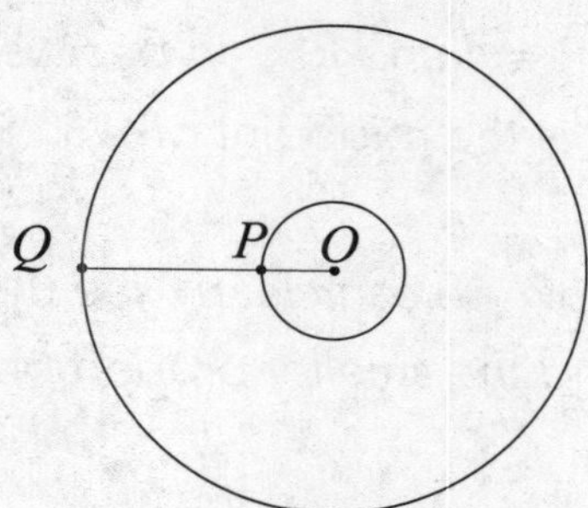

3. In the figure above, O is the center of both circles. If the length of $\overline{QO}$ is 14 and the ratio of $\overline{QP}$ to $\overline{PO}$ is 4 to 3, what is the circumference of the smaller circle?

A. 8π
B. 12π
C. 24π
D. 32π
E. 64π

★★

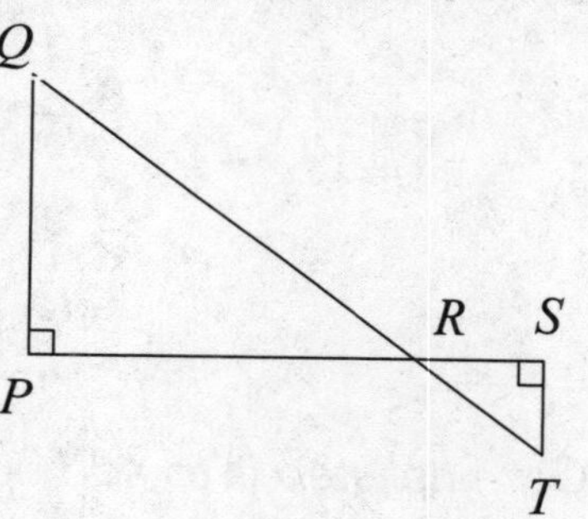

4. In the figure above, $\overline{PQ}$ and $\overline{TS}$ are each perpendicular to $\overline{PS}$. If $\overline{PR} = 12$, $\overline{RS} = 4$, and $\overline{ST} = 3$, what is the length of $\overline{QT}$?

F. 10
G. 12
H. 15
J. 16
K. 20

★★

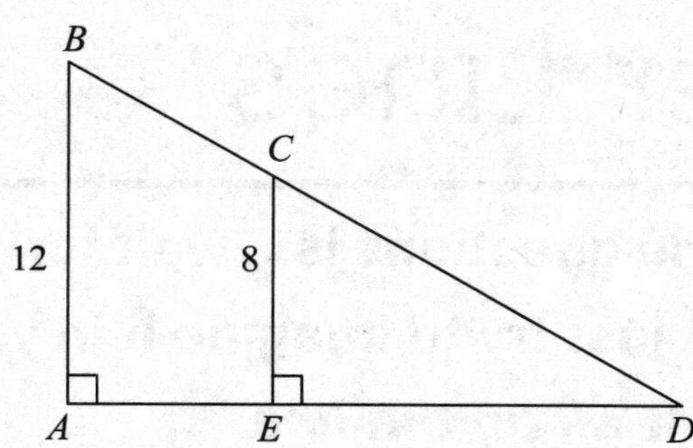

5. In the figure above, what is the value of $\frac{\overline{AE}}{\overline{AD}}$?

A. $\frac{1}{4}$
B. $\frac{1}{3}$
C. $\frac{1}{2}$
D. $\frac{2}{3}$
E. $\frac{3}{4}$

★★

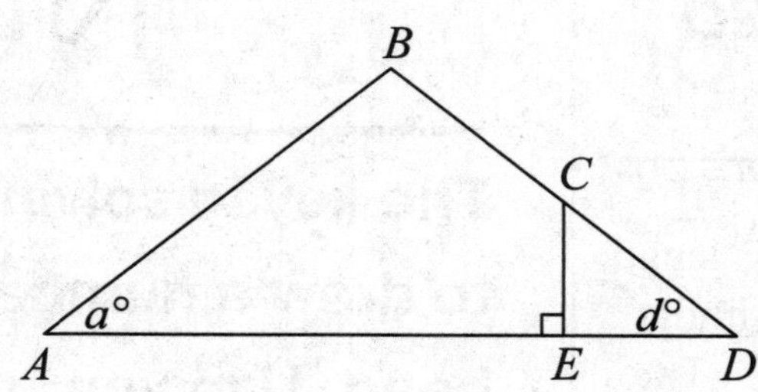

6. In the figure above, $a = d$, $\overline{BC} = \overline{CD}$, and $\overline{ED} = \frac{1}{4}\overline{AD}$. If the area of $\Delta\ CDE$ is 10, what is the area of $\Delta\ ABD$?

F. 40
G. 50
H. 60
J. 80
K. 100

★★★

1%
of all math questions on the ACT

Number Lines

The key to solving number line questions is... wait for it... to draw a number line! Don't just try to imagine it in your head. Use your pencil to lay it *all on the line.*

E1 Points L and M lie on a line in that order. The coordinate of point L is – 6 and the coordinate of point M is 10. If N is located $\frac{1}{4}$ of the way from L to M, what is the coordinate N ?

S *Let's populate our number line and draw the full distance.*

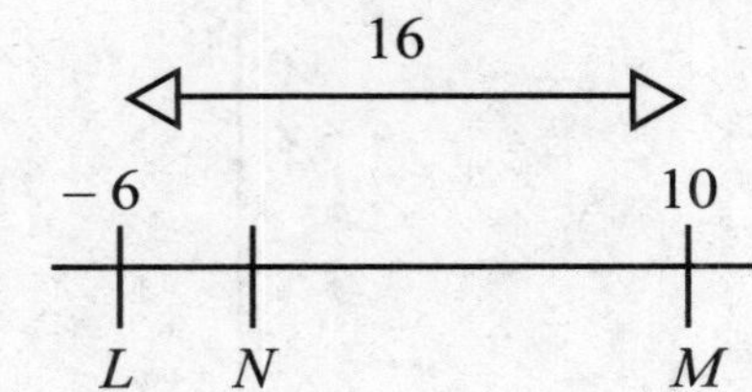

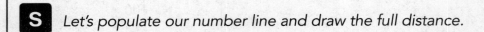

Total distance = 10 – (– 6) = 16

We're told that segment $\overline{LN}$ is $\frac{1}{4}$ of the total distance.

$\frac{1}{4}$ total distance = $\frac{1}{4}$ × 16 = 4

So to get to N, we need to travel **4** *units to the right of* **– 6**.

(–6) + 4 = **–2**

so the coordinate of point N is **(–2)**.

Rest assured "4" will be an answer, and it will be the most commonly selected **wrong** answer.

The question did **not** ask for one fourth of the distance from L to M; it asked for the **coordinate** of N.

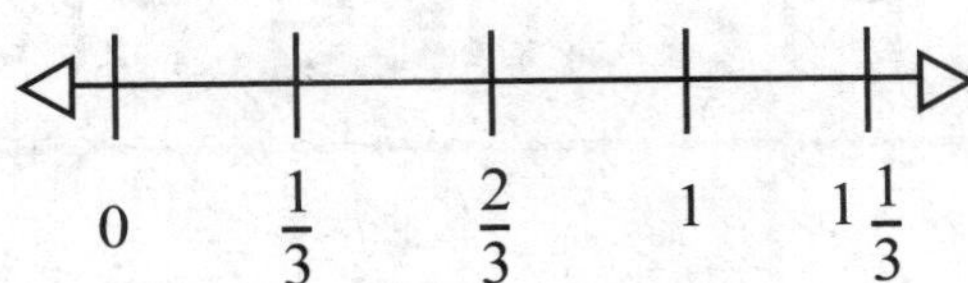

On the number line above, the tick marks are equally spaced, and their coordinates are indicated above. How many tick marks would lie on this number line between the coordinates 11 and 14?

S *Let's draw our number line:*

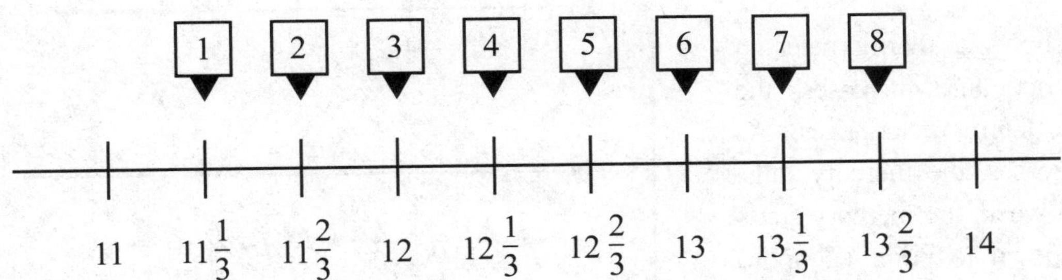

We are counting the ticks ***between*** *11 and 14.*
This means we should NOT count 11 and 14

If we remember to count between the tick marks on either end, we get **(8)**.

Number Line Practice Problems

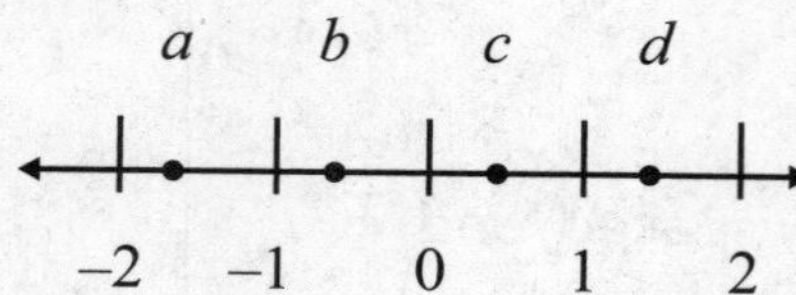

1. The letters a, b, c, and d are coordinates of the points shown on the number line above. Which of the expressions below has the least value ?

A. $a + b$
B. $a + c$
C. $b + c$
D. $c + d$
E. $a \times c$

★

2. The figure below shows a thermometer in Celsius. As the temperature increases, the mercury inside the thermometer rises. As the temperature decreases, the mercury falls. Over the course of a week, the mercury starts at point B, moves down to point C, up to point A, then back down to point D. What is the closest estimate, in degrees Celsius, to the total overall movement of the mercury ?

F. 0
G. 3
H. 15
J. 30
K. 34

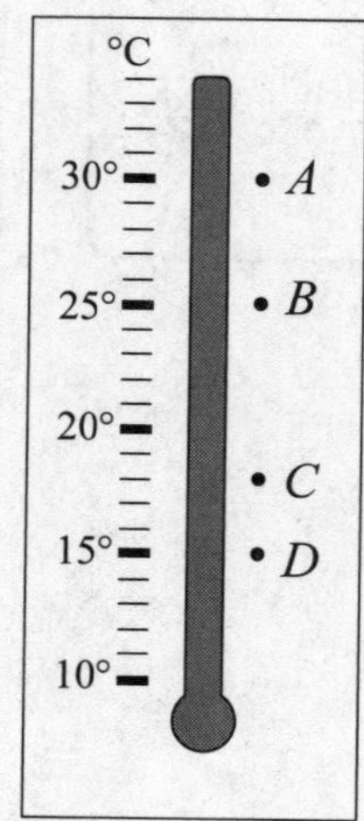

★

$$-7 \leq 2y + 1 < 9$$

3. Which of the following represents all values of y that satisfy the inequality above ?

A.
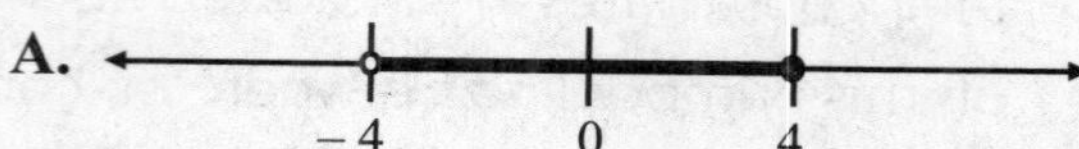

B.
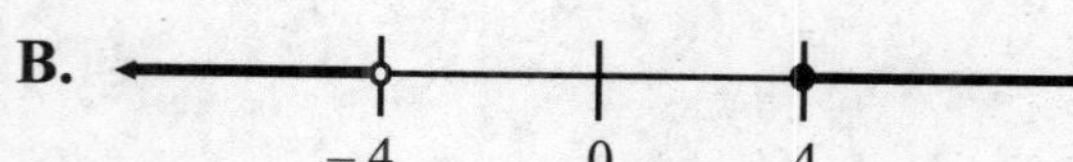

C.
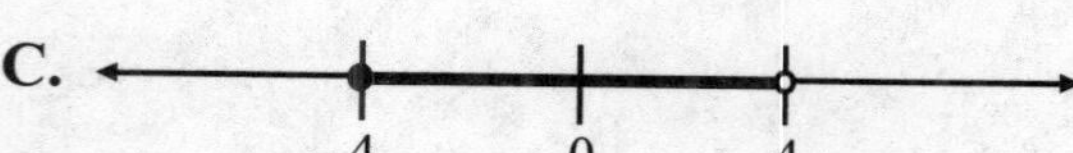

D.
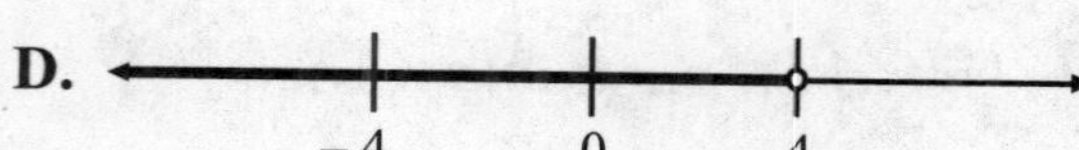

E.
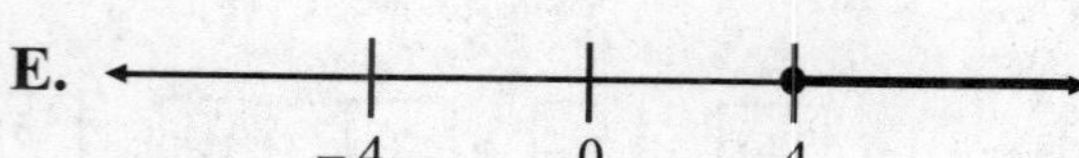

★★

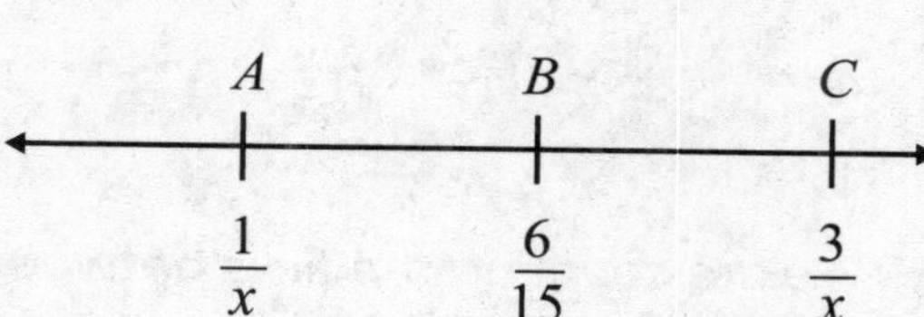

4. In the number line shown above, segment $\overline{AB}$ is equal to segment $\overline{BC}$. What is the length of segment $\overline{AC}$?

F. 15
G. 5
H. 0.6
J. 0.4
K. 0.2

★★

Coordinate Systems

3% of all math questions on the ACT

Coordinate system problems are straightforward on the ACT, but they ALL require a visual.

Remember, in coordinate systems, the x-axis goes across (horizontal) and the y-axis goes up and down (vertical).

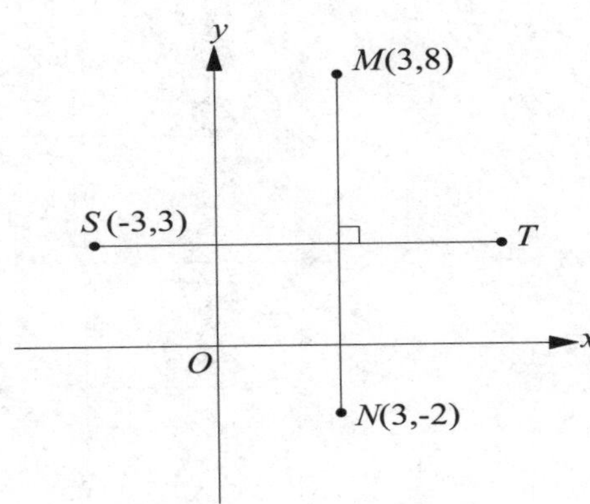

In the figure above, $\overline{ST} = \overline{MN}$. What are the coordinates of point T ?

We need to find both an x and y value for point T.

The length of $\overline{MN}$ is **10** *because we are going up from –2 to +8. Since we are told $\overline{ST} = \overline{MN}$ in the problem, we know $\overline{ST}$ =* **10.**

*To find the x-coordinate of T, begin at the x-coordinate of point S, (***–3***) and add the length of $\overline{ST}$* **(10)**:

x-coordinate = –3 + 10 = +7

Since $\overline{ST}$ is perpindicular to $\overline{MN}$, line $\overline{ST}$ must be horizontal. Therefore, point T and point S have the same y-coordinate: **+3.**

The coordinates of T are **(7,3)**.

Every point on a **horizontal** line has the same **y-value**.

Every point on a **vertical** line has the same **x-value**.

E2 In the (x,y) coordinate plane, what is the perimeter of a rectangle with opposite vertices at $(-3, 3)$ and $(2, -3)$?

S *This is a very simple problem if you graph it.* perimeter = ?

These are opposite vertices. Draw the lines to complete the rectangle, then find and label the side lengths.

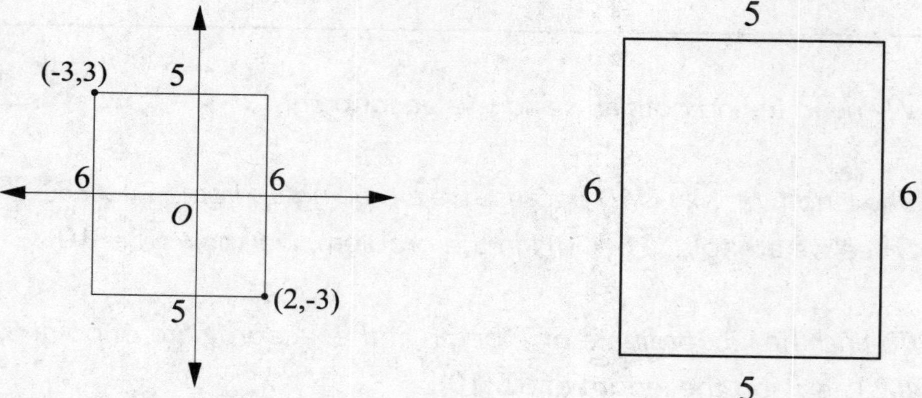

Add the lengths of the sides to find the perimeter.

$5 + 5 + 6 + 6 = \mathbf{22}$

The perimeter is **22**.

E3

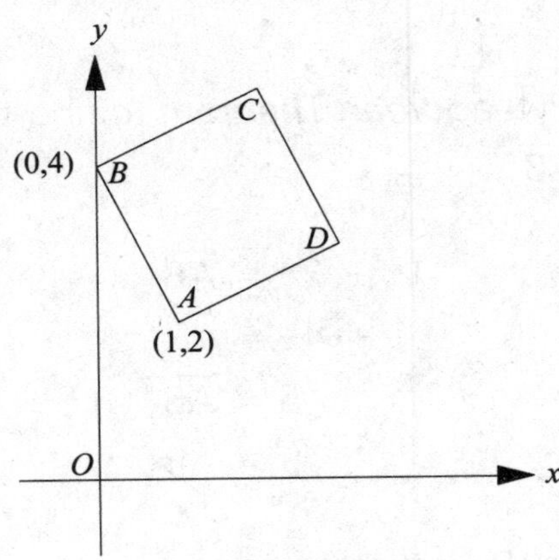

Find the area of square ABCD.

S *This looks tough—no verticals or horizontals!*
Let's draw shapes we know. Do you see the right triangle?

Area = ? ABCD

One great thing that coordinate systems allow you to do is create right triangles. Any diagonal line can be made into a right triangle with two other lines, one parallel to the x-axis and one parallel to the y-axis.

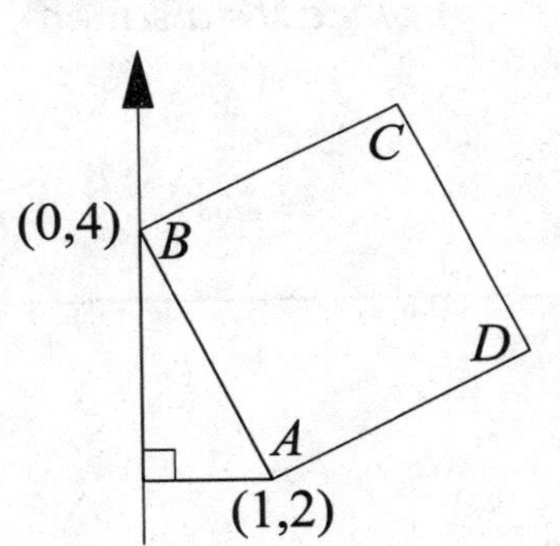

With the two given points, you can find the sides of the right triangle.

$$y_1 - y_2 \rightarrow 4 - 2 = \ \ 2$$
$$x_1 - x_2 \rightarrow 0 - 1 = -1$$

We can drop the negative, because we're dealing with distance.

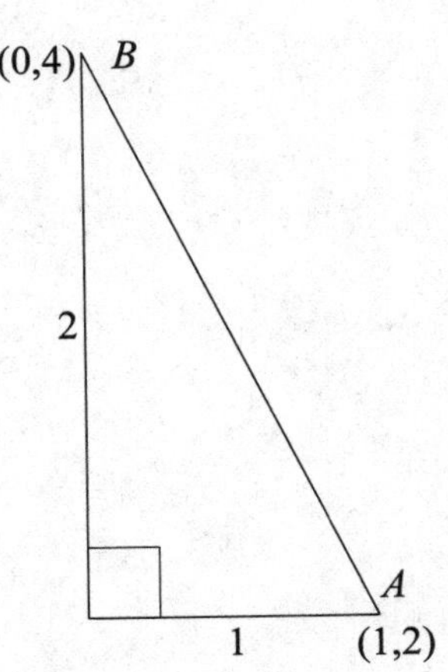

Remember: Right triangles mean use the Pythagorean Theorem!

$a^2 + b^2 = c^2$

Coordinate systems and Pythagoras go hand in hand!

Now, use the Pythagorean Theorem to find the length of our hypotenuse, $\overline{AB}$.

$$1^2 + 2^2 = \overline{AB}^2$$
$$1 + 4 = \overline{AB}^2$$
$$5 = \overline{AB}^2$$
$$\sqrt{5} = \overline{AB}$$

$\overline{AB}$ *is also one side of the* ***square***.

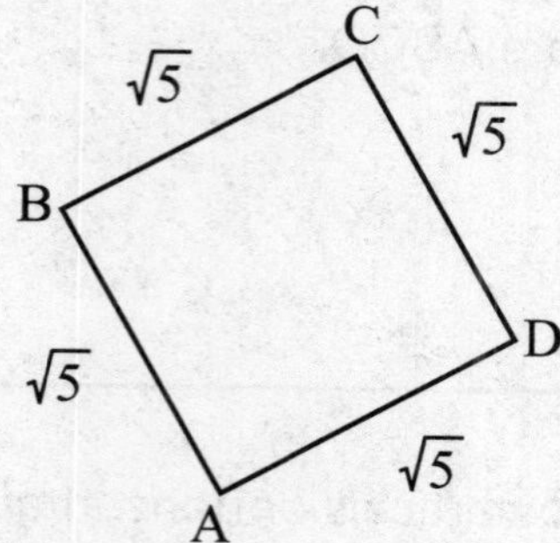

Since it's a square, the area is simply one side squared.

$$\text{area} = (\sqrt{5})^2 = \textcircled{5}$$

Coordinate Systems Practice Problems

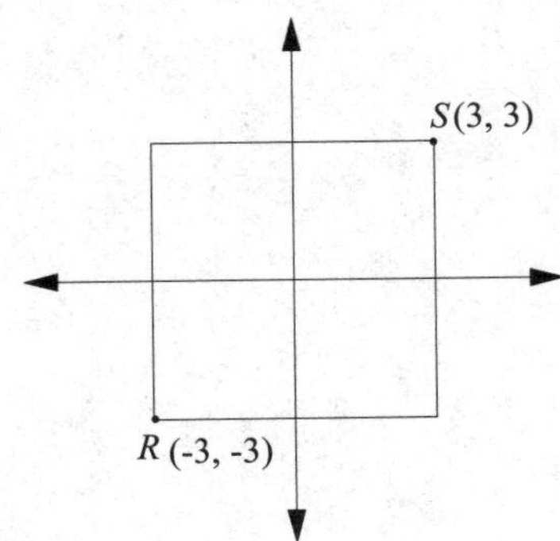

1. In the xy-coordinate system above, points R and S are opposite vertices of a square. Which of the following points could be another vertex of the square ?

   A. (3 , –3)
   B. (–3 , 2)
   C. (3 , –2)
   D. (0 , –3)
   E. (0 , 3)

★

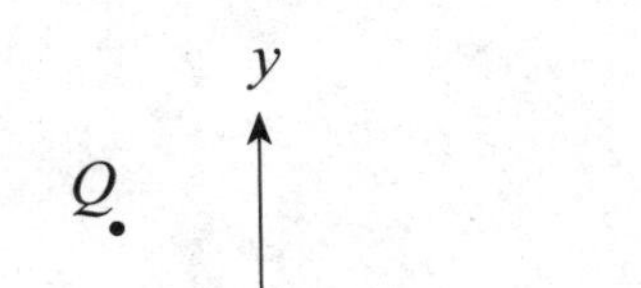

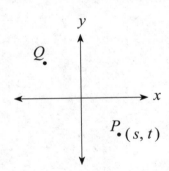

2. In the figure above, point Q is the same distance from the origin as point P is from the origin. Which of the following could be the coordinates of point Q ?

   F. (s , t)
   G. (s , $-t$)
   H. ($-s$, t)
   J. ($-s$, $-t$)
   K. (t , s)

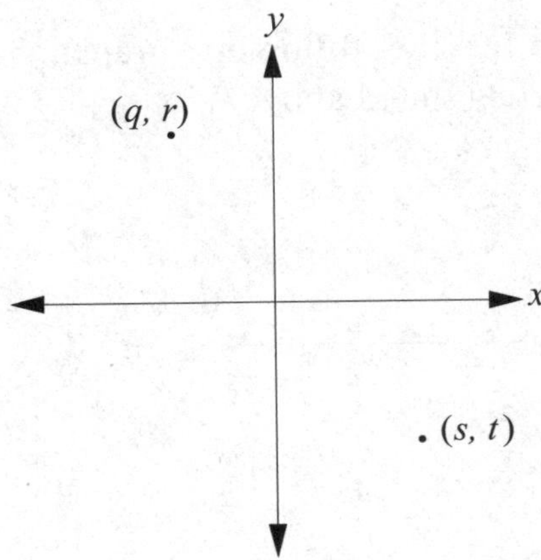

3. Which of the following must be true concerning the figure above ?

   I. $t > s$
   II. $q > s$
   III. $r > t$

   A. I only
   B. II only
   C. III only
   D. II and III
   E. I, II, and III

★★

4. The x-coordinate is greater than the y-coordinate for each point on the graph. The x-coordinate of every point on the graph is positive. No two points on the graph have the same x-coordinates.

Which of the following graphs has the properties stated above ?

F.

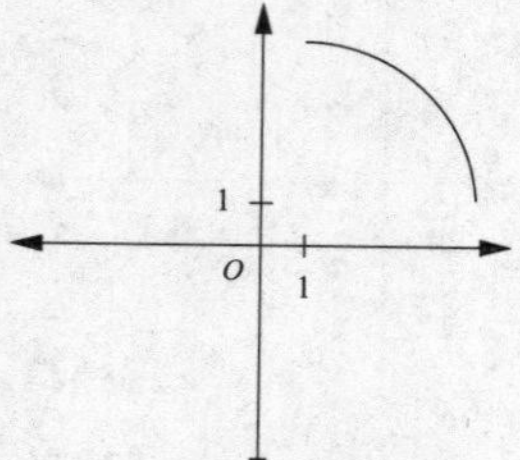

G.

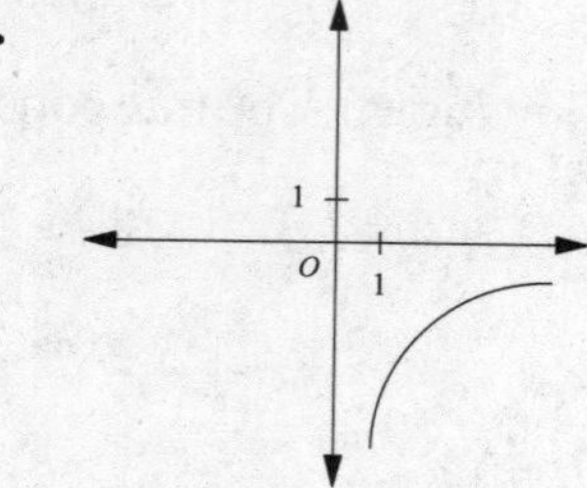

H.

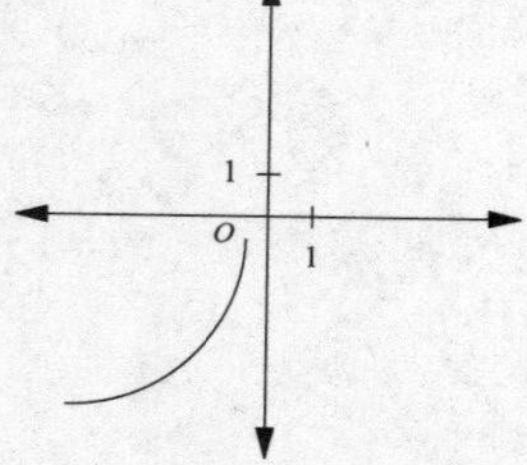

J.

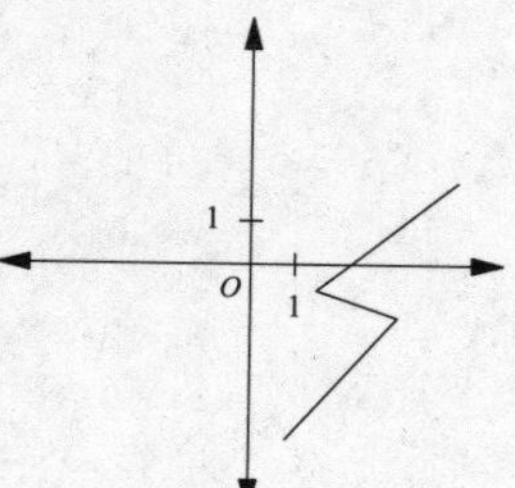

K.

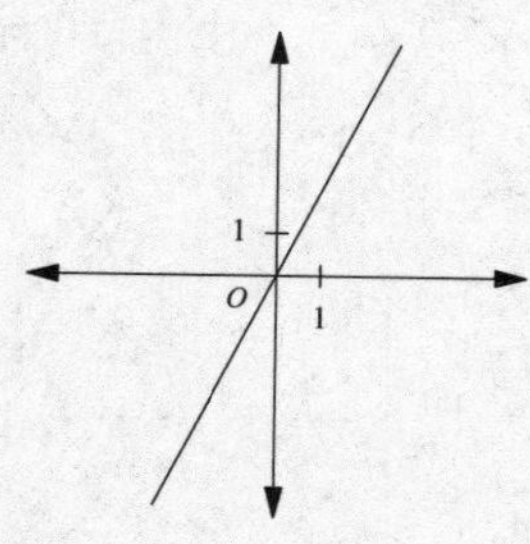

★★

5. What is the x-intercept of the line given by the equation $3y = -(6x - 12)$?

A. -4
B. -2
C. 0
D. 2
E. 4

★★

Slope

Slope can best be described as rise over run, or change in *y* over change in *x*. When you have two points on a line, use the formula:

$$\text{Slope} = m = \frac{\text{rise}}{\text{run}} = \frac{y_2 - y_1}{x_2 - x_1} =$$

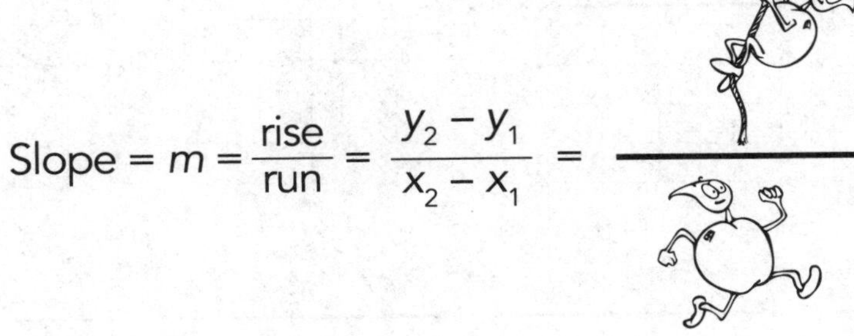

E1

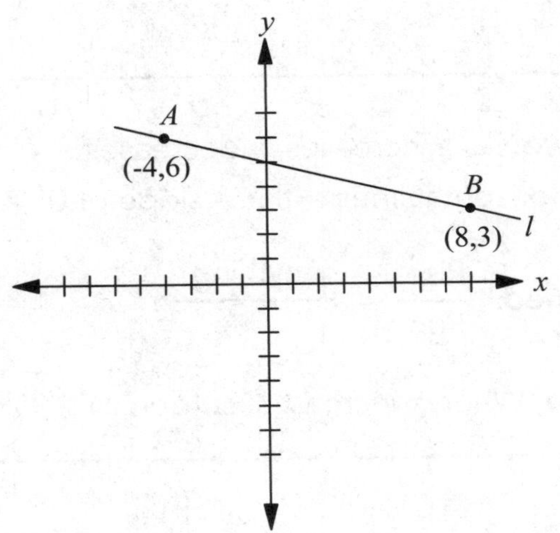

Two points, A and B, lie on line *l* as shown above. What is the slope of line *l*?

S *We need to work with the slope equation:*

Slope = ?

$$m = \frac{(y_2 - y_1)}{(x_2 - x_1)}$$

Let's use our 2 points $(\overset{x_1}{-4}, \overset{y_1}{6})$ *and* $(\overset{x_2}{8}, \overset{y_2}{3})$.

$$m = \frac{(y_2 - y_1)}{(x_2 - x_1)} = \frac{(3-6)}{(8-(-4))} = \frac{-3}{12} = -\frac{1}{4}$$

1% of all math questions on the ACT

In this equation, m is the slope and each *x* and *y* pair represents a point on the line, i.e. (2,1) or (4, –3).

Slope Identification

Slopes are either **positive**, **negative**, **zero**, or **undefined**.
Test your knowledge of slope types by labelling the following graphs:

A

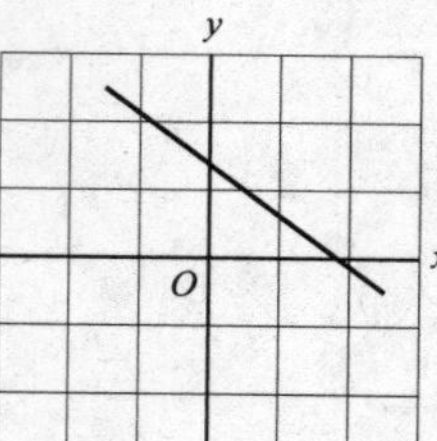

B

C

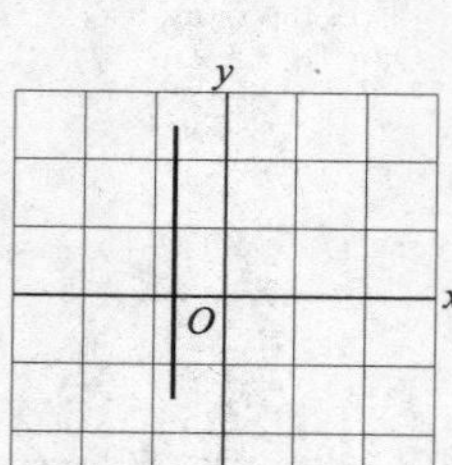

D

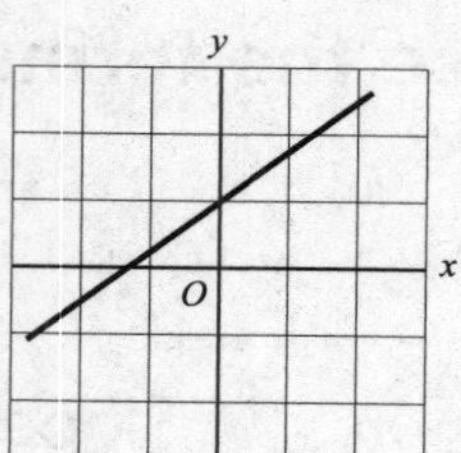

__________ __________ __________ __________

S

A: **Negative**: As x increases, y decreases.

B: **Zero**: Horizontal lines = flat = slope of 0.

C: **Undefined**: $\frac{\text{Rise}}{\text{Run}} = \frac{\text{Anything}}{0}$

D: **Positive**: When x increases, so does y.

Parallel Slopes

Two lines that are parallel have the **same** slope.

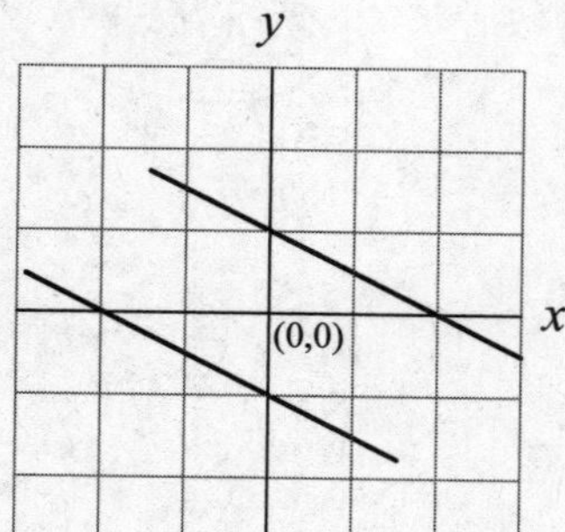

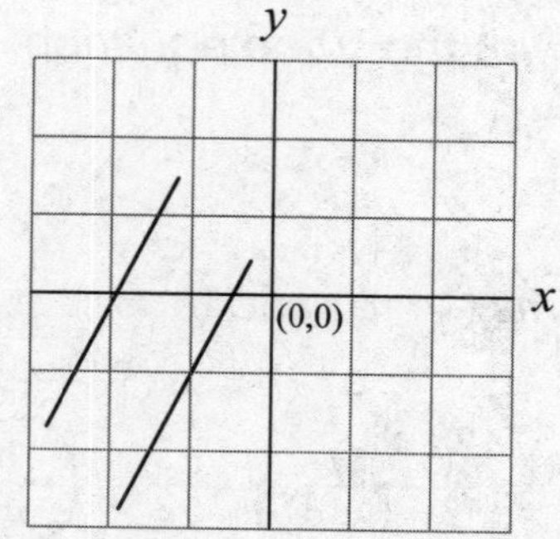

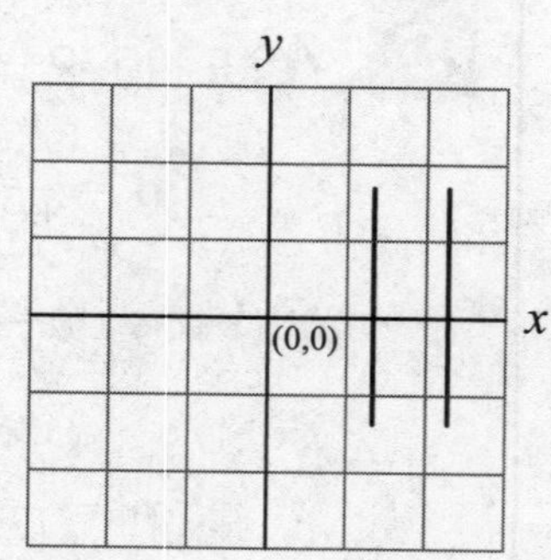

Perpendicular Slopes

Two lines that are perpendicular (meet at a 90° angle) have slopes that are **negative reciprocals** of each other.

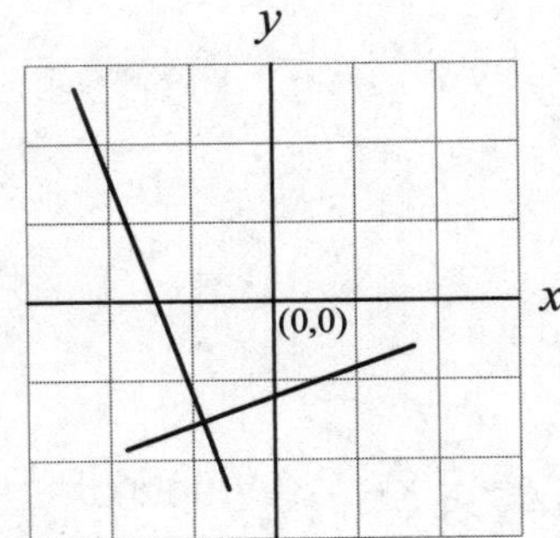

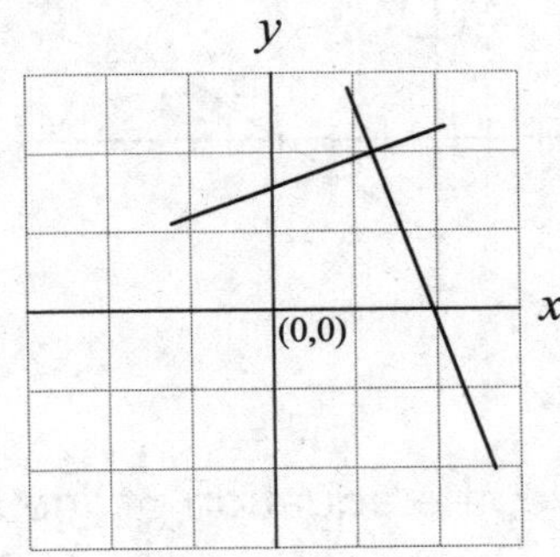

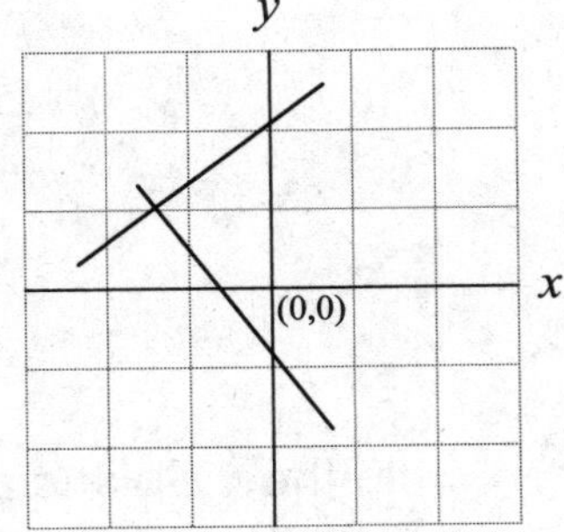

To find the **negative reciprocal** of a fraction:

1. Flip the fraction $\frac{1}{2} \rightarrow \frac{2}{1}$
2. Flip the sign $+\frac{2}{1} \rightarrow -\frac{2}{1}$

So if a line has a slope of $\frac{1}{2}$, a perpendicular line would have a slope of **−2**.

And if a line has a slope of −3, a perpendicular line would have a slope of $\mathbf{\frac{1}{3}}$.

Slope-Intercept Form

The ACT often presents equations for lines using the **Slope-Intercept Form.** The **Slope-Intercept Form** is:

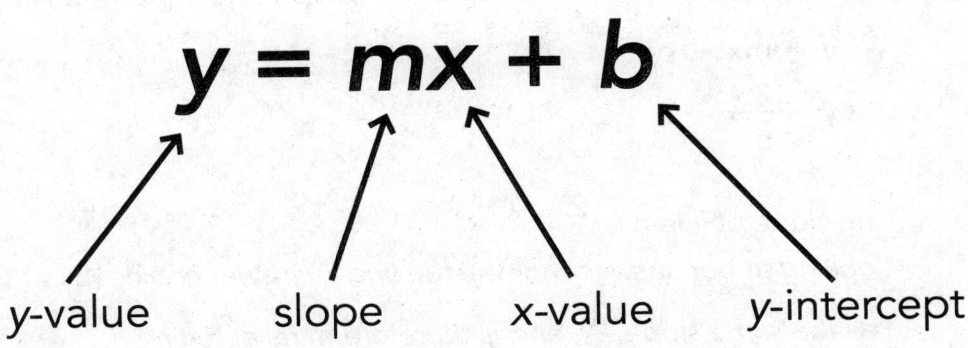

Remember, the *y*-intercept is the point where the line crosses the *y*-axis.

Put another away, the *y*-intercept is what *y* equals if you plug zero in for *x*!

E2

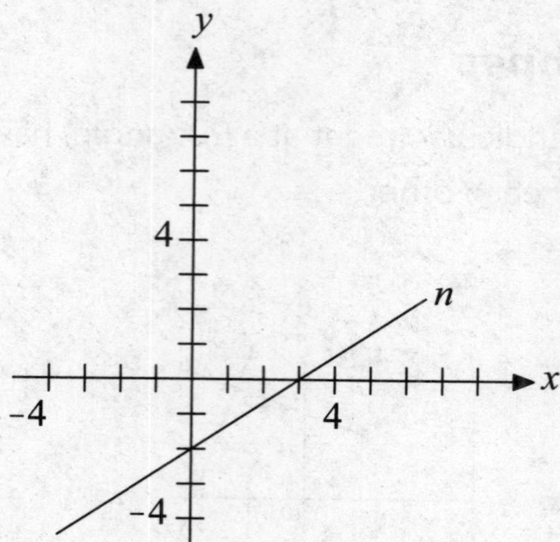

In the xy-plane above, the equation of line n is $y = \frac{2}{3}x - 2$. Which of the following is the equation of a line that is parallel to line n?

A. $y = 2x + 8$

B. $y = -\frac{3}{2}x - 2$

C. $y = -\frac{3}{2}x + 12$

D. $y = \frac{3}{2}x - 4$

E. $y = \frac{2}{3}x + 1$

S

Line n has the equation $y = \frac{2}{3}x - 2$

*A **parallel** line would have the **exact same slope**.*

*We can find the slope of line **n** using the slope-intercept formula.*

$$y = \mathbf{m}x + b$$

$$y = \mathbf{\frac{2}{3}}x - 2$$

The slope of line n is $\frac{2}{3}$.

Looking at our answer choices, the line in answer choice (E) *has the same slope,* $\frac{2}{3}$, *and is therefore parallel to line n.*

E3 Which of the following is the equation of a line in the *xy*-plane that passes through the point (6, 3) and is perpendicular to the line $y = -3x - 1$?

F. $y = 3x + 3$

G. $y = -3x + 6$

H. $y = \frac{1}{3}x - 1$

J. $y = \frac{1}{3}x + 1$

K. $y = -\frac{1}{3}x - 3$

S *When you see the word* ***perpendicular****, you will need to find the slope of the line and then determine the negative reciprocal of that slope.*

$$y = -3x - 1$$

We are already in slope-intercept form, so our slope is ***–3****.*

The negative reciprocal of $-\frac{3}{1} = +\frac{1}{3}$

The only answer choices that have a slope of $\mathbf{\frac{1}{3}}$ *are* **H** *and* **J***. We must determine which of these two lines passes through the point* **(6, 3)***. Let's plug that point into each equation:*

H

$$y = \frac{1}{3}x - 1$$
$$3 = \frac{1}{3}(6) - 1$$
$$3 = 2 - 1$$
$$\mathbf{3 \neq 1}$$

Nope, (6,3) is not a point on this line in H!

J

$$y = \frac{1}{3}x + 1$$
$$3 = \frac{1}{3}(6) + 1$$
$$3 = 2 + 1$$
$$\mathbf{3 = 3}$$

That's it! J is our answer!

If you plug any point (x, y) on a line into the equation of the line, you will get a true result.

E4

$$6y - rx = 9$$

The equation above is the equation of a line in the *xy*-plane, and *r* is a constant. If the slope of the line is 3, what is the value of *r*?

S *First we need to get our equation into slope-intercept form. Let's isolate y.*

r = ?

$$6y = 9 + rx$$
$$y = \frac{9}{6} + \left(\frac{r}{6}\right)x$$
$$y = \left(\frac{r}{6}\right)x + \frac{3}{2}$$
$$\mathbf{y = mx + b}$$

From the problem, we know the slope of our line, $\frac{r}{6}$, equals 3. We can now solve for r.

$$\frac{r}{6} = 3$$
$$r = 3(6) = \mathbf{18}$$

E5 In the xy-plane, the line $4x + 7y = t$ passes through the point (–9, 4). What is the value of t?

S *Let's plug the point (–9, 4) into the line equation* $4x + 7y = t$.

t = ?

$$4x + 7y = t$$
$$4(-9) + 7(4) = t$$
$$-36 + 28 = t$$
$$\mathbf{-8} = t$$

Slope Practice Problems

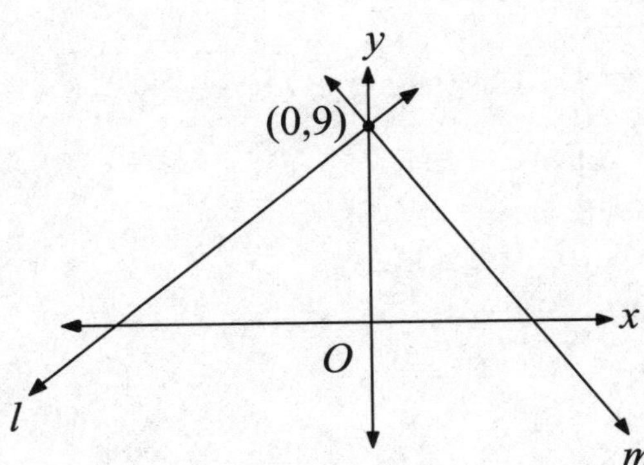

1. The equation of line m in the figure above is $y + 2x = b$. If line l is perpendicular to line m, which of the following could be the equation for line l ?

A. $y = 2x + 9$

B. $y = -\frac{1}{2}x + 9$

C. $y = -\frac{1}{2}x - 9$

D. $y = \frac{1}{2}x + 9$

E. $y = -x - 9$

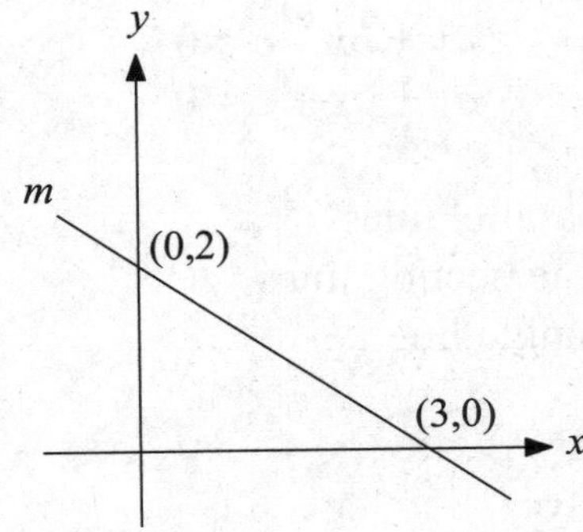

2. In the figure above, what is the slope of line m ?

F. $-\frac{3}{2}$

G. $-\frac{2}{3}$

H. $\frac{2}{3}$

J. $\frac{3}{4}$

K. $\frac{3}{2}$

★

3. Which of the following slope-intercept equations is parallel to $4y + x - 24 = 0$ and passes through coordinate point (4, 11) ?

A. $y = -\frac{1}{4}x + 6$

B. $y = -\frac{1}{4}x - 6$

C. $y = 4x + 9$

D. $y = -4x - 9$

E. $y = -\frac{1}{4}x + 12$

★★

4. The two equations below are graphed in the same, standard (x, y) coordinate plane. If a, b, and c are positive integers, which of the following statements describes the graph of at least one such system of equations?

$$ay + bx - c = 0$$
$$ay + bx + c = 0$$

I. 2 parallel lines
II. 2 intersecting lines
III. A single line

F. I only
G. II only
H. III only
J. I or III
K. I, II, or III

5. Which of the following is an equation of a line in the (x, y) coordinate plane that passes through the point (4, 1) and is parallel to the line $y = 3x - 4$?

A. $y = -\frac{1}{3}x$

B. $y = -3x - 4$

C. $y = 3x - 11$

D. $y = 3x + 4$

E. $y = 3x + 13$

★★

6. In the (x, y) coordinate plane, lines l and m are perpendicular. Line l contains the point (0, 0) and has a slope of 2. Line m contains the points (4, 2) and $(x, 0)$. What is the value of x ?

F. −8
G. −4
H. 0
J. 4
K. 8

★★★

7. In the (x, y) coordinate plane, lines r and p are the diagonals of a square. If the points (0, 3) and (6, 9) lie on line r and the points (1, 8) and $(7, n)$ lie on line p, what is the value of n ?

A. −2
B. −1
C. 1
D. 2
E. 3

★★★

Equation of a Circle

1% of all math questions on the ACT

Once every two tests, the ACT authors test your memory of the Equation of a Circle.

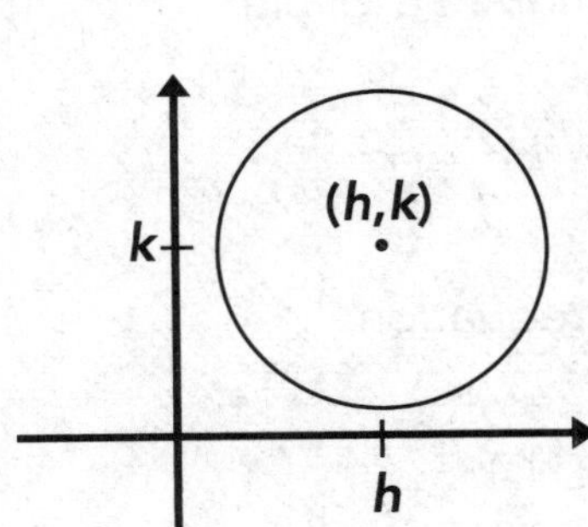

The equation of a circle looks intimidating at first, but it's cheez–on–taters once you know what the variables stand for.

$$(x-h)^2+(y-k)^2=r^2$$

(h,k) = center of the circle

r = radius of the circle

The ACT rarely tests more than your basic understanding of this equation. The writers will give you an equation and ask you to give the **radius**, the **center**, or **both**. Or, if they are feeling particularly frisky, the test writers will give you the radius and center of a circle and ask for its **equation**.

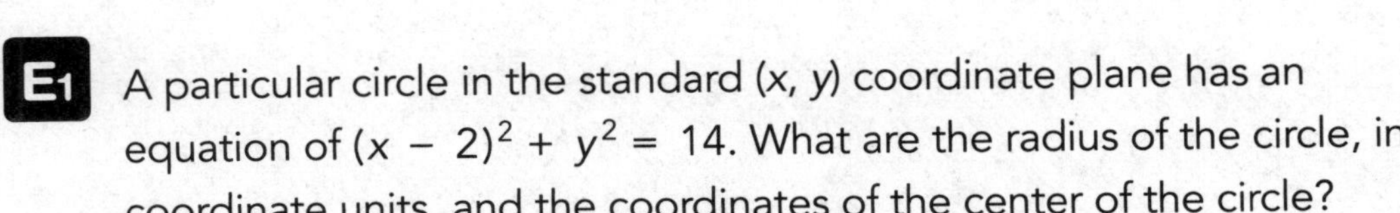

E1 A particular circle in the standard (x, y) coordinate plane has an equation of $(x - 2)^2 + y^2 = 14$. What are the radius of the circle, in coordinate units, and the coordinates of the center of the circle?

	radius	center
A.	7	(−2,0)
B.	7	(2,0)
C.	14	(2,0)
D.	$\sqrt{14}$	(−2,0)
E.	$\sqrt{14}$	(2,0)

S *All you have to do is read the formula. You don't have to draw the circle, unless it makes you feel warm and fuzzy inside.*

radius = ?
center = ?

Let's look at the Equation of a Circle:

$$(x - h)^2 + (y - k)^2 = r^2$$

and compare it to our equation:

$$(x - 2)^2 + y^2 = 14$$

*Comparing these equations, we see that the **h** term has been replaced with a **2**, and the **k** term has disappeared. It must be **zero**! This puts the center of our circle at* **(2,0)**.

*The right side of the equation is now a **14**, which means*

$$r^2 = 14$$

$$\text{so } r = \boxed{\sqrt{14}}$$

***E** is our answer!*

Equation of a Circle Practice Problems

1. In the standard (x, y) coordinate plane, a graph of a circle with a center of $(-3, 4)$ and a radius of 4 coordinate units has which of the following equations?

A. $(x-3)^2+(y-4)^2=4$
B. $(x+3)^2+(y-4)^2=16$
C. $(x+3)^2+(y+4)^2=16$
D. $(x-3)^2+(y-4)^2=16$
E. $(x-3)^2+(y+4)^2=16$

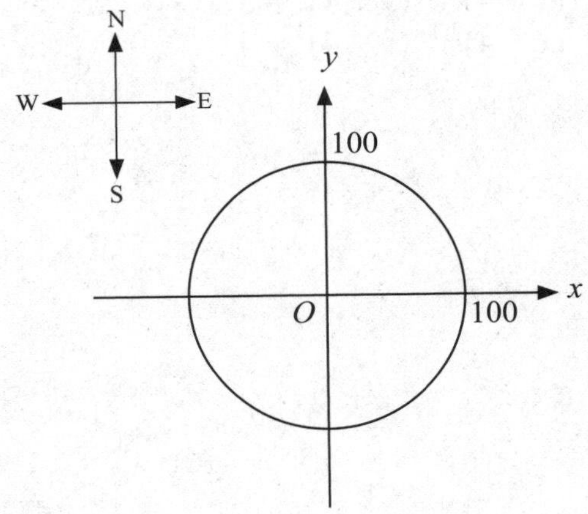

2. A ship sends out a radio signal that has a range of 100 miles in every direction. If the ship's radio signal range is plotted on a coordinate plane, with the ship's radio at the origin and 1 coordinate unit representing 1 mile, which of the following equations represents the circle shown above?

F. $x+y=100$
G. $(x+y)^2=100$
H. $(x+y)^2=100^2$
J. $x^2+y^2=100$
K. $x^2+y^2=100^2$

★★

3. What is the center of the circle with equation $(x+5)^2+(y-5)^2=5$ in the standard (x, y) coordinate plane?

F. $(-\sqrt{5}, \sqrt{5})$
G. $(5, -5)$
H. $(\sqrt{5}, -\sqrt{5})$
J. $(-5, 5)$
K. $(5, 5)$

★★

4. A particular circle has an equation of $(x-7)^2+y^2=22$ in the standard (x, y) coordinate plane. What are the radius of the circle, in coordinate units, and the coordinates of the center of the circle?

	radius	center
F.	$\sqrt{22}$	$(7, 0)$
G.	11	$(7, 0)$
H.	22	$(7, 0)$
J.	$\sqrt{22}$	$(-7, 0)$
K.	11	$(-7, 0)$

★★

5. In the standard (x, y) coordinate plane, a circle is tangent to the x–axis at 4 and tangent to the y–axis at 4. Which of the following is the equation of the circle?

A. $x^2 + y^2 = 4$
B. $x^2 + y^2 = 16$
C. $(x - 4)^2 + (y - 4)^2 = 4$
D. $(x - 4)^2 + (y - 4)^2 = 16$
E. $(x + 4)^2 + (y + 4)^2 = 16$

★★

6. A square has vertices with coordinates (0, 0), (0, 8), (8, 8), and (8, 0) in the standard (x, y) coordinate plane above. Which of the following is an equation of the circle inscribed in the square?

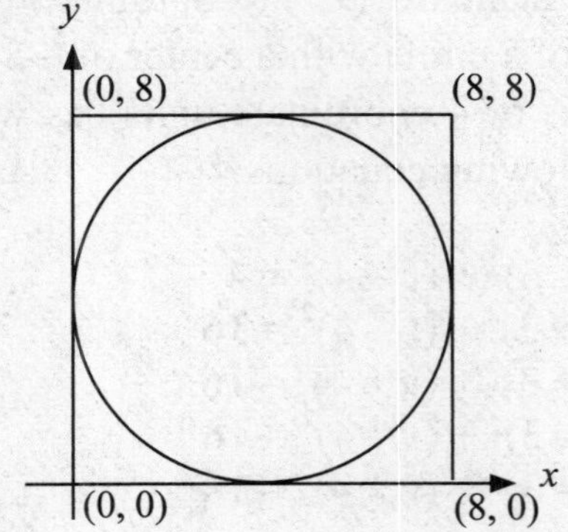

F. $(x - 4)^2 + (y - 4)^2 = 16$
G. $(x - 4)^2 + (y - 4)^2 = 4$
H. $(x + 4)^2 + (y + 4)^2 = 16$
J. $(x + 4)^2 + (y + 4)^2 = 8$
K. $(x + 4)^2 + (y + 4)^2 = 4$

★★

Shifting Graphs

1% of all math questions on the ACT

Let's use the Standard Formula for a parabola to illustrate the basic rules of shifting graphs.

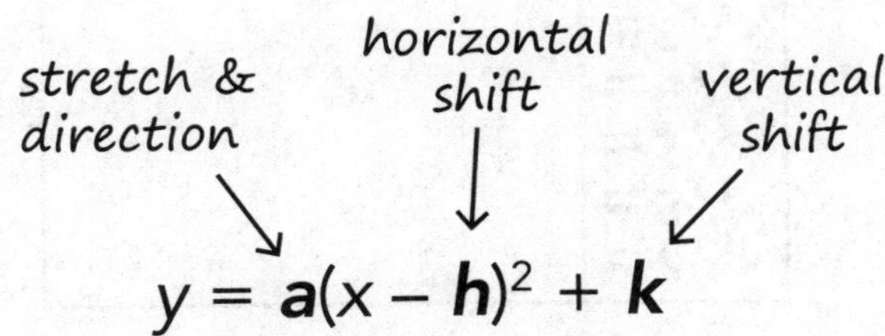

+/– = direction

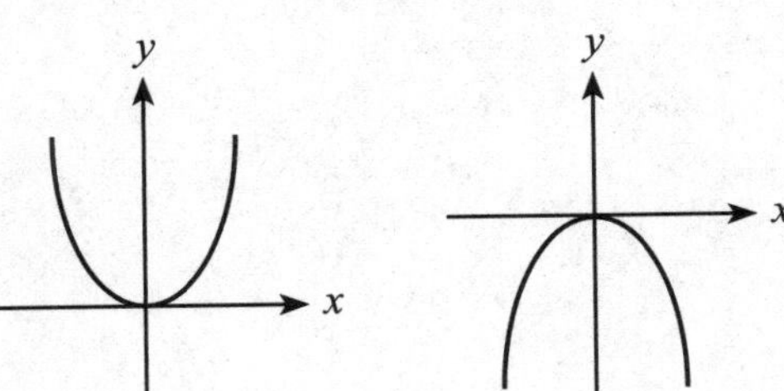

$f(x) = x^2$
a = positive
original equation

$f(x) = -x^2$
a = negative
graph flips down

a = stretch

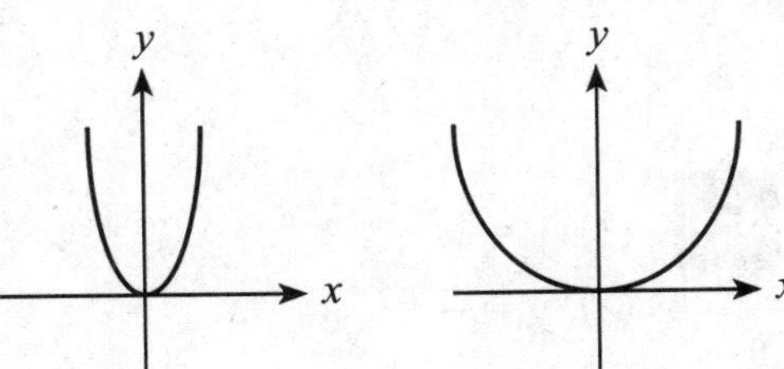

$f(x) = \mathbf{3}x^2$
a = integer
graph narrows

$f(x) = \frac{\mathbf{1}}{\mathbf{3}}x^2$
a = fraction
graph widens

h = horizontal shift

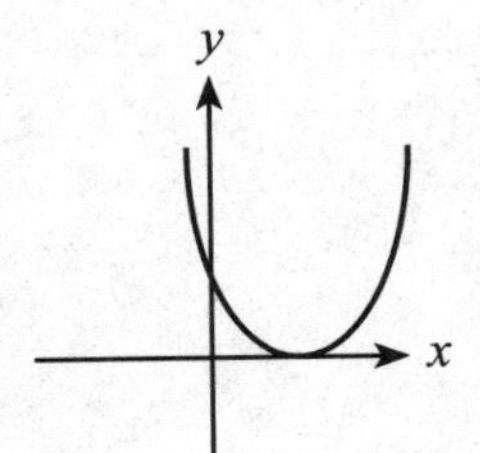

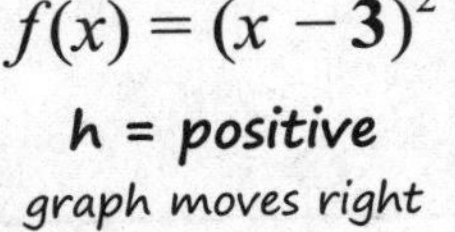

$f(x) = (x - \mathbf{3})^2$
h = positive
graph moves right

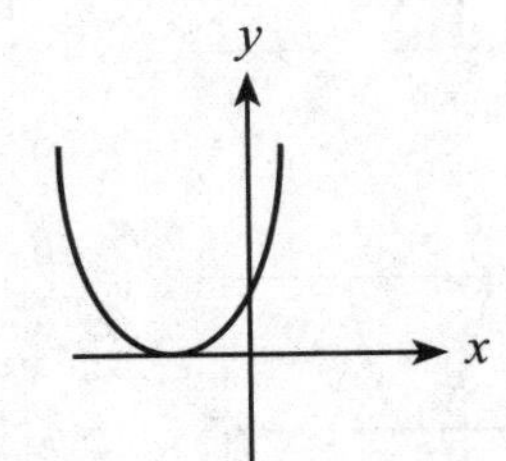

$f(x) = (x + \mathbf{3})^2$
h = negative
graph moves left

k = vertical shift

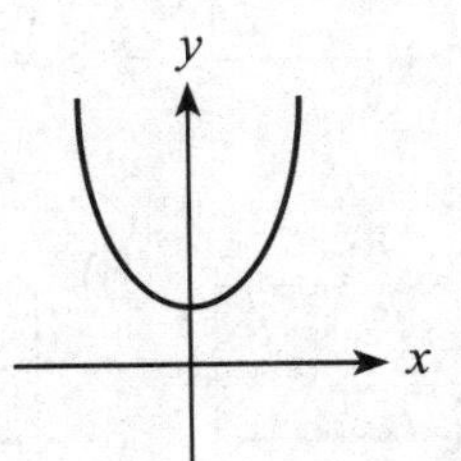

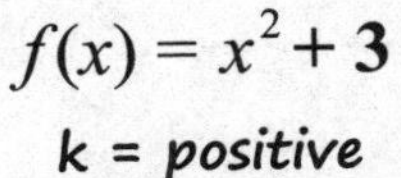

$f(x) = x^2 + \mathbf{3}$
k = positive
graph moves up

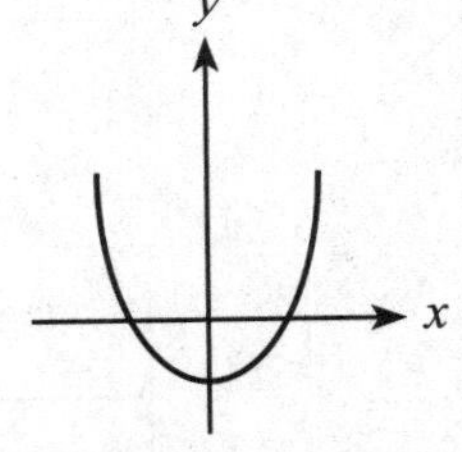

$f(x) = x^2 - \mathbf{3}$
k = negative
graph moves down

Shifting graphs on a calculator

The absolute best strategy to use if you ever forget these rules is to break out your TI and jump to the graphing section. Press the **[y =]** button (below the screen, on the left).

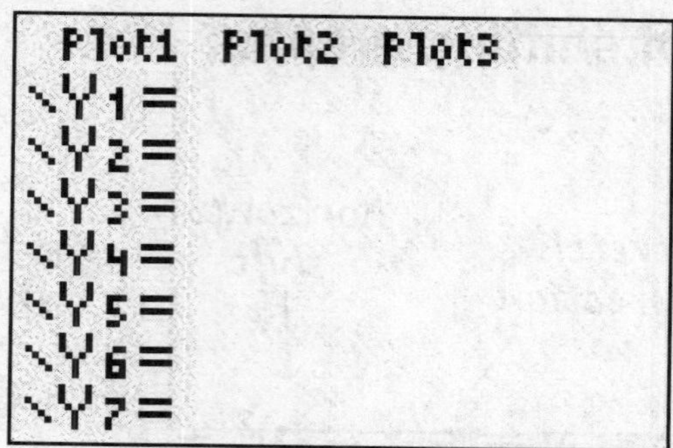

You can refresh all of the shifting graph rules in a matter of seconds using the graphing function. Plug in the following equations, one by one, to refresh the rules:

E1
(1) $y = x^2$
(2) $y = -x^2$
(3) $y = 2x^2$
(4) $y = x^2 + 2$
(5) $y = (x - 2)^2$

S

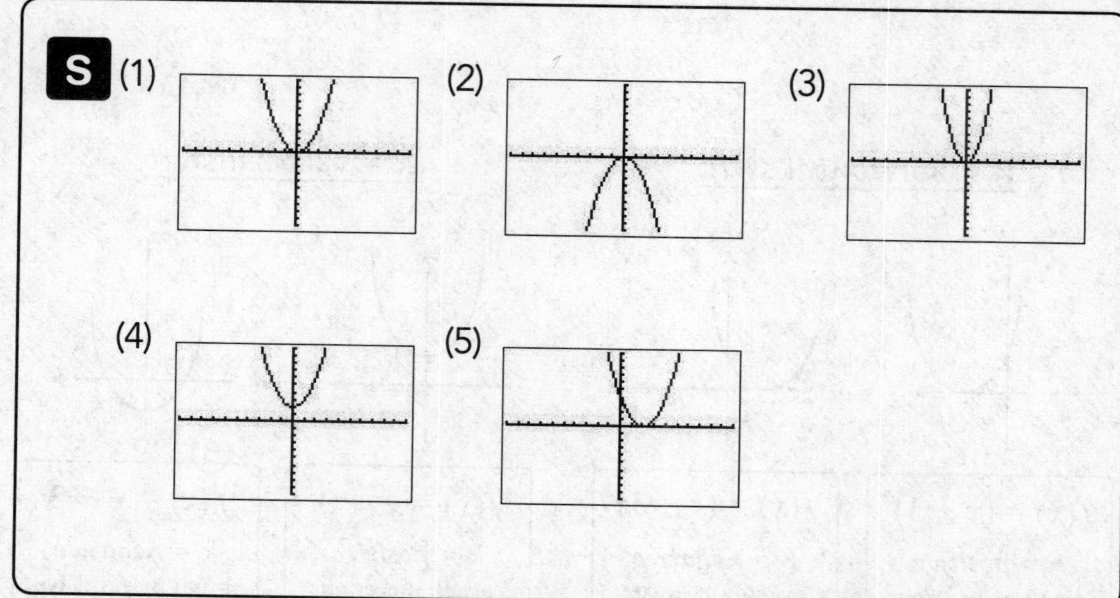

E2

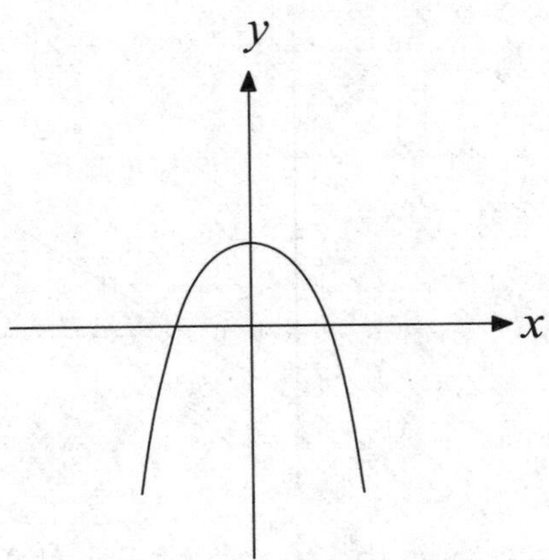
y
x

The graph above is a parabola with the equation $y = -ax^2 + 6$, where a is a constant. If $y = -a(x - 1)^2 + 8$ is graphed on the same axes, which of the following best describes the resulting graph as compared with the graph above?

A. It will be wider.
B. It will be moved 1 unit to the right and 2 units upward.
C. It will be narrower and moved 8 units upward.
D. It will be moved 2 units upward.
E. It will be moved 1 unit to the left and 2 units downward.

S *When you line the equations up, it's clear what is happening:*

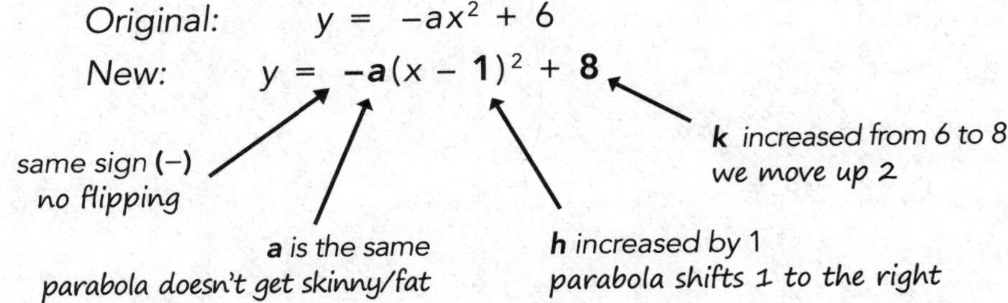
Original: y = −ax² + 6
New: y = −a(x − 1)² + 8
same sign (−)
no flipping
a is the same
parabola doesn't get skinny/fat
h increased by 1
parabola shifts 1 to the right
k increased from 6 to 8
we move up 2

Looking through our options, we see that the answer is **(B)**.

E3

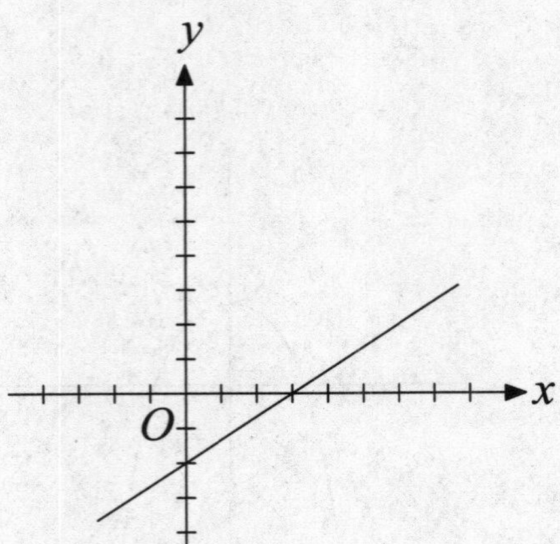

The figure above shows the graph of $y = f(a)$. Which of the following is the graph of $y = |f(a)|$?

A.

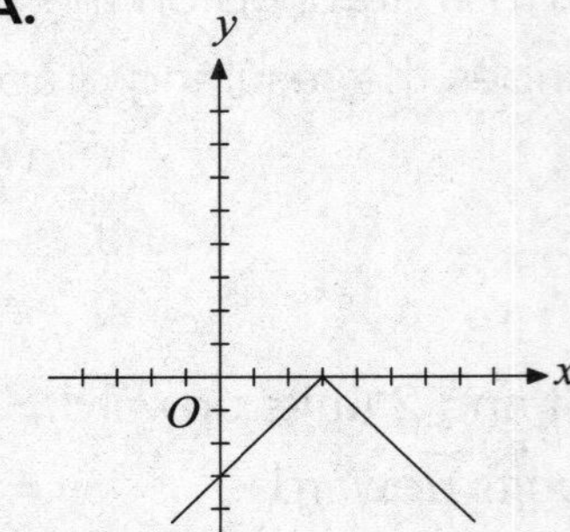

B.

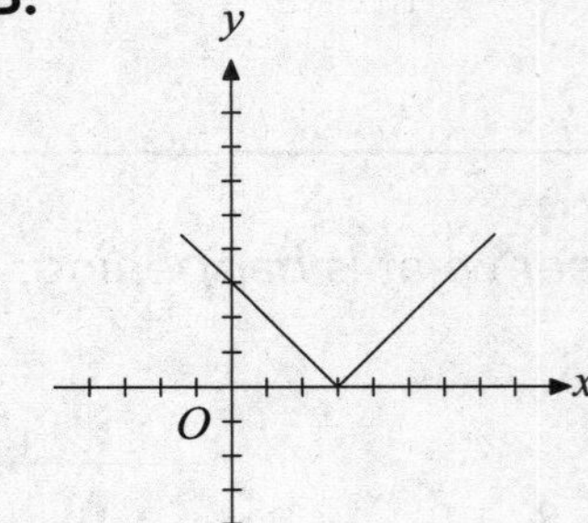

C.

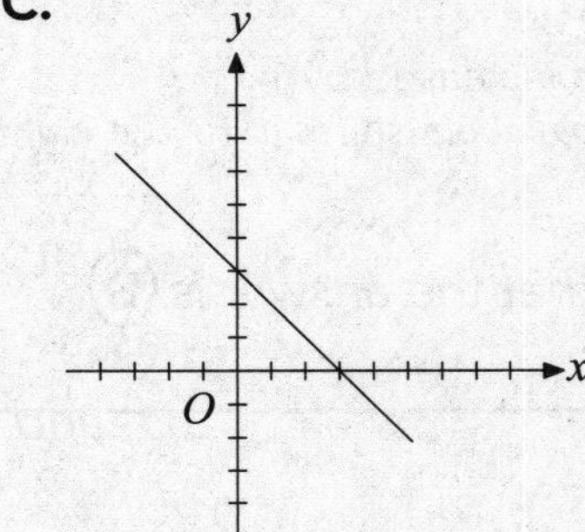

D.

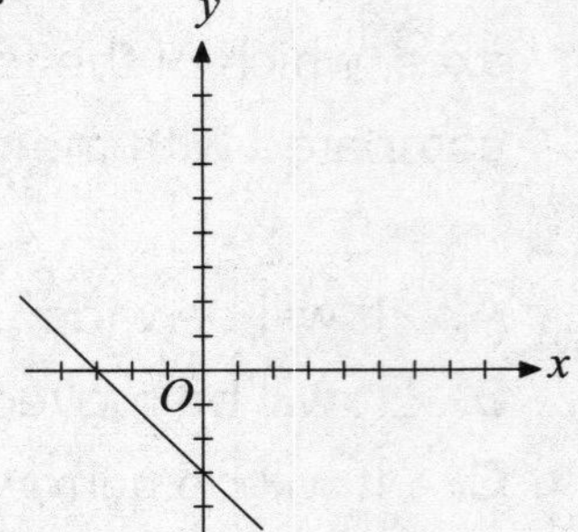

E.

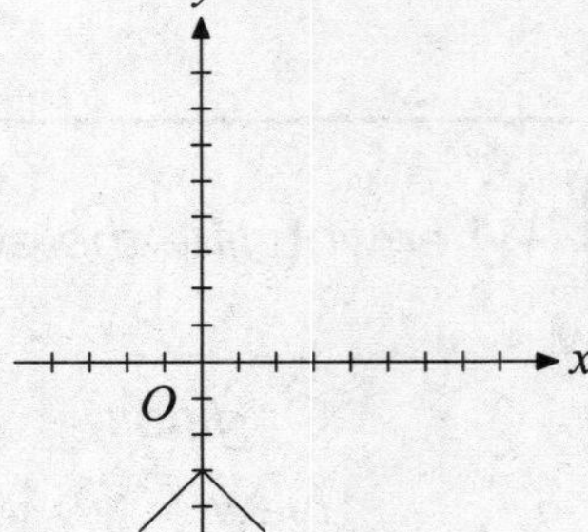

S *Our current graph is $y = f(a)$:*

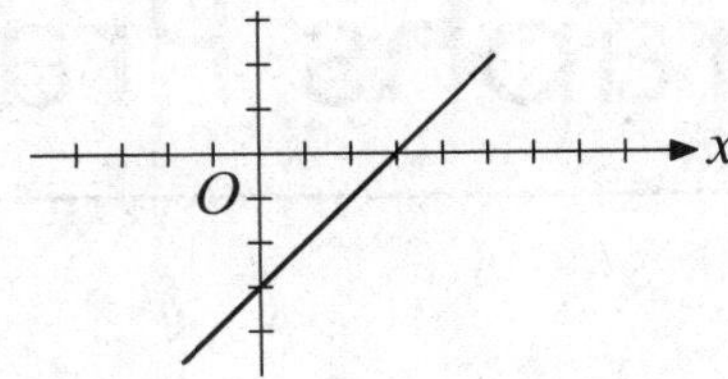

*Our new graph is $y = |f(a)|$ which is the **absolute value** of our original graph.*

Remember, absolute value leaves positive values alone, but it brings everything negative to the positive side:

$|3| = 3$ *Positive stays positive.*

$|-3| = 3$ *Negative becomes positive.*

*Since the absolute value of f(a) is equal to **y**, we know the absolute value sign will impact our y-values, **turning all negative y-values positive**.*

*Looking at our graph, we can see that the portion of our line **under the x-axis** will be moving.*

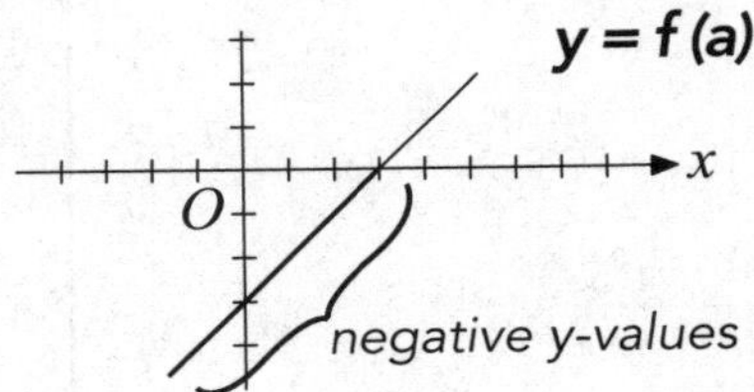

*To graph the absolute value, we **flip** the negative y-values and turn them into positive y-values, **reflecting** them over the x-axis.*

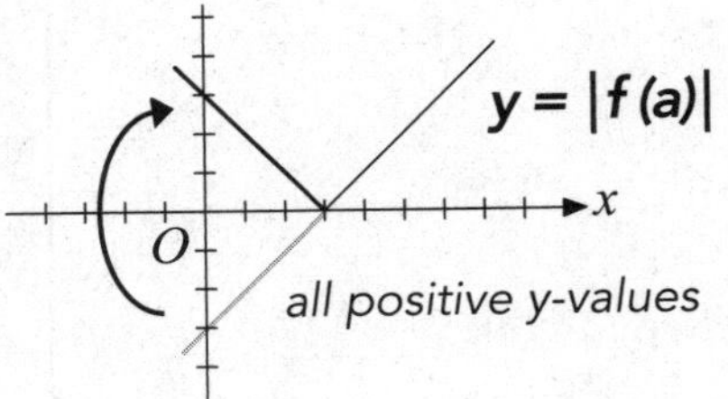

Our positive y-values remain unchanged.

*Additionally, using the process of elimination, we can look at all of the answer choices and cross off anything which has negative y-values. That would instantly knock off **A**, **C**, **D**, and **E**, leaving us with our answer, (**B**.) This matches our graph!*

Absolute value reflects only the negative portion of the line over the x-axis.

Shifting Graphs Practice Problems

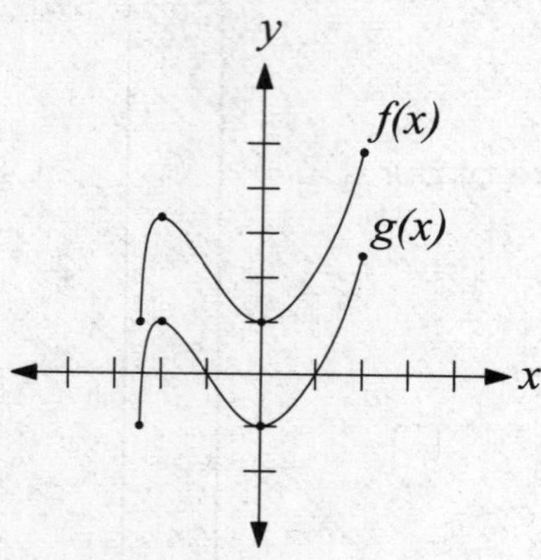

1. The graphs of the functions f and g in the interval from $x = -2.5$ to $x = 2$ are shown above. Which of the following expresses g in terms of f?

A. $g(x) = f(x) + 2$
B. $g(x) = f(x + 2)$
C. $g(x) = f(x) - 2$
D. $g(x) = f(x - 2)$
E. $g(x) = f(x - 2) + 2$

★★

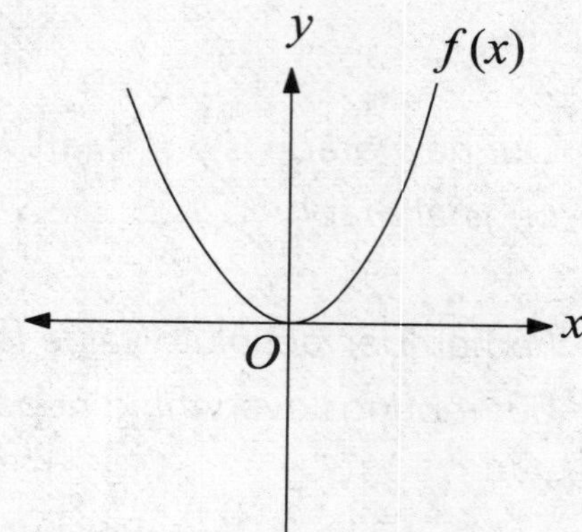

2. The figure above shows the graph of the function $f(x)$. If $g(x) = 2f(x)$ for all values of x, which of the following statements must be true about the graph of g in comparison with the graph of f?

F. It is the same width as $f(x)$ and opens downward.
G. It is wider than $f(x)$ and opens downward.
H. It is narrower than $f(x)$ and opens upward.
J. It is wider than $f(x)$ and opens upward.
K. It is the same width as $f(x)$ and opens upward.

★★

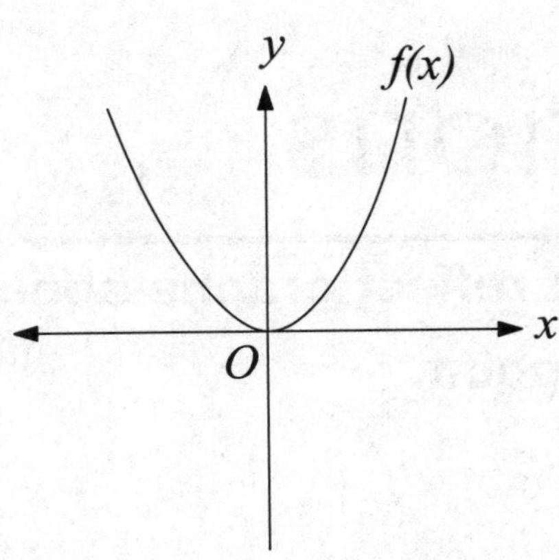

3. The figure above shows the graph of $y = f(x)$. Which of the following is the graph of $f(x-2)+1$?

A.
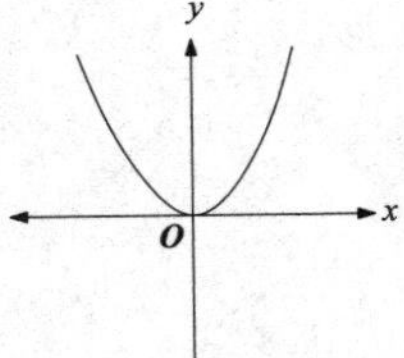

B.
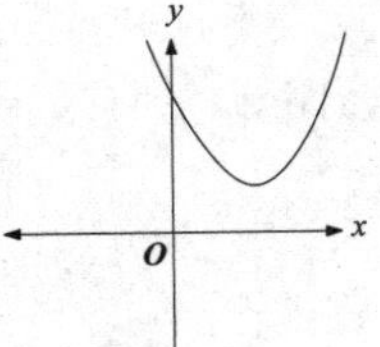

C.
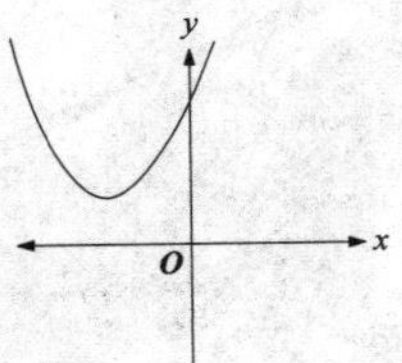

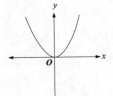

D.
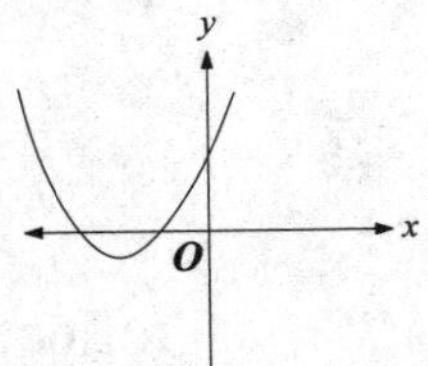

E.
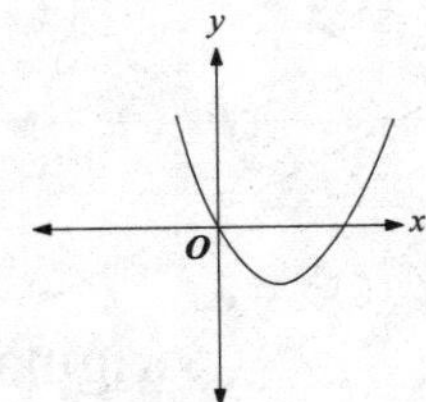

★★

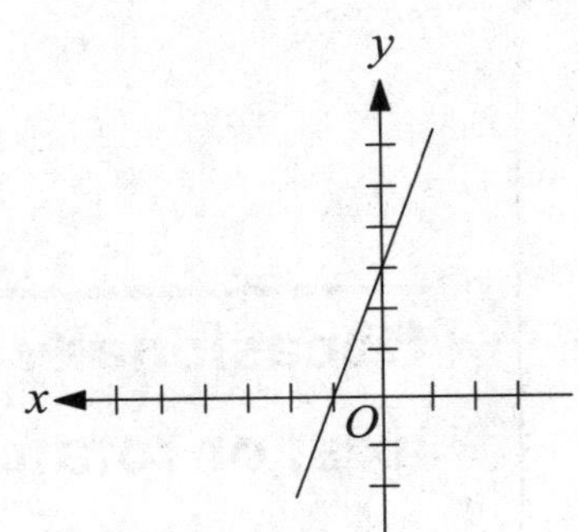

4. The equation of the line in the figure above is $y = 3x + 3$. Which of the following is the graph of $y = |3x + 3|$?

F.
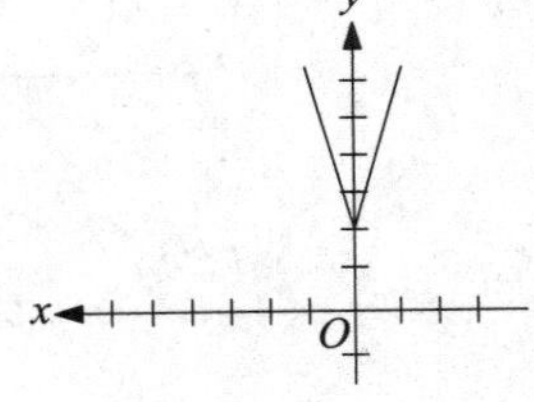

G.
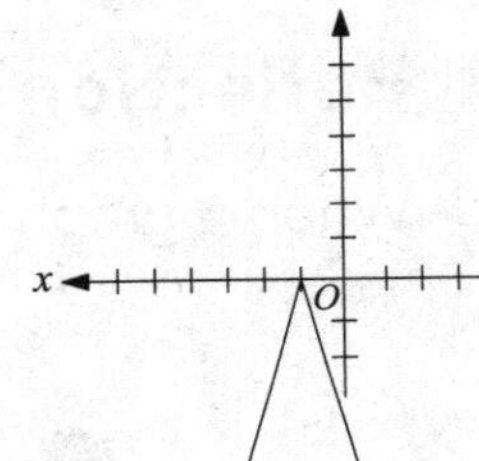

H.
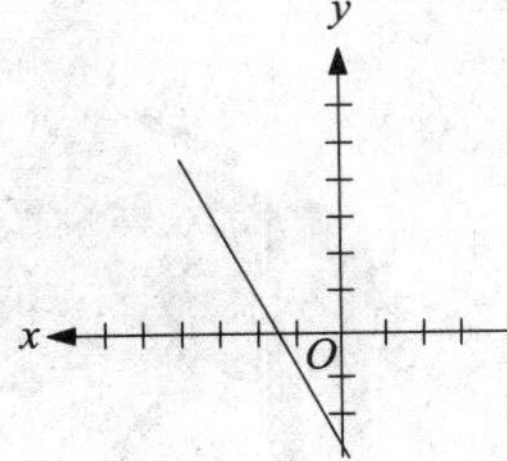

J.
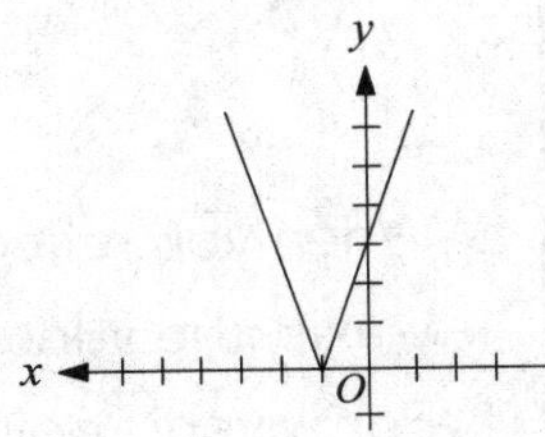

K.
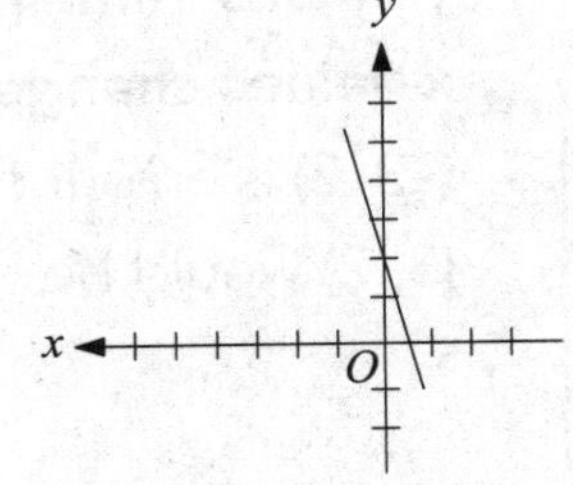

★★

1%
of all math questions on the ACT

Reflections

Occasionally you'll be asked to reflect graphs about an axis, or rotate graphs around a point.

Reflection across the y-axis

When a graph is reflected across/about the **y-axis**, it does this:

When you reflect a line across the y-axis, the y-intercept stays constant. For every point on the line, the **y-values remain the same**, but the **x-values change sign**. So if the point (–3, 2) is on our original line, the point (3, 2) would be on the reflected line.

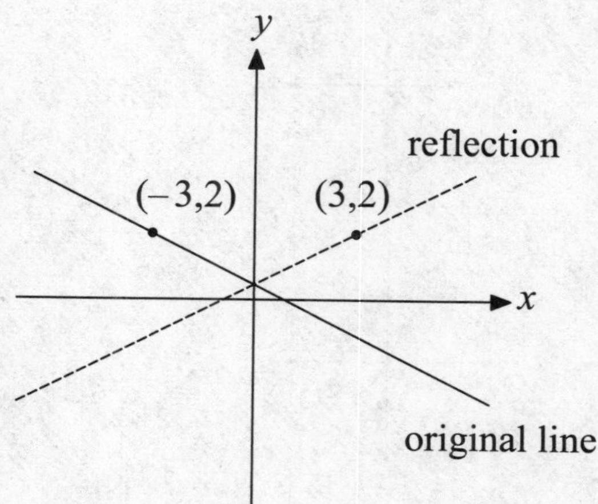

Reflection across the x-axis

When a graph is reflected across/about the x-axis, it does this:

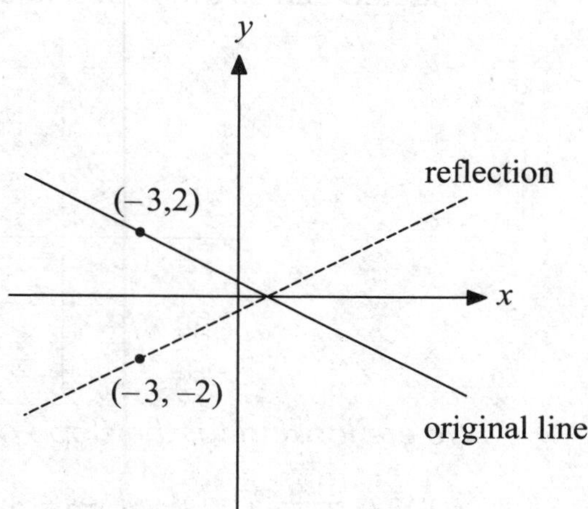

When you reflect a line across/about the x-axis, the x-intercept remains constant. For every point on the line, the **x-values remain the same**, but the **y-values change sign**. So if the point (–3, 2) is on our original line, the point (–3, –2) would be on the reflected line.

E1 In the *xy*-coordinate plane, line *r* is the reflection of line *s* about the *x*-axis. If the slope of line *r* is $\frac{3}{4}$, what is the slope of line *s* ?

A. $-\frac{4}{3}$

B. $-\frac{3}{4}$

C. $\frac{3}{4}$

D. 1

E. $\frac{4}{3}$

S *Line* ***r*** *is the reflection of line* ***s****. When a line is reflected across the x-axis, it looks like this:*

slope = ?

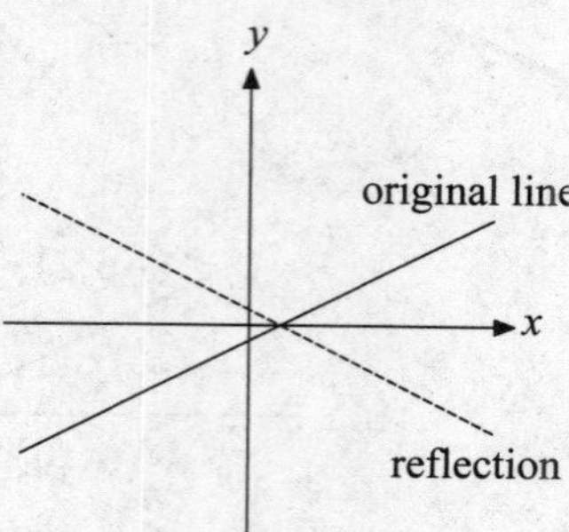

We are looking for the slope of the ***reflected*** *line.*

Slope is $\frac{\textbf{rise}}{\textbf{run}}$*. The x-values stay the same, so the "run" does not change and remains* **4**. *The y-values, however, switch signs, so the "rise" flips from 3 to* **– 3**. *Our new slope is* $\left(-\frac{3}{4}\right)$, ***B.***

E2

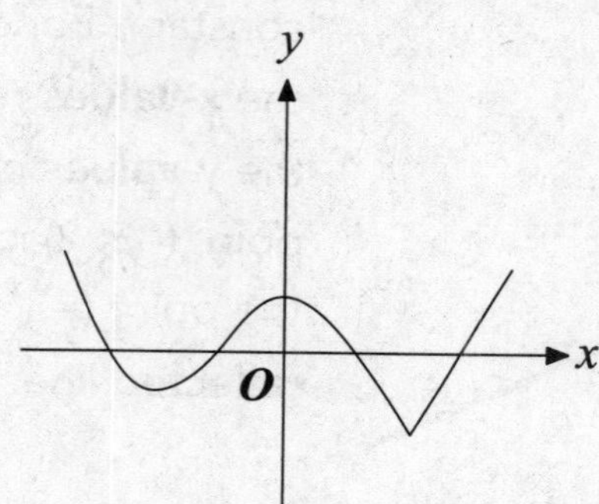

Which of the following graphs is the reflection of the graph above about the x-axis?

F.

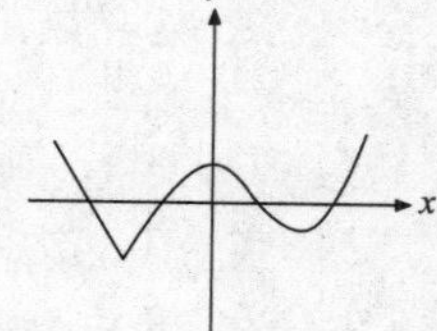

G.

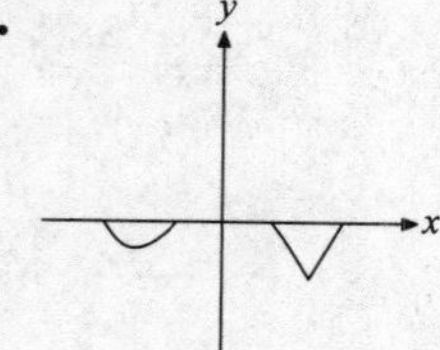

H.

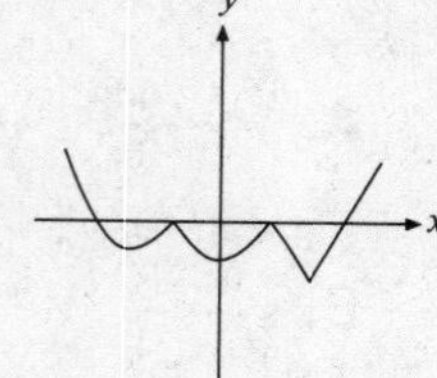

J.

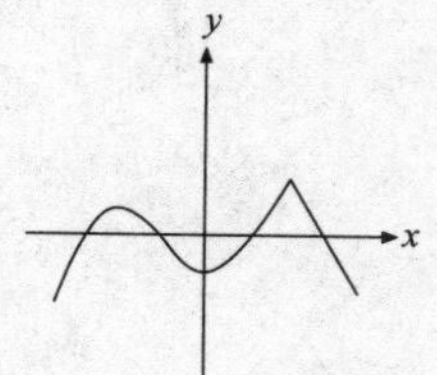

K.

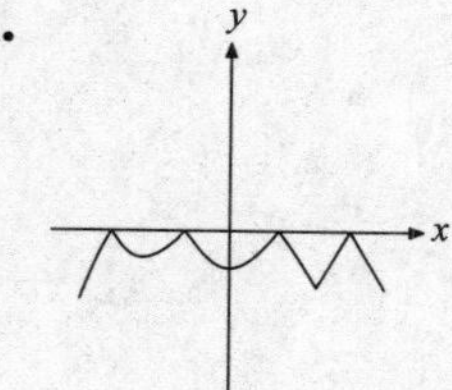

S *Remember our horse! Reflecting about the x-axis flips the image upside down. Our graph will flip just like the horse.*

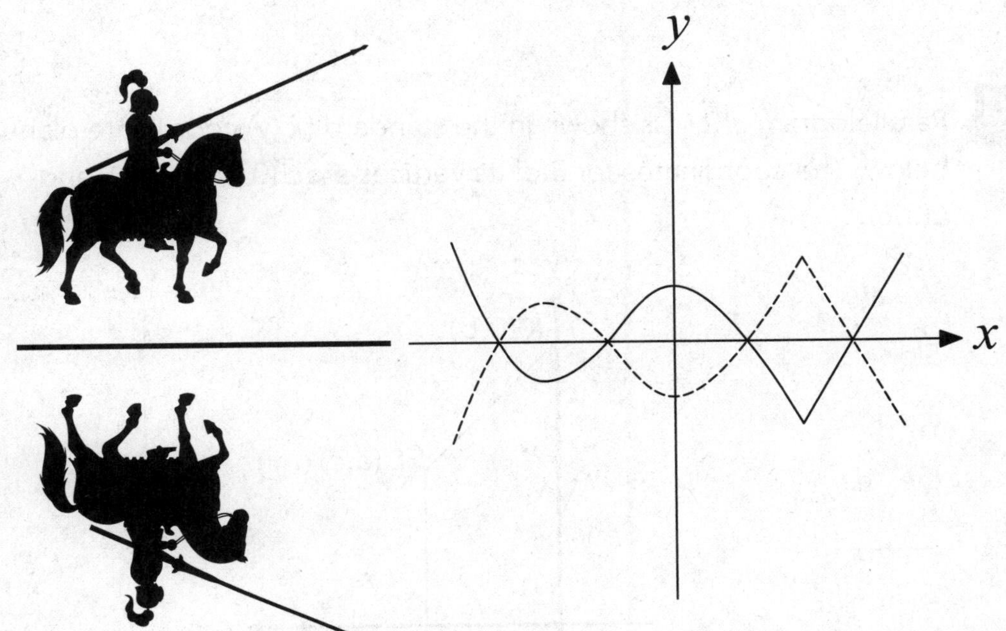

We are looking for the answer choice that looks like the dotted graph. That would be answer choice **J** .

Rotating Graphs

Some ACT questions will ask you to **rotate** a shape around a given point on a graph. This can require some mental acrobatics. Stay grounded by drawing it out.

E3 Parallelogram *JKLM* is shown in the standard (x, y) coordinate plane below. The coordinates for 3 of its vertices are $J(0,0)$, $K(0,b)$, and $L(a,c)$.

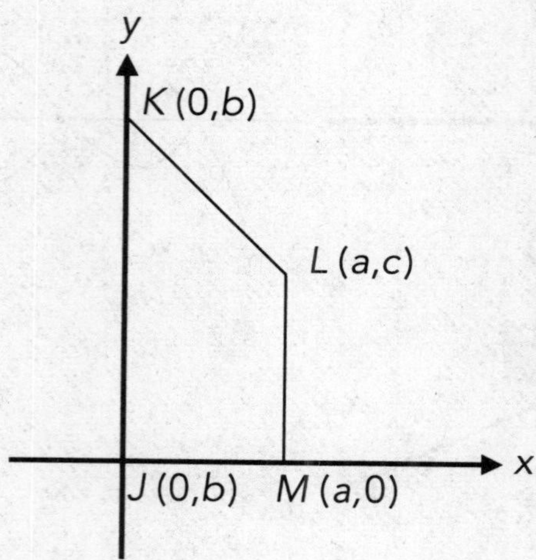

Parallelogram *JKLM* is rotated clockwise (↻) by 90° about the origin. What are the coordinates of point *L* after the rotation?

A. $(a, 0)$
B. $(-a, 0)$
C. (c, a)
D. $(c, -a)$
E. $(b, 0)$

S *First we need to get our bearings. The question tells us to spin the shape clockwise 90° around the origin. We can draw the result to help us find the new coordinates for point L.*

Imagine the shape as the blade of a pinwheel centered on the origin. When the pinwheel spins clockwise 90°, the shape turns on its side and drops down a quadrant:

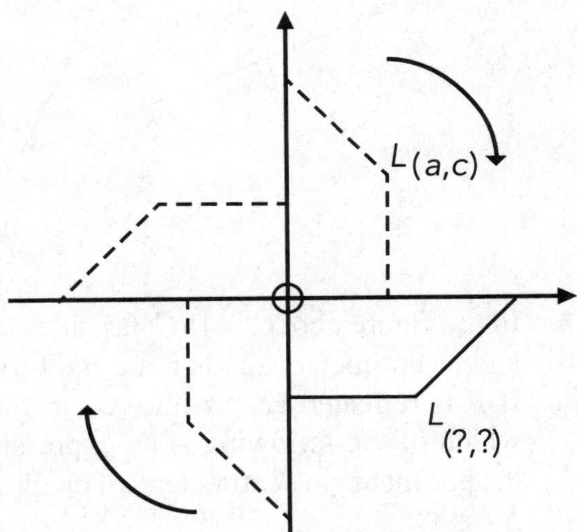

So if the original point L was

a units ***right***
c units ***up***

After spinning clockwise 90°, our new point L is

a units ***down***
c units ***right***

*If we go **right c units** and **down a units**, then we end up at the coordinates **(c, -a)**.*

*Our answer is **D**!*

Reflections Practice Problems

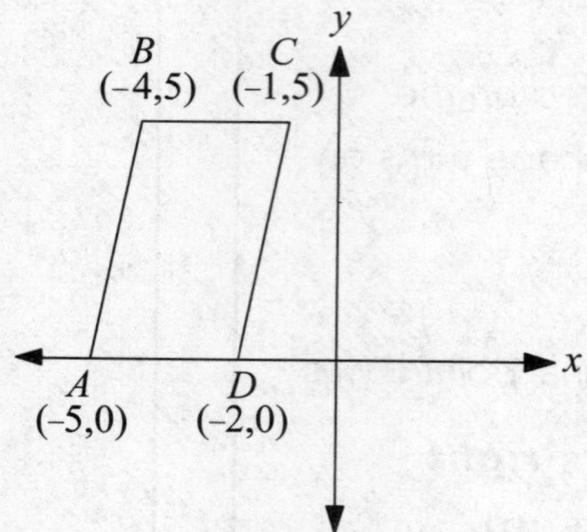

1. If the figure above were reflected about the x-axis, on what coordinates would the new point B lie ?

   A. (– 4, 5)
   B. (4, –5)
   C. (– 4, –5)
   D. (4, 5)
   E. (– 1, 5)

★★

2. In the xy-coordinate plane, line r is the reflection of line s about the x-axis. If the equation of line s is $y = 2x - 3$, which of the following is the equation of line r ?

   F. $y = -0.5x + 3$
   G. $y = -2x - 3$
   H. $y = -2x + 3$
   J. $y = 2x$
   K. $y = 0.5x + 3$

★★

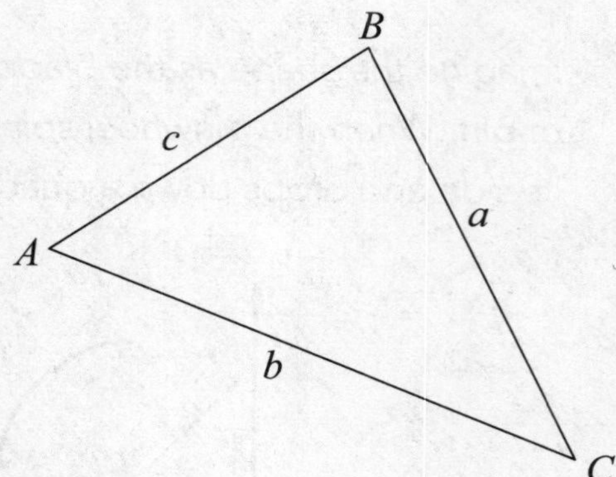

3. In the figure above, ΔABC has sides of a, b, and c centimeters and is not a right triangle. If B is reflected across line $\overline{AC}$ to form B', which of the following is an expression for the perimeter, in centimeters, of quadrilateral $B'CBA$?

   A. $2c + a + b$
   B. $2(a + b + c)$
   C. $2a + 2b$
   D. $2c + 2a + b$
   E. $2c + 2a$

★★

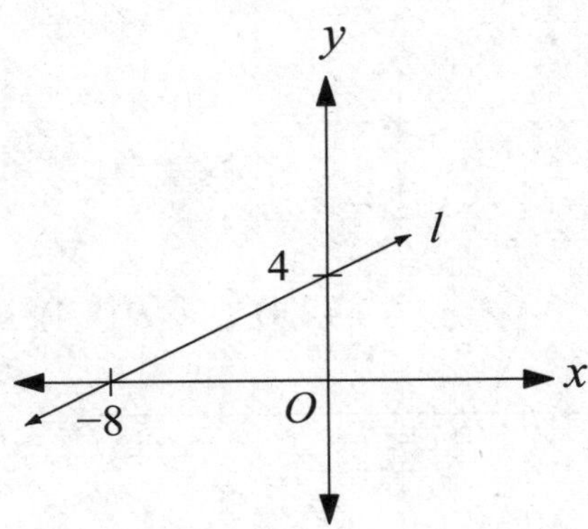

4. Line l is shown above in the standard (x, y) coordinate plane. If line n (not shown) is the reflection of line l about the x-axis, what is the equation of line n ?

F. $y = \frac{1}{2}x - 4$

G. $y = \frac{1}{2}x + 4$

H. $y = -\frac{1}{2}x - 4$

J. $y = -\frac{1}{2}x + 4$

K. $y = -\frac{1}{4}x - 4$

★★

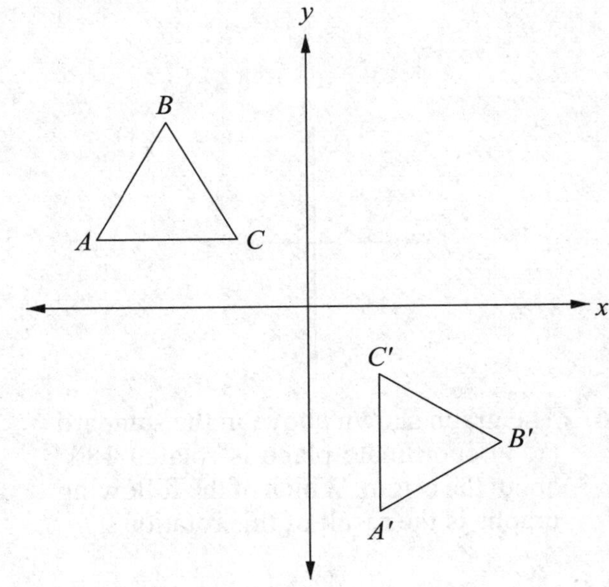

5. In a standard (x, y) coordinate plane, ΔABC is reflected across a line to form $\Delta A'B'C'$. Which of the following lines of reflection would best describe this transformation?

A. $y = 0$

B. $x = 0$

C. $y = -x$

D. $x = y$

E. $y = \frac{1}{2}$

★★★

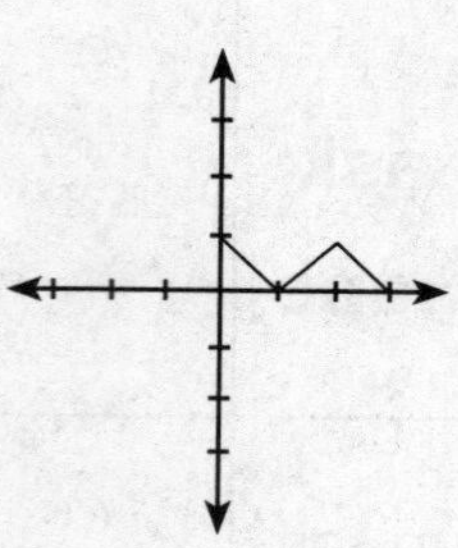

6. The graph shown above in the standard (x, y) coordinate plane is rotated 180° about the origin. Which of the following graphs is the result of this rotation?

F.

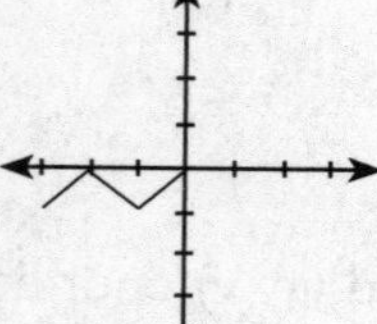

G.

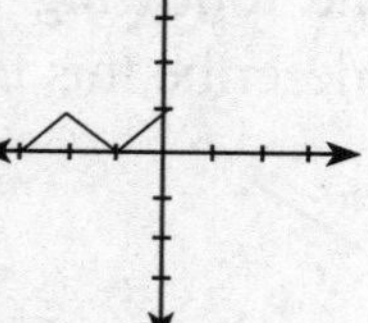

H.

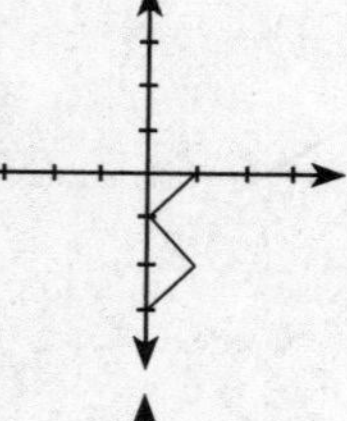

J.

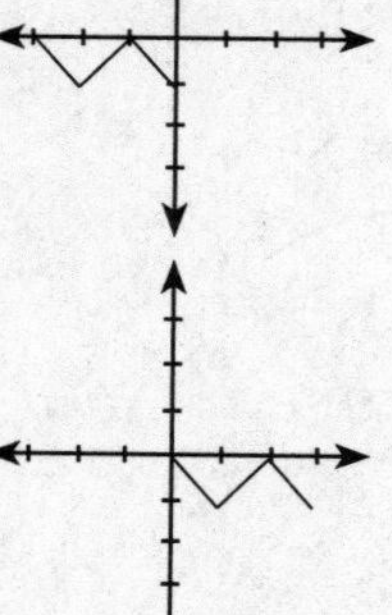

K.

★★

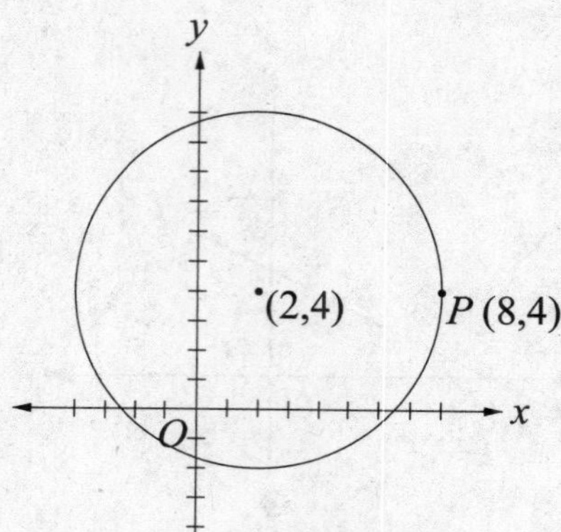

7. Point P (8, 4) lies on the circle with center (2, 4) and radius of 6 coordinate units, as shown in the standard (x, y) coordinate system above. If the circle is rotated 90° clockwise about the center of the circle, what are the coordinates of the image of P ?

A. $(-8, -4)$
B. $(-4, 4)$
C. $(2, -2)$
D. $(6, -1)$
E. $(2, 4)$

★★★

Diagonals and Symmetry

<1% of all math questions on the ACT

Get ready to draw! Some geometry questions ask you to count the diagonals or lines of symmetry in shapes.

These questions are a cinch if you are willing to draw and mark up some shapes. Don't make the mistake of trying to do these in your head.

Lines of Symmetry

A **line of symmetry** is a line that you can draw through a shape such that **a mirror image** is created.

Here are some examples of lines of symmetry:

How many lines of symmetry do each of these basic shapes have?

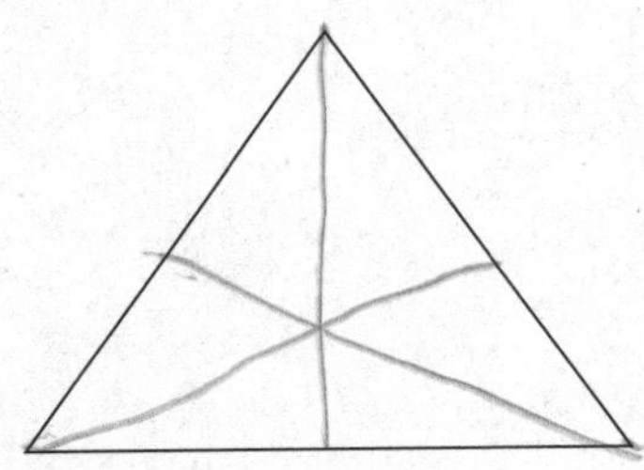

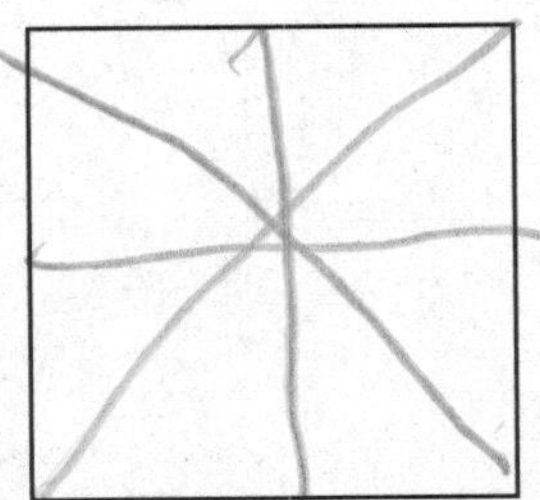

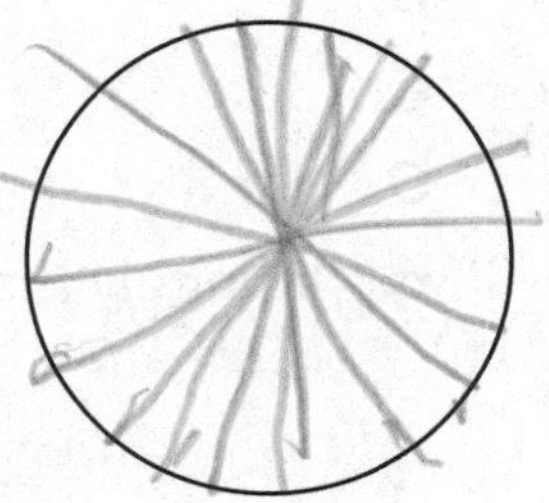

Don't be afraid of infinity (∞) or think that infinity is an automatic wrong answer. Some questions, especially those involving circles, have infinity as the right answer.

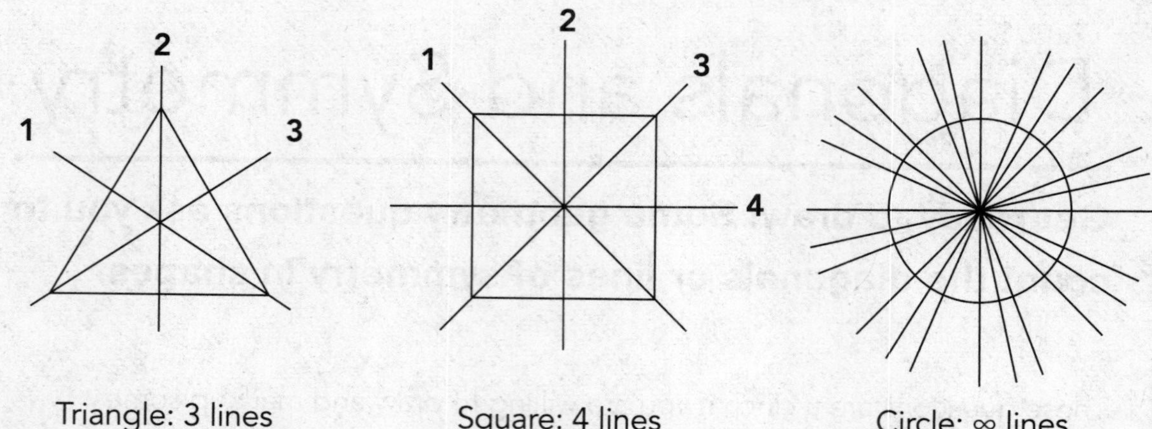

Triangle: 3 lines   Square: 4 lines   Circle: ∞ lines

Be careful not to double count your lines! This is a frequent error. The best practice is to draw each line of symmetry all the way through the shape and then label it.

E1

The figure shown above has how many lines of symmetry?

A. 0
B. 1
C. 3
D. 6
E. Infinitely many

S

This is a little sneaky, but not ***too*** *bad. A circle, by itself, has infinite lines of symmetry. But this triangle only has three.*

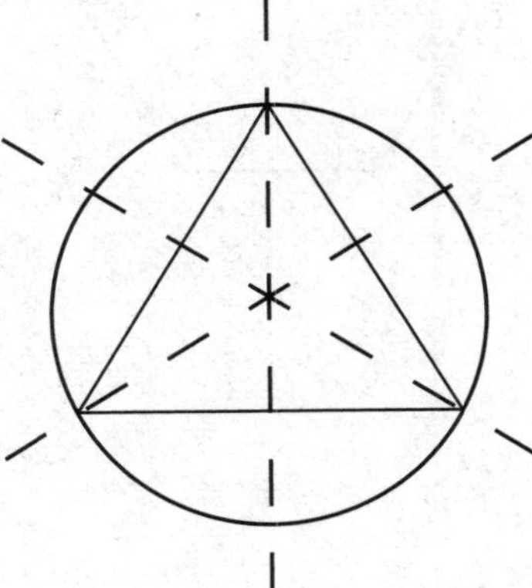

The triangle is a limiting factor. By placing a triangle in our circle, we max out at three lines of symmetry. ***C*** *is our answer!*

Diagonals

Diagonals are straight lines connecting vertices (points) of a shape. Diagonals must cross the interior space of the shape. If you are tracing the side of the shape, you are not drawing a diagonal!

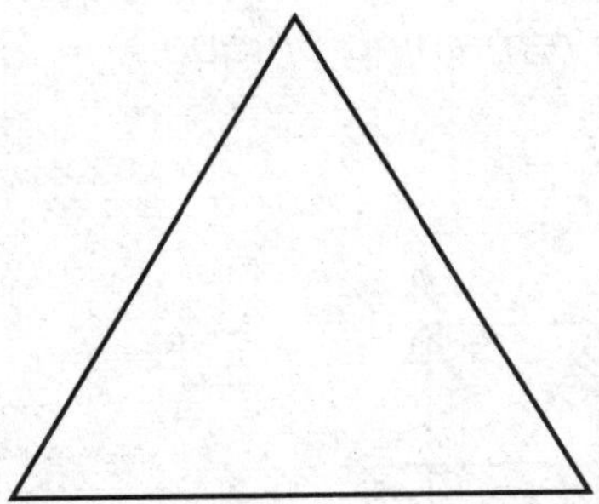

No diagonals!

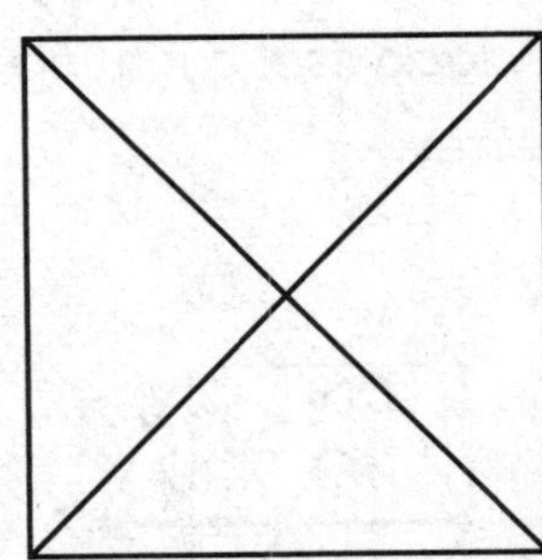

Dos diagonales!

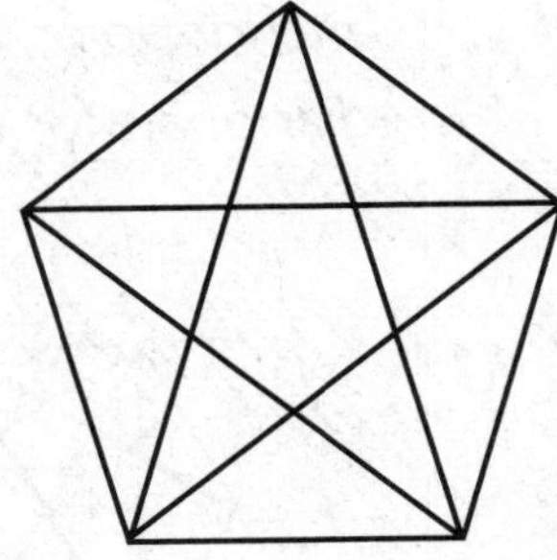

Muchos diagonales!

The only way to solve questions about diagonals is to carefully draw and count them. Just as in symmetry questions, you must be very careful not to double count or under–count your lines.

E2 How many diagonals does the hexagon shown below have?

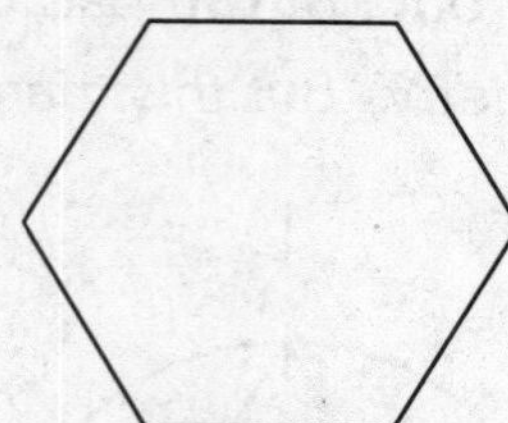

A. 3
B. 6
C. 9
D. 18
E. 30

S *Let's **anchor** at the top left point and draw diagonals one at a time.*

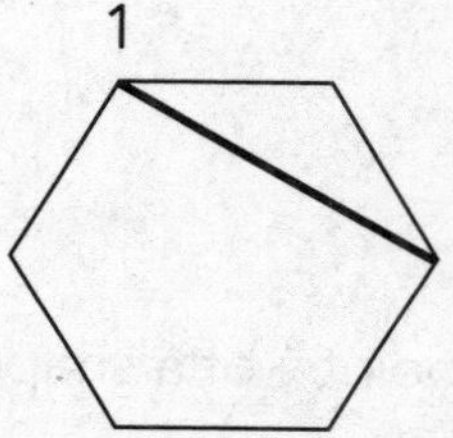

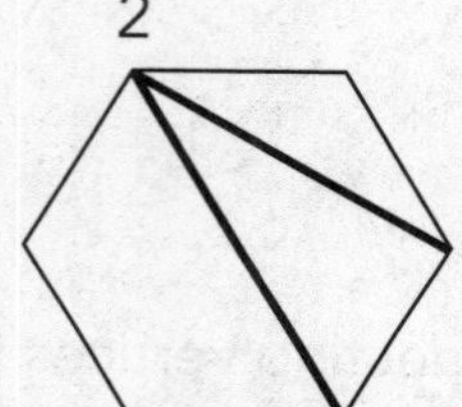

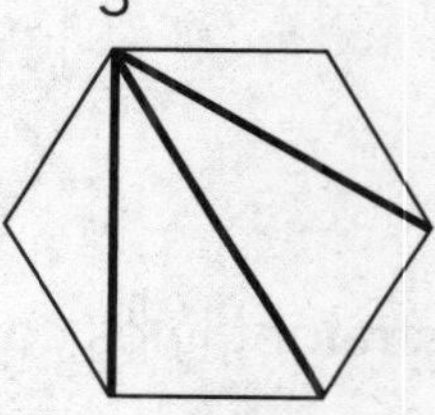

So we have three diagonals coming off that top left point. We can write a "3" by that point to help us keep track. From this anchor point, we go clockwise, counting the remaining unique diagonals for each vertex.

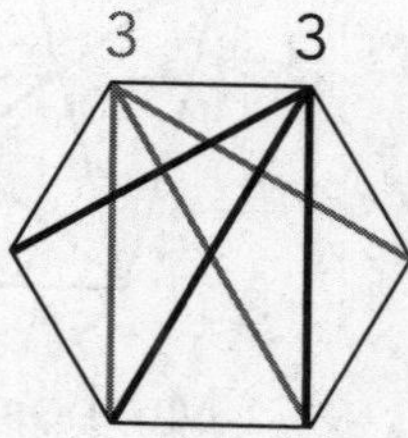

3 3 2

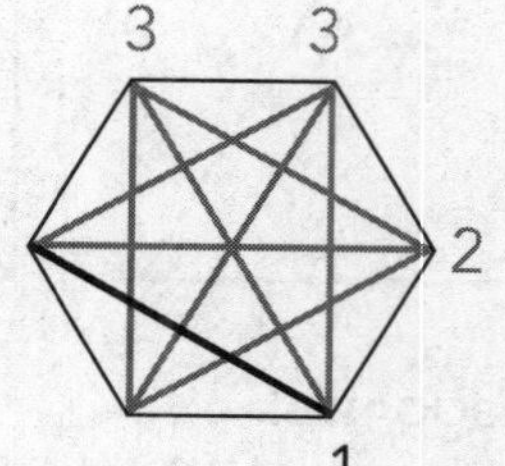

3 + 3 + 2 + 1 = (9)

If we try to draw any more, we'll just be tracing old lines.
***C** is our answer!*

Diagonals and Symmetry Practice Problems

1. How many diagonals does the octagon below have?

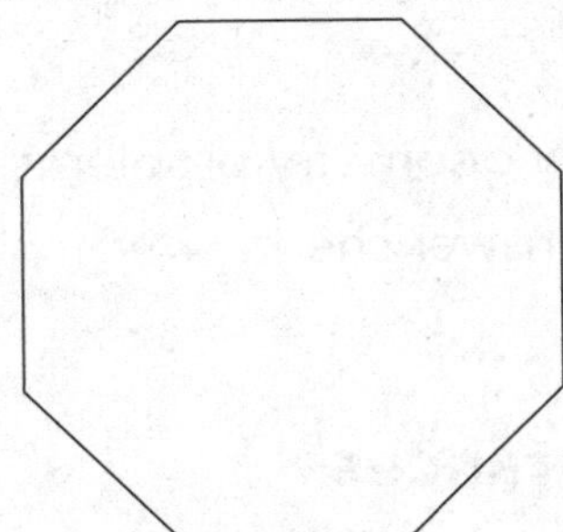

A. 8
B. 16
C. 20
D. 30
E. 32

★

2. An artist has a block of wood in the shape of a regular hexagon. He will create a design for which he must draw lines from each vertex of the hexagon to another vertex, without drawing lines along the edge of the hexagon. If he does not repeat any lines, how many lines will he need to draw to create his design?

F. 3
G. 5
H. 7
J. 9
K. 18

★★

3. The figure below shows a certain jewler's design for a necklace pendant. How many lines of symmetry are there in the jeweler's design?

A. 2
B. 3
C. 5
D. 9
E. 18

★★

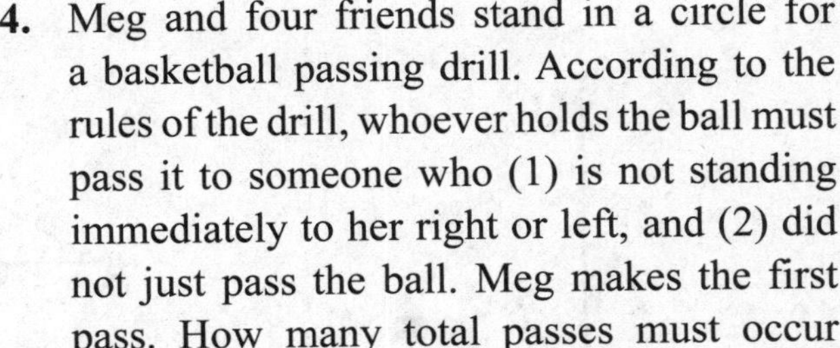

4. Meg and four friends stand in a circle for a basketball passing drill. According to the rules of the drill, whoever holds the ball must pass it to someone who (1) is not standing immediately to her right or left, and (2) did not just pass the ball. Meg makes the first pass. How many total passes must occur before she holds the ball again?

F. 4
G. 5
H. 6
J. 7
K. 8

★★

Measuring

Although the ACT warns you that the diagrams are not always drawn to scale, they frequently are! You can use this to your advantage.

The corner of your answer sheet is a 90° angle. Bisect that to get two 45° angles, and from there you can estimate almost any angle you're given.

When you are stuck, you can solve some tricky geometry problems by measuring **side lengths** or **angles** with your answer sheet.

Requirements for Measuring Distances

In order to use this tactic on the ACT, you must be:

1. given a **2-dimensional** diagram (distances get funky in 3D);
2. given the **length of a line** in the diagram;
3. asked to find the length of **another line** on the diagram.

Let's see this in action.

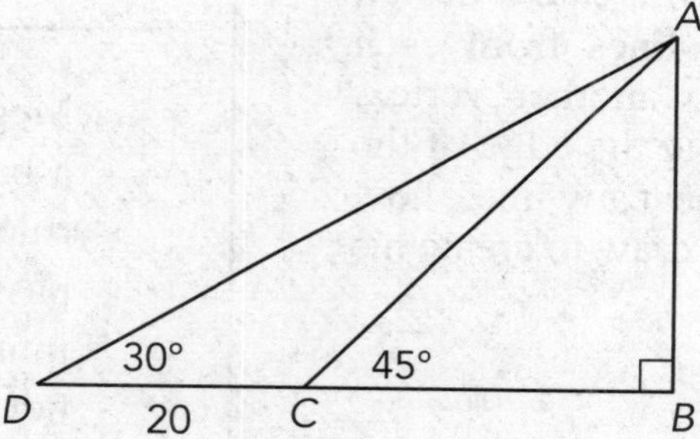

E1 In the diagram above line segment $\overline{DC}$ = 20 inches. To the nearest inch, how long is line segment $\overline{AD}$?

A. 40
B. 48
C. 55
D. 75
E. 80

S 1 Line the answer sheet up with the **known length**

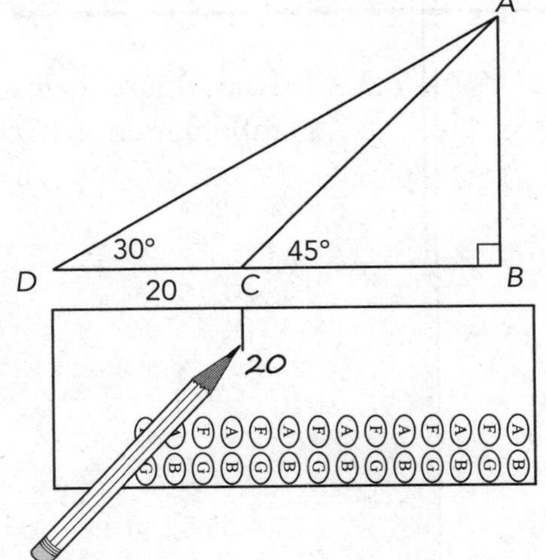

2 Establish **midpoints** and **multiples**

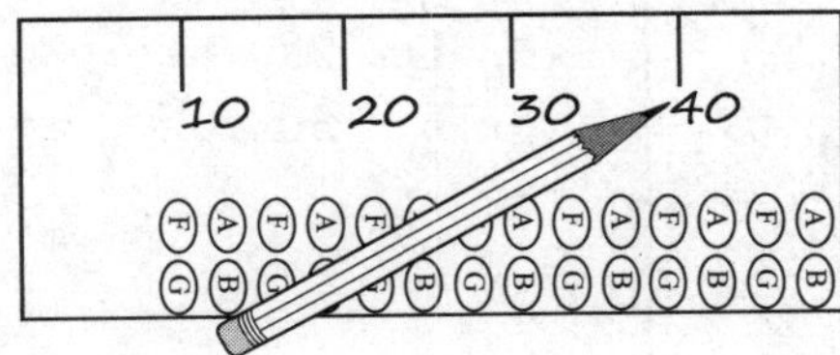

3 **Measure** side and **compare** to answer choices

A. 40 *too low!*
B. 48 *too low!*
(C.) 55 ***bingo!***
D. 75 *too high!*
E. 80 *too high!*

That's all there is to it! Sure enough, **C** *is the correct answer. This can be a quick way to pick up an extra point if you're not sure how to tackle the problem head-on.*

This question normally requires knowledge of special triangles and the use of some clever algebra.

Geometry Review

1. What is the volume, in cubic inches, of a rectangular box measuring 5 inches wide, 10 inches long, and 12 inches tall?

   A. 60
   B. 78
   C. 245
   D. 600
   E. 729

★

2. In the right triangle below, $\overline{AB} = 12$ inches and $\overline{AB} = \overline{BC}$. What is the length, in inches, of $\overline{AC}$?

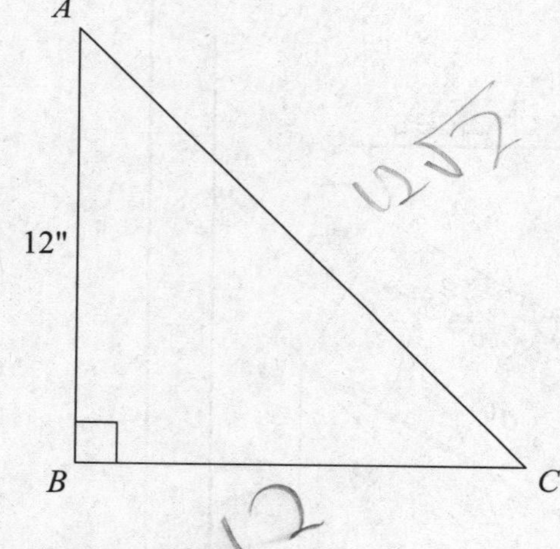

   F. 6
   G. 12
   H. 24
   J. $4\sqrt{6}$
   K. $12\sqrt{2}$

★

3. In the figure below, what is the area of parallelogram $ABCD$?

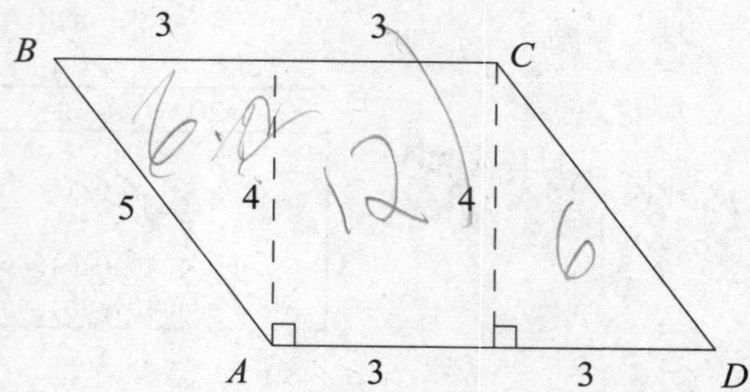

   A. 12
   B. 22
   C. 24
   D. 28
   E. 30

★

4. For the number line below, the ratio of the length of $\overline{JK}$ to the length of $\overline{KL}$ is 4:3. If it can be determined, what is the ratio of the length of $\overline{JK}$ and the length of $\overline{JL}$?

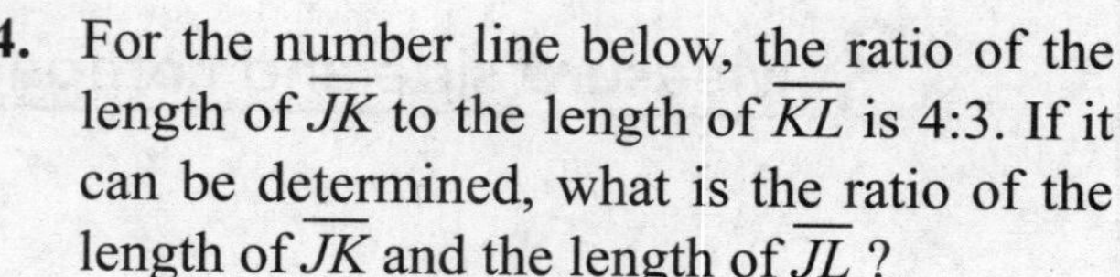

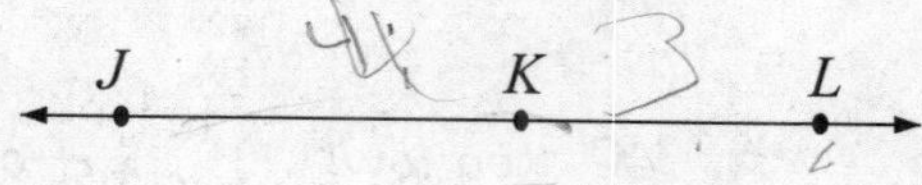

   F. 4:1
   G. 4:7
   H. 3:4
   J. 3:7
   K. Cannot be determined from the given information.

★★

5. The figure below shows line $\overline{AD}$ with point E between points A and D. If two rays, $\overrightarrow{EB}$ and $\overrightarrow{EC}$ extend from point E, which of the following statements must be true about the measures of the angles formed?

(Note: The figure below shows 1 possible arrangement of these points.)

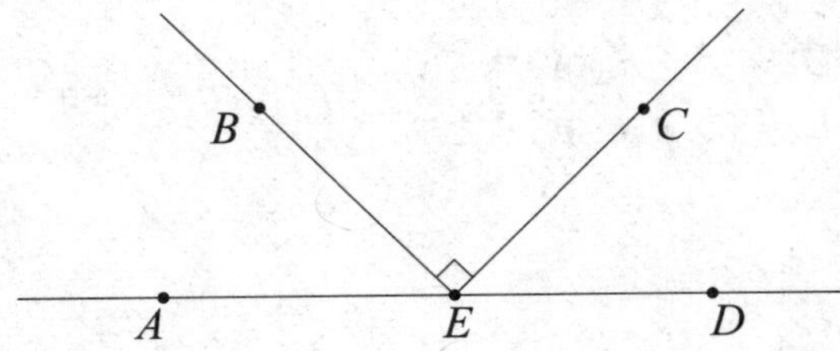

A. The measure of $\angle AEB$ is less than 45°
B. The measure of $\angle CED$ is less than 45°
C. The measure of $\angle AEB$ is 90°.
D. The sum of the measures of $\angle AEB$ and $\angle CED$ is 180°.
E. The sum of the measures of $\angle AEB$ and $\angle CED$ is 90°.

★★

6. A triangle has sides of lengths 7 inches, 16 inches, and 18 inches, respectively. In a second triangle similar to the first, the longest side is 24 inches. To the nearest tenth of an inch, what is the length of the shortest side of the second triangle?

F. 6.2
G. 7.0
H. 9.3
J. 14.0
K. 16.2

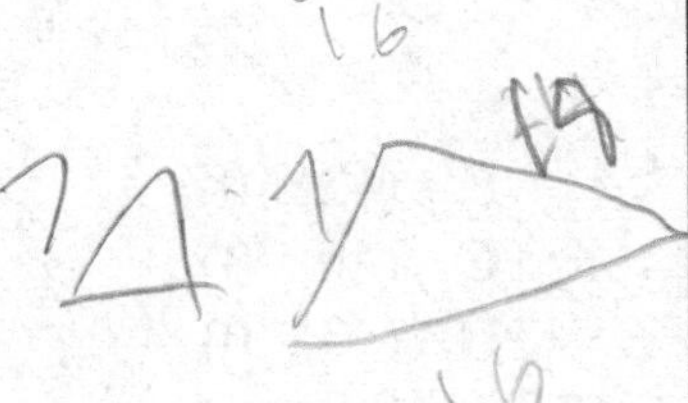

★★

7. What is the y-intercept of the graph of $6x + 3y = 18$?

A. 3
B. 6
C. 9
D. 12
E. 18

★

8. Which of the following is the slope of a line perpendicular to the line $y = -\frac{1}{3}x + 5$ in the standard (x, y) coordinate plane?

F. 5

G. 3

H. 1

J. $\frac{1}{3}$

K. $-\frac{1}{3}$

★★

9. An equilateral triangle with side lengths of 5 inches long is inscribed in a standard (x, y) coordinate system. If one vertex is at (3, 2), which of the following points could also be a vertex of the triangle?

A. (10, 6)
B. (2, –3)
C. (–3, 2)
D. (3, 6)
E. (3, 7)

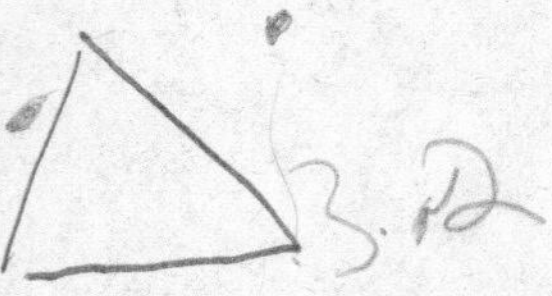

★★★

10. A circle is defined by the equation $(x - 7)^2 + y^2 = 24$ in the standard (x, y) coordinate plane. In coordinate units, what are the radius of the circle and the coordinates of the center of the circle?

	Radius	Center
F.	12	(–7,0)
G.	12	(7,0)
H.	24	(7,0)
J.	$\sqrt{24}$	(–7,0)
K.	$\sqrt{24}$	(7,0)

★★

11. The number line graph below is the graph of which of the following inequalities?

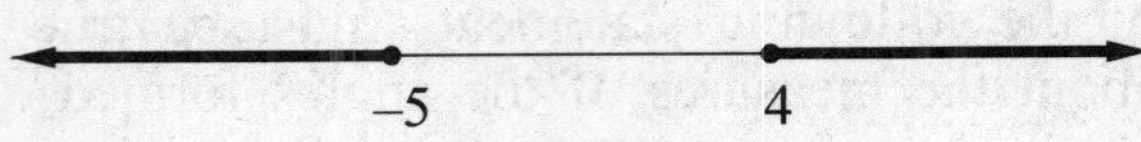

A. $-5 \le x$ and $4 \le x$
B. $-5 \le x$ and $4 \ge x$
C. $-5 \le x$ or $4 \le x$
D. $-5 \ge x$ or $4 \le x$
E. $-5 \ge x$ or $4 \ge x$

★

12. The triangle, shown in the standard (x, y) coordinate plane below, is reflected along the line $y = x$, not shown. If point A has a coordinate value of (0, 3), what is the value of the new point A' ?

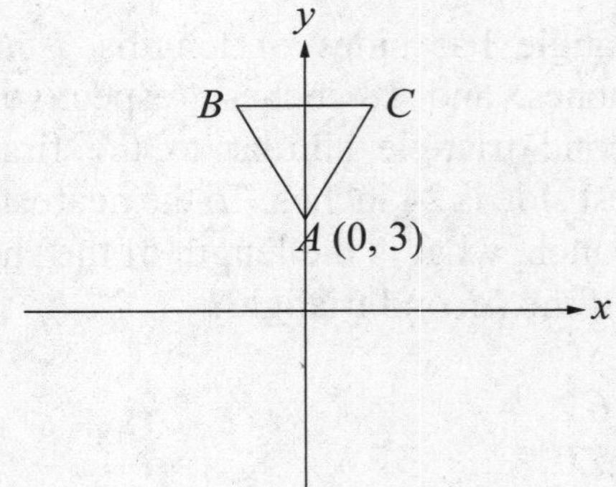

F. (–3, 0)
G. (0, –3)
H. (3, 0)
J. (3, 3)
K. (6, 0)

★★★

13. A circle with a circumference of 20 inches has four points, Q, R, S, and T which lie on the circle. Point S is 6 inches clockwise from Q along the circle, point T is 6 inches counterclockwise from point Q, and point R is 6 inches counterclockwise from point T. Starting at point Q and moving clockwise around the circle, what is the order of the points?

A. Q, R, S, T
B. Q, R, T, S
C. Q, S, T, R
D. Q, S, R, T
E. Q, T, S, R

★★

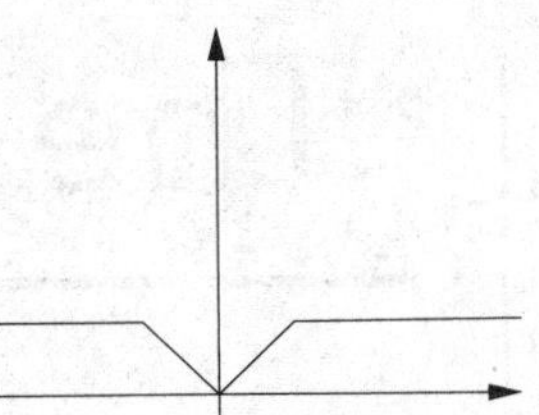

14. The graph in the standard (x, y) coordinate plane above is the graph of $y = f(x)$. One of the following graphs is the graph of $y = f(x - 4) - 6$. Which one is it ?

F.

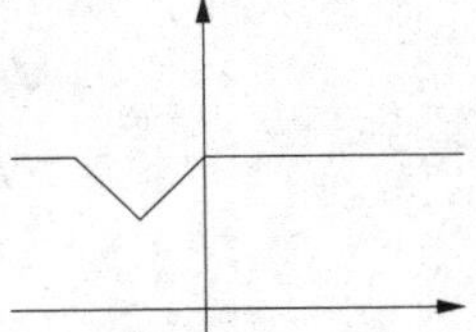

G.

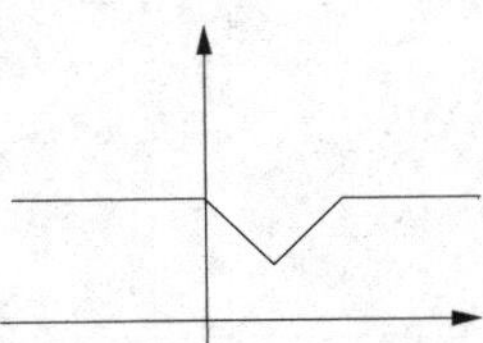

H.

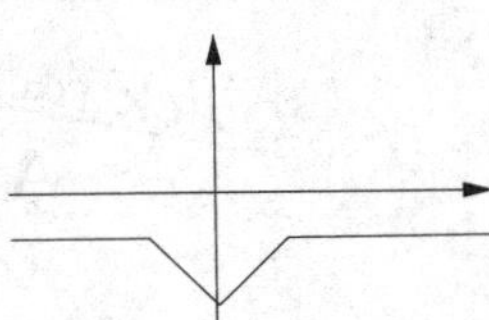

J.

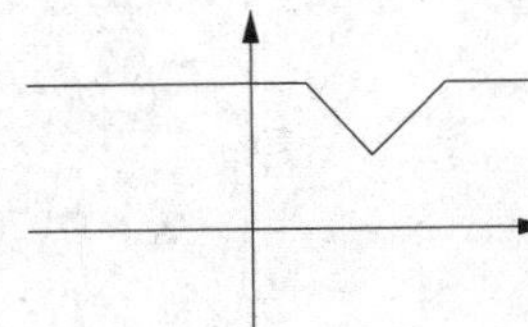

K.

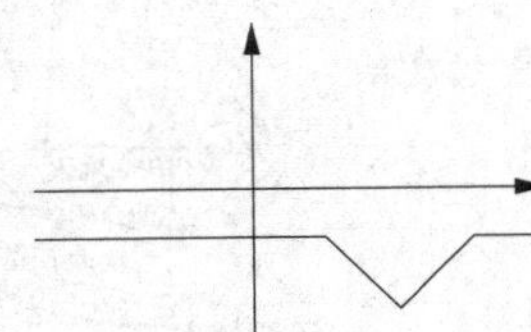

★★

The Geometry Short List

1 Angles

Quick facts

Angles in a **triangle** add up to **180°**
Angles on one side of a **line** add up to **180°**
Angles in a **quadrilateral** add up to **360°**
Vertical angles are equal
With parallel lines, **BIG = BIG** and **small = small**

If a shape is funky, divide it into triangles and rectangles!

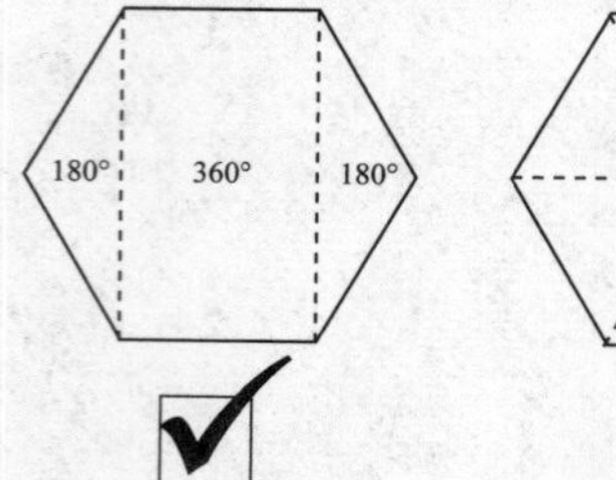

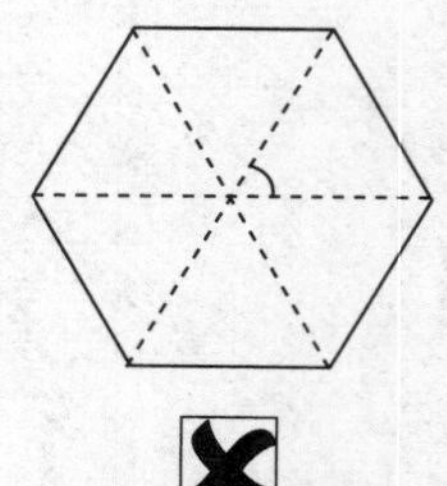

2 Triangles

Quick facts

Area = $\frac{1}{2}bh$
Isosceles triangles have **two equal sides** and **two equal angles**.
Equilateral triangles have **three equal sides** and **three 60° angles.**

*When you see a **right triangle**, think pythagorean theorem.*

Pythagorean Theorem

$$a^2 + b^2 = c^2$$

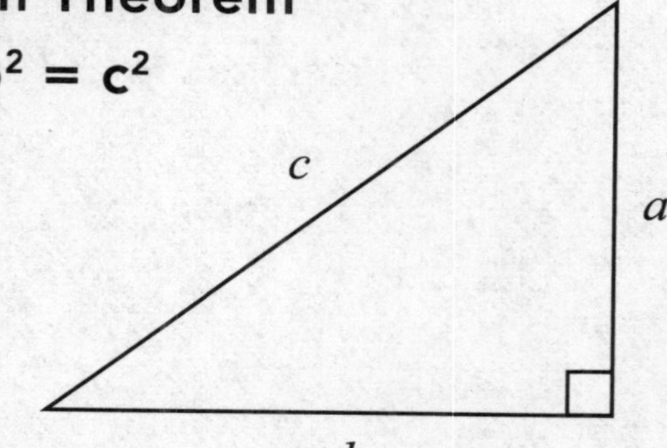

Special Right Triangles

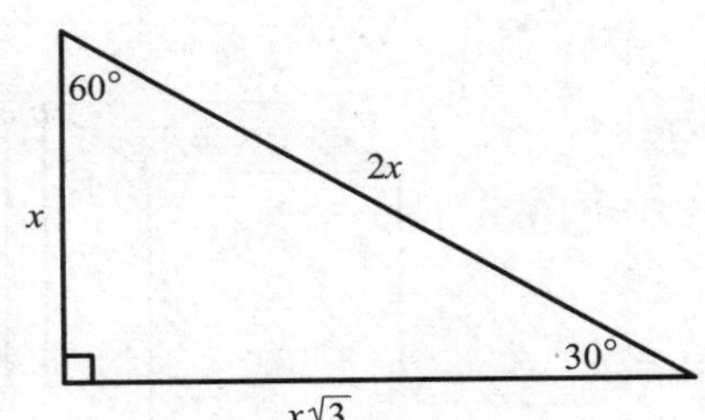

30°– 60°– 90° Triangle

The one with **3** different angles is the one with $\sqrt{3}$

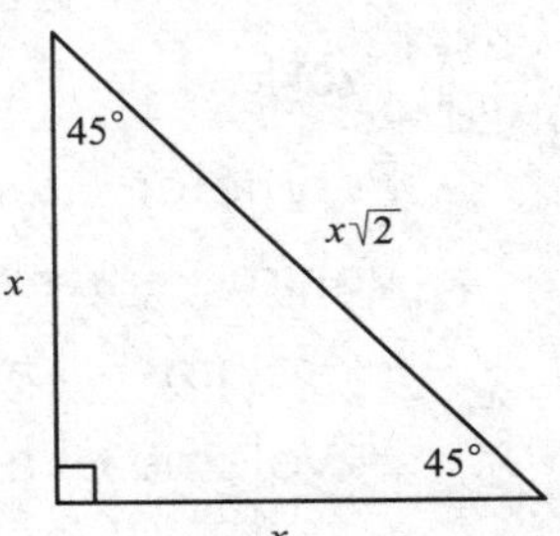

45°– 45°– 90° Triangle

The one with **2** different angles is the one with $\sqrt{2}$

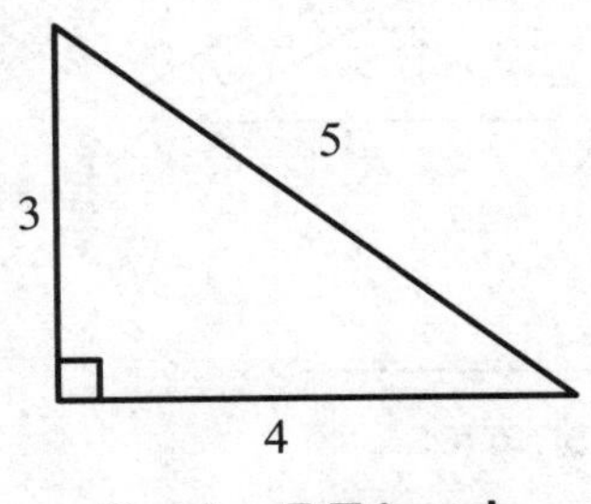

3 – 4 – 5 Triangle

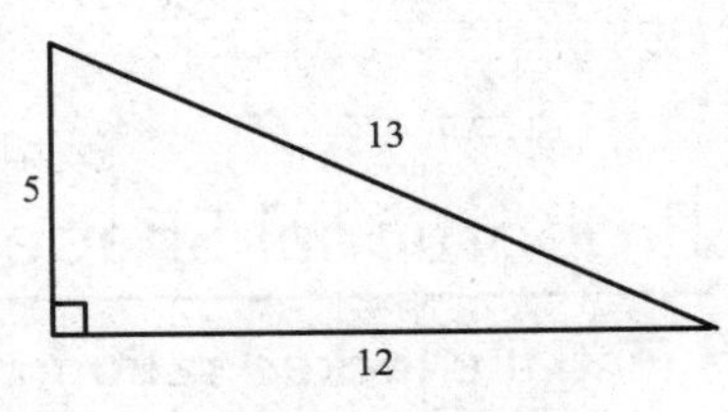

5 – 12 – 13 Triangle

3 Circles

Quick facts

Area = πr^2

Circumference = $2\pi r$

There are **360°** in a circle

A line tangent to the circle forms a **90°** with the radius.

$$\frac{\text{Piece}}{\text{Whole}} = \frac{\text{Angle measure}}{360^\circ} = \frac{\text{Arc length}}{\text{Circumference}} = \frac{\text{Wedge area}}{\text{Circle area}}$$

PIECE / WHOLE = x° / 360° = ABC / C = 2πr = A = πr²

4 Perimeter, Area, and Volume

Quick facts

Perimeter = length of **outside** edges

Volume = **area** of shape on end × **height**

Volume of a **cube** = s × s × s

Volume of a **box** = l × w × h

Volume of a **cylinder** = πr^2 × h

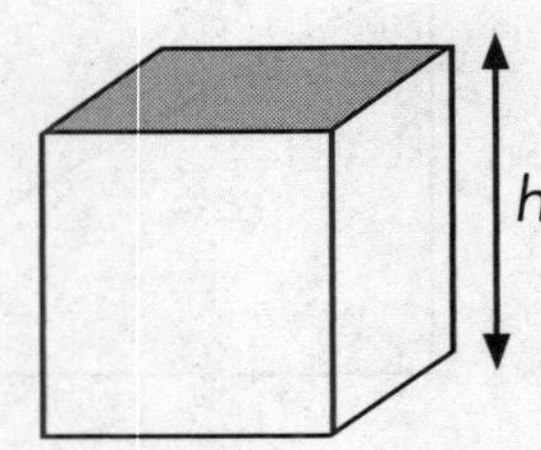

Surface area is the sum of the area of every side

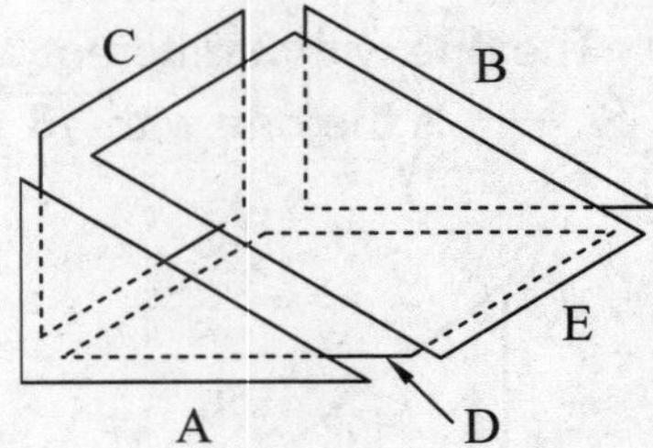

5 Proportional Shapes

Find the **locked ratio** for similar/proportional shapes.

1. Use **two known sides** to find the ratio
2. Use ratio to find the **missing side**

If two triangles have equal angle measurements, the triangles are proportional.

$$\frac{AD}{AE} = \frac{AC}{AB} = \frac{EB}{DC}$$

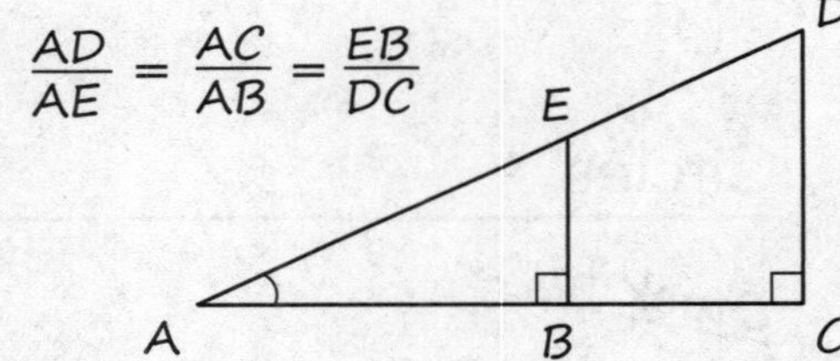

6 Slope

Quick facts

The equation of a line is ***y = mx + b*.**

Parallel lines have the same slope.

The slopes of **perpendicular** lines are **(–) reciprocals.**

(x, y) = point on the line
m = slope
b = y-intercept

$$\text{Slope} = m = \frac{\text{rise}}{\text{run}} = \frac{\Delta y}{\Delta x} = \frac{y_2 - y_1}{x_2 - x_1}$$

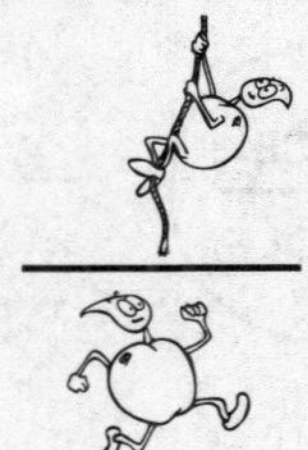

7 Equation of a Circle

$$(x-h)^2+(y-k)^2=r^2$$

(h,k) = center of the circle

r = radius of the circle

8 Shifting Graphs

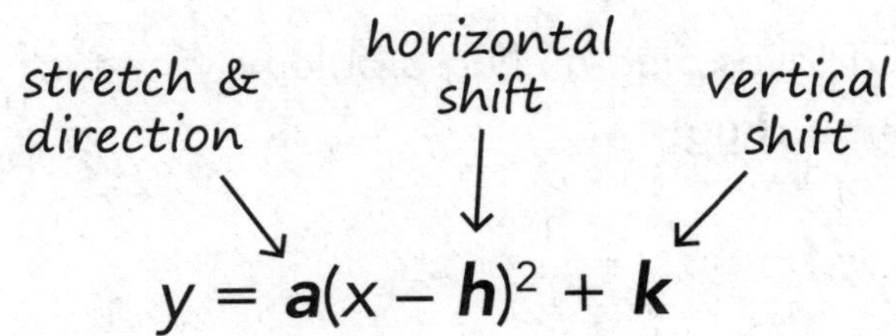

9 Reflections

Quick facts

When you **reflect** over the **x-axis**,
the y-values change but the x-values stay the same.

When you **reflect** over the **y-axis**,
the x-values change but the y-values stay the same.

10 Abstract Geometry

Quick facts

A **line of symmetry** creates a **mirror image**.
A **diagonal** connects two vertices of a shape.

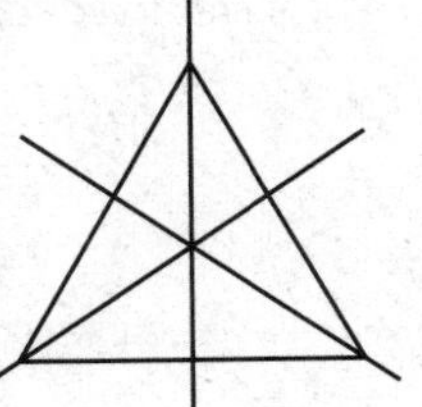

When drawing diagonals, pick a starting point and count for each vertex.

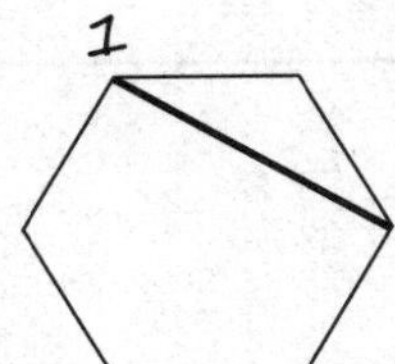

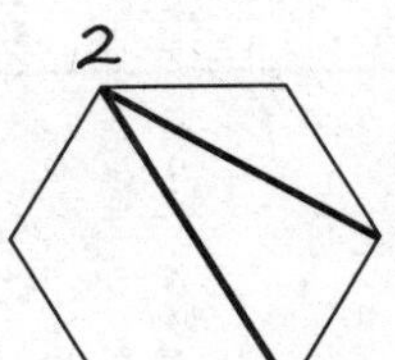

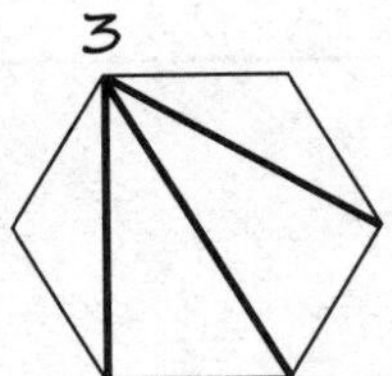

Basic Algebra

The most common algebra question type on the ACT simply tests your ability to substitute numbers for variables in an equation.

Plug-n-chug

In other words, the ACT loves *plug-n-chug* problems. The trick is to work step-by-step. **Plug before you chug!**

E1 If $p = 6$, $r = 3$, and $s = -2$, what does $(p + s)(r + p - s)$ equal?

S *First we* ***plug****:*

$$(p + s)(r + p - s) = ?$$
$$(6 + (-2))(3 + 6 - (-2)) = ?$$

Then we ***chug****:*

$$(6 - 2)(3 + 6 + 2) = ?$$
$$4(11) = \boxed{44}$$

Simplifying Equations

Often, the test writers will ask you to simplify an equation. These questions are not particularly difficult if you remember your **order of operations: PEMDAS.**

Please Excuse My Dear Aunt Sally

Parentheses

Exponents

Multiplication

Division

Addition

Subtraction

Students lose easy points when they neglect those **parentheses**! Try solving this next example using just your calculator.

$$\frac{48}{16 + 2 \cdot 4} - 4(2 + 3) = ?$$

As a rule, it's good to keep numerators and denominators in their own parentheses.

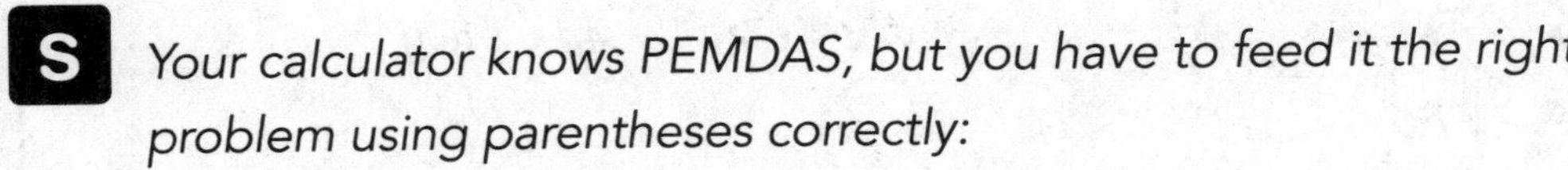

Your calculator knows PEMDAS, but you have to feed it the right problem using parentheses correctly:

$$48 \div (16 + 2 \times 4) - 4(2 + 3) = \boxed{-18}$$

Look at the variety of errors that occur if you omit parentheses:

- $48 \div 16 + 2 \times 4 - 4(2 + 3) =$ **−9**
- $48 \div (16 + 2 \times 4) - 4 \times 2 + 3 =$ **−3**
- $48 \div (16 + (2 \times 4) - 4(2 + 3) =$ **ERROR**

E3 If $\frac{3x - y}{x + y} = \frac{3}{2}$, then $\frac{x}{y} = ?$

S 1 Simplify the equation

$\frac{x}{y} = ?$

*Since we have two fractions set equal to each other, we can **cross multiply**.*

$$\frac{3x - y}{x + y} \quad \frac{3}{2}$$

$2(3x - y) = 3(x + y)$ *distribute*

$6x - 2y = 3x + 3y$ *simplify*

$3x = 5y$ *much simpler!*

2 Solve

Now we need to get $\frac{x}{y}$ by itself.

$3x = 5y$

$\frac{3x}{y} = 5$ *divide each side by y*

$\frac{3x}{3y} = \frac{5}{3}$ *divide each side by 3*

$\frac{x}{y} = \boxed{\frac{5}{3}}$ *done and done!*

E4 The formula $S = N(1 + 0.01r)^t$ is used to calculate the final value, S dollars, of N dollars invested at r% interest, compounded annually for t years. Which of the following is an expression for N in terms of r, s, and t?

A. $\frac{(1 + 0.01r)^t}{s}$

B. $(\frac{s}{1 + 0.01r})^t$

C. $\frac{s + 4}{(1 + 0.01r)^t}$

D. $s - 0.01r^t$

E. $s + 0.01r^t$

S *This problem might look tough at first, but all we're asked to do is simplify the equation. We need to get **N** by itself.*

$$S = N(1 + 0.01r)^t$$

$$(\frac{1}{(1 + 0.01r)^t})\,S = N\,\frac{\cancel{(1 + 0.01r)^t}}{1} \times \frac{1}{\cancel{(1 + 0.01r)^t}}$$

$$\frac{S}{(1 + 0.01r)^t} = N$$

C *is our answer!*

Basic Algebra Practice Problems

1. Which of the following is a simplified form of the expression $3(4 + 7x) + 8 - 3x$?

A. $4x + 20$
B. $11x + 17$
C. $18x + 20$
D. $30x + 8$
E. $38x$

★

2. For the equation $7a + b = c$, which of the following expressions gives a in terms of b and c ?

F. $\frac{c-b}{7}$

G. $\frac{c-7}{b}$

H. $\frac{c+b}{7}$

J. $\frac{b-c}{7}$

K. $c - b - 7$

★

3. If $-9 + 2x = 13$, then $3x = ?$

A. 2
B. 6
C. 11
D. 26
E. 33

★

4. A grocery store sells 3 bottles of water for \$1.99. At this price, how much would the store charge for 2 bottles of water, rounded to the nearest cent?

F. \$1.33
G. \$1.25
H. \$1.00
J. \$0.67
K. \$0.66

★

5. Which of the following is a simplified expression for $4(2x + 5) - 5(3x - 1)$?

A. $x - 4$
B. $-2x + 3$
C. $-7x + 3$
D. $-7x + 25$
E. $13x + 23$

★

6. Indigo is installing a rectangular pool in his backyard. A diagram of the pool is shown below. Which of the following expressions gives the perimeter of Indigo's pool?

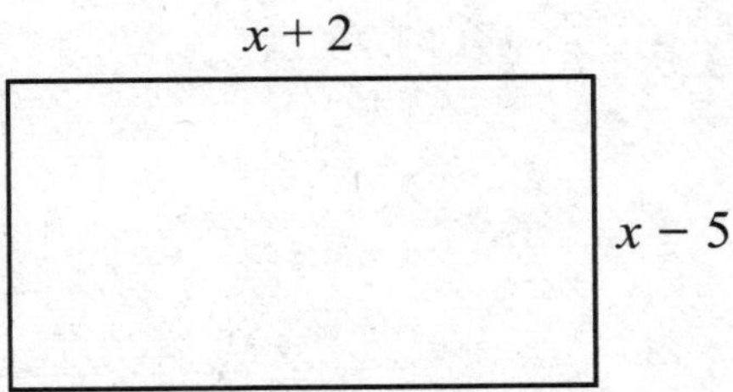

F. $2x - 3$
G. $2x + 7$
H. $4x - 6$
J. $4x + 14$
K. $x^2 - 3x - 10$

---

7. Which of the following is the value of the expression $(x - y)^2$ when $x = 3$ and $y = -4$?

A. -7
B. -1
C. 1
D. 7
E. 49

★

8. Which of the following is equivalent to $(3x^2 + x + 1) + (2x - 1) - (3x + 2x + x)$?

F. $3x^2 + 3x$
G. $3x^2 - 3x + 2$
H. $3x^2 - 3x$
J. $6x^2$
K. $6x^2 - 3x$

★★

---

9. On the day that Sam bought a parakeet, he taught it to say 4 new words. On each day after that, he taught it 3 new words. Which of the following expressions gives the number of words Sam has taught his parakeet after x days if $x > 2$?

A. $3(x - 1) - 4$
B. $4(x - 1) - 3$
C. $7(x - 1)$
D. $4(x - 1) + 3$
E. $4 + 3(x - 1)$

★★

Polynomials

4% of all math questions on the ACT

Polynomial questions ask you to simplify complicated algebra equations. Whether you are substituting, factoring, or FOILing, careful written work is key.

E1 If $2x + 2y = 10$, $x + z = 13$, and $3z = 9$ what is the value of y?

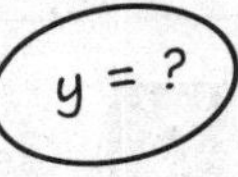

S

1 Solve the **simplest** equation

$3z = 9$

$z = \boxed{3}$ *Bingo! We have a replacement for z!*

2 **Substitute** new value into second equation

$x + z = 13$ *Plug in 3 for z....*

$x + 3 = 13$

$x = \boxed{10}$ *...and we have a replacement for x!*

3 **Substitute** new value into third equation

$2x + 2y = 10$ *Plug in 10 for x....*

$2(10) + 2y = 10$

$20 + 2y = 10$

$2y = -10$

$y = \mathbf{-5}$ (circled) *...and we have our answer!*

Factoring Quadratics

A **quadratic** is an expression containing a squared variable, for example:

$$x^2 + 6x + 9$$

Most ACT quadratic problems require you to **FOIL** the factors of a quadratic.

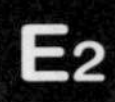

$$(3x + 5)^2 = ?$$

S *Get out your roll of FOIL, because it's time for some good, old fashioned **F**irst **O**uter **I**nner **L**ast!*

$$(3x + 5) \times (3x + 5) = (3x + 5)^2$$

First	$(\mathbf{3x} + 5) \times (\mathbf{3x} + 5)$	$= 3x \cdot 3x = \mathbf{9x^2}$
Outer	$(\mathbf{3x} + 5) \times (3x + \mathbf{5})$	$= 3x \cdot 5 = \mathbf{15x}$
Inner	$(3x + \mathbf{5}) \times (\mathbf{3x} + 5)$	$= 5 \cdot 3x = \mathbf{15x}$
Last	$(3x + \mathbf{5}) \times (3x + \mathbf{5})$	$= 5 \cdot 5 = \mathbf{25}$

Now we just need to sum our products:

$$9x^2 + 15x + 15x + 25$$

Then we simplify to get our answer:

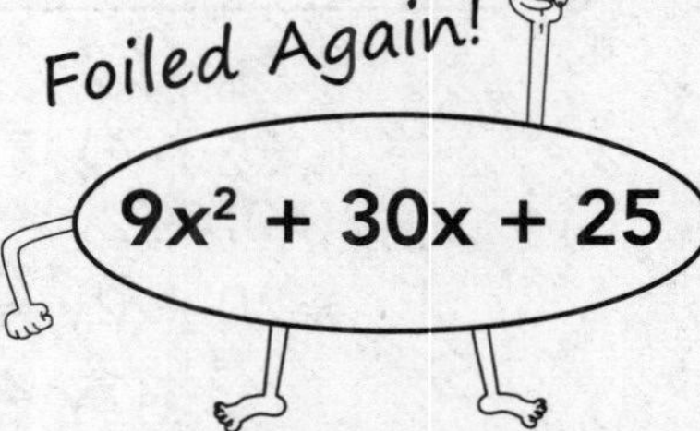

Difference of Squares

Frequently, when you are asked to factor quadratics, you will come across a common identity: the **Difference of Squares**. Any time you have two perfect squares separated by a minus sign, you are in D.O.S. land!

$$x^2 - y^2 = (x + y)(x - y)$$

$$b^2 - 16 = (b + 4)(b - 4)$$

$$16x^4 - 36 = (4x^2 + 6)(4x^2 - 6)$$

Any time you recognize a Difference of Squares, immediately factor it out.

$$x^4 - 16$$

Which of the following is not a factor of the expression above?

A. $(x + 2)$
B. $(x + 4)$
C. $(x^2 - 4)$
D. $(x - 2)$
E. $(x^2 + 4)$

S *We have two perfect squares separated by a minus sign! Difference of Squares, here we go!*

$$x^4 - 16 = (x^2 + 4)(x^2 - 4)$$

Hold on, we're not done factoring yet! We have another D.O.S. staring us in the face!

$$x^4 - 16 = (x^2 + 4)\,\mathbf{(x^2 - 4)}$$

$$x^4 - 16 = (x^2 + 4)\,\mathbf{(x + 2)(x - 2)}$$

*The elusive **Double D.O.S.**!*

The only choice that doesn't show up in our factored equations is **(x + 4).**

***B** is our answer!*

E4 For all x in the domain of the function $\frac{x+2}{x^3 - 4x}$, this function is equivalent to:

F. $\frac{1}{2x^2} - \frac{1}{2x^3}$

G. $\frac{1}{2x^2} - \frac{1}{2x}$

H. $\frac{1}{2x^2 - 4}$

J. $\frac{1}{x^2 - 2x}$

K. $\frac{1}{2x^3}$

S *We're dealing with a thinly veiled Difference of Squares. We can start by factoring out an* **x** *from the denominator.*

$$\frac{x+2}{x^3-4x} = \frac{x+2}{x(x^2-4)}$$

In this form, we see our D.O.S. clearly: $\mathbf{x^2 - 4}$

$$\mathbf{(x+2)(x-2)}$$

Once we factor the D.O.S., we can simplify to find our answer.

$$\frac{x+2}{x(x^2-4)} = \frac{\cancel{x+2}}{x\cancel{(x+2)}(x-2)} = \frac{1}{x(x-2)} = \boxed{\frac{1}{x^2-2x}}$$

***J** is our answer!*

Polynomials Equal to Zero

When the ACT writers ask you for multiple solutions to a polynomial equation, you'll need to **set the equation equal to zero** and then **factor**.

E5 What values of x are solutions for $x^2 + 4x = 12$?

A. −6 and 2
B. −2 and 0
C. −2 and 6
D. −6 and −2
E. 0 and −4

x = ?

S

First, we need to set up our equation for factoring. Bring everything to one side and set it all equal to zero.

$$x^2 + 4x = 12$$
$$x^2 + 4x - 12 = 0$$

Now we can rock and roll. We are working with $\mathbf{x^2}$ *so we will have two terms. Our final term is* **−12***, which tells us we are multiplying a (+) integer by a (−) one. Our middle term,* **+4x***, tells us that the (+) integer is larger than the (−) one.*

Let's factor 12 and look for a difference of 4 between the factors:

Factors of 12	Difference
1 × 12	11
2 × 6	**4**
3 × 4	1

Aha! Our terms are 2 and 6. Since the larger of the two terms needs to be positive, we must be working with **−2 and +6***.*

Time to set up our equation.

$$x^2 + 4x - 12 = 0$$
$$(x + 6)(x - 2) = 0$$
$$x = \mathbf{-6} \text{ or } \mathbf{2}$$

We can set x to either **−6** *or* **+2** *to give us a zero term.*

Our answer is ***A!***

E6 In the equation below, for which of the following values of k does x have only one real solution?

$$x^2 - 12x + k = 0$$

F. −3
G. 4
H. 12
J. 24
K. 36

Get to work! Setting up your work can help you see what to do next.

k = ?

*We have a poly equal to zero, so we know we need to factor. In our **standard** form, we usually end up with **2 answers**:*

$$(x + a)(x + b) = 0$$ x could be −a or −b

*If we only have **one** answer, we need a **perfect square** form:*

$$(x + a)(x + a) = 0$$ x could be −a only

*Let's **foil** this form and compare to our original equation:*

$$(x + a)(x + a) = x^2 - 12x + k$$
$$x^2 + 2ax + a^2 = x^2 - 12x + k$$

*We can compare our **middle terms** to find **a**:*

$$x^2 + \mathbf{2ax} + a^2 = x^2 \mathbf{- 12x} + k$$
$$2ax = -12x$$
$$2a = -12$$
$$a = \boxed{-6}$$

*Now we can compare our **final terms** to find **k**:*

$$x^2 + 2ax + \mathbf{a^2} = x^2 - 12x + \mathbf{k}$$
$$a^2 = k$$
$$(-6)^2 = k$$
$$36 = k$$

Here's an example of a poly with only one solution:

$$x^2 + 6x + 9 = 0$$
$$(x + 3)(x + 3) = 0$$
$$x = \mathbf{-3}$$

Cubic Equations

The ACT writers may give you a **cubic** equation with a missing term, such as:

$$2x^3 - 4x^2 + 2kx + 12$$

Don't worry, you don't actually have to factor these equations! The writers will give you a factor you can use to find **one possible value of x**. All you have to do is set the equation equal to zero, plug in x, and solve for the missing term.

Questions like these will only show up at the very end of the test.

E7 What is the value of k if $x + 2$ is a factor of $3x^3 + 3x^2 - 3kx + 6$?

A. −6
B. −3
C. 0
D. 1
E. 8

S *We're told that **(x + 2)** is a factor of our crazy equation. Let's set our equation equal to zero to see how this helps us.*

$k = ?$

$$3x^3 + 3x^2 - 3kx + 6 = 0$$
$$(x + 2)(\textit{other factors}) = 0$$

*No matter what the **other** factors of the equation are, we know from our given factor that one possible value for x is **−2**.*

$$(\mathbf{-2} + 2)(\textit{other factors}) = 0$$
$$(0)(\textit{other factors}) = 0$$

*We can plug **−2** in for x in our original equation to solve for **k**:*

$$3x^3 + 3x^2 - 3kx + 6 = 0$$
$$3(\mathbf{-2})^3 + 3(\mathbf{-2})^2 - 3k(\mathbf{-2}) + 6 = 0$$
$$3(-8) + 3(4) - (-6)k + 6 = 0$$
$$-24 + 12 + 6k + 6 = 0$$
$$-6 + 6k = 0$$
$$6k = 6$$
$$k = \textcircled{1}, \textbf{ D.}$$

Quadratic Formula

Once in a blue moon, the ACT will throw in a problem testing your knowledge of the quadratic formula. This is straight memorization.

For $\mathbf{a}x^2 + \mathbf{b}x + \mathbf{c} = 0$

$$x = \frac{-b \pm \sqrt{b^2 - 4ac}}{2a}$$

If the ACT asks you to apply the quadratic formula, your job is simply to spot the answer choice that puts the negative signs and digits in the right places.

For $\mathbf{4}x^2 + \mathbf{3}x + \mathbf{12} = 0$

$$x = \frac{-\mathbf{3} \pm \sqrt{\mathbf{3}^2 - 4(\mathbf{4})(\mathbf{12})}}{2(\mathbf{4})}$$

Infinite Solutions

When two seemingly different equations turn out to be the **exact same equation**, there are an infinite number of solutions.

1) $x + y = 4$
2) $2x + 2y = 8$

The two equations above look different enough, but the the second equation is just the first in disguise! You can reveal this hidden truth by multiplying both sides of the first equation by 2:

1) $2(x + y) = 4(2)$ ⟶ 1) $2x + 2y = 8$
2) $2x + 2y = 8$ 2) $2x + 2y = 8$

These "two" equations have every single point in common! There are therefore an **infinite** number of solutions.

Polynomials Practice Problems

1. The dimensions of the right triangle shown below are in inches. What is the area, in square inches, of the triangle?

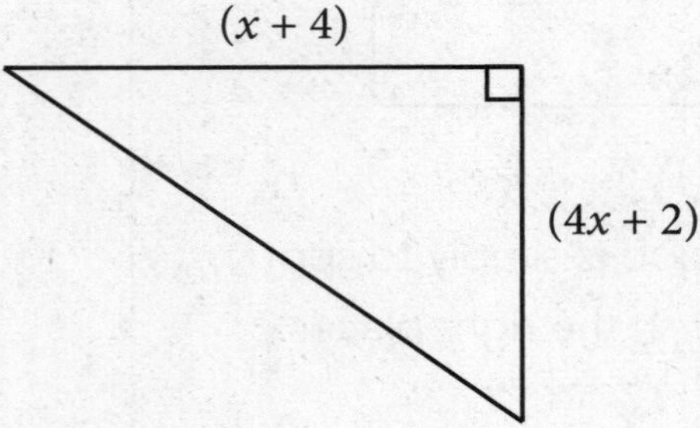

A. $x^2 + 6$
B. $2x^2 + 4$
C. $4x^2 + 8$
D. $2x^2 + 9x + 4$
E. $4x^2 + 18x + 8$

★

---

2. What values of x are solutions for $x^2 - x = 12$?

F. 4 and –3
G. –4 and 0
H. –4 and 3
J. 0 and 4
K. 11 and 12

★

3. What is the sum of the two solutions of the equation $x^2 - 6x - 27 = 0$?

A 9
B. 6
C. 0
D. –3
E. –27

---

4. Which of the following is a solution to the equation $x^2 - 16x = 0$?

F. 32
G. 16
H. 8
J. 6
K. –6

---

5. Which of the following is a simplified version of the equation $(x + 3a)(x - 4b) = 0$?

A. $x^2 - 12ab = 0$
B. $x^2 - x(3a - 4b) - 12ab = 0$
C. $x^2 - x(3a + 4b) + 12ab = 0$
D. $x^2 + x(3a - 4b) - 12ab = 0$
E. $x^2 + x(3a + 4b) + 12ab = 0$

★★

6. The equation $ax^2 + bx + c = 0$, has two solutions of $x = \frac{3}{4}$ and $x = \frac{1}{2}$. Which of the following could be factors of $ax^2 + bx + c$?

F. $(4x - 3)$ and $(2x - 1)$
G. $(4x - 1)$ and $(2x - 3)$
H. $(4x + 1)$ and $(2x + 3)$
J. $(4x + 3)$ and $(2x + 1)$
K. $(4x + 3)$ and $(2x - 1)$

7. Which of the following could be the equation for the parabola graphed in the standard (x, y) coordinate plane below?

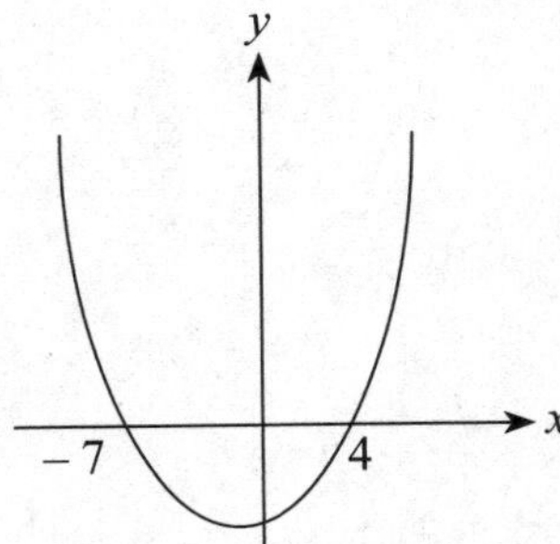

A. $y = (x + 7)(x - 4)$
B. $y = (x - 7)(x + 4)$
C. $y = -(x - 7)(x + 4)$
D. $y = -(x - 7)(x - 4)$
E. $y = -(x + 7)(x + 4)$

8. Which of the following equations has solutions at $-\frac{3}{2}, \frac{1}{3}, i$, and $-i$?

F. $(2x + 3)(3x - 1)(x^2 + 1) = 0$
G. $(2x + 3)(3x - 1)(x^2 - 1) = 0$
H. $(2x - 3)(3x - 1)(x^2 + 1) = 0$
J. $(2x - 3)(3x - 1)(x^2 - 1) = 0$
K. $(2x - 3)(3x + 1)(x^2 + 1) = 0$

★★★

9. Which of the following is the least common denominator for $\frac{1}{(3x - 9)} + \frac{1}{(x^2 - 9)}$?

A. $(x - 3)$
B. $3(x + 3)$
C. $(x - 3)(x + 3)$
D. $3(x - 3)(x + 3)$
E. $(3x - 9)(x^2 - 9)$

10. Mrs. Findlay wants to explain to her class the volume of geometric shapes using variables. She draws a rectangular prism with a length of $x + 4$ meters, a width of $x - 2$ meters, and a height of $x + 6$ meters. Which of the following expresses the volume, in cubic meters, of the rectangular prism?

F. $3x + 8$
G. $3x + 12$
H. $x^3 + 83x + 8$
J. $x^3 + 2x^2 - 8x + 6$
K. $x^3 + 8x^2 + 4x - 48$

★★

11. In the standard (x,y) coordinate plane, which of the following numbers CANNOT be the x-coordinate of a point on the graph of $y = \frac{x^2 + x - 1}{x^2 - 9}$?

A. 2
B. 1
C. 0
D. −2
E. −3

---

12. For what value of c would the following system of equations have infinitely many solutions?

$$6x + 2y = 20$$
$$24x + 8y = 5c$$

F. 4
G. 16
H. 20
J. 80
K. 100

★★★

13. What is the value of a if $x + 1$ is a factor of $2x^3 + x^2 - ax + 4$?

A. −4
B. −3
C. 0
D. 2
E. 8

★★★★

Mean, Median, and Mode

3% of all math questions on the ACT

Mean (Average) $= \dfrac{\textbf{Sum}}{\textbf{Number of Items}}$

Median: When a set of numbers is arranged in **ascending or descending order**, the median (like the median of a highway) is the **middle** term.

Mode: The **most commonly occurring** term in a list.

E1 For the numbers 1, 4, 7, 12, 34, 34, and 83, find the mean, median, and mode.

S **Mean** $= \dfrac{\textbf{Sum}}{\textbf{\# of items}} = \dfrac{1+4+7+12+34+34+83}{7} = \dfrac{175}{7} = (25)$

Median = 1, 4, 7, (12), 34, 34, 83

MEDIAN

Mode = (34)

The Average Box

When working with averages, **always**, **always** find the grand total and the number of items. A nice tool to help with averages is the **average box.**

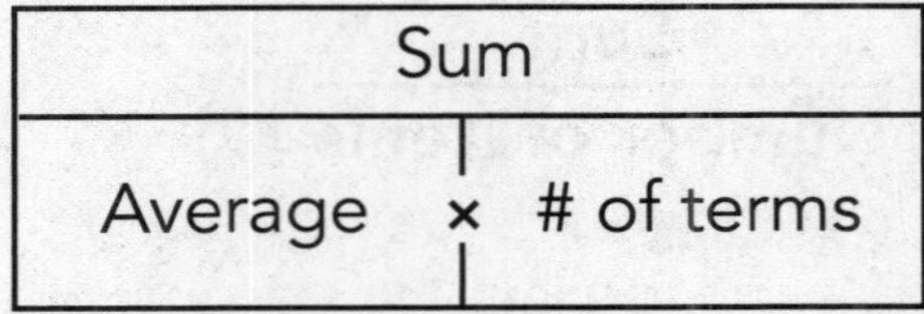

To use this tool, simply cover the term you are looking for (sum, average, or number of terms) and then solve. If the average of 6 terms is 14, to find the **sum** simply fill in the average box and do the math:

Sum	
14 × 6	= **84**

E2 Greta, Adelaide, and Pooky own a total of 174 purses. If Adelaide owns 112 of them, what is the average (arithmetic mean) number of purses owned by Greta and Pooky?

A. 31
B. 56
C. 57
D. 58
E. 62

S *We are looking for the average of Greta and Pooky's purses, so we need to first find their **sum**, then use the average box.*

$$G + A + P = 174$$
$$G + 112 + P = 174$$
$$G + P = \mathbf{62}$$ *found the sum! box time!*

Sum of G and P	→	62	
(Average) × # of terms	→	(Avg) × 2	$= \frac{62}{2} =$ (31), **A.**

E3 Erik has completed 4 of the 5 equally weighted homework projects in his Theoretical Horticulture class this semester, and he has an average grade of 72. How many points does he need to earn on the 5th and final test to bring his average grade up to exactly 75?

F. 97
G. 95
H. 90
J. 87
K. 75

S *We see the word **average** again, so we need to find the **sum**. So far Erik has **4** grades and an average of **72**. Box it!*

Sum after 4 grades	
Average	× # of terms

→

Sum		
72	×	4

= **288**

*So before his 5th and final project, Erik has a **sum** of 288 points. After he receives one more score, his new sum will be 288 **plus** whatever that score is: **288 + x**. And his average will be **75**.*

Sum after 5 grades	
Average	× # of terms

→

288 + x		
75	×	5

= **375**

Put it together: $288 + x = 375$

$x = \boxed{87}$, **J.**

E4

14, 23, 8, y, 16, 19, 28, 22, 14, 25, 16

For the set of numbers above, the median is 16. Each of the following could be the value of y EXCEPT:

A. 3
B. 8
C. 10
D. 11
E. 17

S *Because we see the word **median**, we need to set everything up in **ascending order**.*

8, 14, 14, 16, 16, 19, 22, 23, 25, 28, ...and y

Term: 1 2 3 4 5 6 7 8 9 10

(Terms 1–4: 4 terms; terms 6–10: 5 terms)

*We have more terms on the right of 16 than on the left. So to make 16 the **middle term**, y needs to go on the **left**.*

y, 8, 14, 14, 16, (16), 19, 22, 23, 25, 28,

Term: 1 2 3 4 5 6 7 8 9 10 11

(Terms 1–5: 5 terms; terms 7–11: 5 terms)

Any number ≤ 16 will work just fine.
*The only answer choice greater than 16 is (**17.**)*

***E** is our answer!*

Mean, Median, and Mode Practice Problems

1. Suhail's average score for 4 of 5 English tests, each worth the same number of points, is 74.0 points. What score does he need to earn on the 5th test to bring his average score up to exactly 78.0 points?

A. 94
B. 90
C. 86
D. 80
E. 75

★

Pollen Levels in Sweet Home, OR

Day	Pollen Levels
Monday	7.8
Tuesday	8.5
Wednesday	9.5
Thursday	9.5
Friday	9.4
Saturday	9.4
Sunday	8.2

2. As shown in the table above, the pollen level in Sweet Home, Oregon was recorded each day for a one-week period. What was the average (arithmetic mean) pollen level for the period?

F. 7.8
G. 7.9
H. 8.9
J. 9.4
K. 9.5

★

3. Dori and her 3 siblings used a total of 6,780 minutes of their family's shared cell phone minutes last month. If Dori used 2,310 of the minutes, what is the average (arithmetic mean) number of minutes used by each of her 3 siblings last month?

A. 1,480
B. 1,490
C. 1,695
D. 2,260
E. 3,030

★★

4. The average (arithmetic mean) of 12 consecutive even numbers is 67. If each of these 12 numbers is multiplied by 3, what is the average of the new set?

F. 33.5
G. 67
H. 168
J. 201
K. 402

★★

5. For which of the following sets is the average (arithmetic mean) of the set equal to the median of the set?

I. {1, 2, 3, 3, 3, 7}
II. {1, 2, 3, 5, 6, 7}
III. {2, 4, 6, 8, 10}

A. I only
B. III only
C. I and II only
D. II and III only
E. I, II, and III

★★

6. An American football team recorded the number of touchdowns it scored for each of the 38 games it played in a season, as shown in the table below. What is the average number of touchdowns it scored per game, to the nearest 0.1 touchdown?

Total touchdowns	Number of games with this total
0	3
1	8
2	12
3	9
4	5
5	1

F. 1
G. 2.2
H. 3
J. 5.4
K. 12.8

★★

7. Mr. Sanchez deletes the lowest quiz grade for a semester and then calculates the average of the remaining quiz grades. André took all 7 quizzes and earned the following grades in Mr. Sanchez's class this semester: 65, 73, 78, 82, 84, 86, 89. What was André's overall quiz score for Mr. Sanchez's class this semester?

A. 74.3
B. 77.0
C. 79.6
D. 82.0
E. 85.7

★★

Function Notation

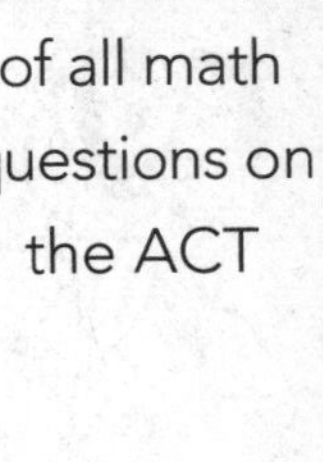

1.5%
of all math
questions on
the ACT

An equation is in Function Notation when it is written in the form f(*x*) = *y*. You plug something in for *x*, and you get something out on the other side.

If we plug a number in for *x* on the **left** side of the equation, we plug the same number in for *x* on the **right** side:

$$\begin{aligned} f(\mathbf{x}) &= \mathbf{x}^2 + 2 \\ \hline f(\mathbf{3}) &= \mathbf{3}^2 + 2 \\ f(\mathbf{-5}) &= (\mathbf{-5})^2 + 2 \\ f(\mathbf{2a}) &= (\mathbf{2a})^2 + 2 \\ f(\mathbf{a+1}) &= (\mathbf{a+1})^2 + 2 \end{aligned}$$

E1 A group of high school students painted houses to raise money. The profit *R*, in dollars, raised by painting *m* houses is given by the function $R(m) = 90m - 75$. If the students painted a total of 6 houses, what was their profit?

A. \$75
B. \$150
C. \$450
D. \$465
E. \$540

Important! f (x) is not the same thing as f · x.

S 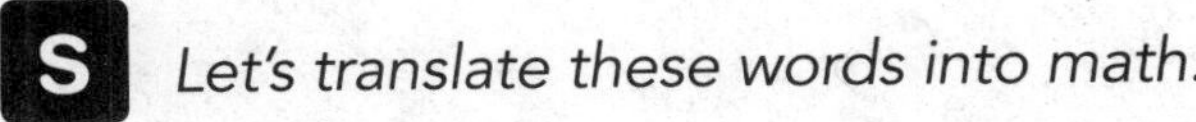
Let's translate these words into math.

profit = ?

R = profit
m = number of houses
$R(m) = 90m - 75$

Since we're told the students painted 6 houses, we know $\mathbf{m = 6}$.

***R*(6)** is just another way of saying "R when m is 6", or "Profit when 6 houses are painted."

*Now we can plug **6** in for m to find our profit, R.*

$$R(\boldsymbol{m}) = 90\boldsymbol{m} - 75$$
$$R(\boldsymbol{6}) = 90(\boldsymbol{6}) - 75$$
$$R(\boldsymbol{6}) = 540 - 75$$
$$R(\boldsymbol{6}) = \boxed{\$465}$$

*Our answer is **D!***

E2 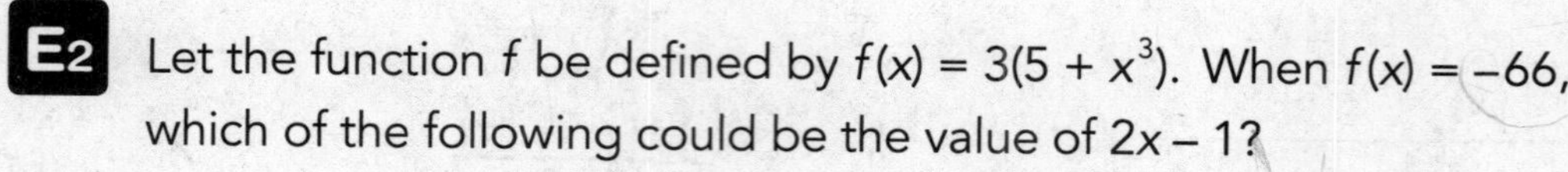
Let the function f be defined by $f(x) = 3(5 + x^3)$. When $f(x) = -66$, which of the following could be the value of $2x - 1$?

F. −21
G. −7
H. −3
J. 3
K. 7

Don't forget to keep the negative when you take the **cubed** root of a negative!

S 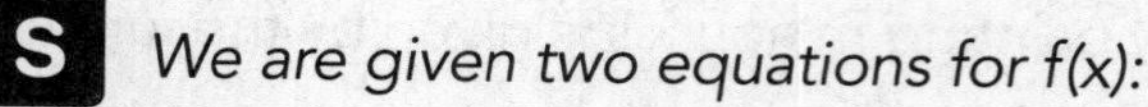
We are given two equations for f(x):

2x − 1 = ?

1. $f(x) = \mathbf{3(5 + x^3)}$
2. $f(x) = \mathbf{-66}$

Since both equal f(x), we can set the right sides equal to each other:

$$3(5 + x^3) = -66$$
$$15 + 3x^3 = -66$$
$$3x^3 = -81$$
$$x^3 = -27$$
$$\sqrt[3]{x^3} = \sqrt[3]{-27}$$
$$x = -3$$

*We aren't done yet! We need to find **2x − 1**. Let's plug in our x:*

$2(-3) - 1 = \boxed{-7}$, **G.**

E3 Let the function h be defined by $h(t) = 3t - c$, where c is a constant. If $h(8) + h(4) = 12$, what is the value of c?

A. 3
B. 4
C. 6
D. 12
E. 18

S

1 Copy what we know

$$h(t) = 3t - c$$
$$h(8) - h(4) = 12$$

Let's take it piece by piece.

2 Solve for $h(8)$ and $h(4)$

*Let's plug our first t value, **8**, into the h function.*

$$h(\mathbf{t}) = 3\mathbf{t} - c$$
$$h(\mathbf{8}) = 3(\mathbf{8}) - c$$
$$h(\mathbf{8}) = \boxed{24 - c}$$

*Now let's plug our second t value, **4**, into the h function.*

$$h(\mathbf{4}) = 3(\mathbf{4}) - c$$
$$h(\mathbf{4}) = \boxed{12 - c}$$

3 Substitute and solve for c

$$h(8) + h(4) = 12$$
$$(24 - c) + (12 - c) = 12$$
$$36 - 2c = 12$$
$$-2c = -24$$
$$c = \textcircled{12}, \text{ D.}$$

E4 The function g is defined by $g(x) = x^2 - bx + 8$, where b is a constant. In the xy-plane, the graph of $y = g(x)$ crosses the x-axis where $x = 4$. What is the value of b?

Remember f(x) = y, or in this case g(x) = y. This is our most basic rule for advanced algebra.

F. -6
G. -2
H. 0
J. 4
K. 6

S *Let's first write down our equations:*

b = ?

$$g(x) = x^2 - bx + 8$$
$$g(x) = y = x^2 - bx + 8$$

The graph of g(x) crosses the x-axis where x = 4.
Aha! This gives us a point to work with. If our function crosses the x-axis at x = 4, then we know that point (4,0) lies on the graph g(x).

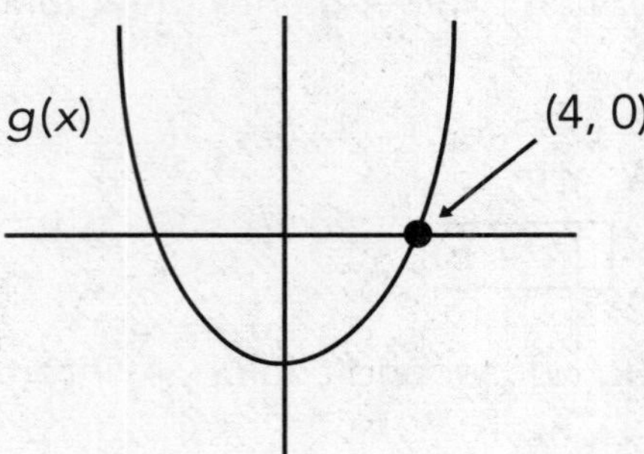

"Plugging in a point" is an extremely helpful tool on the ACT.

Now we can ***plug our point*** *(4,0) back into the function to find b. At point (4, 0) our* ***x = 4*** *and our* ***y = 0****.*

$$y = x^2 - bx + 8$$
$$0 = 4^2 - 4b + 8$$
$$0 = 16 + 8 - 4b$$
$$0 = 24 - 4b$$
$$4b = 24$$
$$b = \textcircled{6}$$, **K.**

Function Notation Practice Problems

1. If $f(x) = x^2 - 18$, then $f(-2) =$

A. –20
B. –14
C. – 4
D. 4
E. 16

★

$f(x)$	x
0	15
1	a
a	c

2. The table above defines a linear function. If $f(x) = \frac{1}{3}x - 5$, what is the value of c ?

F. – 6.55
G. 18
H. 24
J. 49
K. 69

★★

3. If the function f is defined by $f(x) = 2x - 5$, then $3f(x) - 5 =$

A. $2x - 10$
B. $2x - 15$
C. $6x - 10$
D. $6x - 15$
E. $6x - 20$

★★

4. Which of the following equations gives a function $f(x)$ that satisfies $f(8) = 14$?

F. $f(x) = 2x + 2$
G. $f(x) = x - 6$
H. $f(x) = 8x + 14$
J. $f(x) = x^2 - 2$
K. $f(x) = x^2 - 50$

★★

5. If $f(x) = 3x - 9$, what is $f(7) - f(5)$?

A. $f(2)$
B. $f(3)$
C. $f(5)$
D. $f(12)$
E. $f(18)$

★★

6. Let the function h be defined by $h(x) = 2x^2 + r$, where r is a constant. If $h(6) + h(4) = 140$, what is the value of r?

F. 6
G. 9
H. 18
J. 41
K. 81

---

7. Let the function f be defined by $f(x) = x - 2$. What is the value of $f(3w) - 3f(w)$?

A. -8
B. -6
C. -4
D. 0
E. 4

★★★

8. A bank uses a formula to determine what interest it will return to a member who puts a certain amount into a retirement account for an extended period of time. The formula is $A = P(1 + r)^n$, where A is the current value of the amount invested, P is the initial amount deposited, r is the rate of interest per year, expressed as a decimal, and n is the number of years since the initial depost. Which of the following amounts is closest to the value of a retirement account after 20 years if \$5,000 is deposited at 5% annual interest compounded yearly?

F. \$5,250
G. \$13,266
H. \$16,626
J. \$18,000
K. \$25,000

★★★

---

9. If $f(x + 2) = x^2 + 4x + 4$, then $f(x) =$

A. x^2
B. $x^2 + 2$
C. $x^2 + 8x + 16$
D. $x^2 + 4x + 2$
E. $x^2 + 4x + 6$

★★★★

Composite Function Notation

1%
of all math questions on the ACT

If you can solve normal function problems, then you can solve composite function problems with a little help from our good friend, PEMDAS.

First let's get some practice working with multiple functions at once.

E1 If $f(x) = x^2 + 6$ and $g(x) = 2x^2 - 3$, then $f(3) + g(4) =$

A. 15
B. 37
C. 44
D. 47
E. 76

S *This is simply* ***two*** *function notation problems rolled into one:*

1

$f(\mathbf{x}) = \mathbf{x}^2 + 6$
$f(\mathbf{3}) = (\mathbf{3})^2 + 6$
$f(\mathbf{3}) = 9 + 6$
$f(\mathbf{3}) = 15$

2

$g(x) = 2x^2 - 3$
$g(\mathbf{4}) = 2(\mathbf{4})^2 - 3$
$g(\mathbf{4}) = 32 - 3$
$g(\mathbf{4}) = 29$

Now we can ***substitute*** *to find our answer:*

$f(3) + g(4) = ?$
$15 + 29 = \mathbf{44}$, **C.**

It doesn't matter if you're working with f(x), g(x), or q(x); you solve all functions the same way.

E2

x	g(x)
−2	10
−1	7
0	6
1	10
2	15
3	22
4	31

Several values of the function g are shown above. The function h is defined by $h(x) = g(4x - 10)$. What is the value of $h(3)$?

F. 6
G. 10
H. 15
J. 22
K. 31

S

$$h(x) = g(4x - 10)$$
$$h(3) = ?$$

$h(3) = ?$

*To find **h(3)**, we can plug **3** in for **x** on each side of the equation:*

$$h(x) = g(4x - 10)$$
$$h(3) = g(4(3) - 10)$$
$$h(3) = g(12 - 10)$$
$$h(3) = g(2)$$

*Now we can reference our table and find the solution for **g(2)**.*

According to the table, when our x value is 2,

$g(2) = 15$

*Our answer is **H!***

x	g(x)
−2	10
−1	7
0	6
1	10
2	15
3	22
4	31

The most advanced composite functions that the ACT can throw at you are the "function in a function" problems. Keep **PEMDAS** by your side!

E3 If $f(x) = 2x - 15$ and $g(x) = 3x^2 - x + 3$, what is $f(g(2))$?

S 1 Copy what you know

$f(x) = 2x - 15$
$g(x) = 3x^2 - x + 3$
$f(g(2)) = ?$

The key to the "function in a function" problems is to begin ***inside*** *the parentheses and* ***work your way out****.*

2 Solve the **inside** function:

$g(\mathbf{x}) = 3\mathbf{x}^2 - \mathbf{x} + 3$
$g(\mathbf{2}) = (3)(\mathbf{2})^2 - \mathbf{2} + 3$
$g(2) = 12 - 2 + 3$
$g(2) = 13$

3 Plug in and solve the **outside** function

$f(g(2)) = f(13)$
$f(x) = 2x - 15$
$f(13) = (2)(13) - 15$
$f(13) = 26 - 15 = \textcircled{11}$

Composite Function Notation Practice Problems

1. If $f(x) = 6x - 3$ and $g(x) = 2x + 10$, what is the value of $f(g(5))$?

A. 43
B. 67
C. 89
D. 117
E. 215

★★

2. If $f(x) = x^2 - 2$ and $g(x) = \frac{x}{2} - 1$, then $g(f(10)) = ?$

F. 47
G. 48
H. 49
J. 50
K. 98

★★

3. If $f(x) = \sqrt{x}$ and $g(x) = 3x - b$. In the standard (x, y) coordinate plane, if $y = f(g(x))$ passes through (6,5), what is the value of b?

A. 25
B. 18
C. 1
D. -1
E. -7

★★★

Logarithms

1% of all math questions on the ACT

Logarithms, or "logs", are simply another way of writing out exponential equations.

$4^3 = 64 \longleftrightarrow \log_4(64) = 3$

Both of the equations above are saying, "4 raised to the power of 3 is 64."

The Swoop

You can read log form by simply remembering the **swoop:**

$\log_4(64) = 3$ "4...

$\log_4(64) = \mathbf{3}$ ...raised to the power of 3...

$\log_4(\mathbf{64}) = 3$ ...is 64."

If you remember **the swoop**, you'll have logs in the bag!

$2^3 = 8$ $\quad$ $3^2 = 9$ $\quad$ $4^2 = 16$

$\log_2(8) = 3$ $\quad$ $\log_3(9) = 2$ $\quad$ $\log_4(16) = 2$

E1 Write each of the following log equations in exponent form.

$\log_4(1) = 0 \longrightarrow$ $4^0 = 1$

$\log_x(z) = y \longrightarrow$ ________

$\log_2(8) = 3 \longrightarrow$ ________

$\log_{11}(14641) = 4 \longrightarrow$ ________

S

$\log_4(1) = 0 \longrightarrow 4^0 = 1$

$\log_x(z) = y \longrightarrow x^y = z$

$\log_2(8) = 3 \longrightarrow 2^3 = 8$

$\log_{11}(14641) = 4 \longrightarrow 11^4 = 14641$

E2 Which of the following is a value of x that satisfies the equation $\log_x 64 = 2$?

A. 4
B. 6
C. 8
D. 16
E. 32

S *This is straight forward logging. Swoop n' solve!*

x = ?

$\log_x 64 = 2 \longrightarrow x^2 = 64$

$\sqrt{x^2} = \sqrt{64}$

$x = ⑧$

E3 If $\log_x a = 6$ and $\log_x b = 2$, then $\log_x(ab) = ?$

F. 4
G. 6
H. 8
J. 16
K. 64

S *Let's clear out these logs one at a time.*

$\log_x(ab) = ?$

$$\log_x a = 6 \longrightarrow x^6 = a$$
$$\log_x b = 2 \longrightarrow x^2 = b$$
$$\log_x(ab) = ? \longrightarrow x^? = ab$$

Aha! Now it's just a test of exponent rules. Substitute and solve.

$$x^? = ab$$
$$x^? = (x^6)(x^2) = x^{6+2} = x^{\mathbf{8}}$$

Our answer is ***H***.

Classic
Log-a-rhythms

Classic
Al-gore-rhythms

Advanced Log Rules

Occasionally, you will be asked to add or subtract logs with like bases. To do this, you will need to memorize the two rules below.

$\log_x A - \log_x B = \log_x \frac{A}{B}$	*Subtracting logs leads to division*
$\log_x A + \log_x B = \log_x (AB)$	*Adding logs leads to multiplication*

E4 What is the real value of x in the equation $\log_4 48 - \log_4 3 = \log_3 x$?

S *On the left side of the equation, we are* ***subtracting*** *logs with like bases, so we can simplify!*

$x = ?$

$$\log_x A - \log_x B = \log_x \frac{A}{B}$$

$$\log_4 48 - \log_4 3 = \log_4 \frac{48}{3}$$

$$\log_4 48 - \log_4 3 = \log_4 16$$ *Hm.. let's swoop and simplify.*

$$\log_4 48 - \log_4 3 = \log_4 16 = \mathbf{2}$$ *Aha! The equation simply equals 2!*

Let's go back to our original equation and set it equal to ***2****.*

$$\log_4 48 - \log_4 3 = \log_3 x = 2$$

$$\log_3 x = 2$$

$$3^2 = x$$

$$\textcircled{9} = x$$

Swoop Loggy Log and Dr. Dre know how to **drop da base**.

$$\mathbf{Log_D R = E}$$

D = Da Base
R = Result
E = Exponent

Logarithms Practice Problems

1. For which value of x does $\log_x 64 = 2$?

A. 4
B. 8
C. 9
D. 16
E. 32

★★

2. What is the real value of x in the equation $\log_3 27 - \log_3 3 = \log_4 x$?

F. 3
G. 16
H. 24
J. 72
K. 81

★★★

3. If $x > 3$, $\log(x - 3) + \log(x) =$

A. $\log(-3)$

B. $\log(2x - 3)$

C. $\log(x^2 - 3x)$

D. $\log(\frac{x-3}{x})$

E. $\log(\frac{x}{x-3})$

★★★

4. What is the value of k if $\log_k \frac{1}{64} = -3$ and k is a positive integer?

F. 4

G. 8

H. 67

J. $\frac{1}{4}$

K. $\frac{1}{8}$

★★★

5. If $\log_a r = b$ and $\log_a s = c$, then $\log_a (rs)^2 =$?

A. $2(b + c)$
B. $b + c$
C. $2bc$
D. $4bc$
E. bc

★★★

Max and Min

1% of all math questions on the ACT

The ACT sometimes asks questions that require you to find the least possible value or the greatest possible value given a certain situation.

- If you are asked for the **greatest** possible value of one term, **minimize** all of the ***other*** terms.
- If you are asked for the **least** possible value of one term, **maximize** all of the ***other*** terms.

E1 What is the largest value of x for which there exists a real value of y such that $x^2 + y^2 = 289$?

S *We have two terms,* ***x*** *and* ***y****. In order to find the* ***largest*** *possible value of x, we need to* ***minimize y****.*

$$\overset{\uparrow}{\mathbf{x}^2} + \underset{\downarrow}{\mathbf{y}^2} = 289$$

Let's minimize y all the way down to ***zero****:*

$$\mathbf{x}^2 + (\mathbf{0})^2 = 289$$
$$x^2 = 289$$
$$\sqrt{x^2} = \sqrt{289}$$
$$x = \textcircled{17}$$

Note that in this problem, picking zero makes y^2 smaller than if we had picked a **negative** number.

E2 Cheetah Population at the Canseco Nature Reserve

Year	Number of Cheetahs
1983	88
1984	x
1985	84
1986	81
1987	82

The table above shows the number of cheetahs living in captivity in the Canseco nature reserve from 1983 through 1987. If the median cheetah population for the five years was 82, and no two years had the same population, what is the greatest possible value for x?

S $max_x = ?$

To begin, because we are working with a ***median****, we need to line up our terms in order from least to greatest:*

median

? 81 **(82)** 84 88

For 82 to be the median, it must be the ***middle*** *term. We need to pick the greatest number we can for our term on the* ***left*** *to push 82 to the center.*

We can't pick 81, because every year needs to have a different population. And don't pick 80.4 either! Have you ever seen 0.4 cheetah? I didn't think so.

That's one sorry excuse for a cheetah.

We need **(80)** *whole cheetahs!*

E3 A teacher distributes a note card to each of her four students. She asks each student to write a positive integer less than 100 on his or her card. If the average (arithmetic mean) of these integers is 23, what is the greatest possible integer that any one of the students could have written?

S *We see **average**, so let's fill what we know into an Average Box:*

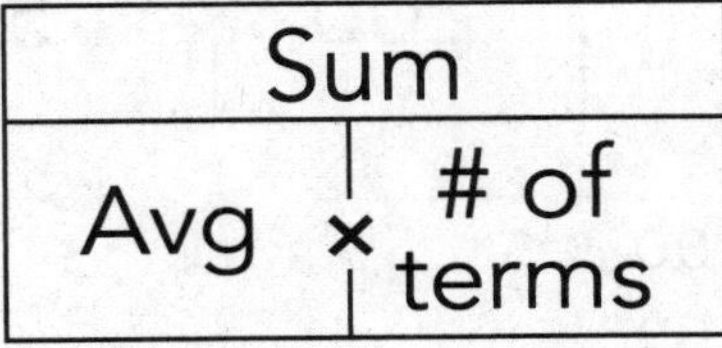

→

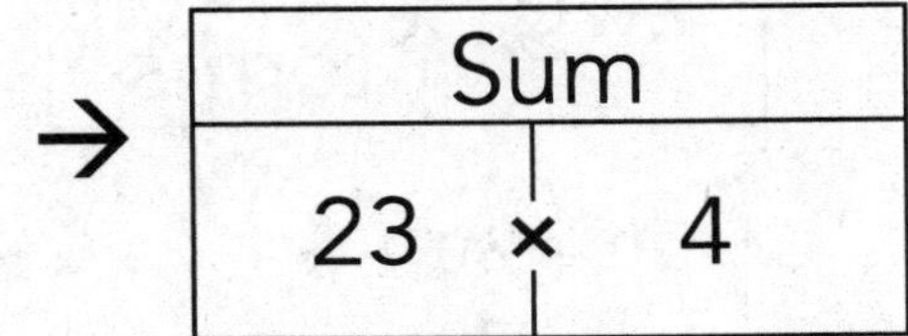

Let's find the sum.

$23 \times 4 = \mathbf{92}$

Now, set up the problem. Four numbers sum up to 92:

_____ + _____ + _____ + _____ = 92

*To max out one of these numbers, **minimize** the other three. The smallest **positive integer** is 1:*

1 ↓ + 1 ↓ + 1 ↓ + ⓧ ↑ = 92

$1 + 1 + 1 + x = 92$

$3 + x = 92$

$x = \boxed{89}$

Pay attention to whether or not the numbers have to be different. If the problem doesn't say that the numbers must be "distinct" or "different," use the same number.

E4 The average (arithmetic mean) of five positive integers is 200. Two of the integers are 20 and 60, and each of the other integers is greater than 60. If all five integers are different, what is the greatest possible value for any one of the five integers?

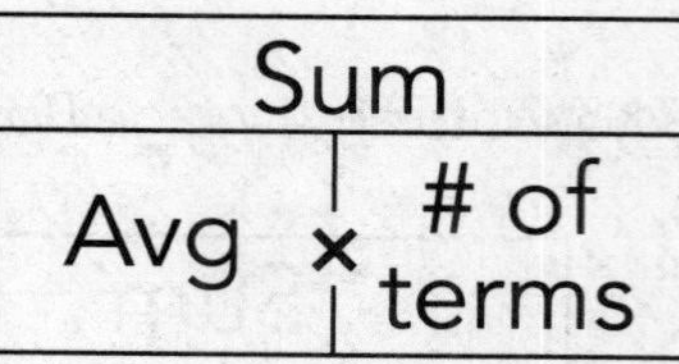

S

Sum	
Avg ×	# of terms

→

20 + 60 + x + y + z	
200 ×	5

$$20 + 60 + x + y + z = 200 \times 5$$
$$80 + x + y + z = 1000$$
$$x + y + z = \mathbf{920}$$

Now we have our sum!

In order to maximize one term, we must ***minimize*** *the other two.*

$$\overset{\uparrow}{\underline{ⓧ}} + \underset{\downarrow}{\underline{y}} + \underset{\downarrow}{\underline{z}} = \mathbf{920}$$

We need to pick the ***smallest*** *numbers that are:*

1) **distinct** integers
2) bigger than **60**

So… ***61*** *and* ***62****!*

$$x + 61 + 62 = 920$$
$$x + 123 = 920$$
$$x = \boxed{797}$$

Pay close attention when a problem says different or distinct: you are being set up to fall into a wrong answer trap.

Max and Min Practice Problems

1. An actor has 30 pages to memorize over 5 days. On the first and second day, he memorized 3 and 10 pages, respectively. If he memorizes at least 1 page for each of the remaining days, what is the greatest number of pages he could have left to memorize on the last day?

A. 8
B. 11
C. 15
D. 18
E. 135

★★

2. The average of 4 positive integers is 160. If 1 of the integers is 240, and all the integers are different, what is the maximum value for any one of the other 3 integers?

F. 1

G. $26\frac{2}{3}$

H. 40

J. 397

K. 460

★★

3. On a basketball team, there are 8 sophomores, 12 juniors and 10 seniors. What is the minimum number of sophomores that must be added to make the team at least 50% sophomores?

A. 10
B. 12
C. 14
D. 18
E. 22

★★

4. If $y \neq 0$, what is the smallest value of x such that $x^2 + y^2 = 197$?

F. -14
G. -1
H. 0
J. 1
K. 14

★★

2%
of all math questions on the ACT

Distance, Rate, and Time

Distance, Rate, and Time questions test your knowledge of a basic formula:

Distance = Rate × Time

Just think it through in terms of driving. If you drive at a rate of 30 miles per hour for two hours, you'll travel a total distance of:

30 mph	×	2 hours	=	60 miles
Rate	×	Time	=	Distance

E1 Driving at a constant speed, Tareeq traveled 270 miles in 6 hours. At this rate, how many miles did Tareeq travel in 5 hours?

S

1 Use the **first** equation to find Tareeq's **R**ate

D = R × T
270 miles = R × 6 hours
45 mph = R

2 **Plug** Tareeq's Rate into a **second** equation

D = R × T
D = 45 mph × 5 hours
D = (225)

E2

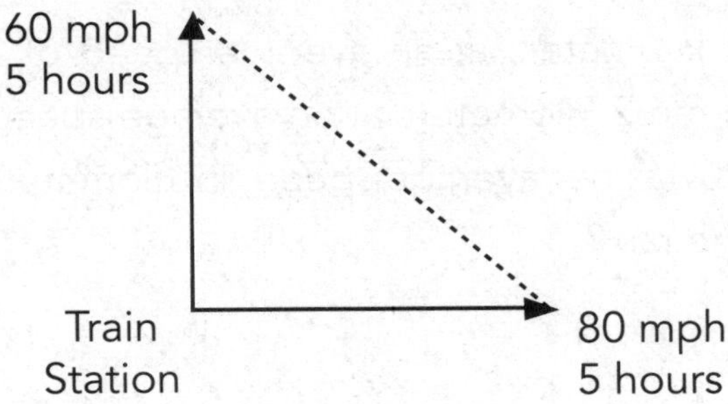

Two trains leave a station at the same time and travel for 5 hours. The first train travels due north at an average rate of 60 mph. The second train travels due east at an average rate of 80 mph. What is the straight line distance between them, in miles, at the end of the 5 hours?

S *This is a combo **D = RT** and **Pythagorean Theorem** question. The **distance** between the 2 trains is a **hypotenuse**. We can use Pythag's theorem once we find two sides of the triangle!*

<u>Distance for Train 1:</u>

$D_1 = R \times T$

$D_1 = 60 \times 5$

$D_1 = 300$ miles

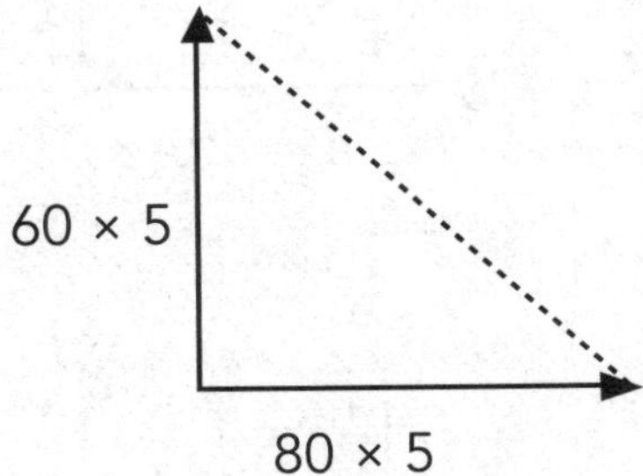

<u>Distance for Train 2:</u>

$D_2 = R \times T$

$D_2 = 80 \times 5$

$D_2 = 400$ miles

*Now that we have both sides, we can find our **hypotenuse**:*

$$A^2 + B^2 = C^2$$
$$300^2 + 400^2 = C^2$$
$$90{,}000 + 160{,}000 = C^2$$
$$250{,}000 = C^2$$
$$\sqrt{250{,}000} = \boxed{500}$$

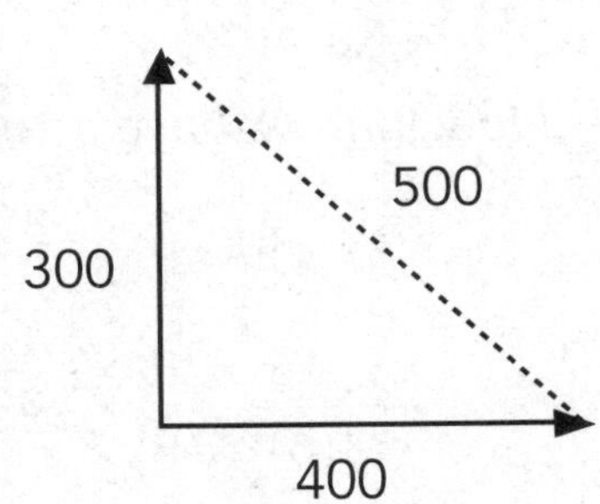

E3 Jennifer ran 4 kilometers at an average speed of 20 kilometers per hour and then ran 2 kilometers at an average speed of 15 kilometers per hour. What was her average speed, in kilometers per hour, for the 6 kilometers she ran?

A. 6
B. 12
C. 17.5
D. 18
E. 24

Don't make the mistake of assuming you can just take the average of 15 and 20! We need totals!

S *Jennifer is booking it! In order to find her average speed for the* ***total*** *run, we need to find the* ***total distance*** *and the* ***total time****.*

$$\text{Total Distance} = \text{Average Rate} \times \text{Total Time}$$

We know the total distance is ***6 km****, but we'll need to piece together the total time from the two legs of her run:*

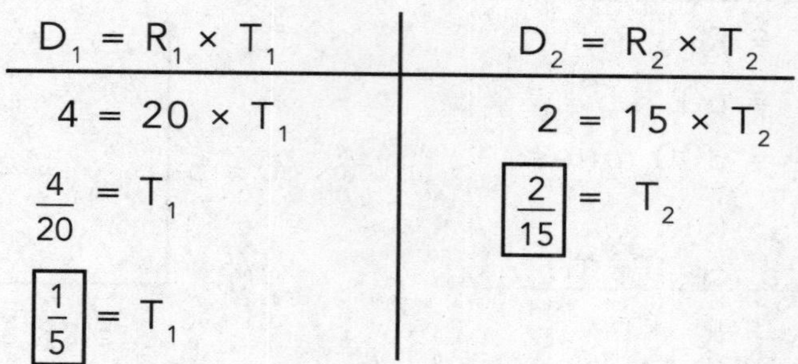

$D_1 = R_1 \times T_1$	$D_2 = R_2 \times T_2$
$4 = 20 \times T_1$	$2 = 15 \times T_2$
$\frac{4}{20} = T_1$	$\boxed{\frac{2}{15}} = T_2$
$\boxed{\frac{1}{5}} = T_1$	

$$\text{Total time} = \frac{1}{5} + \frac{2}{15}$$

$$\text{Total time} = \frac{3}{15} + \frac{2}{15} = \frac{5}{15} = \frac{1}{3} \textit{ of an hour!}$$

Logic Check
This makes sense! She ran the longer leg at 20 km/hr, and 18 is closer to 20 than it is to 15!

Now that we have a ***total time*** *and* ***total distance****, we can solve:*

$$D = R \times T$$

$$6 = R \times \frac{1}{3}$$

$$3(6) = R$$

$$\textcircled{18} = R$$

Distance, Rate, and Time Practice Problems

1. If a cyclist travels at a constant rate of 18 miles per hour, what distance (in miles) will she travel in 40 minutes?

A. 10
B. 12
C. 14
D. 18
E. 24

★

2. In a typing class, Marshall typed 75 words in 20 minutes, and Emma typed 96 words in 3 minutes. If the students maintained this typing speed, how many more words would Emma type in 1 hour than Marshall?

F. 171
G. 225
H. 375
J. 1,695
K. 1,920

★

3. Car A traveled 100 miles in two hours. Car B traveled half as far in four hours. What was Car B's average speed in miles per hour?

A. 10
B. 12.5
C. 15
D. 25
E. 50

★★

4. Yoder, Kansas is 200 miles from Speed, Kansas. If a car travels from Yoder to Speed at an average rate of 60 miles per hour and returns at an average rate of 40 miles per hour without stopping, what will be the car's average rate, in miles per hour, for the entire trip?

F. 58
G. 50
H. 48
J. 36
K. 24

★★

5. On a 1,000 mile trip from New York City to Peoria, Illinois, Samantha drove 5 hours each day for the first 2 days. If she drove at an average rate of 75 mph the first day and 65 mph the second day, at what rate, in miles per hour, must she drive the third day to finish her trip in exactly 5 hours?

A. 45
B. 50
C. 55
D. 60
E. 65

★★

6. It took Linda a total of 6 hours to paddle from one end of a lake to the other and back again along the same path. If she averaged 3 miles per hour for the first leg and 2 miles per hour coming back, how many miles was it from one end of the lake to the other?

F. 2.4
G. 3.6
H. 6.0
J. 7.2
K. 8.6

★★★

Complex Word Problems

7% of all math questions on the ACT

The ACT loves complex word problems. Almost every math concept you have studied so far can pop up in a word problem. Just take it one step at a time, translating words into math as you go.

E1 Jenny and eight of her friends picked up pieces of trash for two days. Each individual kept track of how many pieces she picked up each day and in total for the two days. The totals for the nine friends were 184, 201, 192, 176, 154, 168, 180, 161, and Jenny's total, which was the average (arithmetic mean) of the nine totals. If Jenny picked up 91 pieces on the first day, how many pieces of trash did she pick up on the second day?

S *Yowsers that's a lot to translate!*
Jenny and 8 others collected trash.

Jenny's Day 2 = ?

Total collected over 2 days =
184 + 201 + 192 + 176 + 154 + 168 + 180 + 161 + Jenny

Total = 1416 + J

We also know Jenny's total (J) is the average. Let's show that:

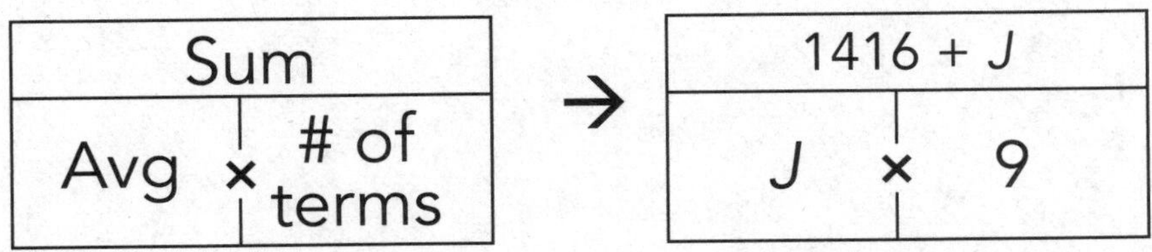

We are not done when we find Jenny's total! We need to find the amount she gathered on Day 2!

1416 + *J*	
J	× 9

We can use this information to solve for J:

$$1416 + J = 9J$$
$$1416 = 8J$$
$$177 = J$$

*We know that Jenny picked up **91** pieces on day 1 and **177** total. So on day 2, Jenny picked up:*

177 – 91 = (86) pieces!

E2 192 riders started the Tour de France in 1990. At the end of the seventh stage of the 21-stage race, only 144 riders remained. If the number of riders decreased by the same percentage every seven stages, what fraction of the starting number of riders remained at the end of the race?

A. $\frac{1}{4}$

B. $\frac{81}{256}$

C. $\frac{27}{64}$

D. $\frac{83}{191}$

E. $\frac{1}{2}$

S *There are originally 192 riders. After stage 7, 144 riders remain.*

Net loss in riders: 192 – 144 = 48.

What is the ***percentage decrease*** *in riders?*

$$\frac{\text{Change}}{\text{Original}} = \frac{48}{192} = 0.25, \text{ or } \mathbf{25\%\ decrease.}$$

So we lose 25% of our riders every 7 stages.

Stage 7: 144 Riders
Stage 14: 144 × 0.75 = 108 riders
Stage 21: 108 × 0.75 = 81 riders

At the end of the race 81 of 192 riders remain: $\frac{81}{192} = 0.421875.$

Let's find that decimal among our answer choices, using our calculator. The ***Math Frac*** *function is helpful here.*
We have our value 0.421875 entered on our calculator.
Next we press the following sequence of buttons:

Math → Frac → Enter → Enter

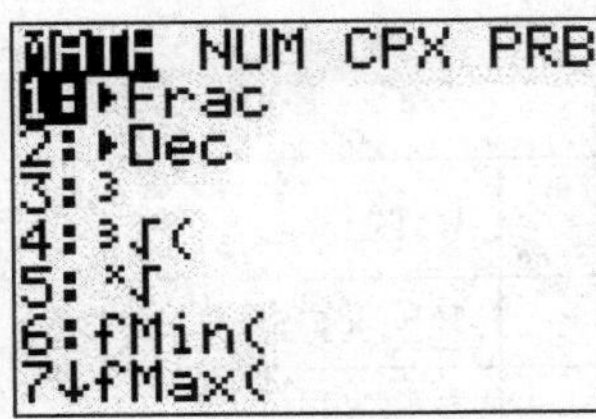

81/192
.421875
Ans▸Frac

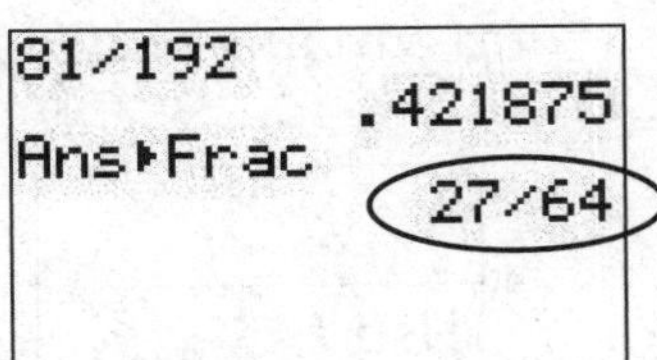

And the answer $\frac{27}{64}$ *appears in* ***choice C!***

Remember that we are decreasing by the same percentage each interval, not by the same number of riders. If you fall into that trap, you will lose 48 × 3 riders and end up with answer A, which is wrong.

E3 A car dealership has 12,000 vehicles on its lot, and the ratio of used vehicles to new vehicles on the lot is 3 to 5. All of the vehicles are either cars or trucks. If 7,500 of the vehicles are cars and 4,000 of the cars are new, how many of the vehicles on the lot are used trucks?

S *There are **12,000** vehicles in total.*

\# of used trucks = ?

*The **ratio** of used to new is **3** to **5**:*

$$\frac{\text{Used Vehicles}}{\text{New Vehicles}} = \frac{3}{5}$$

*When we see the word **ratio**, we know to find the **sum of parts**:*

used $\frac{3 : 5}{8}$ *new* $\frac{3 : 5}{8}$

$$\text{Used} = \frac{3}{8} \times 12{,}000 = \mathbf{4{,}500}$$

$$\text{New} = \frac{5}{8} \times 12{,}000 = \mathbf{7{,}500}$$

Don't forget that you can sometimes solve these problems by picking numbers and working backwards!

Now we enter the Matrix. This problem is much easier if we set up a matrix and input our given values.

	Cars	Trucks	Total
Used	?	?	4,500
New	4,000	?	7,500
Total	7,500	?	12,000

Now we do simple subtraction to fill in the missing values:

	Cars	**Trucks**	Total
Used	3,500	1,000	4,500
New	4,000	3,500	7,500
	7,500	4,500	12,000

Used trucks → Find the corresponding row and column: **1,000**

Complex Word Problem Practice Problems

1. A car salesman works Wednesday through Saturday, spending 1 hour on the phone, 5 hours selling on the lot, 1 hour at lunch, and 1 hour doing paperwork each day. What fraction of the total number of working hours in these 4 days does he spend on the phone or doing paperwork?

A. $\frac{1}{8}$

B. $\frac{1}{7}$

C. $\frac{1}{4}$

D. $\frac{1}{3}$

E. $\frac{1}{2}$

★

2. For expected patronage between 100 and 150 customers, the amount, in dollars, a shop owner expects to make is modeled by the equation $P(c) = c(18 - 0.04c)$, where P is the profit earned and c is the number of customers for that day. The numbers of customers expected on Saturday and Sunday are 120 and 140 respectively. According to this model, how much more is the shop owner expected to make on Sunday than on Saturday?

F. $125
G. $152
H. $1,584
J. $1,736
K. $3,320

★★☆

3. The members of a marching band arrange themselves on a field such that the number of columns they form is the same as the number of band members in each column. Which of the following could be the total number of band members on the field?

A. 15
B. 24
C. 38
D. 49
E. 54

★★☆

4. Philip's starting salary is $30,000 per year; he is given a 10 percent raise at the end of each year. His salary n years from his starting date is given by the function $S(n) = 30{,}000\left(\frac{11}{10}\right)^n$. How many years from his starting date will Philip first make more than $40,000 per year?

F. 1
G. 2
H. 3
J. 4
K. 5

★★☆

5. An archer shoots an arrow into the air at a certain speed. The height of the arrow, in meters, is given by the formula $h(t) = 50t - 12t^2$ where $h(t)$ represents the height of the arrow t seconds after it is released for $0 \le t \le 4.17$. What will be the height of the arrow, in meters, 2 seconds after it is released?

A. 12
B. 19
C. 48
D. 52
E. 76

★★

6. An art studio has a sale on all of its small paintings. Each small painting is discounted 12% off the marked price. Agatha wants to create an equation with her calculator that will give her the discounted price when she inputes the marked price. Which of the following is an expression of the discounted price on a marked price of d dollars?

F. $d - 0.12d$
G. $d - 0.12$
H. $d - 12d$
J. $d - 12$
K. $0.12d$

★★

7. One student stands on a balcony 25 feet above the ground and drops a balloon that drops at a constant rate of 3 feet per second. Another student 3 feet above the ground releases a helium-filled balloon that ascends at a constant rate of 5 feet per second. To the nearest tenth of a second, after how many seconds will the balloons be at the same height above the ground?

A. 0.3
B. 0.8
C. 2.8
D. 3.5
E. 14.0

★★★

Charts, Tables and Graphs

7%
of all math questions on the ACT

On the ACT you must be able to read graphs and see trends and changes over time.

E1

Slug Movement (In Inches) Over Time

Time	11:00	12:00	1:00	2:00	3:00	4:00	5:00
Total Distance Traveled	0	18	36	54	72	90	108

The chart above shows the progress of a racing slug. If the slug began a race at 11:00 and moved at a constant rate until it finished the race at 5:00, which of the graphs below best describes the given data?

A.

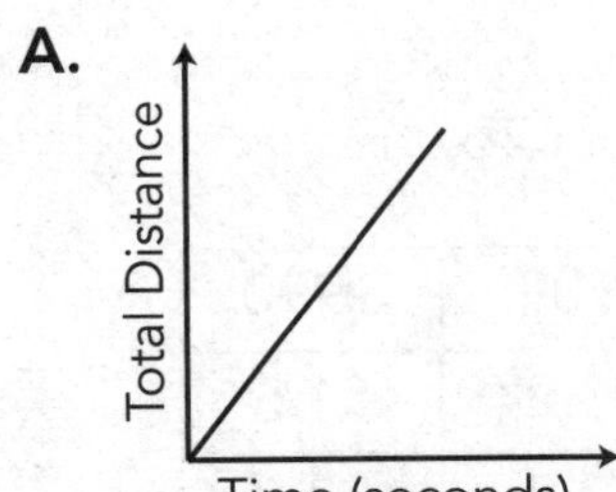

B.

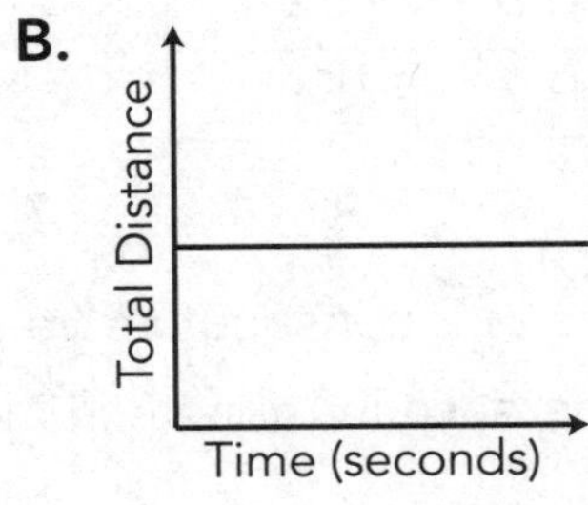

C.

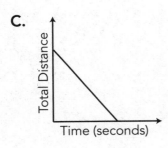

Total Distance
Time (seconds)

D.

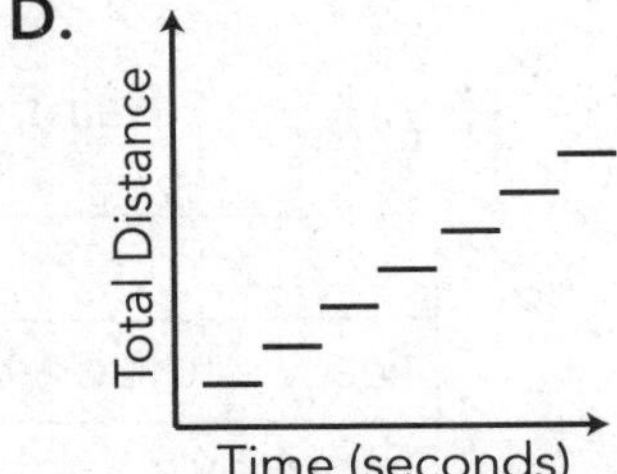

E.

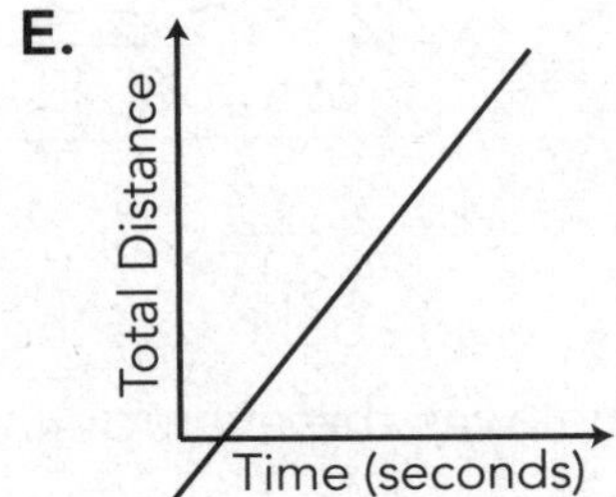

S *There are several key words that inform our answer choice. One of them is "**constant.**" If the slug is racing along at a **constant** rate, we need a **straight** line. So we can eliminate **D**.*

*Next we can see from the chart that the slug **only moves forward** from the starting line. It's a race. No looking back, slug. We need a line with a **positive slope**. So we can eliminate **B** and **C**.*

*Finally, from the chart, we see that the slug's **starting position** at 11:00 is **0 inches**. So our line needs to begin where distance = 0, at the base of the y-axis. Choice E puts the slug at a negative starting point.*

*It's just not right to handicap the slug! We can eliminate E, leaving us with choice **A** as our answer!*

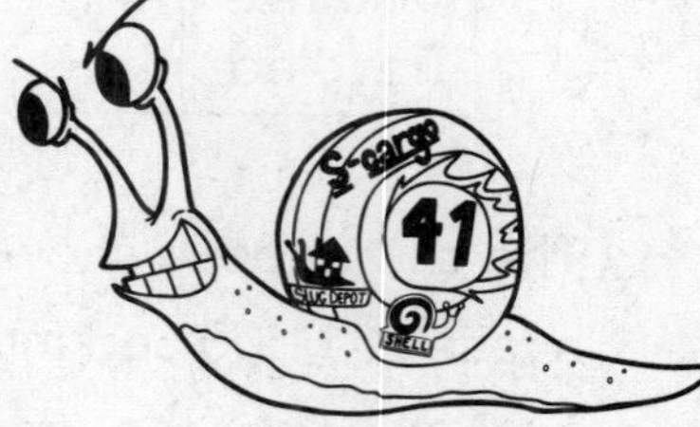

E2

Rainfall (in inches) for Four Towns

	1989	1990
Mary's Igloo, AK	50.2	51.5
Monkey's Eyebrow, AZ	52.8	53.0
Hygiene, CO	60.8	62.1
Frostproof, FL	49.2	51.2

The table above lists the rainfall for 4 towns in 2 consecutive years. What was the average (arithmetic mean) increase in rainfall, in inches, for these four towns from 1989 to 1990 ?

F. 0.6
G. 1.2
H. 1.6
J. 2.4
K. 4.8

S *First we need to calculate the difference between the years and create a* ***third column:***

	1989	1990	Increase
Mary's Igloo, AK	50.2	51.5	1.3
Monkey's Eyebrow, AZ	52.8	53.0	0.2
Hygiene, CO	60.8	62.1	1.3
Frostproof, FL	49.2	51.2	2.0

Our final step is to find the ***average*** *increase.*

Average × # of terms = Sum

Average × 4 = 1.3 + 0.2 + 1.3 + 2.0

Average × 4 = 4.8

Average = (1.2), ***G.***

E3

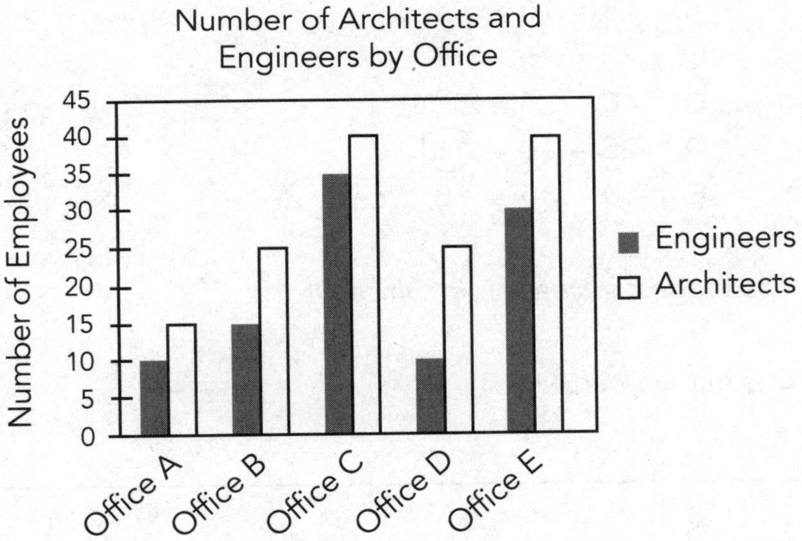

Number of Architects and Engineers by Office

According to the graph above, in which office is the difference between the number of engineers and the number of architects the greatest?

A. Office A
B. Office B
C. Office C
D. Office D
E. Office E

S *In this instance it's helpful to label each bar with its numeric value.*

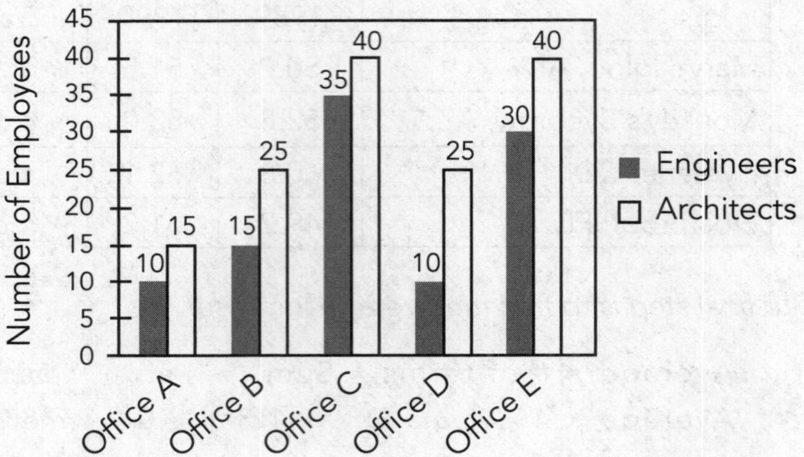

Now we need to calculate the differences for each office:

A. 15 − 10 = 5
B. 25 − 15 = 10
C. 40 − 35 = 5
D. 25 − 10 = (15)
E. 40 − 30 = 10

The biggest increase is in Office D!

***D** is our answer!*

Office D Architects Win!

E4

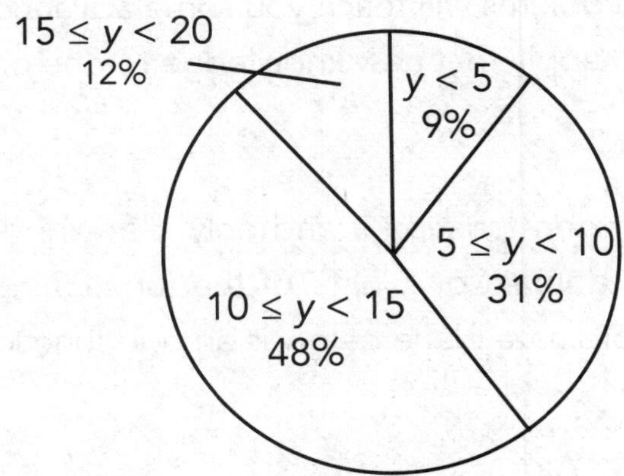

The chart above shows the results when 600 people were asked, "How many hours per week do you spend on the Internet?" The response they gave is represented by y. How many people said that they spend at least 5 hours per week on the Internet?

F. 54
G. 72
H. 288
J. 474
K. 546

S *We need to find all the people who responded with a weekly internet usage of **5 hours or greater**.*

*Of the 4 groups, only **one** group had members who reported a y value less than 5. That group accounted for 9% of the sample. So the remaining **91%** spend 5 hours or greater on the net.*

91% × 600 people = (546), K.

Advanced Graph Reading

Some higher level math problems will teach you some advanced graphing vocabulary and ask you to apply that new knowledge to one or more graphs.

E5 A function f is an *odd* function if and only if $f(-x) = -f(x)$ for every value of x in the domain of f. One of the functions graphed in the standard (x,y) coordinate plane below is an odd function. Which one?

A.

D.

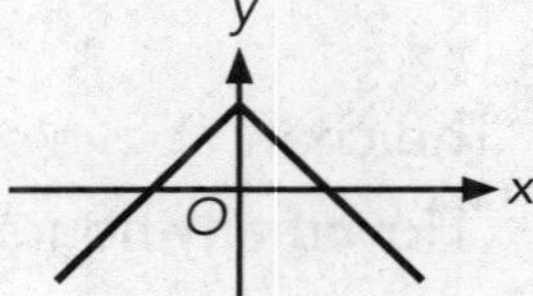

B.

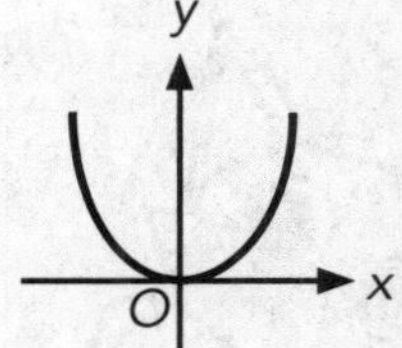

E.

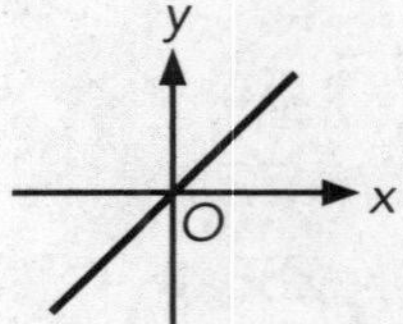

C.

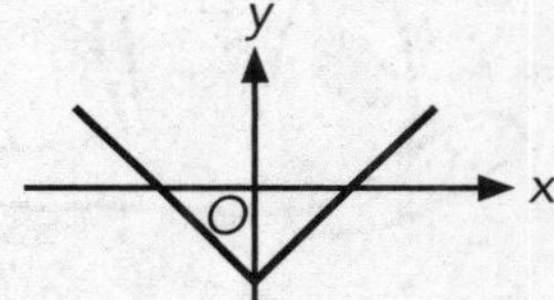

Wowza, that can be tough to wrap your head around. Let's pick some numbers!

S *This is a tough question. We know that* ***f(x) = y****.*
If we plug in an x-value, we get a y-value. Got it.

Let's look at the equation for an ***odd*** *function:*

$$f(-x) = -f(x) = y$$

To understand what's going on here, we need some points.

Let's focus on the left side of the equation: **f(–x) = y.**
Let's keep it simple and pick the point: **f(–1) = 2**

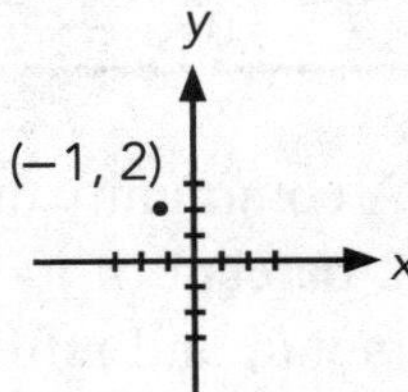

To get our second point, let's plug our chosen x-value, **1**, *in for x on the other side of the equaiton:*

$$f(-x) = -f(x) = y$$
$$f(-\mathbf{1}) = -f(\mathbf{1}) = 2$$

Now we can solve for f(1) to get our next point:

$$-f(\mathbf{1}) = 2$$
$$f(\mathbf{1}) = \mathbf{-2}$$

We have a new point: **(1, –2)**. *Let's add that to our graph.*

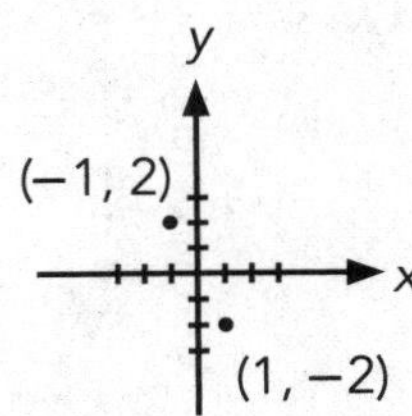

Let's connect the dots to see what this bad boy looks like.

y
(–1, 2)
x
(1, –2)

I ain't lyin... that looks like a line.

Looking at our answers, choice E is the only straight line!

E *is our answer!*

Charts, Tables and Graphs Practice Problems

Type of Shoe	# of Shoes in each Display	# of Displays in Store
Running Shoe	19	2
Sandal	23	3

1. The table above shows the number of shoes on display by type of shoe in a certain store. According to the table, how many more sandals than running shoes are on display?

A. 1
B. 4
C. 31
D. 69
E. 107

★

2. A community drains its swimming pool by 2 percent of its volume at the end of each month and refills the pool when the water volume reaches 90 percent of the original volume. If the volume is measured once per day, which of the following graphs could represent the water volume over a 7-month period?

F.

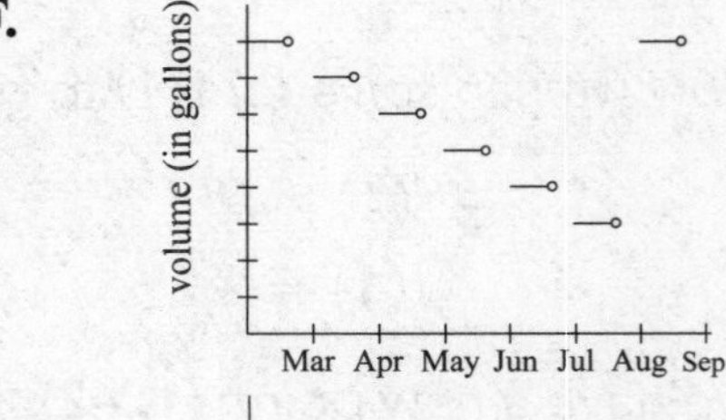

G.

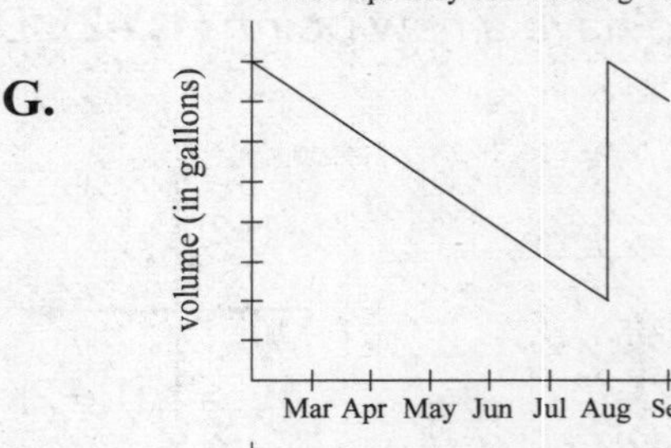

H.

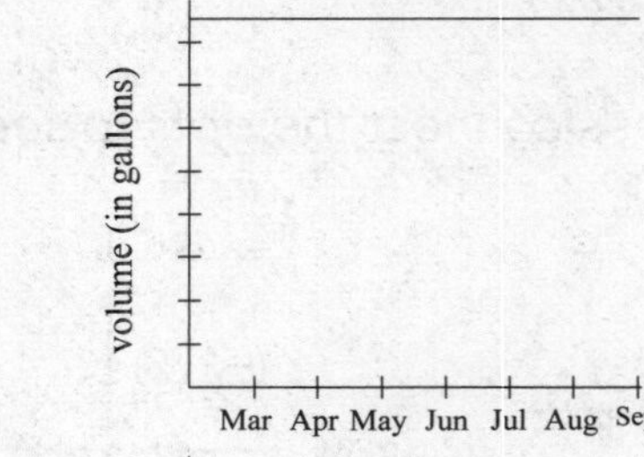

J.

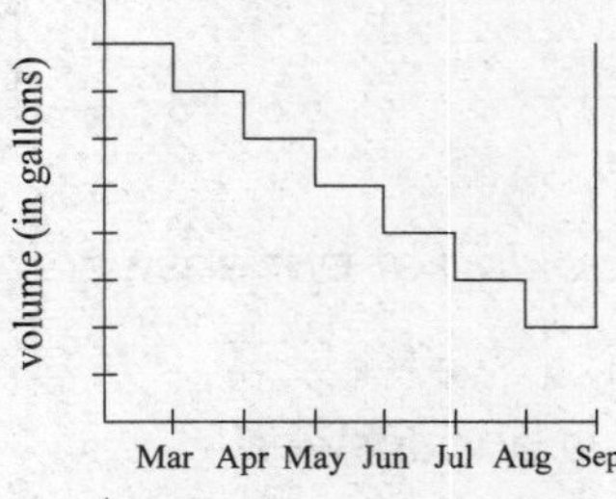

K.

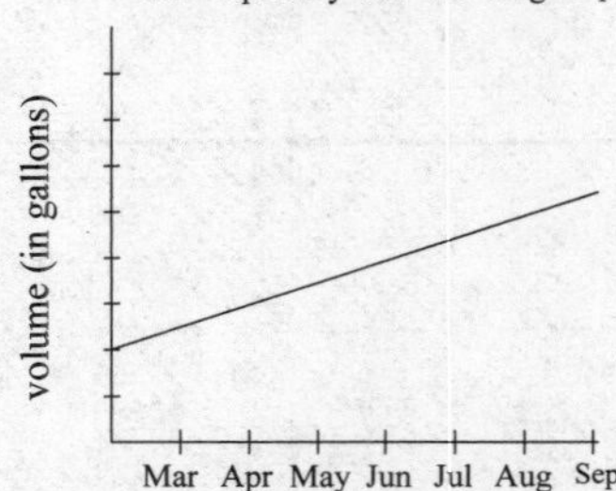

★★

n	p
4	13
6	19
8	25
10	31

3. The table above defines points along a line. Which of the following is the equation of the line?

A. $p = 3n - 1$
B. $p = 5n + 5$
C. $p = 3n + 1$
D. $p = 4n - 9$
E. $p = 2n - 3$

★

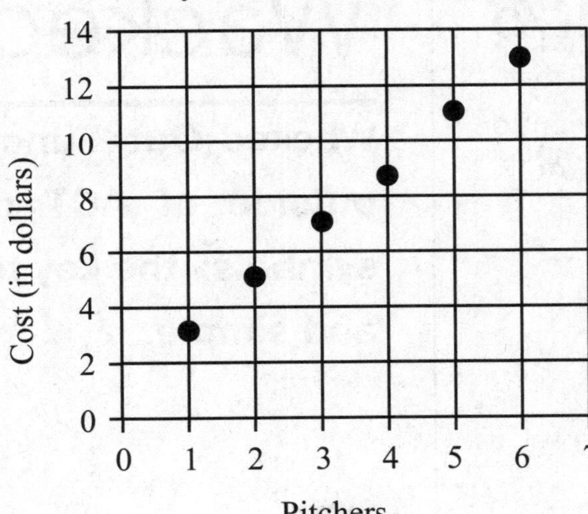

4. Emily runs a lemonade stand. Her cost of production of lemonade is shown on the graph above for 1-pitcher intervals. If c represents the cost in dollars and p represents the number of pitchers, which of the following equations best describes the data shown?

F. $c = p + 3$

G. $c = 2p + 1$

H. $c = 3p - 2$

J. $c = 5p + 3$

K. $c = p^2 - 1$

★★

1% of all math questions on the ACT

Wacked-Out Functions

Wacked-Out Functions have no meaning whatsoever outside of ACT math. Don't worry about the funky symbols; the key to these problems is substitution, plain and simple.

E1 If $\boxed{x \mid y} = x^y - y(x-y)$, then what is the value of $\boxed{4 \mid 2}$?

A. 8
B. 12
C. 16
D. 24
E. 28

S

1 **Copy** the Wacked-Out Function

$$\boxed{x \mid y} = x^y - y(x-y)$$

$$\boxed{4 \mid 2} = ?$$

2 **Substitute** like crazy

x *replaced* ***4****. So everywhere you see an* ***x****, drop in a* ***4****.*
y *replaced* ***2****. So everywhere you see a* ***y****, drop in a* ***2****.*

$$\boxed{x \mid y} = x^y - y(x-y)$$

$$\downarrow\ \downarrow \qquad\qquad \downarrow$$

$$\boxed{4 \mid 2} = 4^2 - 2(4-2)$$

$$= 16 - 2(2)$$

$$= 16 - 4$$

$$= \textcircled{12}, \textbf{B.}$$

The ACT made up its own function! All by itself!

E2 If t, x, and h are integers, let $(t, x)h$ be defined to be true only if $x > t > h$. If $(t, 1) - 6$ is true, which of the following could be a possible value of t?

I. 2
II. 0
III. -6

F. I only
G. II only
H. III only
J. II and III
K. I, II, and III

S *This is a lot to handle. We need to break the problem into parts.*

t, x, and h are integers
$(t, x)h$ is true only if $x > t > h$

*Now we need to do some **substitution:***

$(t, x)\,h$ is true only if $x > t > h$
$(t, \mathbf{1})\,\mathbf{-6}$ is true only if $\mathbf{1} > t > \mathbf{-6}$

*So the only acceptable t values are **between 1 and – 6**.*
*That eliminates **2** and **– 6**, leaving only **0.***

***G** is our answer!*

In this problem, the wacked-out function is **(t , x) h**.

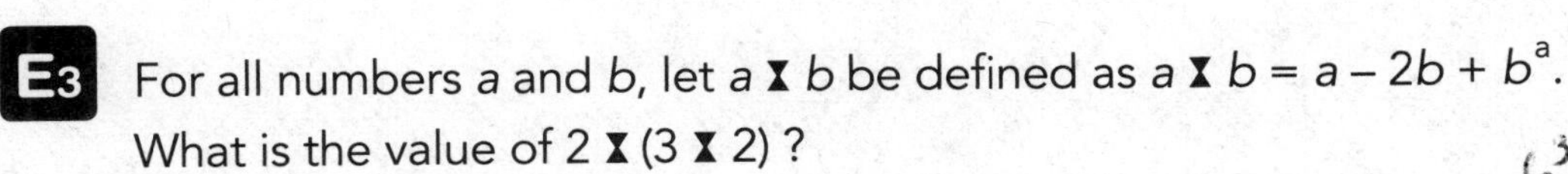

E3 For all numbers a and b, let a ⧗ b be defined as a ⧗ $b = a - 2b + b^a$. What is the value of 2 ⧗ (3 ⧗ 2) ?

A. 8
B. 16
C. 37
D. 61
E. 116

S 1 **Copy** the Wacked-Out Function

$a \between b = a - 2b + b^a$

$2 \between (3 \between 2) = ?$

No sweat - this is essentially a composite function problem. We need to start inside the parentheses and work our way out.

2 Solve the W.O.F. **inside** the parentheses

$a \between b = a - 2b + b^a$

$3 \between 2 = 3 - 2(2) + 2^3$

$3 \between 2 = 3 - 4 + 8$

$3 \between 2 = \mathbf{7}$

So the junk inside the parentheses is ***7****! Now we can solve.*

3 **Substitute** and solve

$2 \between (3 \between 2) = 2 \between 7$

$a \between b = a - 2b + b^a$

$2 \between 7 = 2 - 2(7) + 7^2$

$2 \between 7 = 2 - 14 + 49 = \textcircled{37}$, **C.**

Wacked-Out Functions Practice Problems

1. For all positive integers a and b, let a ♀ b be defined as $a^2 - b^2$. What is the value of 6 ♀ 3 ?

A. -27
B. -25
C. 9
D. 25
E. 27

2. For all integers m and n, let m ☼ n be defined as m ☼ $n = m^2n$. What is the value of 4 ☼ 2 ?

F. 4
G. 8
H. 16
J. 32
K. 48

★★

3. The positive integer $n!$ is defined as the product of all the positive integers less than or equal to n. For example, $3! = (3)(2)(1) = 6$. What is the value of the expression $\frac{7!}{4!3!}$?

A. 1
B. 3
C. 21
D. 35
E. 210

★★

4. For all numbers a and b, let $a \lozenge b$ be defined as $a \lozenge b = a^2 - 2ab + b^2$. What is the value of $(2 \lozenge 3) \lozenge 1$?

F. -17
G. -1
H. 0
J. 1
K. 25

★★★

5. For all positive numbers x and y where $x \neq y$, let $x \ \Theta \ y$ be defined as $x \ \Theta \ y = \frac{xy}{x^2y^2}$. For all positive numbers r and s, which of the following must be true?

I. $r \ \Theta \ s = \frac{r}{r^2} - \frac{s}{s^2}$

II. $r \ \Theta \ s = \frac{r}{r+s} \times \frac{s}{r-s}$

III. $r \ \Theta \ s = s \ \Theta \ r$

A. I only
B. II only
C. III only
D. II and III only
E. I, II, and III

★★★

6. The operation ▲ is defined with pairs of ordered pairs of integers by the following: $(a, b) ▲ (c, d) = \frac{ad - bc}{cd - ab}$. What is the value of $(7, 3) ▲ (4, 2)$?

F. $-\frac{2}{13}$

G. $-\frac{2}{7}$

H. $\frac{2}{7}$

J. 2

K. 7

★★★

Direct/Inverse Proportions

1%
of all math questions on the ACT

When two variables, x and y, are proportional to one another, they are locked into a fixed relationship.

1 If x and y are **Directly Proportional**

when x increases, y increases.

$$y = (k)(x)$$

In these formulas, *k* is a constant, specific to each problem.

2 If x and y are **Inversely Proportional**

when x increases, y decreases.

$$y = \frac{k}{x}$$

Solve for k, then Plug-n-Chug

Whenever you see the words **directly** or **inversely proportional** on the ACT, immediately write down the corresponding formula. Your job is to first solve for k, and then use k to solve for a missing variable.

E1 If x is inversely proportional to *y* and *x* = 5 when *y* = 21, what is the value of *y* when *x* = 15?

S 1 Solve for **k**

$x = 15, y = ?$

We see inversely proportional, so our formula is:

$$y = \frac{k}{x}$$

We know x = 5 when y = 21. Let's plug that in:

$$21 = \frac{k}{5}$$

$$(21)(5) = k$$

$$\mathbf{105} = k$$

2 **Plug in** k and solve for y

When x = 15:

$$y = \frac{k}{x} = \frac{105}{15}$$

$$y = \textcircled{7}$$

E2

x	$\frac{1}{3}$	$\frac{1}{2}$	?	3	5
y	90	60	40	10	6

In the table above, x and y are inversely proportional. What is the value of x when y is 40?

A. $\frac{3}{4}$

B. 1

C. $\frac{4}{3}$

D. 2

E. 18

S 1 Solve for **k**

($y = 40, x = ?$)

We can choose any x, y pair from the table to begin solving.

Let's pick an easy relationship:

$y = 10$

$x = 3$

Now, we need to solve for our constant, k.

$$y = \frac{k}{x}$$

$$10 = \frac{k}{3}$$

$$(10)(3) = k$$

$$\mathbf{30} = k$$

2 **Plug in** k and solve for y

When y = 40:

$$40 = \frac{30}{x}$$

$$(40)(x) = 30$$

$$x = \frac{30}{40}$$

$$x = \boxed{\frac{3}{4}}$$, **A.**

Directly/Inversely Proportional Practice Problems

1. On a certain map, 1 inch represents 50 miles. How many miles are represented by 4.3 inches?

A. 150
B. 200
C. 215
D. 225
E. 250

★

$$y = Cx$$

2. In the equation above y is directly proportional to x and C is a constant. If y is 20 when x is 5, what is x when $y = 100$?

F. 9
G. 12
H. 15
J. 18
K. 25

★★

3. Which of the following equations shows the pressure P varying directly as the volume V and inversely as the square of the temperature T ?

A. $P = \frac{3T^2}{V}$

B. $P = \frac{3V}{T^2}$

C. $P = \frac{3}{VT^2}$

D. $P = 3VT^2$

E. $P = 3\left(\frac{V}{T}\right)^2$

★★

4. If $r \neq 0$ and r is directly proportional to t, which of the following is inversely proportional to $\frac{1}{r^4}$?

F. $\frac{1}{t^4}$

G. $-\frac{1}{t^4}$

H. $\frac{1}{t}$

J. t

K. t^4

$$F = kD$$

5. The force required to stretch a spring past its natural length is determined by the equation above where F is the force, in pounds, D is the distance stretched, in inches, and k is a constant. If a force of 10 pounds stretches the spring 6 inches, what is the force (in pounds) required to stretch the same spring 2 feet?

A. 3.3
B. 6.7
C. 14.4
D. 24.0
E. 40.0

★★★

Algebra Review

1. Which of the following expressions is a factor of the polynomial $x^2 + x - 20$?

A. $x + 5$
B. $x + 4$
C. $x - 3$
D. $x + 2$
E. $x + 1$

★

2. If $x + y = 36$ and $\frac{x}{y} = \frac{5}{7}$, what is $\frac{x+y}{xy}$?

F. $\frac{4}{35}$
G. $\frac{12}{35}$
H. $\frac{35}{35}$
J. $\frac{14}{5}$
K. $\frac{35}{4}$

★★

3. Which of the following expressions is equivalent to $(x + 3)(x + 2)(x - 4)$?

A. $3x + 1$
B. $3x + 9$
C. $x^2 - 24$

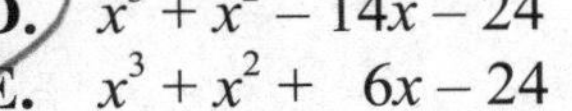

D. $x^3 + x^2 - 14x - 24$
E. $x^3 + x^2 + 6x - 24$

★★

4. Anna works a job that pays \$7.00 for every hour she works up to 40 hours per week. For every hour she works over 40 hours in a week, Anna is paid $1\frac{1}{2}$ times her regular pay. How much does Anna earn for a week in which she works 47 hours?

F. \$164.50
G. \$329.00
H. \$304.50
J. \$353.50
K. \$421.50

★

5. Which of the following equations gives a function $f(x)$ that satisfies $f(-3) = 14$?

A. $f(x) = 2x^2 - 4$
B. $f(x) = 2x^2 + 4$
C. $f(x) = x - 17$
D. $f(x) = 6x - 4$
E. $f(x) = 14x + 3$

★

Questions 6 and 7 refer to the chart below.

The grades of 4 students for 3 of 4 English papers were organized into the table below. Each paper was given a score of an integer between 0 and 100.

Student A	Student B	Student C	Student D
78	85	92	81
82	88	87	79
83	89	91	86

6. Which student has the greatest range in scores for the English papers, and what is that range, in points?

F. Student A; 4
G. Student A; 5
H. Student B; 4
J. Student C; 6
K. Student D; 7

★

7. After the table was created, the English teacher assigned a 4th paper and returned the grades to the students. The information will be added to the table and an average of the scores will be found. If Student C earned 90 points on the 4th paper, what is the minimum grade that Student B must earn to have a higher average paper score than Student C across the 4 papers?

A. 82
B. 90
C. 95
D. 98
E. 99

★★

8. If 4 times a number n is subtracted from 16, the result is negative. Which of the following equations shows all possible value(s) for n?

F. $n = 0$
G. $n = 4$
H. $n = 12$
J. $n > 4$
K. $n < 4$

★★

9. The functions $f(x)$ and $g(x)$ are defined such that $f(x) = \frac{x+4}{3-x}$ and $g(x) = x^2 + 4x - 2$. What is the value of $f(g(-3))$?

A. -8

B. -5

C. $-\frac{1}{8}$

D. $\frac{1}{2}$

E. $\frac{44}{9}$

★★★

10. The table below shows the price of different quantities of bagels at a bakery. What is the least amount of money needed to purchase exactly 20 bagels if there is no tax charged for bagels?

1 Bagel	6 Bagels	12 Bagels
$0.95	$5.25	$10.25

F. $19.00
G. $17.85
H. $17.40
J. $16.70
K. $15.30

★★

11. When a machine is running at 74% of its operating power, it produces 15,000 sheets of paper in 1 hour. When the machine is running at 80% of its operating power, it produces 16,750 sheets of paper in 1 hour. The number of sheets of paper produced is linearly related to the percent of the operating power. Which of the following is the best estimate of the number of sheets of paper produced per hour when the machine is running at 70% of its operating power?

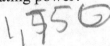

A. 7,349
B. 8,726
C. 9,382
D. 10,285
E. 13,833

★★★

12. Which of the following is equivalent to the expression $\frac{\log_8(512)}{\log_2(32)}$?

F. $\frac{1}{5}$

G. $\frac{3}{5}$

H. 4

J. $\log_4(16)$

K. $\log_6(16)$

★★★

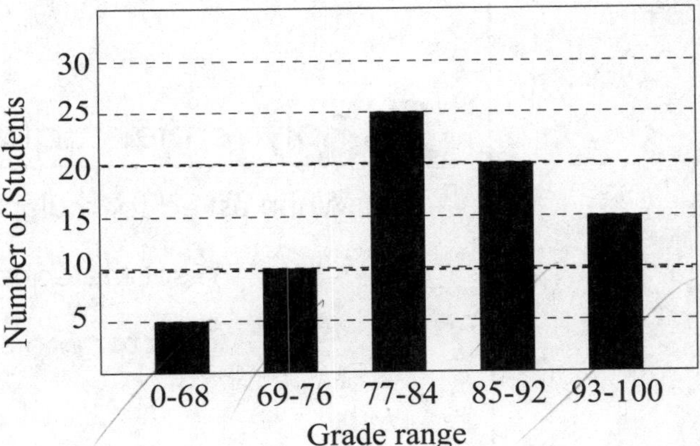

13. When 75 students were given a test, their grades for that test were represented in the bar graph above. What is the highest possible value for the median score for these 75 students on this test?

(Note: The median of an odd number of grades is the middle grade when the grades are ordered from least to greatest.)

A. 76
B. 77
C. 80
D. 84
E. 87

★★

The Algebra Short List

1 Order of Operations

Please Excuse My Dear Aunt Sally

Parentheses
Exponents
Multiplication
Division
Addition
Subtraction

2 Polynomials Equal to Zero

When asked for multiple solutions to a polynomial:

1. set the equation **equal to zero**
2. **factor** and solve

Always remember to pack some FOIL!

First
Outer
Inner
Last

3 Difference of Squares

If you ever see **two perfect squares separated by a minus sign**, factor that turkey immediately!

$$x^2 - y^2 = (x + y)(x - y)$$

$$b^2 - 16 = (b + 4)(b - 4)$$

$$16x^4 - 36 = (4x^2 + 6)(4x^2 - 6)$$

4 Mean, Median, and Mode

Quick facts

Median: middle term of an ordered sequence of numbers

Mode: most commonly occuring term

Mean = $\frac{\text{Sum}}{\text{\# terms}}$

Sum	
Avg ×	# of terms

Always, always find the sum!

5 Function Notation: $f(x) = y$

Plug something in for x, get something out the other side!

For **composite functions**, start inside the parentheses and work your way out.

For **wacked-out functions**, follow the example and substitute carefully!

$f(\mathbf{x}) = \mathbf{x}^2 + 2$

$f(\mathbf{3}) = \mathbf{3}^2 + 2$

$f(\mathbf{2a}) = (\mathbf{2a})^2 + 2$

$f(\mathbf{a+1}) = (\mathbf{a+1})^2 + 2$

6 Logarithms

$\mathbf{Log_2 x = 3}$

$\mathbf{2^3 = x}$

$\mathbf{8 = x}$

To unpack logs, Swoop Loggy Log!

$\log_x A - \log_x B = \log_x \frac{A}{B}$ *Subtracting logs leads to division*

$\log_x A + \log_x B = \log_x (AB)$ *Adding logs leads to multiplication*

7 Max and Min

When asked for the **greatest** possible value of one term, **minimize** all of the other terms.

When asked for the **least** possible value of one term, **maximize** all of the other terms.

8 Distance = Rate × Time

When asked to calculate distance/production, rate, or time, write:

$$D = R \times T$$

If you are dealing with two equal distances, substitute:

$$D_1 = D_2$$
$$R_1T_1 = R_2T_2$$

9 Direct/Inverse Proportions

Directly proportional: when x increases, ***y* increases.**

$$y = (k)(x)$$

Inversely proportional, when x increases, ***y* decreases.**

$$y = \frac{k}{x}$$

Exponents

Exponents are used to show that a number is multiplied by itself a certain number of times.

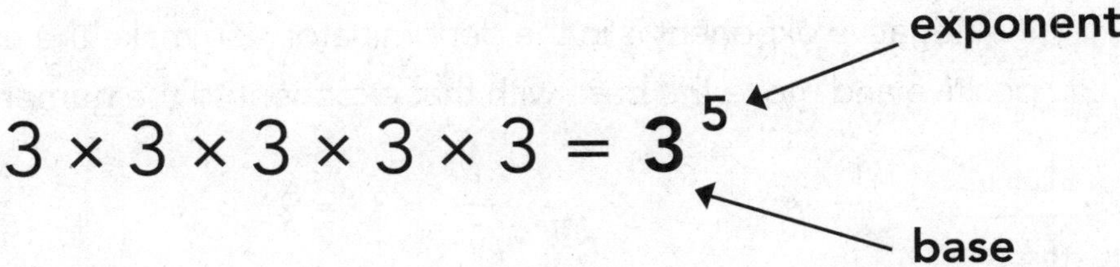

4%
of all math questions on the ACT

Exponent Rules

Let's look at the basic rules of exponents:

1 When you **multiply like bases**, you **add** the exponents.

$$(x^y) \times (x^z) = x^{y+z}$$
$$(3^4) \times (3^2) = 3^{4+2} = 3^6 = 729$$

2 When you **divide like bases**, you **subtract** the exponents.

$$\frac{x^y}{x^z} = x^{y-z} \qquad \frac{x^6}{x^4} = x^{6-4} = x^2$$

3 You **cannot** add or subtract like bases with different exponents!

$$(x^y) + (x^z) \neq x^{y+z}$$
$$x^3 + x^2 \neq x^5$$

Use your calculator to check this!

$3^4 + 3^2$ is the same as 81 + 9, or **90**.

But 3^6 = **729!**

4 When you raise a **power to a power**, you **multiply** exponents.

$$(x^y)^z = x^{yz}$$
$$(3^3)^4 = 3^{(3 \times 4)} = 3^{12} = 531{,}441$$

You can apply this rule backwards by **factoring out** an exponent.

$$x^{\frac{y}{z}} = (x^{\frac{1}{z}})^y$$
$$x^{\frac{3}{2}} = (x^{\frac{1}{2}})^3$$

5 When you have a **negative exponent**, you make that exponent **positive** and put the whole thing **under 1**.

$$x^{-y} = \frac{1}{x^y} \qquad 3^{-2} = \frac{1}{3^2} = \frac{1}{9}$$

If a negative exponent is in the denominator, you make the exponent positive and move the base with that exponent to the **numerator**.

$$\frac{1}{x^{-y}} = x^y \qquad \frac{1}{3^{-2}} = 3^2 = 9$$

You cannot distribute an exponent to items within parentheses if they are separated by an addition or subtraction sign. $(x + y)^2$ does NOT equal $x^2 + y^2$.

6 When you raise a number to the $\frac{1}{2}$ **power**, you take the **square root**.

$$x^{\frac{1}{2}} = \sqrt{x}$$
$$4^{\frac{1}{2}} = \sqrt{4} = 2$$

7 You can **distribute** exponents to numbers **multiplied** in parentheses.

$$(xy)^z = x^z y^z$$
$$(3 \times 2)^2 = (3^2)(2^2) = (9)(4) = 36.$$

8 You can **distribute** an exponent to numbers **divided** in parentheses.

$$\left(\frac{x}{y}\right)^z = \frac{x^z}{y^z} \qquad \left(\frac{2}{3}\right)^3 = \frac{2^3}{3^3} = \frac{8}{27}$$

Notice that when you raise a fraction to an exponent, the fraction gets smaller.

9 Any number **raised to the 0 power** is equal to **1**.

$$x^0 = 455^0 = 1255^0 = -32^0 = \mathbf{1}$$

10 Zero raised to **any power** is still **zero**.

$$0^x = 0^1 = 0^{10} = 0^{468} = \mathbf{0}$$

Working with Like Bases

When you are working with exponents that have like bases, you can **create an equation** from just the exponents and greatly simplify things.

$$(2^x)(2^3) = 2^5$$
$$2^{(x+3)} = 2^5$$
$$\cancel{2}^{(x+3)} = \cancel{2}^5 \quad \textit{Drop da base!}$$
$$x + 3 = 5$$
$$x = \mathbf{2}$$

We don't need the bases at all! Since the bases on each side are equal, the exponents must also be equal.

When working with exponents with like bases—focusing only on the exponents saves lots of time.

$4^{2n} \times 4^3 = 4^{15}$, what is the value of n ?

A. 2.5
B. 3
C. 5
D. 6
E. 12

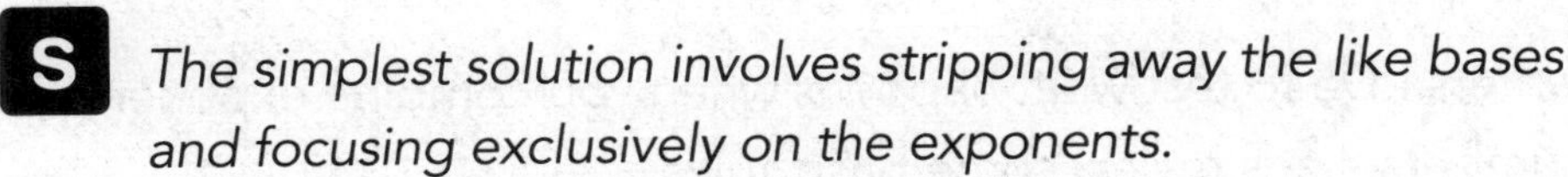

The simplest solution involves stripping away the like bases and focusing exclusively on the exponents.

$$4^{\textcircled{2n}} \times 4^{\textcircled{3}} = 4^{\textcircled{15}}$$
$$2n + 3 = 15$$
$$2n = 12$$
$$n = \textcircled{6}, \textit{ choice } \mathbf{D}.$$

Easy! If you forget this rule, it's just as easy to work backwards from the answer choices. Remember, start in the middle:

C. $4^{2(5)} \times 4^3 = 4^{10} \times 4^3 = \mathbf{4^{13}} \neq \mathbf{4^{15}}$ *too small, let's try D*

D. $4^{2(6)} \times 4^3 = 4^{12} \times 4^3 = \mathbf{4^{15}} = \textcircled{\mathbf{4^{15}}}$ *There it is!*

Remember, when you multiply like bases, you add the exponents.

Creating Like Bases

The toughest exponent problems require you to **create** like bases. The question will give you an equation that might seem impossible at first:

If $3^6 = 9^x$, what is x?

However, with some **clever substitution** we can get right back to like bases:

$$3^6 = 9^x$$
$$3^6 = (3^2)^x$$
$$3^6 = 3^{2x}$$
$$6 = 2x$$
$$③ = x$$

Be on the lookout for opportunities to create like bases. Equations with 2's, 4's, and 8's, or equations with 3's, 9's, and 81's are prime candidates for this trick. Once you find a common base, the rest is simple.

Even/Odd and Positive/Negative

The ACT writers love to test what happens when you combine exponents with negative numbers. Let's review some basic rules:

1 A **positive** base raised to **any** power **=** a **positive** number

$3^2 = 3 \times 3 = \mathbf{9}$

$3^3 = 3 \times 3 \times 3 = \mathbf{27}$

2 A **negative** base raised to an **even** power **=** a **positive** number

$(-2)^2 = (-2)(-2) = \mathbf{4}$

3 A **negative** base raised to an **odd** power **=** a **negative** number

$(-2)^3 = (-2)(-2)(-2) = (4)(-2) = -8$

Substituting with Exponents

The ACT often tests your ability to remember exponent rules while substituting one variable for another. Use parentheses to keep everything straight.

If $a = b^2$ for all positive integers b, and $c = a^4 - a$, then which of the following must be equivalent to c?

F. b^6
G. $b^6 - b^2$
H. $b^8 - b^2$
J. $b^2 - b$
K. $b^2 - b^8$

Notice that all of our answer choices are in terms of b.
We need to solve for c, converting all the ***a*** *terms into* ***b*** *terms.*
This will require ***substitution****. Let's line up our two givens:*

$c = ?$

1) $c = a^4 - a$
2) $a = b^2$

Now let's substitute, replacing each ***a*** *with a* $\mathbf{b^2}$

$c = a^4 - a$
$c = (b^2)^4 - b^2$

Time for an exponent rule! We have a *<u>power raised to a power</u>.*
We need to ***multiply exponents!***

$c = (b^2)^4 - b^2$
$c = \mathbf{b^8 - b^2}$ That's it– no more work necessary!

Our answer is ***H****!*

Parentheses are your best friends! Invite them to your next birthday party.

Exponents Practice Problems

1. Which of the following is equal to $(4x^2y^5)^3$?

A. $4x^6(y^3)^5$
B. $4x^6y^{15}$
C. $12x^6y^{15}$
D. $64x^5y^8$
E. $64x^6y^{15}$

★

2. If $4^{r+1} \times 4^3 = 4^8$, what is the value of r ?

F. 0
G. 1
H. 2
J. 4
K. 16

★

3. If $\frac{a^x}{a^y} = a^2$ for all $a \neq 0$, which of the following must be true?

A. $x - y = 2$
B. $x + y = 2$
C. $x \div y = 2$
D. $x \times y = 2$
E. $\sqrt{xy} = 2$

★★

4. If $3^5 = 9^x$, then $x =$

F. 5
G. 3
H. $\frac{2}{5}$
J. $\frac{5}{2}$
K. 2

★★

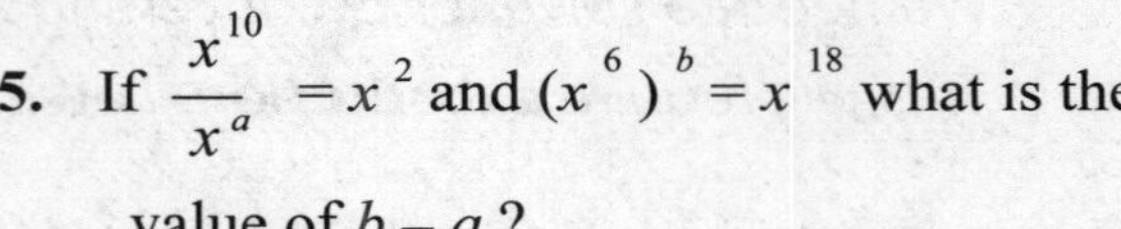

5. If $\frac{x^{10}}{x^a} = x^2$ and $(x^6)^b = x^{18}$ what is the value of $b - a$?

A. -5
B. -2
C. 4
D. 7
E. 10

★★

6. In the set of real numbers, what is the solution of the equation $16^{(3x+2)} = 4^{(1-x)}$?

F. $-\frac{1}{7}$

G. $-\frac{1}{3}$

H. $-\frac{3}{7}$

J. $-\frac{1}{2}$

K. $\frac{1}{2}$

★★

7. If $x = 2^{2a+1}$ and $y = 4$, then $\frac{x}{y} =$

A. 2^{2a+1}

B. 2^{2a}

C. 2^{2a-1}

D. $2^{\frac{a+1}{2}}$

E. $(\frac{1}{2})^{2a+2}$

★★

8. If $a^2 = 16$ and $b^2 = 36$, which of the following CANNOT be a value of $a + b$?

F. −10
G. −2
H. 2
J. 10
K. 52

9. If x, y, and z are real numbers and $x^2y^3z^4 < 0$, which of the following must be less than 0 ?

A. x^2y
B. xy
C. xz
D. xyz
E. yz

★★★

10. If $x^{\frac{3}{4}} = y$, what does x^3 equal in terms of y ?

F. $y^{\frac{4}{3}}$

G. $y^{\frac{3}{2}}$

H. y^4

I. y^6

J. y^8

★★★

11. If $r^{-\frac{3}{2}} = m^3$ and $s^{\frac{3}{4}} = n^6$, what is $(rs)^{\frac{1}{2}}$ in terms of m and n ?

A. 0

B. $n^4 m$

C. $\frac{n^4}{m}$

D. $\frac{m}{n^4}$

E. $\frac{1}{n^4 m}$

★★★

Inequalities

If you see a < or > symbol in a question, you have an inequality on your hands. Let's review a few basic rules:

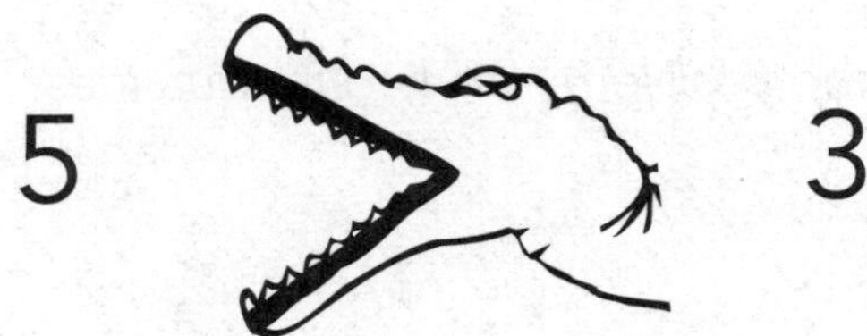

> is the "greater than" sign. Whatever is to the left of this symbol is larger than what is to the right of the symbol. The above reads, "5 is greater than 3."

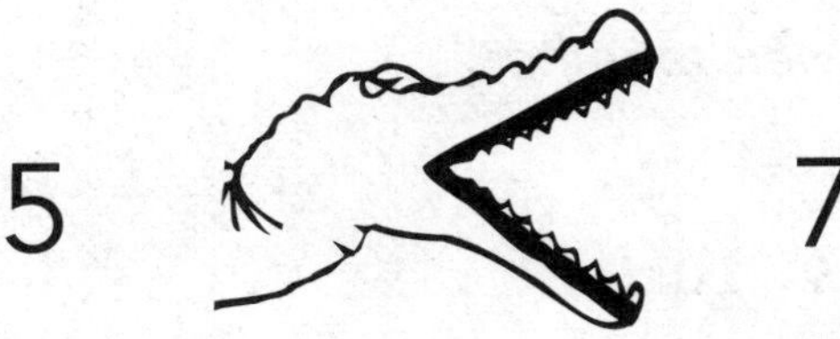

< is the "less than" sign. Whatever is to the left of this symbol is smaller than what is to the right of the symbol. The above reads, "5 is less than 7."

Working with Inequalities

There are two things to remember about solving inequalities:

1 If the equation is a complex inequality, break the problem up into **two different inequalities** and solve each piece separately.

$$3x - 4 < 6x < 3x + 8 \longrightarrow \begin{cases} 6x > 3x - 4 \\ 6x < 3x + 8 \end{cases}$$

2 When multiplying or dividing inequalities by negative numbers, we have to **switch the direction of the sign**.

$$-3x < 9 \xrightarrow{\text{Flip!}} x > -3.$$

3%
of all math questions on the ACT

Remember the old alligator trick from elementary school: The gator always wants to eat the bigger of the two things!

$\geq$ means greater than or equal to.

$\leq$ means less than or equal to.

E1 For how many integer values of x does $8 < 2x - 4 < 18$?

S *First let's break the problem into two inequalities.*

$$2x - 4 > 8$$
$$2x - 4 < 18$$

Next, solve each inequality:

$2x - 4 > 8$	$2x - 4 < 18$
$2x > 12$	$2x < 22$
$\mathbf{x > 6}$	$\mathbf{x < 11}$

Now put the answers together:

$$6 < x < 11$$

6 **7 8 9 10** 11

We have four choices for x: 7, 8, 9, or 10.
Our answer is ④*!*

E2 If $0 < 2x < y$, which of the following is the greatest?

A. 0
B. y
C. $2x$
D. $-x$
E. $\frac{y}{2}$

S *First, let's break up the complex inequality:*

$$0 < 2x < y \quad \rightarrow \quad 2x > 0, \quad 2x < y$$

Let's try picking numbers for x and y.
We know that 2x must be greater than 0; let's pick **x = 3**.
Likewise, y must be greater than twice x. Let's pick **y = 7**.

Now we plug in our chosen numbers:

A. 0
B. $y = 7$
C. $2x = 2(3) = 6$
D. $-x = -3$
E. $\frac{y}{2} = \frac{7}{2} = 3.5$

Our largest option is (7).
***B** is our answer!*

E3 If $5 < a < 9$ and $-3 < b < 4$, which of the following is the set of all possible values of ab ?

F. $ab = 36$
G. $-15 < ab < 36$
H. $-3 < ab < 13$
J. $-3 < ab < 9$
K. $-27 < ab < 36$

S *Watch out! The* **–3** *makes this one tricky!*

To find the extreme values for **ab**, *we have to multiply* **both** *of the extreme values of* **a** (5 *and* 9) *by* **both** *of the extreme values of* **b** (–3 *and* 4).

The four boundary possibilities of ab are:

1 smallest a (5) × smallest b (–3)

$(5)(-3) = \mathbf{-15}$

2 smallest a (5) × largest b (4)

$(5)(4) = \mathbf{20}$

3 largest a (9) × smallest b (– 3)

$(9)(-3) = \mathbf{-27}$

4 largest a (9) × largest b (4)

$(9)(4) = \mathbf{36}$

Now we pick the lowest and highest numbers as our boundaries:

K. $-27 < ab < 36$

If you picked **G** as your answer, you probably assumed that multiplying the **smallest a** by the **smallest b** would equal the **smallest ab**. That would be true if we weren't dealing with a **negative 3**!

Absolute Value Inequalities

Quite often the ACT likes to combine absolute value problems with inequalities.

$$|x + a| > b$$

To solve this kind of problem, just split the inequality into a positive form and a negative form:

$$(x + a) > b \quad \text{and} \quad -(x + a) > b$$

Then solve as you normally would.

E4 Find the range of x values possible for the following equation:

$$|x-2| < 6$$

S *First, split the equation into positive and negative forms:*

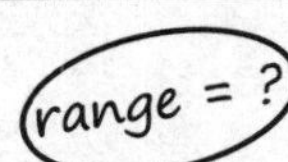

$$(x-2) < 6 \quad \text{and} \quad -(x-2) < 6$$

Next, solve each equation.

$$(x-2) < 6 \quad \text{and} \quad -(x-2) < 6$$

$$x < 8 \qquad\qquad -x + 2 < 6$$

$$-x < 4$$

$$x > -4$$

Combine into one statement: $\boldsymbol{-4 < x < 8}$

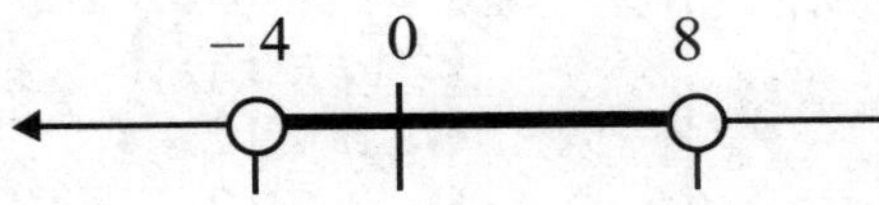

Remember to flip the sign when multiplying or dividing by a negative.

Inequalities Practice Problems

1. The inequality $5(x + 2) > 4(x - 2)$ is equivalent to which of the following inequalities?

A. $x > -18$
B. $x < 2$
C. $x < 12$
D. $x < 22$
E. $x < 32$

★

2. If $x > y$, which of the following must be true?

F. $x^2 > y^2$
G. $y > -x$
H. $x > -y$
J. $-x < -y$
K. $-x > -y$

★★

3. If a, b, and c are positive even integers where $ab = 8$, $bc = 24$, and $ac = 48$, which of the following must be true?

A. $a < b < c$
B. $a < c < b$
C. $b < a < c$
D. $b < c < a$
E. $c < a < b$

★★

4. If $a + b = 24$ and $b < 12$, then which of the following must be true?

F. $a = 13$
G. $a < 12$
H. $a > 12$
J. $b > 13$
K. $b = 0$

★

5. If x is a positive even integer and $40 < 4x + 6 < 50$, what is the value of x ?

A. 9
B. 10
C. 11
D. 44
E. 45

★

6. To be elected for a 2nd term, a president of a student council must receive more than two-thirds of the student votes. If 171 students voted in the election, which of the following expressions gives v, the number of votes needed for the president to be elected for a 2nd term?

F. $v < 57$
G. $v = 57$
H. $v > 58$
J. $v < 114$
K. $v > 114$

★★

7. When $-5 \leq x \leq 2$ and $-3 \leq y \leq 4$, what is the least possible value for xy?

A. –20
B. –15
C. –6
D. 8
E. 20

★★

8. Which of the following is equivalent to the expression $\frac{2-4x}{3} + 2 > 0$?

F. $x > 0$

G. $x > \frac{1}{2}$

H. $x < 1$

J. $x < 2$

K. $x > 2$

★★

3% of all math questions on the ACT

Fractions

For some ACT questions you will need to add or multiply fractions or find a common denominator between them.

Occasionally, the ACT will push fraction problems to a higher level of difficulty, requiring you to **manipulate**, **cross multiply** or **split fractions** into parts.

E1 If $\frac{6}{(r+2)} = \frac{8}{(3-2r)}$, what is the value of r?

A. -4

B. 0

C. $\frac{1}{10}$

D. $\frac{1}{5}$

E. $\frac{8}{5}$

S *Whenever you see 2 fractions set equal to each other, you know you will need to* ***cross multiply***.

$r = ?$

$$\frac{6}{(r+2)} \times \frac{8}{(3-2r)}$$

$$6(3 - 2r) = 8(r + 2)$$
$$18 - 12r = 8r + 16$$
$$2 = 20r$$
$$\frac{2}{20} = r$$
$$\frac{1}{10} = r$$

***C** is our answer!*

E2 If $\frac{t}{r} = 6$ and $\frac{r}{s} = 3$, what is the value of $\frac{(t + r + s)}{r}$?

F. $7\frac{1}{3}$

G. $7\frac{2}{3}$

H. $8\frac{1}{6}$

J. 9

K. 10

S *What are we given?* $\frac{t}{r} = 6$ and $\frac{r}{s} = 3$

What do we need to find? $\frac{(t + r + s)}{r}$

More than likely, we will need to get everything down to one variable so we can solve. Let's simplify.

$$\frac{r}{s} = 3$$

$$r = \boxed{3s}$$ A replacement for r!

And we also know:

$$\frac{t}{r} = 6$$

$$t = 6r$$ Aha! We can plug in our replacement for r!

$$t = 6(3s)$$

$$t = \boxed{18s}$$

So r = 3s, and t = 18s! Now we can just plug-in and simplify:

$$\frac{(t + r + s)}{r}$$

$$\frac{(18s + 3s + s)}{3s} = \frac{22s}{3s} = \frac{22}{3} = 7\frac{1}{3}$$

***F** is our answer!*

Notice that we never solved for any of the variables, but that was not a requirement of the problem. Don't get hung up on solving for things you do not need to solve for! Stick with the problem.

Least Common Denominator

In order to add two fractions together, you need to find a common denominator. Occasionally, the ACT tests this skill directly by asking you to find the **lowest common denominator** of multiple fractions.

E3 Which of the following is the least common denominator for the expression below?

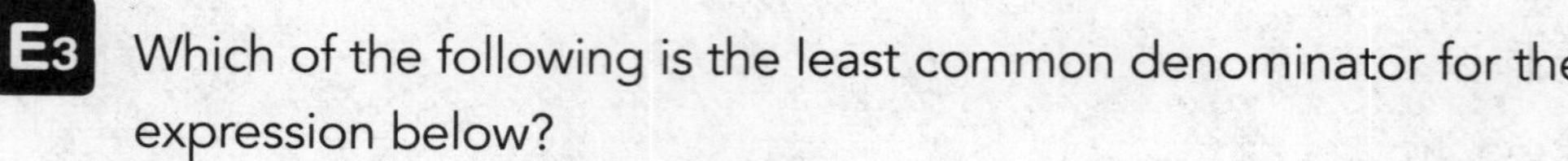

$$\frac{1}{11^2 \cdot 13 \cdot 23} + \frac{1}{13^2 \cdot 23} + \frac{1}{13 \cdot 23^3}$$

A. $13 \cdot 23$
B. $11 \cdot 13 \cdot 23$
C. $11^2 \cdot 13 \cdot 23$
D. $11^2 \cdot 13^2 \cdot 23^3$
E. $11^2 \cdot 13^4 \cdot 23^5$

Since every numerator is already 1, we know we can't **reduce** the fractions at all.

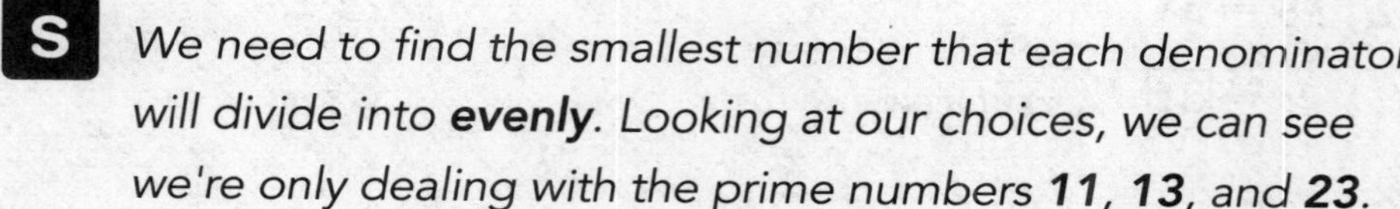

S *We need to find the smallest number that each denominator will divide into* ***evenly****. Looking at our choices, we can see we're only dealing with the prime numbers* ***11, 13****, and* ***23****.*

To find the lowest common denominator (LCD), we can count how many times 11, 13, and 23 appear in each fraction.

	11	13	23
$11^2 \cdot 13 \cdot 23$	**2**	1	1
$13^2 \cdot 23$	0	**2**	1
$13 \cdot 23^3$	0	1	**3**

$$\mathbf{11^2 \cdot 13^2 \cdot 23^3}$$

So to make room for each of the denominators, our LCD needs to have ***two 11's****,* ***two 13's****, and* ***three 23's****.*

D *is our answer!*

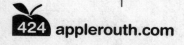

Fractions Practice Problems

1. If $\frac{2}{3}$ of a number is 16, what is $\frac{1}{2}$ of the number?

   A. $\frac{1}{12}$

   B. $\frac{1}{3}$

   C. 8

   D. 12

   E. 24

★

2. If a movie is 6 hours long, what fraction of the movie is completed 45 minutes after it is begun?

   F. $\frac{1}{16}$

   G. $\frac{1}{12}$

   H. $\frac{1}{8}$

   J. $\frac{1}{6}$

   K. $\frac{1}{3}$

★★

3. If $\frac{4}{(3v+6)} = \frac{4}{(v-2)}$, what is the value of v?

   A. -4
   B. -2
   C. 0
   D. 2
   E. 4

★★

4. What is the least common denominator for the sum of the fractions $\frac{5}{27}+\frac{7}{45}+\frac{13}{21}$?

   F. 105
   G. 315
   H. 945
   J. 2,835
   K. 25,515

★

5. Which of the following is the least common denominator for the expression below?

$$\frac{1}{13 \cdot 29^2 \cdot 19} + \frac{1}{13^2 \cdot 19} + \frac{1}{13 \cdot 19^2}$$

   A. $13 \cdot 19$
   B. $13 \cdot 19 \cdot 29$
   C. $13 \cdot 19 \cdot 29^2$
   D. $13^2 \cdot 19^2 \cdot 29^2$
   E. $13^4 \cdot 29^2 \cdot 19^4$

★★★

4%
of all math questions on the ACT

Percentages

Generally, it's a good idea to convert all percentages or fractions to decimals, which are easier to work with. If you need to convert to a fraction, simply treat the % symbol like the number ($\frac{1}{100}$).

So if you need to convert 5% to a fraction, you'd simply multiply and reduce:

$$5\% = 5 \times \left(\frac{1}{100}\right) = \frac{5}{100} = \frac{1}{20}$$

Using the [FRAC] function on your graphing calculator will turn decimals into fractions.

Percent of a number

In questions that require you to translate words into math, "percent of" translates into $\frac{1}{100}$ and "a number" translates into a variable, like "*x*" or "*y*."

"Forty percent of a number" is:

40%	of	a number	is
$40\left(\frac{1}{100}\right)$	$\times$	y	$=$

$$40\left(\frac{1}{100}\right)(y) =$$

E1 The price of a dress is reduced by 20%. If the original price of the dress was \$70, what is the new price?

S 1 Find the amount the dress was **discounted** *new price = ?*

20% of a $70 dress is:

$$.20(\$70) = \$14$$

2 **Subtract** the reduction from the original price

$$\$70 - \$14 = \$56$$

Shortcut: *if a dress is being reduced by 20%, it is quicker to multiply the original amount by (100% – 20%), or 80%.*

So $70 × 0.80 = **$56**. *Same answer and we save a step!*

E2 What percent of 4 is 5?

A. 75%
B. 80%
C. 125%
D. 150%
E. 180%

S 1 **Translate** into an equation

What	*percent*	*of*	4	*is*	5?
(x)	$(\frac{1}{100})$	×	4	=	5

2 Solve for **x**

$$x(\frac{1}{100})(4) = 5$$

$$x(\frac{1}{100}) = \frac{5}{4}$$

$$x(\frac{1}{100}) = 1.25 = 125\%$$, **C.**

It is usually easier to work with decimals on your calculator than with fractions. Here we changed $\frac{5}{4}$ to 1.25.

E3 65 percent of 90 is the same as 50 percent of what number?

S *Translate:* $0.65 \times 90 = 0.5x$

$$x = 0.65\left(\frac{90}{0.5}\right)$$

$$\mathbf{x} = \boxed{117}$$

E4 A store charges $180 for a TV. The price is 25% more than the amount it costs the store to buy the television. At the close-out sale, store employees can purchase all merchandise at 40% off the store's cost. How much would it cost an employee to purchase the television at this sale?

Remember multiplying by 0.6 (AKA 60%) is the same as taking 40% off.

S

employee price = ?

1 Set up the equation.

Store charges = 125% (cost of TV)

Store charges = 1.25 (cost of TV)

2 Solve for cost of TV.

1.25 (cost of TV) = $180

$$\text{cost of TV} = \frac{\$180}{1.25}$$

cost of TV = $144

3 Find employees' price at sale.

$144 (0.60) = **$86.40**

E5 A $10 mug is reduced by 15% per week for 2 weeks in a row. What is the final price?

Remember multiplying by 0.85 (aka 85%) is the same as taking 15% off.

S *The first part is easy: %15 off the original price of $10.* (final $$ = ?)

$10 × 0.85 = $8.50

Now for the tricky part: we need to take 15% off the ***new*** *price.*

$8.50 × 0.85 = **$7.23** (rounded)

Percent Increase/Decrease

Use the same formula for both percent increase and percent decrease problems! The key to these problems is this simple formula:

$$\frac{\textbf{(New number – Old number)}}{\textbf{Old number}} \times 100 \quad \text{or} \quad \frac{\textbf{Change}}{\textbf{Original}} \times 100$$

The most common rookie mistake is to reduce by $1.50 each week, forgetting that there is a new price each week **after the discount.** That would give you a final price of $7.00, the most common wrong answer.

E6 A certain stock had a price of $7 in May and rose to a price of $11 in June. The stock price in June is what percent greater than the stock price in May?

S

$$\frac{\text{Change}}{\text{Original}} \times (100\%) = \frac{11-7}{7} \times (100\%)$$

$$= \frac{4}{7} \times (100\%)$$

$$= \boxed{57.1\%}$$

E7 The price of a \$20 purse was first increased by 25%, and then the new price was decreased by 20%. The final price is what percent less than the original price?

S

1 *First there was a 25% increase in price for the \$25 purse.*

$\$20 \times (125\%) = \text{new price}$

$\$20 \times (1.25) = \mathbf{\$25}$

2 *Next the new price was decreased by 20%,*

$\$25 \times 80\% = \text{final price}$

$\$25\ (0.80) = \mathbf{\$20}$ *the original price!*

We're back to where we started! The answer is ***zero!***

E8 Drew has won 40% of the 10 debate tournaments he has entered this year. If Drew wins 70% of the remaining 20 tournaments, what will be his final winning percentage?

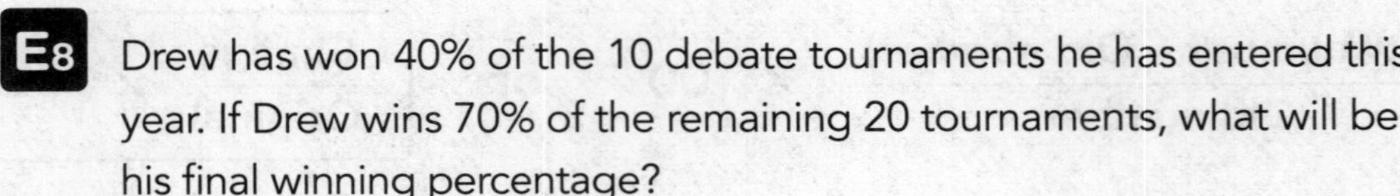

S

1 *Find how many tournaments Drew has already won.* final % = ?

$(0.40) \times 10 = 4$

2 *Figure out how many he will win for the rest of the season.*

$(0.70) \times 20 = 14$

3 *Divide total wins by total tourneys and convert to percent:*

$$\frac{(14 + 4)}{30} = \frac{18}{30} = 0.6 = \mathbf{60\%}$$

Percentages Practice Problems

1. 13 is what percent of 65?

A. 10%
B. 15%
C. 20%
D. 25%
E. 30%

★

2. Which of the following is equal to 40% of y ?

F. $\frac{4y}{100}$

G. $\frac{2y}{5}$

H. $4y$

J. $400y$

K. $\frac{y}{4}$

★

3. There are 638 students enrolled at Winter Park High School. If 108 of these students are graduating, approximately what percentage of students will **NOT** be graduating?

A. 17%
B. 64%
C. 82%
D. 83%
E. 90%

★

4. In Sidney's fish tank, 35% of the fish are Angelfish. If there are 28 Angelfish in the tank, how many fish total does Sidney have?

F. 52
G. 78
H. 80
J. 96
K. Cannot be determined from the information provided.

★★

5. What is the product of 300 percent of 1 and 150 percent of 4 ?

A. 2
B. 3
C. 9
D. 12
E. 18

★★

6. If a coat is on sale for 80% of the original price, by what percent must the sale price be increased to obtain the original price?

F. 15%
G. 20%
H. 23%
J. 25%
K. 27%

★★

7. A class of 50 students is made up of b boys and g girls. In terms of g, what percentage of the class is made up of boys?

A. $50 - g$

B. $50 + g$

C. $100 - 2g$

D. $100 + 2g$

E. $\frac{g}{50}$

★★

8. A coffee company sells 150 different varieties of coffee. Of the 150 varieties, 6% of the varieties are decaffeinated, and 15 of the caffeinated coffee varieties are grown in South America. How many coffee varieties are caffeinated and are NOT grown in South America?

F. 141
G. 135
H. 132
J. 126
K. 121

9. A company's profits increased by 20% from 2005 to 2006 and by 30% from 2006 to 2007. By what percent did its profit increase from 2005 to 2007 ?

A. 56%
B. 50%
C. 30%
D. 25%
E. 5%

★★

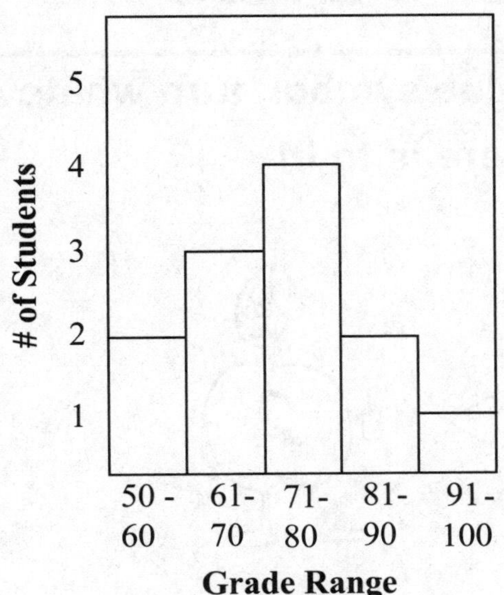

10. The graph above shows the distribution of grades in Mr. Barry's Physics class. If all grades are integers, what percentage of students earned grades between 71 and 90, inclusive?

F. 33.33%
G. 40.00%
H. 50.00%
J. 66.66%
K. 91.66%

★★

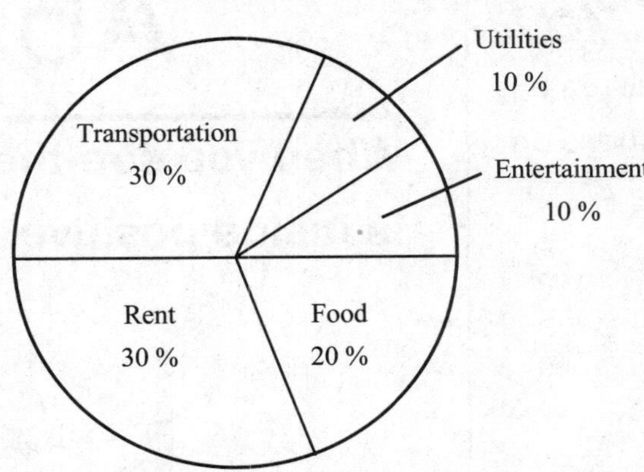

11. The pie graph above shows the allocation of Frank's budget. The amount Frank pays for transportation is only part of the total transportation cost for the car he uses, because Frank carpools with 3 other people. If Frank's total monthly budget is \$1000, and the carpoolers split the cost evenly, what is the total transportation cost for Frank's car each month?

A. \$300
B. \$600
C. \$900
D. \$1200
E. \$1500

★★

---

12. If x is 45% of y, then 110% of y is what percent of x, rounded to the nearest percent ?

F. 155%
G. 190%
H. 220%
J. 244%
K. 450%

★★★

2%
of all math questions on the ACT

Absolute Value

When you see the absolute value symbol, turn whatever is inside positive. That's all there is to it!

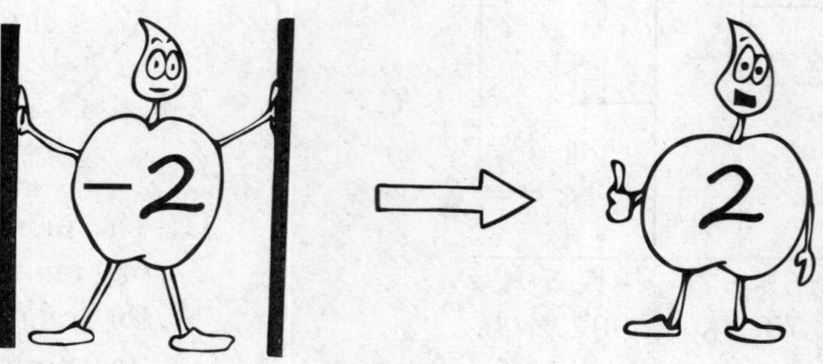

E1 If $y = |7 - 3x|$, what is the value of y when $x = 3$?

S *We know that $x = 3$; let's plug it in and simplify.*

$y = ?$

$$y = |7 - 3x|$$
$$y = |7 - 3(3)|$$
$$y = |7 - 9|$$
$$y = |-2|$$

Now we just take **−2** *and turn it positive.*

$\mathbf{y = 2}$

Absolute Value Equations

When you're asked to find possible values for a variable inside an absolute value, you will need to solve **two** equations: one where the contents of the absolute value are **positive** and one where they are **negative**.

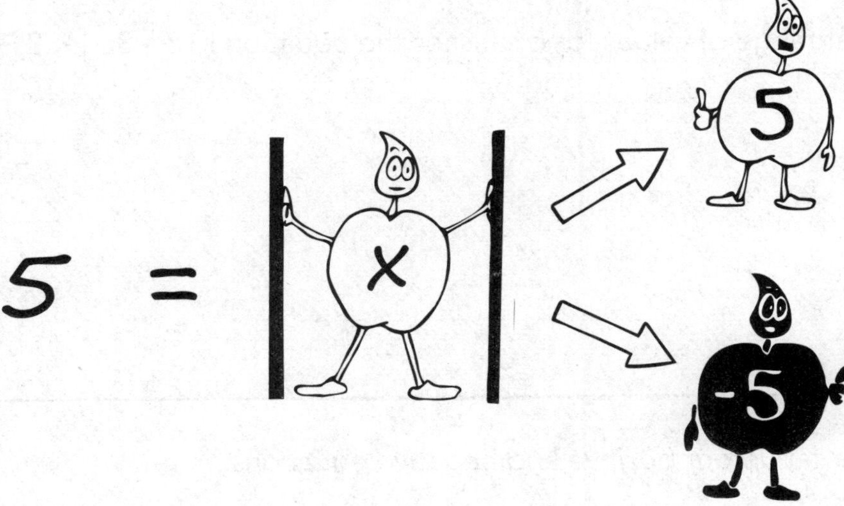

E2 What are all of the solutions for $|5x - 3| = 8$?

Remember,
$|5x - 3| = |-(5x - 3)|$

S *Let's write out our positive and negative forms, and solve for x:*

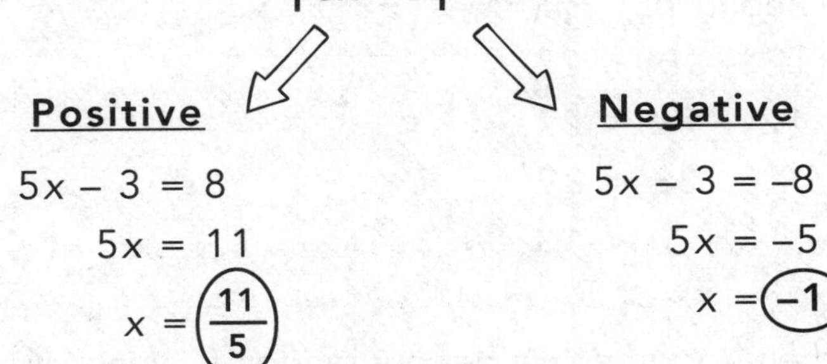

$$|5x - 3| = 8$$

Positive

$$5x - 3 = 8$$
$$5x = 11$$
$$x = \frac{11}{5}$$

Negative

$$5x - 3 = -8$$
$$5x = -5$$
$$x = -1$$

Absolute Values and Inequalities

Often the ACT will combine absolute values and inequalities. There are no fancy new tricks to learn here: just follow the rules for each and work carefully.

E3 What range of values for b satisfies the equation $|12 - 3b| < 27$?

 *Let's set up our positive and negative equations:*

$$|12 - 3b| < 27$$

Positive	**Negative**
$12 - 3b < 27$	$-(12 - 3b) < 27$

Now let's solve.
Start with the positive:

$$12 - 3b < 27$$
$$-3b < 15$$
$$\mathbf{b > -5}$$

Now the negative:

$$-(12 - 3b) < 27$$
$$-12 + 3b < 27$$
$$3b < 39$$
$$\mathbf{b < 13}$$

Putting them together, we get our range of values for b:

$$\mathbf{-5 < b < 13}$$

E4 If $|8 - 4x| > 30$, which of the following could equal x ?

A. −5
B. −2
C. 0
D. 9
E. 10

S *We find a range by solving our positive and negative equations, but let's see if we can save time by simply plugging in the answer choices until we find one that works.*

A. $|8 - 4(\mathbf{-5})| > 30$
$|28| > 30$
$28 > 30$ False! A doesn't work.

B. $|8 - 4(\mathbf{-2})| > 30$
$|16| > 30$
$16 > 30$ Nope, B's wrong too.

C. $|8 - 4(\mathbf{0})| > 30$
$|8| > 30$
$8 > 30$ Incorrect! C's out.

D. $|8 - 4(\mathbf{9})| > 30$
$|-28| > 30$
$28 > 30$ Close, but wrong.

E. $|8 - 4(\mathbf{10})| > 30$
$|-32| > 30$
$32 > 30$ True! E is the answer!

Absolute Value Practice Problems

1. If $x = 11$, then $|7 - x| =$

A. -18
B. -6
C. -4
D. 4
E. 18

★

$$|x + 4| < 7.5$$

2. If x is a positive integer, what is the least possible value of x that satisfies the equation above?

F. -3
G. -2
H. 1
J. 2
K. 3

★★

3. If $7 < |-x + 6| < 9$ which of the following could be the value of x?

A. -3
B. -2
C. 0
D. 2
E. 3

★★

4. A wrestling team for Springfield High School requires that a wrestler's weight cannot vary more than 10 pounds from p pounds. Which of the following inequalities gives the range of a wrestler's weight, w, in pounds?

F. $|w - p| \leq 10$
G. $|w + p| \leq 10$
H. $|w - p| < 10$
J. $w - 10 < p$
K. $w + 10 < p$

★★★

Sequences

4%
of all math questions on the ACT

Arithmetic Sequence

In this type of sequence, the difference between any two consecutive terms is the same.

2, 5, 8, 11, 14

+3 +3 +3 +3

Geometric Sequence

In this type of sequence, each term after the first is found by multiplying the previous term by a fixed number.

2, 8, 32, 128, 512

× 4 × 4 × 4 × 4

The ACT likes to combine elements of arithmetic and geometric sequences. If the sequence is relatively short (fewer than 10 terms), it's best to write it out.

2, 4, 10...

In the sequence above, the first term is 2, and each term after the first is 2 less than 3 times the preceding term. What is the 7th term of the sequence?

A. -61
B. 28
C. 244
D. 730
E. 1458

S *With only 7 terms, it's easiest to simply write them all down, being careful to label each term of the sequence.*

7th term = ?

	×3 − 2	×3 − 2	×3 − 2	×3 − 2	×3 − 2	×3 − 2	
Value	2	4	10	28	82	244	(730)
Term	**1**	**2**	**3**	**4**	**5**	**6**	**7**

***D** is the answer!*

E2 The first term of a sequence of numbers is – 2. If each term after the first is the product of – 3 and the preceding term, what is the 5th term of the sequence?

Watch your signs! You need to keep careful watch on signs when your multiplier is a negative number.

S *Since we only have 5 terms, let's write them out:*

5th term = ?

	×(−3)	×(−3)	×(−3)	×(−3)	
Value	−2	6	−18	54	(−162)
Term	**1**	**2**	**3**	**4**	**5**

Repeating sequences

Some ACT problems ask you to find terms of a sequence such as the 192nd term. Good luck writing out 192 terms! The key to problems like these is to **find the repeat**. You need to physically write/draw out the sequence only until you find the repeat or pattern, and then you can solve.

E3

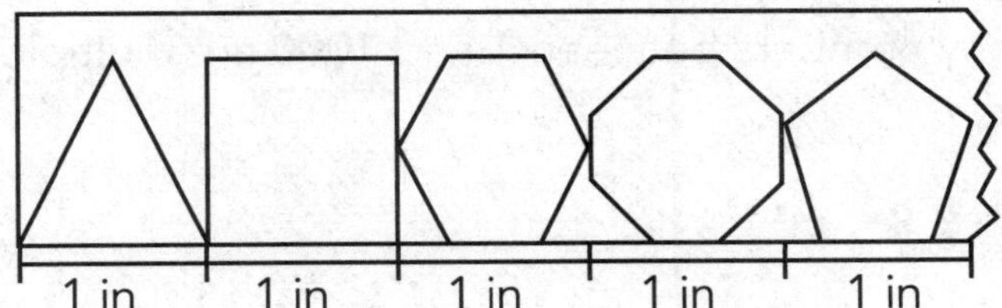

One end of a 128 inch-long piece of fabric is shown above. A student cuts out these 5 shapes from the fabric, over and over, starting with the shape on the left and continuing in order from left to right. If the student uses all of the available fabric and leaves no space between shapes, what will be the number of sides of the last shape the student cuts from the fabric?

F. Three
G. Four
H. Five
J. Six
K. Eight

S *We need the 128th term. No way we are expected to draw out that many shapes! Let's draw out a few to help find the pattern.*

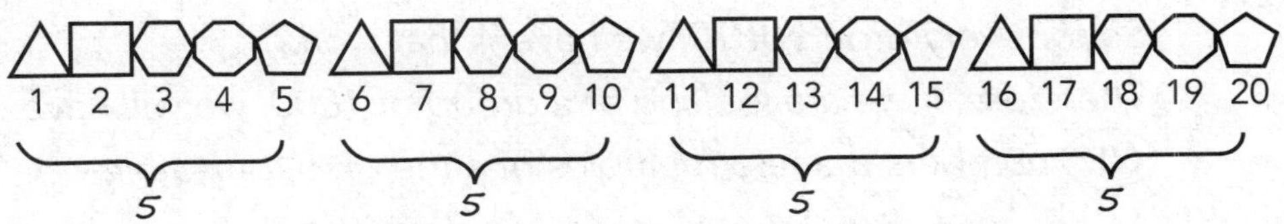

We can see that our pattern repeats every 5 shapes. The 5th term is a , as is the 10th, 15th and 20th term! Since we know that every multiple of 5 will be a , we can jump way ahead to the multiple of 5 closest to 128! Let's jump to 125 and resume our pattern:

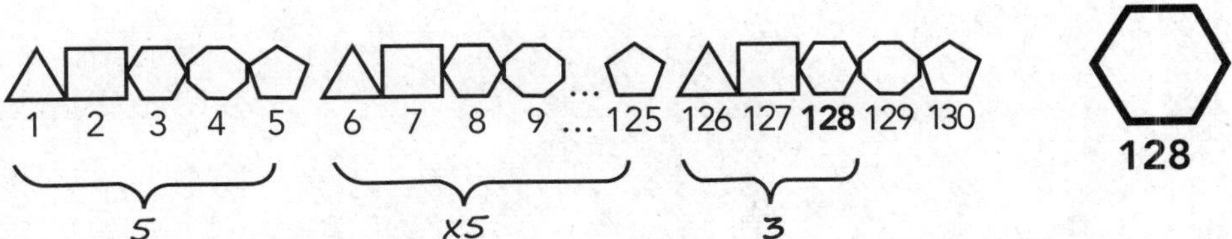

Found it! Skipping ahead to 125, we count 3 more terms and find the 128th shape, a ***hexagon****.* ***J*** *is the answer!*

If you end up with a remainder of 0, the desired term is the last term of the repeat; in this case, that would be a .

E4 How many numbers between 1 and 1000 are multiples of either 4, 5, or both?

S *Let's write down terms that fit our criteria until we see a pattern:*

1, 2, 3, (4), (5), 6, 7, (8), 9, (10) *4 so far*

11, (12), 13, 14, (15), (16), 17, 18, 19, (20) *another 4*

And if we continue, we notice that for every 10 integers, 4 match our criteria:

4, 5, 8, 10,	12, 15, 16, 20	24, 25, 28, 30	32, 35, 36, 40
1 - 10	11 - 20	21 - 30	31 - 40

So for every group of 10, we have 4 that work.
Therefore, if we are looking at a group of 1000, we will have ***(400)*** *numbers that are multiples of either 4, 5, or both.*

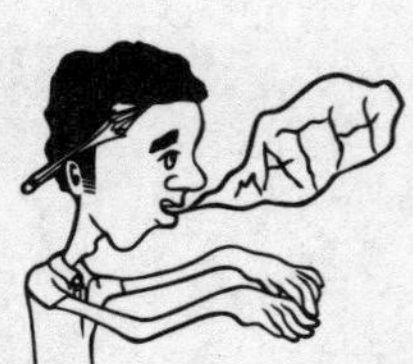

Remember: find the pattern and you're half way there!

Sequences Practice Problems

1. How many terms are there between 18 and 45, exclusive, in the arithmetic sequence below?

12, 15, 18,…, 45

A. 0
B. 8
C. 9
D. 27
E. 44

★

2. How many integers between 3 and 39 can be divided by 4 with a remainder of zero?

F. 8
G. 9
H. 10
J. 11
K. 12

★

3. The first 3 terms of a geometric sequence are 9, 12, and 16. What is the next term in the sequence?

A. 19

B. $21\frac{1}{3}$

C. 28

D. 32

E. 38

4. A jogger began a month by running 7 miles on the first day. On every day after that, he ran 4 miles. How many miles, in total, did he run after 15 days?

F. 26
G. 60
H. 63
J. 74
K. 109

★

5. The sum of an infinite geometric series with first term a and common ratio $r < 1$ is given by $\frac{a}{1-r}$. The sum of a given infinite geometric series is 100, and the common ratio is .3. What is the second term of this series?

A. 21
B. 30
C. 69.7
D. 70
E. 99.7

6. The repeating decimal $0.\overline{734}$ is equivalent to the fraction $\frac{734}{999}$. What is the 72nd digit to the right of the decimal?

F. 2
G. 3
H. 4
J. 7
K. 9

★★

5, 16, 27, 38 . . .

7. The first four numbers in a sequence are shown above. Each term after the first is obtained by adding d to the preceding term. Which term in this sequence is equal to $5 + (17 - 1)d$?

A. 5th
B. 11th
C. 16th
D. 17th
E. 18th

★★★

8. What is the sum of the first 4 terms of the arithmetic sequence in which the 5th term is 8 and the 9th term is 15?

F. 8.25
G. 10.75
H. 14.5
J. 18
K. 32.5

★★★

Ratios

When you are working with ratio problems, you must always add the individual parts to find the whole.

2% of all math questions on the ACT

E1 In a certain city the ratio of the number of men to women is 3 to 2. What fraction of the population is female?

A. $\frac{2}{5}$

B. $\frac{3}{5}$

C. $\frac{2}{3}$

D. $\frac{5}{3}$

E. $\frac{3}{2}$

S

1 *Add the parts to find the whole:* $3 + 2 = \boxed{5}$ *fraction female = ?*

2 *Place the ratio of the parts over the whole:*

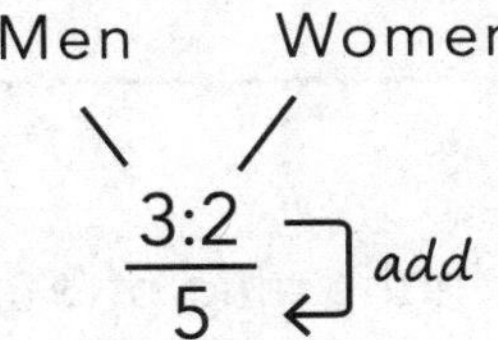

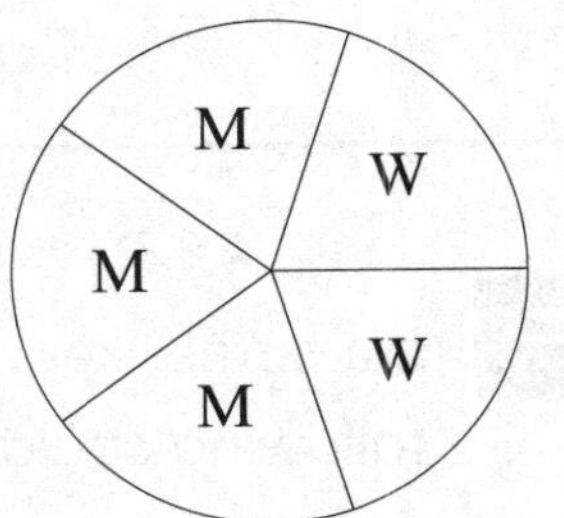

3 *Circle your fraction:*

Men

$\frac{3:2}{5}$

Women

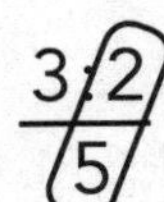

The fraction of the population that is male is $\frac{3}{5}$, *and the fraction of the population that is female is* $\frac{2}{5}$.

When you're working with ratios, think of a **pie**. Find the total number of pieces in the pie, and you're good to go.

E2 If a \$345,000 prize was divided among three game show contestants in the ratio 2 to 7 to 9, what was the largest amount awarded to any one contestant, rounded to the nearest dollar?

F. \$7,041
G. \$38,333
H. \$134,167
J. \$172,500
K. \$345,000

S

Smallest Largest

largest prize = ?

$\frac{2:7:9}{18}$ *add*

Smallest $\frac{2:7:9}{18}$

Middle $\frac{2:7:9}{18}$

Largest $\frac{2:7:9}{18}$

The largest prize awarded is $\frac{9}{18}$, or half of the total prize.

$\frac{1}{2}$ of \$345,000 = **\$172,500**, *choice* **J.**

E3 If a farmer keeps only cows and pigs in the ratio of 3 to 4, each of the following could be the number of animals on the farm EXCEPT

A. 7
B. 10
C. 28
D. 42
E. 84

S

Cows Pigs

$\frac{3:4}{7}$ add

Cows

$\frac{3:4}{7}$

Pigs

$\frac{3:4}{7}$

*Unless we want to have fractions of animals, we need our grand total to be a **multiple of 7**. So cold-cuts aside, we need to see totals such as 7, 14, 21, 28, etc.*

For example, if the farmer had 28 animals, $\frac{3}{7}$ would be cows and $\frac{4}{7}$ would be pigs.

Cows $\longrightarrow \frac{3}{7} \times 28 = 12$ cows.

Pigs $\longrightarrow \frac{4}{7} \times 28 = 16$ pigs.

All whole animals. All good!

So the only odd-ball answer in our current problem is **B**. *If we have 10 animals, we get animal parts:*

Cows $\longrightarrow \frac{3}{7} \times 10 = 4.29$ cows

Pigs $\longrightarrow \frac{4}{7} \times 10 = 5.71$ pigs

We want our animals whole! Our answer is **(B.)**

Ratios Practice Problems

1. A catering order calls for Greek and Caesar salads in the ratio of 4:5. If there are 54 salads in the order, how many are Caesar salads?

A. 4
B. 5
C. 24
D. 30
E. 54

★

2. Which of the following is equal to the ratio 3.5 to 14 ?

F. 1 to 2
G. 1 to 3
H. 8 to 2
J. 2 to 8
K. 2 to 80

★

3. In the wild, the ratio of male peacocks to female peacocks is 3 to 5. What percent of peacocks in the wild are female?

A. 32.5%
B. 35.0%
C. 37.5%
D. 60.0%
E. 62.5%

★

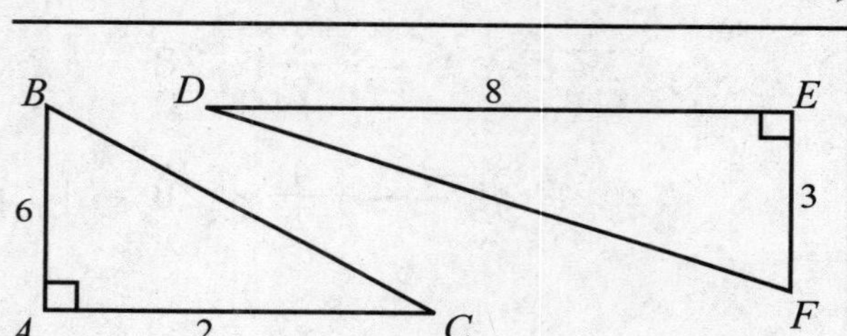

4. In the figure above, what is the ratio of the area of triangle *ABC* to the area of triangle *DEF* ?

F. 1:2
G. 1:3
H. 1:4
J. 2:3
K. 2:5

★

5. If Kara only owns drama and comedy movies and the ratio of dramas to comedies in her DVD collection is 3:2, which of the following could be the total number of DVDs in her collection?

A. 15
B. 16
C. 17
D. 18
E. 19

★★

6. When 30 students were asked who they would vote for in an upcoming class election, their results were put into the table shown below:

Candidate	Number of Voters
Sam	7
Ruth	12
Jordan	11

If the student responses are indicative of how the 500 students in the class will vote in the actual student election, which of the following best estimates the votes that Ruth will receive in the election?

F. 100
G. 150
H. 200
J. 250
K. 300

★★

7. In a parking lot with 168 spaces, there were 48 more filled spaces than empty spaces. What was the ratio of filled spaces to empty spaces?

A. 5 to 9
B. 9 to 5
C. 2 to 1
D. 5 to 2
E. 11 to 3

★★

8. The ratio of x to y is 1 to 3, and the ratio of y to z is 2 to 3. What is the ratio of x to z ?

F. 1 to 2
G. 1 to 3
H. 2 to 3
J. 1 to 9
K. 2 to 9

★★★

2% of all math questions on the ACT

Probability

Probability represents the likelihood that a particular event will occur. It is expressed as a value from 0 to 1.

A probability of 1 tells you: *It's a sure thing!*

A probability of 0 tells you: *It's just not going to happen.*

The formula is simple:

$$\text{Probability} = \frac{\text{\# of outcomes that meet the requirements}}{\text{Total \# of possible outcomes}}$$

E1 A shelf contains only plastic toys and wooden toys. If 6 out of 15 toys on the shelf are plastic, what is the probability that a toy selected at random will be wooden?

S *So 6 out of our 15 toys are plastic; the remaining 9 toys must be wooden. To find the probability that a toy chosen at random will be wooden, we use this equation:*

p(wooden) = ?

$$\frac{\text{\# that meet requirements}}{\text{\# of total possible}} = \frac{\text{Wooden Toys}}{\text{Total Toys}} = \frac{9}{15}$$

E2 A bag has only pearls and emeralds inside. There are three times as many pearls as emeralds. The pearls are either white or black, and 8 times as many pearls are white as are black. If one jewel is drawn at random from the bag, what is the probability that the jewel drawn will be a black pearl?

S *We can solve this problem by using a probability tree. Build the tree* ***starting at the top*** *with the most generic detail (total) down to the most specific detail (White or Black).*

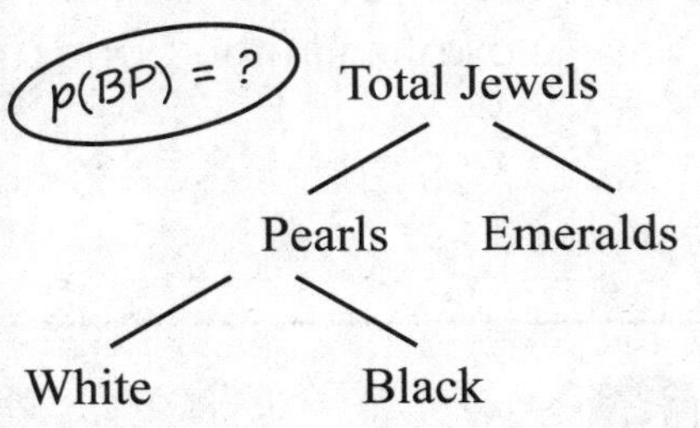

Now let's fill in the information, ***starting from the bottom:***

1 *Starting at the lowest level, we have 8 white pearls for each black pearl. This gives us* ***9 pearls total.***

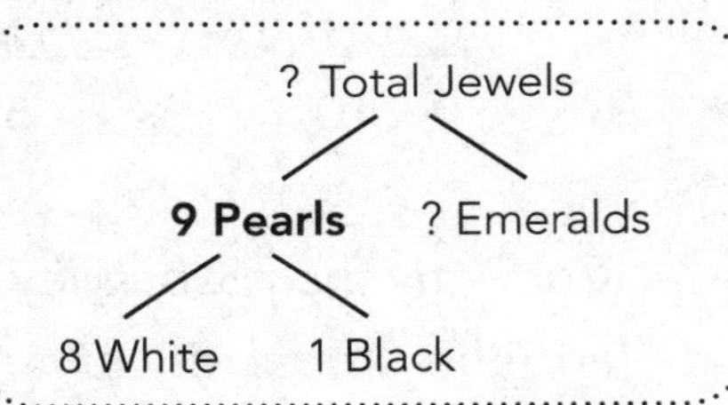

2 *Moving up the tree, we have 3 pearls for every emerald. Since we have 9 pearls, we must have* ***3 emeralds.***

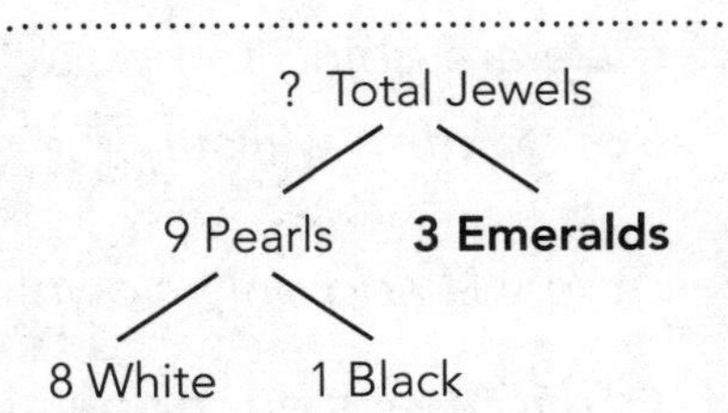

3 *Moving up the tree, we know we have 9 pearls and 3 emeralds. That makes a* ***total of 12 jewels.***

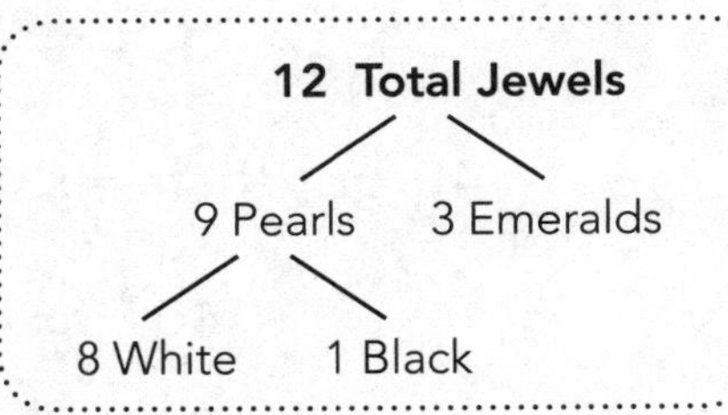

Looking at our tree, it's easy to see that out of 12 jewels, the probability of drawing 1 black pearl is $\frac{\text{Black Pearl}}{\text{Total Jewels}} = \frac{1}{12}$.

Changing Probabilities

Whenever you have a probability problem where one component is changing while the other stays the same, **focus on the element that is not changing.**

E3 There are 90 fish in a pond. 40 are goldfish and 50 are clownfish. If clownfish are added to the pond until the probability of randomly catching a clownfish becomes $\frac{2}{3}$, what will be the total number of clownfish in the pond?

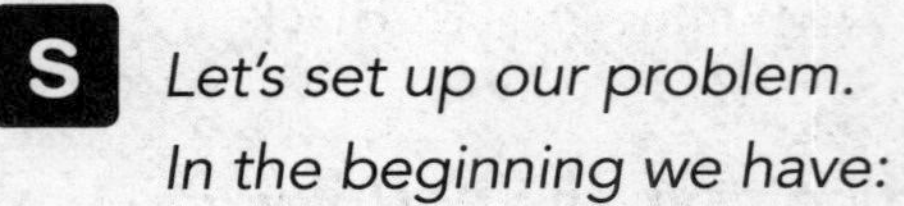

S *Let's set up our problem.*
In the beginning we have:

clown = ?

Goldfish	Clownfish	Total (T)
40	50	90

Currently the probability of randomly catching a goldfish is $\frac{40}{90}$. *and the probability of randomly catching a clownfish is* $\frac{50}{90}$.

We are going to be adding clownfish, but the number of goldfish will stay the same. So let's focus on the ***goldfish.***

We will add only clownfish until we have $\frac{2}{3}$ *clownfish in the pond. That means our* ***original 40 goldfish*** *will now account for* $\frac{1}{3}$ *of the total fish in the pond. Let's write that out and solve:*

40 goldfish = $\frac{1}{3}$ of the new total.

$$40 = \frac{1}{3} \times T$$

$$120 = T$$

120 total fish – 40 goldfish = **80 clownfish**

E4 An artist is planning to hold a private art show. Of the pieces he has already completed, 20 are sculptures and 40 are oil paintings. If the artist does not complete any more oil paintings, how many more sculptures must he complete in order to ensure that the probability of seeing a sculpture at the show is $\frac{4}{5}$?

S *In the beginning we have:*

additional sculptures = ?

Sculptures	Paintings	Total (T)
20	40	60

Currently $\frac{20}{60}$ *(or* $\frac{1}{3}$*) of the pieces are sculptures.*

We are going to be adding only sculptures until $\frac{4}{5}$ *of the total pieces are sculptures and* $\frac{1}{5}$ *are paintings.*

Let's focus on the ***paintings****, since they are the unchanging factor.*

When all the works are completed, 40 paintings will comprise $\frac{1}{5}$ *of the total pieces in the show.*

$$40 = \frac{1}{5} \times T$$

$$200 = T$$

200 total pieces – 40 paintings = 160 sculptures

We're not done yet! The question asks how many ***more*** *sculptures must he create. Starting from a base of 20, he will need to knock out:*

160 – 20 = **140 additional sculptures**

Probability Practice Problems

1. In a certain store, there are 3 blue sweaters, 4 red sweaters, 7 green sweaters, and 4 white sweaters for sale. If these are the only sweaters in the store, what is the probability that a sweater randomly selected from this store is blue?

A. $\frac{1}{6}$

B. $\frac{1}{3}$

C. $\frac{1}{2}$

D. $\frac{11}{18}$

E. $\frac{2}{3}$

★

2. Every student in Mr. Smith's class plays exactly one sport. The probability that a student chosen at random from the class plays baseball is $\frac{1}{8}$. If exactly 3 students play baseball, what is the total number of students in the class?

F. 6
G. 12
H. 18
J. 24
K. 30

★

3. A drawer contains only white, black and brown socks. If the probability of randomly selecting a white sock from the drawer is $\frac{1}{5}$ and the probability of selecting a black sock is $\frac{1}{4}$, which of the following could **NOT** be the total number of socks in the drawer?

A. 20
B. 25
C. 40
D. 60
E. 80

★

4. The Atlanta Zoo has 3 monkeys that are 10 years old, 6 monkeys that are 6 years old, 2 monkeys that are 4 years old, and 4 monkeys that are 2 years old. What is the probability that a monkey selected at random will be less than 6 years old?

F. $\frac{2}{5}$

G. $\frac{4}{15}$

H. $\frac{3}{5}$

J. $\frac{11}{15}$

K. $\frac{4}{5}$

★★

Number of Computers per Home in Johnstown

Computers per Home	Number of Homes
0	4
1	16
2	20
3	12
4	8

5. A survey revealed the data shown in the table above. What is the probability that a home chosen at random from Johnstown will contain exactly 3 computers?

A. $\frac{1}{5}$

B. $\frac{1}{4}$

C. $\frac{1}{3}$

D. $\frac{1}{2}$

E. $\frac{2}{3}$

★★

---

6. If two of the positive factors of 6 are multiplied together, what is the probability that the result will be a multiple of 2 ?

F. $\frac{1}{6}$

G. $\frac{1}{3}$

H. $\frac{1}{2}$

J. $\frac{2}{3}$

K. $\frac{5}{6}$

★★★

	Male	Female
Age 0 – 20	35	93
Age 21 – 40	55	49
Age 41 – 60	60	48

7. The table above shows demographic information for 340 customers at City Mall. What is the probability that a randomly selected person at this mall is a male whose age is 21 or greater?

A. $\frac{39}{289}$

B. $\frac{55}{340}$

C. $\frac{23}{68}$

D. $\frac{15}{34}$

E. $\frac{127}{170}$

★★

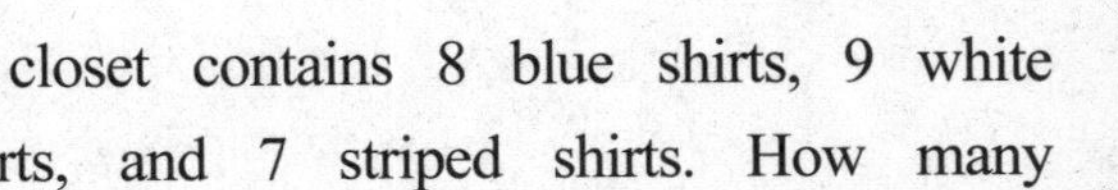

8. A closet contains 8 blue shirts, 9 white shirts, and 7 striped shirts. How many additional blue shirts must be added to the 24 shirts in the closet so that the probability of selecting a blue shirt at random is $\frac{3}{7}$?

F. 2
G. 4
H. 6
J. 8
K. 10

★★★

9. An integer from 500 through 1000, inclusive, will be selected at random. What is the probability that the number selected will have 1 as at least 1 digit?

A. $\frac{11}{501}$

B. $\frac{36}{501}$

C. $\frac{96}{501}$

D. $\frac{101}{501}$

E. $\frac{201}{1000}$

★★★

10. A school held a raffle contest to raise money for a local soup kitchen. The circle graph below shows the distribution of raffle tickets that students purchased according to their grade. A raffle ticket holder is selected randomly from this group to win a prize. What are the odds (in the grade range:not in the grade range) that the person with the winning ticket is in grade 10, 11, or 12 ?

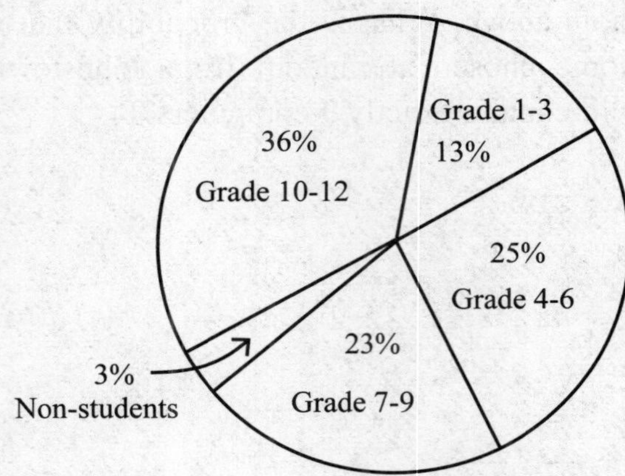

F. 1 : 3
G. 9 : 16
H. 9 : 37
J. 18 : 33
K. 36 : 25

★★

Matrix

1% of all math questions on the ACT

It's the question that brought you here. The question that drives us: *What is the matrix?*

$$\begin{bmatrix} 23 & 34 & 23 \\ 34 & 55 & 7 \\ 4 & 56 & 32 \end{bmatrix}$$

A matrix is simply a group of numbers, organized in a rectangle. Matrices allow you to quickly add or multiply a series of numbers in an organized way. Don't be intimidated by their complicated appearance! Behind the matrix, it's all just simple arithmetic.

Sam and Diane work in a health food store. Each week, they compete to see who can sell the most herbal tea. The herbal tea sold in the store comes in boxes of three different sizes (A, B, and C). The matrices below show the number of boxes sold by Sam and Diane last week and the cost for each size box. What is the total value of the herbal tea sold by Sam and Diane last week?

$$\begin{array}{l} \\ \text{Sam} \\ \text{Diane} \end{array}\begin{array}{c} \begin{array}{ccc} \text{A} & \text{B} & \text{C} \end{array} \\ \begin{bmatrix} 75 & 150 & 125 \\ 95 & 40 & 80 \end{bmatrix} \end{array} \qquad \begin{array}{l} \text{A} \\ \text{B} \\ \text{C} \end{array}\begin{array}{c} \text{Cost} \\ \begin{bmatrix} \$\ 5 \\ \$10 \\ \$15 \end{bmatrix} \end{array}$$

A. $2,400
B. $2,495
C. $3,550
D. $3,925
E. $5,825

Brackets let you know that you have entered the matrix.

S *Welcome to the matrix! We need to combine the sales information from the left table with the cost information from the right. If Sam sold 75 of size "A" boxes, and size "A" boxes cost $5 each, it makes sense to multiply "75" by "$5." We simply need to do this math for each combination:*

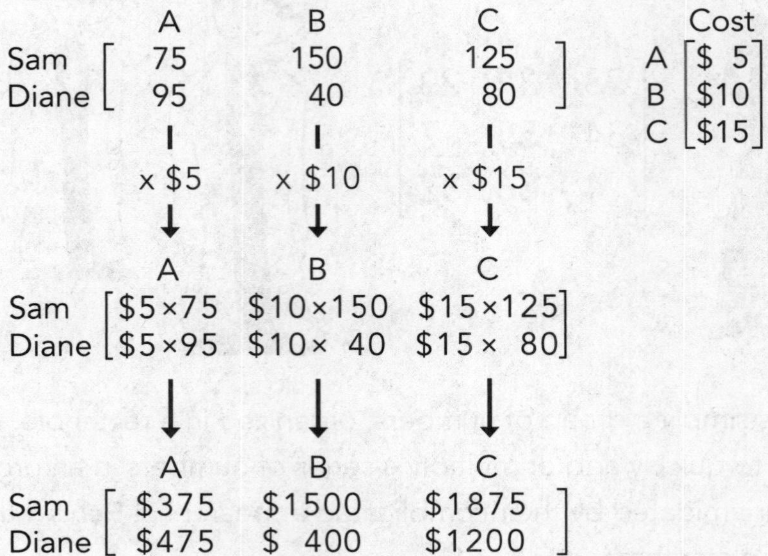

A B C Cost
Sam 75 150 125 A $ 5
Diane 95 40 80 B $10
C $15
x $5 x $10 x $15
A B C
Sam $5×75 $10×150 $15×125
Diane $5×95 $10× 40 $15× 80
A B C
Sam $375 $1500 $1875
Diane $475 $ 400 $1200

If you missed this problem, don't sweat it. No one ever makes their first jump.

Now we need to sum up the grand total for Sam and Diane. We can create an extra column on the right to help with this.

$$\begin{array}{l} \\ \text{Sam} \\ \text{Diane} \end{array} \begin{array}{c} \text{A} \qquad\quad \text{B} \qquad\quad \text{C} \\ \left[\begin{array}{l} \$375 + \$1500 + \$1875 = \mathbf{\$3750} \\ \$475 + \$\ \ 400 + \$1200 = \underline{\mathbf{\$2075}} \end{array}\right] \\ \qquad\qquad\qquad\qquad\qquad \boxed{\mathbf{\$5825}} \end{array}$$

***E** is our answer!*

You can see how a matrix can actually make your work easier! If you match the rows from one matrix with the columns from another, the rest is just multiplication, addition, and subtraction.

Determinant

Occasionally you will see a matrix problem that involves a specific concept known as a *determinant*. Don't sweat having to memorize anything new here. The writers will give you the formula: follow it and you're golden.

E2 The *determinant* of a matrix $\begin{bmatrix} a & b \\ c & d \end{bmatrix}$ equals $ad - cb$.

What must be the value of x for the matrix $\begin{bmatrix} x & 3 \\ 2x & x \end{bmatrix}$ to have a determinant of -9?

F. -3

G. $-\frac{3}{2}$

H. $-\frac{9}{2}$

J. $-\frac{9}{4}$

K. 3

S *Easy peasy. Finding the determinant here is like solving two fractions across an equal sign. Just cross multiply!*

$x = ?$

$$\begin{bmatrix} a & b \\ c & d \end{bmatrix} = ad - cb$$

$$\begin{bmatrix} x & 3 \\ 2x & x \end{bmatrix} = x^2 - 6x$$

Now we need to set our determinant to −9, as is given in our instructions:

$$x^2 - 6x = -9$$

$$x^2 - 6x + 9 = 0$$

$$(x - 3)(x - 3) = 0$$

$x = 3$, K.

Matrix Product

When you multiply two matrices together, your outcome is a **brand new matrix**! As you are multiplying terms, you just need to remember to fill in the products from top to bottom, and left to right. Let's see this in action.

E3 What is the matrix product $\begin{bmatrix} a \\ 2a \\ 4a \end{bmatrix} \begin{bmatrix} -1 & 0 & 1 \end{bmatrix}$?

A. $\begin{bmatrix} -a & 0 & a \\ -2a & 0 & 2a \\ -4a & 0 & 4a \end{bmatrix}$

B. $\begin{bmatrix} -a & -2a & -4a \\ 0 & 0 & 0 \\ a & 2a & 4a \end{bmatrix}$

C. $\begin{bmatrix} -2a & 0 & 2a \end{bmatrix}$

D. $\begin{bmatrix} -7a & 0 & 7a \end{bmatrix}$

E. $\begin{bmatrix} 0 \end{bmatrix}$

S *To help us visualize our matrix product, we can set up a multiplication table where the given matrices act as labels.*

	[−1	**0**	**1]**
[a			
2a			
4a]			

With our table in place, we simply need to do some basic multiplication. When we're done, we'll have a brand new matrix:

	−1	**0**	**1**
a	$(a) \times (-1)$	$(a) \times (0)$	$(a) \times (1)$
2*a*	$(2a) \times (-1)$	$(2a) \times (0)$	$(2a) \times (1)$
4*a*	$(4a) \times (-1)$	$(4a) \times (0)$	$(4a) \times (1)$

	−1	**0**	**1**
a	$-a$	0	a
2*a*	$-2a$	0	$2a$
4*a*	$-4a$	0	$4a$

Our answer is A!

The product of two matrices is another (bigger) matrix. Choices C, D, and E can be crossed out immediately!

Adding and Subtracting Matrices

Occasionally, you will be asked to add two similar matrices together. To accomplish this feat, simply add corresponding terms:

$$\begin{bmatrix} 2 & 3 \\ 2 & 3 \end{bmatrix} + \begin{bmatrix} 1 & 3 \\ 2 & 4 \end{bmatrix} = \begin{bmatrix} 2+1 & 3+3 \\ 2+2 & 3+4 \end{bmatrix} = \begin{bmatrix} 3 & 6 \\ 4 & 7 \end{bmatrix}$$

That's all there is to it! Subtracting matrices works in the exact same way. No matter how big or small the matrices are, just match terms and subtract:

$$\begin{bmatrix} 4 & 4 & 4 \\ 3 & 3 & 3 \\ 2 & 2 & 2 \end{bmatrix} - \begin{bmatrix} 4 & 4 & 4 \\ 3 & 2 & 3 \\ 2 & 2 & 2 \end{bmatrix} = \begin{bmatrix} 0 & 0 & 0 \\ 0 & 1 & 0 \\ 0 & 0 & 0 \end{bmatrix}$$

I believe...
I have found...
The One.

Matrix Practice Problems

1. Bill owns two used bookstores (X and Y) which sell 3 types of books (A, B, and C). The matrices below show the number of each type of book in each bookstore and the cost of each type of book. What is the total value of Bill's inventory of books at his two bookstores?

$$\begin{array}{c} \\ X \\ Y \end{array}\begin{array}{c} \begin{array}{ccc} A & B & C \end{array} \\ \begin{bmatrix} 20 & 5 & 15 \\ 15 & 35 & 10 \end{bmatrix} \end{array} \qquad \begin{array}{c} A \\ B \\ C \end{array}\begin{bmatrix} \$10 \\ \$12 \\ \$15 \end{bmatrix}$$

A. $572
B. $680
C. $935
D. $1,098
E. $1,205

★★

2. The number of packages of different types of beans that a factory processes daily is shown in the following matrix:

$$\begin{array}{ccc} \text{Lima} & \text{Black} & \text{Pinto} \end{array}$$
$$\begin{bmatrix} 440 & 375 & 300 \end{bmatrix}$$

The quality control officer estimates the proportion of packages that will not pass inspection according to the following matrix:

$$\begin{array}{c} \text{Lima} \\ \text{Black} \\ \text{Pinto} \end{array}\begin{bmatrix} 0.05 \\ 0.04 \\ 0.03 \end{bmatrix}$$

Given these matrices, what is the quality control officer's estimate for the total number of packages that will be rejected?

F. 37
G. 42
H. 45
J. 46
K. 54

★★

3. What is the matrix product of $\begin{bmatrix} a \\ 2a \end{bmatrix}$ and $\begin{bmatrix} 12 & 2a \end{bmatrix}$?

A. $\begin{bmatrix} 12a \\ 4a^2 \end{bmatrix}$

B. $\begin{bmatrix} 24a & 12a \\ 2a^2 & 4a^2 \end{bmatrix}$

C. $\begin{bmatrix} 12a & 2a^2 \\ 24a & 4a^2 \end{bmatrix}$

D. $\begin{bmatrix} 12 & a \\ 2a & 2a \end{bmatrix}$

E. $\begin{bmatrix} 12a & 4a^2 \end{bmatrix}$

★★

4. Given the matrix equation shown below, what is $\frac{t}{s}$?

$$\begin{bmatrix} 4! \\ 3! \end{bmatrix} + \begin{bmatrix} 3! \\ 2! \end{bmatrix} = \begin{bmatrix} s \\ t \end{bmatrix}$$

(Note: Whenever n is a positive integer, the notation $n!$ represents the product of the integers from n to 1. For example, $3! = (3)(2)(1)$.)

F. $\frac{4}{15}$

G. $\frac{5}{7}$

H. $\frac{9}{8}$

J. $\frac{15}{4}$

K. 3

★★★

1% of all math questions on the ACT

Scientific Notation

Scientific notation is a shorthand method for writing very large or very small numbers without having a boatload of zeroes. You will be moving decimals and multiplying your nonzero value by 10 raised to an exponent.

To refresh your memory on exponents and decimals, take a quick look at the following table:

(+) exponent	**(−) exponent**	**# of zeros**
$10^1 = 10$	$10^{-1} = 0.1$	1
$10^2 = 100$	$10^{-2} = 0.01$	2
$10^3 = 1{,}000$	$10^{-3} = 0.001$	3
$10^4 = 10{,}000$	$10^{-4} = 0.0001$	4
$10^5 = 100{,}000$	$10^{-5} = 0.00001$	5
$10^6 = 1{,}000{,}000$	$10^{-6} = 0.000001$	6

When you multiply a number by 10 raised to an exponent, you move its decimal to the left or to the right. This is the foundation of scientific notation.

Shortening Big Numbers

Say you're a busy scientist who wants to write the following number in scientific notation:

5,340,000

Your first step is to **move the decimal to the left** until it lands just to the right of the first non–zero number, and count the number of moves:

Six moves! Your next step is to drop all those zeros and multiply your number (5.34) by 10 raised to the number of moves (six):

$$5.34 \times 10^{6}$$

Shortening a Small Number

Using scientific notation to shorten a very small number works in almost exactly the same way. Say you want to write **.00000534** in scientific notation. Move the decimal to the **right** until it is immediately to the right of the first non–zero number; then count the number of moves:

Six moves again! You know the next step: drop all those zeros and multiply your number (5.34) by 10 raised to the number of moves (six). The one difference is that you need to make the exponent **negative**:

$$5.34 \times 10^{-6}$$

Remember: (+) exponents make numbers bigger, while (-) exponents make numbers smaller.

Now let's practice translating numbers into scientific notation:

E1

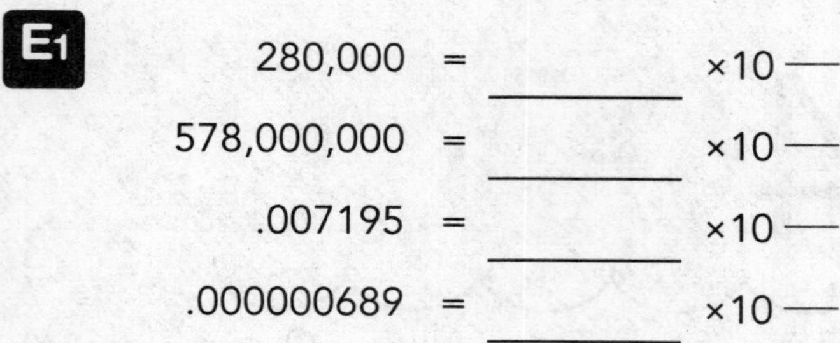

280,000 = ________ ×10 —

578,000,000 = ________ ×10 —

.007195 = ________ ×10 —

.000000689 = ________ ×10 —

S

Move the decimal until it is immediately to the right of the first non-zero number and count your moves:

$$280{,}000 = 2.8 \times 10^{5}$$
$$578{,}000{,}000 = 5.78 \times 10^{8}$$
$$.007195 = 7.195 \times 10^{-3}$$
$$.000000689 = 6.89 \times 10^{-7}$$

Moving from scientific to standard notation is as simple as shifting the decimal to the left or right according to the exponent over the 10:

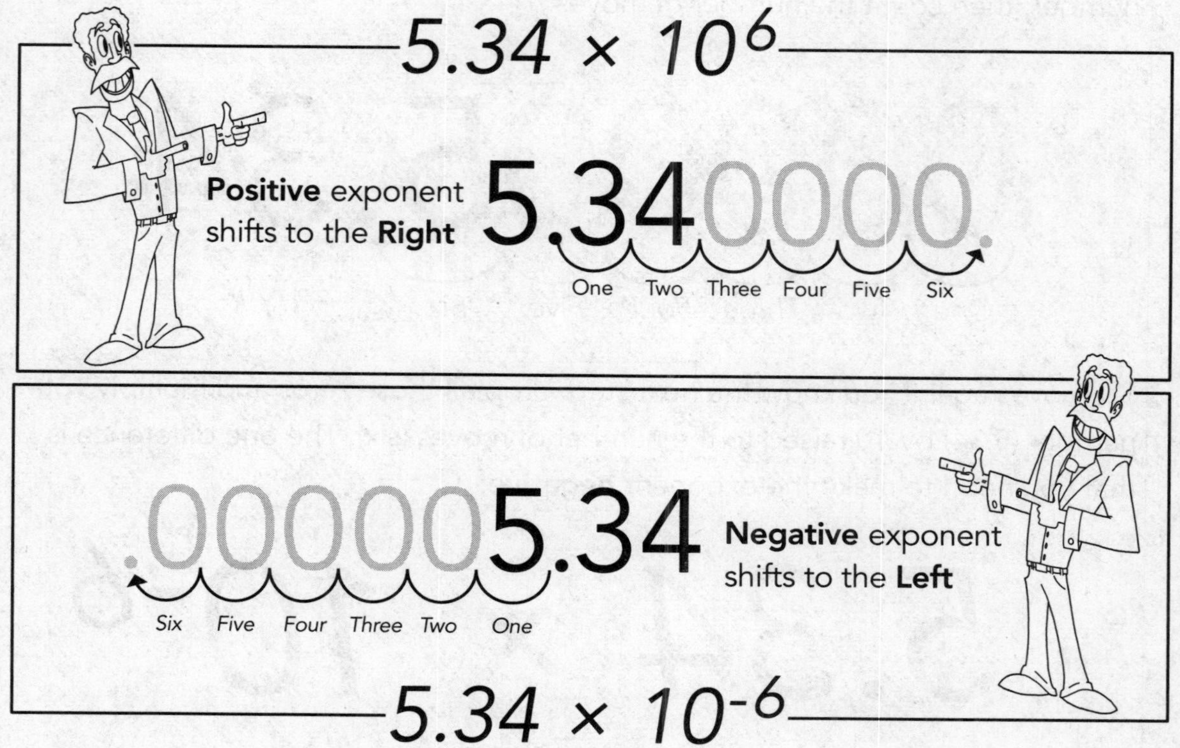

Let's see how the ACT tests scientific notation.

E2 What is 12% of 2.63×10^5 ?

F. 3,156,000
G. 315,600
H. 31,560
J. 2,191.70
K. 219.17

S *All we need to do is convert from scientific notation back into standard form.*

$$2.63 \times 10^5 = 263{,}000$$

Now we multiply by 12% and we have our answer.

$$263{,}000 \times .12 = \mathbf{31{,}560}$$

***H** is our answer!*

Scientific Notation Practice Problems

1. Which of the following is equivalent to 4.328671×10^4 ?

   A. 43.28671
   B. 432.8671
   C. 4,328.671
   D. 43,286.71
   E. 432,867.1

★

2. If 100 cubic meters of compost can fertilize 0.04 square kilometers of soil, how many square kilometers of soil can be fertilized by 10^7 cubic meters of compost?

   F. 400
   G. 4,000
   H. 40,000
   J. 400,000
   K. 4,000,000

★★

3. If a spaceship travels at 175,000 miles per hour, how far does it travel in 3 days?

   A. 4.20×10^{-6}
   B. 4.20×10^{6}
   C. 1.26×10^{7}
   D. 1.26×10^{-7}
   E. 6.30×10^{8}

★★

4. If there are 3.84 grams of copper for every 10,000 gallons of drinking water, what is the amount of copper, in scientific notation, in 1 gallon of drinking water?

   F. 3.84×10^{4}
   G. 3.84×10^{2}
   H. 3.84×10^{-3}
   J. 3.84×10^{-4}
   K. 3.84×10^{-5}

5. What is 17% of 5.32×10^7 ?

   A. 90,440,000
   B. 9,044,000
   C. 904,400
   D. 53,200
   E. 532

★★

Logic Tests

1%
of all math questions on the ACT

The ACT has begun to venture into the world of pure logic. If you love Socrates and snow cones, then you will love logic tests.

The key is to translate all the text into simple logical statements. You may find it handy to use basic **if–then statements**, which are at the core of logic:

If a person eats fries,
then that person will dance.

so **If** you see me munchin' fries,
then guess what's next?

E1 At Spick–n–Spaniel Dog Hotel, a dog cannot be boarded overnight if that dog does not weigh more than 10 pounds. If Susan boarded her dog, Venture, today, then which of the following may be logically concluded?

A. Venture weighs at most 9 pounds.
B. Venture weighs less than 10 pounds.
C. Venture weighs exactly 10 pounds.
D. Venture weighs more than 10 pounds.
E. Venture weighs at least 11 pounds.

S *Time to flex our art of translation skills. Let's start by focusing on the if-then statement:*

If dog is **not** 10 pounds or more
then dog **cannot** be boarded

*In other words: my dog needs to weigh at least 10 lbs to board! That double negative of **not** and **cannot** is confusing, so let's say this statement in a positive way:*

If dog <u>is boarded</u>
then dog is <u>more than 10 pounds</u>

Much easier to understand! Now let's take care of Susan's dog:

If Susan's dog <u>is boarded</u>
then what can be concluded?

So Venture made the cut.
Clearly he must weigh more than 10 lbs!

***D** is our answer!*

As you can see, logic tests boil down to some very simple ideas. Whenever you see a logic question:

1. Put the question into your own words
2. Focus on the IFs and THENs

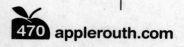

E2 Consider the 3 statements below to be true:

All animals that can hear the whistle are dogs.
Animal A is not a dog.
Animal B can hear the whistle.

Which of the following statements is necessarily true?

F. Animal A is a dog that cannot hear the whistle.
G. Animal A is a dog that can hear the whistle.
H. Animal A can hear the whistle.
J. Animal B cannot hear the whistle.
K. Animal B is a dog.

S *It's time to translate sentences into simple, logical statements:*

1. *All animals that can hear the whistle are dogs.*
   ***If** it hears the whistle,*
   ***then** it is a dog.*

2. *Animal A is not a dog.*
   A ≠ dog.

3. *Animal B can hear the whistle.*
   B hears the whistle

*We know that **if** you hear the whistle, **then** you are a dog. By simple logic, we know that **if** B hears the whistle, **then** B must be a dog.*

K is our answer!

Logic Tests Practice Problems

1. All of the girls in a class have brown hair. Some of the boys in the class have blonde hair. Which of the following statements must be true?

A. A student with brown hair must be a girl.
B. Some of the boys in the class have brown hair.
C. No girl in the class has blonde hair.
D. Some boys and girls have red hair.
E. No boys have hair that is not blonde.

★★

2. A company offers three reimbursement programs for its employees. All members of Blue Healthcare receive 100% coverage. Some members of Red Healthcare receive over 80% coverage. No members of Green Healthcare receive less than 90% coverage. If an employee has 85% coverage, which statement must be true?

F. The employee is not a member of Red Healthcare.
G. The employee is a member of Blue Healthcare.
H. The employee is not a member of Green Healthcare.
J. The employee may be a member of Blue Healthcare.
K. The employee is a member of Green Healthcare.

★★

3. An individual must be over 12 years old to buy a movie ticket on his/her own. If Sallie buys a movie ticket, which of the following statements must be true?

A. Sallie is at least 11 years old.
B. Sallie is not 11 years old.
C. Sallie is between 12 and 15 years old.
D. Sallie is 13 years old.
E. Sallie is not 18 years old.

★★

4. Amy's coach made the true statement below:

If it is storming, then the game is off.

Which of the following statements is logically equivalent to the coach's statement?

F. If the game is off, then it is storming.
G. If the game is not off, then it is not storming.
H. The game is off if and only if it is storming.
J. If it is not storming, then the game is off.
K. If it is not storming, then the game is not off.

Combinations and Permutations

1% of all math questions on the ACT

When you are asked to determine the number of possible arrangements of different elements, you can use a trusty tool called the Slot Method.

E1 If 5 people are to be seated in five chairs, how many different seating arrangements are possible?

S *Let's meet our five friends:*

1 Draw a slot for every **decision point**

*We have 5 chairs to fill, so we have **5 decisions** to make!*

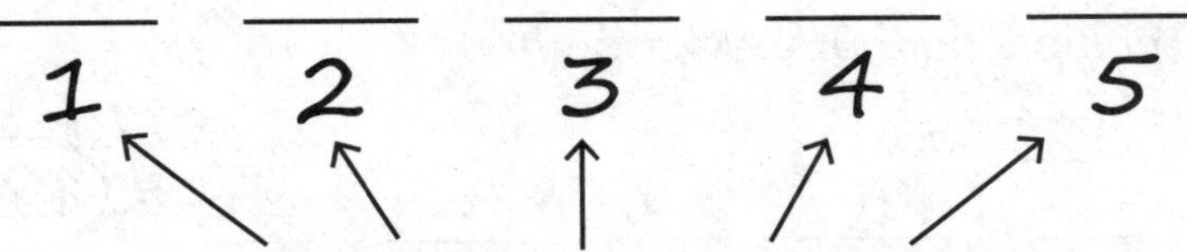

Now that we've drawn our slots, let's focus on Slot 1.

2 Write the number of **options** for each slot

How many options do we have for Slot 1?

5				
1	2	3	4	5

Let's say we pick 'Fro Boy. How many options for Slot 2?

5	4			
1	2	3	4	5

*Since we picked 'Fro Boy for Slot 1, we only have **four** options for Slot 2! This pattern will continue until we only have 1 choice for Slot 5:*

5	4	3	2	1
1	2	3	4	5

3 **Multiply** the options together

To find the total number of arrangements, we simply multiply our numbers together:

$$\underset{1}{5} \times \underset{2}{4} \times \underset{3}{3} \times \underset{4}{2} \times \underset{5}{1} = \boxed{120}$$

E2 A class field trip will go from the school to the Triassic Park on 1 of 4 roads, from the park to a safety bunker by 1 of 6 trails, and from the bunker to a helipad by 1 of 3 escape routes. How many routes are possible for the class to go from the school to the park to the bunker to the helipad?

S

1 Draw a slot for every **decision point**

Every time we have a route to pick, we need a slot!

School _____ Park _____ Bunker _____ Helipad

2 Write the number of **options** for each slot

Simply write in the number of routes given in the problem:

School 4 Park 6 Bunker 3 Helipad

3 **Multiply** the options together

Time to multiply!

$4 \times 6 \times 3 = 72$

Combinations and Permutations Practice Problems

1. A certain restaurant serves 4 different entrees with 6 different sides. How many different entree-side combinations are possible at this restaurant?

A. 10
B. 12
C. 16
D. 20
E. 24

★

2. Erica has 7 shirts, 3 sweaters, and 4 skirts. How many different outfits, each consisting of a shirt, a sweater, and a skirt, can Erica choose?

F. 14
G. 33
H. 64
J. 84
K. 218

★

3. Jenny must choose a three-digit number to be the combination for her gym locker. If the first digit is prime, the second digit is odd and the third digit is even (non zero), how many different possibilities are there for her combination?

A. 20
B. 40
C. 60
D. 80
E. 100

★★

4. A student can bike from his house into town by 1 of 3 roads, and from town to school by 1 of 5 roads. How many possible routes can the student take from his house to town to school and back without taking the same road twice?

F. 8
G. 15
H. 30
J. 60
K. 120

★★

Square Roots

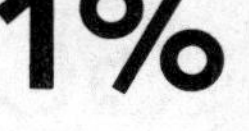

of all math questions on the ACT

Roots are the opposite of squares. To get rid of a radical (AKA the square root symbol), simply square the term.

$$16 = 4^2 \text{ and } (-4)^2$$

$$\sqrt{16} = 4 \text{ and } -4$$

General Rules

1. You can add and subtract square roots as long as they have the same number under the radical.

$$4\sqrt{2} + 6\sqrt{2} = 10\sqrt{2}$$

2. You can multiply or divide square roots as long as everything stays under the radical.

$$\sqrt{2} \times \sqrt{8} = \sqrt{16} = 4$$

If you ever see a negative under a radical, simply factor out an *i*.

$$\sqrt{-2} = i\sqrt{2}$$
$$\sqrt{-8} = 2i\sqrt{2}$$

E1 If $\sqrt{7} = 2s - 12$, what is the value of $(2s - 12)^2$?

A. $\sqrt{2}$
B. $\sqrt{7}$
C. 7
D. 26
E. 49

S *We know that* $\sqrt{7} = 2s - 12$, *and we are looking for* $(2s - 12)^2$. *Square both sides.*

$$\sqrt{7} = 2s - 12$$
$$(\sqrt{7})^2 = (2s - 12)^2$$
$$\boxed{7} = (2s - 12)^2$$

Our answer is **C**!

SQUARE ROOTS!

Square Roots Practice Problems

1. What is the value of x for which $5\sqrt{x} + 15 = 30$?

A. 3
B. 9
C. 15
D. 27
E. 81

★

2. If $y = 3\sqrt{x} + 4\sqrt{x}$, then $3y\sqrt{x} = ?$

F. $36x^2$
G. $12x^2$
H. $7x$
J. $21x$
K. $36x\sqrt{x}$

★★

$$\sqrt{54} = x\sqrt{y}$$

3. If x and y are both positive integers, what is the value of xy ?

A. 3
B. 9
C. 15
D. 18
E. 36

4. Which of the following complex numbers is a sum of $\sqrt{-72}$ and $\sqrt{-8}$?

F. $-8\sqrt{2}$
G. $-6\sqrt{2}$
H. $6i\sqrt{2}$
J. $8i\sqrt{2}$
K. $12i\sqrt{2}$

★★★

Arithmetic Review

1. If x, y, and z are positive integers, which of the following expressions is always equivalent to $xzyz$?

A. $(xy)z$
B. $(xyz)z$
C. $(x + y)z$
D. $(x + y)2z$
E. $x(y)z$

★★

2. The product of $(3a^4b^2)(4a^2b)$ is equivalent to:

F. $7a^6b^3$
G. $7a^8b^2$
H. $12a^6b^2$
J. $12a^6b^3$
K. $12a^8b^3$

★

3. Which of the following inequalities is equivalent to $-\frac{7x}{3} + 4 < 11$?

A. $x < -\frac{49}{3}$

B. $x < -\frac{28}{3}$

C. $x < -3$

D. $x > -3$

E. $x > 3$

★

4. Bill and Jasmine are baking cupcakes for a school bake sale. They start with 5 cups of sugar. Bill used $\frac{3}{4}$ cup of sugar and Jasmine used $1\frac{1}{2}$ cups of sugar. How much sugar was left after they baked their cupcakes?

F. $2\frac{1}{4}$

G. $2\frac{1}{2}$

H. $2\frac{3}{4}$

J. $3\frac{1}{2}$

K. $4\frac{1}{4}$

★

5. Susan bought a sweater for \$18.00. If this price included a 20% sales tax, how much was the tax?

A. \$0.90
B. \$1.80
C. \$3.00
D. \$3.60
E. \$4.50

★★

6. What is the value of $|-7|-|8-32|$?

F. -31
G. -17
H. 17
J. 31
K. 47

★

7. When a bowling ball is dropped onto a trampoline, the height to which the ball bounces is directly proportional to its initial height before it was dropped. If the bowling ball falls from an initial height of 20 feet, it bounces up to a height of 15 feet after hitting the trampoline for the first time. The ball would then fall from this height and bounce a second time. If this sequence continued, and the heights of each bounce were arranged in the order in which they occurred, the sequence would be:

A. arithmetic with common difference of 5 ft

B. arithmetic with common difference of –5 ft

C. geometric with common ratio of $\frac{3}{4}$

D. geometric with common ratio of $\frac{4}{3}$

E. neither arithmetic nor geometric

★★★

8. The ratio of red to blue to green marbles in a jar is 1 to 3 to 4, respectively. What fraction of the marbles in the jar is blue?

F. $\frac{1}{8}$

G. $\frac{1}{4}$

H. $\frac{3}{8}$

J. $\frac{1}{2}$

K. $\frac{5}{8}$

★

9. A square with a side length of 2 is inscribed in a circle so that its 4 vertexes lie on the circle's circumference. If a point is chosen at random within the circle, what is the probability that the point lies within the square?

A. $\frac{1}{2}$

B. $\frac{2}{\pi}$

C. $\frac{\pi}{3}$

D. $\frac{3\pi}{2}$

E. $\frac{3}{4}$

★★★

10. What is the least common multiple of 50, 90, and 130 ?

F. 90
G. 270
H. 585
J. 5850
K. 585,000

★★

11. Coach Harold must pick the starting point guard, center, shooting guard, and forward from a team of 13 students. If he already knows that Rachel will be the starting point guard, how many different lineups could he choose for the remaining positions?

A. 33
B. 36
C. 1320
D. 1716
E. 17160

★★

12. What is the solution to matrix equation below?

$$\begin{bmatrix} 2x & 4 & x \\ 4x & 6 & 2x \end{bmatrix} + \begin{bmatrix} -x & -4 & -x \\ 4x & 2 & x \end{bmatrix} = ?$$

F. $12x + 8$

G. $\begin{bmatrix} -x & 2 \\ 2x & -4 \\ 4x & 6 \end{bmatrix}$

H. $\begin{bmatrix} -2x^2 & -16 & x^2 \\ 16x^2 & 12 & 2x^2 \end{bmatrix}$

J. $\begin{bmatrix} 3x & 8 & 2x \\ 8x & 8 & 3x \end{bmatrix}$

K. $\begin{bmatrix} x & 0 & 0 \\ 8x & 8 & 3x \end{bmatrix}$

13. If $753 \times 10^x = 0.000753$, what is x ?

A. −4
B. −5
C. −6
D. −7
E. −8

★★

14. Which of the following statements is a logical conclusion from the 3 true statements given below?

All flarps are peeps.
All droops are peeps.
All shirps are flarps.

F. No droops are flarps.
G. No droops are shirps.
H. All shirps are peeps.
J. All droops are flarps.
K. All flarps are droops.

★★★

15. If $\sqrt{-45x} - 3\sqrt{-5x} = \sqrt{x}$, then $x = ?$

A. 0
B. 2
C. 3
D. 5
E. 9

★★★

The Arithmetic Short List

1 Exponents

Quick facts

When you **multiply** like bases, **add** the exponents.

When you **divide** like bases, **subtract** the exponents.

When you **don't** have like bases, try to **get 'em**.

If you **can't** get like bases, **let 'em be**.

Use your calculator to refresh on exponent rules during the test!

2 Inequalities

If you **divide or multiply by a negative....**

3 Percentages

To take 20% off a number, just **multiply by .8!**

$$\textbf{\% Change} = \frac{\text{(New number} - \text{Old number)}}{\text{Old number}} \times 100$$

4 Absolute Value

Every equation with an absolute value is actually **two equations.**

5 Sequences

Quick facts

Geometric sequences – **multiply or divide** to get the next term

Arithmetic sequences – **add or subtract** to get the next term

Looooong sequences – **find the repeat!**

6 Probability

$$\frac{\text{\# of outcomes that meet the requirements}}{\text{Total \# of possible outcomes}}$$

7 Ratios

To turn a ratio into a fraction, find the **total number** of parts

1. add the parts
2. put the total in the denominator
3. circle your fraction

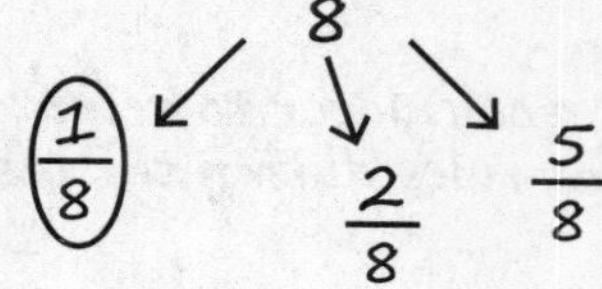

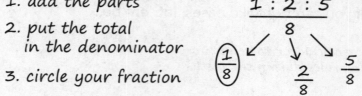

8 Matrix

When you **multiply matrices**, your result is a **bigger matrix.**
When you **add/subtract matrices**, your result is the same size.

$$\begin{bmatrix} a \\ b \\ c \end{bmatrix} \times \begin{bmatrix} -1 & 0 & 1 \end{bmatrix} = \begin{bmatrix} -a & 0 & a \\ -b & 0 & b \\ -c & 0 & c \end{bmatrix}$$

9 Scientific Notation

A **positive exponent** kicks the decimal to the right.
A **negative exponent** kicks the decimal to the left.

10 Combinations

Draw a **slot** for every **decision** you have to make.
Write the **number of options** for each slot.
Multiply the slots!

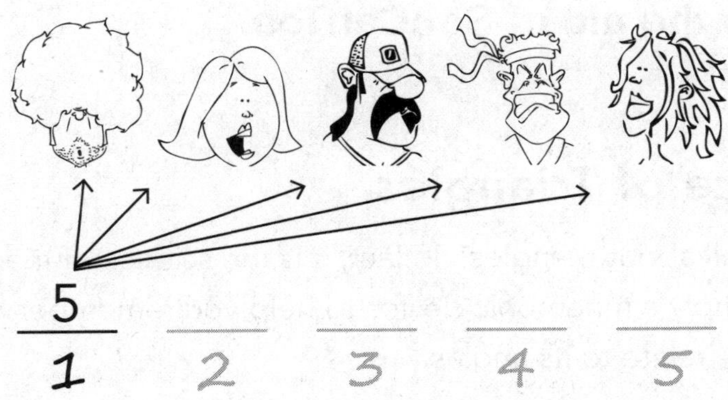

5
___ ___ ___ ___ ___
1 2 3 4 5

11 Square Roots

Quick facts

You can **multiply** two square roots together.

$$\sqrt{3} \times \sqrt{6} = \sqrt{18}$$

To **simplify** square roots, **factor out** a perfect square.

$$\sqrt{18} = \sqrt{9} \times \sqrt{2}$$
$$\sqrt{18} = 3\sqrt{2}$$

To get rid of a **negative** beneath a square root, **factor out an *i*.**

$$\sqrt{-7} = i\sqrt{7}$$
$$\sqrt{-8} = 2i\sqrt{2}$$

SohCahToa

In most cases, you will face four Trigonometry questions on the ACT. At least two of these can be solved by simply calling upon the aid of SohCahToa.

The Science of Triangles

Trigonometry is all about triangles. In fact, it is the science of triangles. **SohCahToa** is simply a mnemonic device to help you remember the way the sides of a triangle relate to its angles.

Let's begin with our beloved right triangle.
We have 3 angles and 3 sides:

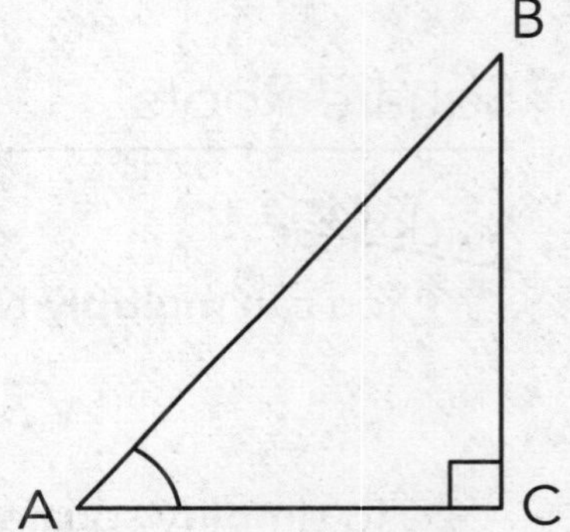

	Angles	Sides
1.	$\angle A$	$\overline{BC}$
2.	$\angle B$	$\overline{AC}$
3.	$\angle C$	$\overline{AB}$

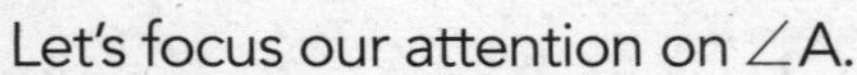

"Adjacent" is just another word for "touching."

Your angle in a trig problem will always be formed by an adjacent side and the hypotenuse.

Let's focus our attention on $\angle A$.
We can describe the way each side relates to $\angle A$ by giving the sides new names:

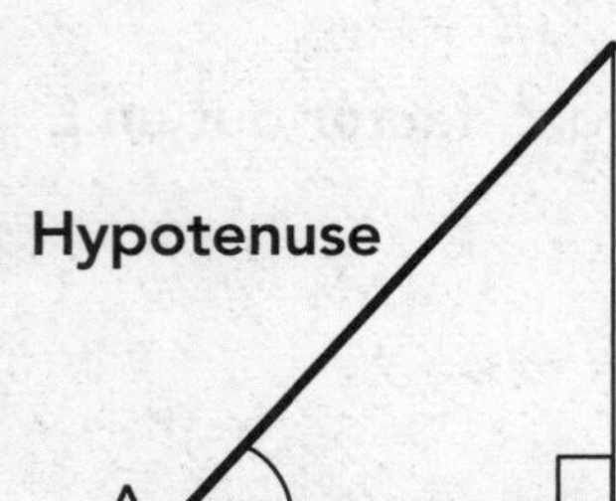

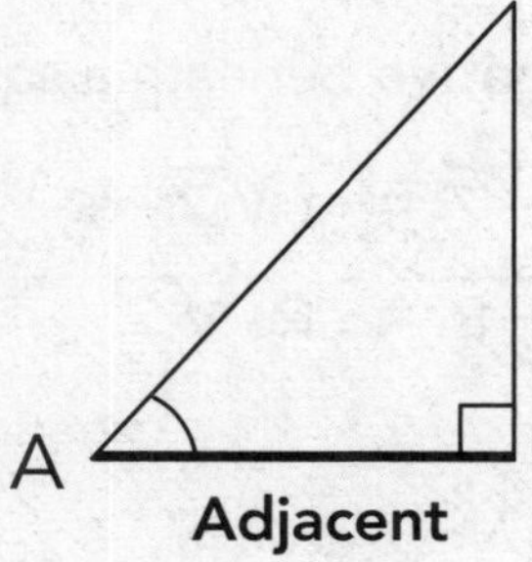

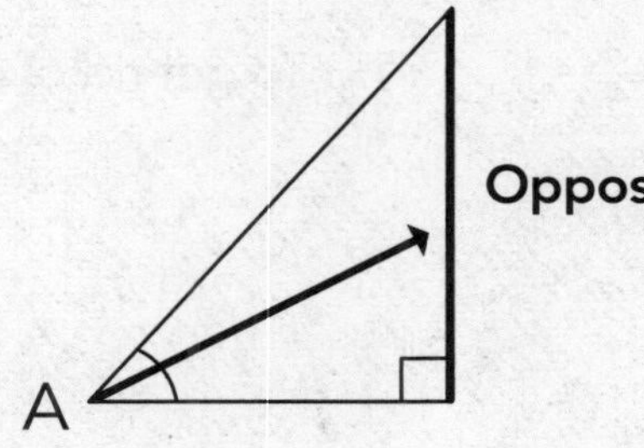

the **hypotenuse**, the side **adjacent** to $\angle A$, and the side **opposite** $\angle A$.

Once you get used to these new names, you can start working some trig magic.

Sine, Cosine, and Tangent

When the ACT authors talk about the **sin**, **cos**, or **tan** of an angle in a triangle, they are actually talking about the relationship between the *sides* of the triangle:

sin We get the **Sine** of ∠A when we divide the side **Opposite** ∠A by the **Hypotenuse.**

cos We get the **Cosine** of ∠A when we divide the side **Adjacent** ∠A by the **Hypotenuse.**

tan We get the **Tangent** of ∠A when we divide the side **Opposite** ∠A by the side **Adjacent** ∠A.

If you see sin, cos, or tan in your problem, you can be sure that you're in the world of trigonometry!

If this seems complicated, never fear! You need only memorize one super word:

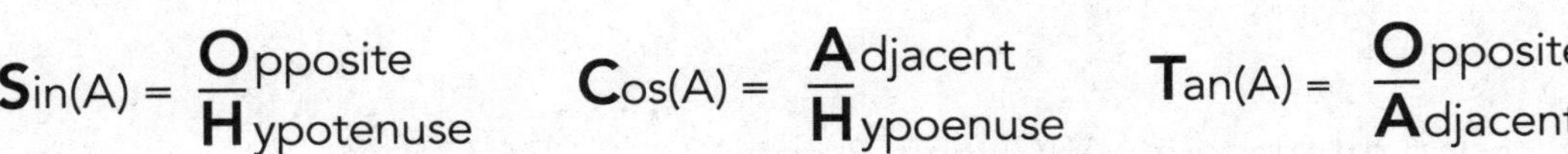

SohCahToa to the rescue! Write this word down as soon as you spot a trig problem.

SohCahToa in Action

To see SohCahToa in action, let's use the Big Daddy of all right triangles, our old friend: 3, 4, 5.

$$\text{Sine}\angle A = \frac{\text{Opposite}}{\text{Hypotenuse}} = \frac{3}{5}$$

$$\text{Cosine}\angle A = \frac{\text{Adjacent}}{\text{Hypotenuse}} = \frac{4}{5}$$

$$\text{Tangent}\angle A = \frac{\text{Opposite}}{\text{Adjacent}} = \frac{3}{4}$$

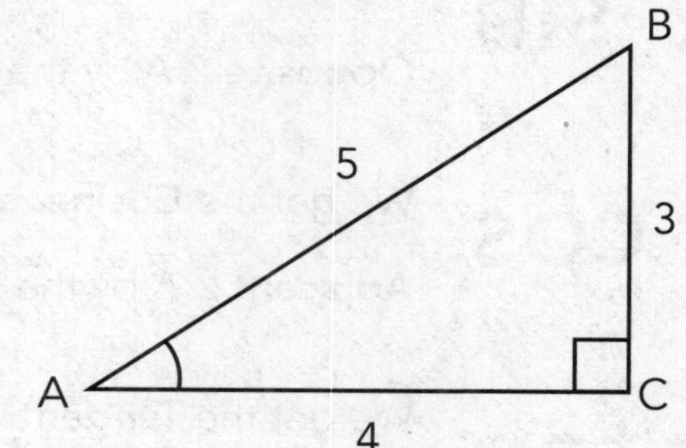

If you were asked for Sin, Cos, or Tan values of ∠B instead of ∠A, no problem! Your opposite and adjacent sides switch, but the hypotenuse stays constant:

$\text{Sin}\angle B = \frac{4}{5}$ $\text{Cos}\angle B = \frac{3}{5}$ $\text{Tan}\angle B = \frac{4}{3}$

Now let's practice using SohCahToa to solve some common ACT trig problems.

Simple Pythagorean Theorem

Many SohCahToa problems require you to first use the pythagorean theorem to find a missing side.

E1 For right triangle ΔABC, what is cos A?

A. $\frac{7}{11}$

B. $\frac{11}{7}$

C. $\frac{7}{\sqrt{72}}$

D. $\frac{\sqrt{72}}{7}$

E. $\frac{\sqrt{72}}{11}$

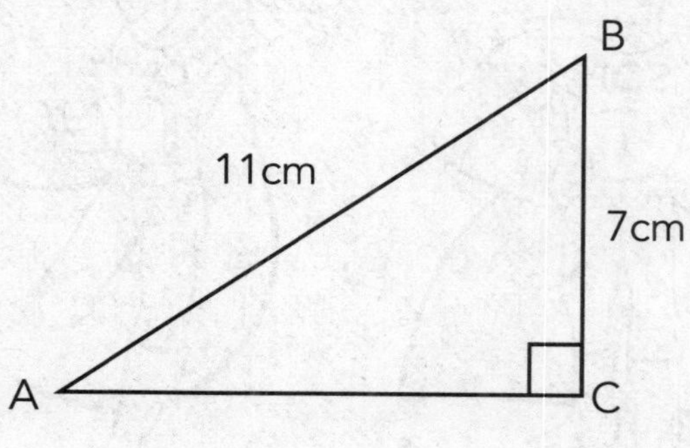

S *Since we see a trig word, we should immediately write down SohCahToa. We are looking for* **cos**, *so we focus on* **Cah**.

$$\text{Cos}(A) = \frac{\textbf{A}\text{djacent}}{\textbf{H}\text{ypotenuse}}$$

We need ***adjacent*** *and* ***hypotenuse****! We know that the hypotenuse is* **11**, *but we need to use Pythag's theorem to find our missing adjacent side:*

$$a^2 + b^2 = c^2$$
$$a^2 + 7^2 = 11^2$$
$$a^2 + 49 = 121$$
$$a^2 = 72$$
$$a = \sqrt{72}$$

Now we have our missing side. To finish up, we simply need to drop our side lengths into SohCahToa:

$$\text{Cos}(A) = \frac{\textbf{A}}{\textbf{H}} = \frac{\sqrt{72}}{11}$$

E *is our answer!*

Hidden Right Triangles

Sometimes the right triangle in a SohCahToa problem is not readily apparent.

You will need to draw the right triangle, which may be as simple as dropping a line and completing a partial shape.

These questions can come in a number of different forms. Just remember: if you see **sin**, **cos**, or **tan**, there must be a triangle hiding somewhere!

Hidden Triangles: Coordinate Systems

Whenever you are dealing with a coordinate system, a triangle is staring you right in the face!

E2 In the figure below, $\sin \theta = ?$

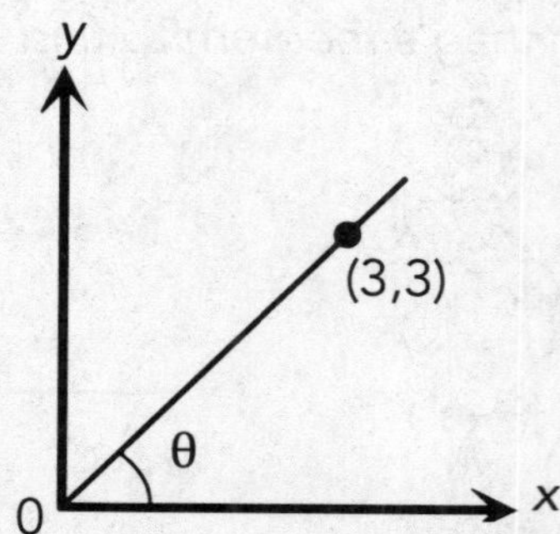

F. 9

G. $3\sqrt{2}$

H. 3

J. $\sqrt{2}$

K. $\frac{\sqrt{2}}{2}$

Dropping a straight line to an axis creates a right triangle.

S *We can't work any SohCahToa magic until we have a right triangle. Luckily, there's always one hiding in a coordinate system.*

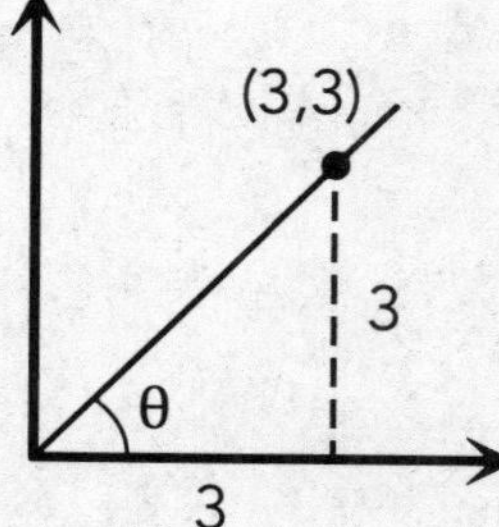

By dropping a line to the x-axis, we have a right triangle with two sides of length 3.

Because this is a 45°– 45°– 90° right triangle, we know that our missing hypotenuse is $\mathbf{3\sqrt{2}}$.

Now we turn to ***SohCahToa*** *to finish the job.*

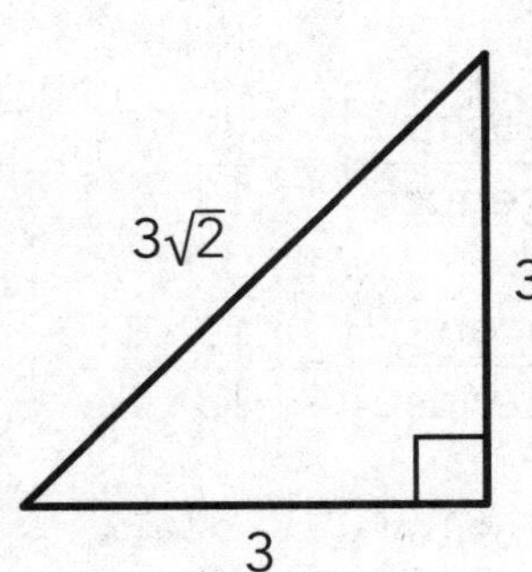

$$\text{Sin } \theta = \frac{\text{Opposite}}{\text{Hypotenuse}} = \frac{3}{3\sqrt{2}} = \frac{1}{\sqrt{2}}$$

We need to clean up that radical in the denominator by multiplying our term by $\frac{\sqrt{2}}{\sqrt{2}}$

$$\frac{1\,(\sqrt{2})}{\sqrt{2}\,(\sqrt{2})} = \frac{\sqrt{2}}{\sqrt{4}} = \boxed{\frac{\sqrt{2}}{2}}$$

K is our answer!

Hidden Triangles: Draw from Scratch

Often the ACT writers will describe a triangle and leave the drawing up to you.

The variable "θ" is often used instead of *x* when speaking about angles. You can read it as "theta" or simply "an angle."

An angle in a right triangle has measure θ. If $\cos \theta = \frac{12}{13}$ and $\sin \theta = \frac{5}{13}$, then $\tan \theta = ?$

A. $\frac{5}{12}$

B. $\frac{12}{13}$

C. $\frac{5}{\sqrt{119}}$

D. $\frac{5}{\sqrt{119}}$

E. $\frac{12}{5}$

S *We can use SohCahToa to draw and label our triangle:*

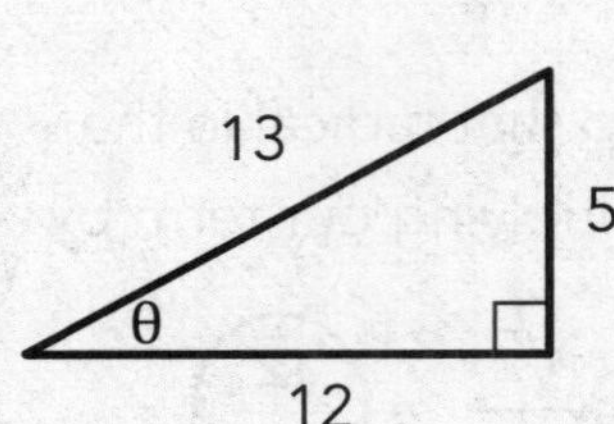

$$\text{Sin } \theta = \frac{\text{Opposite}}{\text{Hypotenuse}} = \frac{5}{13}$$

$$\text{Cos } \theta = \frac{\text{Adjacent}}{\text{Hypotenuse}} = \frac{12}{13}$$

$$\text{Tan } \theta = \frac{\text{Opposite}}{\text{Adjacent}} = \frac{?}{?}$$

To find **tan θ**, *we can simply apply SohCahToa to our triangle:*

$$\textbf{T}\text{an } \theta = \frac{\textbf{O}\text{pposite}}{\textbf{A}\text{djacent}} = \boxed{\frac{5}{12}}$$

A is our answer!

E4 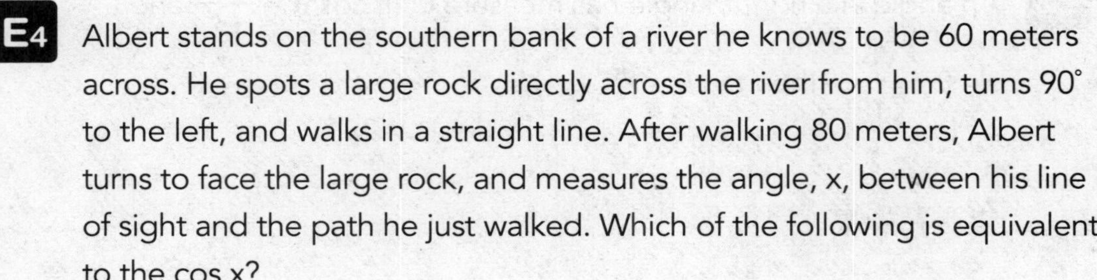
Albert stands on the southern bank of a river he knows to be 60 meters across. He spots a large rock directly across the river from him, turns 90° to the left, and walks in a straight line. After walking 80 meters, Albert turns to face the large rock, and measures the angle, x, between his line of sight and the path he just walked. Which of the following is equivalent to the cos x?

F. $\frac{4}{5}$

G. $\frac{5}{4}$

H. $\frac{\sqrt{80}}{13}$

J. $\frac{5}{32}$

K. $\frac{10}{\sqrt{80}}$

S *We need to get busy drawing! Let's take it line by line: Albert stands on the southern bank of a river he knows to be 60 meters across.*

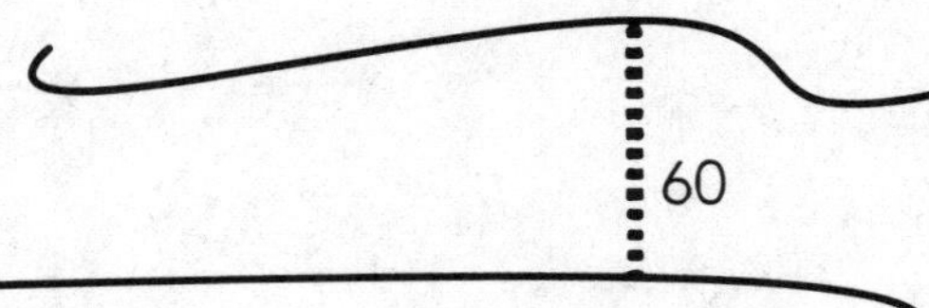

He spots a large rock directly across the river from him, turns 90° to the left, and walks in a straight line.

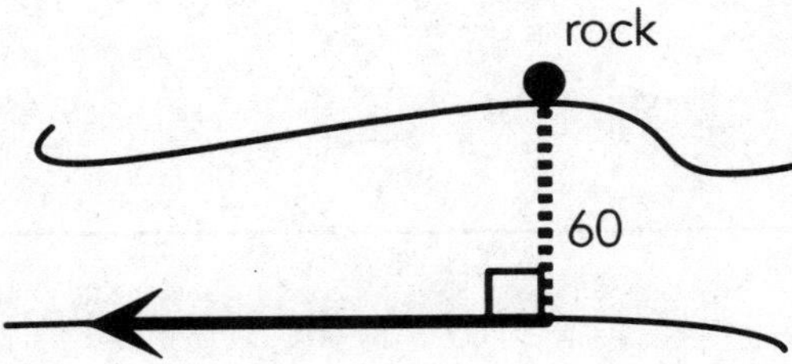

After walking 80 meters, Albert turns to face the large rock and measures the angle, x, between his line of sight and the path he just walked.

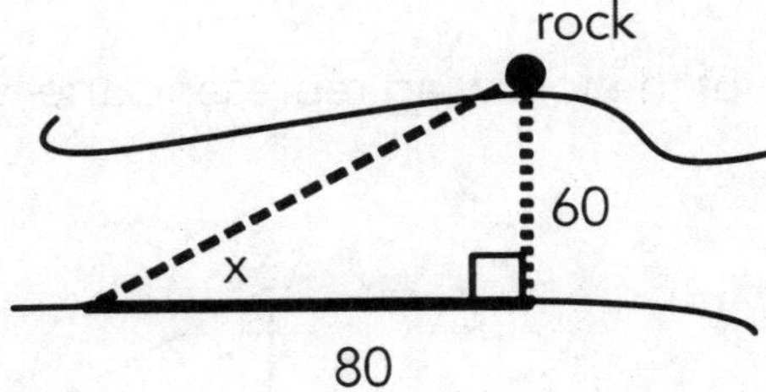

And now we have our triangle!

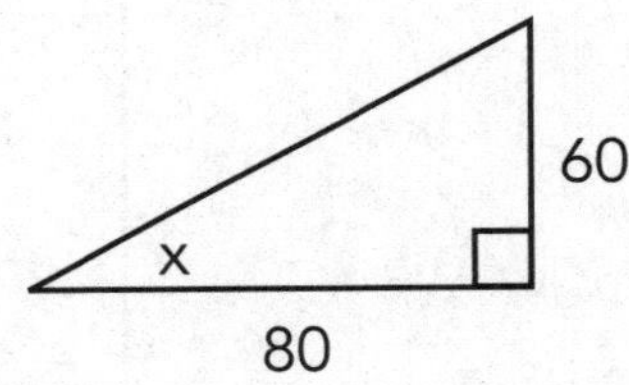

To solve for **cos x** *we need to find the hypotenuse.*

Let's look to Pythagoras for some help here:

$$A^2 + B^2 = C^2$$
$$60^2 + 80^2 = C^2$$
$$3600 + 6400 = C^2$$
$$10000 = C^2$$
$$\sqrt{10000} = C$$
$$100 = C$$

Now we can find ***cos x***

$$\text{Cos}(x) = \frac{\text{Adjacent Side}}{\text{Hypotenuse}} = \frac{80}{100} = \frac{8}{10} = \frac{4}{5}$$

***F** is our answer!*

Alternately we could have seen our trusty 3, 4, 5 hiding behind the scenes. 3, 4, 5 is a slight step from 6, 8, 10, which is only a hop away from 60, 80, 100.

Solving for Sides

When you are given an angle and asked to solve for a side, you can use **sin**, **cos**, and **tan** as variables in an equation.

E5 For the polygon below, which of the following represents the length, in meters, of $\overline{AB}$?

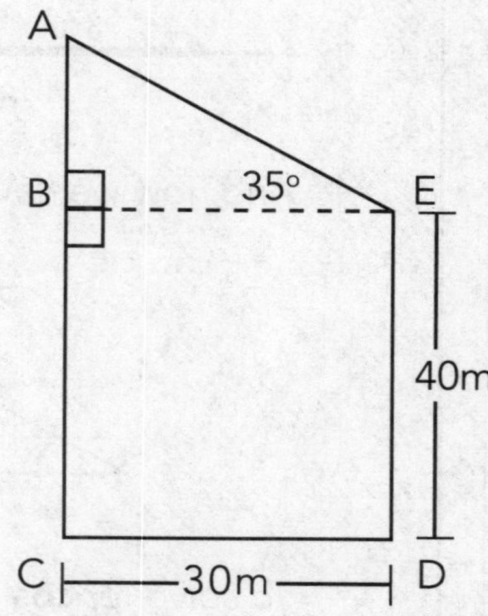

A. 30

B. 50

C. 30 tan 35°

D. $\frac{40}{\tan 35^\circ}$

E. tan 35°

S *I see the word **tan**: clearly, we are playing the triangle game. Let's isolate our triangle and fill in what we know.*

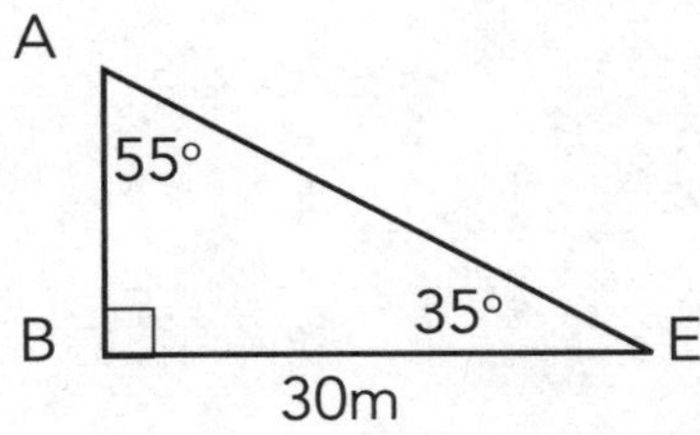

*We can pull up the **30m** from $\overline{CD}$ to give us the length of $\overline{BE}$. But we still do not know $\overline{AB}$ or $\overline{AE}$.*

SohCahToa, you're our only hope!

*Looking at the answer choices, it's clear **tan 35°** may play a role.*

$$\text{Tan (E)} = \frac{\text{Opposite Side}}{\text{Adjacent Side}} \qquad \text{Tan } (35°) = \frac{\overline{AB}}{30}$$

Aha!! *So we are solving for $\overline{AB}$. Let's isolate $\overline{AB}$ in our equation.*

30 tan 35° = AB ***C is our answer!***

Playing with SohCahToa

Sometimes, the test writers will play with SohCahToa rules directly.

E6 Which of the following is equivalent to $\tan\theta \times \cos\theta$?

F. $\sin\theta$

G. $\dfrac{\sin^2\theta}{\cos\theta}$

H. $\dfrac{\sin\theta}{\cos\theta}$

J. 1

K. $\dfrac{1}{\sin\theta}$

We don't need no stinking triangle! We see **tan** and **cos** and we know exactly who to send in. Sock it to 'em, SohCahToa!

S *We are looking for* **tan** θ × **cos** θ AKA:

$$\frac{\textbf{O}\text{pposite}}{\textbf{A}\text{djacent}} \times \frac{\textbf{A}\text{djacent}}{\textbf{H}\text{ypotenuse}}$$

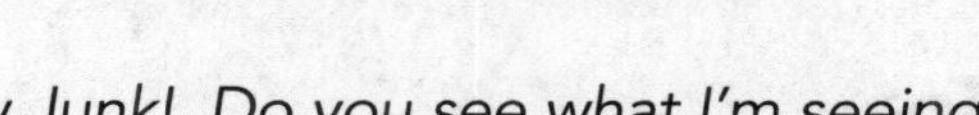

Awww Junk! Do you see what I'm seeing?

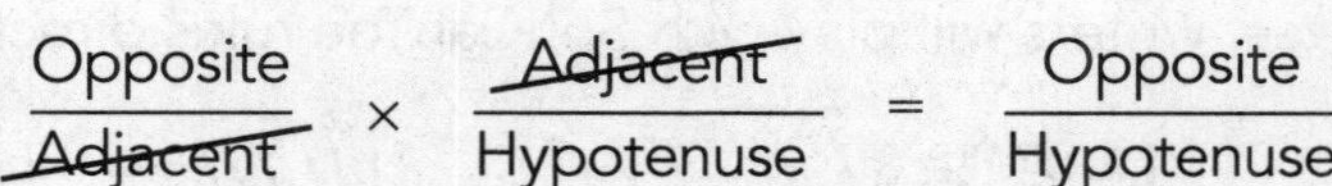

$$\frac{\text{Opposite}}{\cancel{\text{Adjacent}}} \times \frac{\cancel{\text{Adjacent}}}{\text{Hypotenuse}} = \frac{\text{Opposite}}{\text{Hypotenuse}}$$

(Awww Junk)^2*! I can see the* **Sin** $= \dfrac{\textbf{O}\text{pposite}}{\textbf{H}\text{ypotenuse}}$

So $\tan\theta \times \cos\theta =$ **sin θ**.

If it helps with the problem, you can always replace **tan** with $\frac{\sin}{\cos}$.

Shortcut Alert

There is a handy identity that can save you time on the test:

$$\boxed{\tan\theta = \frac{\sin\theta}{\cos\theta}} = \frac{\frac{\mathbf{O}}{\mathbf{H}}}{\frac{\mathbf{A}}{\mathbf{H}}} = \frac{O}{\cancel{H}} \times \frac{\cancel{H}}{A} = \frac{O}{A} = \tan\theta$$

SohCahToa Practice Problems

1. For the right triangle ΔABC, what is $\sin \angle A$?

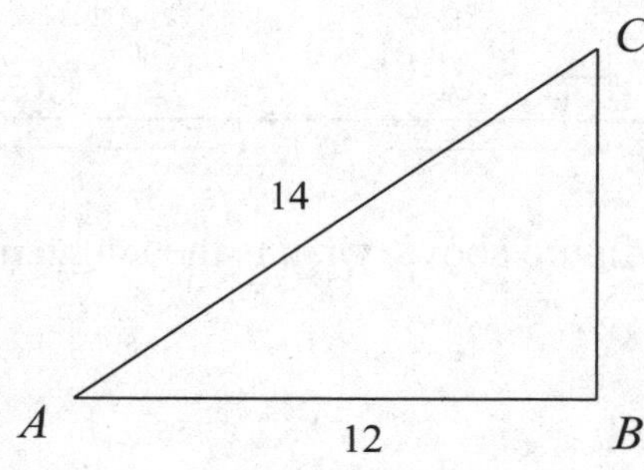

A. $\frac{12}{14}$

B. $\frac{14}{12}$

C. $\frac{\sqrt{52}}{12}$

D. $\frac{12}{\sqrt{52}}$

E. $\frac{\sqrt{52}}{14}$

★★

---

2. A right triangle has an angle of b. If $\tan b = \frac{12}{5}$ and $\cos b = \frac{5}{13}$, which of the following is equivalent to $\sin b$?

F. $\frac{12}{13}$

G. $\frac{5}{12}$

H. $\frac{5}{\sqrt{119}}$

J. $\frac{5}{\sqrt{313}}$

K. $\frac{13}{5}$

★★

3. In the figure below, what is $\cos \theta$?

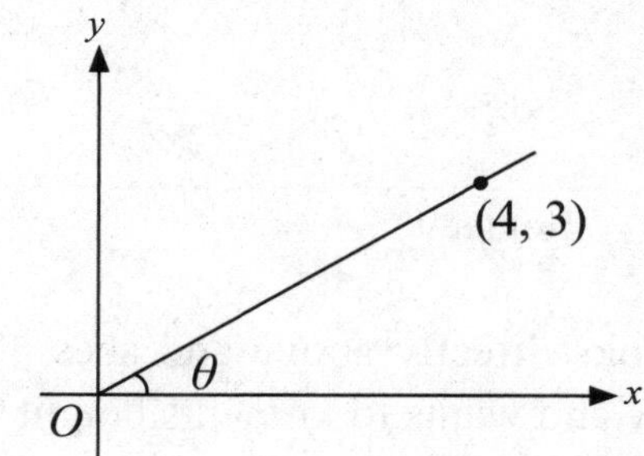

A. $\frac{3}{4}$

B. $\frac{4}{3}$

C. $\frac{5}{3}$

D. $\frac{3}{5}$

E. $\frac{4}{5}$

★★

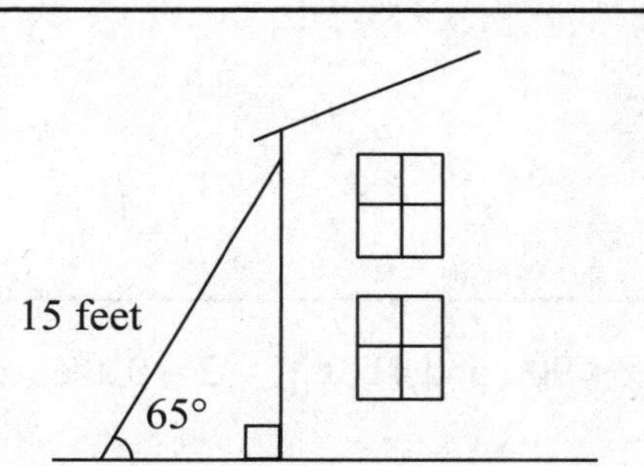

4. A 15-foot-tall ladder leans against a house at a 65° angle, as show above. Which of the following expressions gives the height, in feet, at which the ladder touches the house?

F. $15 \sin 65°$

G. $15 \cos 65°$

H. $15 \tan 65°$

J. $\frac{15}{\sin 65°}$

K. $\frac{15}{\tan 65°}$

★★

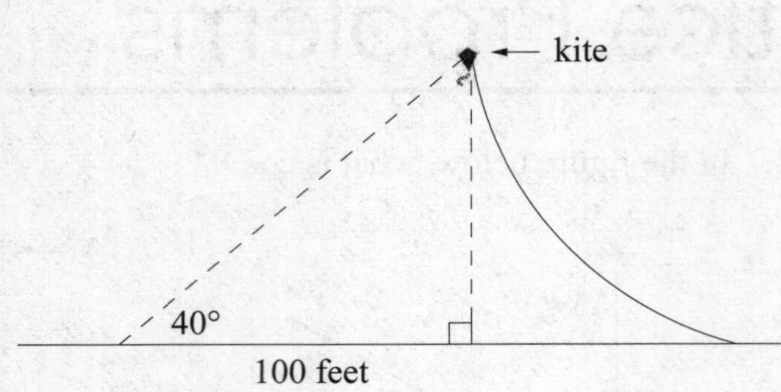

5. Susan looks directly above and sees a kite in the sky and wants to know its height. She walks 100 feet away from the kite and then faces the kite again. She measures the angle between her line of sight and the ground and finds it to be 40°, as shown above. Which of the following is the closest measurement, in feet, of the the height of the kite?

(Note: $\sin 40° \approx 0.67$, $\cos 40° \approx 0.77$, $\tan 40° \approx 0.84$)

A. 67
B. 84
C. 77
D. 134
E. 148

6. If $0° < x < 90°$, and $4 \cos x° - 2 = 0$, then $x° = ?$

F. 0°
G. 15°
H. 30°
J. 45°
K. 60°

★★★

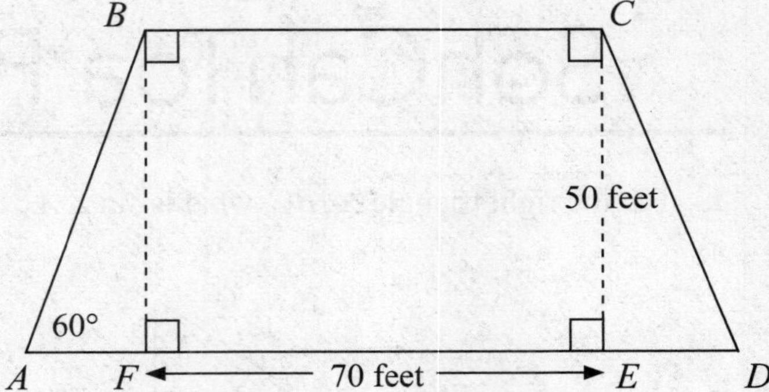

7. In the figure above, what is the length, in feet, of $\overline{AF}$?

A. 50

B. 20

C. $\frac{50}{\tan 60°}$

D. $\frac{20}{\tan 60°}$

E. $\tan 60°$

8. The figure below shows the dimensions of a right triangle. Which of the following is equivalent to $\tan \theta \times \cos \theta$?

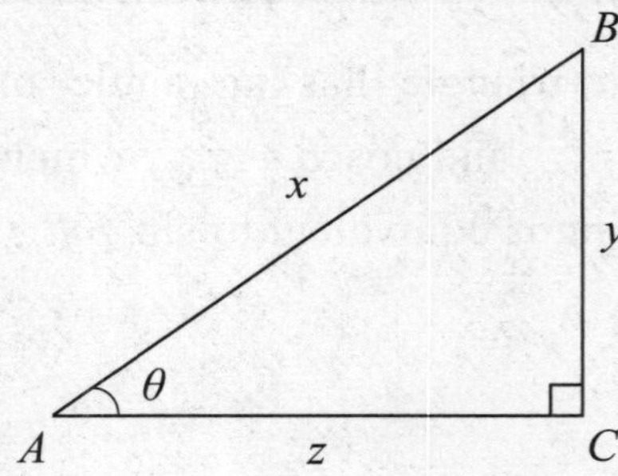

F. $\frac{y}{x}$

G. $\frac{x}{y}$

H. $\frac{z^2}{yx}$

J. $\frac{yz}{x}$

K. $\frac{x}{yz}$

★★★

9. A national park wants to build an observation deck so that its visitors can enjoy a full view of a 15-mile-long mountain range through their binoculars. The binoculars have a fixed setting that requires them to be placed at a certain distance from an object in order for that object to be in focus. The observation deck is placed directly in front of the mountain range, as shown in the diagram below. What is the distance, in miles, between the observation deck and the mountain range?

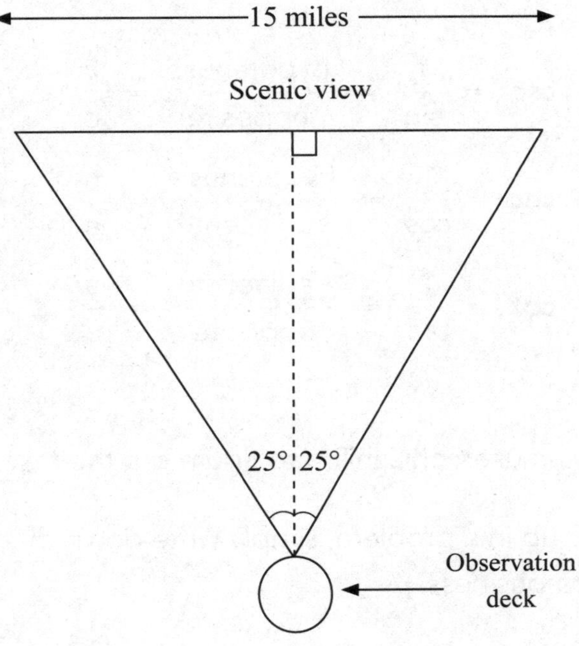

A. $\frac{7.5}{\tan 25°}$

B. $\frac{7.5}{\tan 50°}$

C. $7.5 \tan 25°$

D. $7.5 \tan 50°$

E. $15 \tan 25°$

★★★

10. A power line connects a house with a transformer across the street, as shown in the diagram below. The power line is attached to the top of a 1-foot mast on the house's roof, and connects to the transformer at a point that is level with the base of the roof. Given the measurements in the diagram below, what is the length of the power line?

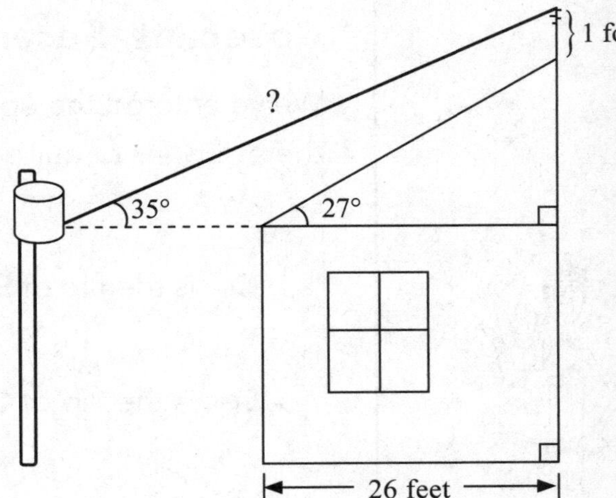

F. $\frac{\tan 35° + 1}{26 \cos 27°}$

G. $26 \tan 27°$

H. $\frac{\tan 27° + 1}{26 \sin 35°}$

J. $26(\tan 27°)(\sin 35°)$

K. $\frac{26 \tan 27° + 1}{\sin 35°}$

★★★

Advanced Trig Identities

The ACT writers will occasionally test your knowledge of some more advanced trig identities. Memorize these and you'll be fine.

Cosecant, Secant, and Cotangent

We've entered the upside-down world of Csc, Sec, and Cot! Think of these as the evil twins of our good friends Sin, Cos, and Tan:

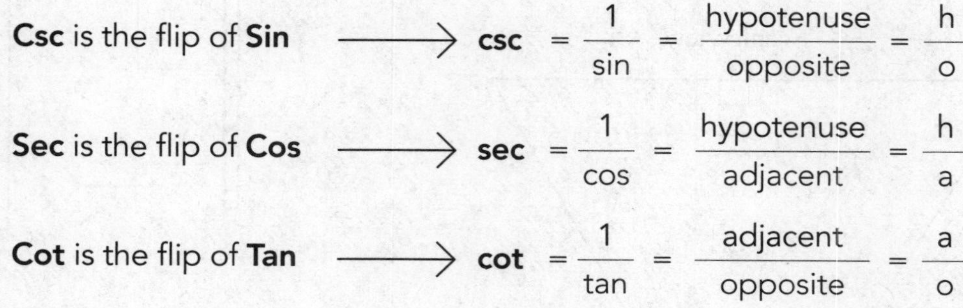
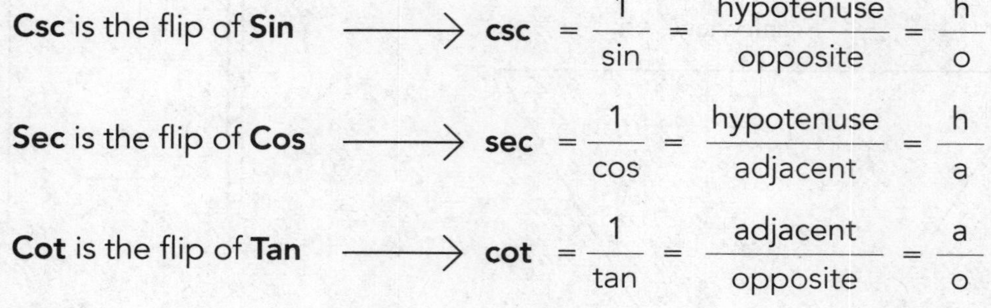

Csc is the flip of **Sin** $\longrightarrow$ $\textbf{csc} = \frac{1}{\text{sin}} = \frac{\text{hypotenuse}}{\text{opposite}} = \frac{\text{h}}{\text{o}}$

Sec is the flip of **Cos** $\longrightarrow$ $\textbf{sec} = \frac{1}{\text{cos}} = \frac{\text{hypotenuse}}{\text{adjacent}} = \frac{\text{h}}{\text{a}}$

Cot is the flip of **Tan** $\longrightarrow$ $\textbf{cot} = \frac{1}{\text{tan}} = \frac{\text{adjacent}}{\text{opposite}} = \frac{\text{a}}{\text{o}}$

Be careful! Although it would be nice if Cosecant was the flip of Cosine, this is not the case!

Once you memorize your flips, you can use SohCahToa to figure out the rest.

If you see any of these evil twins pop up in a problem, simply write down the "flips" and go about your SohCahToa business.

Cos

Sec

E1 A certain rectangle, shown below, has a length of a inches, width of b inches, diagonal of c inches, and angle measurement x°. Which of the following trigonometric equations is valid?

A. $\csc x = \frac{c}{a}$

B. $\sec x = \frac{a}{b}$

C. $\cot x = \frac{a}{b}$

D. $\sin x = \frac{c}{a}$

E. $\tan x = \frac{b}{c}$

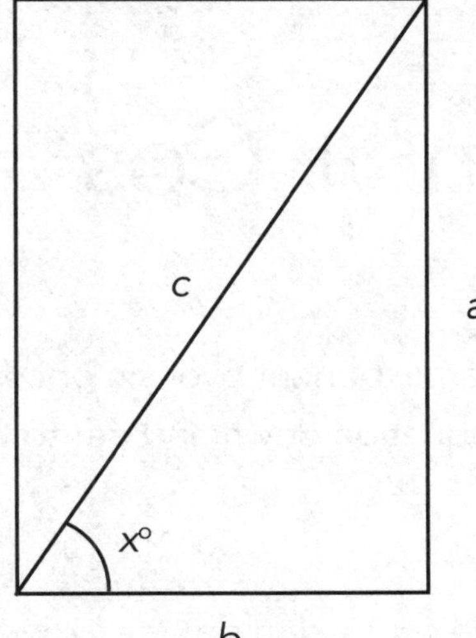

S *Before we do anything else, we should label our sides. Focusing on angle x, our sides are:*

Opposite: ***a*** *Adjacent:* ***b*** *Hypotenuse:* ***c***

Now we're set up for SohCahToa. But wait! I see **csc**, **sec**, *and* **cot** *in the answer choices. We'll need to get rid of these evil twins.*

We can change Choice A from **csc x** *to* **sin x** *if we flip the other side of the equation as well.*

$\csc x = \frac{c}{a}$

$\sin x = \frac{a}{c}$

Much better! SohCahToa tells us that **sin x** *is* $\frac{\text{opposite}}{\text{hypotenuse}} = \frac{a}{c}$!

Choice ***A*** *is correct!*

$\text{Sin}^2 + \text{Cos}^2 = 1$

Anytime you see **Sin²** or **Cos²**, you can bet your money the ACT writers are testing your knowledge of this ancient equation:

$$\text{Sin}^2 + \text{Cos}^2 =$$

If you see an exponent over sin or cos, write this equation down and get to work!

E2 The expression $\sin^2\theta - (25 - \cos^2\theta)$ is equivalent to:

F. −26
G. −25
H. −24
J. 24
K. 26

S *I see* **Sin²** *and* **Cos²**! *Ain't no doubt about it:* ***Sin² + Cos² = 1***. *Let's start things off by distributing that negative:*

$$\sin^2\theta - (25 - \cos^2\theta)$$
$$\sin^2\theta + \cos^2\theta - (25)$$

Now we can apply our rule: ***Sin² + Cos² = 1***.

$$(\sin^2\theta + \cos^2\theta) - 25$$
$$(1) - 25 = \boxed{-24}$$

H *is our answer!*

E3 The expression $\dfrac{(\sin^4\theta - \cos^4\theta)}{(\sin^2\theta - \cos^2\theta)}$ is equivalent to:

A. 2
B. 1
C. $\sin\theta - \cos\theta$
D. $\sin^2\theta - \cos^2\theta$
E. Cannot be determined from the given information

S *The test writers are surely calling into play* ***Sin² + Cos² = 1****.* *On top of this, they are layering another classic. Did you see it?* **The Difference Of Squares!** *Here's a quick refresher:*

DIFFERENCE OF SQUARES:

$$x^2 - y^2 = (x + y)(x - y)$$
$$64x^2 - 49y^2 = (8x + 7y)(8x - 7y)$$
$$A^4 - B^4 = (A^2 + B^2)(A^2 - B^2)$$

Now let's see how the D.O.S. helps here:

$$\frac{(\text{Sin}^4\theta - \text{Cos}^4\theta)}{(\text{Sin}^2\theta - \text{Cos}^2\theta)} = \frac{(\text{Sin}^2\theta + \text{Cos}^2\theta) \times (\text{Sin}^2\theta - \text{Cos}^2\theta)}{(\text{Sin}^2\theta - \text{Cos}^2\theta)}$$

Look at those like terms! Let's work our magic!

$$\frac{(\text{Sin}^2\theta + \text{Cos}^2\theta) \times \cancel{(\text{Sin}^2\theta - \text{Cos}^2\theta)}}{\cancel{(\text{Sin}^2\theta - \text{Cos}^2\theta)}}$$

$$\frac{(\text{Sin}^2\theta + \text{Cos}^2\theta)}{1} = \frac{1}{1} = \textcircled{1}$$

And that's our favorite trig identity!

B *is our answer!*

Whenever you see a squared term subtracted from another squared term, the D.O.S is never far behind!

Inverse Trig Functions

The ACT writers sometimes ask you to use SohCahToa in reverse. You can spot these questions by $\mathbf{sin^{-1}}$, $\mathbf{cos^{-1}}$, $\mathbf{tan^{-1}}$, or **arcsin, arccos, arctan**.

Arcsin and $\sin^{-1}$ are just two names for the same thing.

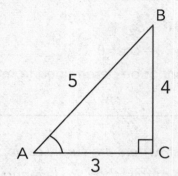

$$\sin \angle A = \frac{4}{5}$$

$$\sin^{-1}\left(\frac{4}{5}\right) = A$$

$$\arcsin\left(\frac{4}{5}\right) = A$$

$$\sin^{-1}\left(\frac{3}{5}\right) = B \qquad \arccos\left(\frac{3}{5}\right) = A \qquad \tan^{-1}\left(\frac{3}{4}\right) = B$$

Notice that if you see inverse trig functions you still use SohCahToa! Just remember to work backwards!

E4 A seaplane departs from an island and rises at a fixed angle of ascent ($x°$) so that the plane will reach a height of 20,000 feet when the plane has flown 30 miles from the island, as illustrated in the figure below. Which of the following expressions gives the angle of ascent? (Note: 1 mile = 5,280 feet)

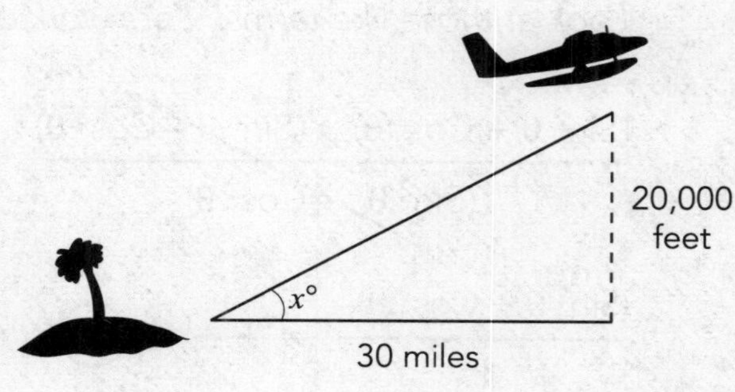

F. $\arcsin\left(\dfrac{20{,}000}{30(5{,}280)}\right)$

G. $\arccos\left(\dfrac{20{,}000}{30(5{,}280)}\right)$

H. $\arctan\left(\dfrac{30(5{,}280)}{20{,}000}\right)$

J. $\arctan\left(\dfrac{20{,}000}{30(5{,}280)}\right)$

K. $\arcsin\left(\dfrac{30}{20{,}000}\right)$

*When you see junk like **arcsin** or **cos⁻¹**, you know you're dealing with a simple SohCahToa problem, with a minor twist.*

*In this case, we're given the side **O**pposite our angle (20,000 feet) and **A**djacent to our angle (30 miles). We are most likely in tangent land.*

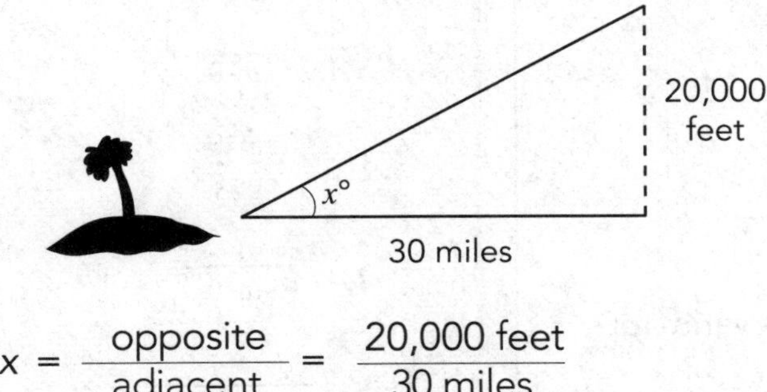

$$\tan x = \frac{\text{opposite}}{\text{adjacent}} = \frac{20{,}000 \text{ feet}}{30 \text{ miles}}$$

To convert all our units to feet, we can multiply 30 by 5,280.

$$\tan x = \boxed{\frac{20{,}000}{30\,(5{,}280)}}$$

Looking at our answer choices, this looks just like choice J! ***Arctan*** *(aka* ***tan⁻¹****) is simply the inverse of tangent. All the parts are the same, they just come in a different order:*

$$\tan(x) = \frac{20{,}000}{30\,(5{,}280)} \qquad \arctan\left(\frac{20{,}000}{30\,(5{,}280)}\right) = x$$

***J** is our answer!*

Time Saver!
A quick glance at the answer choices can give you an idea of where to start!

Advanced Trig Identities Practice Problems

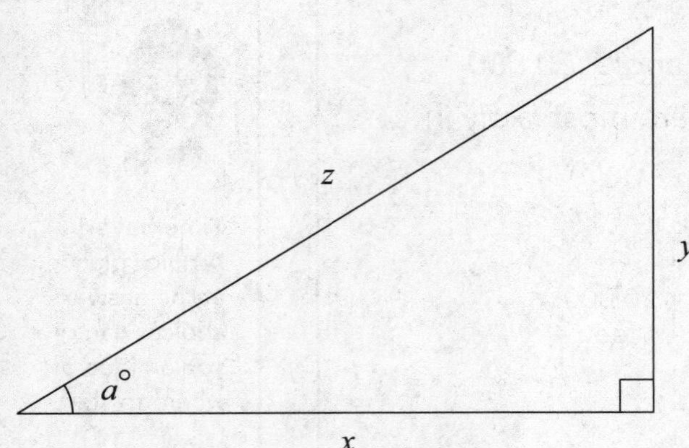

1. Which trigonometric equation is valid for the right triangle shown above?

A. $\cos a = \frac{y}{z}$

B. $\cot a = \frac{y}{x}$

C. $\sec a = \frac{x}{y}$

D. $\csc a = \frac{z}{y}$

E. $\tan a = \frac{x}{y}$

★★★

2. Whenever $\frac{\sec \theta}{\tan \theta}$ is defined, it is equivalent to:

F. $\frac{1}{\cos \theta}$

G. $\frac{1}{\sin \theta}$

H. $\frac{\sin^2 \theta}{\cos \theta}$

J. $\frac{1}{\sin^2 \theta}$

K. $\frac{1}{(\sin \theta)(\cos \theta)}$

3. The expression $\cos^2(x) - 3 + \sin^2(x)$ is equivalent to which of the following?

A. -4
B. -3
C. -2
D. 2
E. 3

★★★

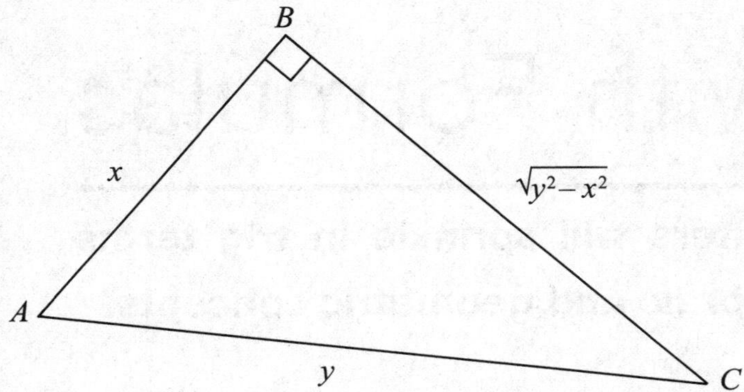

4. The figure above shows a right triangle with lengths of x, y, and $\sqrt{y^2 - x^2}$, with $x > 1$ and $y > 1$. Which of the following expressions gives the cotangent of $\angle C$?

F. $\sqrt{y^2 - x^2}$

G. $\dfrac{\sqrt{y^2-x^2}}{y}$

H. $\dfrac{y}{x}$

J. $\dfrac{x}{\sqrt{y^2-x^2}}$

K. $\dfrac{\sqrt{y^2-x^2}}{x}$

★★★

5. For all x such that $0° < x° < 90°$, the expression $(\sqrt{1-\cos^2 x})(\csc x) + (\sqrt{1-\sin^2 x})(\sec x)$ is equivalent to which of the following?

A. 0
B. 1
C. 2
D. $-\tan\theta$
E. $\sin 2\theta$

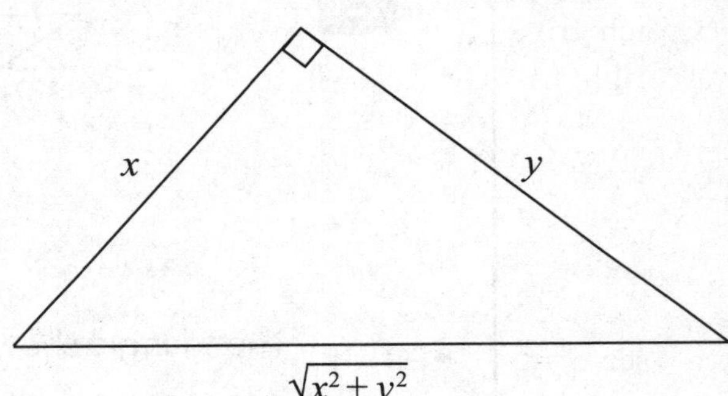

6. In the right triangle above, x and y are positive real numbers. If one of the triangle's angle measures is $\tan^{-1}(\frac{x}{y})$, what is $\sin(\tan^{-1}(\frac{x}{y}))$?

F. $\dfrac{x}{y}$

G. $\dfrac{y}{x}$

H. $\dfrac{x}{\sqrt{x^2+y^2}}$

J. $\dfrac{y}{\sqrt{x^2+y^2}}$

K. $\dfrac{\sqrt{x^2+y^2}}{x}$

Working with Formulas

Sometimes the ACT writers will sprinkle in trig terms while testing basic algebraic and geometric concepts.

The writers are not testing your knowledge of trig here; they are merely seeing if you are comfortable enough with the terms to keep your cool and solve the given algebra or geometry problem.

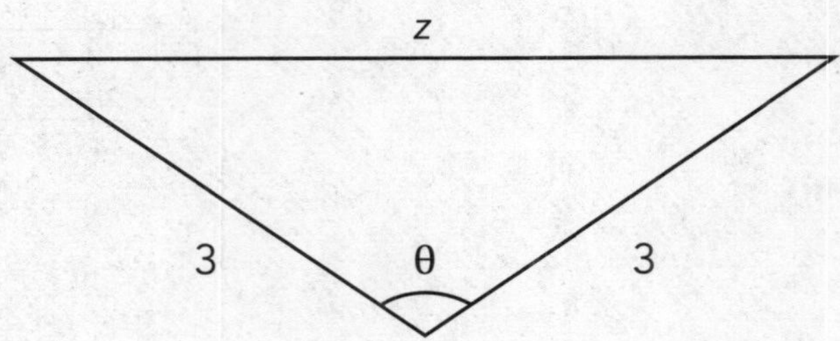

The triangle shown in the figure above has 2 sides, each of length 3 centimeters, and a 3rd side of length *z* centimeters. The measure of the angle between the 2 sides that are 3 centimeters long is θ. In terms of *z*, cos θ = ?

(Note: For any triangle, if *a*, *b*, and *c* are the lengths of the sides opposite angles *A*, *B*, and *C*, respectively, then $a^2 = b^2 + c^2 - 2bc\cos\angle A$.)

A. $\frac{(z^2-6)}{18}$

B. $\frac{(z^2+18)}{18}$

C. $\frac{(z^2-18)}{18}$

D. $\frac{(6-z^2)}{18}$

E. $\frac{(18-z^2)}{18}$

S *Let's look more closely at our given formula:*

$$a^2 = b^2 + c^2 - 2bc \cos\angle A$$

The note tells us that angle A corresponds with opposite side "a", angle B with opposite "b", and so on. The angle we are interested in is θ, which corresponds with opposite side z. Both of the other sides have a length of ***3****, which we can substitute in for* **b** *and* **c**.

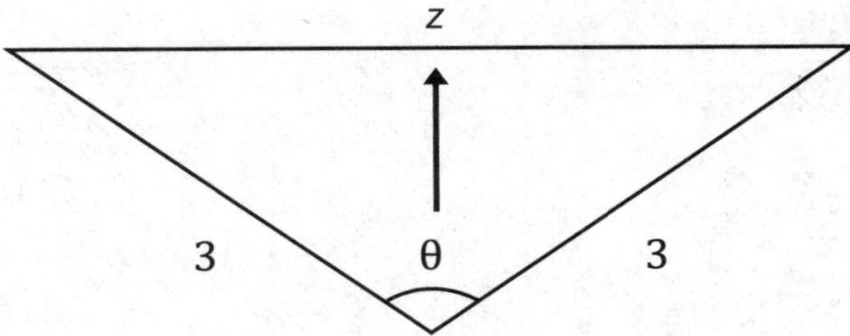

Let's plug our values into the provided formula and simplify:

$$a^2 = b^2 + c^2 - 2bc \cos\angle A$$
$$z^2 = 3^2 + 3^2 - 2(3)(3)\cos\theta$$
$$z^2 = 9 + 9 - 18\cos\theta$$
$$z^2 = 18 - 18\cos\theta$$

Now we just need to solve for cos θ:

$$z^2 = 18 - 18\cos\theta$$
$$z^2 - 18 = -18\cos\theta$$
$$\frac{(z^2 - 18)}{-18} = \cos\theta$$
$$\frac{(-z^2 + 18)}{18} = \cos\theta$$
$$\frac{(18 - z^2)}{18} = \cos\theta$$

E is our answer!

Be careful when distributing that negative from the −18 term. If you are not careful, you will fall headfirst into a wrong answer trap

E2 In $\Delta\ DEF$, the measure of $\angle D$ is 32°, the measure of $\angle E$ is 68°, and the length of side $\overline{EF}$ is 29 centimeters. Which of the following is an expression for the length, in centimeters, of side $\overline{DF}$?

(Note: The law of sines states that that for any triangle, the ratios of the lengths of the sides to the sines of the angles opposite those sides are equal.)

F. $\dfrac{\sin 32^\circ}{29 \sin 68^\circ}$

G. $\dfrac{\sin 68^\circ}{29 \sin 32^\circ}$

H. $\dfrac{29 \sin 32^\circ}{\sin 68^\circ}$

J. $\dfrac{29 \sin 68^\circ}{\sin 32^\circ}$

K. $\dfrac{(\sin 32^\circ)(\sin 68^\circ)}{29}$

S *First let's translate the "law of sines" into math:*

$$\frac{(\text{Side } A)}{(\sin \angle A)} = \frac{(\text{Side } B)}{(\sin \angle B)} = \frac{(\text{Side } C)}{(\sin \angle C)}$$

Next we need to draw our triangle using the information given:

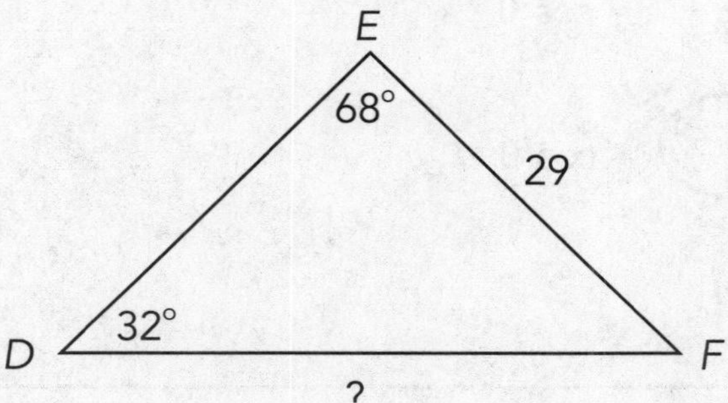

Now we're set to work! We are asked to solve for side $\overline{DF}$, which corresponds with, or is opposite to, the 68° angle.

Let's plug everything we know into our law of sines equation:

$$\frac{\text{Side } D\ (\overline{EF})}{(\sin \angle D)} = \frac{\text{Side } E\ (\overline{DF})}{(\sin \angle E)} = \frac{\text{Side } F\ (\overline{DE})}{(\sin \angle F)}$$

$$\frac{29}{(\sin 32^\circ)} = \frac{\overline{DF}}{(\sin 68^\circ)} = \frac{\overline{DE}}{(\sin \angle F)}$$

We can ignore side/angle F and focus on side/angle D and E to solve the equation. We must isolate $\overline{DF}$ to solve. We can do this by multiplying each side by sin 68°.

$$\frac{29}{(\sin 32^\circ)} = \frac{\overline{DF}}{(\sin 68^\circ)}$$

$$\frac{\mathbf{29\ (\sin 68^\circ)}}{\mathbf{(\sin 32^\circ)}} = \overline{DF}$$

***J** is our answer!*

Working with Formulas Practice Problems

1. In ΔABC shown below, $\angle Q$ is 65°, $\overline{QS}$ = 16 feet, and $\overline{QR}$ = 10 feet. Which of the following is the length, in feet, of $\overline{RS}$) ?

(Note: For a triangle with sides of length a, b, and c and opposite angles $\angle A$, $\angle B$, and $\angle C$, respectively, the law of sines states $\frac{\sin \angle A}{a} = \frac{\sin \angle B}{b} = \frac{\sin \angle C}{c}$ and the law of cosines states $c^2 = a^2 + b^2 - 2ab\cos \angle C$.)

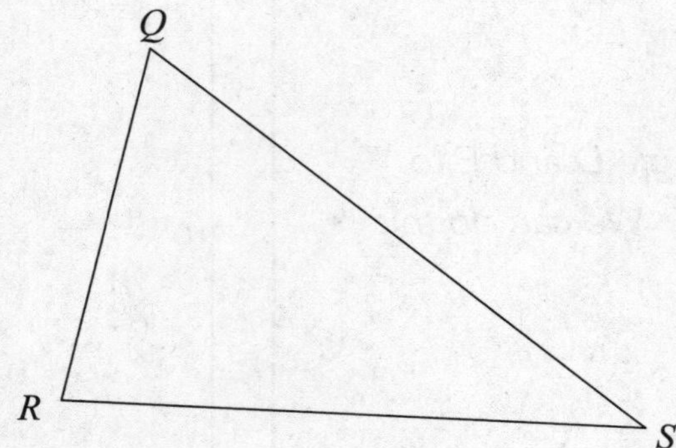

A. $16\sin 65°$
B. $10\sin 65°$
C. $\sqrt{16^2 - 10^2}$
D. $\sqrt{16^2 + 10^2 - 2(16)(10)\sin 65°}$
E. $\sqrt{16^2 + 10^2 - 2(16)(10)\cos 65°}$

★★

2. What is $\sin\frac{\pi}{6}$ given that $\frac{\pi}{6} = \frac{\pi}{2} - \frac{\pi}{3}$ and $\sin(\alpha - \beta) = (\sin \alpha)(\cos \beta) - (\sin \beta)(\cos \alpha)$?

(Note: You may use the following table of values.)

θ	$\sin \theta$	$\cos \theta$
$\frac{\pi}{4}$	$\frac{\sqrt{2}}{2}$	$\frac{\sqrt{2}}{2}$
$\frac{\pi}{3}$	$\frac{\sqrt{3}}{2}$	$\frac{1}{2}$
$\frac{\pi}{2}$	1	0

F. 0
G. $\frac{1}{2}$
H. 1
J. $\frac{\sqrt{2} - 2}{2}$
K. $\frac{\sqrt{3}}{2}$

★★★

3. If $\sin x = -\frac{1}{2}$, what is the value of $\cos 2x$?

(Note: $(\sin x)^2 = \frac{1}{2}(1 - \cos 2x)$.)

A. $-\frac{1}{2}$

B. 0

C. $\frac{1}{2}$

D. 1

E. 2

★★★

4. In ΔABC, $\angle A$ has an angle measure of 37°, $\angle B$ has an angle measure of 78°, and $\overline{BC}$ has a length of 13 inches. Which of the following is an expression of the length, in inches, of $\overline{AC}$?

(Note: The law of sines states that for any triangle, the ratios of the lengths of the sides to the sines of the angles opposite those sides are equal.)

F. $\frac{\sin 37°}{13\sin 78°}$

G. $\frac{\sin 78°}{13\sin 37°}$

H. $\frac{13\sin 37°}{\sin 78°}$

J. $\frac{13\sin 78°}{\sin 37°}$

K. $\frac{\sin 37° \sin 78°}{13}$

★★★

Unit Circle

Some SohCahToa questions require you to first draw a triangle on the Unit Circle diagram shown below:

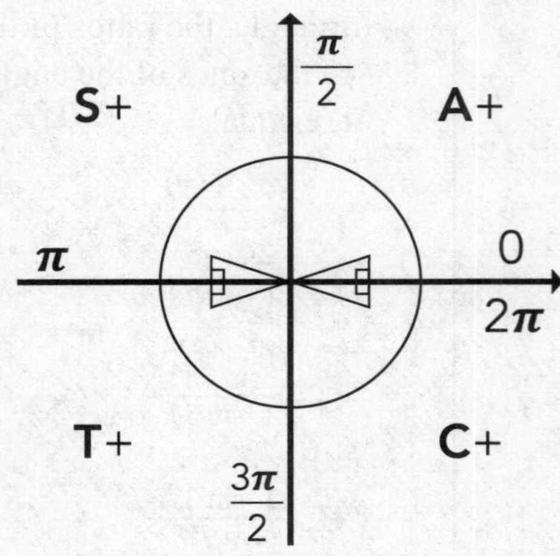

All Students Take Calculus:

All are positive in Quadrant 1

Sin is positive in Quadrant 2

Tan is positive in Quadrant 3

Cos is positive in Quadrant 4

To remember the letters in the Unit Circle, memorize the simple phrase: "**A**ll **S**tudents **T**ake **C**alculus."

You will use the **radians** (the $\boldsymbol{\pi}$ numbers) to figure out where to draw your triangle. The **letters** (A, S, T, C) will tell you if your SohCahToa product should be positive or negative.

You already know how to describe a circle in terms of **degrees**:

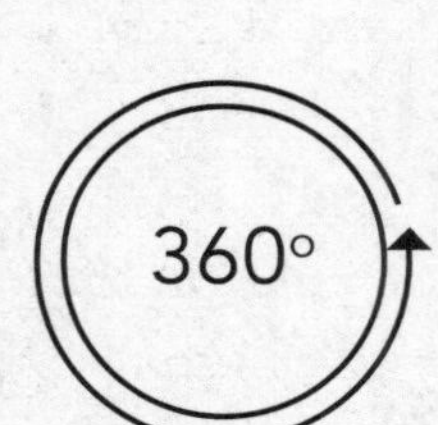

a circle is 360°

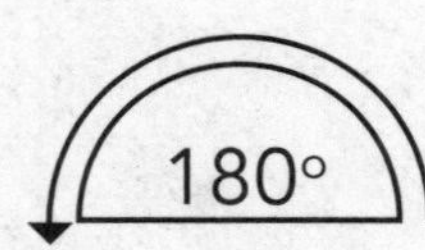

a half circle is 180°

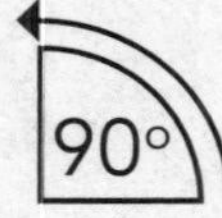

a quarter circle is 90°

If you remember that **a full circle is 2π**, you can work backwards to figure out the rest!

For the purposes of trig, we can also describe a circle in terms of **radians**:

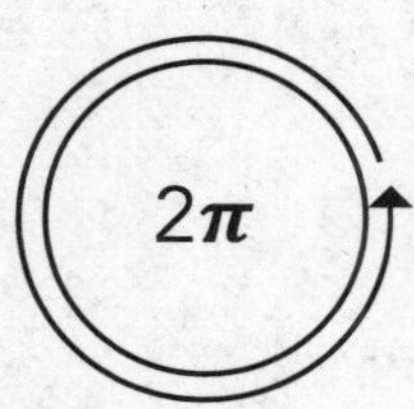

a circle is 2π

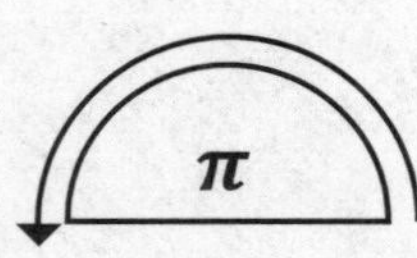

a half circle is π

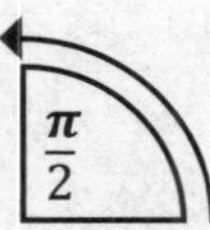

a quarter circle is $\frac{\pi}{2}$

If you are asked to convert degrees to radians, you can simply multiply the number of degrees by $\frac{\pi}{180}$:

90° becomes $\frac{\pi}{2}$ $\quad 90 \times \frac{\pi}{180} = \frac{90\pi}{180} = \frac{\pi}{2}$

180° becomes π $\quad 180 \times \frac{\pi}{180} = \frac{180\pi}{180} = \pi$

270° becomes $\frac{3\pi}{2}$ $\quad 270 \times \frac{\pi}{180} = \frac{270\pi}{180} = \frac{3\pi}{2}$

360° becomes 2π $\quad 360 \times \frac{\pi}{180} = \frac{360\pi}{180} = 2\pi$

If you ever see radians in a question, you can be sure you're dealing with a Unit Circle question. Draw out your diagram and get ready to plot your triangle!

Drawing Your Triangle

Now that you understand radians, you're ready to draw your triangle on the Unit Circle. The test writers will point you to a particular quadrant by giving you a range of radians.

The four possible triangles are seen in the mini bowtie shape in the Unit Circle diagram.

Notice that the x-axis will always be your adjacent side!

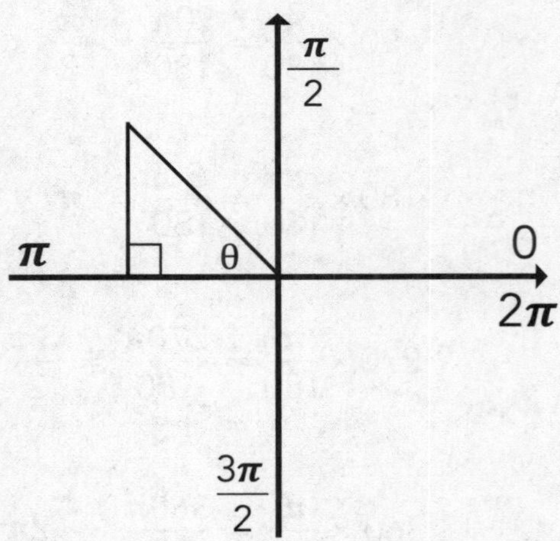

For example, if we are told:

$$\frac{\pi}{2} < \theta < \pi$$

we know that we are in **Quadrant 2.**

We can draw our triangle directly on the x-axis, label our sides, and get ready to SohCahToa!

All Students Take Calculus

The final step in a Unit Circle problem is to solve the positive/negative question. This part is easy as pie:

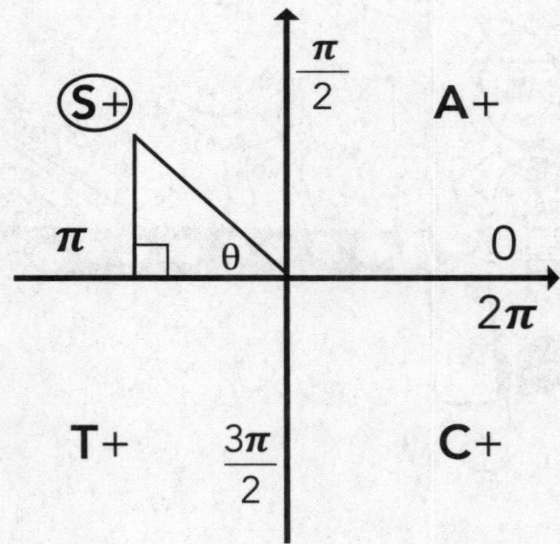

Since we are in Quadrant 2, we are in the land of sine! The letter "S" tells us that **only sin θ will be positive.**

Alternatively, if our triangle were in Quadrant 1, the letter "A" tells us that we'd have a bonanza of positivity on our hands!

That's it! Once the radians and letters are sorted, the rest is straight SohCahToa.

E1 If $\sin\theta = -\dfrac{3}{5}$ and $\pi < \theta < \dfrac{3\pi}{2}$, then $\tan\theta = ?$

A. $-\frac{5}{4}$

B. $-\frac{3}{4}$

C. $-\frac{3}{5}$

D. $\frac{3}{4}$

E. $\frac{4}{5}$

S *I see radians! Unit Circle time! Our range of* $\pi < \theta < \dfrac{3\pi}{2}$ *points us to* **Q3**. *Let's draw our triangle:*

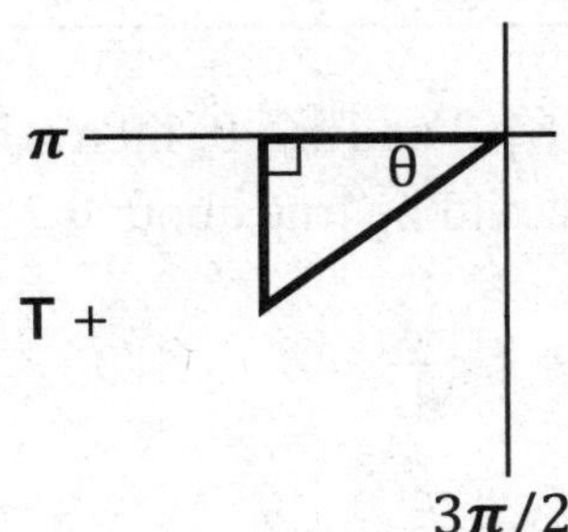

Now we're in business.
Before we can find tan θ, we need side lengths. Luckily, the question gives us what we need.

We know that $\sin\theta = -\dfrac{3}{5}$.

SohCahToa, bring the heat! $\quad \text{Sin} = \dfrac{\text{Opposite}}{\text{Hypotenuse}} = -\dfrac{3}{5}$

So our opposite side is 3 and our hypotenuse is 5.
Ohhhhhhhh no you didn't! 3-4-5 in the house!

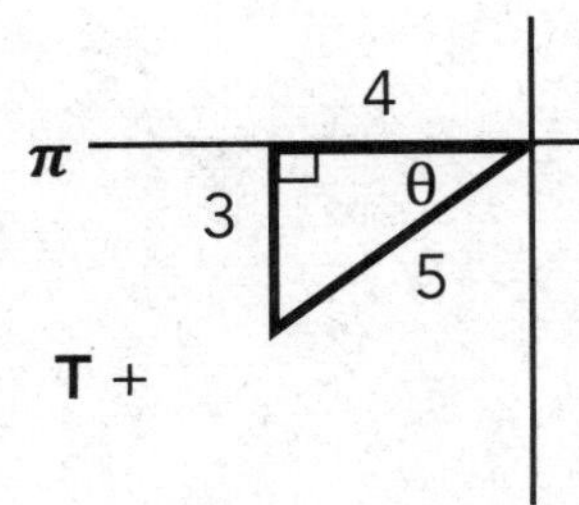

Now we can finally find tan θ:

$$\text{Tan}\,\theta = \frac{\textbf{O}\text{pposite}}{\textbf{A}\text{djacent}} = \frac{3}{4}$$

Since our **T***an is in Q3, it's positive!*

***D** is our answer!*

Don't fret over where to place that (–) sign just yet. We'll let our letters settle the positive/negative question at the end.

Unit Circle Practice Problems

1. If $\sin\theta = -\frac{3}{5}$ and $\frac{3\pi}{2} < \theta < 2\pi$, then $\cos\theta = ?$

A. $\frac{4}{5}$

B. $\frac{3}{4}$

C. $-\frac{3}{5}$

D. $-\frac{3}{4}$

E. $-\frac{4}{5}$

2. If $\tan\theta = \frac{r}{s}$, $r > 0$, $s > 0$, and $0 < \theta < \frac{\pi}{2}$, what is $\sin\theta$?

F. $\frac{r}{s}$

G. $\frac{s}{r}$

H. $\frac{r}{\sqrt{r^2+s^2}}$

J. $\frac{s}{\sqrt{r^2+s^2}}$

K. $\frac{\sqrt{r^2+s^2}}{s}$

★★★

3. For what value of θ is $\frac{\sin\theta}{\cos\theta} = 1$?

A. $\frac{\pi}{4}$

B. $\frac{\pi}{3}$

C. $\frac{\pi}{2}$

D. $\frac{3\pi}{2}$

E. π

4. If $\sin^{-1}(-x) = \theta$ and $x > 0$, then which of the following could be true about θ ?

F. $0 \leq \theta < \frac{\pi}{4}$

G. $\frac{\pi}{4} \leq \theta < \frac{\pi}{2}$

H. $\frac{\pi}{2} \leq \theta < \frac{3\pi}{4}$

J. $\frac{3\pi}{4} \leq \theta < \pi$

K. $\pi \leq \theta < \frac{3\pi}{2}$

★★★

Sin/Cos Graphs

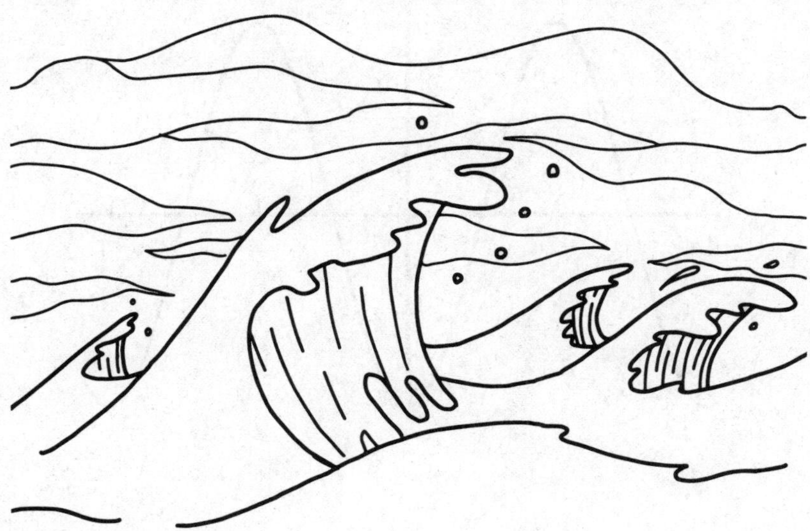

When the ACT writers wish to test your graph reading skills, they frequently use the graphs of sine and cosine "waves:"

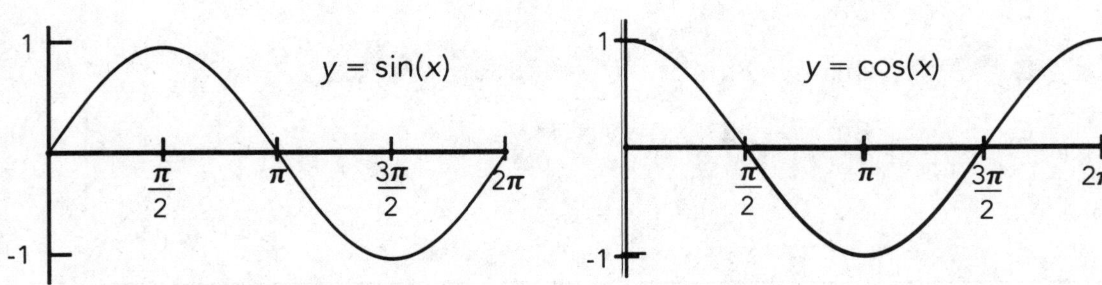

The ACT will use these graphs to test your knowledge of two key concepts: **period** and **amplitude**. Think of these as the width and height of a graph:

1. The **period** of a sine/cosine wave is the horizontal distance it travels before completing a full cycle. Both of the graphs seen above have a **period of 2π.**

2. The **amplitude** of a sine/cosine wave is the vertical distance between the *x*-axis and the wave's peak. Both of the graphs seen above have an **amplitude of 1.**

E1 The graph of the trigonometric function $y = -2\cos(\frac{1}{2}x)$ is shown below. What are the amplitude and the period of this function?

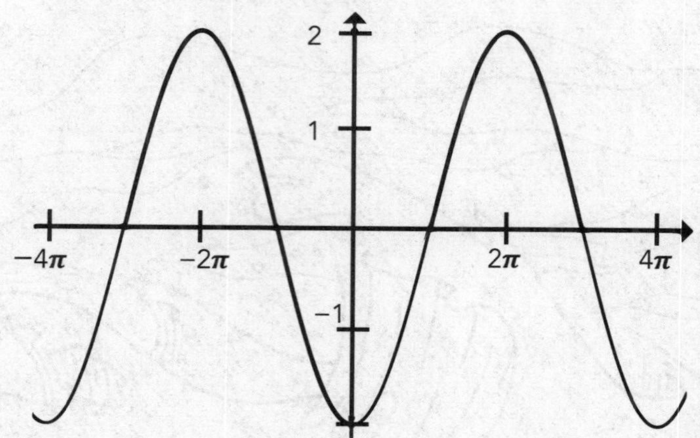

	amplitude	period
A.	0	2
B.	4	2π
C.	2	4π
D.	4π	8π
E.	8π	8

S *Nothing to do but measure our period and amplitude!*

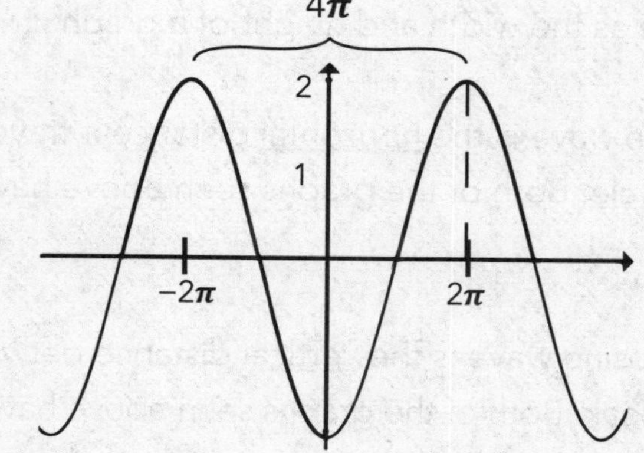

It looks like the graph peaks at 2 on the y-axis, so our ***amplitude is 2.***

The graph peaks at $x = -2\pi$ and again at $x = 2\pi$, giving the wave a ***period of 4π.***

C *is our answer!*

E2 Two functions, *f*(x) and *g*(x), are plotted in the graph below.

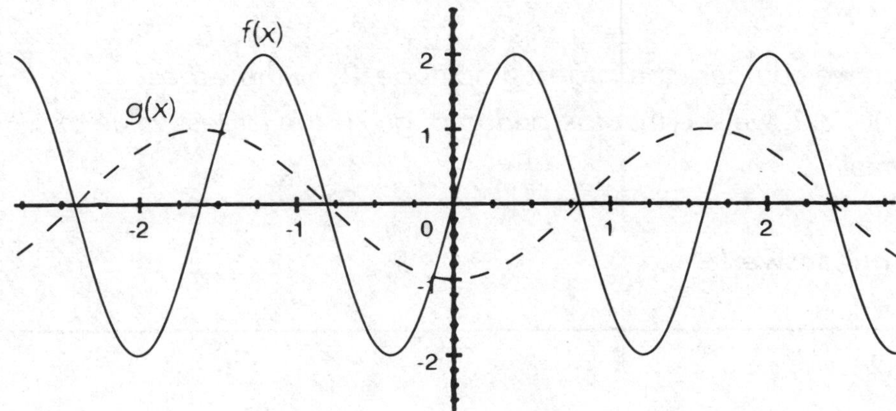

Which of the following is the largest?

F. The amplitude of *f*(x)
G. The period of *f*(x)
H. The amplitude of *g*(x)
J. The period of *g*(x)
K. Cannot be determined from the given information.

S *Let's use the process of elimination.*

1 *Which of the functions has the larger* ***period****?*

F(x) starts a cycle at the **origin** *and completes the pattern when x is roughly* **1.6***. Thus, the* ***period of f(x)*** *is about* **1.6.**

G(x) crosses the x–axis at **–0.8** *and completes the pattern when x is roughly* **2.4***. So the* ***period of g(x)*** *is 2.4 – (–.8) =* **3.2.**
That's clearly bigger than 1.6! Choice G is out.

2 *Which of the functions has a larger* ***amplitude****?*

Visually, it's clear that f(x) is the big winner. From the x–axis to the peak of f(x), the distance is **2***: this is the largest amplitude.*

So we're down to two contenders: the amplitude of f(x) and the period of g(x).

When we compare the largest amplitude, ***2****, to the largest period,* ***3.2****, we see that the period of g(x) is the largest value of them all.*

J is our answer!

Use Your Calculator, Turkey!

If you're talking about SIN, COS, or TAN, you're talking about graphs. If you are ever stuck on a trig problem asking you whether the graph of **sin 2x** or **sin x** has a bigger amplitude or period, you can just break out your calculator!

1. Hit the **Y= button** in the top left corner

2. Enter sin(2x) into the $\mathbf{Y_1}$**=** field

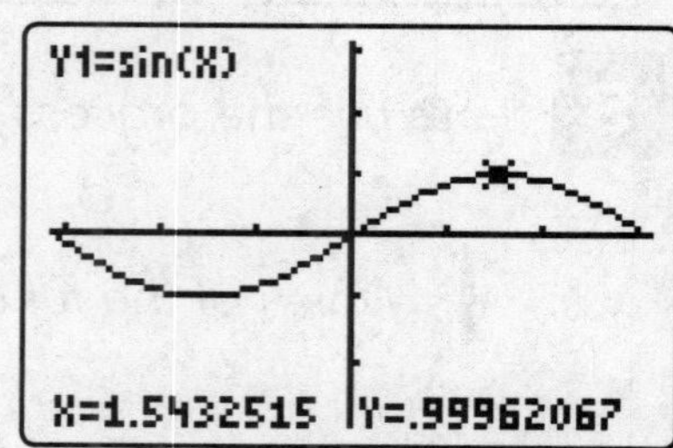

3. Enter 2sin(x) into the $\mathbf{Y_2}$**=** field

4. Press the **[GRAPH] button** in the top right corner

Sin/Cos Graphs Practice Problems

1. The graphs of $f(x)$ and $g(x)$ are shown below in the standard (x, y) coordinate plane below. If $f(x) = \sin x$, which of the following transformations is applied to $f(x)$ to graph $g(x)$?

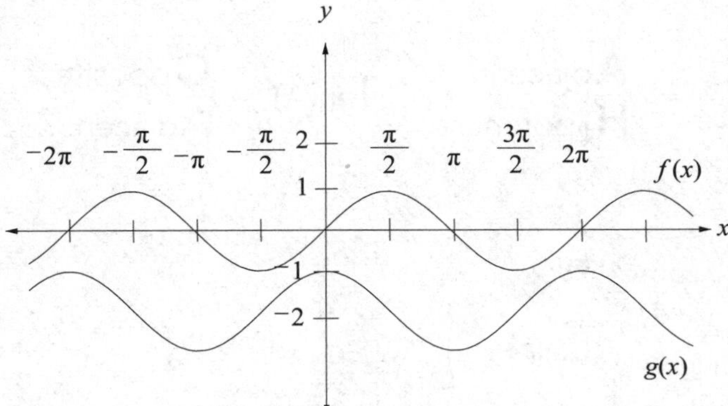

A. Shift $f(x)$ 2 units up and $\frac{\pi}{2}$ units left.

B. Shift $f(x)$ 2 units up and $\frac{\pi}{2}$ units right.

C. Shift $f(x)$ 2 units down and $\frac{\pi}{2}$ units left.

D. Shift $f(x)$ $\frac{\pi}{2}$ units up and 2 units right.

E. Shift $f(x)$ $\frac{\pi}{2}$ units down and 1 unit left.

★★★

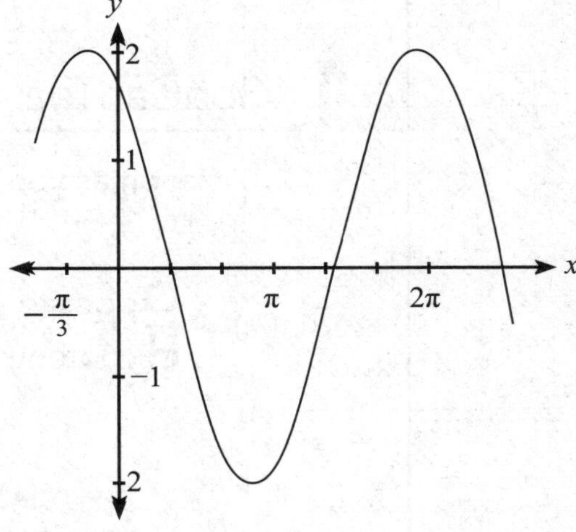

2. The graph of a the trigonometric function $f(x) = a\cos(x - b)$ is shown above. Which of the following accurately describes p, the period of the function?

F. $\frac{\pi}{6} < p < \frac{\pi}{3}$

G. $\pi < p < 2\pi$

H. $p > 2\pi$

J. $p = 2\pi$

K. $p = 2$

★★★

The Trigonometry Short List

1 SohCahToa

As soon as you spot a trig function, write down SOHCAHTOA

$$\textbf{S}\text{in(A)} = \frac{\textbf{O}\text{pposite}}{\textbf{H}\text{ypotenuse}} \qquad \textbf{C}\text{os(A)} = \frac{\textbf{A}\text{djacent}}{\textbf{H}\text{ypotenuse}} \qquad \textbf{T}\text{an(A)} = \frac{\textbf{O}\text{pposite}}{\textbf{A}\text{djacent}}$$

*If you see **Sin**, **Cos**, or **Tan**, a right triangle is somewhere nearby!*

And where there's a right triangle, Pythagoras can't be far!

2 Advanced Trig Identities

Quick facts

Csc is the flip of **Sin**
Sec is the flip of **Cos**
Cot is the flip of **Tan**

Most of the work in Trig Identities problems is still plain ol' SohCahToa.

Sin^{-1} and **arcsin** are **SohCahToa in reverse**.

$$\text{Sin}^2 + \text{Cos}^2 =$$

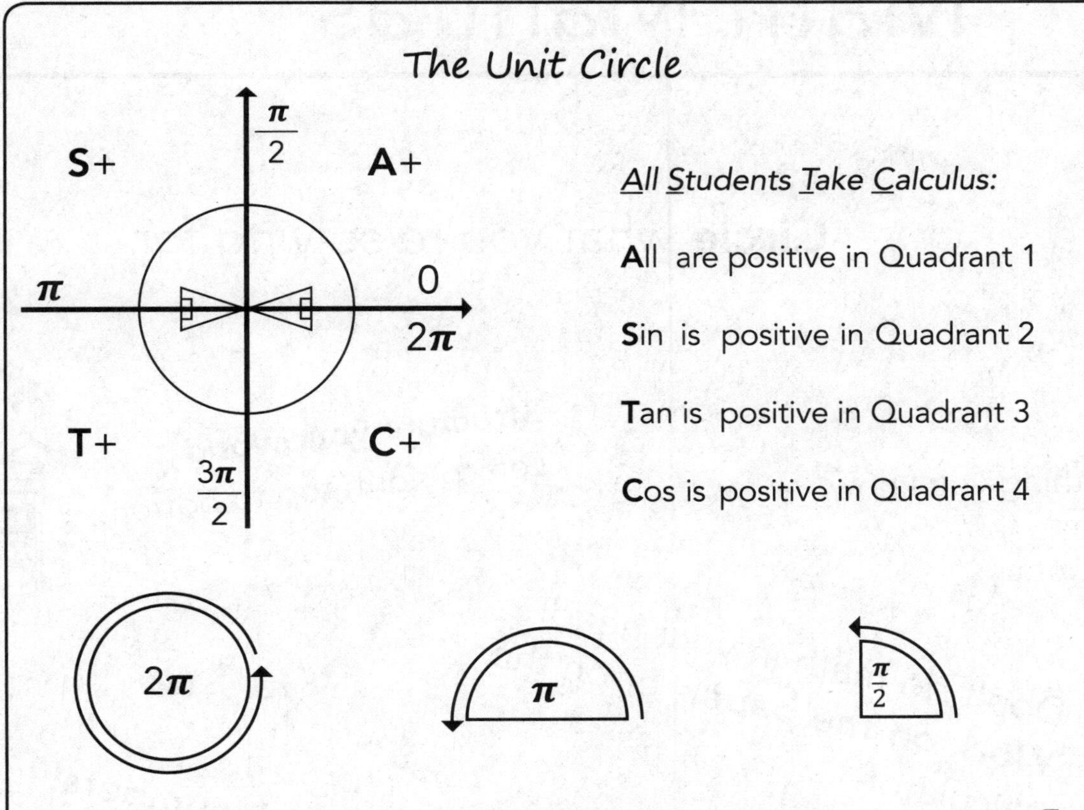
The Unit Circle
S+
A+
T+
C+
$\frac{\pi}{2}$
π
0
2π
$\frac{3\pi}{2}$
All Students Take Calculus:
All are positive in Quadrant 1
Sin is positive in Quadrant 2
Tan is positive in Quadrant 3
Cos is positive in Quadrant 4
2π
π
$\frac{\pi}{2}$
a circle is 2π
a half circle is π
a quarter circle is $\frac{\pi}{2}$

3 Sin/Cos Graphs

Quick facts

The **period** of a sine/cosine wave is the **horizontal** distance it travels before completing a **full cycle**.

The **amplitude** of a sine/cosine wave is the **vertical** distance between the **x-axis** and the wave's **peak**.

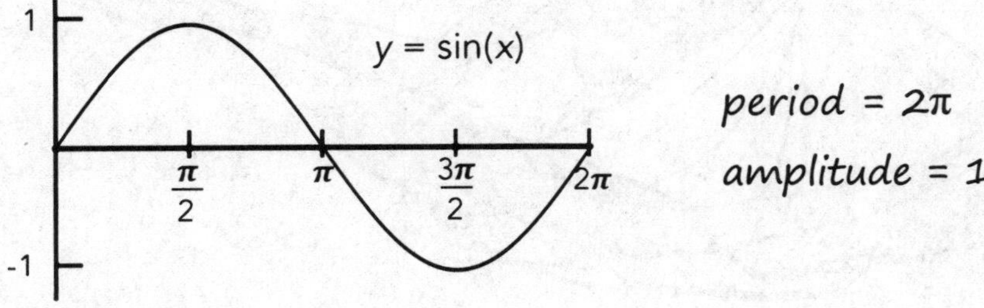
1
-1
$y = \sin(x)$
$\frac{\pi}{2}$
π
$\frac{3\pi}{2}$
2π

period = 2π

amplitude = 1

Math Mantras

Circle what you're solving for.

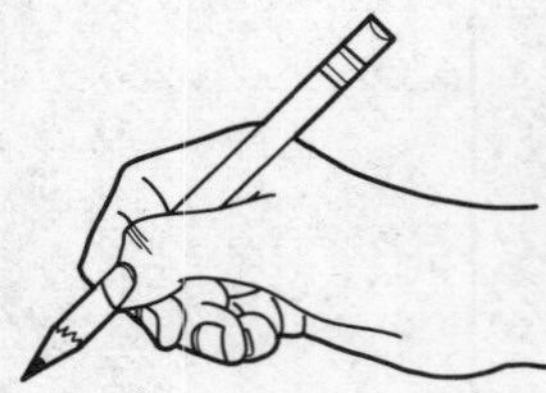

Label everything.
Write down everything you know.

Structure your work!
Left to right, top to bottom.

Don't do math in your head!
Work on the paper, or on the calculator!

When in doubt, **pick numbers!**

If you can't work forward,
Work Backwards!

Actively read and translate the problem **one line at a time.**

Math Answers

The Basics

Art of Translation
1. D
2. F
3. B
4. H
5. B
6. J
7. B
8. G

Working Backwards
1. D
2. J
3. B
4. K
5. B
6. J
7. D

Properties of Numbers
1. E
2. H
3. E
4. J
5. A
6. J
7. E
8. J
9. B
10. G
11. B
12. H
13. E
14. G
15. D
16. H

Picking Numbers
1. D
2. K
3. A
4. J
5. A
6. K
7. C

Geometry

Angles
1. C
2. F
3. D
4. H
5. D
6. K
7. B
8. F

Triangles
1. D
2. J
3. B
4. G
5. D
6. G
7. C
8. H
9. A
10. H
11. B
12. J

Circles
1. D
2. G
3. C
4. G
5. B
6. K
7. D
8. H
9. D
10. J
11. C
12. K
13. D
14. G

Perimeter, Area, and Volume
1. C
2. H
3. D
4. K
5. C
6. J
7. E
8. K
9. B
10. H
11. E
12. J
13. D
14. K

Proportional Shapes
1. B
2. K
3. B
4. K
5. B
6. J

Number Lines
1. A
2. K
3. C
4. J

Coordinate Systems
1. A
2. J
3. C
4. G
5. D

Slope
1. D
2. G
3. E
4. F
5. C
6. K
7. D

Equation of a Circle
1. B
2. K
3. J
4. F
5. D
6. F

Shifting Graphs
1. C
2. H
3. B
4. J

Reflections
1. C
2. H
3. E
4. H
5. D
6. J
7. C

Diagonals and Symmetry
1. C
2. J
3. D
4. G

Geometry Review
1. D
2. K
3. C
4. G
5. E
6. H
7. B
8. G
9. E
10. K
11. D
12. H
13. D
14. K

Algebra

Basic Algebra
1. C
2. F
3. E
4. F
5. D
6. H
7. E
8. H
9. E

Polynomials
1. D
2. F
3. B
4. G
5. D
6. F
7. A
8. F
9. D
10. K
11. E
12. G
13. B

Mean, Median, and Mode
1. A
2. H
3. B
4. J
5. D
6. G
7. D

Function Notation

1. B
2. K
3. E
4. K
5. C
6. H
7. E
8. G
9. A

Composite Function Notation

1. D
2. G
3. E

Logarithms

1. B
2. G
3. C
4. F
5. A

Max and Min

1. C
2. J
3. C
4. F

Distance = Rate × Time

1. B
2. J
3. B
4. H
5. D
6. J

Complex Word Problems

1. C
2. G
3. D
4. J
5. D
6. F
7. C

Charts, Tables, and Graphs

1. C
2. F
3. C
4. G

Wacked-Out Functions

1. E
2. J
3. D
4. H
5. C
6. F

Direct/Inverse Proportions

1. C
2. K
3. B
4. K
5. E

Algebra Review

1. A
2. F
3. D
4. J
5. A
6. K
7. E
8. J
9. C
10. H
11. E
12. G
13. D

Arithmetic

Exponents

1. E
2. J
3. A
4. J
5. A
6. H
7. C
8. K
9. A
10. H
11. C

Inequalities

1. A
2. J
3. C
4. H
5. B
6. K
7. A
8. J

Fractions
1. D
2. H
3. A
4. H
5. D

Percentages
1. C
2. G
3. D
4. H
5. E
6. J
7. C
8. J
9. A
10. H
11. D
12. J

Absolute Value
1. D
2. H
3. B
4. F

Sequences
1. B
2. G
3. B
4. H
5. A
6. H
7. D
8. H

Ratios
1. D
2. J
3. E
4. F
5. A
6. H
7. B
8. K

Probability
1. A
2. J
3. B
4. F
5. A
6. K
7. C
8. G
9. C
10. G

Matrix
1. E
2. J
3. C
4. F

Scientific Notation
1. D
2. G
3. C
4. J
5. B

Logic Test
1. C
2. H
3. B
4. G

Combinations
1. E
2. J
3. D
4. K

Square Roots
1. B
2. J
3. D
4. J

Arithmetic Review
1. B
2. J
3. D
4. H
5. C
6. G
7. C
8. H
9. B
10. J
11. C
12. K
13. C
14. H
15. A

Trigonometry

SohCahToa

1. E
2. F
3. E
4. F
5. B
6. K
7. C
8. F
9. A
10. K

Advanced Trig Identities

1. D
2. G
3. C
4. K
5. C
6. H

Working with Formulas

1. E
2. G
3. C
4. J

Unit Circle

1. A
2. H
3. A
4. K

Sin/Cos Graphs

1. C
2. H

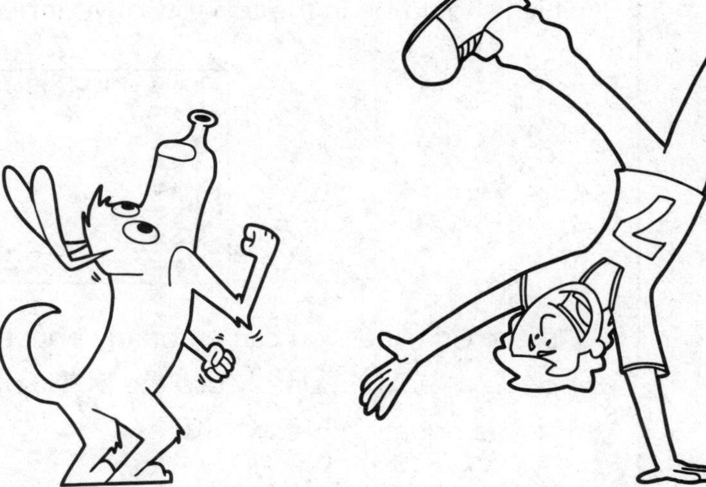

Graphing Calculator Guide

Your calculator is your friend. Use your calculator. Don't use your friends. The calculator is the archnemesis of carelessness. Every chance you get, use your calculator and write down what you discover.

This tutorial will mainly deal with the TI-84, but it is applicable to most graphing calculators.

Graphing Basic Equations

Frequently, you will be asked to find where two graphs intersect, or where one graph crosses an axis. You can use your calculator to find this point, often faster than it would take to do the algebra!

First, let's get acquainted with your graphing screen. Hit the **[Y=] button**, which should be in the top row of your buttons.

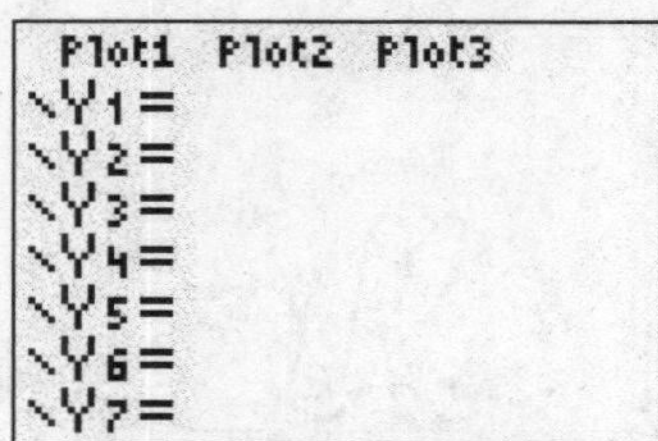

On each **Y**= line, you can enter any equation you want to see graphically. To include a variable, simply use the [**X**,**T**,θ,**n**] button. Let's get some practice with the equation below.

$$y = 5x^3 - 4x^2 + 2x - 5.$$

Graphing Equations

$$y = 5x^3 - 4x^2 + 2x - 5.$$

Isolate your y-variable on one side of your equation before you enter it into the calculator.

1 Enter the equation into the Y_1= field

```
Plot1 Plot2 Plot3
\Y1=5X^3-4X^2+2X
-5
\Y2=
\Y3=
\Y4=
\Y5=
\Y6=
```

2 Hit the **[GRAPH] button** in the top right corner

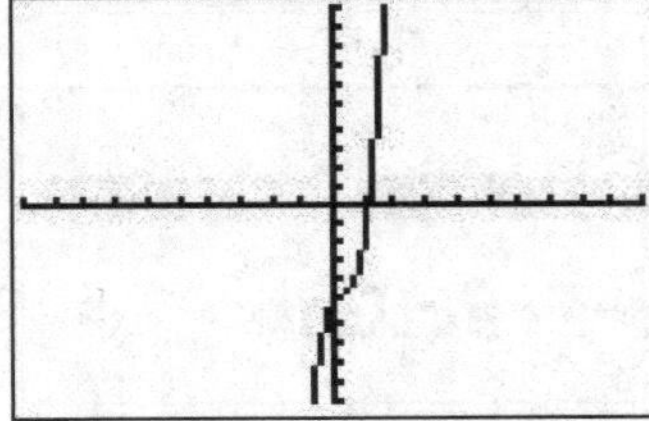

*To zoom in on a specific point, you can keep zooming in using the **[ZOOM]** function, or you can get there faster by setting parameters with the **[WINDOW]** function.*

3 Hit the **[WINDOW] button** in the top row of buttons

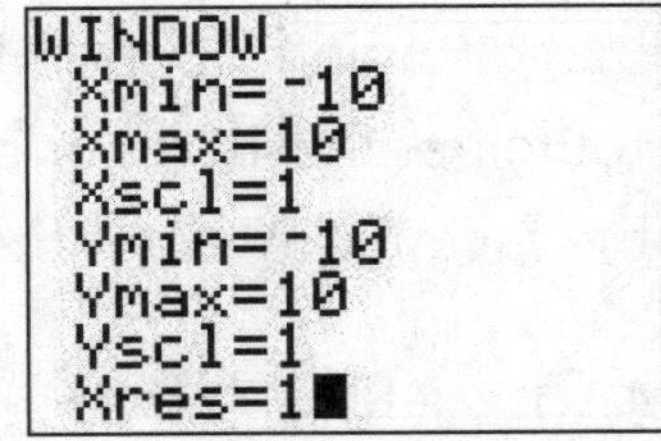

*Now we can define what part of the graph we want to look at. **Xmin** is the left-most point shown on the screen. **Xmax** is the right-most point. **Ymin** and **Ymax** are your top and bottom.*

*Change your x values to **Xmin = −2** and **Xmax = 2.***
Your graph should look now like:

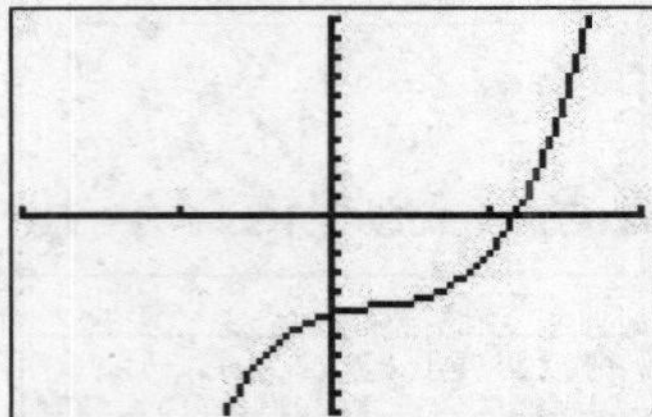

This same trick can be used to find where two graphs intersect!

Simply enter the second equation into the **Y_2=** field and trace to the point where the graphs cross.

4 Use the **ARROW keys** to trace the graph

*Using the Up, Down, Left, and Right buttons, you can hover over a point and **simply read the (x,y) points** along the graph!*

Turning Decimals into Fractions

If you find yourself lost in Decimal Land, looking for a route back home to Fractionville, there's a handy tool called **MATHFRAC**. Enter your decimal (try .0625), then hit:

MATH → 1 (Frac)

This turns your decimal into its fraction equivalent!

"4!" is shorthand for multiplying every integer from 1 to 4:

4! = 4×3×2×1
4! = 24

Factorials

Occasionally you will see exclamation points on the Math section: 3! 4! 5! The writers are not showing you their enthusiasm for counting; they're asking you to find a **factorial**. To find the factorial **9!** enter the number "9", then press:

MATH → PRB → 4 (!)

This drops the exclamation point after the 9. Press enter to see your solution!

Calculators permitted during testing are:

- graphing calculators
- scientific calculators
- four-function calculators (not recommended)

You are not required to clear the memory on your calculator.

Calculating devices NOT permitted during test are:

- **Texas Instruments:** All model numbers that begin with TI-89 or TI-92 and the TI-Nspire CAS (The TI-Nspire (non-CAS) **is** permitted.)
- **Hewlett-Packard:** HP 48GII and all model numbers that begin with HP 40G, HP 49G, or HP 50G
- **Casio**: Algebra fx 2.0, ClassPad 300 and ClassPad 330, and all model numbers that begin with CFX-9970G
- Smart Phones or Cell Phones
- Any kind of laptop or tablet computer
- Calculator that has QWERTY (typewriter-like) keypad, uses an electrical outlet, makes noise, or has a paper tape

Visit www.act.org for more information.

Calculator Tips

Always check your batteries the night before the ACT.
Always bring extra batteries to the testing center.
Do NOT let the calculator be a substitute for writing down your work.
Do NOT use a fancy calculator that you have never seen before on test day. This is not the time to learn new skills.

Math Glossary

Absolute Value the distance that an equation or number is from zero; always a positive number.

Adjacent in geometry, an angle that is directly next to and shares a common side with your reference angle (the one you are working with).

Angle a figure formed by two lines that meet at one point.

Arc a distance on the circumference of a circle from one point to another; different from a chord because it travels along the circumference, not through the interior of the circle.

Arcsin, Arccos, Arctan the inverse function of sine, cosine, and tangent; the angle that has a sine, cosine, or tangent equal to the given number.

Area the amount of space within a given boundary, in square units.

Average (Arithmetic Mean) the sum of a set of numbers divided by the number of terms in the set.

Binomial an algebraic expression with two terms, one of which must be a variable, connected by a + or – sign; e.g. $(2x + 3)$.

Chord a straight line that connects two points on the circumference of a circle and travels through the interior of the circle.

Circle a geometrical figure where all points are equidistant from a central point.

Circumference the perimeter of a circle; measured using 1-dimensional units (e.g. cm).

Consecutive numbers or terms that are the next step in a pattern: *Three **consecutive** even integers are 2,4,6.*

Constant a quantity that is unchanging: *In the slope-intercept formula $y = mx + b$, m and b are both **constants**.*

Coordinate one of a set of numbers used to show the position of a point on a line or graph.

Cube a 3-dimensional figure where length = width = height.

Denominator the bottom number in a fraction; what you are dividing the top number (the numerator) by.

Diagonal a straight line that connects two vertices of a polygon that are not next to each other.

Diameter a chord that passes through the center of the circle; it is the largest possible chord.

Directly Proportional This term indicates that two or more values have a constant ratio, so that $y = xk$, where k is a constant. If x is **directly proportional** to y, when x triples, y will triple. Note that this only uses the operations of **division** and **multiplication**. If you add 3 to x, you do NOT just add 3 to y.

Distinct numbers or symbols or values that are different in some way.

Domain the x-values over which a function, or a part of a function, is defined.

Equilateral Triangle a triangle that has three equal angles, each measuring 60°, and three equal sides.

Exterior Angle the outside angle formed when a side of a polygon is extended.

Factor a factor of n is a number which divides evenly into n without a remainder.

FOIL method used to multiply binomials (First, Outer, Inner, Last).

Function a defined relationship between a set of x-values and a set of y-values: *In a **function** each x-value can ONLY correspond to a single y-value.*

Greatest Common Factor the largest factor that two numbers have in common.

Hexagon a 6-sided polygon.

Hypotenuse the side opposite of the right angle in a right triangle; also the longest side of a right triangle; only right triangles have hypotenuses.

Imaginary Number the square root of a negative; represented by the letter i where $i^2 = -1$.

Inclusive This term indicates that the endpoints of a set of numbers are included in the evaluation. This is represented on a number line by filled in circles at the endpoints of a line or can be expressed algebraically using the greater than or equal to sign ($\geq$) or the less than or equal to sign ($\leq$).

Inscribed This term indicates that a geometric figure has been produced within another figure so that the points of intersection are maximized without any part of the inscribed figure lying outside the other figure.

Integer any whole number, whether positive, negative, or zero.

Interior Angle the angle on the inside of a polygon.

Inversely Proportional This term indicates that two or more values have a constant ratio so that $y = \frac{k}{x}$, where k is a constant. If x is **inversely proportional** to y, when x triples, y will be a third of its original value. Note that this only uses the operations of **division** and **multiplication**. If you add 3 to x, you do NOT just subtract 3 from y.

Irrational Numbers a number that cannot be completely expressed as a simple fraction; an **infinite decimal without repetition** and the **square root of a non-perfect square** are irrational numbers.

Isosceles Triangle a triangle with two equal sides and two equal angles; the angles opposite the equal sides are equal.

Least Common Multiple the smallest number (not zero) that is a multiple of two numbers.

Line a graphical representation of the equation $y = mx + b$, where m is the **slope**, which is always constant, and b is the **y-intercept.**

Line of Symmetry a line that can be drawn through the plane of a geometric shape such that two, mirrored halves are created.

Linear Function an algebraic representation of a line that conforms to the equation $y = mx + b$.

Logarithm (Log) the exponent of the power to which a base number must be raised to equal a given number; if $\log_x(12) = 3$, then base number x must be raised to the exponent 3 to equal 12.

Matrix a rectangular array of numbers organized in rows and columns.

Median When a set of terms is arranged in ascending or descending order, the **median** (like the median of a highway) is the middle term.

Midpoint a point that lies exactly half-way between two other points.

Mode the value that occurs most frequently in a set of numbers.

Multiple the product of any quantity by an integer.

Numerator the top number in a fraction; the number being divided.

Octagon an 8-sided polygon.

Ordered Pair a point in the xy-coordinate plane, whose the first value is the x-coordinate and the second value is the y-coordinate.

Origin the point (0,0) in the xy-plane.

Parabola an equation with the general form of $y = Ax^2 + Bx + C$ where A, B, and C are constants; another form of the parabola equation used for graphing is $y = a(x - h)^2 + k$, where (h, k) is the vertex of the parabola and a is a stretch factor.

Parallel lines that have the same **slope** and never intersect.

Parallelogram a quadrilateral where sides opposite each other are **parallel.**

PEMDAS order of operations: Parentheses, Exponents, Multiplication and/or Division, Addition and/or Subtraction.

Pentagon a 5-sided polygon.

Percent Increase/ Percent Decrease $\frac{\text{(New number – Old number)}}{\text{Old number}} \times 100$

Perimeter a 1-dimensional measurement of the outer edge of a figure.

Perpendicular Bisector a straight line that intersects another line at its midpoint at a right angle.

Perpendicular Lines two lines that intersect at a right angle and have slopes that are negative reciprocals (e.g. if line 1's slope = m, then line 2's slope = $-\frac{1}{m}$).

Prime Number a number greater than 1 that is divisible only by 2 distinct numbers, 1 and itself; 2 is the lowest and only even prime number.

Probability $\dfrac{\text{\# of outcomes that meet the requirements}}{\text{Total \# of possible outcomes}}$

Product a quantity obtained by multiplying two or more terms together.

Proportion a fancy term for **ratio.**

Pythagorean Theorem an equation that relates the lengths of the legs of a right triangle to the length of its hypotenuse: $a^2 + b^2 = c^2$.

Radical the sign that indicates a square root ($\sqrt{\ }$).

Radius of a Circle the distance from the center of a circle to the circumference.

Range the y-values of a function over a specified domain.

Ratio a comparison of two numbers using division; usually represented by a fraction or with the word "to."

Real Numbers any number, whether rational or irrational, that is not imaginary and, therefore, does not contain the term i.

Remainder the whole number left after division.

Right Triangle a triangle that contains a 90° angle.

Sector a piece of the area of a circle.

Semicircle one half of a circle.

Similar Triangles 2 or more triangles where the ratio of the three sides is equal; also, the corresponding angles are congruent: *Two triangles that have sides 3, 4, 5 and 6, 8, 10 are* **similar** *since they both have side ratios of 3:4:5.*

Slope rise over run; also known as change in y divided by the change in x; constant in a line.

Slope-Intercept Form $y = mx + b$, where m is the slope and b is the y-intercept.

SohCahToa a mnemonic device used to remember the identities of trig functions **sine** (**o**pposite over **h**ypotenuse), cosine (**a**djacent over **h**ypotenuse), and tangent (**o**pposite over **a**djacent).

Square a 2-dimensional figure where all four sides are equal and all four angles are 90°.

Square Root the **square root** of a number is a number which multiplied by itself, gives you the original number; e.g.$\sqrt{9}$ is 3 or -3 because $3 \times 3 = 9$ and $-3 \times -3 = 9$.

Sum a quantity obtained by adding two or more terms together.

Surface Area the area of all the polygons that are on the surface of a 3-dimensional figure; all measurements should be in square units.

Tangent (to) touching at a single point in relation to a curve or surface. *Note: two lines do not lie tangent to each other.*

Variable a value that can change; typically variables are indicated by the letters x, y or z.

Vertex A point of intersection for any 2 sides of any polygon or 3-dimensional figure.

Volume a 3-dimensional measurement of space occupied by an object; measured in cubed units (e.g. cm^3).

Whole Number any number that is not a fraction or a decimal; also known as an **integer.**

X-Intercept the point where a function crosses the x-axis; where the y-coordinate of the point is 0.

Y-Intercept the point where a function crosses the y-axis; where the x-coordinate of the point is 0.

Math Quick Reference

Geometry

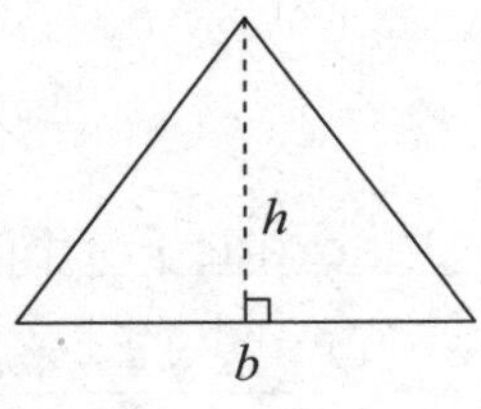

180°

Area $= \frac{1}{2}bh$

Perimeter $= s_1 + s_2 + s_3$

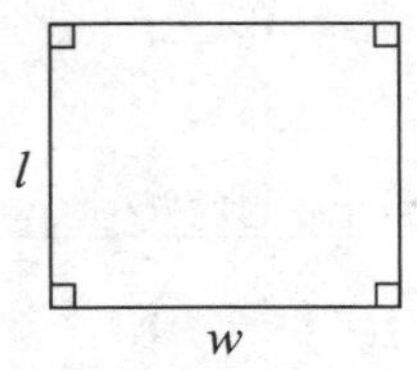

360°

Area $= lw$

Perimeter $= 2l + 2w$

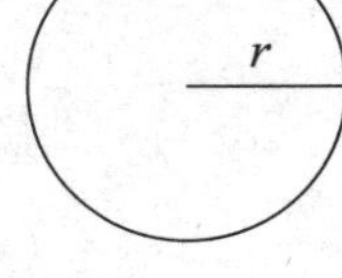

360°

Area $= \pi r^2$

Circumference $= 2\pi r$

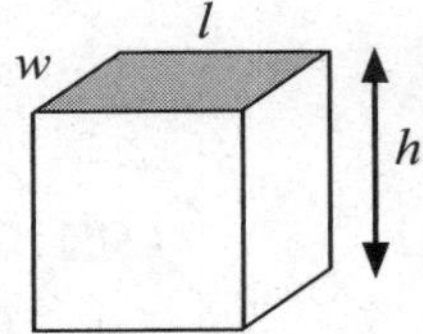

Volume $= lwh$

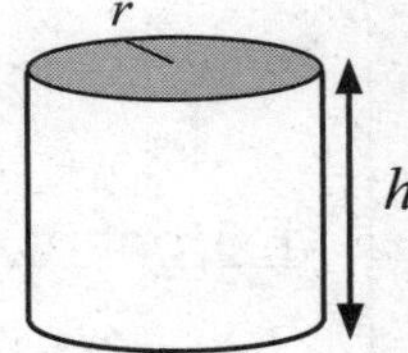

Volume $= \pi r^2 h$

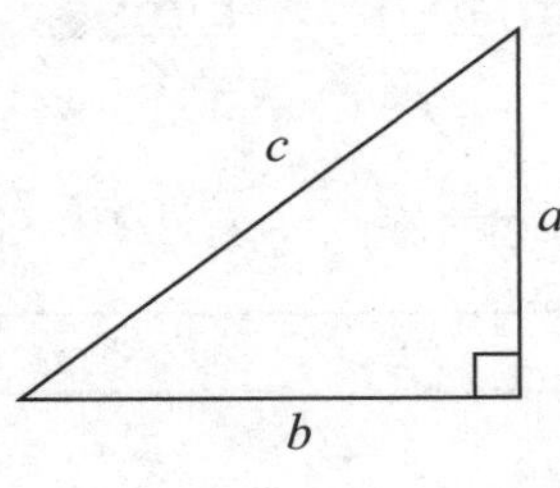

$a^2 + b^2 = c^2$

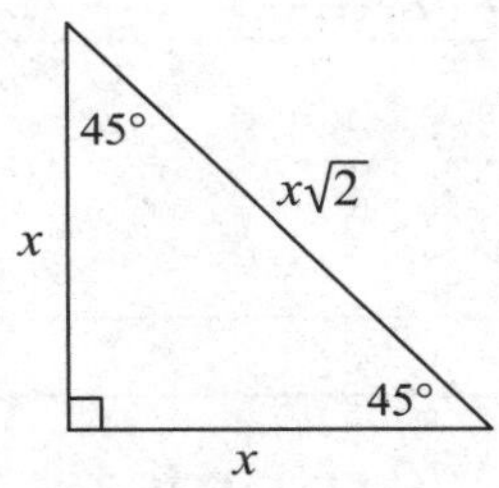

45°– 45°– 90° Triangle

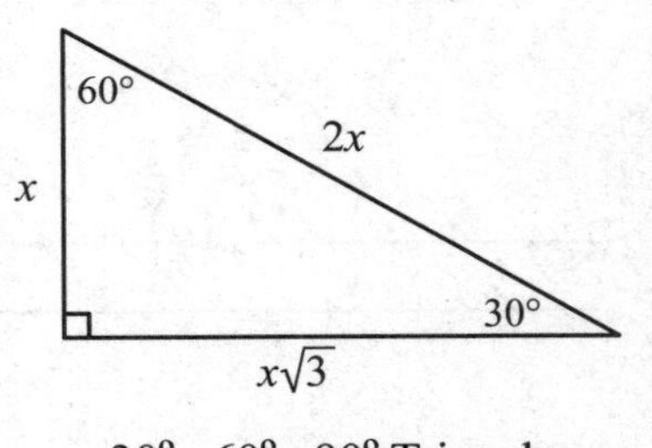

30°– 60°– 90° Triangle

Trigonometry

$\sin\theta = \frac{\text{opposite}}{\text{hypotenuse}}$ $\qquad \csc = \frac{1}{\sin}$

$\cos\theta = \frac{\text{adjacent}}{\text{hypotenuse}}$ $\qquad \sec = \frac{1}{\cos}$ $\qquad \sin^2 + \cos^2 = 1$

$\tan\theta = \frac{\text{opposite}}{\text{adjacent}}$ $\qquad \cot = \frac{1}{\tan}$

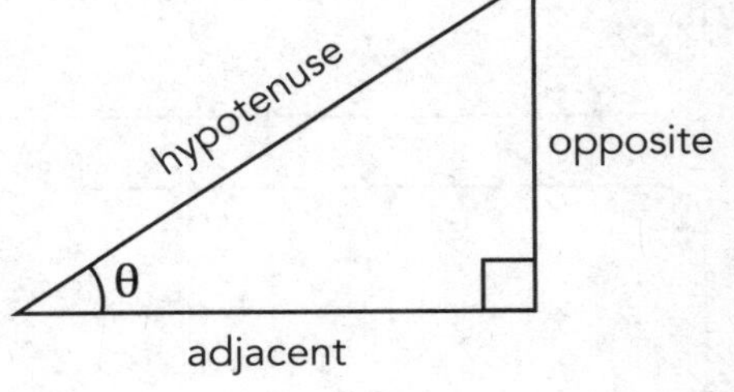

Radians

$90° = \frac{\pi}{2}$

$180° = \pi$

$270° = \frac{3\pi}{2}$

$360° = 2\pi$

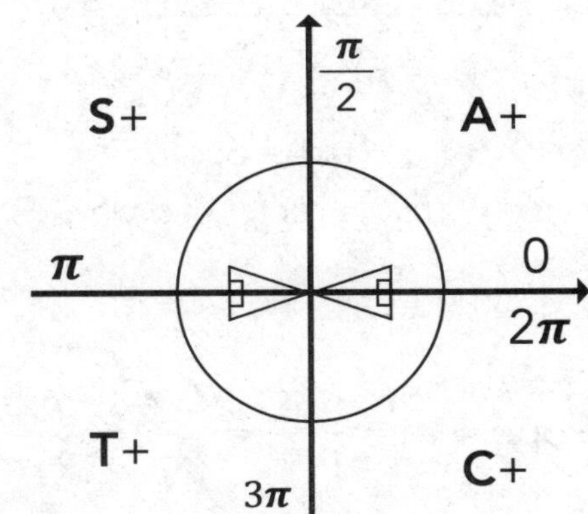

All Students Take Calculus:

All are positive in Q1

Sin is positive in Q2

Tan is positive in Q3

Cos is positive in Q4

Math Quick Reference

Algebra

Exponent Rules

$(x^a)(x^b) = x^{a+b}$

$(x^a)^b = x^{ab}$

$\frac{x^a}{x^b} = x^{a-b}$

Logarithms

$\log_x A - \log_x B = \log_x \frac{A}{B}$

$\log_x A + \log_x B = \log_x (AB)$

Difference of Squares

$(x^2 - y^2) = (x + y)(x - y)$

Quadratic Formula

$x = \frac{-b \pm \sqrt{b^2 - 4ac}}{2a}$

Directly Proportional

$y = kx$

Inversely Proportional

$y = \frac{k}{x}$

Imaginary Number

$i = \sqrt{-1}$

$i^2 = -1$

Arithmetic

$$\% \text{ Change} = \frac{\text{(New number – Old number)}}{\text{Old number}} \times 100$$

$$\text{Average} = \frac{\text{Sum}}{\text{\# terms}}$$

Sum		
Avg	×	# of terms

$$\text{Probability} = \frac{\text{\# of outcomes that meet the requirements}}{\text{Total \# of possible outcomes}}$$

Coordinate Systems

Equation of a Line

$y = mx + b$

m = slope

b = y-intercept

(x,y) = point on the line

Equation of a Circle

$(x - h)^2 + (y - k)^2 = r^2$

r = radius of circle

(h,k) = center of circle

Perpendicular lines

$m_1 = -\frac{1}{m_2}$

Parallel lines

$m_1 = m_2$

$$\text{Slope} = m = \frac{\text{rise}}{\text{run}} = \frac{\triangle y}{\triangle x} = \frac{y_2 - y_1}{x_2 - x_1}$$

Reading

Reading

The ACT Reading section assesses your ability to quickly read large blocks of interesting or wildly boring text (you will have both!) and answer specific and inference questions from that text.

You only have 8 minutes 45 seconds to move through each of the four passages and knock out all the accompanying questions. There is a balance you must achieve between spending time reading the passage and answering the questions. With practice, you will find the balance that is right for you.

Passage Types

The test writers have chosen four passage types in the hope that you will like at least one of them. The passages come in the following order:

Passage 1: Prose/Fiction

For the fiction lovers out there, you will naturally be drawn to this dialogue-rich format. This section is largely drawn from **novels, plays, and short-stories**. To nail this passage type you must get into the heads of several people: the principal characters, the narrator, and occasionally the author. It's all about telling the difference between the various **perspectives** presented in the passage.

Passage types you like will generally be easier to understand.

Passage 2: Social Science

If you like meeting new people and learning about what makes them tick, you are going to love the wide selection of social science passages. You'll learn about inventors, tribes in the Amazon, political revolutionaries, civil rights movements, cultural developments, and potential vacation destinations. Prepare to expand your **cultural horizons**!

Passage 3: Humanities

Awaken your inner artist and come learn about the great **creative innovators** of our time. Study the painters who changed our perspective, the writers who revolutionized the written word. Humanities passages read like biographies. They single out an artist or a group of artists working during a particular point in history.

Passage 4: Natural Science

Asteroids, invertebrates, and epidemics, oh my! Science lovers of the world unite! This is your chance to explore the most **cutting-edge scientific discoveries** of our time, to play in the dirt and reach for the stars! This straightforward section offers you more specific details and **jargon** to wade through, but if you look past the big words, the skills tested are the same as those tested in the other passage types.

Don't Be So Passive

When students struggle with the Reading section, it is often because they are used to reading passively. Whether out of boredom or habit, they simply scan the passages and hope to absorb all the important information. This is a sure-fire way to struggle on ACT Reading!

Be a Hawk for Details

To beat the ACT you will need to adjust your reading style. You need to become a hawk for **details** and **specific language**. Right or wrong answers frequently hinge upon a single word. Don't get fresh! Stick with the words on the page.

Let's take a closer look at the hawk-like reading that is the key to success.

Active Reading

Reading on the ACT is not a passive activity. To master the ACT Reading passages, you must become a hunter of specific words and details.

The Hunt

When you read for the ACT, you need to:

- **Narrow your focus** to the words on the page, forgetting everything else.
- **Track the author** and try to understand her every move. What is she trying to achieve? What's her point? How is she building her argument?
- Actively **translate the author's words** into your own words and constantly check your understanding as you go.
- **Become alert** for subtle shifts or transitions in the text.

Reading With Your Pencil

As you make your way through a passage, your pencil should be marking up and dissecting the passage. You will need to refer back to the passage, and it will be so much easier if you have already identified the important information. When you finish actively reading, your tracks will be everywhere: words will be **circled**, **starred**★, and **underlined**; **arrows** will be drawn showing connections between sections; **notes** will be in the margins.

true dat!

Cure for Boredom
When you read actively, it is much harder to become bored or lose your focus!

But do I have time for all of this?

Surprisingly, yes! It turns out that, although this active reading process at first seems cumbersome, it will actually **speed you up**! Most students rush through the passage without using their pencil at all— without making meaning of the text. When they come to the questions, they hit a brick wall and end up having to read the same material over and over to pull out the necessary information.

When you read actively, you wisely trade all that re-reading for some **quick pencil movements** early on.

The key is to invest your time on the front end, and reap the return once you arrive at the questions. By interacting with the text at a deeper level on your first read-through, you will come to more fully understand the text as soon as possible. Then, you can rocket through the questions!

The Art of Active Reading

Let's look at how you can **read with your pencil** to increase comprehension.

Don't fall into the trap of underlining everything.

If you do that, you will have made no progress distinguishing truly important information from distracting information.

1 Underline Key Ideas

Most information in a passage plays only a supporting role, and some is simply there to distract you. You only need to underline content that conveys the main points and key ideas of the author. In general, you will underline roughly 20 to 30 percent of the words in a passage.

2 Circle Logic Words

Many authors will signal that their main point is coming by using a logic word. Words like **but**, **however**, **although**, and **despite** let you know that the author is about to tell you what he or she really thinks. When you see logic words like these, circle them!

3 Star Main Ideas

When the author lays out the essence of the argument, put a star (★) next to it. When you get to a question asking for the main idea, let these stars guide you home.

4 Use Notations to Summarize Key Ideas

When you come across key ideas in a passage, translate them into your own words and write a brief summary statement of 10 words or less in the margin. These "Cliff's Notes™" will be extremely useful when you tackle the questions.

Now that you are familiar with the art of Active Reading, let's see it in action.

Passage 1

It is highly doubtful that the Allied forces would have won World War II without the help of Polish mathematician Marian Rejewski. At age fourteen, Rejewski enrolled in a secret cryptology course for German speakers. Soon his full-time occupation was decoding the German *Enigma* machine. Combining his usage of pure mathematics with information provided by French intelligence, Rejewski succeeded in decoding the *Enigma*, and consequently, the Allied forces were able to intercept German intelligence transmissions for six years. Historian David Kahn says that Rejewski's stunning achievement "elevates him to the pantheon of the greatest cryptanalysts of all time." On the 100th anniversary of his birthday, a sculpted memorial was presented to his hometown of Bydgoszcz, Poland.

Passage 1

★ It is highly doubtful that the Allied forces would have won World War II without the help of Polish mathematician Marian Rejewski. At age fourteen, Rejewski enrolled in a secret cryptology course for German speakers. Soon his full-time occupation was decoding the German *Enigma* machine. Combining his usage of pure mathematics with information provided by French intelligence, Rejewski succeeded in decoding the *Enigma*, and consequently, the Allied forces were able to intercept German
★ intelligence transmissions for six years. Historian David Kahn says that Rejewski's stunning achievement "elevates him to the pantheon of the greatest cryptanalysts of all time." On the 100th anniversary of his birthday, a sculpted memorial was presented to his hometown of Bydgoszcz, Poland.

Polish kid, greatest cryptanalyst—helped win war, memorial

1 Underline Key Ideas

If we strip away all the supporting text, we are left with:

doubtful —Allied forces —won World War II without—mathematician Marian Rejewski—fourteen—secret cryptology course—German speakers—decoding—German *Enigma* machine—mathematics—French intelligence—decoding the *Enigma*—Allied forces—intercept German intelligence—Rejewski's stunning achievement—greatest cryptanalysts—memorial

So we underlined 38 out of 116 words: **roughly 32% of the passage.**

2 Circle Logic Words

We did not have any key logic words like **however** or **although** to circle in this passage.

3 Star Main Ideas

★ It is highly **doubtful** that the **Allied forces** would have **won World War II without** the help of Polish **mathematician Marian Rejewski**.

★ Historian **David Kahn says** that **Rejewski's** stunning achievement "elevates him to the pantheon of the **greatest cryptanalysts of all time**."

4 Use Notations to Summarize Key Ideas

Polish kid, greatest cryptanalyst—helped win war, memorial

These eight words help summarize the key ideas of the passage. By translating these ideas into our own words, we check our understanding of the passage. Bring on the questions!

E2 **Passage 2**

Coleman Hawkins, one of the first great saxophonists of the Harlem Renaissance, was a consistently modern improviser who possessed an encyclopedic knowledge of music. Hawkins was a giant of the jazz scene for more than forty years. His musical odyssey began in front of the keys of a piano at the age of five; he moved on to the cello before settling on the tenor saxophone. In the 1920s and 30s, the saxophone was primarily considered a novelty instrument used in marching bands. However, Hawkins saw a greater potential for this instrument. His lyrical tones and innovative style helped usher in a new age of avant-garde jazz known as Bebop and placed the saxophone at the center of the new jazz aesthetic. Succeeding generations of saxophonists, whose members included Sonny Rollins, Lester Young, and John Coltrane, acknowledged the profound influence that "Hawk" had on their musical styles.

S

Passage 2

Coleman Hawkins, one of the first great saxophonists of the Harlem Renaissance, was a consistently modern improviser who possessed an encyclopedic knowledge of music. Hawkins was a giant of the jazz scene for more than forty years. His musical odyssey began in front of the keys of a piano at the age of five; he moved on to the cello before settling on the tenor saxophone. In the 1920s and 30s, the saxophone was primarily considered a novelty instrument used in marching bands. However, Hawkins saw a greater potential for this instrument. His lyrical tones and innovative style helped usher in a new age of avant-garde jazz known as Bebop and placed the saxophone at the center of the new jazz aesthetic. Succeeding generations of saxophonists, whose members included Sonny Rollins, Lester Young, and John Coltrane, acknowledged the profound influence that "Hawk" had on their musical styles.

Hawkins, Jazz great, Saxophone innovator, influential

The Importance of Practice

This process will naturally slow you down in the beginning. But the more you practice, the faster you will eventually become.

Attacking Questions

Here are a few principles to keep in mind when attacking ACT Reading questions.

Forget Everything You Know!

Don't be distracted by what you know about the outside world. When you read for the ACT, you are like a horse with blinders. All that exists, all that matters, are the words on the page directly in front of you.

Turn Off Your Brain!

Don't overthink! If you find yourself using any of the following words to justify an answer choice, **it is likely the wrong choice!**

Ya' know...

Hmm...

That **may** have happened...

That **could** be right..

click

It's **possible** that is true...

Maybe...

Well, I **could maybe** see...

Well...

That **kind of** makes sense...

Potentially... I guess?

Strategy

On a basic level, every Reading question can be solved the same way.

1 **Paraphrase** the question

The first step to answering a question is knowing what it's asking. To check your understanding, put the question into your own words.

2 Come up with your **own** answer

The ACT writers will set up numerous traps for you in the answer choices. To avoid these well-laid traps, start off by **covering** the answer choices. If possible, take the time to answer the question **in your own words** before you even look at the answer choices.

3 **Read** the answer choices

It's easier to understand the answer choices when you read them in context. Read each choice as a **complete sentence** beginning with your paraphrased question. If you read a choice that matches your own answer exactly, choose it!

4 Eliminate **wrong answers** as you go

Focusing on individual words, cross out answer choices that are not supported by the passage. Find your right answer through the magical **process of elimination**.

Pay attention: This is the most important concept in the Reading section of this book.

Throw-aways

The key to a high Reading score is to focus on the WRONG answers. If you eliminate all the junk, you will be left with the correct answer.

The essence of a wrong answer lies in a tiny word or series of words that is not supported by evidence from the passage. We call these words **throw-aways.** EVERY wrong answer choice has:

1 a string of familiar, **good-sounding** words

2 at least one **throw-away**

A wrong answer looks something like this:

A. Good word great word, good phrase filler word **throw-away** amazing word.

ACT writers expect you to be mesmerized by all of the gleaming, beautiful, right-sounding words. Then, while your guard is down, they sneak in a throw-away that makes the choice completely wrong.

If you look for good sounding words, you'll find them everywhere! Instead, focus on throwaways!

Students are often so drawn to the familiar language in an answer choice ("Oh, I saw that word/phrase!") that they ignore the throw-away. To avoid falling into this trap, you need to **narrow your focus** and **hunt for throw-aways**.

Speedy Hunting

Hunting for throw-aways will save you time. The instant you see a completely foreign or unsupported word in an answer choice, you can eliminate that answer choice without reading any further.

Let's practice hunting for throw-aways!

Passage 1

It is highly doubtful that the Allied forces would have won World War II without the help of Polish mathematician Marian Rejewski. At age fourteen, Rejewski enrolled in a secret cryptology course for German speakers. Soon his full-time occupation was decoding the German *Enigma* machine. Combining his usage of pure mathematics with information provided by French intelligence, Rejewski succeeded in decoding the *Enigma*, and consequently, the Allied forces were able to intercept German intelligence transmissions for six years. Historian David Kahn says that Rejewski's stunning achievement "elevates him to the pantheon of the greatest cryptanalysts of all time." On the 100th anniversary of his birthday, a sculpted memorial was presented to his hometown of Bydgoszcz, Poland.

1. The author most likely mentions historian David Kahn (line 7) in order to:

- **A.** introduce a lighthearted digression.
- **B.** offer evidence to support a prior claim.
- **C.** offer an anecdote revealing the flaw in a popular misconception.
- **D.** suggest the value perceived in a historical event.

2. The primary purpose of the passage is to.

- **F.** explain how the *Enigma* machine was decoded.
- **G.** illustrate the principles of cryptology.
- **H.** highlight the contribution of a noted mathematician to the war effort.
- **J.** provide insight into the motivations of a renowned cryptanalyst.

Remember to read the paraphrased sentence stem before each and every answer choice.

"The author mentions Dave to introduce a lighthearted digression."

S

1. The author most likely mentions historian David Kahn (line 8) in order to:
Author mentions Dave to...

~~A.~~ introduce a lighthearted digression.
Lighthearted... Are you laughing? Digressing... Have we changed topics, or is this essential to our passage? Both of these are throw-aways.

~~B.~~ offer evidence to support a prior claim.
Evidence? What evidence is Kahn bringing to the table? He's simply saying the event was important; that's not new evidence.

~~C.~~ offer an anecdote revealing the flaw in a popular misconception.
*What part of this answer is **not** wrong? **Anecdote**, **flaw**, and **misconception** are clear throw-aways. But it sure is confusing when you see all these words together. Take it one word at a time.*

(D.) suggest the value perceived in a historical event.
Nothing outlandish here! This is the best choice!

2. The primary purpose of the passage is to:
The author wrote the passage to...

~~F.~~ explain how the *Enigma* machine was decoded.
*Do you see an explanation? Did you learn how the machine worked? Could you build one now? The word **how** is the throw-away.*

~~G.~~ illustrate the principles of cryptology.
*Quick - name the principles... still waiting... Don't beat yourself up; they weren't in the passage! We saw **cryptology**, but no principles!*

(H.) highlight the contribution of a noted mathematician to the war effort.
Nothing glaringly wrong with this answer; let's move on.

~~J.~~ provide insight into the motivations of a renowned cryptanalyst.
*We know what Rejewski did, but we have no clue **why** he did it.*

E2 Passage 2

Coleman Hawkins, one of the first great saxophonists of the Harlem Renaissance, was a consistently modern improviser who possessed an encyclopedic knowledge of music. Hawkins was a giant of the jazz scene for more than forty years. His musical odyssey began in front of the keys of a piano at the age of five; he moved on to the cello before settling on the tenor saxophone. In the 1920s and 30s, the saxophone was primarily considered a novelty instrument used in marching bands. However, Hawkins saw a greater potential for this instrument. His lyrical tones and innovative style helped usher in a new age of avant-garde jazz known as Bebop and placed the saxophone at the center of the new jazz aesthetic. Succeeding generations of saxophonists, whose members included Sonny Rollins, Lester Young, and John Coltrane, acknowledged the profound influence that "Hawk" had on their musical styles.

3. The passage supports which of the following statements about Hawkins?

A. He broke new ground for jazz saxophonists.
B. His innovative lyrics helped usher in a new musical era.
C. His music earned international acclaim for many decades.
D. His modernist style alienated more traditional musicians.

4. The author references Hawkins' "odyssey" (line 3) in order to

F. enumerate the steps he took to develop his saxophone technique.
G. suggest the many challenges he faced in his musical training.
H. convey an appreciation for an artist's journey of self-expression.
J. reveal that Hawkins was not initially drawn to the saxophone.

S

3. The passage supports which of the following statements about Hawkins?

I read that Hawkins...

(A.) He broke new ground for jazz saxophonists.
Nothing sticking out here.

~~B.~~ His innovative lyrics helped usher in a new musical era.
Lyrics? He played the saxophone! Singing while playing the sax is a feat achieved by few musicians. Lyrics is a clear throw-away.

~~C.~~ His music earned international acclaim for many decades.
He was definitely acclaimed. But international? We don't know. It's not mentioned in the passage. Watch your assumptions!

~~D.~~ His modernist style alienated more traditional musicians.
The passage never mentions the reaction of traditional musicians. For all we know, they were huge fans!

S **4.** The author references Hawkins' "odyssey" (line 3) in order to:

The author mentions "odyssey" to...

~~**F.**~~ enumerate the steps he took to develop his saxophone technique.

These lines mention piano and cello – not sax technique.

~~**G.**~~ suggest the many challenges he faced in his musical training.

*Didn't see anything about **challenges**. He seemed like a natural!*

~~**H.**~~ convey an appreciation of an artist's journey toward self-expression.

Haha! Love that one. Self-expression? Appreciation of the journey? Assumption anyone?

(J.) reveal that Hawkins was not initially drawn to the saxophone.

We read that— piano first, then cello. Nothing wrong here.

E3 **Passage 3**

Walter Alvarez, the fourth in a line of eminent and successful scientists, was practically destined for distinction in the world of science. Even with his pedigree, no one could have predicted the magnitude of his contributions to the study of dinosaurs. Alvarez ventured into the field of geology and discovered a significant amount of iridium in the layer of the Earth's crust containing the last fossilized remains of many dinosaur species. Because iridium commonly appears in asteroids, Alvarez concluded that an asteroid must have driven the dinosaurs to extinction. His theory is now the most widely-believed answer to the most widespread of questions: what killed the dinosaurs?

5. The author primarily references Alvarez's "pedigree" (line 2) in order to:

A. illustrate the level of fame attained by prominent scientists.
B. suggest his tendency toward progressive ideas.
C. show that he was entrenched in the scientific theories of the day.
D. imply that Alvarez was almost certain to achieve scientific renown.

6. The statement in lines 7–8 ("His... dinosaurs?") serves primarily to underscore the:

F. popular appeal of a theory.
G. impressionability of the public.
H. general public's fascination with dinosaurs.
J. level of celebrity achieved by scientists.

5. The author primarily references Alvarez's "pedigree" (line 2) in order to:
The author mentions "pedigree" to...

A. illustrate the level of fame attained by prominent scientists.
B. suggest his tendency toward progressive ideas.
C. show that he was entrenched in the scientific theories of the day.
(D.) imply that Alvarez was almost certain to achieve scientific renown.

6. The statement in lines 7-8 ("His…dinosaurs?") serves primarily to underscore the:
The statement is there to show the...

(F.) popular appeal of a theory.
G. impressionability of the public.
H. general public's fascination with dinosaurs.
J. level of celebrity achieved by scientists.

Passage 4

Whether as an African-American child in the segregated South or as a young single mother, Maya Angelou never failed to transcend her surroundings. A gifted artist, Angelou has achieved worldwide recognition as an author, poet, playwright, professional stage and screen producer, director, performer, and singer. Sidonie Ann Smith of *Southern Humanities Review* attributes Angelou's acclaim to "her ability to recapture the texture of the way of life in the texture of its idioms, its idiosyncratic vocabulary and especially its process of image-making." The same indomitable spirit that helped her overcome early challenges allowed Angelou to succeed in the literary world, becoming the second poet ever invited to speak at a Presidential inauguration.

7. The author most likely refers to events in Angelou's early life (lines 1–2) in order to:

A. indicate the specific hardships African Americans faced in the South.
B. highlight some of the struggles Angelou has had to overcome.
C. account for her international literary appeal.
D. give historical background for the content of Angelou's art.

8. The primary purpose of the quotation in lines (5–7) is to:

F. explain the appeal of Angelou's early work.
G. critically evaluate Angelou's work.
H. evoke sympathy for Angelou's hardships.
J. illustrate how Angelou's early life influenced her writing.

S

7. The author most likely refers to events in Angelou's early life (lines 1–2) in order to:

A. indicate the specific hardships African Americans faced in the South.
B. highlight some of the struggles Angelou has had to overcome.
C. account for her international literary appeal.
D. give historical background for the content of Angelou's art.

8. The primary purpose of the quotation in lines (5–7) is to:

F. explain the appeal of Angelou's early work.
G. critically evaluate Angelou's work.
H. evoke sympathy for Angelou's hardships.
J. illustrate how Angelou's early life influenced her writing.

Picking an Answer

You've hunted for throw-aways, you've eliminated two choices, and now you're staring down the last two possible answers. What do you do?

When you reach this point, you have **two** options.

1 Focus on **throw-aways**

If you feel **confident** about the passage, keep your eyes on the choices! None of the words were glaringly wrong on your first pass, but you know one word **must** be a throw-away. **Pick the worst word**, and eliminate that answer choice.

2 Focus on **evidence**

If you **don't feel fully qualified** to pick a throw-away, return to the passage. Look for "evidence" in the passage that supports one of the answer choices. Find words in the passage that match words in the answer choice, and pick the choice that is the **clearest match**.

Evidence

When throw-aways alone can't finish the job, turn to evidence. Evidence consists of words from the passage that match words in the answer choices.

Sometimes, choices are ripped directly from the passage; usually, evidence takes the more subtle form of **synonyms**.

The Proof is in the Passage

Every single RIGHT answer:

1 Lacks **throw-aways**

2 Contains **evidence**

In this courtroom, you are the judge. Since you couldn't make the call by looking for throw-aways, it's time to gather some evidence.

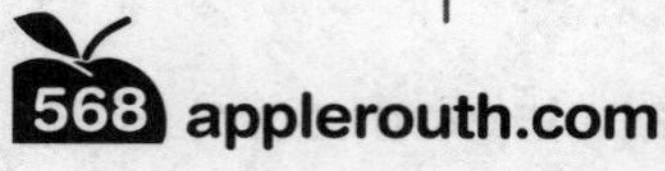

The Great Synonym Hunt

To find evidence, start with the words in the remaining answer choices, and begin the wonderful game of **Word Match** or **Synonym Hunt**. If you can't point to specific words that support an answer choice, you've got no proof. Cross out that sorry excuse for an answer choice!

Drawing Connections

When you are hunting for synonyms, you can draw a **synonym chain** directly linking answer choices with evidence in the passage.

The parakeet would not be caged. He was as rambunctious as a red-footed mongoose, as feral as a ginger-fed jackrabbit, and he was the bane of the existence of Marvin, the beleaguered janitor of Humberto's Krumping Clown Academy.

1. The author characterizes the parakeet as:
   I. an undomesticated nuisance.

synonym chain

In the example above, **feral** is *evidence* for **undomesticated** and **bane** is *evidence* for **nuisance**.

It's important that you **keep moving** and don't get hung up on one little question.

Remember, each question is only worth one 'raw score' point.

Practice drawing synonym chains in the following examples.

Passage 1

Although it is in our nature to be superstitious, cultural and environmental factors clearly influence how superstitious an individual actually is. For example, when we feel we are losing control over our lives, we tend to become more superstitious. One study found that people living in high-risk areas of the Middle East, such as Tel Aviv, are much more likely to carry a lucky charm than are other people. Nobody is immune. "We can all shift our supernatural inclination depending on the circumstances," says Bruce Hood, cognitive psychologist from the University of Bristol.

1. The author supports his argument by:
   - **A.** quoting an authority with whom he disagrees.
   - **B.** exploring a controversial scientific theory.
   - **C.** presenting the findings of a study.
   - **D.** disproving an alternate hypothesis.

2. The actions of the people in Tel Aviv (lines 4-6) primarily suggest that:
   - **F.** certain groups of people are inherently superstitious.
   - **G.** environmental factors impact our level of superstitious behavior.
   - **H.** the collective power of superstition is reinforced by heightened anxiety.
   - **J.** people who feel frightened rely more on supernatural interventions.

Passage 1

Although it is in our nature to be superstitious, cultural and environmental factors clearly influence how superstitious an individual actually is. For example, when we feel we are losing control over our lives, we tend to become more superstitious. One study found that people living in high-risk areas of the Middle East, such as Tel Aviv, are much more likely to carry a lucky charm than other people. Nobody is immune. "We can all shift our supernatural inclination depending on the circumstances," says Bruce Hood, cognitive psychologist from the University of Bristol.

synonym chain

S

1. The author supports his argument by:
The author backs up his argument by...

~ **A.** quoting an authority with whom he disagrees.
*A psychologist is an **authority**! I see a **quote**! Nothing about agreement or disagreement.*

~~B.~~ exploring a controversial scientific theory.
*No direct evidence for **controversy**.*

✓ (C.) presenting the findings of a study.
***Findings** matches **found**. **Study** matches **study**!*

~~D.~~ disproving an alternate hypothesis.
The author does not bring up any alternative explanation or hypothesis.

synonym chain

Passage 1

Although it is in our nature to be superstitious, cultural and environmental factors clearly influence how superstitious an individual actually is. For example, when we feel we are losing control over our lives, we tend to become more superstitious. One study found that people living in high-risk areas of the Middle East, such as Tel Aviv, are much more likely to carry a lucky charm than other people. Nobody is immune. "We can all shift our supernatural inclination depending on the circumstances," says Bruce Hood, cognitive psychologist from the University of Bristol.

synonym chain

S

2. The actions of the people in Tel Aviv (lines 4-6) primarily suggest that:

We learn from the Tel Aviv folks that...

~F. certain groups of people are inherently superstitious.

The author writes that we are **all** superstitious by nature, not just certain groups.

(G.) environmental factors impact our level of superstitious behavior.

These phrases are taken directly from the passage.

H. the collective power of superstition is reinforced by heightened anxiety.

Watch your assumptions! We can't connect either of these phrases to specific words in the passage.

J. people who feel frightened rely more on supernatural interventions.

These words seem on-topic, but frightened has no direct synonym in the passage. It's an assumption.

Passage 2

At a time when natural resources such as oil, coal, and natural gas are being depleted at an alarming rate, "alternative energy" seem to be the magic words at the tip of everyone's tongue. One of the most exciting proposals for generating renewable energy comes from an old idea: the solar updraft tower. Conceived in 1903, the solar tower, designed like a giant chimney, draws heated air into openings at its base. Once inside the hollow tower, the heated air rises, accelerating to speeds of 35 mph. As the air rushes upward, dozens of wind turbines turn, generating electricity. A solar updraft tower as high as 1,000 meters with a diameter as large as 7 kilometers could eventually power as many as 200,000 typical households.

3. The phrase "magic words" (lines 2-3) most directly emphasizes the:

A. unsubstantiated belief in a proposed solution.

B. inevitability of an ecological crisis.

C. ability of language to capture the public's attention.

D. perceived appeal of a solution.

4. The last sentence of the passage (lines 8-10) serves to:

F. convey the importance of a problem.

G. highlight the potential benefits of an invention.

H. speculate about the likelihood of an outcome.

J. defend a widely accepted practice.

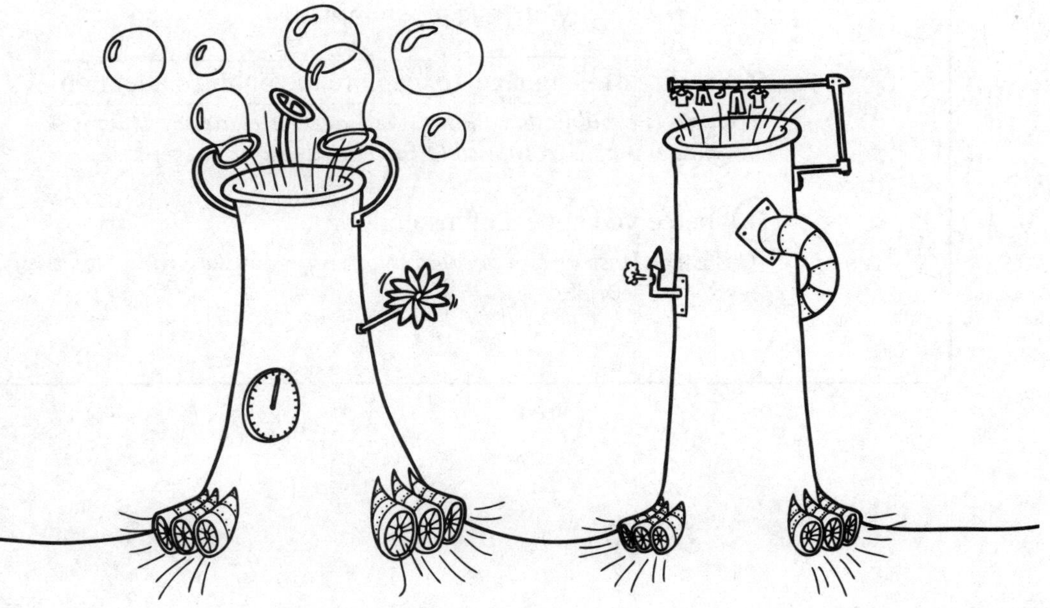

Passage 2

At a time when natural resources such as oil, coal, and natural gas are being depleted at an alarming rate, "alternative energy" seem to be the magic words at the tip of everyone's tongue. One of the most exciting proposals for generating renewable energy comes from an old idea: the solar updraft tower. Conceived in 1903, the solar tower, designed like a giant chimney, draws heated air into openings at its base. Once inside the hollow tower, the heated air rises, accelerating to speeds of 35 mph. As the air rushes upward, dozens of wind turbines turn, generating electricity. A solar updraft tower as high as 1,000 meters with a diameter as large as 7 kilometers could eventually power as many as 200,000 typical households.

S

3. The phrase "magic words" (lines 2-3) most directly emphasizes the:

From the phrase "magic words" we learn about the

~ **A.** unsubstantiated belief in a proposed solution.

The passage does not say whether the proposal is substantiated.

B. inevitability of an ecological crisis.

No evidence that there is a crisis afoot, even if you believe that's the case. Watch your assumptions.

C. ability of language to capture the public's attention.

Though the public is talking, we have no evidence that it's ***language*** *that is responsible for capturing its attention.*

D. perceived appeal of a solution.

This is the least wrong answer. Nothing brazenly wrong. It's the best of our options.

Passage 2

At a time when natural resources such as oil, coal, and natural gas are being depleted at an alarming rate, "alternative energy" seem to be the magic words at the tip of everyone's tongue. One of the most exciting proposals for generating renewable energy comes from an old idea: the solar updraft tower. Conceived in 1903, the solar tower, designed like a giant chimney, draws heated air into openings at its base. Once inside the hollow tower, the heated air rises, accelerating to speeds of 35 mph. As the air rushes upward, dozens of wind turbines turn, generating electricity. A solar updraft tower as high as 1,000 meters with a diameter as large as 7 kilometers could eventually power as many as 200,000 typical households.

S

4. The last sentence of the passage (lines 8–10) serves to:

The last sentence is there to...

F. convey the importance of a problem.

This is not about the problem but about a proposed ***solution.***

Synonym chain

G. highlight the potential benefits of an invention.

Bingo - this is perfect. Exactly what the passage says.

H. speculate about the likelihood of an outcome.

We are not speculating about the ***probability*** *of this taking place, just what might happen.*

J. defend a widely accepted practice.

We are not ***defending*** *anything, nor is the practice widely accepted.*

The Least Wrong Answer

What if there is no clearly right answer? If you find yourself in a situation where you have crossed off A, B, and C, don't force D!

The fact that A through C looked wrong does **not** mean that D is automatically right. On your first pass use a **single cross** to mark wrong answers:

Single Cross

~~A.~~ Completely ridiculous answer
~~B.~~ Doesn't look right
~~C.~~ I don't like it
~~D.~~ Not a chance this could be it

On the second pass, use a **double cross** for choices that are **clearly ridiculous:**

Double Cross

~~A.~~ Completely ridiculous answer
~~B.~~ Mostly wrong, don't love it
~~C.~~ I don't like it, but maybe
~~D.~~ Still utterly, offensively wrong

Once you go through this process, you will often be left with one or two unpleasant answer choices that are not great but are also not totally ridiculous. Pick the **Least Wrong Answer** and move on to the next question.

The Sparrow Answer

More often than not, correct answers are surprisingly simple— so simple, in fact, that students tend to overlook them in their search for scholarly-sounding answers.

We call an unassuming, unpretentious, simple answer choice a **Sparrow**. A Sparrow does not call attention to itself. It blends in. The key to a Sparrow is that by saying so little, it makes no bold statements that can be attacked. The result: no throw-away in sight.

Let's compare a **Sparrow** to a more flashy, **but still correct**, answer choice.

It is highly doubtful that the Allied forces would have won World War II without the help of Polish mathematician Marian Rejewski. Rejewski and his team cracked the code of the German *Enigma* machine, allowing the Allies to intercept and decode encrypted messages sent between the Axis forces. Historian David Kahn says that Rejewski's stunning achievement "elevates him to the pantheon of the greatest cryptanalysts of all time."

1. The main purpose of the passage is to:

sparrow — highlight the contribution of a noted mathematician to the war.

flashy — praise the history-changing work of one of the best cryptanalysts of all time.

Notice how much more **specific** and **dramatic** the right answer could have been. The test writers decided to understate things and create a Sparrow.

Sparrow Spotting

It's all about soft language! Let's look at some more examples of how ACT writers can word a Sparrow answer.

- The primary purpose of the passage is to challenge the findings of a **particular group of people**

  How perfect! A particular group of people. It's hard to argue with that. It would be easy to poke holes in an answer such as "challenge the **outrageous** findings of **overqualified** scientists." All of those adjectives can be sources of potential weakness. But "a particular group of people" is a very hard phrase to attack.

- The author mentions x in line y in order to explore **possible** explanations for a phenomenon

  Again, flawless. There are no grand claims here. **Possibility** is difficult to challenge. Anything's possible!

- The author describes x most likely to defend a position that **might be** challenged

  This answer screams Sparrow! This is very far from an absolute position. It **might**, **could**, **possibly, may** be challenged. This is a nice qualified position. Easy to defend. Hard to attack.

- Lines x–y serve primarily to **suggest** the origins of a field of research

  Words like **suggest** or **highlight** are qualified so as not to offend. These words often start off a Sparrow answer.

Now it's your turn to practice spotting Sparrows!

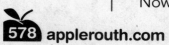

E3 **Passage 3**

Popular tastes in art, music, and politics are often as changeable as the wind. But nothing is as capricious as the fashion industry. Witty Victorian writer Oscar Wilde once said, "Fashion is a form of ugliness so intolerable that we have to alter it every six months." Whimsical as it is, fashion is more than a superficial craze. From pencil skirts to bell-bottoms, oversized sweaters to ruffled dress shirts, clothing signals everything from socioeconomic status to stage in life. For many, fashion is a form of self-expression, and individual personalities have been conveyed through fabric for centuries.

5. This passage indicates that fashion has been:

A. championed as a superficial symbol of individuality.
B. the primary means of expressing one's individual identity.
C. a means of self-expression throughout history.
D. influenced by changes in art, music and politics.

6. The list in lines 5–6 ("From...shirts") primarily serves to:

F. provide specific examples to illustrate a point.
G. exaggerate the changeable nature of fashion.
H. celebrate the diverse ways to express one's self through fashion.
J. reveal how quickly fashion trends become outdated.

S

5. This passage indicates that fashion has been:

A. championed as a superficial symbol of individuality.

B. the primary means of expressing one's individual identity.

(C.) a means of self-expression throughout history.

Short and uncomplicated: "fashion is a form of self-expression" straight from lines (7-8). "Throughout history" lines up with "have been conveyed through fabric for centuries" Perfect answer!

D. influenced by changes in art, music and politics.

6. The list in lines 5–6 ("From …shirts") primarily serves to:

(F.) provide specific examples to illustrate a point.

This is the perfect Sparrow answer. Doesn't offend or stand out, or try to show off. A harmless little statement- it gives examples to make a point. How could this be wrong?

G. exaggerate the changeable nature of fashion.

H. celebrate the diverse ways to express one's self through fashion.

J. reveal how quickly fashion trends become outdated.

E4 **Passage 4**

As wind instruments go, folded vegetation seems a little on the primitive side. Orangutans have been found to blow through leaves to modulate the sound of their alarm calls, making them the only animal apart from humans known to use tools to manipulate sound. The orangutan's music, if you can call it that, is actually an alarm call known as a "kiss squeak." "When you're walking the forest and you meet an orangutan that is not habituated to humans, they'll start giving kiss squeaks and breaking branches," says Madeleine Hardus, a primatologist at the University of Utrecht in the Netherlands, who documented the practice among wild apes in Indonesian Borneo. She contends that orangutans use leaves to make kiss squeaks to deceive predators, such as leopards, snakes, and tigers, as to their actual size – a deeper call indicating a larger animal.

7. The author references "wind instruments" (line 1) and "music" (line 4) primarily in order to:

A. offer a possible explanation for the orangutan's complex behavior.
B. question the aesthetic validity of the orangutan's sound manipulations.
C. indicate that orangutans are more sophisticated than originally thought.
D. place the orangutan's kiss squeaks in a larger context.

8. The last sentence primarily serves to:

F. place a natural behavior in its original context.
G. propose an explanation for a behavior.
H. defend the use of deception as a means of survival.
J. underscore the origins of an evolutionary adaptation.

S

7. The author references "wind instruments" (line 1) and "music" (line 4) primarily in order to:

A. offer a possible explanation for the orangutan's complex behavior.
B. question the aesthetic validity of the orangutan's sound manipulations.
C. indicate that orangutans are more sophisticated than originally thought.

D. place the orangutan's kiss squeaks in a larger context.

8. The last sentence primarily serves to:

F. place a natural behavior in its original context.

G. propose an explanation for a behavior.
H. defend the use of deception as a means of survival.
J. underscore the origins of an evolutionary adaptation.

E5 **Passage 5**

The year-long Montgomery Bus Boycott, the response to Rosa Parks' arrest for refusing to comply with Alabama's racial segregation laws in 1955, is probably the most famous social protest campaign in U.S. history. Popularized during the American Civil Rights movement, boycotting—refusing to cooperate as a means of protesting unjust political, social, or economic conditions—originated well before the 1950s. Almost seventy years earlier in a small town in Ireland, a similar movement was launched. Objecting to worker exploitation, a unified group of laborers refused to harvest the estate of a local earl. When a former military officer attempted to undermine the protest, the Irish Land League launched a campaign of isolation against him. Shops refused to serve him, neighbors openly ignored him and the postman even refused to deliver his mail. The former army captain's name was Charles Boycott.

9. The passage indicates that boycotting is

A. a unified social movement that transcends class boundaries.
B. a popular way to promote minority interests.
C. a method of protest against unjust conditions.
D. a means of effecting change only fully appreciated in modern times.

10. The author mentions Charles Boycott in order to

F. compare modern social protest with that of the past.
G. reveal the historical origins of a term.
H. illustrate the international appeal of organized social protest.
J. offer an example of effective social protest.

S

9. The passage indicates that boycotting is:

A. a unified social movement that transcends class boundaries.

B. a popular way to promote minority interests.

C. a method of protest against unjust conditions.

D. a means of effecting change only fully appreciated in modern times.

10. The author mentions Charles Boycott in order to:

F. compare modern social protest with that of the past.

G. reveal the historical origins of a term.

H. illustrate the international appeal of organized social protest.

J. offer an example of effective social protest.

Reading for Recall

Reading for recall is a skill. Believe it or not, there are things you can do to drastically improve your reading comprehension and recall.

Wait, what did
I just read??

Pinball Reading

For many students, reading can be a frustrating endeavor. They bounce back and forth between the questions and the passage, never feeling like they have a real grasp of what's going on.

They feel rushed, inefficient, and **frustrated**. And they wonder how other students can keep all that information in their heads.

Students struggle on Reading when they read **passively**. Their eyes scan the page like a paint brush, passing over each word without fully processing the meaning underneath. When it comes time to answer questions on the text, they are not able to recall key information and must go back to read yet again.

Skillful Reading

Students perform much better on Reading when they read actively. They work with the passage; they use their pencil, they paraphrase, and they engage their imagination. As a result, when it comes time to answer questions on the text, they are able to recall enough information to quickly move toward the right answer.

Let's look in more detail at the different levels of Reading for Recall:

1 Use your pencil

You already know this as Active Reading: your hand is moving, underlining, starring, and notating. The reason this is effective is you are making choices, prioritizing the text, and establishing a hierarchy. This "analysis in action" aids recall.

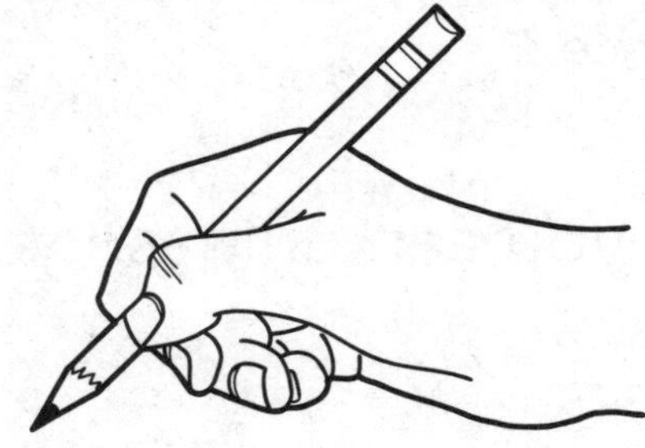

2 Paraphrase

It's easier to remember your own words.

Hard phrase to remember:
The collective efforts of the anguished artists yielded few enduring results.

Easy phrase to remember:
The artists achieved nothing.

When you translate the author's language into your own, you make the phrases "stickier" for your mind. Simplify and personalize: it's like Velcro for the brain.

3 Engage your imagination

If you've ever read a book you loved or heard a friend tell a riveting story, you've let your imagination loose and pictured a story as it unfolded. This is incredibly beneficial for remembering the story later. Images are the stickiest things of all. If you bring your imagination to the test room, watch your reading score rise.

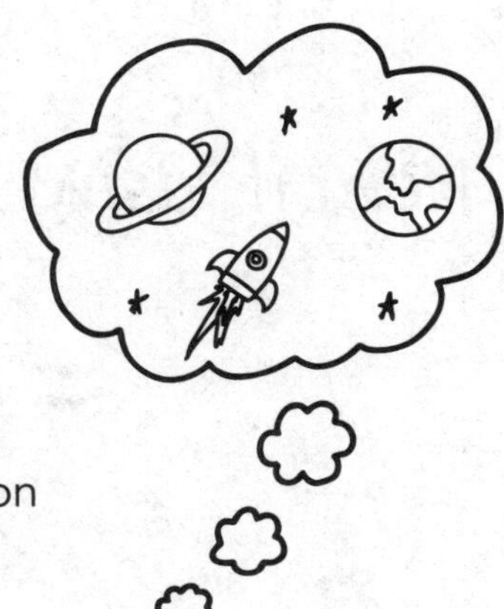

If you improve in **any** of these three areas, your ability to recall text will improve, and your score will increase. If you work all three at once...

...you can unleash your **inner ACT Reading Beast!**

Pencil Usin' + Paraphrasin' + Imaginin'

= BEAST

Reading Styles

All great readers actively engage with the passage, but not all readers have the same reading style. To maximize your score, find the style that works best for you.

Let's look at three readers and see what strategies they use to recall the text.

Reader 1: Picture Patterson

Patterson is a super-visual reader. He remembers pictures better than words. Since the ACT doesn't have any pictures, he **makes his own mental images** to help remember what he reads.

When he hears the word **cow**, he doesn't just think "cow: bovine, milk-giving mammal" or see the word **COW**, he actually **imagines** a cow. He will likely be able to tell you what color the cow is!

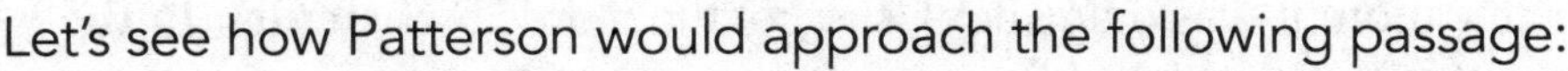

Let's see how Patterson would approach the following passage:

> My father was a St. Bernard, my mother was a Collie, but I am a transcendentalist. This is what my mother told me, I do not know these nice distinctions myself. To me they are only fine large words meaning nothing. My mother had a fondness for such words; she liked to say them, and see other dogs look surprised and envious, wondering how she got so much education. But, indeed, it was not real education; it was only show: she got the words by listening in the dining-room and drawing-room when there was company, and by going with the children to Sunday-school and listening there.

The Picture Patterson Approach

My father was a **St. Bernard**, my mother was a **Collie**, but I am a **transcendentalist**.

This is what my mother told me, I do not know these nice distinctions myself. To me they are only fine large words meaning nothing. My mother had a fondness for such words; **she liked to say them**, and **see other dogs look surprised and envious**, wondering how she got so much education.

But, indeed, it was not real education; it was only show: she got the words by **listening in the dining-room** and drawing-room when there was company,

The Picture Patterson Approach

Do you like Patterson's approach? If you pictured things in a similar way, you might be a Picture Patterson kind of reader. Breaking out this skill on the test may be your pathway to a higher score.

Picture Patterson says:

Feed your imagination.

Reader 2: Movie Melissa

Melissa has a cinematic imagination. When she reads about a field, she pictures herself **in** the field, she can smell the grass, feel the texture of the flowers: she **brings it to life**.

Melissa doesn't picture static images like Patterson. Instead she pictures an unfolding narrative in which **she's the star**, or at least the best supporting actress. Making **a movie in her mind** helps her recall the sequence of information from the passage.

Let's see how Melissa tackles the following passage.

Once upon a time, when the most advanced piece of technology in the typical office was a fax machine, "work" was somewhere you went – typically from 9-5, dressed in a suit and a tie. There was a clear delineation between "work" and "home," and that boundary helped most people define a balance between productivity and play. Now, "work" is no longer a place you go, but something you do. It can be done from anywhere – and typically is.

It's time that our cities and our public spaces began responding to these social changes. Stuffy, outdated office parks full of empty cubicles should give way to more flexible spaces that invite productivity without demanding it. Desks need not be replaced entirely, but should give way to couches, countertops, and comfortable chairs. Communal areas and conference rooms should be granted more space in the office, since increasingly people are coming in expressly for meetings. Coffee shops should be supplemented with productivity centers where nomadic workers can stop for an hour or an afternoon for a small fee. Parks should offer WiFi. And the kind of technology you'd typically find in an office – from high-res scanners to high-speed printers – should be available on every corner.

Not only would these changes assist nomadic workers in attaining greater productivity on a daily basis, they'd make things easier on those who still do the 9-5, by cutting down on traffic and congestion, and making the freelancers and contractors they collaborate with easier to reach.

The Movie Melissa Approach

Once upon a time, when the most advanced piece of technology in the typical office was a fax machine, "**work**" was somewhere you went – typically from **9-5**, dressed in a **suit and a tie**. There was a clear delineation between "work" and "home," and that boundary helped most people define a balance between productivity and play.

Now, "work" is **no longer a place you go**, but something you do. It can be done from **anywhere** – and typically is.

The Movie Melissa Approach

It's time that our cities and our public spaces began responding to these social changes. **Stuffy, outdated office parks full of empty cubicles...**

...should give way to **more flexible spaces** that invite productivity without demanding it. Desks need not be replaced entirely, but should give way to **couches**, countertops, and **comfortable chairs**. Communal areas and **conference rooms** should be granted more space in the office, since increasingly people are coming in expressly for meetings.

The Movie Melissa Approach

Coffee shops should be supplemented with productivity centers where nomadic workers can stop for an hour or an afternoon for a small fee. **Parks should offer WiFi**. And the kind of technology you'd typically find in an office – from high-res scanners to high-speed printers – should be available on every corner.

Not only would these changes assist **nomadic workers** in attaining greater productivity on a daily basis, they'd make things easier on those who still do the 9-5, by **cutting down on traffic and congestion**, and making the freelancers and contractors they collaborate with easier to reach.

Reader 3: Paraphrase Paul

Paul is not really a visual guy. He's more of a word guy. He's all about **logic**, ideas and keeping things simple.

When his friends tell him, "Paul, we've deliberated amongst ourselves and come to the conclusion that we want to travel to the House of Pies," he responds, "You're hungry. Got it."

Paul was **born** to paraphrase.
He's been doing it since he was a baby.

Read the following passage and practice your active reading skills. On the next page, Paul will show you how he breaks a passage down into his own words.

The one good thing society can do for the artist is to leave him alone. Give him liberty. The more completely the artist is freed from the pressure of public taste and opinion, from the hope of rewards and the menace of morals, from the fear of absolute starvation or punishment, and from the prospect of wealth or popular consideration, the better for him and the better for art, and therefore the better for everyone.

Liberate the artist: here is something that those powerful and important people who are always assuring us that they would do anything for art can do. They might begin the work of encouragement by disestablishing and disendowing art; by withdrawing funding from art schools, and confiscating the moneys misused by the Royal Academy.

The case of the schools is urgent. Art schools do nothing but harm, because they must do something. Art is not to be learned; at any rate it is not to be taught. All that the drawing-master can teach is the craft of imitation. In schools there must be a criterion of excellence and that criterion cannot be an artistic one; the drawing-master sets up the only criterion he is capable of using—fidelity to the model.

The Paraphrase Paul Approach

The **one good thing** society can do for the artist is to leave him **alone**.

Leave artists alone.

Give him **liberty**. The more completely the **artist is freed from the pressure** of public taste and opinion, from the hope of rewards and the menace of morals, from the fear of absolute starvation or punishment, and from the prospect of wealth or popular consideration, the better for him and the **better for art**, and therefore the better for everyone.

Leave alone = better art, happier people.

Liberate the artist: here is something that those powerful and important people who are always assuring us that they would do anything for art can do. They might begin the work of encouragement by disestablishing and disendowing art; by **withdrawing funding from art schools**, and confiscating the moneys misused by the Royal Academy.

Cut $$ from art schools.

The case of the schools is urgent. Art schools do nothing but harm, because they must do something. Art is not to be learned; at any rate it is not to be taught.

Art can't be taught.

All that the drawing-master can teach is the craft of imitation. In schools there must be a criterion of excellence and that criterion cannot be an artistic one; the drawing-master sets up the only criterion he is capable of using—fidelity to the model.

Teachers turn artists into imposters.

Okay easy. Leave artists alone to get better art. Cut schools. Teachers make imposters. Got it.

Paul broke it down! These few **sticky words** help Paul remember all the key information.

Translating As You Read

Patterson, Melissa, and Paul each have their own unique approach to reading a passage. All three students, however, have one crucial thing in common: they **translate what they read into their own language**. This language is easier for them to understand as they read, and easier to remember when they get to the questions.

The ACT rewards each of them with a **higher Reading score!**

Find Your Style

It's your turn. Use the next passage to practice translating into your own language. Whether that means picturing like Patterson, imagining like Melissa, or paraphrasing like Paul (or your own unique blend), take a few minutes to find what works for **you**.

Engage more with the passage, and your recall (and score) **will** improve.

Your Personal Approach

The new guy, Zeke, had started at the coffee shop ten days ago, and things were different since he arrived. It was hard to put into words. But the machines kept malfunctioning, the faucet would suddenly turn scalding when it was supposed to run cold, and the milk kept mysteriously going bad. It was like a force field; everything around Zeke went strange.

Zeke messed things up indirectly

(space for your notes or illustrations)

The customers could feel it too. They didn't stay as long; they shifted awkwardly in their seats, gulped their drinks, and left. Students complained that their laptops were acting up – turning on, turning off, blue screen of death… that kind of thing. We didn't mind that so much. No one wanted a bunch of table-hogging kids who bought a cup of joe for $1.85, then parked themselves in prime real estate for three hours.

Zeke himself was totally average: the surfer type, slightly built with broad shoulders and skinny legs. He was tan, with shoulder-length yellow hair, bleached by the sun. He tended to look away when he spoke to you, fidgeting with the edge of his striped hoodie, digging into the pocket of his khaki shorts. He was nice, but it was hard to draw him out. "So tell me about yourself, Zeke," I asked him one day when the shop was slow. Zeke shook his head. "I don't know, nothing much to tell," he mumbled, then slunk away to clean out the espresso machine.

Your Personal Approach

I'd been working at the coffee shop for two years, so I was an old pro; I knew all the regulars (and their drinks). I also knew that our cranky old espresso machine broke down once a month like clockwork; until Zeke showed up. Then it started breaking down every other day.

Odd sorts started coming into the shop. They wore long, dingy coats that almost touched the floor, and long, dingy hair that lay limp and greasy on their shoulders. Their faces were pale and shiny, as if overly scrubbed, and they didn't say much. They counted their money very carefully, fingering each coin as if trying to remember it. They bought drinks but didn't drink them.

But that wasn't the strangest thing about them. The strangest thing was this: I saw them come in all the time. But I never once saw one of them leave. They'd go into the bathroom. Then they'd just disappear. You probably think I'm crazy, but I know what I saw. Finally I decided I was going to investigate. For some reason the odd sorts – I'd begun calling them "irregulars" – always came in when we were extra busy, so for a while it was hard to find the time. They'd sneak into the bathroom when I was busy with a customer, then next thing I knew their table was empty and they were gone.

Your Personal Approach

But finally I caught one. He was my father's age. He wore an oversized tan trench coat; it was tattered, with faded stains like coffee and mustard. He wore a childlike expression, lost and vacant. I saw him go into the men's room; I ran over to the door and waited outside, arms crossed. Several minutes passed, then several more. I banged on the door, but no one answered. Then I heard a strange swelling of music, like smooth jazz mixed with the scary music they play at the beginning of a horror movie mixed with old radio announcements in loud cheerful tones. I heard a muffled scream. I banged on the door again, then tried the knob. It opened freely. There was no one inside.

Zeke walked up behind me and cleared his throat. "Something VERY weird is going on," I said. He rubbed his ear thoughtfully, then brushed his long hair out of his eyes for the nineteenth time that day. "The espresso machine is broken again," he said, and walked away.

Common Question Types

At a basic level, all questions on the Reading section of the ACT fall into one of two broad categories: specific questions and general questions.

You will need to learn strategies for both of these question types. Let's look at how often each question type shows up on the test.

9 out of 10 questions on the ACT are **specific** questions!

This means the ability to hunt for specific details will nab you **90%** of the possible points!

A broad understanding of the content is required for a mere 4 out of 40 questions.

Question Type	% of questions	Avg # of questions
Specific Questions	**90%**	**36**
Specific Detail	55%	22
Inference	28%	11
Vocabulary in Context	7%	3
General Questions	**10%**	**4**
Purpose of a Paragraph	5%	2
Primary Purpose/ Description of Passage	2%	1
Author's Point of View	2%	1
Structure of the Passage	0.5%	0-1
Effective Summary	0.5%	0-1
Total	**100%**	**40**

Specific Questions

Specific questions have a narrowly defined focus, frequently involving an isolated detail in the passage. Here are a few examples of specific questions:

- The narrator states that she felt close to her coworkers because...
- Which of the following questions does the passage NOT answer?
- Which of the following does the passage suggest had happened...
- As it is used in line 21, the word *circumvent* most nearly means...

Only 25 percent of questions will direct you to specific lines in a passage. For the rest of the questions, you will need to locate relevant details from the passage. The more actively you read the passage, the easier it will be to locate details!

Reading in Context

If you are given a line reference, you will generally need to read five lines above and five lines below the specified lines. If you are directed to lines 19-21, read lines 14-26. On occasion, you may need to read another line or two beyond this range to find the answer. But do not deviate too far. The writers pointed you to lines 19-21 because the answer is nearby.

Scanning for Specific Words

If you are pointed to a specific detail but are not given a line reference, you must do a quick visual scan of the passage to find the word or words in question. Once you isolate the detail mentioned in the question, read in context, five up and five down, to acquire enough information to answer the question.

The snaggletoothed dancing man was wild-eyed and crazed from hours and hours of impromptu dancing, flailing about like a **willow tree** caught in the middle of a class 5 hurricane. He imagined himself caught up in the storm, the great storm, the mindless, soul-drenching storm.

Bracketing

Use brackets to focus your attention on relevant information. In the margins of the passage, draw brackets around the five lines above and below the specified lines. Brackets tell you: "Look in this range." Also underline the word or lines specified by the question.

1. In line 15, the phrase "dancing…time" suggests

Occasionally you will need to read a few additional lines beyond the brackets, but in general, the brackets will focus your attention on the meaningful content.

The snaggletoothed dancing man was wild-eyed and crazed from hours and hours of impromptu dancing, flailing about like a willow tree caught in the middle of a Category 5 hurricane. He imagined himself caught up in the storm, the great storm, the mindless, soul-drenching storm. He felt himself dancing his way through time, around time, over and through and between time. He danced the dance of his forefathers, his forbearers, his pallbearers and ring bearers and grudge bearers. His was a dance that knew neither time nor place. A dance conceived before culture gave birth to the very idea of dancing. As the hours passed and his dancing grew more frenzied, more urgent, he felt himself merging with the elements, with the universe, as physical boundaries melted away.

Types of Specific Questions

Specific Detail

Roughly **half** of the 40 questions will fall into this category. Specific Detail questions direct you to a word or small phrase. Find your evidence and always read in context.

- The passage states that the Aethiopian Sea is home to...
- According to the passage, Ares envisioned himself working as...
- The passage supports which of the following about Humberto's school?

Inference

The second most common question type is the **inference** question. Roughly 10 of the 40 questions, 25 percent of the Reading section, will fall into this category. There are two main kinds of inference questions.

1 Suggests/Implies

- Which of the following does the passage suggest had happened?
- It can reasonably be inferred from the passage that the author believes...
- The passage's author most strongly implies...
- The passage suggests that Heisenberg most valued...

2 Primarily serves to

- The author uses the events named in lines 82-86 primarily to...
- The author most likely includes the third paragraph (lines 45-63) to...
- The reference to the "flaming snack-pack" (line 8) primarily serves to...

Inference questions are fairly straightforward. Use your standard rules of evidence, looking for synonyms and watching out for throw-aways. And **always** read in context.

Vocabulary in Context (VIC)

Roughly 2 or 3 of the 40 questions will fall into this category.

- As it is used in line 62, the word *advantage* most nearly means...
- As it is used in line 32, the word *hollow* most nearly means...
- As it is used in line 18, the word *exalted* most nearly means...

Here are some of the relatively simple words the ACT has used in the past:

coppers, revolution, conventions, battery, humor, concentrated, unwinds, carve up, popular, read, consumers, liability, novel, import, engendered, radical, workers, tempered, compensation, ravages, miracle, circumscribed, Australopithecus

Few of these words are particularly challenging, but frequently the ACT will use these easy words in a novel or unusual way. Even if you know the most common definition of a word, don't automatically assume it is the correct answer. You need to **read in context** to determine how the ACT is using these words.

If you come to the end of a paragraph while reading five up or down, you do not need to read further for a VIC question.

Strategy for VIC questions

Step 1	Read the **question**.
Step 2	Find the line specified in the passage containing the vocabulary word. Read in context, **five lines up and down**.
Step 3	Replace the word with your **own prediction**.
Step 4	**Eliminate** any choices that don't match your guess.
Step 5	**Plug** the remaining choices into the sentence in the passage, one at a time, to see which ones make sense in context.
Step 6	Using the process of elimination, **choose an answer**.

Let's see this VIC strategy in action.

1 Read the question

In line 26, *peculiar* most nearly means:

A. abnormal
B. specific
C. uncustomary
D. fantastic

2 Read in context

Read 5 lines up and 5 lines down (lines 21-31)

Traveling opens up doors and expands horizons. It is a means of enriching one's knowledge and expanding one's conception of the world. Additionally, travel can greatly expand one's understanding of the many ways in which cultures interpret language. For many travelers, unaccustomed to the cultural milieu of a particular destination, they will need clarification of the terminology <u>peculiar</u> to a particular region and its history. For the meaning of a phrase may be isolated to a particular region. Travel thirty miles outside of one locale, and the same phrase may have a completely different connotation.

All meaning is locally defined. If you don't know where you are...

3 Make your prediction

"The terminology *peculiar* to a particular region. "

The meaning of *peculiar* has to do with the word "particular." When terminology is "particular to" a region, it is "linked to" it.

My guess is *"linked to."*

Eliminate choices that don't match your guess

Now we need to go and see which words might work.

~~A.~~ abnormal *Does not mean "linked to." Nix it.*
~ **B.** specific *This has some potential, let's keep it.*
~~C.~~ uncustomary *This is almost the opposite of "linked to." Nix it.*
~ **D.** fantastic *hmm... sounds funny, but not as wrong as the others; keep it for now.*

5 Plug in the remaining answer choices

Next we plug the remaining answer choices back **into** our original sentence, replacing the word *peculiar* with the words from the answer choice:

B. specific "terminology ***specific*** to a particular region"
D. fantastic "terminology ***fantastic*** to a particular region"

6 Choose your answer

After reading the two options in context, *"specific"* seems to be a better match.

The answer is **B. specific.**

General Questions

Not all Reading questions direct you to a specific detail in a passage. Many questions involve multiple parts of a passage, overarching themes in a passage, or an analysis of the passage as a whole.

Here are a few examples of general questions:

- One of the **main ideas** established by the passage is that...
- The **point of view** from which the passage is told is...
- Which of the following best describes the **structure** of the passage...
- Would the statement above be an **effective summary** of the passage?

When you are dealing with general questions, you must integrate information from various parts of the passage. These questions require a broader view.

Purpose of a Paragraph

Roughly 2 of the 40 questions will fall into this category.

- The primary purpose of the fourth paragraph (lines 65-74) is to...

To answer this question, you need to understand how the paragraph functions in the context of the passage. What **job** is it doing? Clarifying a point? Adding evidence? Offering a contrast? You will need to read the five lines preceding and following the paragraph in addition to reading the paragraph itself.

Be on the lookout for **transitions**. Circle words or phrases like **although**, **however**, or **in spite of**, which indicate such transitions.

Purpose of the Passage

Occasionally, 1 of the 40 questions will fall into this category.

- Which of the following best expresses the main idea of the passage?
- Would the above quote be an effective summary of the passage?

Remember that we are looking for the **main theme** of the passage. Do not get stuck in the weeds, in the details, or in the content of one isolated paragraph. The primary purpose must be the dominant theme of the **entire passage**.

Bookending

A good strategy to determine the primary purpose of a passage is **bookending**. You skim the first and last sentence, the "bookends," of each paragraph. You are not reading for detail but merely to get a **general sense of each paragraph.** You can bookend a passage quickly to get its "gist" and solve these questions.

> Björk conducted almost 1,000 interviews while traveling across Europe. In an interview in Rome, renowned pop singer Björk was asked about her identity as an Icelandic artist living in England. Her reply—"When I was a teenager in Iceland people would throw rocks and shout abuse at me because they thought I was weird. I never got that in London no matter what I wore." Björk is forever associated with her Icelandic homeland, and her music is infused with the sounds and rhythms of her native soil. However, she has found a new home and a greater degree of acceptance in London.

Point of View

Occasionally, 1 of the 40 questions will fall into this category.

- The point of view from which the passage is told is best described as...

Don't confuse the characters and the narrator if you are working with a **Prose/ Fiction** passage. As always, use throw-aways to eliminate wrong answers.

Structure of the Passage

Occasionally, 1 of the 40 questions will fall into this category.

- Which of the following best describes the structure of the passage?
- It is most accurate to say that the information about glaciers in the passage is organized in a way that is...
- The author's main technique in the passage is to...

When it comes to structure questions, you need to step **way** back from the content and look at the **"skeleton" of the passage**. How is the passage organized? Do we start off with a hypothesis which is then analyzed? Does the author state a problem and propose several solutions? Does the author outline a process or procedure?

Effective Summary

Occasionally, 1 of the 40 questions will fall into this category.

- Would the statement above be an effective summary of the passage?

Effective Summary questions are best answered by **bookending** and focusing on **throw-aways**. What was the focus of the passage? Does the offered summary cover the entire passage? As with all General questions, you need to take a **broad view** of the passage to answer these questions.

ACT Reading Outlaws

The characters below are trouble. They are bad role models. Do you see yourself in any of them? If so, don't worry. There's a fix for every bad habit!

Notorious for:
Making assumptions not supported by passage. Overthinking.

Last heard saying:
*"I can see how that could **possibly** be true..."*

Advised action: Focus on **throw-aways**!

Notorious for:
Refusing to underline, notate, or cross out throw-aways. Insisting that's "just how she reads."

Last heard saying:
*"But I don't have **time** to underline..."*

Advised action: Practice **active** reading!

Notorious for:
Not balancing time between passage and questions. Spinning his wheels on hard questions.

Last heard saying:
"FIVE MINUTES LEFT?! ....WHAT?!"

Advised action: Timing drills! And **watch the clock!**

Notorious for:
Skimming the surface; reading without really reading. Having to re-read the passage over and over.

Last heard saying:
"Wait... What did I just read???"

Advised action: Use active reading to stay focused! Pause after each paragraph to **check understanding**.

Notorious for:
Missing the big picture; mistaking details for themes. Frequently missing general questions.

Last heard saying:
*"Line 6 clearly mentions squirrels. **Hello, main idea!**"*

Advised action: Step back. Count how **often** ideas show up in the passage, and rely on throw-aways!

Notorious for:
Losing points by misreading the question. Rushing past words like EXCEPT.

Last heard saying:
"Gotta go fast, gotta go fast, gotta go fast..."

Advised action: Slow down. Underline words in the question. Use **timing drills** to find a comfortable pace.

Notorious for:
Having "buyer's remorse" after picking an answer. Wasting time before committing to an answer.

Last heard saying:
*"Junk, I **knew** that was the right answer!"*

Advised action: Cross out throw-aways. Pick an answer and stick with it. Trust your instinct!

Managing Your Time

For many students, effective time management is the key to attaining a high score on the Reading section of the ACT.

There are several things you can do to help you manage your pacing on the Reading section.

Keep your eye on the clock

You have 8:45 per passage. That's it. It's good to write down the start and finish time for a given passage directly on the passage. This will anchor you in to the appropriate pacing. Know that this 8:45 needs to be allocated across the passage **and** the questions.

Most of our students will complete the passage in **4 minutes** and use the remaining time for questions. If you cannot finish reading the passage in roughly 4 minutes, you need to practice timing drills until this pace becomes more comfortable. Once you move from the passage to the questions, you can expect to have roughly **30 seconds** per question. Some questions are obviously faster than others, but you should never, for any reason, spend more than a minute on a single question.

Actively read

If you read the passage deeply on the first pass, you will save a ton of time on the questions!

Stay on Task

There are four steps, and only four steps, to approaching Reading questions.

1 Throw-aways

2 Evidence

3 Guess

4 Move on

Repeat these to yourself until you have the steps memorized.

Throw-aways, evidence, guess, move on.
Throw-aways, evidence, guess, move on.

There's no time for anything else! Once you've finished one step, move on to the next. You don't need to add anything else into the mix. Staying on task will keep you fast.

Don't Spin Your Wheels

You have 30 seconds per question. Once you have narrowed down the choices using throw-aways, you can only ponder for a few seconds. Weigh the remaining choices. Trust your gut. Guess. And move on!

Reading Walkthrough

It's time to practice your skills. In the pages that follow, you will find two ACT Reading passages—one Prose Fiction, the other Natural Science. After each passage, we will walk through the correct answers, step by step.

Compare your work to the solutions to find areas that need improvement. Learn from your mistakes and work to improve on the second passage. Remember the keys to acing the ACT Reading section:

1 **Actively** read

Keep your pencil moving! Underline, circle logic words, star main ideas, and take notes!

2 Translate into your **own language**

Whether you are a Movie Melissa, a Picture Patterson, or a Paraphrase Paul, actively engage with the passage and flex your imagination!

3 Stay on **task**

Throw-aways, evidence, guess, move on.
Throw-aways, evidence, guess, move on.
Don't spin your wheels!

4 Manage your **timing intervals**

A single passage should take, at most, **8 minutes and 45 seconds**. If you're taking too long, find out why! Did you spend over half of your time reading? Did you spin your wheels and spend a whole minute on a single question?

READING WALKTHROUGH 1

8 Minutes 45 Seconds — 10 Questions

Passage I

PROSE FICTION

The summer I was twelve came to be known as the "Summer of the Sandwich," at least between my brother and me. He was ten, just old enough to be interested in sandwiches.

We lived in the city. It was hot and muggy and sweaty during the summertime, especially inside the dim confines of our cramped apartment. Our mother was tired of listening to our arguments and kept sending us off to the park. It was hot there, too, the air flat and moist and still, like underneath the bed. We'd throw the Frisbee around a couple times before collapsing in the shade, sluggish and annoyed.

Our only hope for enjoying the summer lay in De Luca's, the deli three blocks north and four blocks west. De Luca's specialized in sandwiches; the big chalkboard behind the counter listed three dozen different kinds, maybe more. The sandwiches were named after friends and family members, old TV shows, puns and plays on words. De Luca's also served soft drinks in slim glass bottles, which made the plain old soda seem more sophisticated, and very cold lemonade that was both mouth-numbingly sour and deliciously sweet. Best of all, they had air conditioning.

Tommy De Luca, the deli owner, still sliced the ham, fried the eggs, and sautéed the onions behind the counter. He could recount the history of every deli in the city, and detail the anatomy of each sandwich served on their menus. He described himself as "one of the last true hoagie connoisseurs." This summer, he was running an intriguing special. If a customer could invent their own completely unique, delicious sandwich – along with the clever, play-on-words name that would sum up all that sandwich offered to the world – and if Tommy chose this sandwich as one of his "Featured Sandwiches," to be written up on the chalkboard, along with all the other great sandwiches that had gone before it – that customer would be allowed to eat half-price for the duration of the summer. We were hooked.

This invitation was extended to all, written in a flowing script on an A-shaped blackboard propped up just inside the door. But we may have given our parents the impression that Mr. De Luca had taken one look at us and realized we were sandwich pioneers in the making, and therefore issued us this sandwich challenge specifically. Of course, after this our parents had no choice but to support us in our endeavors.

So we embarked on a journey of innovation. The first thing, of course, was to stop by De Luca's and meticulously copy down each menu item into our college-ruled notebook, to ensure we didn't cover any familiar ground. We studied this notebook over the next couple days, and then began brainstorming our own concoctions. We narrowed these hypothetical delicacies down to a few likely candidates. Then we began assembling the chosen few.

Most were disappointments. Grilled cheese with banana peppers and bologna was a particular low point; also, peanut butter and pickles sound good together in theory, but leave a lot to be desired in practice.

Despite our parents' desire to see us succeed, they were also showing signs of discomfort over our new hobby. Our frequent trips to the grocery store exceeded our allowance and we had to beg our mother for cash. Meanwhile, our methodical approach in the kitchen tended to yield huge messes as well as scientific data. Since my brother was only ten he was pretty oblivious to our parents' growing annoyance, but I could see the writing on the wall: if we didn't invent the perfect sandwich soon, they were going to shut this whole operation down.

And then we found it. Slightly stale raisin bread, thinly sliced Granny Smith apple, and extra sharp cheddar cheese: it was sweet and simple, and best of all, it wasn't on the menu. Tommy De Luca would be impressed; we were sure of it. We couldn't decide between the names 'Green-Eyed Monster' or 'Cheesy Granny.' We felt both were good. We created a beautiful specimen, complete with toothpick, and carried it to De Luca's.

It was the hot, boring part of the afternoon, between lunch and dinner, when no one was particularly hungry. Tommy sat in the dining area, reading a newspaper. He looked with mild interest at our sandwich, then listened to our pitch. We held our breath as he took a bite – slowly chewed – nodded – took another bite – nodded again.

"It's pretty good," he said. "Pretty good. Not too bad, kids. But, I don't know – it just doesn't scream De Luca's to me. Know what I mean?"

We wandered home, disappointed but determined. My brother kept harping on about how we should have tried the meatball-grilled cheese he'd suggested. Secretly, I agreed, although I steadfastly refused to admit it. Anyway, this was no time for blame or regrets. It was time to go back to the cutting board. It was time to invent a better sandwich.

1. The point of view from which the passage is told is best described as that of:
   A. a twelve year old describing the events of his summer.
   B. an adult reminiscing about a summer when he was young.
   C. a deli owner explaining how he gets his ideas.
   D. a parent who wants to encourage his children's hobby.

2. According to the passage, the children wanted to create a sandwich because:
   F. their mother wanted them to find a way to keep busy.
   G. they would be able to eat half-price at De Luca's.
   H. Tommy De Luca issued a special challenge to them.
   J. they wanted to win the respect of the other customers.

3. According to the passage, which condition did the winning sandwich NOT need to fulfill?
   A. Unique combination of ingredients
   B. Chosen by Tommy De Luca
   C. Apt and witty name
   D. A type of classic hoagie

4. It can most reasonably be inferred from the passage that "peanut butter and pickles" was a sandwich the brothers:
   F. considered, but immediately decided against.
   G. liked, but Tommy De Luca did not.
   H. made, but were unhappy with the results.
   J. would have made, but did not have the ingredients.

5. The main purpose of the last paragraph is to:
   A. demonstrate the siblings' sense of disappointment.
   B. indicate that the siblings should have pursued another idea.
   C. show that the siblings' resolve had not been broken.
   D. explain why this incident made an impact on the narrator.

6. As it is used in lines 26-27, the word *connoisseur* most nearly means:
   F. expert.
   G. chef.
   H. inventor.
   J. businessman.

7. The passage makes clear that the brothers liked eating at De Luca's deli because:
   A. it was close to the park and had delicious food.
   B. it offered air conditioning along with food.
   C. Tommy De Luca was a neighborhood friend.
   D. it led to their journey of innovation.

8. It can reasonably be inferred from the passage that the parents' discomfort with the contest was most likely due to:
   F. the brothers' constant arguments about sandwiches.
   G. the mess the boys were making in the kitchen.
   H. the boys spending too much time indoors.
   J. the potential for the boys to face great disappointment.

9. The passage implies that which of the following is most likely to result from De Lucas' decision?
   A. The parents will put an end to the sandwich project.
   B. The boys will take a more methodical and scientific approach.
   C. The boys will return to the process of brainstorming new creations.
   D. The boys will go shopping to obtain new ingredients.

10. According to the passage, the boys used the college-ruled notebook in order to:
   F. organize all of their recipes.
   G. reference De Luca's existing sandwiches.
   H. keep track of their shopping expenditures.
   J. record the results of their experiments.

READING WALKTHROUGH 1

Explanations

Passage I

PROSE FICTION

Past summer

The summer I was twelve came to be known as the "Summer of the Sandwich," at least between my brother and me. He was ten, just old enough to be interested in sandwiches.

Hot

We lived in the city. It was hot and muggy and sweaty during the summertime, especially inside the dim confines of our cramped apartment. Our mother was tired of listening to our arguments and kept sending us off to the park. It was hot there, too, the air flat and moist and still, like underneath the bed. We'd throw the Frisbee around a couple times before collapsing in the shade, sluggish and annoyed.

Deli = A/C

Our only hope for enjoying the summer lay in De Luca's, the deli three blocks north and four blocks west. De Luca's specialized in sandwiches; the big chalkboard behind the counter listed three dozen different kinds, maybe more. The sandwiches were named after friends and family members, old TV shows, puns and plays on words. De Luca's also served soft drinks in slim glass bottles, which made the plain old soda seem more sophisticated, and very cold lemonade that was both mouth-numbingly sour and deliciously sweet. Best of all, they had air conditioning.

De Luca — *sandwich contest* — *$$$*

Tommy De Luca, the deli owner, still sliced the ham, fried the eggs, and sautéed the onions behind the counter. He could recount the history of every deli in the city, and detail the anatomy of each sandwich served on their menus. He described himself as "one of the last true hoagie connoisseurs." This summer, he was running an intriguing special. If a customer could invent their own completely unique, delicious sandwich – along with the clever, play-on-words name that would sum up all that sandwich offered to the ★ world – and if Tommy chose this sandwich as one of his "Featured Sandwiches," to be written up on the chalkboard, along with all the other great sandwiches that had gone before it – that customer would be allowed to eat half-price for the duration of the summer. We were hooked.

parents ok

This invitation was extended to all, written in a flowing script on an A-shaped blackboard propped up just inside the door. But we *may* have given our parents the impression that Mr. De Luca had taken one look at us and realized we were sandwich pioneers in the making, and therefore issued us this sandwich challenge specifically. Of course, after this our parents had no choice but to support us in our endeavors.

notebook

So we embarked on a journey of innovation. The first thing, of course, was to stop by De Luca's and meticulously copy down each menu item into our college-ruled notebook, to ensure we didn't cover any familiar ground. We studied this notebook over the next couple days, and then began brainstorming our own concoctions. We narrowed these hypothetical delicacies down to a few likely candidates. Then we began assembling the chosen few.

Most were disappointments. Grilled cheese with banana peppers and bologna was a particular low point; also, peanut butter and pickles sound good together in theory, but leave a lot to be desired in practice.

$$$ — *hurry*

Despite our parents' desire to see us succeed, they were also showing signs of discomfort over our new hobby. Our frequent trips to the grocery store exceeded our allowance and we had to beg our mother for cash. Meanwhile, our methodical approach in the kitchen tended to yield huge messes as well as scientific data. Since my brother was only ten he was pretty oblivious to our parents' growing annoyance, but I could see the writing on the wall: if we didn't invent the perfect sandwich soon, they were going to shut this whole operation down.

Success!

★ And then we found it. Slightly stale raisin bread, thinly sliced Granny Smith apple, and extra sharp cheddar cheese: it was sweet and simple, and best of all, it wasn't on the menu. Tommy De Luca would be impressed; we were sure of it. We couldn't decide between the names 'Green-Eyed Monster' or 'Cheesy Granny.' We felt both were good. We created a beautiful specimen, complete with toothpick, and carried it to De Luca's.

It was the hot, boring part of the afternoon, between lunch and dinner, when no one was particularly hungry. Tommy sat in the dining area, reading a newspaper. He looked with mild interest at our sandwich, then listened to our pitch. We held our breath as he took a bite – slowly chewed – nodded – took another bite – nodded again.

"It's pretty good," he said. "Pretty good. Not too bad, kids. But, I don't know – it just doesn't scream De Luca's to me. Know what I mean?" *Not quite.*

We wandered home, disappointed but determined. My brother kept harping on about how we should have tried the meatball-grilled cheese *he'd* suggested. Secretly, I agreed, although I steadfastly refused to admit it. Anyway, this was no time for blame or regrets. It was time to go back to the cutting board. It was time to invent a better sandwich.

Hot summer, brothers try to invent sandwich for deli contest.

Close, but no salami.

1. The point of view from which the passage is told is best described as that of:

A. a twelve year old describing the events of his summer.
B. an adult reminiscing about a summer when he was young.
C. a deli owner explaining how he gets his ideas.
D. a parent who wants to encourage his children's hobby.

1. What is the POV of this passage?

In the very first line we see "when I was twelve..."

A. The narrator **was** twelve. Not any more!
B. This one looks good so far. Keep it.
C. **Deli owner** is a character in the story, not the narrator.
D. Same trick here - the **parent** was just a character.

---

2. According to the passage, the children wanted to create a sandwich because:

F. their mother wanted them to find a way to keep busy.
G. they would be able to eat half-price at De Luca's.
H. Tommy De Luca issued a special challenge to them.
J. they wanted to win the respect of the other customers.

2. Why did the children enter the contest?

If we look to our notes, we can see $$$ was a factor in entering the contest.

F. **Mother**? They had their own reasons!
G. **Half-price** matches our $$$ note. Keep G.
H. The contest was open to all, not just the kids.
J. Not a shred of evidence for **respect**.

---

3. According to the passage, which condition did the winning sandwich NOT need to fulfill?

A. Unique combination of ingredients
B. Chosen by Tommy De Luca
C. Apt and witty name
D. A type of classic hoagie

3. Which was NOT in the contest rules?

Our "sandwich contest" note tells us to look in paragraph four for the rules.

A. Evidence: "completely unique sandwich"
B. Evidence: "and if Tommy chose..."
C. Evidence: "clever, play-on-words name"
D. Evidence: None. Bingo! This is our answer.

---

4. It can most reasonably be inferred from the passage that "peanut butter and pickles" was a sandwich the brothers:

F. considered, but immediately decided against.
G. liked, but Tommy De Luca did not.
H. made, but were unhappy with the results.
J. would have made, but did not have the ingredients.

4. What probably happened with the peanut butter and pickles sandwich?

In line 53, we see this sandwich "sounded good in theory" but not "in practice."

F. They tried it! No evidence for **immediately**.
G. Did **Tommy** see the sandwich? No evidence for that.
H. No clear throw-aways here.
J. Didn't read that they were short on pickles!

5. The main purpose of the last paragraph is to:

A. demonstrate the siblings' sense of disappointment.
B. indicate that the siblings should have pursued another idea.
(C.) show that the siblings' resolve had not been broken.
D. explain why this experience made an impact on the narrator.

5. What was the main point of the last paragraph?

"We wandered home, disappointed but determined... It was time to invent a better sandwich." So they're going back to the drawing board!

A. **Disappointment** came up, but that was only half the story. What about **determined**?

B. Same problem as A. This might be true, but it doesn't address going back to inventing.

C. That's more like it.

D. Did it ever say **why**? Watch assumptions!

---

6. As it is used in lines 26-27, the word *connoisseur* most nearly means:

(F.) expert.
G. chef.
H. inventor.
J. businessman.

6. What does *connoisseur* mean in context?

*The sentence just before this word says Tommy "could recount the history" of every sandwich. So **knowledge** is a clue.*

F. Bingo! Experts have a lot of knowledge.

G. Chefs **cook**, not "recount histories."

H. **Invention** comes up in the passage, but not in the context of our vocab word.

J. Not even close.

---

7. The passage makes clear that the brothers liked eating at De Luca's deli because:

A. it was close to the park and had delicious food.
(B.) it offered air conditioning along with food.
C. Tommy De Luca was a neighborhood friend.
D. it led to their journey of innovation.

7. Why did the brothers like the deli?

Looking where the deli first came up, we see: "best of all, they had air conditioning," and our note "Deli = A/C"

A. No evidence the food was **delicious**.

B. This matches our note! Keep it.

C. Easy, Assumption Al, we didn't read that Tommy and the boys were **friends**.

D. This takes a leap of logic and an assumption or two. Stick to the words on the page!

8. It can most reasonably be inferred from the passage that the parents' discomfort with the contest was most likely due to:

~~F.~~ the brothers' constant arguments about sandwiches.

(G.) the mess the boys were making in the kitchen.

~~H.~~ the boys spending too much time indoors.

~~J.~~ the potential for the boys to face great disappointment.

8. Why were the parents trippin'?

Parental discomfort comes up around line 55. Nearby, we see "begging for cash" and "messes in the kitchen."

F. No nearby evidence for **arguments**.

G. Aha, we read about messes!

H. **Time indoors** came up at the beginning, before the contest ever came up. Off-base.

J. No evidence the parents were **worried**.

---

9. The passage implies that which of the following is most likely to result from De Lucas' decision?

~~A.~~ The parents will put an end to the sandwich project.

~~B.~~ The boys will take a more methodical and scientific approach.

(C.) The boys will return to the process of brainstorming new creations.

~~D.~~ The boys will go shopping to obtain new ingredients.

9. What is probably going to happen next?

The last sentence makes this one clear: "It was time to invent a better sandwich." More inventions to come!

A. We can't assume this. Focus on evidence!

B. Can you point to words that mean **methodical and scientific**? If not, it's a throw-away!

C. More inventions = more brainstorming! This one is the best so far.

D. Possibly, but this would be an **assumption**.

---

10. According to the passage, the boys used the college-ruled notebook in order to:

~~F.~~ organize all of their recipes.

(G.) reference De Luca's existing sandwiches.

~~H.~~ keep track of their shopping expenditures.

~~J.~~ record the results of their experiments.

10. What was the notebook for?

Scanning our notes, we see "notebook" next to a sentence with "...copy down each menu item into our college-ruled notebook." Aha! It had De Luca's menu!

F. Close, but it was **De Luca's recipes** they were organizing. Don't read too quickly!

G. Winner, Winner, Chicken Dinner.

H. Nope. Nothing about money nearby.

J. Negativo!

READING WALKTHROUGH 2

8 Minutes 45 Seconds—10 Questions

Passage IV

NATURAL SCIENCE

According to ancient Greco-Roman mythology, not only was the goddess Juno the wife of Jupiter, but she also had a special talent: when Jupiter surrounded himself with clouds in order to conceal his illicit activities, only Juno could see through the clouds – and reveal what was really going on. NASA's recent New Frontiers mission to Jupiter draws on this symbolic story as inspiration. Both the mission and the spacecraft are nicknamed Juno. Like the mythological goddess, the Juno mission aims to peer deep into Jupiter's atmosphere, learning more about the planet's origins and evolution.

Classified as a "gas giant," Jupiter boasts a mass two and a half times larger than the rest of the solar system's planets combined. Its massive size and its position on the outer edges of the solar system make it a very different planet than Earth. In fact, the composition of Jupiter's atmosphere is more like that of the Sun's, composed primarily of hydrogen and helium. In the high-pressure, high-temperature environment deep within Jupiter's atmosphere, hydrogen gas condenses into an electricity-conducting liquid that behaves somewhat like a metal. This conducting layer, combined with the planet's fast rotation, produces a powerful magnetic field.

Past missions to Jupiter have provided valuable information about the planet's atmosphere and magnetic field. Now, with information gathered by the Juno mission, scientists hope to learn even more.

One of the Juno mission's main goals is to measure the composition of Jupiter's atmosphere and determine the quantity of oxygen (most commonly present in water). By gaining a better estimate of the amount of water in the atmosphere, scientists can deduce important facts about Jupiter's formation. Did it collapse from an original cloud of gas, or did it begin as a core of ice and rock that attracted hydrogen gas? Or did water arrive in the form of loose space debris carrying loads of ice? Each of these scenarios predicts different amounts of water in Jupiter's atmosphere, and each corresponds to a different theory about how the solar system itself was formed. Thus, by researching the amount of water present in Jupiter's atmosphere, we can learn more about our own planet's origins. We may also be able to develop theories about similar planetary systems throughout the galaxy.

Other objectives include measuring temperature and cloud patterns inside Jupiter's atmosphere, mapping Jupiter's gravity field to learn more about the planet's interior structure, and studying Jupiter's magnetosphere, especially near the poles. The spacecraft is also equipped with a camera that will record images of the planet's surface.

The spacecraft has a long way to go before it arrives. It was launched from the Kennedy Space Center on August 5, 2011; Juno's next step is to swing by Earth for a gravity assist to help boost it into space. It should arrive at Jupiter on October 19, 2016. Upon arrival, Juno will enter Jupiter's orbit and begin transmitting data continuously to NASA. Once Juno has orbited Jupiter for a full year, its mission will be complete. In October 2017, Juno will be de-orbited and crash into Jupiter.

Juno is also the first solar-powered spacecraft to travel to Jupiter, or venture this deeply into space. It's equipped with three solar arrays, which protrude from the body of the spacecraft in a symmetrical fashion, a bit like a three-bladed ceiling fan. Each solar array measures about six feet wide by 27 feet long, providing a total 650 sq. ft. of solar panel. The craft's orbit will ensure that the solar panels are bathed in sunlight at all times. However, once the craft falls into orbit around Jupiter, it will only receive about four percent of the sunlight we receive on Earth. Both the solar cell technology and the instruments on board Juno are designed for maximum efficiency, ensuring that the craft can continue to operate effectively even at these reduced levels of sunlight.

Aboard Juno is a plaque that was gifted to the mission by the Italian Space Agency. The plaque is dedicated to Galileo, who in 1610 sighted the first of Jupiter's largest moons for the first time. The plaque depicts a self-portrait of Galileo, along with a quotation from a passage he wrote during the observation session in question. Translated into English, the text reads: "On the 11th it was in this formation: the star closest to Jupiter was half the size of, and very close to, the other so that during the previous nights all of the three observed stars looked of the same dimension and among them equally afar; it is evident that around Jupiter there are three moving stars that were, until now, invisible to all."

In fact, what Galileo described as "three moving stars" were actually bright moons. Now referred to as the "Galilean moons," they are named Io, Europa, and Callisto. Since Galileo's discovery, astronomers have identified more than 60 moons in orbit around Jupiter, and this number is growing each year. With the information provided by Juno, researchers hope to pierce the mystery shrouding this massive and fascinating planet.

1. Which of the following questions about the Juno mission does the passage NOT directly answer ?
   - **A.** When will Juno reach Jupiter?
   - **B.** How is the Juno spacecraft powered?
   - **C.** How much will the Juno mission cost?
   - **D.** Why are researchers interested in Jupiter?

2. The author does all of the following in the second paragraph (lines 12-23) EXCEPT:
   - **F.** compare Jupiter's atmosphere to the Sun's.
   - **G.** contrast Jupiter's temperature with the Sun's.
   - **H.** relate Jupiter's mass to other solar planets' mass.
   - **J.** describe differences between Jupiter and Earth.

3. According to the author's description, the solar panels on Juno most resemble:
   - **A.** a reflective greenhouse.
   - **B.** a ceiling fan.
   - **C.** a three-leaf clover.
   - **D.** an electromagnetic array.

4. According to the passage, the amount of water present in Jupiter's atmosphere is important because:
   - **F.** it will provide evidence to support certain theories of Jupiter's formation.
   - **G.** it will indicate whether Jupiter is habitable.
   - **H.** oxygen is most commonly found in water.
   - **J.** it could help us identify other "gas giants" like Jupiter.

5. The main focus of the last two paragraphs is the role that Galileo played in:
   - **A.** identifying three nearby stars.
   - **B.** naming Io, Europa, and Callisto.
   - **C.** developing the modern telescope.
   - **D.** discovering Jupiter's largest moons.

6. The passage states that Juno's solar panels and technology were designed to be extremely efficient because:
   - **F.** efficient technology helps save money on the mission.
   - **G.** the amount of sunlight received on Jupiter is much smaller than that on Earth.
   - **H.** the solar array will be momentarily hidden from the Sun during take off.
   - **J.** space debris may obscure the solar panels from sunlight.

7. Which of the following is NOT a mission objective mentioned in the fifth paragraph ?
   - **A.** Measuring atmospheric cloud patterns.
   - **B.** Taking pictures of the planet.
   - **C.** Testing the composition of Jupiter's core.
   - **D.** Mapping the planet's gravity field.

8. According to the passage, Jupiter's electricity-conducting interior and fast rotation produce:
   - **F.** a powerful magnetic field.
   - **G.** a high-pressure, high-temperature environment.
   - **H.** an atmosphere like the Sun's.
   - **J.** a gas giant.

9. According to the passage, the mission will be concluded when Juno:
   - **A.** makes a 1-year orbit around Jupiter.
   - **B.** crashes into Jupiter.
   - **C.** passes by Earth for a gravity assist.
   - **D.** transmits its findings back to NASA.

10. It can reasonably be inferred from the first paragraph that the author believes NASA named the mission Juno in order to:
    - **F.** pay respects to the Greeks and Romans who pioneered astronomy.
    - **G.** honor one of the few female goddesses in ancient mythology.
    - **H.** learn more about the planet's origins and evolution.
    - **J.** draw on the story of Jupiter and Juno to symbolize the goals of the mission.

READING WALKTHROUGH 2

Explanations

Passage IV

NATURAL SCIENCE

Greek Goddess

According to ancient Greco-Roman mythology, not only was the goddess Juno the wife of Jupiter, but she also had a special talent: when Jupiter surrounded himself with clouds in order to conceal his illicit activities, only Juno could see through the clouds – and reveal what was really going on. NASA's recent New Frontiers mission to Jupiter draws on this symbolic story as inspiration. Both the mission and the spacecraft are nicknamed Juno. Like the mythological goddess, the Juno mission aims to peer deep into Jupiter's atmosphere, learning more about the planet's origins and evolution.

Goal of mission ★

Jupiter Info

Classified as a "gas giant," Jupiter boasts a mass two and a half times larger than the rest of the solar system's planets combined. Its massive size and its position on the outer edges of the solar system make it a very different planet than Earth. In fact, the composition of Jupiter's atmosphere is more like that of the Sun's, composed primarily of hydrogen and helium. In the high-pressure, high-temperature environment deep within Jupiter's atmosphere, hydrogen gas condenses into an electricity-conducting liquid that behaves somewhat like a metal. This conducting layer, combined with the planet's fast rotation, produces a powerful magnetic field.

Past missions to Jupiter have provided valuable information about the planet's atmosphere and magnetic field. Now, with information gathered by the Juno mission, scientists hope to learn even more.

Main goal 1

H_2O

One of the Juno mission's main goals is to measure the composition of Jupiter's atmosphere and determine the quantity of oxygen (most commonly present in water). By gaining a better estimate of the amount of water in the atmosphere, scientists can deduce important facts about Jupiter's formation. Did it collapse from an original cloud of gas, or did it begin as a core of ice and rock that attracted hydrogen gas? Or did water arrive in the form of loose space debris carrying loads of ice? Each of these scenarios predicts different amounts of water in Jupiter's atmosphere, and each corresponds to a different theory about how the solar system itself was formed. ★ Thus, by researching the amount of water present in Jupiter's atmosphere, we can learn more about our own planet's origins. We may also be able to develop theories about similar planetary systems throughout the galaxy.

other goals

Other objectives include measuring temperature and cloud patterns inside Jupiter's atmosphere, mapping Jupiter's gravity field to learn more about the planet's interior structure, and studying Jupiter's magnetosphere, especially near the poles. The spacecraft is also equipped with a camera that will record images of the planet's surface.

Journey

The spacecraft has a long way to go before it arrives. It was launched from the Kennedy Space Center on August 5, 2011; Juno's next step is to swing by Earth for a gravity assist to help boost it into space. It should arrive at Jupiter on October 19, 2016. Upon arrival, Juno will enter Jupiter's orbit and begin transmitting data continuously to NASA. Once Juno has orbited Jupiter for a full year, its mission will be complete. In October 2017, Juno will be de-orbited and crash into Jupiter.

Solar

↓ Sun

Juno is also the first solar-powered spacecraft to travel to Jupiter, or venture this deeply into space. It's equipped with three solar arrays, which protrude from the body of the spacecraft in a symmetrical fashion, a bit like a three-bladed ceiling fan. Each solar array measures about six feet wide by 27 feet long, providing a total 650 sq. ft. of solar panel. The craft's orbit will ensure that the solar panels are bathed in sunlight at all times. However, once the craft falls into orbit around Jupiter, it will only receive about four percent of the sunlight we receive on Earth. Both the solar cell technology and the instruments on board Juno are designed for maximum efficiency, ensuring that the craft can continue to operate effectively even at these reduced levels of sunlight.

Plaque

Aboard Juno is a plaque that was gifted to the mission by the Italian Space Agency. The plaque is dedicated to Galileo, who in 1610 sighted the first of Jupiter's largest moons for the first time. The plaque depicts a self-portrait of Galileo, along with a quotation from a passage he wrote during the observation session in question. Translated into English, the text reads: "On the 11th it was in this formation: the star closest to Jupiter was half the size of, and very close to, the other so that during the previous nights all of the three observed stars looked of the same dimension and among them equally afar; it is evident that around Jupiter there are three moving stars that were, until now, invisible to all."

Moons

In fact, what Galileo described as "three moving stars" were actually bright moons. Now referred to as the "Galilean moons," they are named Io, Europa,and Callisto. Since Galileo's discovery, astronomers have identified more than 60 moons in orbit around Jupiter, and this number is growing each year. With the information provided by Juno, researchers hope to pierce the mystery shrouding this massive and fascinating planet.

Juno scoping out Jupiter's atmosphere to teach about planets.

1. Which of the following questions about the Juno mission does the passage NOT directly answer?

A. When will Juno reach Jupiter?
B. How is the Juno spacecraft powered?
C. How much will the Juno mission cost?
D. Why are researchers interested in Jupiter?

1. What don't we find out about Juno?

Our best bet is to scan for each answer choice we don't remember seeing in the passage.

A. Evidence: "It should arrive..." *(line 53)*
B. Evidence: "...first solar-powered..." *(line 59)*
C. Evidence: ??? Scanning for dollar signs comes up with zilch. nada. zip. C it is!
D. Evidence: "...we can learn more about our own planet's origins..." *(line 39)*

---

2. The author does all of the following in the second paragraph (lines 12-23) EXCEPT:

F. compare Jupiter's atmosphere to the Sun's.
G. contrast Jupiter's temperature with the Sun's.
H. relate Jupiter's mass to other solar planets' mass.
J. describe differences between Jupiter and Earth.

2. What doesn't come up in paragraph 2?

Let's scan paragraph 2 for each choice, and cross out any with evidence.

F. "..Jupiter's atmosphere is more like that of the sun..." *(line 17)*
G. The word temperature shows up, but the author doesn't draw a **contrast**. Tricky!
H. "Jupiter boasts a mass two and a half times larger..." *(lines 12-13)*
J. "..very different planet than Earth." *(line 15)*

---

3. According to the author's description, the solar panels on Juno most resemble:

A. a reflective greenhouse.
B. a ceiling fan.
C. a three-leaf clover.
D. an electromagnetic array.

3. How'd the author describe the solar panels?

*Checking our notes, we see a paragraph marked "solar." On **line 62** we see "three-bladed ceiling fan." Bingo!*

A. Nope.
B. Bingo-Bango!
C. Three-leaf instead of three-bladed. Nice try.
D. This came up in a different paragraph.

4. According to the passage, the amount of water present in Jupiter's atmosphere is important because:

(F.) it will provide evidence to support certain theories of Jupiter's formation.

~~G.~~ it will indicate whether Jupiter is habitable.

~~H.~~ oxygen is most commonly found in water.

~~J.~~ it could help us identify other "gas giants" like Jupiter.

4. Why do we care about water on Jupiter?

Next to our note "H_2O", we see:

"by gaining a better estimate of water in the atmosphere... scientists can deduce important facts about Jupiter's formation."

F. **formation**! That's dead-on. Keep F.

G. Easy, Assumption Al! **Inhabiting** Jupiter never came up in the passage.

H. Watch it Wrong-level Walter, **oxygen** was just a side detail.

J. This answer misses the big picture. The whole paragraph was about **formation**.

---

5. The main focus of the last two paragraphs is the role that Galileo played in:

~~A.~~ identifying three nearby stars.

~B. naming Io, Europa, and Callisto.

~~C.~~ developing the modern telescope.

(D.) discovering Jupiter's largest moons.

5. How did Galileo contribute to this topic?

Looking at our note, we can see the last paragraph talks about ***moons****.*

A. Close, but **stars** are not moons!

B. Io, Europa, and Callisto are moons, so this one is closer. But Gallileo didn't **name** them.

C. Be a horse with blinders! This might be true, but it's not in the last two paragraphs.

D. Moons! This one is a clear winner.

---

6. The passage states that Juno's solar panels and technology were designed to be extremely efficient because:

~~F.~~ efficient technology helps save money on the mission.

(G.) the amount of sunlight received on Jupiter is much smaller than that on Earth.

~~H.~~ the solar array will be momentarily hidden from the Sun during take off.

~~J.~~ space debris may obscure the solar panels from sunlight.

6. Why did the panels need to be efficient?

Scanning for the word "efficient", we see in lines 68-71:

"..maximum efficiency, ensuring that the craft can continue to operate effectively even at these reduced levels of sunlight."

Reduced sunlight! To the choices!

F. Probably true, but **money** never comes up!

G. Less sunlight! This looks good.

H. The **take off** is never mentioned.

J. **Space debris** is way off-base.

7. Which of the following is NOT a mission objective mentioned in the fifth paragraph?

A. Measuring atmospheric cloud patterns.
B. Taking pictures of the planet.
C. Testing the composition of Jupiter's core.
D. Mapping the planet's gravity field.

7. What didn't we see in the fifth paragraph?

Synonym chain time!

A. "cloud patterns" (*line 45*)
B. "camera that will record images (*line 49*)
C. No evidence! This is our answer.
D. "mapping Jupiter's gravity field" (*line 45*)

---

8. According to the passage, Jupiter's electricity-conducting interior and fast rotation produce:

F. a powerful magnetic field.
G. a high-pressure, high-temperature environment.
H. an atmosphere like the Sun's.
J. a gas giant.

8. What does Jupiter's rotation produce?

*Let's look to our "Jupiter Info" note and read near the word **rotation**.*

F. **Magnetic field** is in *line 22*, right next to "rotation." That's some strong evidence!
G. Right paragraph, but not near "rotation."
H. Yet another distraction from the paragraph.
J. Well that's silly. Jupiter **is** a gas giant.

---

9. According to the passage, the mission will be concluded when Juno:

A. makes a 1-year orbit around Jupiter.
B. crashes into Jupiter.
C. passes by Earth for a gravity assist.
D. transmits its findings back to NASA.

9. When does Juno's mission end?

*Line 56: once Juno has **orbited** for a full year, its mission is complete.*

A. **Orbit** looks good; no throwaways. Keep A!
B. **Crash** shows up one line **after** our "mission complete" line. The mission ends pre-crash!
C. Here, each word has evidence, but too early in the paragraph!
D. Nope, transmission happens **continuously.**

---

10. It can reasonably be inferred from the first paragraph that the author believes NASA named the mission Juno in order to:

~F. pay respects to the Greeks and Romans who pioneered astronomy.
G. honor one of the few female goddesses in ancient mythology.
H. learn more about the planet's origins and evolution.
J. draw on the story of Jupiter and Juno to symbolize the goals of the mission.

10. Why'd they name the mission **Juno**?

We learn the name in the first paragraph, which tells the Greek myth.

F. Hmm... that takes an assumption or two.
G. How many **goddesses** are there? Didn't say.
H. Tricky one. This is the purpose of the mission, not the rationale for the name!
J. Sparrow! "Draw on" and "symbolize" are both inoffensive, making this a safe choice.

Reading Mantras

Read **Actively**

Forget what you know, and **make no assumptions!**

Put it in your own words: **Paraphrase** the question.

Read for recall. Engage your **imagination**!

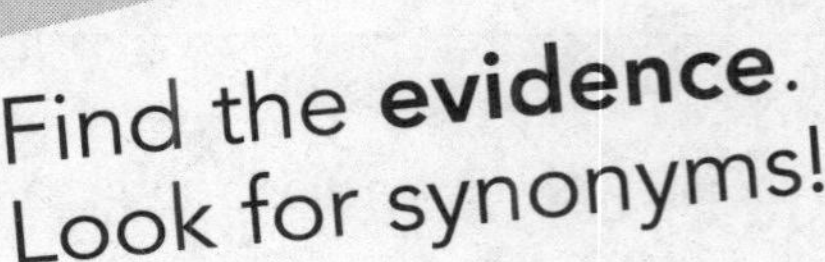

Find the **evidence**. Look for synonyms!

Read 5 lines up and 5 lines down for **context**.

Focus on **throw-aways**. Eliminate what's wrong to find what's right.

Science

Science Intro

If you feel the "need for speed," you will make out like a bandit on the Science section, the ultimate test of your ability to move quickly through charts, tables, and graphs.

The Science section is a bona fide **data bonanza**, consisting of seven passages detailing scientific experiments from the fields of Biology, Physics, Geoscience, and Chemistry. And you only have 35 minutes! At first glance, it's a beast. If you try to tackle this section the way you would a high school Physics test, it's gonna hurt! Never fear! **There is a better way.**

The Secret to Science

Once you know the Secret to Science, you will transform the ACT Science section from a fearsome, lumbering beast... into Jeremy. And he ain't so bad!

You are not expected to read or understand all the supporting information!

Stay on the Surface

You don't need to dive into the deep waters of scientific knowledge in order to conquer ACT Science. It's okay not to fully understand what's happening. You can **ace** a passage without fully understanding its content!

To begin with, much of the information provided by the ACT writers will **not** help you answer the questions, but merely serve to slow you down. You will only need to read a **fraction** of the text and a portion of the tables, charts, and graphs. You will learn to focus on what you need and ignore the rest.

Remember, the ACT Science section is a **data-driven reading test,** not a science test! The vast majority of the questions require no outside scientific knowledge at all.

Speedy by Design

The science section, at its foundation, is a graph and table **speed-reading test.** The writers designed this section to allow you to skip over most of the content. What they really want to determine is how quickly you can plot a point, see a trend, or notice a correlation.

You'll have to move fast, but remember: you do not have much time to read the supporting information because *you were never supposed to in the first place*! In this chapter, you will learn how to use matching to find an answer in **seconds**, how to draw arrows to make trends **pop** out of the data, and how to skillfully - and quickly - tackle **even the toughest problems**. So don't panic!

Stay on the surface and keep moving!

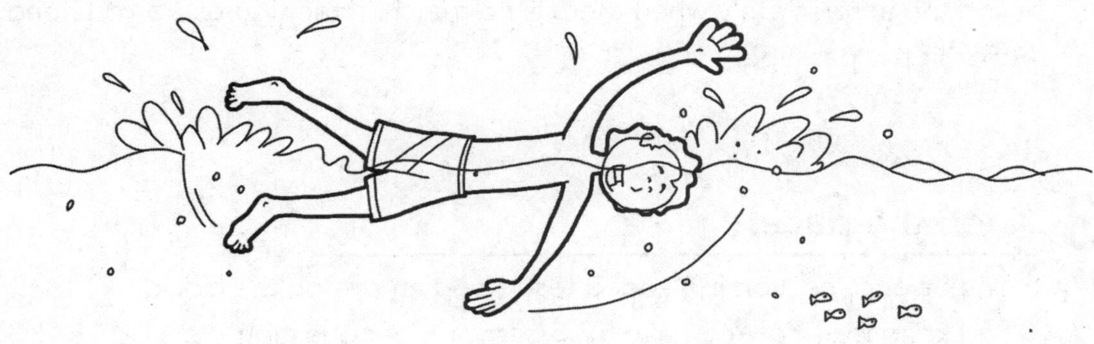

ACT Science Strategy

Let's put what we know about the ACT Science section to use. Follow the strategy below to conquer Science:

1 **Skip** the passage!

Go straight to the questions! If you read all that background information, you are hosed. Save time by letting the questions tell you what's important and what's fluff.

2 Make the **match!**

Your primary job is to match words in the question with words in the figures. For almost three-fourths of the questions, this is all it takes to find the answer. Only when there is no match in the figures do you need to visit the passage.

3 Keep the **pace!**

The Science section is a speed test! Keep an eye on the clock, and keep moving! You have **52.5 seconds** per question. As a rough guide, you can subtract a minute from the number of questions in a given passage to establish a timing goal:

Questions per Passage	Timing Goal
5 questions	4 minutes
6 questions	5 minutes
7 questions	6 minutes

If you finish the passages in the above times, you'll have some time left over and a bit of breathing room.

Passage Types

There are two distinct types of ACT Science passages:

Standard Passage

6 of the 7 passages per test will fall into this category. These passages contain a good deal of data represented in any combination of tables, charts, graphs or diagrams. You will jump right to the questions and let them direct you to the necessary information.

Dueling Scientist Passage

This passage type shows up only once per test. In this format, you are not working with data, but rather with multiple theories attempting to explain a phenomenon. You may be comparing Students 1, 2, 3 or Scientists 1, 2, 3 or Wave Theory vs. Particle Theory vs. String Cheese Theory. Your main task is to simply identify the key elements of each theory.

This is primarily a reading comprehension passage stuck into the science section. Only on the Dueling Scientist passage will you read the passage **first** before moving on to the questions.

QUESTION TYPES

Standard Passages contain 8 primary question types. With practice, you will be able to spot these right away. The more quickly you can identify what a question is asking, the more quickly you can start finding the answer.

#	Question Type	%	
1	Get to the Point	29%	Tables and graphs only!
2	Compare Two Points	11%	
3	Relationships	20%	
4	Expand the Pattern	9%	
5	Read the Passage	16%	Some reading required!
6	Inference	11%	
7	Measurement Adjustment	2%	
8	Outside Knowledge	2%	

Notice that 5 of 8 question types and about 70% of all questions require no knowledge of the passage! This illustrates why reading the passage first is not the most efficient use of your time.

Let us begin by diving into the 8 question types involved in the Standard Passage. We'll start with the first question type: Get to the Point.

Get to the Point

The most basic (and easiest) type of Science question is the *Get to the Point* question. The ACT writers ask you to simply report one piece of data shown in the figures. That's it!

The Matching Game

Get to the Point questions—and there are many of them—are all about one thing: **matching**. The test writers give you information in the question, and your job is to match it with the corresponding information in the figures. You are following a very simple treasure map with clear directions. Take it **one piece at a time** and don't be distracted by the scenery. If you go step by step, you will land at the proper coordinates.

Know your Graphs

Though you answer all *Get to the Point* questions in the same way (matching), the figures themselves can take a variety of different forms—some of which appear vastly more complicated than others:

1. Tables
2. Basic Line Graphs
3. Triple Line Graphs
4. Region Graphs
5. Crazy Graphs

Let's take a tour of all of the different ways the ACT writers can represent data, and practice using simple matching to *Get to the Point*.

Get to the Point

Tables

Fact: The easiest *Get to the Point* questions involve finding a point in a table.

Tables are your friends. To Get to the Point, you'll match words and numbers from the question with those in the table.

Table 1

Water content of:		Humidity Levels (%) at different altitudes 3000 ft	5000 ft	7000 ft
Sage	4%	4	6	3
	23%	12	18	17
	36%	42	50	44
	89%	68	66	70
Chamisa	4%	3	13	8
	23%	11	21	22
	36%	41	44	55
	89%	64	49	68

Note: Humidity levels measured over 24 hour period.

According to Table 1, a site located at an elevation of 5000 feet with chamisa plants consisting of 36% water would most likely have a humidity level of:

A. 36
B. 42
C. 44
D. 50

S *All we need to do is follow the signs. Time to start matching.*

According to Table 1, a site located at an elevation of **5000 feet** with chamisa plants consisting of 36% water would most likely have a humidity level of:

Table 1

Water content of:		Humidity Levels (%) at different altitudes 3000 ft	**5000 ft**	7000 ft
Sage	4%	4	6	3
	23%	12	18	17
	36%	42	50	44
	89%	68	66	70
Chamisa	4%	3	13	8
	23%	11	21	22
	36%	41	44	55
	89%	64	49	68

Note: Humidity levels measured over 24 hour period.

According to Table 1, a site located at an elevation of **5000 feet** with **chamisa plants** consisting of 36% water would most likely have a humidity level of:

Table 1

Water content of:		Humidity Levels (%) at different altitudes 3000 ft	**5000 ft**	7000 ft
Sage	4%	4	6	3
	23%	12	18	17
	36%	42	50	44
	89%	68	66	70
Chamisa	4%	3	13	8
	23%	11	21	22
	36%	41	44	55
	89%	64	49	68

Note: Humidity levels measured over 24 hour period.

Use your fingers and pencil to point out matches as you zero in on your point!

According to Table 1, a site located at an elevation of **5000 feet** with **chamisa** plants **consisting of 36% water** would most likely have a humidity level of:

Table 1				
		Humidity Levels (%) at different altitudes		
Water content of:		3000 ft	**5000 ft**	7000 ft
Sage	4%	4	6	3
	23%	12	18	17
	36%	42	50	44
	89%	68	66	70
Chamisa	4%	3	13	8
	23%	11	21	22
	36%	41	44	55
	89%	64	49	68
Note: Humidity levels measured over 24 hour period.				

Tables may be tiny or tremendously huge, but the matching game stays the same.

According to Table 1, a site located at an elevation of 5000 feet with chamisa plants consisting of 36% water **would most likely** have a **humidity level** of:

Table 1				
		Humidity Levels (%) at different altitudes		
Water content of:		3000 ft	**5000 ft**	7000 ft
Sage	4%	4	6	3
	23%	12	18	17
	36%	42	50	44
	89%	68	66	70
Chamisa	4%	3	13	8
	23%	11	21	22
	36%	41	**44**	55
	89%	64	49	68
Note: Humidity levels measured over 24 hour period.				

That's how we roll! Our answer is **C**!

Get to the Point

Basic Line Graphs

You are probably already pretty comfortable with basic line graphs. These graphs have two labeled axes (x and y) and often a legend or key. Data is plotted along a line, or multiple lines, and each point has one x-coordinate and one y-coordinate. To Get to the Point, you'll **match** words and numbers from the question with words and numbers in the graph.

Let's see this in action.

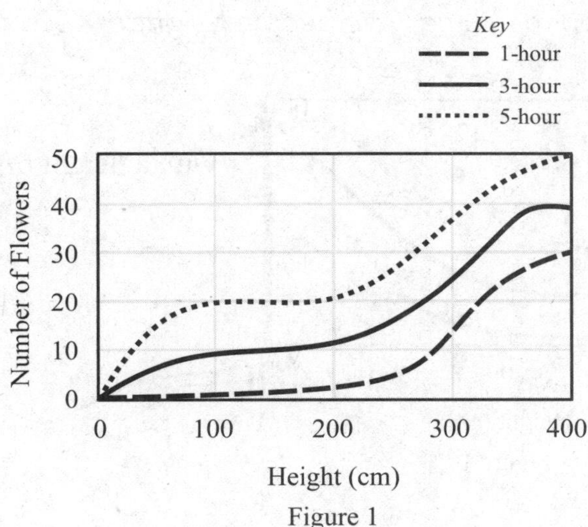

Figure 1

According to Figure 1, a seedling with a height of 400 cm and 30 flowers would most likely have been exposed to how many hours of sunlight per day?

A. 1.0 hours
B. 3.0 hours
C. 5.0 hours
D. 7.0 hours

S

1 *First, we need to get our bearings. We need Figure 1. Let's make sure we're looking at the right graph!*

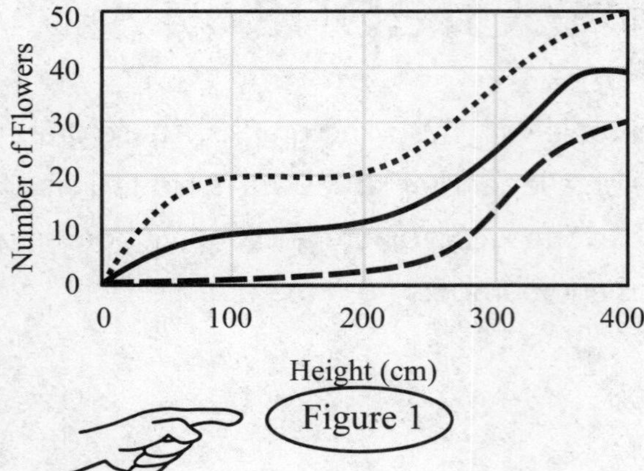

According to **Figure 1**, a seedling with a height of 400 cm and 30 flowers would most likely have been exposed to how many hours of sunlight per day?

2 *Let's keep matching. We need a height of 400 cm.*

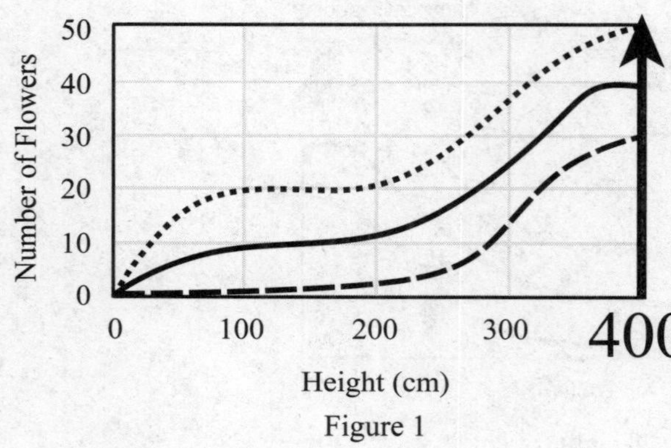

According to Figure 1, **a seedling with a height of 400 cm** and 30 flowers would most likely have been exposed to how many hours of sunlight per day?

3 *Next we need 30 flowers. We can find our match on the y axis.*

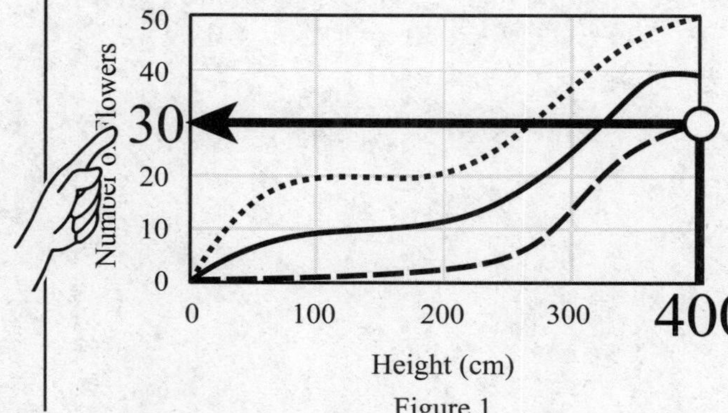

According to Figure 1, a seedling with a height of 400 cm **and 30 flowers** would most likely have been exposed to how many hours of sunlight per day?

4 *Next we need to match our found point with the Key to determine which line we are on.*

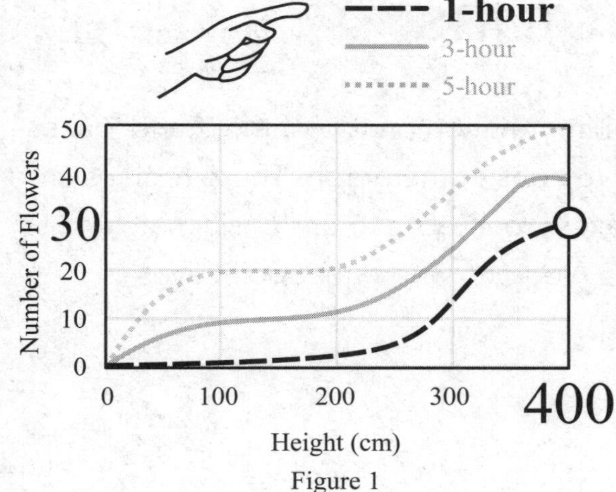

Figure 1

According to **Figure 1**, a seedling with a height of **400 cm** and **30 flowers** would most likely have been exposed to how many **hours of sunlight** per day?

Our point lies on the dashed 1-hour line. Our answer is **A***!*

Get to the Point

Regions

The ACT writers often add a layer of information on top of the X and Y axes by dividing up and defining distinct regions of the graph. These regions are clearly defined and labeled on the axes. Your job is to use basic matching to get to the point, and then report the "region" where that point lives.

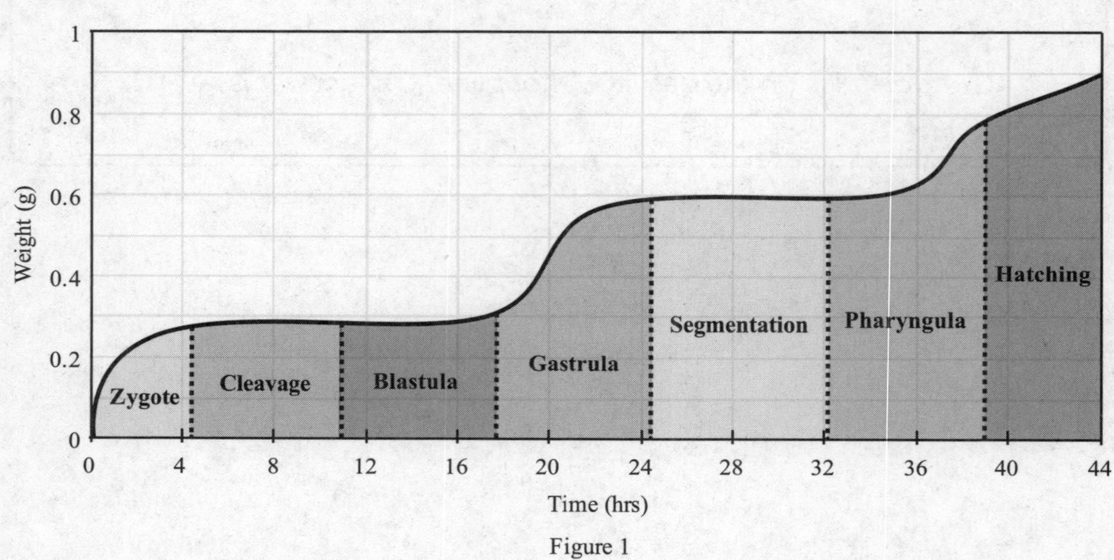

Figure 1

A zebrafish embryo that weighs .4 grams is in which stage of development?

A. Zygote
B. Cleavage
C. Blastula
D. Gastrula

S *We need to find 0.4g, slide to the right until we hit the curve, and read the region below:*

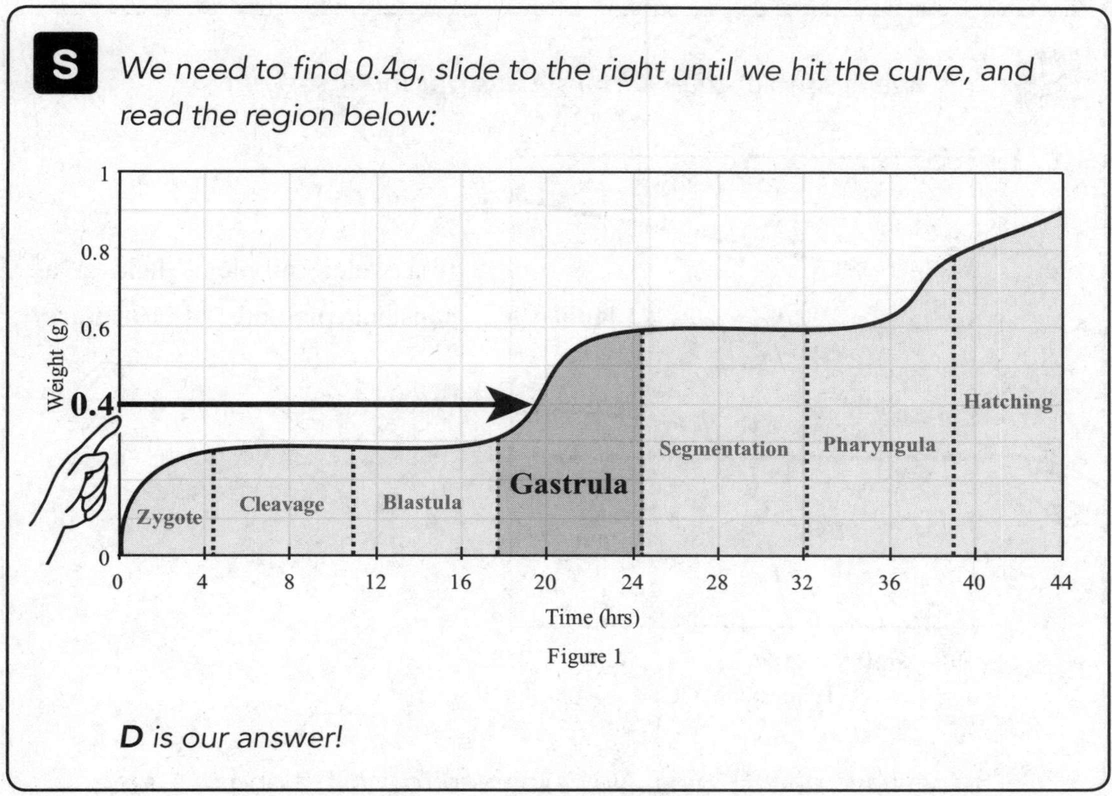

Figure 1

***D** is our answer!*

Let's take it up a level and look at a funkier regions graph.

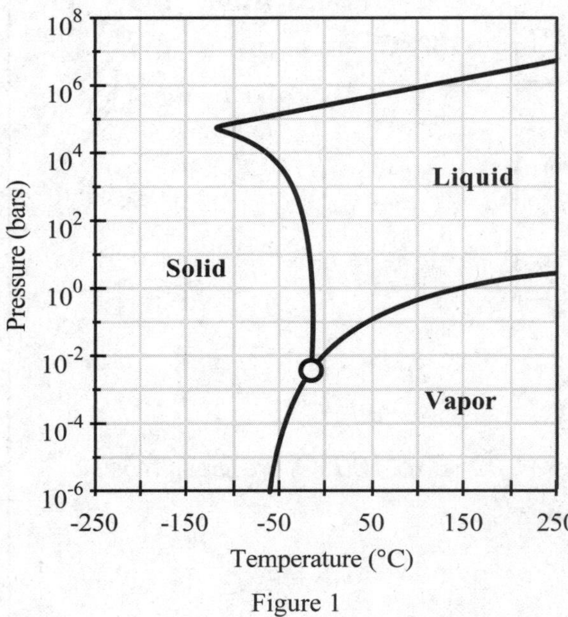

Figure 1

According to Figure 1, if a water sample is held at a constant pressure of 10^{-1} bars and is heated from -100°C to 100°C, which of the following demonstrates the phase shift of the sample.

F. Solid to Liquid
G. Solid to Vapor
H. Vapor to Solid to Liquid
J. Solid to Liquid to Vapor

S *This one is simpler than it looks! Let's get the first point:*

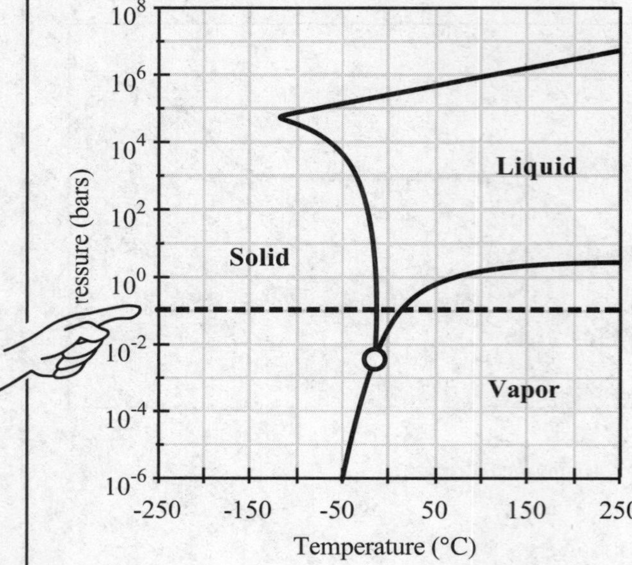

If a water sample is held at a constant pressure of **10^{-1} bars** and is heated from −10 to 100°C, which of the fol demonstrates the phase shif the sample?

Often your point will lie **between** two labels of the x or y axis. Use the tick marks to get to your point!

So we have our 10^{-1} line. Now we need to move along this line from −100°C to 100°C, noting the regions we pass through.

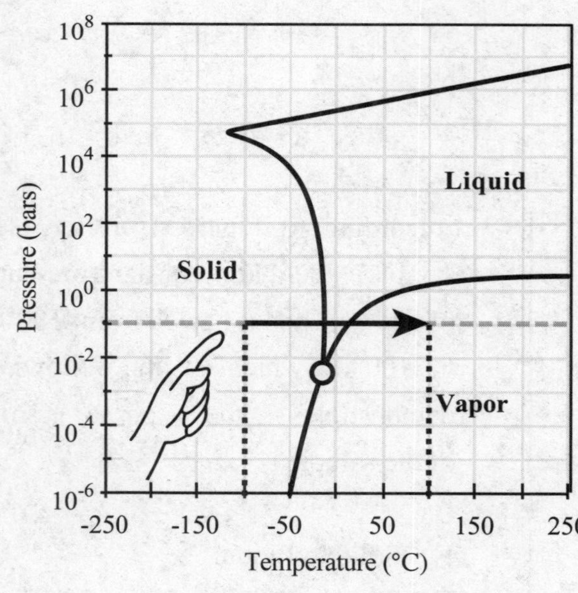

If a water sample is held at a constant pressure of **10^{-1} bars** and is heated **from −100°C to 100°C**, which of the fol ing demonstrates the phase sh the sample?

As we move along our line from −100°C to 100°C, we pass from ***Solid****, through* ***Liquid****, into* **Vapor**.

Our answer is **J***!*

Get to the Point

Triple Axis

Although it may look intimidating at first glance, the triple axis graph is simply a merging of two double-axis graphs.

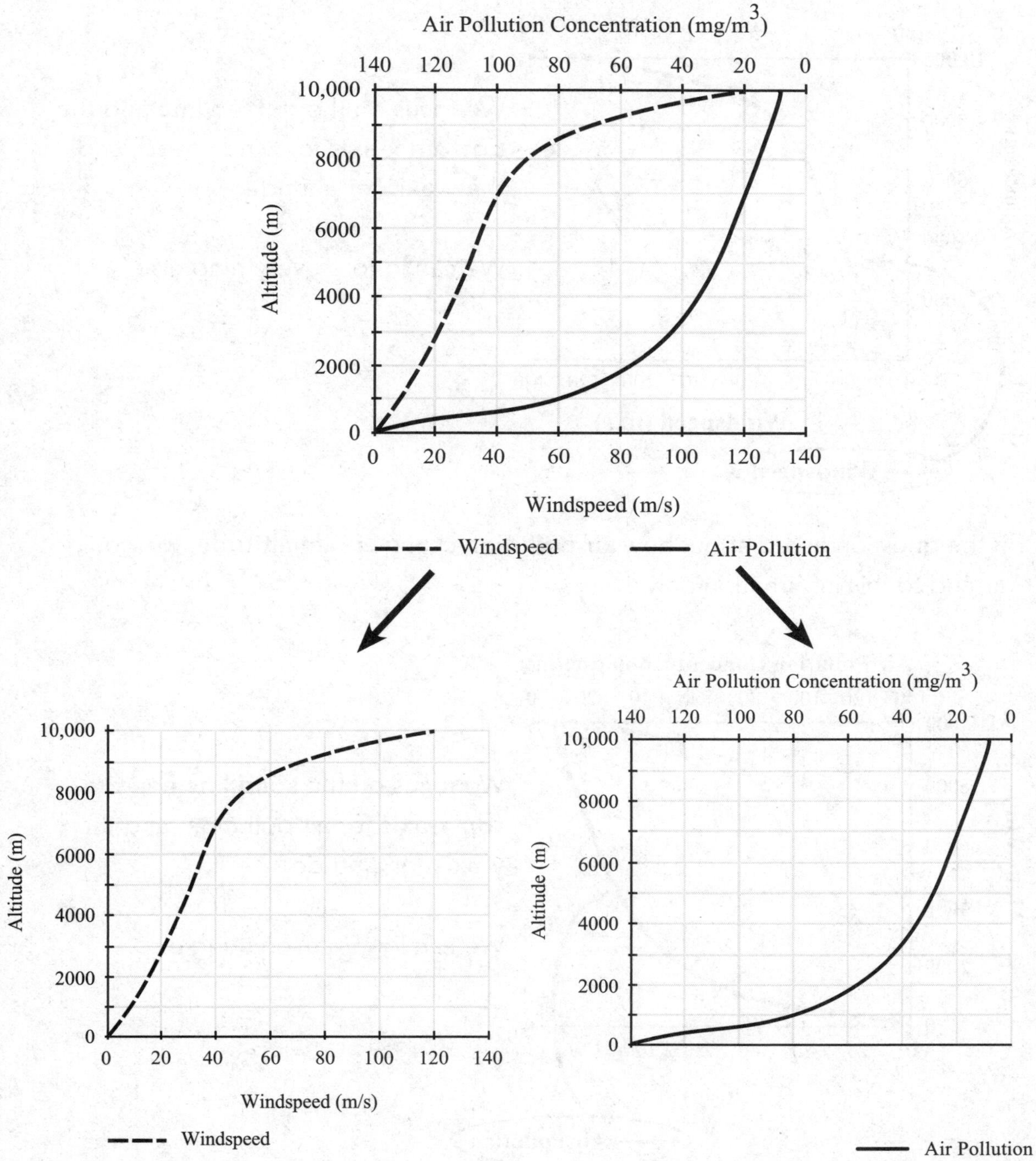

Air Pollution Concentration (mg/m^3)

140 120 100 80 60 40 20 0

Altitude (m)

10,000 8000 6000 4000 2000 0

0 20 40 60 80 100 120 140

Windspeed (m/s)

Windspeed — Air Pollution

Altitude (m)

10,000 8000 6000 4000 2000 0

0 20 40 60 80 100 120 140

Windspeed (m/s)

Windspeed

Air Pollution Concentration (mg/m^3)

140 120 100 80 60 40 20 0

Altitude (m)

10,000 8000 6000 4000 2000 0

Air Pollution

One graph plots pollution versus altitude, the other plots windspeed versus altitude.

The "triple" simply doubles our fun! In one graph, we can see how these 2 variables change with altitude.

Ignore What you Don't Need

To effectively work the triple, you must focus all of your attention on one variable and completely ignore another. The key here is to know what information to **turn on**, and what to **turn off**.

If the question asked about how **wind speed** changes with **altitude**, we would attend to this information only:

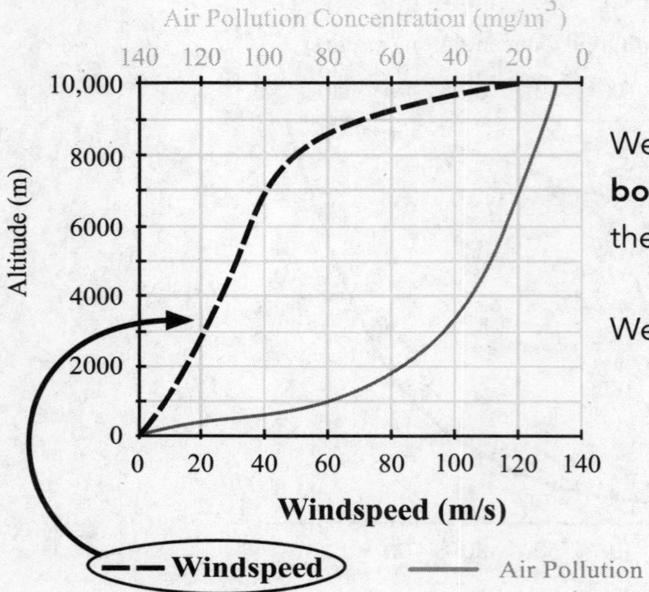

We focus on the **dotted line** and the **bottom x-axis** for wind speed, and the **y-axis** for altitude.

We can ignore everything else.

If the question asked about how **air pollution** changes with **altitude**, we would attend to this information only:

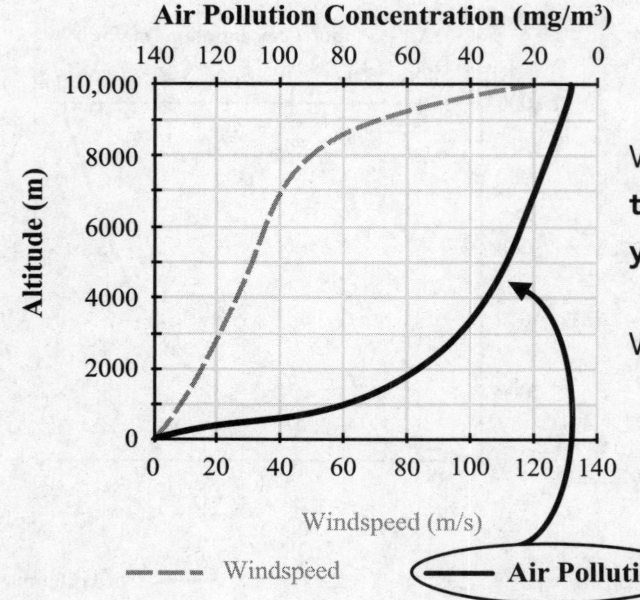

We focus on the **solid line** and the **top x-axis** for air pollution, and the **y-axis** for altitude.

We can ignore everything else.

The key is to selectively attend to some information and ignore the rest. In doing so, we turn the "triple" back into two simpler "doubles."
Let's take a triple for a test-drive:

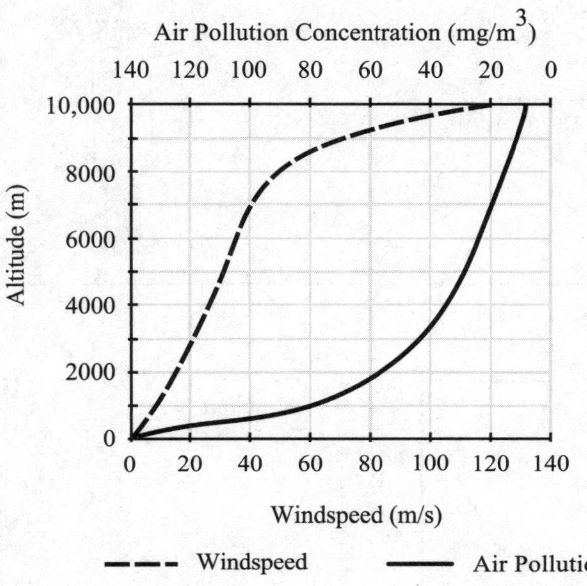

According to the figure, what is the windspeed at an altitude of 3,000 meters?

A. 20 m/s
B. 40 m/s
C. 100 m/s
D. 120 m/s

S *We are directed to* ***3,000 meters****, so our altitude is locked in. The question asks for* ***windspeed****, so we can ignore air pollution.*

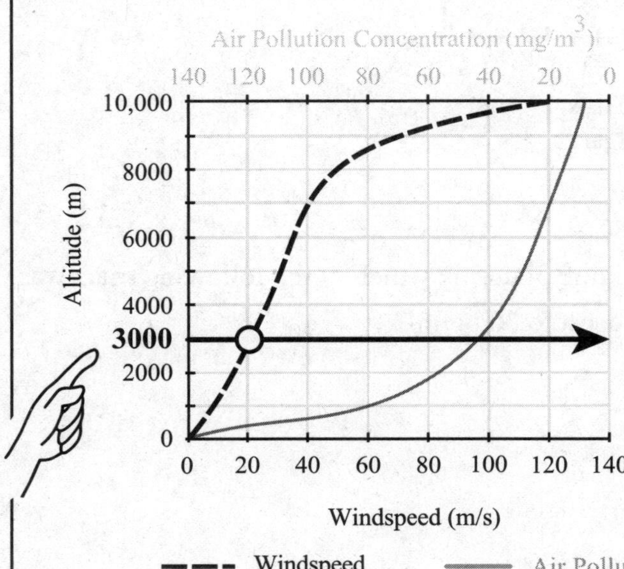

We find ***3000,*** *follow the guideline to the right, and mark where we cross the* ***dotted line****.*

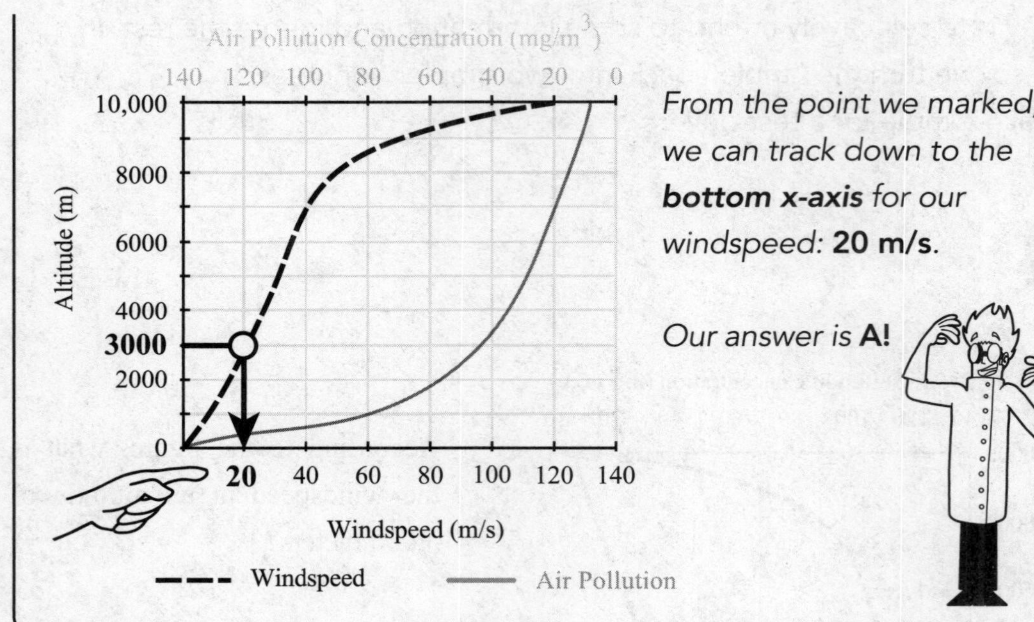

To nail the triple axis, **reduce** it down to a double, ***ignore*** the unneeded information and stay **focused!**

E2

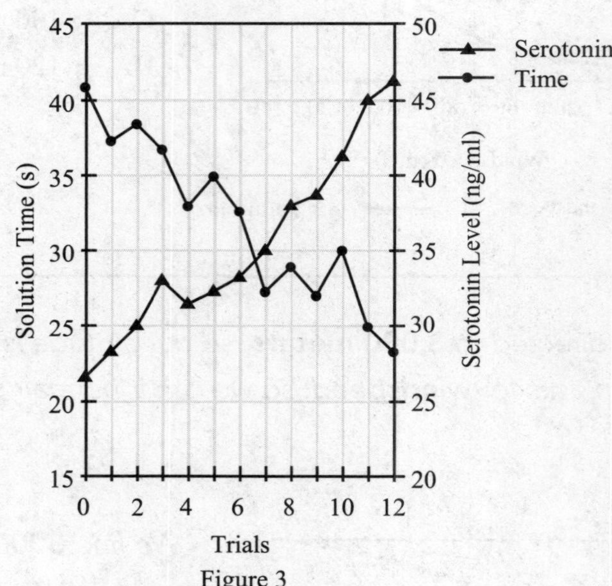

Figure 3

Based on the information in Figure 3, during which of the following trials was the subject's serotonin level closest to 30 ng/ml?

A. 2
B. 4
C. 7
D. 11

S *We are directed to a **serotonin** level of **30 ng/ml.** Serotonin lives on the **right axis**. Place your finger on the right **30** and trace a line to the left until you hit the **serotonin (triangle) line.***

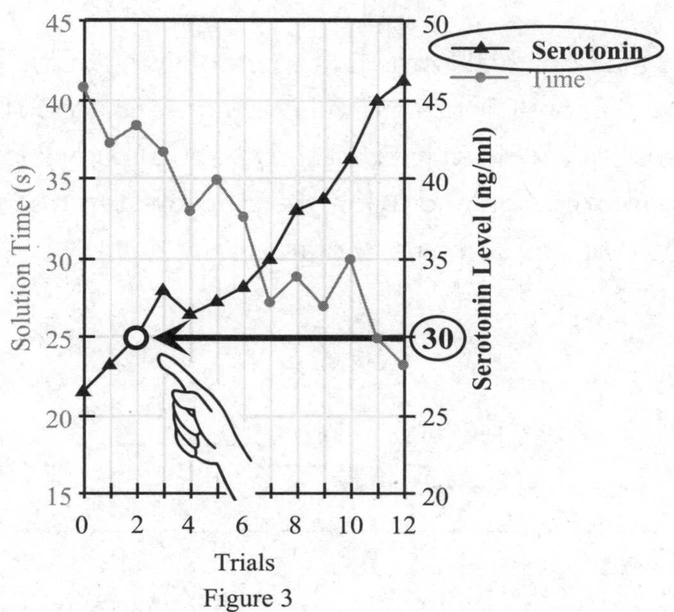

Figure 3

*Now let's get our answer! Using your finger, drop down from our point on the serotonin line down to the **x-axis** to get our trial.*

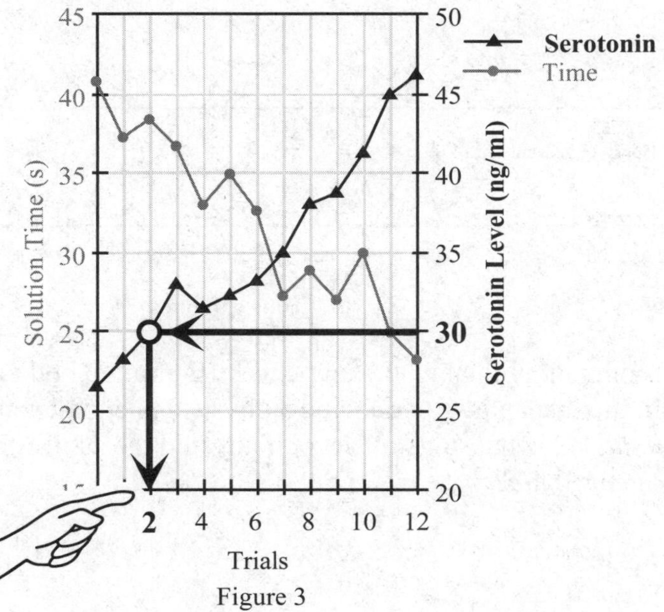

Figure 3

*Trial 2! Our answer is **A!***

Don't fall into the trap of picking the 30 on the left axis. That's ***Solution Time!***

Get to the Point

Crazy Graphs

The graphs that look really scary are a combination of the region graphs and the multi-axis graphs. These are the **crazy graphs**. Don't be intimidated; you have all the skills you need to solve these. You already know to **ignore all distracting information** and follow the **step-by-step matching** guide to Get to the Point. Let's try some crazy graphs!

E1

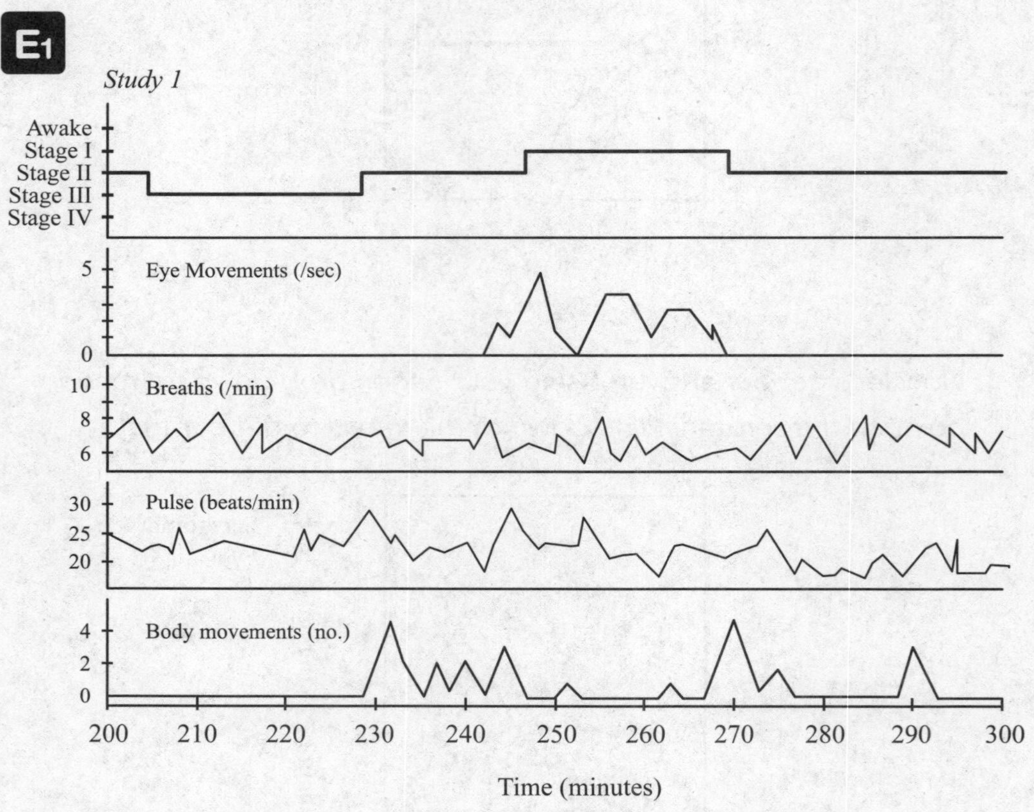

A sleeping individual who experiences 10 or more body movements within a 20 minute-span is experiencing a physical phenomenon known as *hypnic myclonia.* At what stage of sleep, if any, did the subject in Study 1 experience *hypnic myclonia*?

A. Stage I
B. Stage II
C. Stage III
D. Subject did not experience this phenomenon

S *We have our marching orders! We are looking for* **10 or more body movements within 20 minutes.**

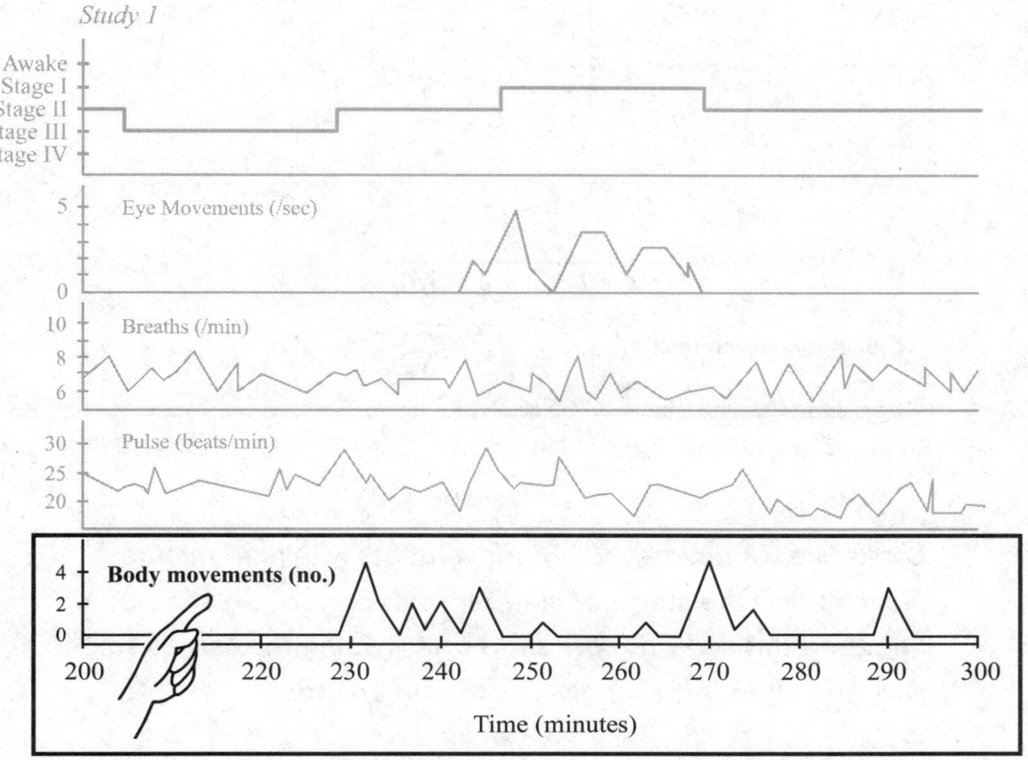

We have found our region! Next we must identify the ***stage of sleep*** *in which we have* ***10+ movements within 20 minutes.***

We need to look at the y-axis to learn how this graph works. Each spike represents 0 to 4 movements. Since we're looking for 10 or more movements in 20 minutes, we need to find the area with ***lots of spikes****.*

It looks like we hit our spikiest region in the 230- 245 minute range.

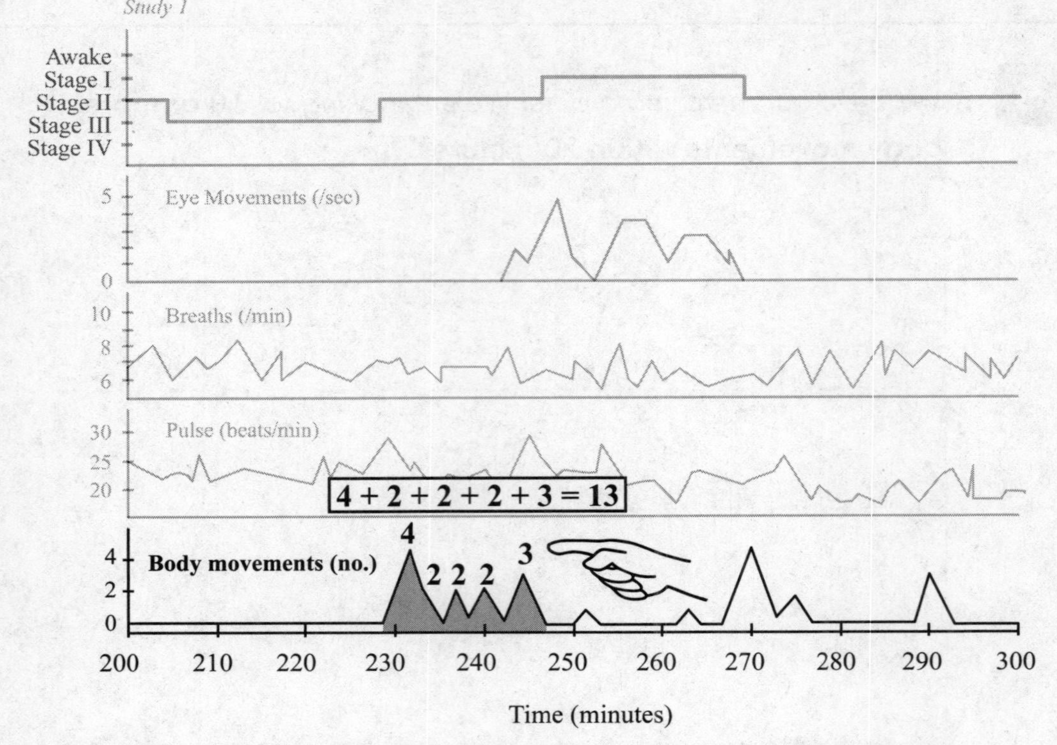

Looks like we have about 13 movements within 20 minutes! Now, to find the ***stage of sleep*** *for this period, we can put our finger on this spiky region,* ***slide up*** *till we hit the "sleep stage" line, and* ***slide left*** *to the y-axis for our answer:*

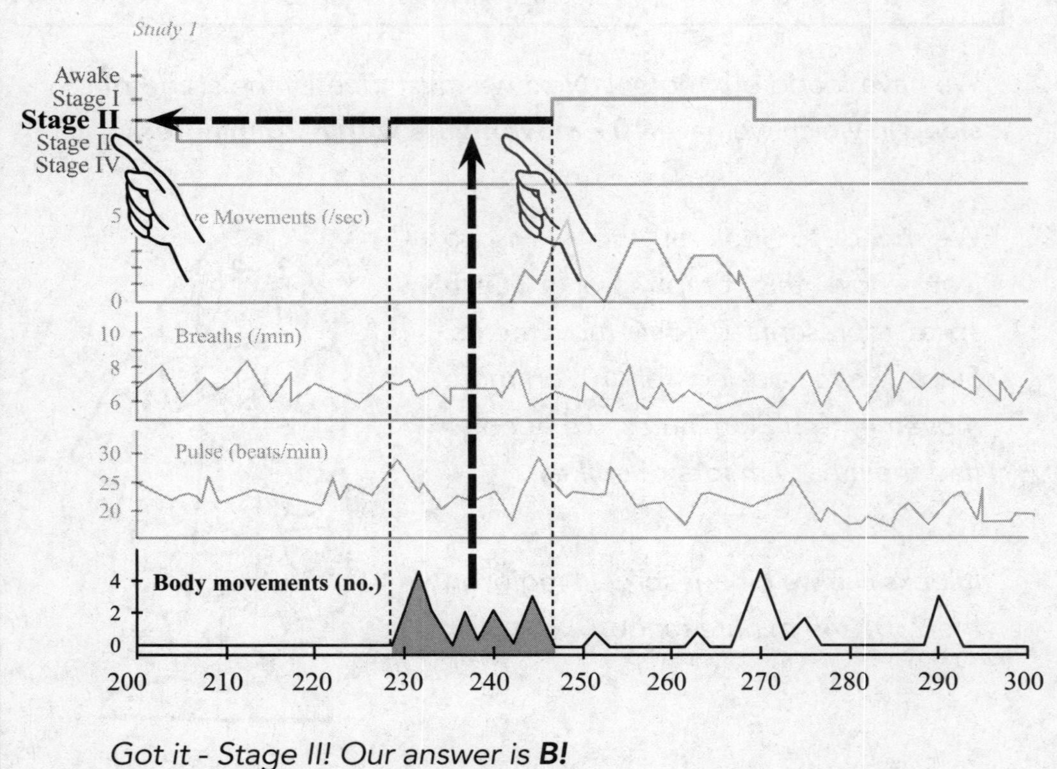

Got it - Stage II! Our answer is ***B!***

E2

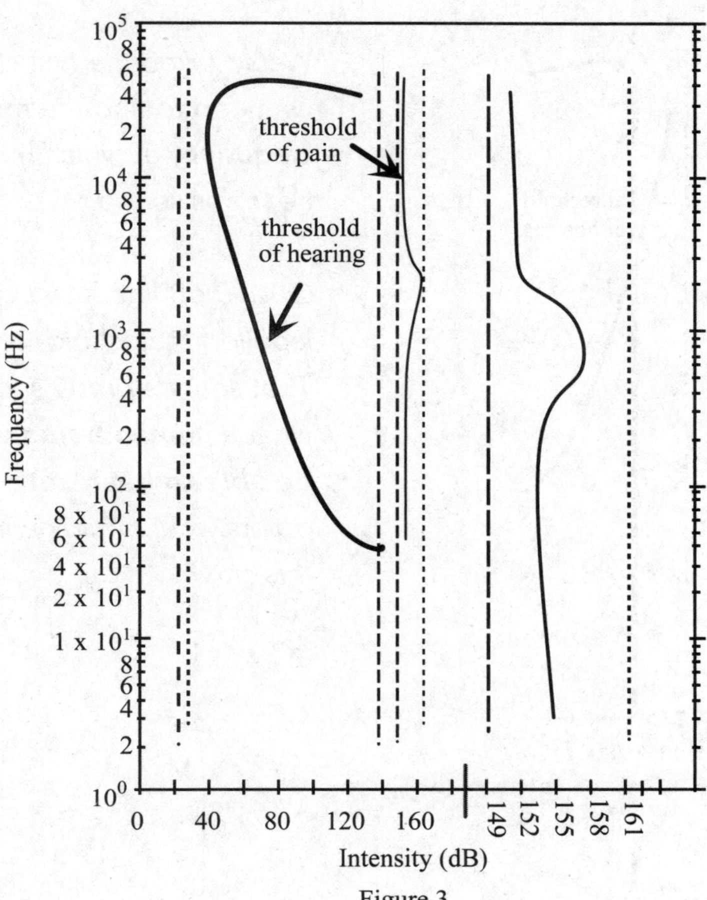

Figure 3

According to Figure 3, what is the minimum frequency at which a human being would be able to hear a 60 decibel (dB) sound?

A. 6×10^1
B. 4×10^2
C. 2×10^3
D. 8×10^4

S *This is a wildly confusing graph! We need to zero in on our target and ignore everything else. Our best clue is* ***60 decibels.*** *We find* ***(dB)*** *on the* ***x-axis****, so let's put our finger at 60 on the x-axis and ignore the right side of the graph.*

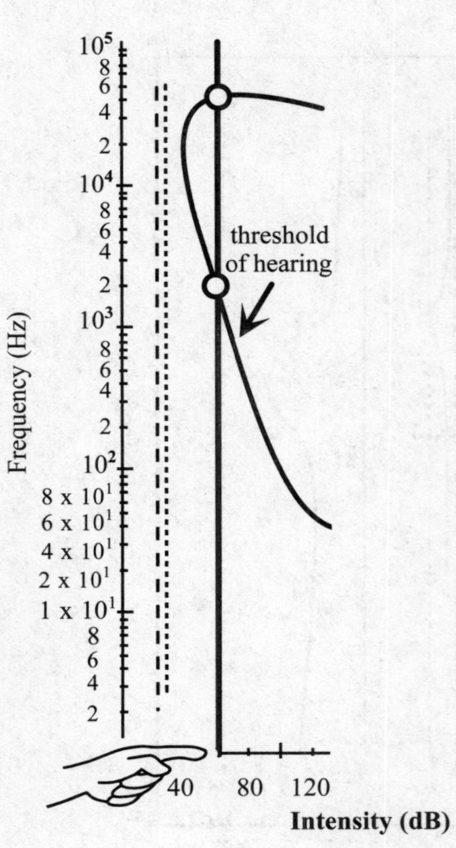

*We've taken the first step. Next we need to find the **minimum frequency** at which humans can **hear** this sound.*

*Our 60 dB line hits a curve labelled "threshold of hearing." That sounds pretty similar to what a **human being would be able to hear**. Let's mark the points where our line intersects this curve.*

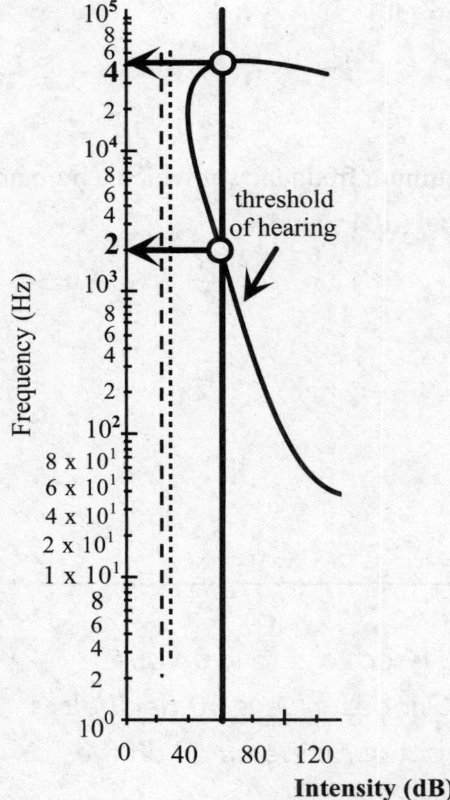

We cross at two distinct points:

1 2×10^3

2 4×10^4

Or, if you were confused by the axis labels, you could estimate:

1 Between 10^3 and 10^4

2 Between 10^4 and 10^5

*Remember, we were asked to find the **minimum frequency.** So we simply take the lower point. The only choice that's bigger than 10^3 and smaller than 10^4 is choice **C!***

Compare Two Points

Now that we know how to get to the point, the next step is to learn how to find two points and compare them.

It's about as easy as it sounds. You will use all of the matching and graph reading skills you've learned so far. As always, take it one step at a time.

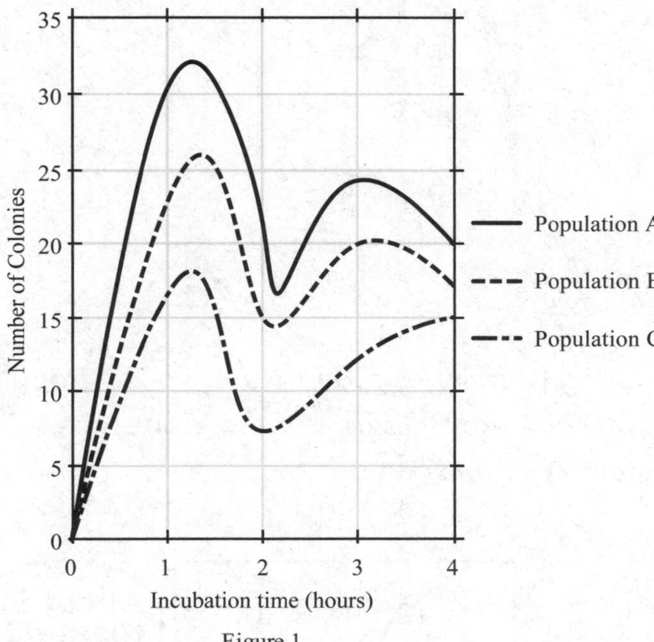

Figure 1

According to Figure 1, the difference in the number of bacterial colonies between population A and C after 3 hours of incubation is approximately:

A. 5
B. 8
C. 12
D. 22

S

1 *Let's get to our points! Line up a vertical at 3 hours.*

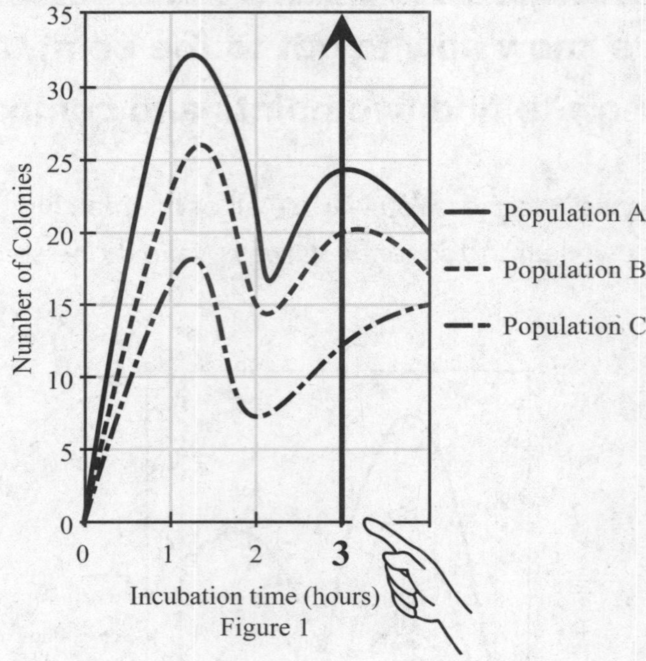

Figure 1

2 *Using your finger,* ***slide up*** *until you hit* ***Population A****, which the key tells us is the solid line. Then simply* ***slide left*** *to get our first point.*

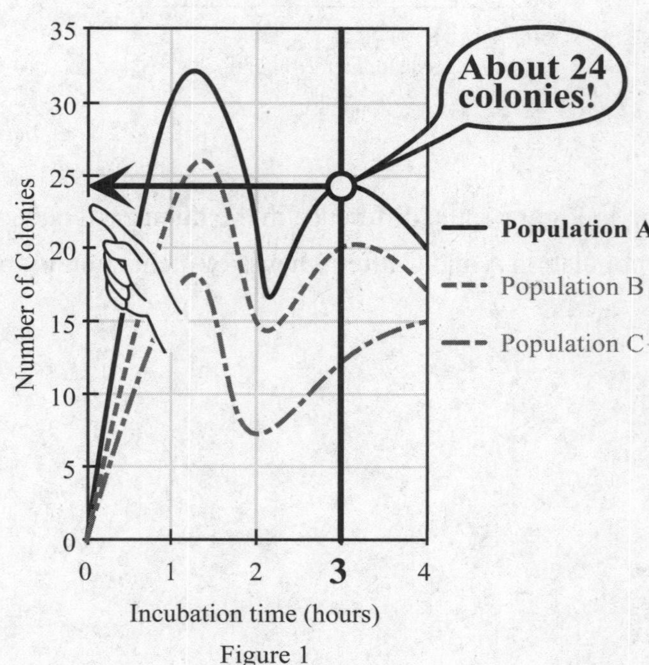

Figure 1

3 *For the second point, repeat the process for Population C.*

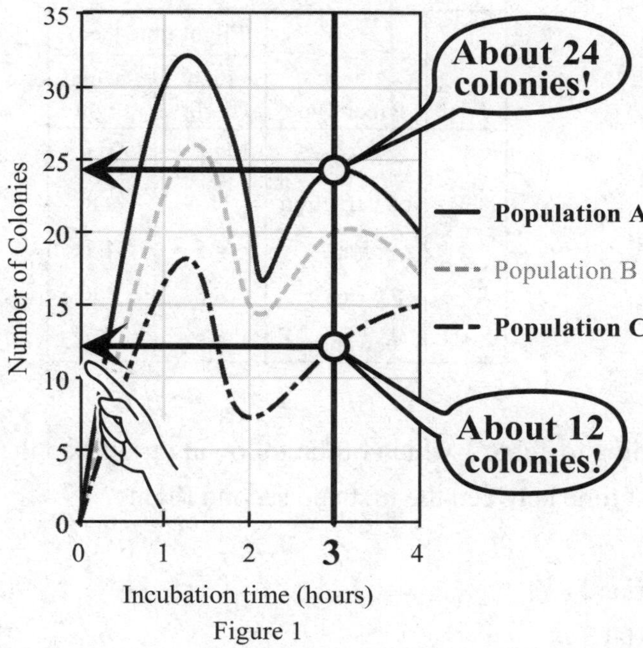

Figure 1

So we have Pop A at **24** *and Pop C at* **12**, *a* ***difference*** *of* **12.**
C *is our answer!*

Comparisons within Tables

Frequently, you'll be asked to compare two points from one or more tables. You will need to **physically write** on the tables to keep your comparisons organized.

For example, if you were asked to use the table below to find which student increased their score more from Test 1 to Test 2, you would **use your pencil to create a new column**:

Table 3			
Student	Test 1	Test 2	increase
Peeta	85	95	10
Katniss	72	99	27

E2

Table 1			
		Flight time (sec)	
Trial	Paper Type	First flight	Second flight
1	résumé	7.6	6.4
2	construction	11.4	9.8
3	wax	4.5	4.3
4	rice	6.5	5.8
5	newsprint	5.8	4.2

According to Table 1 which of the following trials had the smallest decrease in flight time between the first and second flights?

A. Trial 2
B. Trial 3
C. Trial 4
D. Trial 5

S *"Decrease in flight time" tells us we need to do some subtraction! Use your pencil to draw a third column to help compare trials.*

Table 1				
		Flight time (sec)		
Trial	Paper Type	First flight	Second flight	*decrease*
1	résumé	7.6	6.4	*1.2*
2	construction	11.4	9.8	*1.6*
3	wax	4.5	4.3	*0.2*
4	rice	6.5	5.8	*0.7*
5	newsprint	5.8	4.2	*1.6*

We must identify the ***smallest decrease****. Glancing at our new column, that's clearly* **0.2***, from Trial 3. Our answer is* ***B!***

Relationships

Relationship questions ask you to describe how two or more variables relate. You will need to draw arrows on the tables and graphs to help you analyze trends.

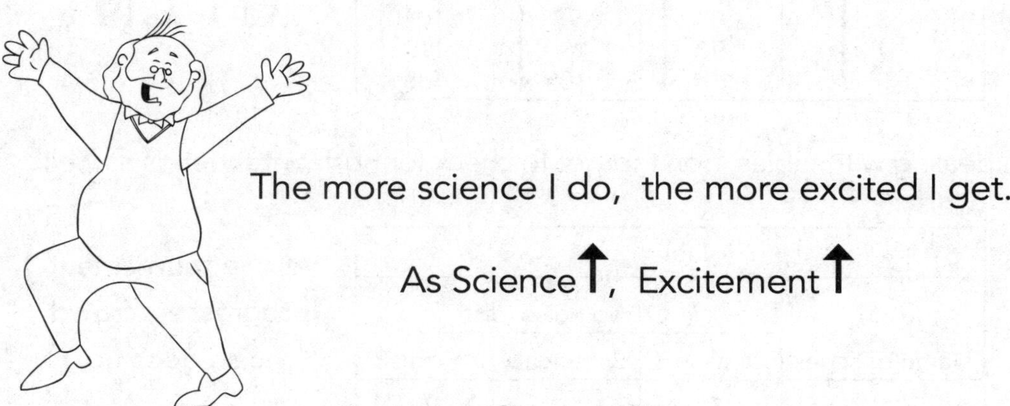

The more science I do, the more excited I get.
As Science ↑, Excitement ↑

As always, you will begin by **matching** words in the questions and figures. The only remaining step is to describe any trends or relationships you find.

Types of Relationships

Let's take a look how you can use **arrows** to illustrate different relationships.

1 **Direct relationship**: as one variable increases, so does the other.

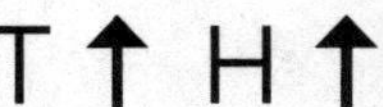

You can use **arrows** to write relationships in shorthand.

Likewise, data is often presented in a **table**. Be sure to **draw arrows** to illustrate the relationships among the different variables in a table.

To keep your arrows consistent, always draw the **head** of the arrow next to the **biggest number**.

1 2 3 4 5 →

Table 1

Game of series	Crowd noise (dB)		
	Qualifiers	Semifinals	Finals
1	79	90	99
2	84	92	103
3	88	98	104
4	90	100	110
5 ↓	101 ↓	105 ↓	135 ↓

As the games of a series progress, crowd noise goes up.

G↑ CN↑

When dealing with tables, don't forget to check for **horizontal** trends as well:

Table 1

Game of series	Crowd noise (dB)		
	Qualifiers	Semifinals	Finals
1	79 →	90 →	99
2	84 →	92 →	103
3	88 →	98 →	104
4	90 →	100 →	110
5	101 →	105 →	135

As the tournament progresses, crowd noise goes up.

T↑ CN↑

2 Inverse relationship: as one variable increases, the other decreases.

As temperature increases, clothing decreases.

T↑ C↓

Let's see what this looks like in a table:

Table 2				
		Accuracy (% bullseye)		
Distance from target (ft)		Not Blindfolded	Blindfolded	
Katniss	100 ↓	100 ↑	95 ↑	
	150	94	82	
	200	89	74	
	250	85	70	
Robin	100 ↓	100 ↑	89 ↑	
	150	91	78	
	200	83	70	
	250	79	62	

As distance increases, accuracy decreases

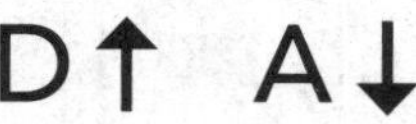

Once you've drawn your arrows, you can spot relationships at a glance!

Direct and Inverse relationships are the most common relationships on the Science section, and are relatively easy to spot. However, for the tougher Relationships questions, you'll need to keep an eye out for **shifting trends**.

3 Shifting Trend: We go up; then we go back down. Or Vice Versa.

What would happen to the diameter of a snake if it ate an elephant?

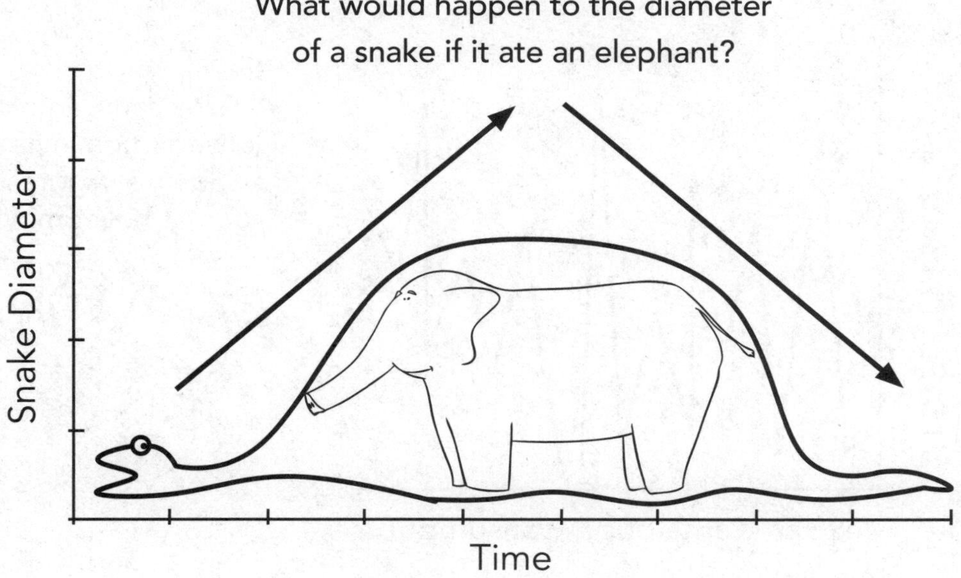

As time goes by, the snake's waistline goes up, then down.

T↑ SD ↑ then ↓

Let's see this phenomenon in a table:

Table 3			
	Energy level (%)		
Time	Jeremy	Julia	Pat
9:00	75	85	69
10:00	65	72	60
11:00	55	63	51
12:00	50	59	45
1:00	60	72	62
2:00	75	85	74
3:00	85	92	89

As time increases, energy level decreases then increases

T↑ EL ↓ then↑

Whenever you have a shifting trend like the one above, pay close attention to **where the shift happens**! It's bound to play a role in an upcoming question. For example, notice how every student gets a boost of energy around 12:00... What might explain this strange phenomenon?

4 **No Relationship:** These things have nothing to do with each other.

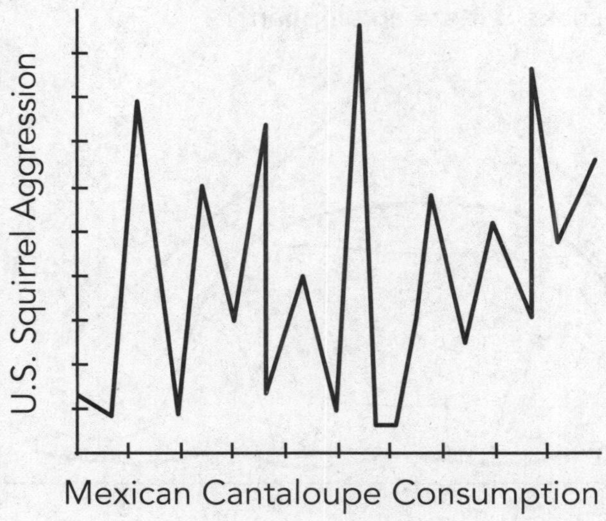

As Mexican Cantaloupe Consumption increases, U.S. Squirrel Aggression... um... never mind.

If you ever have arrows like those in the table below, **there's no relationship!**

Table 4	
Shoe Size (Adult)	Average IQ
6-7	105
7-8	109
8-9	87
9-10	103
10-11	98
11-12	110
12-13	112

There is no relationship between shoe size and IQ!

Nada. Zip. Zilch.

Don't try to find one.

Relationships in Action

Let's get some practice finding relationships! Draw arrows anywhere you see a Direct, Inverse, or Shifting trend. As always, use matching (and your finger) to get to points!

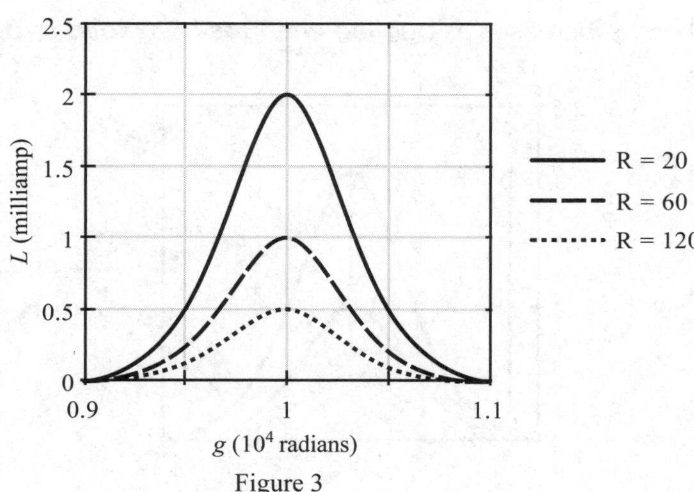

Figure 3

According to Figure 3, does L vary with R?

A. Yes; as R increases, L decreases.
B. Yes; as R increases, L remains the same.
C. No; as R increases, L increases.
D. No; as R increases, L remains the same.

S *We are asked if L **varies with** R. Let's take it step by step:*

1 Use **matching** to find the variables

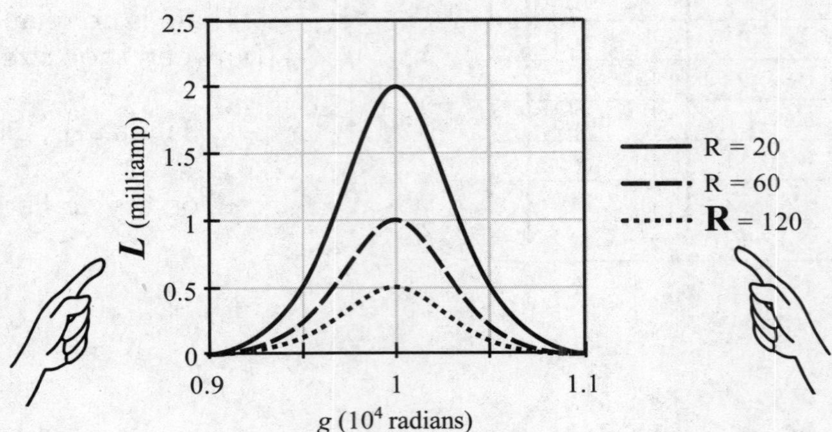

2 Draw **arrows**

*L **increases** as we move **up** the graph.*

*R increases as our **line changes** from **solid** to **dotted**.*

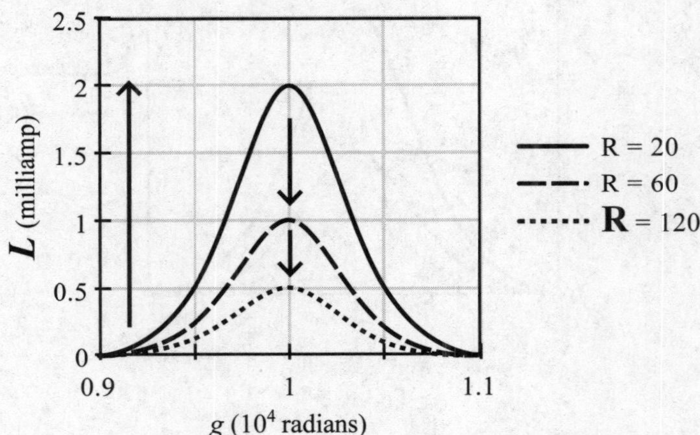

Notice that choice A uses different wording but describes the same **inverse relationship**.

3 Describe **relationship**

Looking at our arrows, we see a relationship: **L ↑ R ↓**

*In other words: **as L increases, R decreases.***

***A** is our answer!*

E2

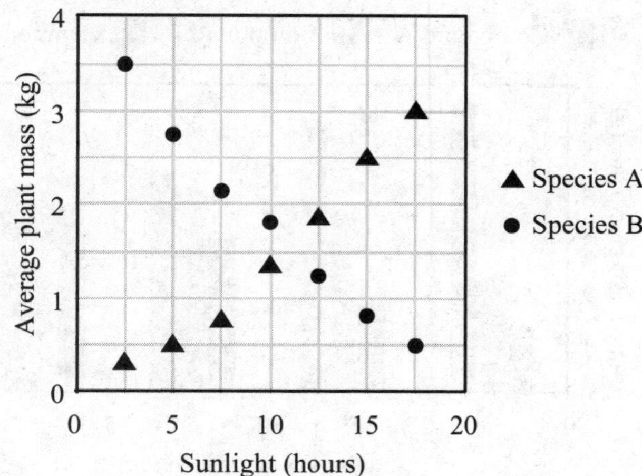

According to the graph above, as the average amount of sunlight increased, the average plant mass

F. increased for Species A, but decreased for Species B.
G. increased for both Species A and Species B.
H. decreased for Species A, but increased for Species B.
J. decreased for both Species A and Species B.

S *We need to connect the dots to find our relationships.*

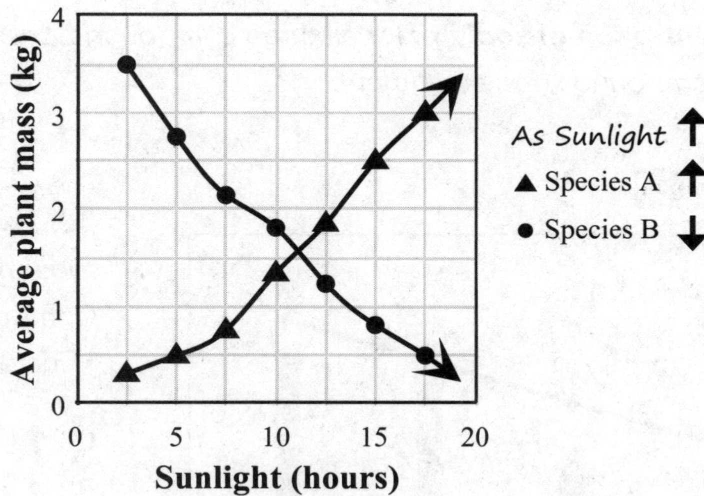

As Sunlight increases, Species A gains mass, and Species B loses mass. Our answer is ***F!***

E3

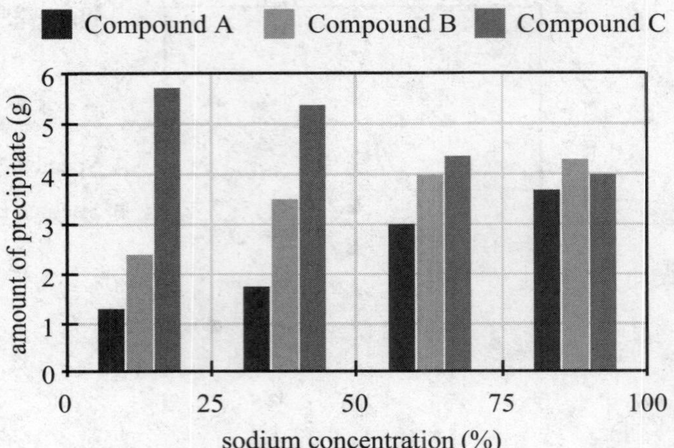

According to the results of Study 1, as the sodium concentration increased, the average amount of crystalline salt that precipitates out from the solution:

A. increased for all 3 compounds.
B. increased for compound A and B, but decreased for compound C.
C. decreased for all 3 compounds.
D. decreased for compound A and B,but increased for compound C.

S *We are looking for the **change in precipitate** as we **increase** the **concentration of sodium**, for all three compounds. Let's tackle the compounds one at a time.*

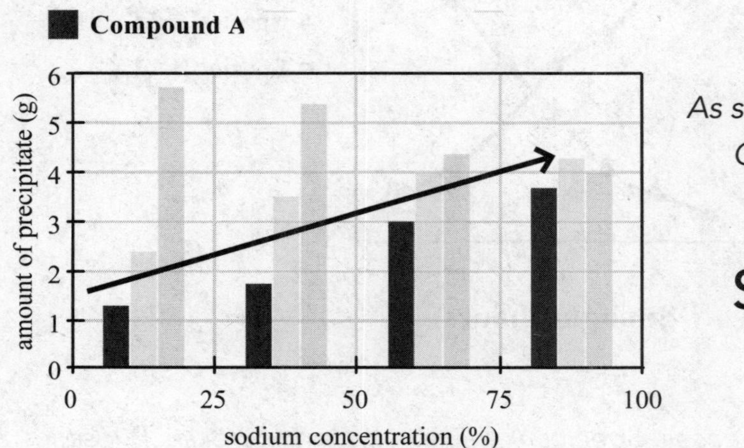

As sodium increases, Compound A increases

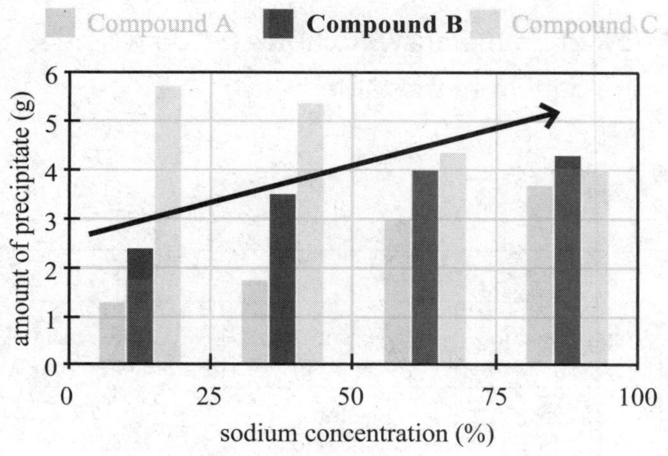

As sodium increases,
Compound B
increases

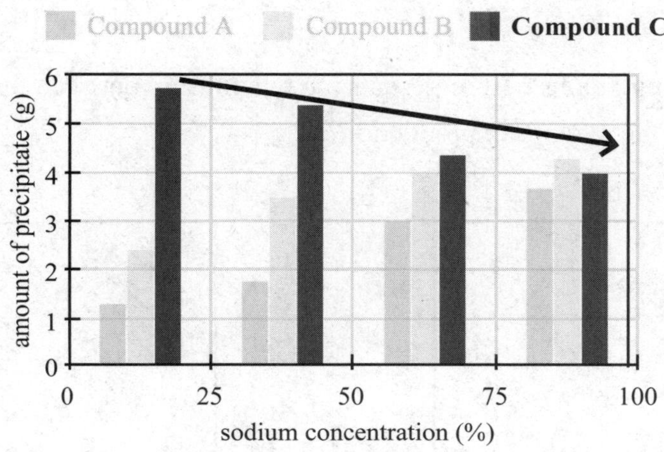

As sodium increases,
Compound C
decreases

S ↑ C ↓

So let's put this all together:

As the sodium concentration increases,
the precipitate levels ***increase*** *for* ***A*** *and* ***B***
and ***decrease*** *for* ***C****.*

Our answer is ***B!***

Graphs in the Answer Choices

Sometimes the graphs will show up in the **answer choices**. You will need to pick the graph that matches the data from the table.

Table 1				
Sequoyah species	Age (yr)	Sap production (cm^3)	Sap production period (yr)	Rate of sap production (cm^3/yr)
A	425	225	300	.75
B	500	336	280	1.2
C	850	420	350	1.2
D	1200	255	340	.75

Which of the following graphs best represents the relationship between the age of the Sequoyah and the rate of sap production?

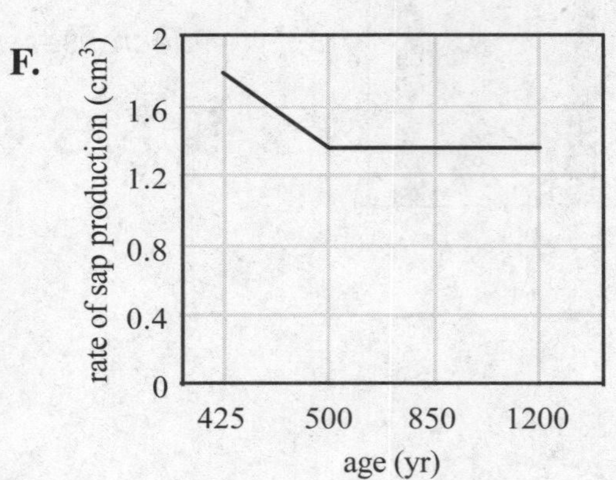

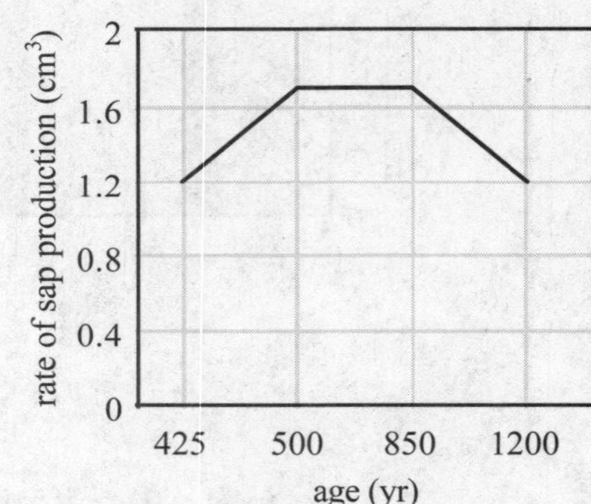

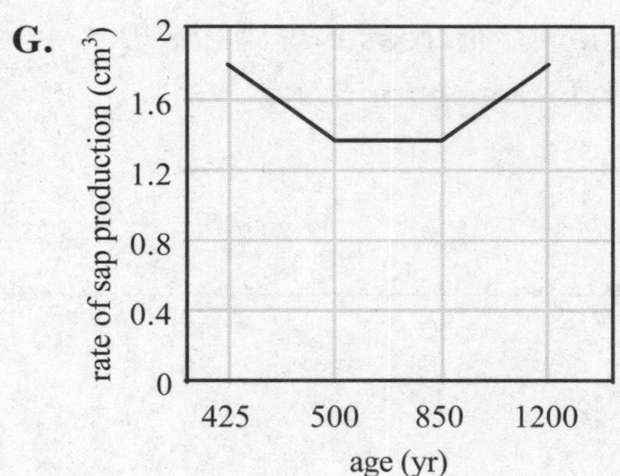

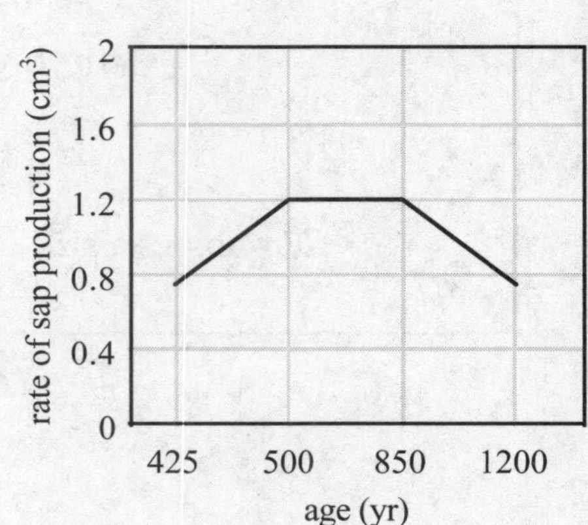

S *We need to find the relationship between* ***age*** *and the* ***rate of sap production****. Let's draw arrows for these variables in our table:*

Table 1				
Sequoyah Species	**Age** (yr)	Sap production (cm^3)	Sap production period (yr)	**Rate of sap production** (cm^3/yr)
A	425 ↓	225	300	↓ .75
	500	336	280	1.2
	850	420	350	↑ 1.2
	1200	255	340	.75

Looking at our arrows we see we're dealing with a ***shifting trend****:*

As age increases,
the rate ***increases****,* ***levels off****,*
and then ***decreases****.*

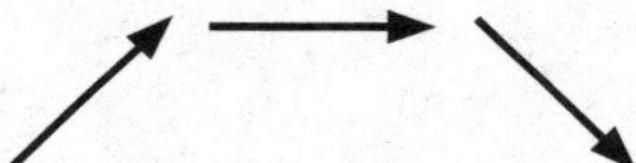

Now let's see if we can match this shape with our choices:

F.

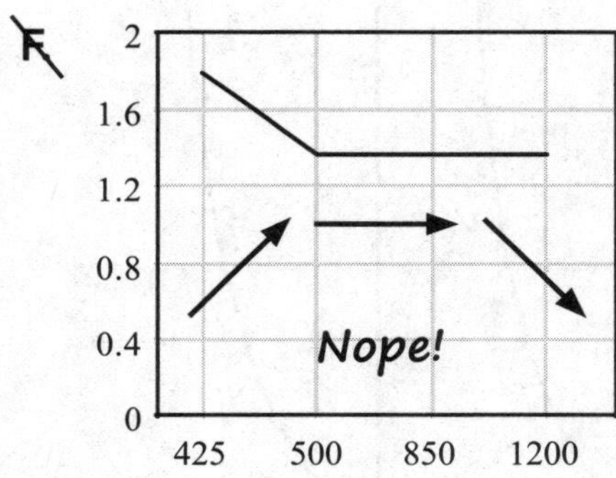

H.

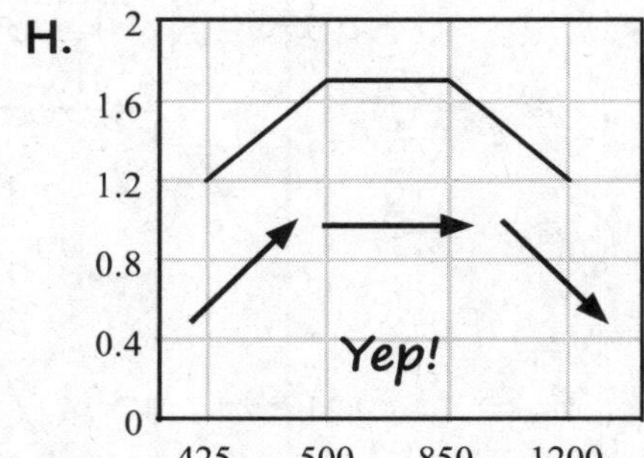

G.

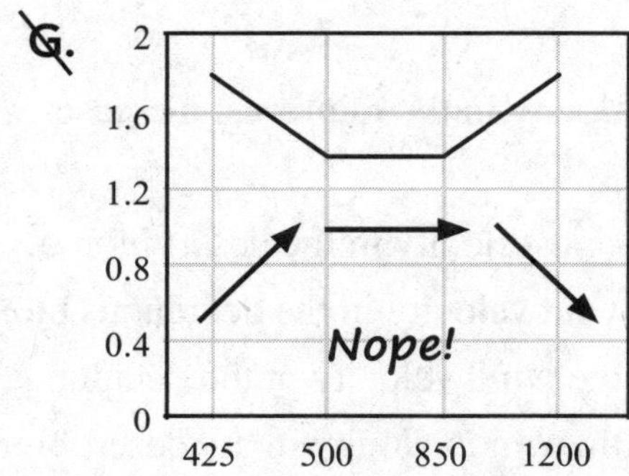

J.

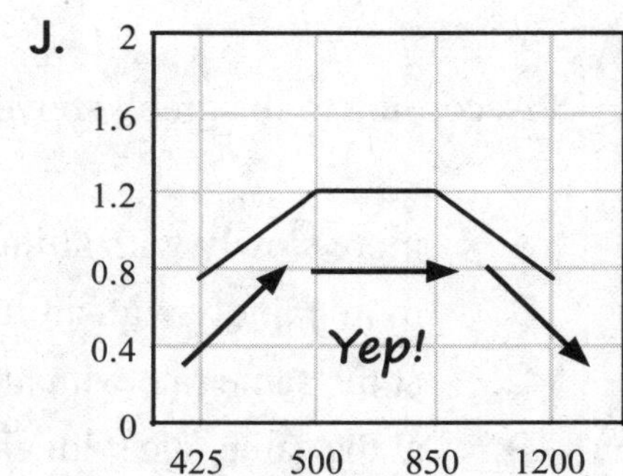

When we compare our shape to the answer choices, it's clear we can eliminate F and G. To pick between H and J, we'll need to look closer at the actual ***numbers****.*

The rate of sap production starts at .75, caps out at 1.2, and then drops back to .75. Choice H has the right shape, but it's in the wrong spot! Our answer is ***J!***

Comparing Relationships: Rates of Change

A very advanced relationship question involves comparing **multiple** relationships. Which variable is changing the most, or the most rapidly? First isolate each relationship, then look at your arrows and numbers to help compare relationships.

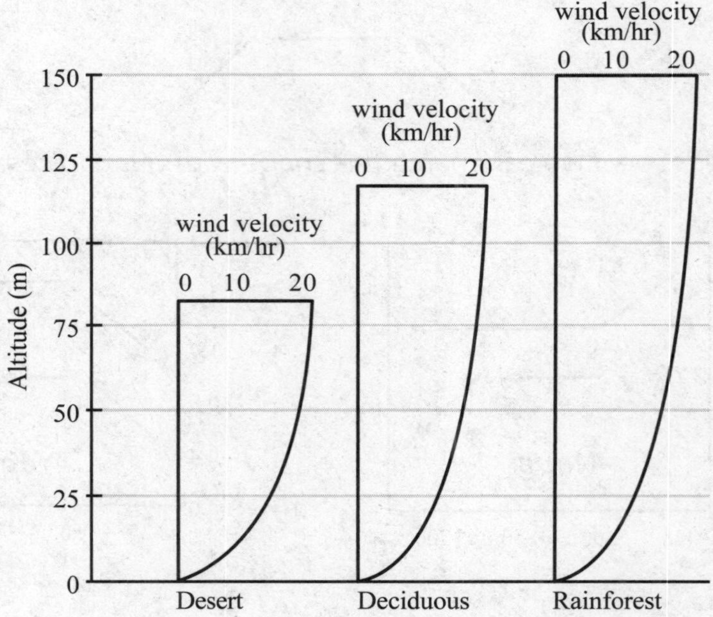

According to the graph above, wind velocity in the rainforest increases:

A. more slowly with altitude than wind velocity in the desert biome.
B. more rapidly with altitude than wind velocity in the deciduous biome.
C. at the same rate with altitude as the wind velocity in the deciduous biome.
D. at the same rate with altitude as the wind velocity in the desert biome.

S *We are dealing with a **crazy graph**! We have 3 curves within a single graph, **all on the same scale**. The curves show velocity increasing from 0 to 20 km/hr for **three different areas**.*

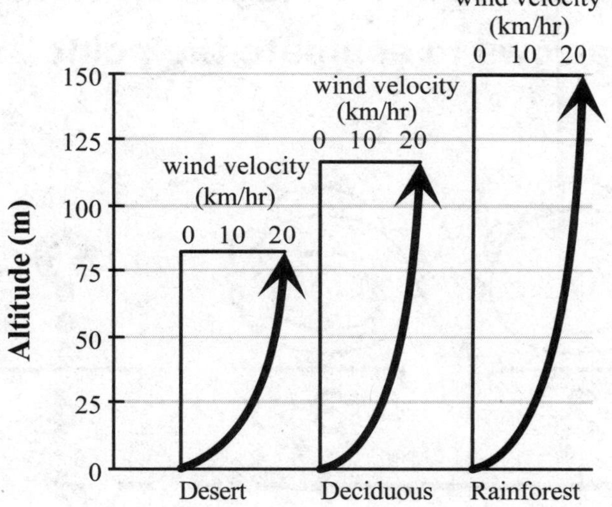

For all 3 areas:

As altitude increases, wind velocity increases

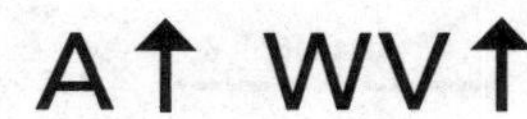

*So what's **different** about these curves?*
*Well, we hit 20 km/hr **faster** with altitude depending on the area.*

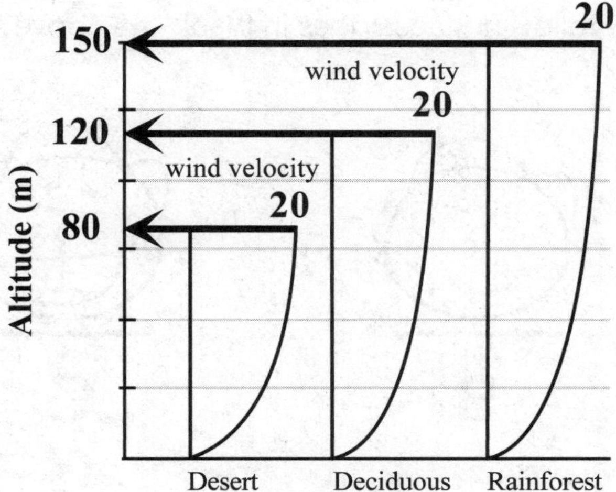

*To hit **20 km/hr** wind velocity, we would have to go up:*

80m in **Desert**
120m in **Deciduous**
150m in **Rainforest**

In the Rainforest, we need to get above all those big trees before the wind really picks up!

*With these numbers, we can compare our relationships! We have to climb **higher** in altitude for the wind to pick up in the Rainforest than in other biomes. In other words, the wind velocity increases **more slowly with altitude** in the Rainforest.*

***A** is our answer!*

Expand the Pattern

Expand the Pattern questions ask you to identify a point that is not explicitly provided in the diagrams. To do this, you will extend your arrows to estimate the point.

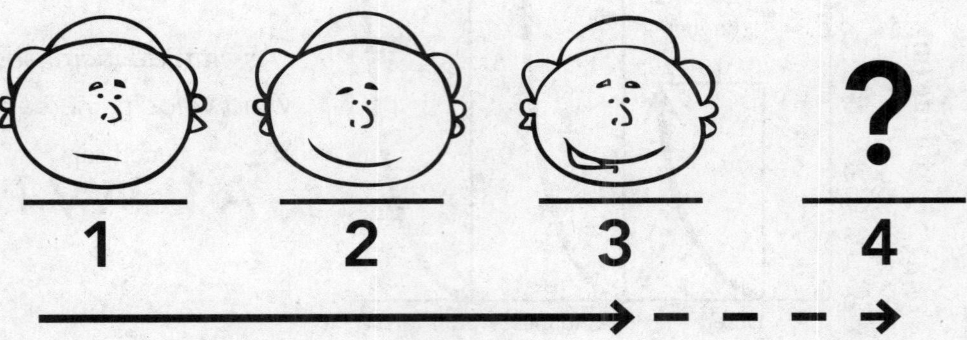

The Power of Deduction

You already **instinctively** know how to figure out something that's not given to you directly. Try it: which of the following faces goes in blank "4" above?

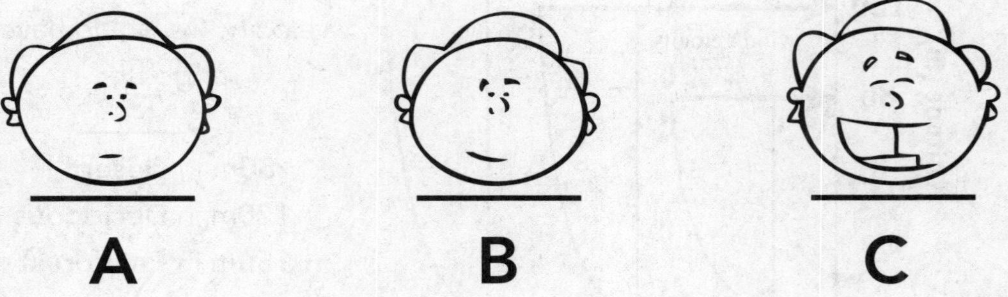

The answer is, of course, C! You knew because you **expanded the pattern!** You noticed that the faces were getting happier, so you looked for the choice that was happier than face #3.

Expanding the pattern is sophisticated stuff as far as the ACT Science section is concerned, yet you do it every day without breaking a sweat!

E1

Table 2				
Sequoyah Species	Age (yr)	Sap Production (cm^3)	Sap production period (yr)	Rate of sap production (cm^3/yr)
E	425	2,500	280	8.9
F	500	3,000	300	10.0
G	850	3,350	340	9.9
H	1200	3,640	350	10.4

Based on the results shown in Table 2, a Sequoyah that produced sap for a period of 370 years would most likely have a sap production:

A. between 2,500 cm^3 and 3,000 cm^3
B. between 3,000 cm^3 and 3,350 cm^3
C. between 3,350 cm^3 and 3,640 cm^3
D. over 3,640 cm^3

S 1 Find the pattern

*We're looking for **production period** and **sap production**. Let's use **matching** and **arrows** to find our pattern:*

Table 2				
Sequoyah Species	Age (yr)	**Sap Production** (cm^3)	**Sap production period** (yr)	Rate of sap production (cm^3/yr)
E		2,500	280	
F	500	3,000	300	10.0
G	850	3,350	340	9.9
H	1200	3,640 ↓	350 ↓	10.4

Reading our arrows, we see a clear, direct relationship:

Period ↑ Sap ↑

2 Expand the pattern

*We are given a sap production period of **370 years**. Let's expand the table to make room for this point:*

Table 2				
Sequoyah Species	Age (yr)	**Sap production** (cm³)	**Sap production period** (yr)	Rate of sap production (cm³/yr)
E	425	2,500	280	8.9
F	500	3,000	300	10.0
G	850	3,350	340	9.9
H	1200	3,640	350	10.4
		?	370	

*Now to find our answer! If we expand the pattern for sap production, we see we need to pick a value that is **bigger than 3,640**:*

Table 2				
Sequoyah Species	Age (yr)	**Sap production** (cm³)	**Sap production period** (yr)	Rate of sap production (cm³/yr)
E	425	2,500	280	8.9
F	500	3,000	300	10.0
G	850	3,350	340	9.9
H	1200	3,640	350	10.4
		>3,640	370	

We don't need to know the exact value when we expand the pattern. The answer choices tend to be greater than / less than statements.

*This makes sense! According to our relationship, as period increases, sap production increases. So if we **increase** the period to a value **over 350**, we need to **increase** the sap production to a value **over 3,640!***

***D** is our answer!*

E2

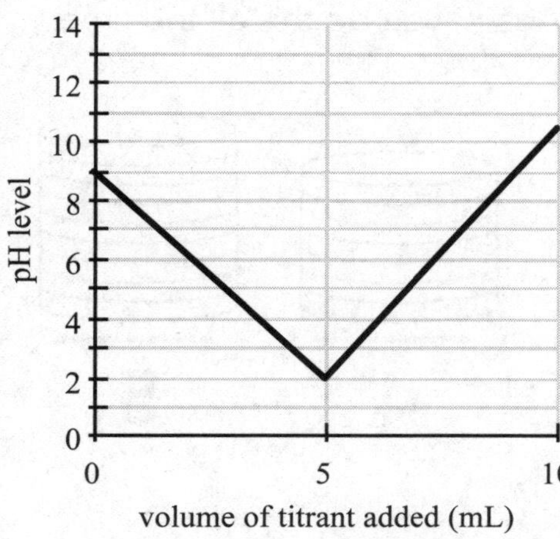

Figure 1

According to Figure 1, if 11.5 mL of titrant had been added to the sample solution, the pH value would most likely have been:

F. less than 4
G. between 4 and 7
H. between 7 and 10.5
J. greater than 10.5

S *The word **titrant** points us to the **x-axis**, but **11.5** is off the graph! We need to expand our pattern. With graphs, this is as simple as extending the line until we hit our new x-value:*

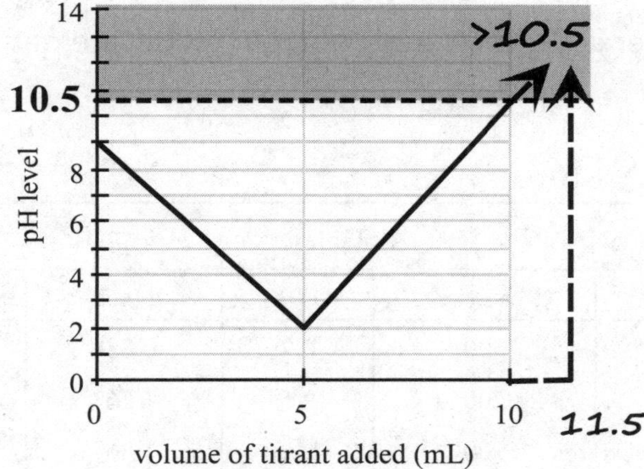

*The original line ended at around **10.5** on the y-axis. If we extend that line to the **right**, we also have to extend it **up**. This means our new pH level will be somewhere **above 10.5**.*

*Lucky for us, we don't need to know the exact value. Looking at our answer choices, we can choose **J** with confidence!*

Reading Between the Lines

Occasionally you will need to predict a value that lies between two points. We call this **reading between the lines.** Again, you do this all the time:

Of course the answer is **B.** You simply need to follow the pattern!

Table 1				
Trial	Mass (kg)	D (m)	P (sec)	g(m/sec^2)
1	500	6.7	0.888	9.8
2	700	9.5	1.267	9.8
3	900	14.6	1.867	9.8

If, in the study above, an additional trial had been conducted with a mass of 600 kg, P would most likely have been:

F. less than 0.888 sec.
G. between 0.888 sec and 1.267 sec.
H. between 1.267 sec and 1.867 sec.
J. greater than 1.867 sec.

S *This is a classic case of reading between the lines. We are asked to find a point that lies between two values in the table.*

1 Find the two nearest points

If, in the Study above, an additional trial had been conducted [...] a **mass of 600 kg**, **P** would most likely hav[...]

Table 1				
Trial	**Mass (kg)**	D (m)	**P (sec)**	g(m/sec2)
1	**500** ↓	6.7	↓ **0.888**	9.8
2	**700**	9.5	**1.267**	9.8
3	900	14.6	1.867	9.8

2 Find the pattern

Our arrows show a direct relationship: as mass increases from 500 to 700, P increases from 0.888 to 1.267.

M↑ P↑

3 Expand the pattern

Table 1				
Trial	**Mass (kg)**	D (m)	**P (sec)**	g(m/sec2)
1	**500**	6.7	**0.888**	9.8
	600 ↓		↓ *?*	
2	**700**	9.5	**1.267**	9.8
3	900	14.6	1.867	9.8

*Since our mass value is **between 500 and 700**, our P value should be **between 0.888 and 1.267**. It's that simple! Our answer is **G**.*

E4

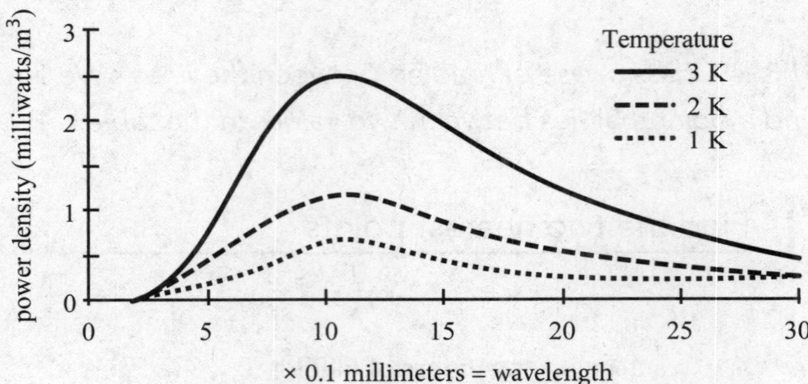

Based on the figure, the maximum power density of the radiation curve will equal 1.7 milliwatts/m^3 when the temperature is closest to:

A. 5 K
B. 1.5 K
C. 2.5 K
D. 3.5 K

S *This one's a bit tricky, so let's start with some careful matching.*

Based on the figure, **the maximum power density** of the radiation curve will equal 1.7 milliwatts/m^3 when the temperature is closest to:

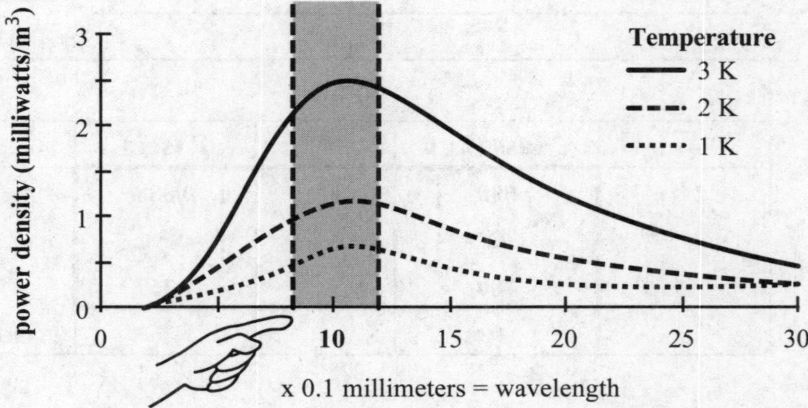

*It looks like the **maximum power density** is where each curve **peaks** in the **shaded area** above. Let's keep matching.*

Based on the figure, **the maximum power density** of the radiation curve will equal **1.7 milliwatts/m³** when the **temperature** is closest to:

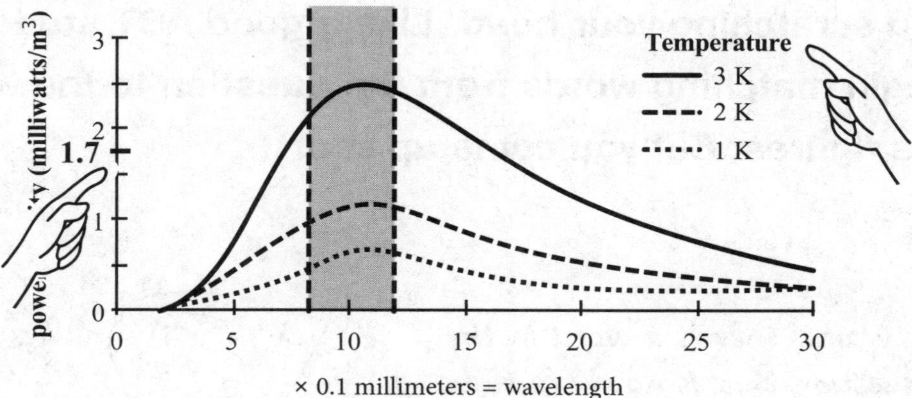

*So the different **curves** are the different **temperatures**, and **1.7 milliwatts** is a point on the **y-axis**. Let's draw a line connecting **1.7** to our shaded area.*

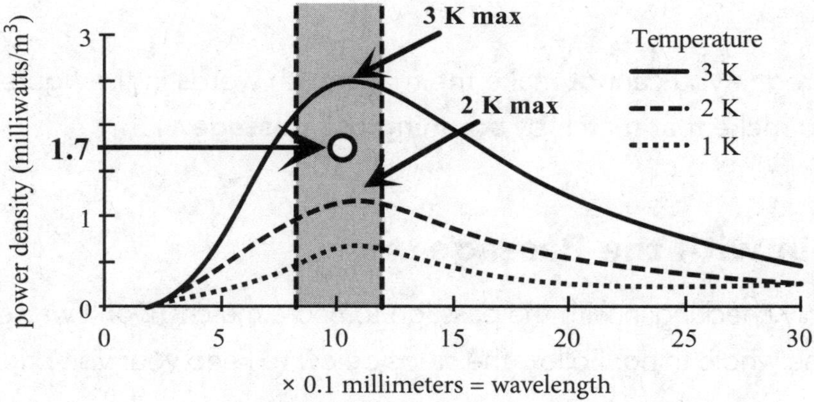

*When we plot our point at **1.7** and move to the right, we hit our **maximum area** somewhere **between the 3 K and 2 K curves.***

*The only choice that falls in this range is **2.5 K**, which looks dead on!*

***C** is our answer!*

Read the Passage

There will come a time when you hit a question that leaves you scratching your head. Like a good ACT student, you begin matching words from the question to the words in the figures. But you come up short.

"Wait... There's a word in the question that is nowhere to be found in the figures!"

Rest assured, if you cannot make the match with words in the figures, you will be able to make that match by **scanning the passage.**

Check-in with the Passage

We are only checking in with the passage to find a match! Don't waste time reading the whole thing. Follow the steps below to keep your visit brief.

1. Start **matching** - *Uh oh! No match in the figures.*
2. **Scan the passage** for a match - *Found my match!*
3. Read the sentence for **context** - *Oh okay, Figure 3 helps.*
4. If necessary, head back to the **figures** - *Found my answer!*

E1

Study 1

Scientists observed multiple species of butterflies in various habitats. The weight, in grams, the wingspan, in centimeters, the habitable temperature ranges, in degrees Celsius, and the preferred habitat for four different species are shown in Table 1.

Table 1

Species	Average weight (grams)	Average wingspan (cm)	Habitable temperature ranges (c)	Preferred habitat
Ithomia mamercus	34	5.8	12-17	Deciduous Forest
Ithomia agnosia	22	4.6	15-21	Rainforest
Ithomia eurimedia	56	7.6	24-34	Rainforest
Ithomia lerida	18	2.5	12-31	Grassland

Study 2

Scientists observed the *Ithomia mamercus* and *Ithomia agnosia* species in the deciduous forest and rainforest biomes over the course of several months to examine the effects of predators on the behavior of the butterflies. They discovered that both species reacted to a seasonal increase in the number of predators by laying more eggs. This allowed the butterflies to maintain a consistent adult population throughout the year, even when threatened.

In a controlled experiment, scientists introduced *Antherium* wasps, a known predator of butterflies, into a habitat of *Ithomia mamercus.* According to Study 2, the most likely result is that:

A. the *antherium* wasps will have no effect on the behavior of the *Ithomia mamercus.*

B. *Ithomia mamercus* will lay more eggs, and its adult population will stay constant.

C. the *Ithomia mamercus* population will decrease.

D. *Ithomia mamercus* will lay more eggs, and its population will increase.

Read the Passage questions often direct you to "Study 1" or "the passage" instead of to a particular table or figure.

S

1 Start **matching**

The question asks us to predict would happen if we added ***predators*** *to a population of* ***ithomia mamercus****. We need to find our matches somewhere in* ***Study 2****.*

2 **Scan the passage** for a match

There is no figure provided for Study 2, so we know we will need to scan the passage for our key words:

> Scientists observed the *ithomia mamercus* and ithomia agnosia species in the deciduous forest and rainforest biomes over the course of several months to examine the effects of predators on the behavior of the butterflies. They discovered that both species reacted to a seasonal increase in the number of **predators** by **laying more eggs**. This allowed the butterflies to maintain a consistent adult population throughout the year, even when threatened.

3 Read the sentence for **context**

So, ***if we bring in predators, we get more eggs.***

P↑ E↑

Choice B and D both mention ***egg laying****. However, they disagree on whether the* ***adult population*** *increases or stays the same. Let's check the passage:*

> ...This allowed the butterflies to maintain a **consistent adult population** throughout the year, even when threatened....

Bingo! Consistent population! That makes ***B*** *our answer!*

Read the Passage Detours

Occasionally, you'll need to **revisit the figures** after scanning the passage.

1 Start **matching**

According to Study 1, how many biscuits did the Albertans consume on Wednesday?

A. 781
B. 1,005
C. 64,543
D. 656,567

This looks easy, I can just check the table for biscuits!

Daily Cookie Consumption in Alberta		
Day	Fig Newton	Peppermint Patty
Monday	17	34
Tuesday	45	6456
Wednesday	435	346
Thursday	5	234
Friday	43	7

Dude, where's my biscuit? I better check the passage...

2 Scan the **passage** for a match

Cookies were invented by Jean rt de Francesco in 1745 BC when a preh was maimed by a Burmes ython had kept as a pet for his own amusem egend has it that Jean Colbert put the P on insi e of the turtle case and screamed, " y God, I have created a Biscuit!!!" **Biscuits came to be known as Cookies** during the Third Peloponnesian war when Empress Cooqueesia announced to her nation that every man, woman, and child...

Biscuits are cookies!!!

Score!

3 Return to the **figures**

Daily ~~Cookie~~ Biscuit Consumption in Alberta		
Day	Fig Newton	Peppermint Patty
Monday	17	34
Tuesday	45	6456
Wednesday	**435**	**346**
Thursday	5	234
Friday	43	7

Biscuits are cookies, so I just need to sum up the row for Wednesday!

According to Study 1, how many biscuits did the Albertans consume on Wednesday?

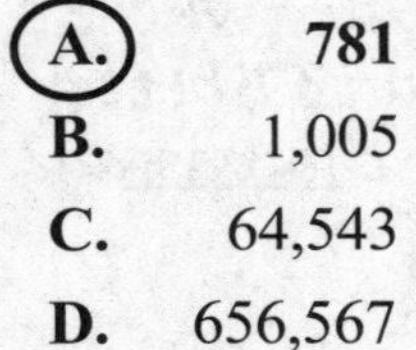

A. 781
B. 1,005
C. 64,543
D. 656,567

435 + 346 = 781

A is the answer!

E2 *Experiment 1*

Flow coefficients (Cv) measure the flow capacities of valves at different sizes. The larger a valve's flow coefficient, the faster liquid can pass through it. Scientists passed 25 gallons of water through four different valves and recorded the flow coefficient and pressure drop (psi) for each. The results are shown in Table 1.

Table 1		
Valve	Pressure drop (psi)	Cv
A	1	25
B	3.5	13.4
C	4.9	11.3
D	530	10.7

Based on the results of Experiment 1, which valve allowed liquid to pass most quickly?

F. Valve A
G. Valve B
H. Valve C
J. Valve D

S 1 Start **matching**

*Our task is to find which **valve** allowed liquid to **pass most quickly**. As always, let's start with the figure to see if we can get everything we need:*

Table 1		
Valve	Pressure drop (psi)	Cv
A	1	25
B	3.5	13.4
C	4.9	11.3
D	530	10.7

*Hm... we have a match for **valve**. But nothing about passing liquid quickly.*

*To the **passage**!*

2 Scan the **passage** for a match

Flow coefficients (Cv) measure the flow capacities of valves at different sizes. The larger a valve's flow coefficient, the faster **liquid can pass** through it. Scientists passed 25 gallons of water through four different valves and recorded the flow coefficient and pressure drop (psi) for each. The results are shown in Table 1.

*Bingo! Reading our sentence for context, we see that a **higher flow coefficient** means the juice is flowin'. Hmm.. we don't have the words **flow coefficient** in the table, either. Let's go back to the passage for another clue:*

Flow coefficients (Cv) measure the flow capacities of valves at different sizes. The larger a valve's flow coefficient, the faster liquid can pass through it.

*Bingo! Our passage tells us **flow coefficient** is **Cv**, and that's right in our table! Time to head back to the figures, applying what we learned from the passage.*

3 Return to the **figures**

*We learned that the larger the Cv, the faster liquid passes through a valve. So we need the **valve** with the **largest Cv!***

Table 1		
Valve	Pressure drop (psi)	**Cv**
A	1	**25**
B	3.5	13.4
C	4.9	11.3
D	530	10.7

***Valve A** has a whopping **25 Cv**!*

*Our answer is **F!***

E3

Scientists tested the ability of different protective surfaces to withstand intense pressure. In each trial, the scientists used a pressurized hammer to strike protective plates of varying surface area, *a*, using varying degree of force, *f*.

The scientists calculated that the pressure $P = \frac{f}{a}$.

The scientists recorded the number of strikes withstood by the protective surfaces before fracturing. The results are shown in Table 1.

Table 1			
Trial	Pressure (newton/m^2)	Surface type	Strikes withstood
1	15	A	56
2	23	A	44
3	15	B	78
4	23	B	67

Based on the introductory information, when *P* was equal to 1, what was the relationship between *f* and *a*?

A. $f = a$
B. $f = 2a$
C. $f = a^2$
D. $a = 2f$

S *We are directed to the* ***introductory information*** *rather than to a particular figure! This is most unusual! Rather than go to the table, let's jump right to the text.*

1 Scan the **passage** for a match

We are looking for the ***relationship*** *between* **f** *and* **a** *when* **P = 1**. *Let's make our match!*

Scientists tested the ability of different protective surfaces to withstand intense pressure. In each trial, the scientists used a pressurized hammer to strike protective plates of varying surface area, *a*, using varying degree of force, *f*.

The scientists calculated that the pressure $\boldsymbol{P} = \dfrac{\boldsymbol{f}}{\boldsymbol{a}}$

Bingo! We have found what we need, and we didn't need the table at all! We are given an equation in the introductory text. We simply need to plug our data into the equation.

2 Use the **equation** from the passage

It's math time! We want to plug **1** *in for* **P**:

$$P = \frac{f}{a}$$

$$1 = \frac{f}{a}$$

$$f = a$$

A *is our answer!*

Inference

Inference questions ask you to think like a scientist. To do this, you will need to dive a little deeper into the depths of scientific thinking.

Starting with **Inference** questions, we begin reading the passages with the same level of scrutiny that we previously applied to the Reading Section of the ACT. Don't panic! We've saved so much time through our efficient match process that when these few questions appear, we have the time we need to dive in and read more carefully to get our answer.

Here are examples of inferences you might be asked to make:

- What was the thought process behind the design of the study?
- What assumptions were made by the scientists?
- What was held constant and what was varied; what was being studied?
- What is the most likely explanation for a particular aspect of the results?

Making an Inference

Though they are among the toughest in the Science section, Inference questions, like Expand the Pattern questions, test a basic skill you use every day.

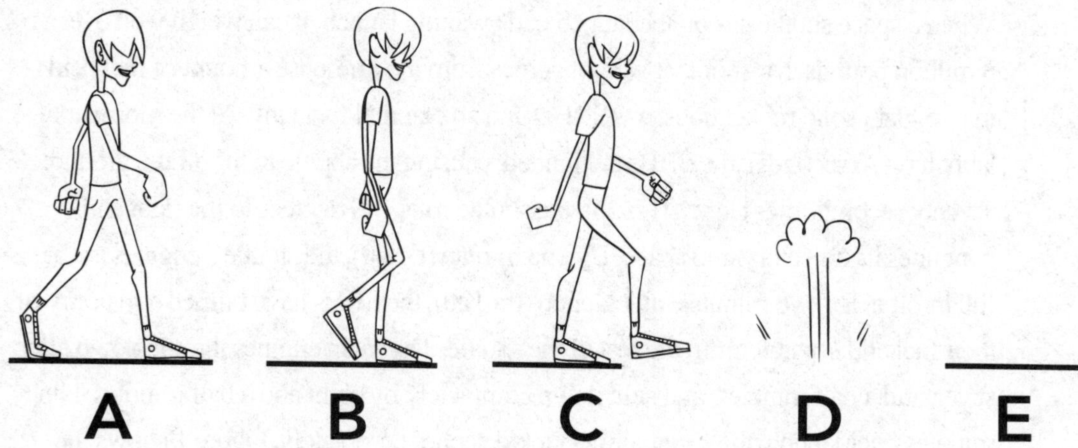

What is the most likely reason the man is missing in **E**?

Even though you didn't see it happen, you can easily make the **inference** that the man above **fell in the hole!** This is a reasonable assumption based on the evidence provided.

Inference Strategy

Inference questions can vary, but every one is solved with a simple strategy:

1. Scan the passage for context
2. If necessary, return to the figures
3. Use common sense to make an inference

E1

Researchers studied the launch of a space shuttle in order to determine how the mass of an object impacts its propulsion through the atmosphere.

When a space shuttle sits on the launch pad awaiting launch, it can weigh well over 4 million pounds. Most of that weight comes from the immense amount of fuel held in two giant solid rocket boosters (SRBs) and an external fuel tank. At the moment of launch (t = 0 seconds), the SRBs are ignited, causing the shuttle to lift off the ground. Twenty seconds after launch (t = 20), the shuttle rolls 180 degrees to the right and continues its trajectory into space. By one minute (t = 60), the shuttle's engines are at full throttle. By two minutes after launch (t = 120), the SRBs have burned a majority of their fuel and separate from the rest of the shuttle. The main engines throttle down after seven and a half minutes, and shut down completely by eight and a half minutes. Nine minutes after launch, the external fuel tank detaches completely. Figure 1 shows the mass of the space shuttle, excluding fuel, at different stages during the launch process.

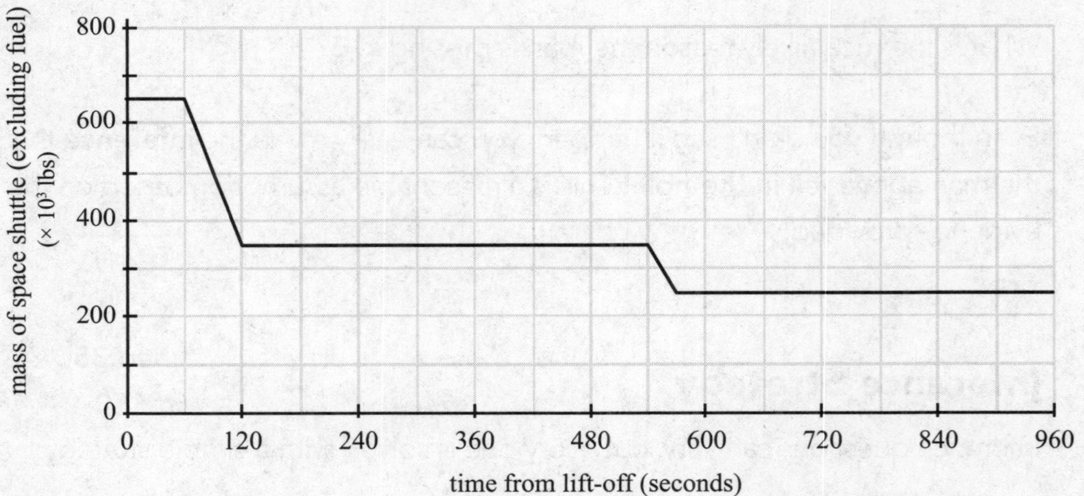

At t = 0, approximately what percent of the mass of the space shuttle was made up by the two solid rocket boosters?

A. 10%
B. 30%
C. 50%
D. 70%

S 1 Scan the **passage** for context

In order to find the percentage of the shuttle's mass that is made up by the ***two solid rocket boosters****, we'll need the mass of the boosters and the shuttle.*

Scanning the passage for ***two solid rocket boosters****, we learn that the boosters separate from the shuttle by* **t = 120.**

2 Return to the **figures**

Let's mark on our graph where the boosters separate and find the mass of the shuttle without the boosters:

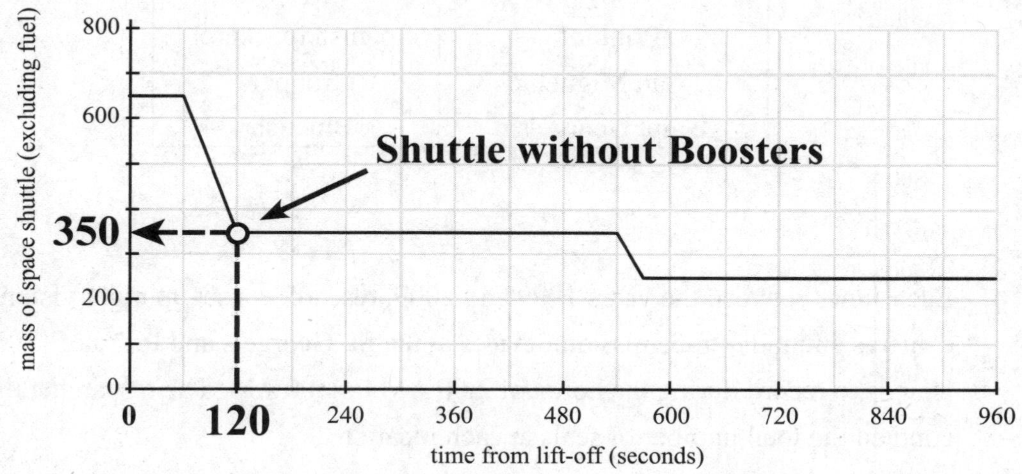

Aha! After the boosters separated, the shuttle weighed **350***.*
Before the separation, at **t = 0,** *the shuttle weighed* **650***.*

3 Use common sense to make an **inference**

We can figure out the mass of the boosters by ***subtracting*** *the mass at* **t = 120** *from the mass at* **t = 0***:*

650 - 350 = (300)

So we can ***infer*** *that the boosters weighed* **300!**
That's about **50%** *of the initial weight.* **C** *is our answer!*

E2

As northern fur seals have faced increasing challenges due to human activity, their populations have dwindled. In order to track the decline in seal populations, researchers monitor large congregations of seals during mating season. The seals mate on only a handful of islands in the Bering Sea, at particular seasons, at particular times, near abundant food sources. All the fur seals studied were mature adults between 175-275 kg in weight, and between 1.8 and 2.3 meters in length. Local islands and their dominant fish populations are shown in Table 1.

Table 1

Bering Sea Islands	Dominant fish populations
Nunivak	Kingfish
Pribolof	Spanish mackerel
San Miguel	Grouper
Saint George's	Bluefish

Study 1

Each June, between the years 1999 and 2009, researchers set up night vision cameras and radio transmission devices at the St. George's and Pribolof Islands to record during the hours of 2:00 AM to 4:00 AM. The researchers counted the total number of seals at each location.

In Study 1, what must the researchers have assumed about the mating and feeding habits of northern fur seals when they set up their recording devices on the specified islands? Northern fur seals:

F. mate at night and feed on bluefish and Spanish mackerel.
G. mate at night and feed on kingfish and grouper.
H. mate during the day and feed on bluefish and Spanish mackerel.
J. mate during the day and feed on kingfish and grouper.

S *The question asks us to determine what the **researchers assumed** about **mating and feeding habits** based on how they set up **recording devices** on certain **islands.***

Let's scan Study 1 for these key words to help make our inference:

1. *The researchers set up **night vision cameras***
2. *on **St. George's and Pribolof Islands***

*Now that we know what the researches **did**, let's figure out **why**:*

*Why would the researchers set up **night vision cameras**? To see at night, obviously! They must have assumed the **seals mate at night.** Looking at our answer choices, we can cross off **H** and **J**.*

*Why would the researchers set up on **St. George's and Pribolof Islands?** Hm, that's less obvious. We need more context! The only other place these islands show up is in Table 1. Let's take a look.*

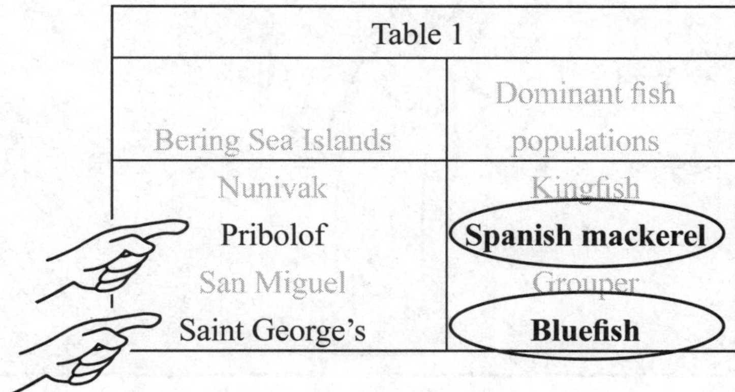

Table 1	
Bering Sea Islands	Dominant fish populations
Nunivak	Kingfish
Pribolof	**Spanish mackerel**
San Miguel	Grouper
Saint George's	**Bluefish**

*Bingo! These islands are home to **Spanish Mackerel** and **Bluefish.** The researchers must have assumed seals snack on these fish!*

***F** is our answer!*

Inference and Experimental Design

Inference questions will occasionally require you to explain how and why the scientists **designed the experiment** the way they did. You will need to know about basic experimental design concepts such as **constants**, **controls** and **independent and dependent variables**.

To help illustrate these concepts, let's pretend we are researchers who have decided to put the **buff** in Science Buff. We want to know which of two protein shakes will help us pack on the muscles: shake A or shake B? Since we are savvy scientists, we decide to design an experiment...

Operation Science Buff

The Question: Is protein shake A or B better at beefin' up a scientist?

The Plan: We give protein shake A to one scientist, protein shake B to a second scientist, and a fruit shake to a third scientist.

1	2	3
Professor Samson	**Professor Hurk U. Lees**	**Professor Atlas**
Sign: Aquarius	Sign: Capricorn	Sign: Gemini
Shake: A	Shake: B	Shake: Fruit
BQ: 34	BQ: 31	BQ: 32

The Procedure: We first measure each scientist's initial Beefcake Quotient (BQ). Every day, for a month, each scientist follows the same routine:

1 **Eat** a bowl of Humberto's Stale Granola Crunch
2 **Run** 2 km to Heisenberg's Fitness Emporium
3 **Lift** a 30 lb medicine ball for 6 hours
4 **Drink** assigned shake
5 Watch Desperate Housewives of **Minnesota**
6 Go to **bed**

The Results: After one month, the scientists were inspected. Their final Beefcake Quotient (BQ) was compared to their initial BQ. The results are shown in Table 1.

Table 1

	Shake	Initial BQ	Final BQ
Prof. Samson	A	34	172
Prof. Hurk U. Lees	B	31	45
Prof. Atlas	Fruit	32	44

Do **not** drink protein shake A.

The Conclusion: Protein shake A is ***dangerously potent!***

Constants, as part of the procedure, are usually found in the passage.

Variables can be quickly identified by looking at the figures.

Scientists **select** different independent variables and **measure** the dependent variable that results.

Variables vs. Constants

Variables: What is **changing** in the study.
In our study: Type of shake and Beefcake Quotient

Constants: What is **NOT changing** in the study.
In our study: The daily routine

Simple! On the ACT, you will need to make a distinction between two different kinds of variables: **Independent** variables and **Dependent** variables.

Independent vs. Dependent Variables

Independent Variable (IV): The input variable manipulated by the scientists.
In our study: Type of Shake

Dependent Variable (DV): The output variable measured by the scientists.
In our study: Beefcake Quotient (BQ)

The scientists learned that if you put in a different type of shake (IV), you get out a different Beefcake Quotient (DV).

Control or Control Groups

Scientists use a **control** or **control group** to ensure that it is their intervention that causes the change in the DV, and not some other factor.

A control group goes through the **same procedure** as every other group, but does NOT receive the experimental intervention administered by the scientists.

In our study, we had Professor Atlas go through the **same procedure** without drinking a protein shake. This allowed us to be confident that it was not the daily routine that caused the terrifying transformation of Professor Samson, but rather protein shake A! Professor Atlas was our one-man **control group.**

Let's get some practice identifying variables, constants, and controls.

E3 *Sarcina aurantiaca* is a type of bacteria that is widely present both in open air and water. It can be grown on nutrient agar basins (NABs) in the laboratory setting after being swabbed on a bacterial lawn. A bacterial lawn is a uniform, even layer of organisms that cover an entire surface. Using a back and forth motion, a sterile swab can be used to cover the surface of a NAB in one direction. Then, the NAB is rotated 90° and swabbed again. After incubation, the bacterial colonies will spread and grow evenly upon the NAB so that a thin, speckled film of bacteria is visible (see Figure 1).

Experiment 1

Students determined if 10 strains (Strains 1 – 10) of *S. aurantiaca* could grow in the presence of certain antibiotics (chemicals that can be used to stop or slow bacterial growth). Cells from Strain 1 were swabbed onto a NAB in order to make a bacterial lawn. An antibiotic dispenser was then used to drop four discs covered with an antibiotic—either Streptomycin (S), Tetracycline (T), Penicillin (P), or Neomycin (N)—and one disc without any antibiotic on top of the nutrient agar and bacteria. After the disc was applied to the bacterial lawn, the NAB was sealed. Once sealed, the NAB was incubated at 90° F for 48 hours to allow the bacterial lawns to grow. This process was repeated with Strains 2 – 10. All NABs were incubated at 90° F for 48 hours and then examined for bacterial growth.

Question 1

Which of the following accurately identifies a factor that was allowed to vary and a factor that was held constant in Experiment 1?

	VARIED	HELD CONSTANT
A.	Incubation Temperature	Antibiotic Type
B.	Antibiotic Type	Incubation Temperature
C.	Bacteria Strain	Antibiotic Type
D.	Incubation Temperature	Bacteria Strain

S *We need to figure out what is **changing** and what is staying **constant**. The answer choices include incubation temperature, antibiotic type, and bacteria strain. Let's scan for these factors one at a time:*

Incubation Temperature - 90° F
Antibiotic Type - either S, T, N, or P
Bacteria Strain - Strains 1 - 10

*We only see **one** temperature, so it must be a constant. Since we see 4 different antibiotic types and 10 different bacteria strains these factors must be variables. **B** is our answer.*

Question 2

Which of the following served as a control in Experiment 1?

F. The strain of *Sarcina aurantiaca* applied to the bacterial lawn.
G. The temperature of the discs.
H. The bacterial lawns exposed to antibiotics.
J. The bacterial lawn exposed to no antibiotic.

S *We are asked to identify the **control** of Experiment 1. We are looking for something that goes through the entire procedure but doesn't receive the experimental intervention.*

> An antibiotic dispenser was then used to drop four discs covered with an antibiotic – either Streptomycin (S), Tetracycline (T), Penicillin (P), or Neomycin (N) – **and one disc without any antibiotic** on top of the nutrient agar and bacteria.

*Bingo! In this experiment, the discs are like our scientists in Operation Science Buff. Only, instead of protein shakes, the discs got antibiotic S, T, P, or N. One disc went through the whole procedure without any antibiotic. That's our control! **J** is the answer.*

Question 3

Before beginning the experiments, the students sterilized the swabs used to create the bacterial lawns. The most likely reason that the swabs were sterilized was to avoid contaminating the:

A. NABs with cells from the *Sarcina aurantiaca*.
B. NABs with cells that were not from the *Sarcina aurantiaca*.
C. swabs with bacteria from the NABs.
D. swabs with antibiotics.

S 1 Scan the **passage** for context

This is a classic Inference question that asks us to get inside the head of the scientists. Why did they sterilize the swab? Let's review what role the swab plays in the procedure:

Step 1. Sterilize **swab**
Step 2. Apply *S. aurantiaca* cells to the **swab**
Step 3. Brush **swab** onto NAB, creating bacterial lawn
Step 4. Drop antibiotic disc onto the bacterial lawn
Step 5. Incubate the bacterial lawn at 90° F
Step 6. Measure bacterial growth

2 Use common sense to make an **inference**

We know scientists ***wanted*** *to put* ***S. aurantiaca*** *on the swab.*
So looking at Step 2 above, Choice A can't be right.

We know they used the ***swab*** *to apply bacteria to the NABs.*
So looking at Step 3 above, Choice C gets it ***backwards****.*

And we know ***antibiotics*** *come* ***after*** *the swab is used.*
So looking at Step 4 above, Choice D couldn't happen.

This leaves us with our answer: Choice ***B!***

Question 4

A complicating factor in interpreting the results of Experiment 1 was that exposing the bacterial lawns to open air while applying antibiotics may have inadvertently:

F. exposed the bacterial lawn to antibiotics.
G. changed the temperature of the sample.
H. exposed the lawn to additional strains of *Sarcina aurantiaca.*
J. desterilized the swab.

S 1 Scan the **passage** for context

*We are looking for a **complicating factor** (aka a **flaw**) in the experimental design. What might a problem be with exposing the lawns to **open air**? We haven't seen "open air" yet - let's scan the passage.*

Sarcina aurantiaca is a type of bacteria that is widely present both in **open air** and water. It can be grown on nutrient agar basins (NABs) in the laboratory setting after being swabbed on a bacterial lawn..

A match! S. aurantiaca is in the open air!

2 Use common sense to make an **inference**

If S. aurantiaca is in the open air, exposing the bacterial lawns to open air also exposes them to S. aurantiaca.

*Do you see the problem? The scientists were so careful to swab only **one strain** of S. aurantiaca onto the lawn, but who knows what other strains were floating around? This is a flaw!*

*Our answer is **H!***

Measurement Adjustment

The toughest ACT questions will ask you to think about how experiments would have turned out differently had the experimental procedure been altered.

To answer these "measurement adjustment" questions, you will need to read the passage enough to understand the **hows**, **whats**, and **whys** of the experiment and then draw an inference about how adjusting one aspect would change the results.

Let's take a look at the most common measurement adjustment questions.

Contaminated Instruments

On occasion, measurement adjustment questions will involve a poorly calibrated or faulty measurement tool which yields erroneous measurements. For example, suppose that scientists used a thermometer to measure the boiling point of different liquids and recorded their results in Table 1 below.

Measurement Adjustment questions require a deeper understanding of the experimental procedure than any other question type. The time you saved getting to the point will come in handy solving these problems.

Table 1	
	Boiling Point (°F)
Liquid A	130
Liquid B	122
Liquid C	107

Suppose the scientists learned that, while measuring the boiling point of Liquid C, the thermometer was contaminated with NO_2, leading to a reported temperature that was 30° cooler than the actual temperature of the liquid. How would this impact the scientists' conclusions about the relative boiling points of the liquids?

Clearly, if your thermometer is off, that's going to impact your conclusions about the boiling points! Measurement C is off by ***30°***, while A and B are correct. To correct your data, you would need to make an adjustment to the initial measurements:

Table 1		
	Measured Boiling Point (°F)	Actual Boiling Point (°F)
Liquid A	130	130
Liquid B	122	122
Liquid C	107 →	137

So the ***actual*** boiling point of Liquid C is the highest of the three liquids measured!

Repeat the Experiment in a Different Environment

Measurement Adjustment questions often ask you to consider what would happen to the results of a study if it were repeated in a different environment.

For example, you may have learned in chemistry that altitude affects the boiling point of a liquid:

A↑ BP↓

If a scientist measured boiling points at sea level, and then repeated the experiment atop Mount Everest, what would happen? Every boiling point would now be lower!

For another example, imagine you are studying how long it takes a 50 gram pendulum to complete a full swing (this is called the **period** of the pendulum), and you know that **higher gravity** means a **shorter period**. What would happen if you replicated this study on the **Moon**?

Repeat the Experiment with More Junk in the Trunk

On occasion, measurement adjustment questions will ask you to repeat the experiment with a different quantity of stuff. For example, if you repeated the pendulum experiment with a **100 gram** pendulum, would the results change?

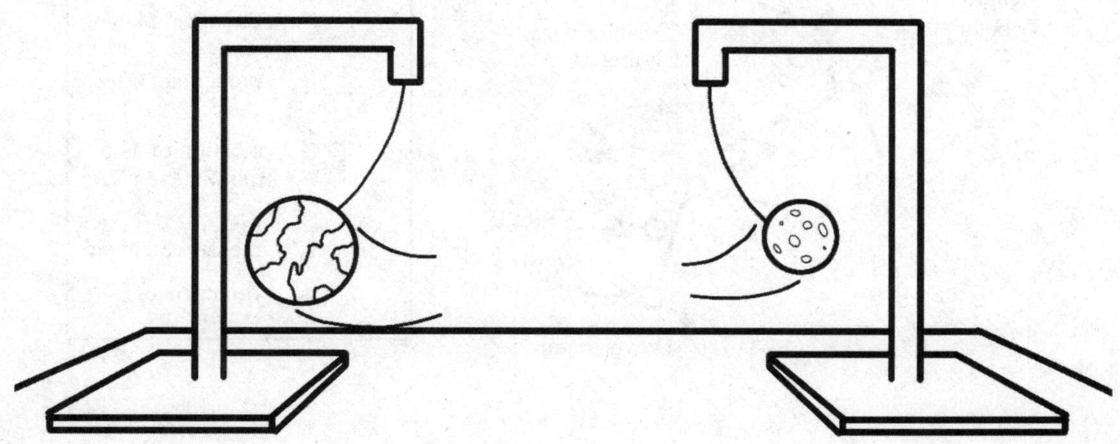

E2

A river's sediment toxicity is the measure of harmful chemicals and volatile compounds which have bound to and settled in the fine particles of the river's floor and depositional areas. This sediment houses organic matter, key to the life cycles of aquatic plants and animals living in the river. Nearby land-dwelling animals – including humans –depend upon the river for both food and drinking water. As a result, high sediment toxicity can negatively impact entire ecosystems surrounding the river.

Factories can increase sediment toxicity directly, by leaking pollutants into the river water, or indirectly, by emitting harmful chemicals into the atmosphere above a river's drainage area. Once in the air, these pollutants can bind to precipitation and fall to the surface as acid rain. The area around a factory where acid rain is most likely to fall is known as the factory's precipitant effect zone.

Researchers conducted a number of studies along the southern leg of the Hosenwurst River in order to determine the effect of five nearby factories on the river's sediment toxicity. (See Figure 1)

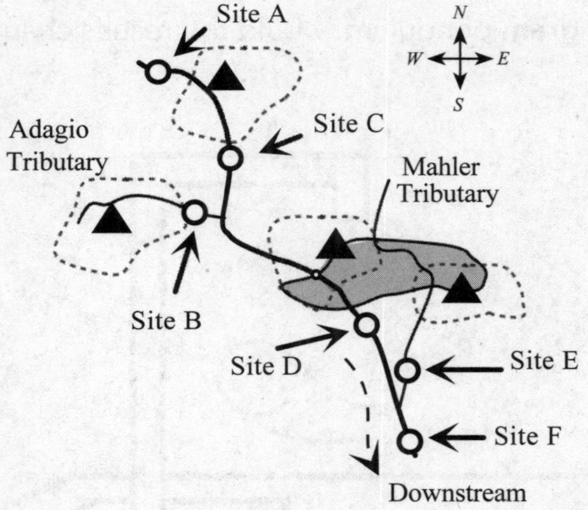

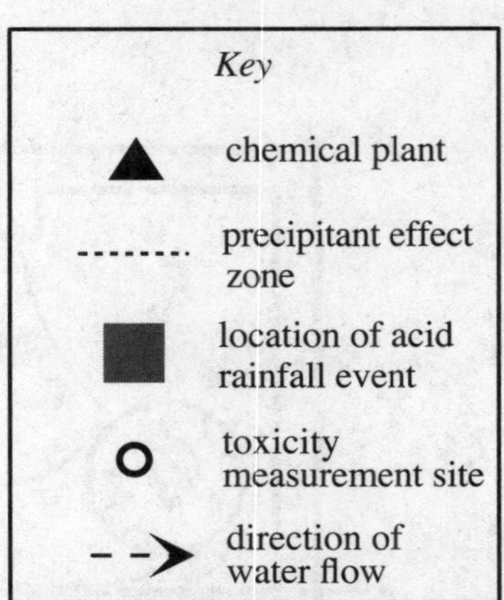

Study 1

Sediment toxicity levels were measured at six sites, labeled Sites A through F, 10 days after a rainfall event over the Hosenwurst River. Scientists extracted a 500 cm^3 sediment sample from each site and measured the toxicity level (TL) of both sediment and surrounding water in ppm (parts per million) for each. Results are shown in Figure 2.

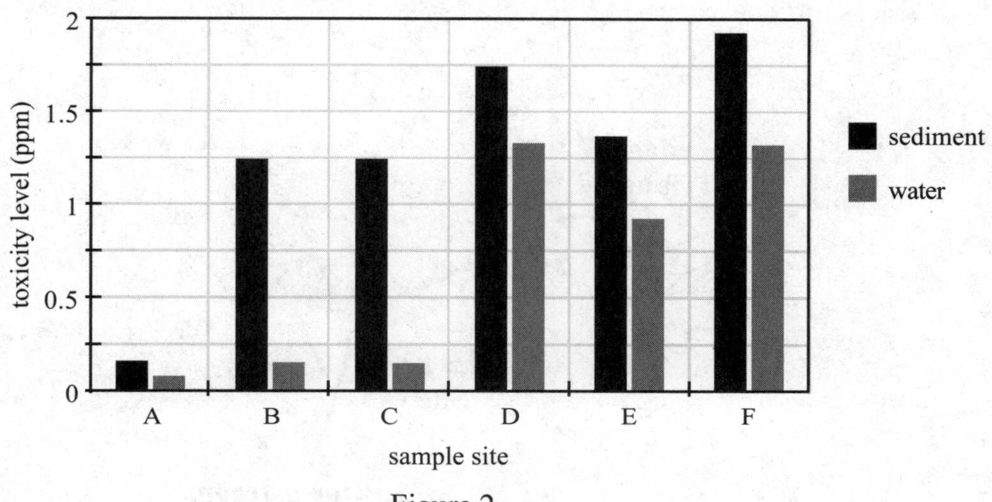

Figure 2

Suppose that the location for Sample Site D had been moved to an area on the Hosenwurst River downstream from where it meets the Adagio tributary but north of where the acid rainfall event occurred. The sediment toxicity level for Site D would most likely have been:

F. less than 1.25 ppm.
G. between 1.25 ppm and 1.75 ppm.
H. between 1.75 ppm and 2 ppm.
J. greater than 2 ppm.

Notice the answer choices! Looks like we might be putting our Expand the Pattern skills to use in this question!

S *We are asked what would happen to the* ***sediment toxicity*** *of* ***Site D*** *if it were moved. First let's find Site D's new home.*

Suppose that the location for Sample Site D had been moved to an area on the Hosenwurst River **downstream from where it meets the Adagio tributary** but north of where the acid rainfall event occurred. The sediment toxicity level for Site D would most likely have been:

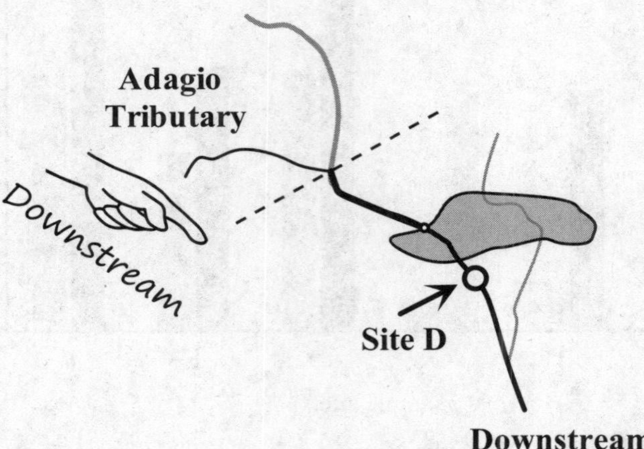

Suppose that the location for Sample Site D had been moved to an area on the Hosenwurst River **downstream from where it meets the Adagio** tributary but **north** of where the **acid rainfall event** occurred. The sediment toxicity level for Site D would most likely have been:

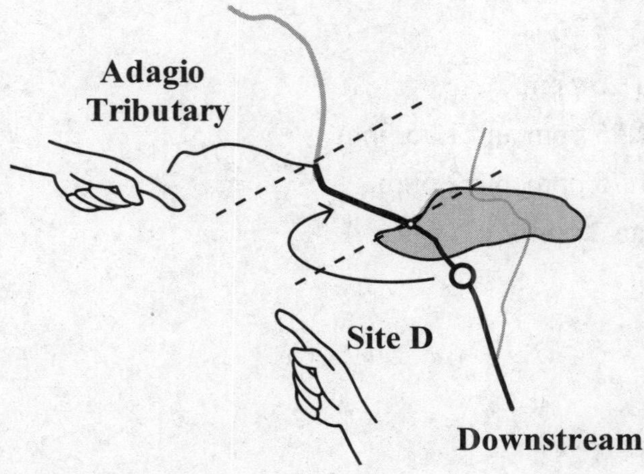

We have our new home for Site D!

*Our task now is to determine what Site D's **new sediment toxicity** would be in its new home. **Toxicity** and **sediment** have matches in Figure 2!*

*Looking at the data, we can see that as we move **downstream,** the sediment toxicity goes **up.***

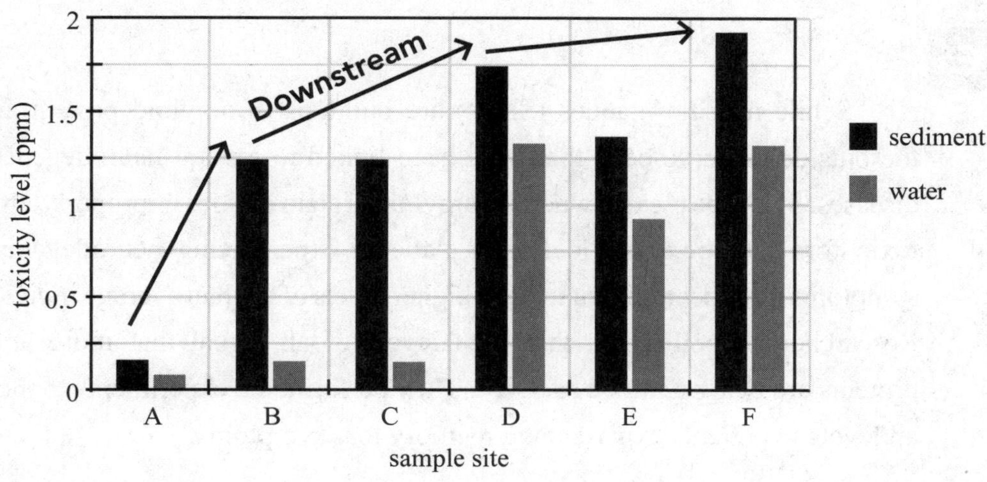

Toxicity builds up as the river flows past factories and acid rain zones.

Understanding at this level certainly helps, but it's not necessary!

*Looking at Figure 1, we can see our new Site D is downstream from Site C but upstream from the old Site D. We need a sediment toxicity **between that of Site C and Site D**.*

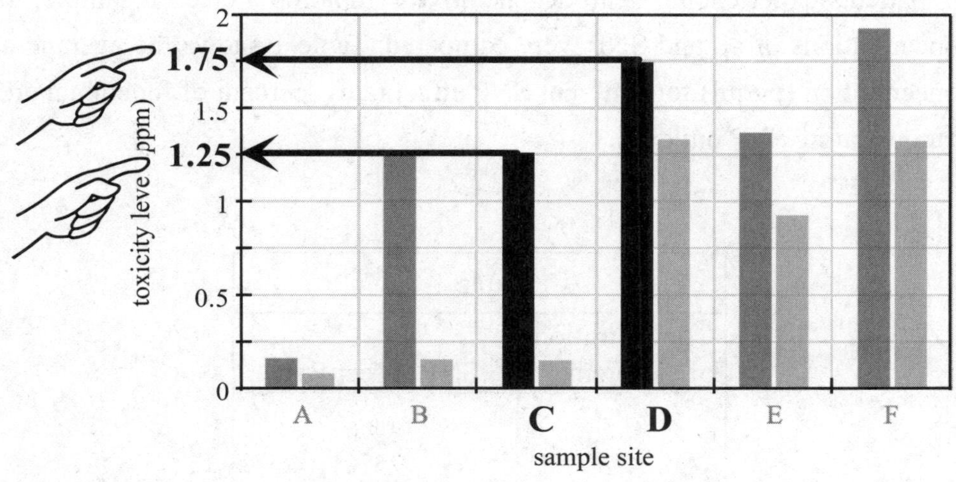

*Our new sediment toxicity lies **between 1.25 and 1.75 ppm**!*

***G** is our answer!*

The Toughest ACT Science Question

The final Measurement Adjustment question is absurd. It is bonkers. Nuts. A question like this should only be attempted by science buffs chasing a 36. For the rest of us, it's good practice for recognizing when it's time to skip a tough problem when there are easy points for the picking elsewhere.

Senile neuritic plaques (SNPs) are buildups of amyloid protein around the outside of nerve cells that have been linked to several neurodegenerative diseases. SNPs are created when the amyloid protein divides improperly, creating toxic forms of beta amyloid (aβ). Patients experiencing neurodegenerative symptoms have been shown to have higher levels of aβ than average individuals. Researchers hypothesized that high levels of aβ signal that more amyloid proteins are being retained as SNPs. They performed 2 experiments to measure aβ levels in patients experiencing memory loss symptoms.

Experiment 1

Samples of 10 mL of cerebrospinal fluid (CSF) were collected from thirty-six patients experiencing neurodegenerative symptoms. For each sample, the concentrations of aβ and SNP were compared. Table 1 shows the average aβ concentration (pg/ml) for different SNP effect rates (percent of functional area demonstrating SNP buildup).

Table 1

Concentration of aβ (pg/ml)	SNP Effect Rate
0.5	0%
4.2	25%
8.5	50%
12.8	75%

Experiment 2

Scientists identified an antibody, AAB, that may help prevent or reverse the protein degradation that leads to SNP formation. To measure natural AAB presence in patients, scientists used a biomarker enzyme—a substance which binds with a target antibody and turns the sample darker. The more of the target antibody present in a sample of CSF, the higher the measured absorbance, and the darker the sample.

Twenty-four samples of 10 mL of CSF were obtained from patients at one of four stages of symptom severity. Patients were classified as Stage 1 (nominal symptoms), Stage 2 (mild symptoms), Stage 3 (moderate symptoms), or Stage 4 (severe symptoms). The samples were each placed in tiny wells on a microtitre plate. Scientists then added 100 μL of diluted biomarker enzyme Eb_{23} to each well and incubated the sample at 90° F. After 2 hours, absorbance and aβ concentration were measured for each sample. Table 2 shows the average aβ concentration, measured absorbance, and estimated AAB concentration for patients from each stage of symptom severity.

Table 2

Symptom Severity	Concentration of aβ (pg/ml)	Measured absorbance	AAB concentration (pg/ml)
Stage 1	2.4	0.780	34.45
Stage 2	7.2	0.710	30.72
Stage 3	12.8	0.590	22.04
Stage 4	14.5	0.285	10.34

If all of the patients tested in Experiment 2 who were experiencing Stage 2 symptom severity were taking antibiotics, and these antibiotics generated a new type of antibody which bound to Eb_{23}, how would the measurements have been affected? Compared to the actual AAB concentrations for these patients, the AAB concentrations apparently measured would be:

A. lower.

B. higher.

C. the same.

D. higher for some Stage 2 patients, lower for others.

Measurement Adjustment questions like this one can be a major time sink, so make sure to answer easier questions first on test day!

S 1 Use **matching** to find a starting point

*We're directed to **Experiment 2**, so we should jump to Table 2. We are going to be adjusting the measurement of **AAB concentration** for **Stage 2** patients.*

Table 2			
Symptom Severity	Concentration of aβ (pg/ml)	Measured absorbance	AAB concentration (pg/ml)
Stage 1	2.4	0.780	34.45
Stage 2	7.2	0.710	**30.72**
Stage 3	12.8	0.590	22.04
Stage 4	14.5	0.285	10.34

*So the measured AAB concentration for Stage 2 is **30.72.** Now for the tough part: we need to figure out if, how, and why this number is changing.*

To do this, we'll have to follow a trail and see how far down the rabbit hole it goes...

2 Scan the **passage** for context

*What would happen if Stage 2 patients had a new antibody which **bound to Eb_{23}?** No clue yet! Let's scan for **Eb_{23}**.*

...The samples were each placed in tiny wells on a microtitre plate. **Scientists then added 100 μL of diluted biomarker enzyme Eb_{23}** to each well and incubated the sample at 90° F.

*Aha! Eb_{23} is a **biomarker enzyme**! What on earth is a biomarker enzyme? We need to go deeper...*

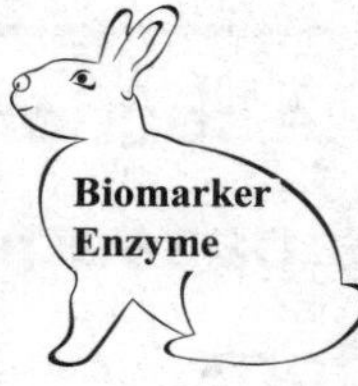

Scientists identified an antibody, AAB, that may help prevent or reverse the protein degradation that leads to SNP formation. To measure natural AAB presence in patients, scientists used a **biomarker enzyme**—a substance which **binds with a target antibody** and **turns the sample darker**. The more of the target antibody present in a sample of CSF, the higher the measured absorbance, and the darker the sample.

Aha! When ***Eb_{23} binds*** *to an antibody, it turns the sample* ***darker****, increasing the* ***measured absorbance****.*

3 Use common sense to make an **inference**

If Stage 2 patients have an extra antibody binding to Eb_{23}, then their samples will be darker than if only AAB were binding to Eb_{23}:

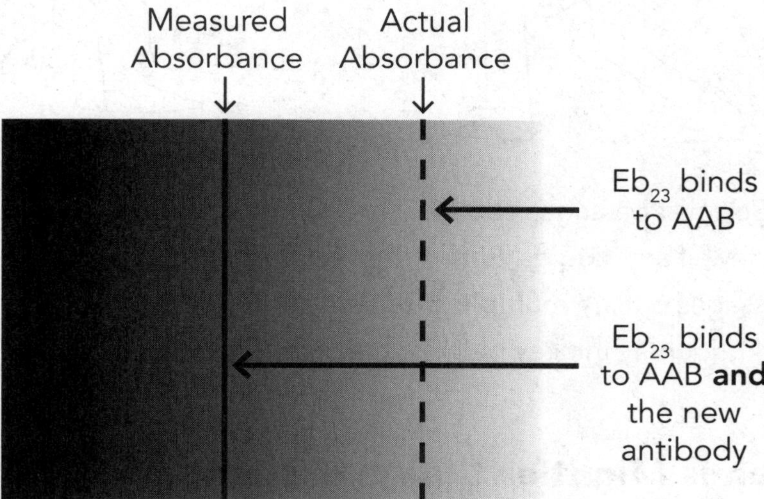

So when scientists see a darker sample (thanks to the extra antibody binding to Eb_{23}) they would ***overestimate*** *the amount of AAB in the sample! In other words, compared to the* ***actual*** *AAB concentration, the* ***measured*** *AAB concentration would be* ***higher****. The answer is* ***B!***

Dueling Scientists

One out of the seven passages in the ACT Science section will be the Dueling Scientists passage. For this passage only, actively read before heading to the questions.

Dueling Scientist passages contain a large amount of text accompanied by relatively few, if any, figures. Rather than describe different studies or experiments, these passages outline **multiple theories** about a scientific phenomenon. Your job is to quickly identify the key points of each theory before moving to the questions.

Dueling Scientist passages always have seven questions— more than any other passage!

The Pen is Mightier than the Sword

As soon as you spot the Dueling Scientist passage, begin to **read actively.** Often, you need only write a single word or phrase to sum up the main idea of each theory. The questions will simply ask you to repeat these main ideas, compare and contrast the different theories, or apply a theory to some basic facts. By glancing at your notes, you will be able to breeze through these easy questions, buying time for those tougher passages ahead.

Let's get some practice answering three different question types.

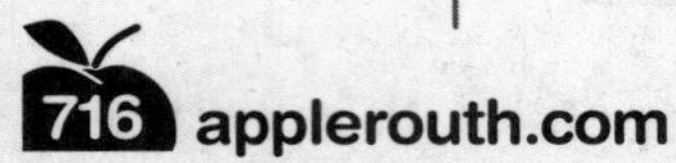

The Great Battle of Fisherman's Grove

A scientific journal published a study detailing an unusual inter-species conflict between a group of *Sciurus carolinensis* squirrels and a group of *Gallus domesticus* chickens in Fisherman's Grove, Wisconsin. Scientists still do not completely understand the cause of this behavioral anomaly. **Three scientists** proposed theories to explain the behavior witnessed on that fateful day, the Eighth of January, 1984.

Scientist 1

The conflict was due to the emotional fragility of the squirrels, sensitive creatures deeply affected by interspecies tensions. The squirrels and chickens of Fisherman's Grove had coexisted for decades under a serene but fragile peace until the Beavers moved into their new ranch home. The delicate balance that had existed between the two species was fractured when the squirrels began to crack under the stress of the Beaver children's tree-house construction. Unable to efficiently store their nuts, the panicked squirrels began to take out their aggression on the fowl bystanders.

Scientist 1 proposes that the squirrels are fighting with the chickens because the squirrels are:

A. emotionally overwhelmed by the increased presence of the Beavers.
B. innately aggressive towards beaked-creatures.
C. entangled in a codependent relationship with the postal workers.
D. defending their historical claim to the half-acre of undeveloped land behind the Beavers' ranch.

Dueling Scientists passages require a bit more reading than Standard passages, but the questions can be answered very quickly. Keep up the pace!

S *This is a **summarize a theory** question. What does Scientist 1 think about this feathery-nutty conflict? Let's check our active reading notes:*

The conflict was due to the **emotional fragility** of the **squirrels, sensitive** creatures deeply affected by interspecies tensions. The squirrels and chickens of Fisherman's Grove had coexisted for decades under a serene but fragile peace until the Beavers moved into their new ranch home. The delicate balance that had existed between the two species was fractured when **the squirrels began to crack under the stress of the Beaver children's tree-house construction.** Unable to efficiently store their nuts, **the panicked** squirrels began to take out their aggression on the fowl bystanders.

emotional squirrels

*Scientist 1 was all about the **emotions** of the squirrels! The squirrels were fragile, stressed, panicked creatures that lashed out against the poultry.*

***A** is our answer!*

Compare/contrast theories

Compare/contrast questions ask you to identify the points on which two scientists agree and disagree. As with all Dueling Scientists questions, active reading is key. Follow these steps when working with multiple theories:

1. Compare **notes** for each theory
2. **Cross off** answer choices that mix up the theories
3. If necessary, **scan** theories for words in remaining choices

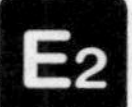

Scientist 2

The conflict occurred because the chickens went into a frenzy when their territory was overrun by the Beavers. The chickens had to take shelter in an abandoned shack when they were displaced from their traditional nesting ground by the Beaver children's Deluxe Swing Set. The new environment was too hot, too crowded, and too cramped for the full brood. A pecking battle ensued which spilled out onto the squirrels' territory, and the squirrels, caught in the cross-fire, were the hapless victims of blind poultry aggression. Simply put, for the squirrels, it was a classic case of wrong place, wrong time.

How does Scientist 2's theory differ from Scientist 1's theory? Scientist 2 claims that the source of the conflict:

F. had its origins in centuries-old land disputes, whereas Scientist 1 claims that the conflict stemmed from recent events.

G. stemmed from the location of the Beaver children's treehouse, whereas Scientist 1 claims that the Deluxe Swing set was the catalyst for the interspecies conflict.

H. had its origin in innate chicken tendencies, whereas Scientist 1 claims that the environmental conditions induced changes in the chicken population.

J. was due to chicken infighting over degraded environmental conditions, whereas Scientist 1 claims that chickens were victims of the panicking squirrel population.

S 1 Compare **notes** for each theory

Scientist 1 - *Those **emotional squirrels** started it!*

Scientist 2 - *Those **displaced, territorial birds** went nuts!*

Now that we have the key idea of each theory, let's check the answer choices.

Wrong answer choices confuse two different theories or pull information out of thin air. Hunt for throwaways!

2 **Cross off** answer choices that mix up the theories

~~F.~~ Scientist 2 claims that the source of the conflict had its origins in centuries-old land disputes, whereas Scientist 1 claims that the conflict stemmed from recent events.

Scientist 2 blamed displaced chickens, not old disputes. Lose F.

~~G.~~ Scientist 2 claims that the source of the conflict stemmed from the location of the Beaver children's **treehouse**, whereas Scientist 1 claims that the **Deluxe Swing Set** was the catalyst for the interspecies conflict.

This is flipped! Scientist 2 mentioned the swing set, not Scientist 1.

~~H.~~ Scientist 2 claims that the source of the conflict had its origin in innate chicken tendencies, whereas Scientist 1 claims that the environmental conditions induced changes in the chicken population.

Scientist 1 is a squirrel man – he hardly mentions chickens. Lose H.

(J.) **Scientist 2** claims that the source of the conflict was due to **chicken** infighting over degraded environmental conditions, whereas **Scientist 1** claims that chickens were victims of the panicking **squirrel** population.

This looks good! S2 = chickens, S1 = squirrels. J is our best match!

Our answer is ***J!***

Apply a Theory

In general, **apply a theory** questions will offer up a new piece of data and ask what one or more of the scientists would think of the data.

There are a number of ways to phrase these questions. You may be asked to:

- explain how a scientist would **likely respond** to new data
- identify data that would **strengthen or weaken** a theory
- choose **which theory or scientist** is supported by the new data

As always, focus on your **active reading** to answer this question type. Use notes to eliminate wrong answer choices, and use common sense if necessary!

Scientist 3

The conflict occurred because the squirrels were deprived of their alpha male when the Beaver children insisted on adopting him as a household pet. When squirrel communities are rendered leaderless, the remaining males will globally increase aggression in order to assert dominance and establish a claim as the new alpha male. Rather than threaten their own population, the squirrels bullied the chickens as a means of displaying physical prowess and superiority over the other males.

Scientist 3's theory would be most weakened if which of the following observations were made?

A. The squirrels had a surplus of nuts for the winter.
B. The new chicken coop was roomier than the chickens' prior nesting ground.
C. All of the squirrels involved in the fighting were female.
D. Alpha battles among leaderless squirrels were observed in neighboring communities.

S *First let's check our notes for a summary of Scientist 3's theory.*

Scientist 3 - *it's an Alpha Male thing.*
Lose the lead male squirrel; chaos breaks out.

*So we need an answer choice that weakens the theory that the squabble was all about **alpha male squirrels.***

~~A.~~ Scientist 3's theory would be most weakened if the squirrels had a surplus of nuts for the winter.

*S1 talked about squirrels going nuts for nuts; S3 is all about **alpha males**. A is wrong.*

~~B.~~ Scientist 3's theory would be most weakened if the new chicken coop was roomier than the chickens' previous nesting ground.

*S2 talked about uncomfy chickens. S3 is about **alpha males**.*

(C.) Scientist 3's theory would be most weakened if all of the **squirrels** involved in the fighting were **female**.

Squirrels and gender! We are on target. And if the fighting squirrels were female, that weakens the Alpha male hypothesis. This looks good!

~~D.~~ Scientist 3's theory would be most weakened if **alpha** battles among leaderless **squirrels** were observed in neighboring communities.

*Topically on target! But would this **weaken** the theory that potential alpha males fight with each other? If it's happening in other places, that **strengthens** S3's theory!*

***C** is the big winner!*

Dueling Scientists Recap

To recap, the Dueling Scientists passage is like the Reading section, only easier. You will NOT skip the passage. Instead, you will **read actively** and **take notes!**

Dueling Scientist questions are a breeze so long as you:

1. Read the passage **actively**
2. **Summarize** each theory using quick **notes**
3. Use notes to **eliminate** wrong answers

Outside Knowledge

The ACT writers will drop in two to four questions that test basic scientific principles and vocabulary. This requires knowledge outside of information in the passage.

Luckily, the writers are relatively predictable in their selection of topics. The two most common topics are genetics and independent/dependent variables.

Genes, Alleles, and Offspring

Some science passages may require you to remember the basics of genetics you learned in Biology class. Let's review some key vocabulary:

- **Genotype:** the genetic makeup of an organism.
  That dog has genotype BB!

- **Phenotype:** the appearance of an organism.
  That dog is round, brown, and gettin' down!

- **Alleles:** the different forms a gene can take.
  Gene B is the Boogie gene. Its alleles are B and b.

Genotypes are short sequences of letters (alleles), like ***Ff***, ***GG*** or ***Hh***.

Phenotypes are simply adjectives, like ***skinny***, ***tall***, ***blue***, or ***funky***.

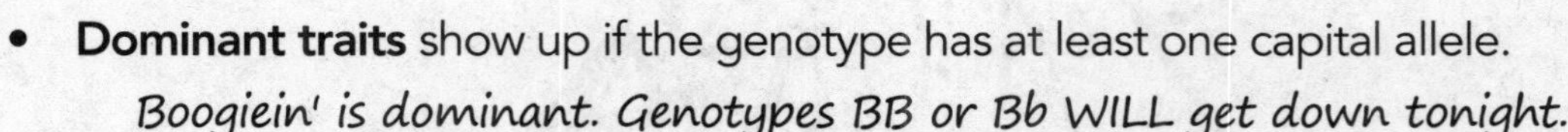

- **Dominant traits** show up if the genotype has at least one capital allele.
  Boogiein' is dominant. Genotypes BB or Bb WILL get down tonight.

- **Recessive traits** show up ONLY if the genotype has two lowercase alleles.
  My dog has genotype bb. He will not be attending the gala.

- **Genetic crosses:** offspring take one allele from each parent.
  So if we crossed a BB genotype with a Bb genotype...

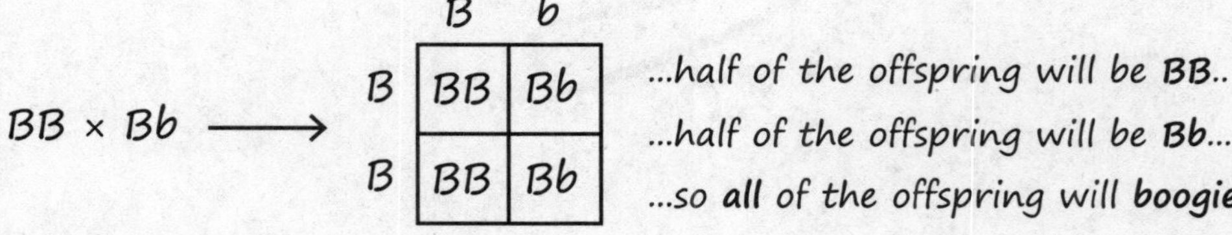

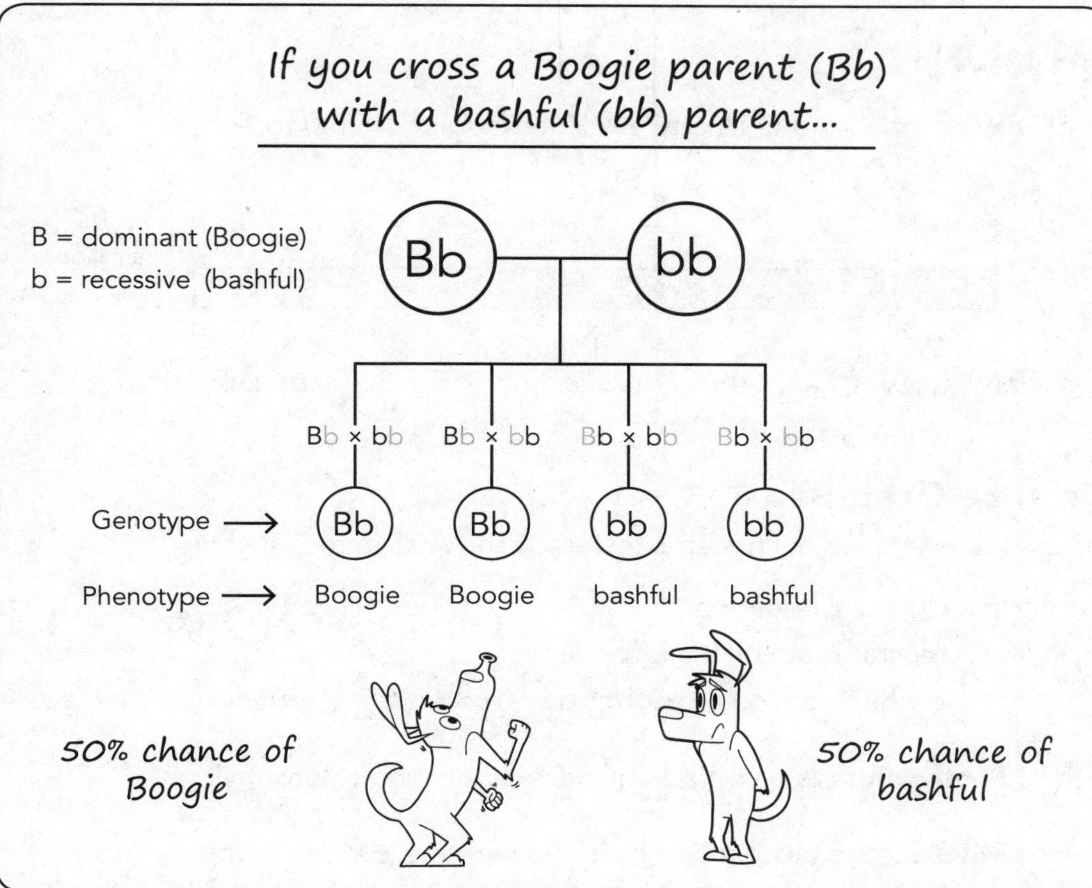

A **homozygous** genotype has two of the same alleles (bb or BB).

A **heterozygous** genotype has one of each allele (Bb).

Dependent and Independent Variables

An Independent Variable is an **input** you are manipulating, and a Dependent Variable is an **output** you are measuring. For example, if you were testing whether your dog's weight changes when you double his daily food ration, the amount of food you give your dog is your **input** (independent variable) and the dog's weight is the **output** (dependent variable). If you were testing whether temperature changes when you increase in altitude, then altitude is your **input** (IV), and temperature is your **output** (DV).

For a refresher on independent and dependent variables, review Operation Science Buff from the **Inference** section.

pH Levels

A pH test is a measure of acidity/alkalinity, ranging from 0 to 14.

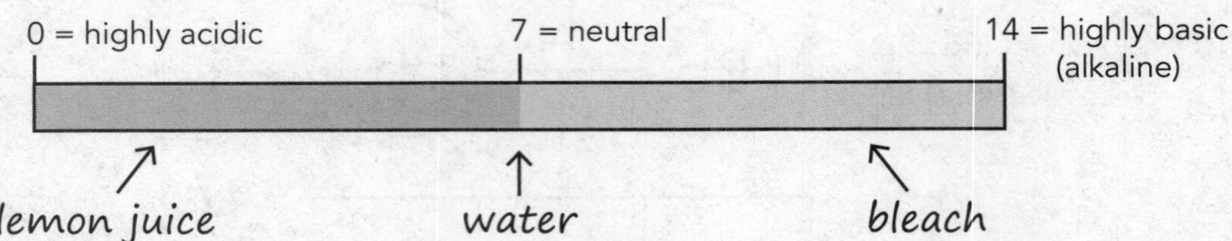

Science Grab Bag

Below are examples of concepts tested by the ACT in recent years:

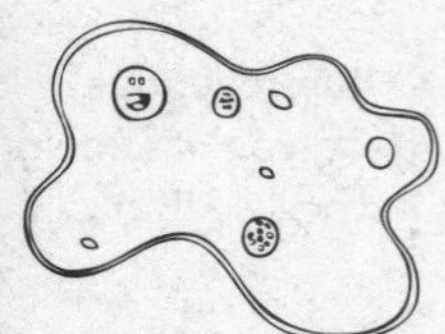

Outside knowledge questions **can** be easy points. But don't panic if you're stumped by one! Simply make an educated guess and move on.

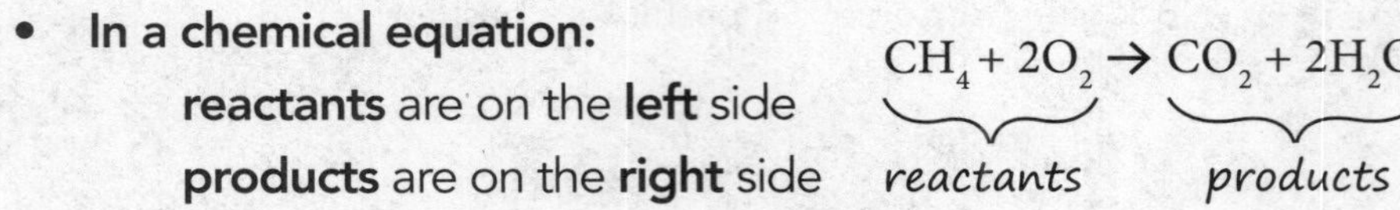

- **In a chemical equation:**
  reactants are on the **left** side
  products are on the **right** side

  $CH_4 + 2O_2 \rightarrow CO_2 + 2H_2O$

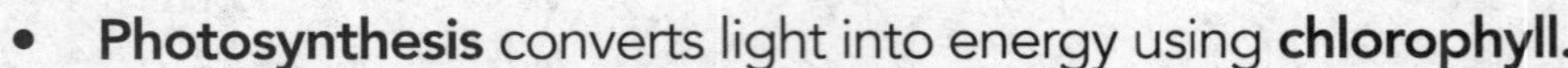

- **Photosynthesis** converts light into energy using **chlorophyll.**
- **Mitosis** is the process by which cells replicate (divide in two).
- **Conductors** like copper conduct and carry electrical currents.
- **Insulators** like plastic oppose electrical currents.
- **Sugars** end in -OSE (e.g., sucr**ose**, fruct**ose**, gluc**ose**, lact**ose**).
  The molecular form of sugar is $\mathbf{C_6H_{12}O_6}$.
- **Molarity** is the degree of concentration in a solution.
  High molarity = higher concentration = more of the substance in a solution
- **Atomic number** is the number of **protons** in the nucleus of an atom.
  The periodic table is arranged in order of ascending atomic number.

Science Walkthrough

Break out your Bunsen burner, whip out your wrist watch, and loosen your labcoat: it's practice time.

Now that you've seen everything ACT Science can throw at you, from expanding tables to interspecies turf wars, you're ready to start practicing in the field.

Practice Makes Perfect

The next 42 pages contain an entire ACT's worth of Science: forty questions over seven passages. After each passage, you'll find fully illustrated answers and explanations. This is your opportunity to practice the two crucial elements to success on the Science section:

1 Identifying Question Types

The faster you can distinguish an Inference question from a Get to the Point question, the faster you can start hunting for your answer! Practice spotting question types by their language, and take note which types give you the most trouble.

2 Keeping the Pace

By far, the toughest part of the Science section is keeping the blazing fast pace of 52.5 seconds/question. Expanding your comfort zone takes practice. Time yourself for each of the seven passages in this walkthrough. There will be a place to write down your speed after each passage to help you track improvement throughout the section. Don't try sprinting out of the gate! Aim to move a little faster each passage without missing more questions.

PASSAGE I

Passage I

Table 1 lists 3 genes found in *Drosophila melanogaster* (a fruit fly), the possible alleles of each gene, and the possible genotypes for each gene.

Table 1

Gene	Allele	Genotype
F	*F, f*	*FF, Ff, ff*
G	*G, g*	*GG, Gg, gg*
H	*H, h*	*HH, Hh, hh*

Table 2 lists various fruit fly genotypes and the phenotype associated with each genotype. Each gene affects only 1 of the 3 phenotypic traits listed.

Table 2

	Phenotype		
Genotype	Wing shape	Body color	Eye color
FFGGHH	long	black	red
FfGGHH	curly	black	red
ffGGHH	short	black	red
FFGgHH	long	striped	red
FFggHH	long	tan	red
FFGGHh	long	black	orange
FFGGhh	long	black	white
FfGGHh	curly	black	orange
FfGGhh	curly	black	white
FfGgHh	curly	striped	orange
ffGghh	short	striped	white
ffgghh	short	tan	white

Table 3 lists 4 fruit fly crosses, the genotypes of the parents, and the number of offspring that displayed each phenotype for the 3 traits listed in Table 2. During each cross, each parent donated 1 allele per gene to each offspring.

Table 3

	Genotype		Number of offspring by phenotype		
Cross	Male parent	Female parent	Wing shape	Body color	Eye color
1	*FFGGHH*	*FFGGHH*	100 long	100 black	100 red
2	*FfggHh*	*FfggHh*	25 long 50 curly 25 short	100 tan	25 red 50 orange 25 white
3	*Ffgghh*	*ffGgHh*	50 curly 50 short	50 striped 50 tan	50 orange 50 white
4	*ffGghh*	*ffGGhh*	100 short	50 black 50 striped	100 white

1. Based on Table 2, which of the 3 genes affects wing shape?

   A. Gene *F* only
   B. Gene *G* only
   C. Gene *H* only
   D. Genes *F*, *G*, and *H*

2. Based on Table 2, a *D. melanogaster* fly with 1 dominant allele for each of the three genes will have which of the following phenotypes?

   F. long wings, black body, white eyes
   G. curly wings, striped body, white eyes
   H. curly wings, striped body, orange eyes
   J. short wings, tan body, orange eyes

3. In Cross 3, what percent of the offspring had genotype *HH*?

   A. 0%
   B. 25%
   C. 50%
   D. 75%

4. The offspring of which of the crosses listed in Table 3 were, for each trait, split evenly between 2 of the 3 possible phenotypes?

   F. Cross 1
   G. Cross 2
   H. Cross 3
   J. Cross 4

5. Based on the information presented, all of the offspring of Cross 2 had tan bodies because each received:

   A. allele *F* from its male parent and allele *f* from its female parent.
   B. allele *G* from its male parent and allele *g* from its female parent.
   C. allele *g* from its male parent and allele *g* from its female parent.
   D. allele *h* from its male parent and allele *H* from its female parent.

6. According to the information given in Table 2, a *D. melanogaster* fly with curly wings, a black body, and white eye color would have which of the following genotypes?

   F. *FfGgHh*
   G. *FfGGhh*
   H. *FfGgHH*
   J. *ffGghh*

GO ON TO THE NEXT PAGE.

1

Based on Table 2, which of the 3 genes affects wing shape?

This is a **Relationship** question. Using Table 2, we must identify the **gene(s)** that, when changed, cause **wing shape** to change.

We can see in the first three rows that changing gene **F** (***FF, Ff, ff***) causes wing shape to change. Conversely, we can see in rows 4-6 that changing gene **G** does not change the wing shape.

A. Gene *F* only

Table 2

Genotype	Phenotype		
	Wing shape	Body color	Eye color
FFGGHH	**long**	black	red
FfGGHH	**curly**	black	red
ffGGHH	**short**	black	red
FFGgHH	long	striped	red
FFggHH	long	tan	red
FFGGHh	long	black	orange
FFGGhh	long	black	white
FfGGHh	curly	black	orange
FfGGhh	curly	black	white
FfGgHh	curly	striped	orange
ffGghh	short	striped	white
ffgghh	short	tan	white

2

Based on Table 2, a *D. melanogaster* fly with 1 dominant allele for each of the three genes will have which of the following phenotypes?

This is a **Get to the Point** question. Remember, **capital letters** indicate a **dominant** allele. Therefore, we are looking for a genotype with **one capital letter in each gene**, or **FfGgHh**.

We find this genotype in the third row from the bottom. Reading off the **phenotype columns** for that row gives us our answer.

H. curly wings, striped body, orange eyes

Table 2

Genotype	Phenotype		
	Wing shape	Body color	Eye color
FFGGHH	long	black	red
FfGGHH	curly	black	red
ffGGHH	short	black	red
FFGgHH	long	striped	red
FFggHH	long	tan	red
FFGGHh	long	black	orange
FFGGhh	long	black	white
FfGGHh	curly	black	orange
FfGGhh	curly	black	white
FfGgHh	**curly**	**striped**	**orange**
ffGghh	short	striped	white
ffgghh	short	tan	white

3

In Cross 3, what percent of the offspring had Genotype *HH*?

This **Outside Knowledge** question is simply testing your **genetics** skills. We need to find Cross 3 in Table 2, cross gene *H*, and count outcomes.

Cross 3: *Ffgghh* × *ffGgHh*

	H	*h*
h	*Hh*	*hh*
h	*Hh*	*hh*

No HH offspring!

A. 0%

4

The offspring of which of the crosses listed in Table 3 were, for each trait, split evenly between 2 of the 3 possible phenotypes?

This is a **Get to the Point** question. We are directed to the "offspring phenotype" columns of Table 3. We need to find the row with **2 phenotypes in each trait column.** Only the third row matches!

Table 3

Cross	Number of offspring by phenotype		
	Wing shape	Body color	Eye color
1	100 long	100 black	100 red
2	25 long 50 curly 25 short	100 tan	25 red 50 orange 25 white
3	**50 curly 50 short**	**50 striped 50 tan**	**50 orange 50 white**
4	100 short	50 black 50 striped	100 white

H. Cross 3

5

Based on the information presented, all of the offspring of Cross 2 had tan bodies because each received:

This is an **Inference** question. "Information" is vague, so every table is fair game. We need to find out what causes **tan bodies**.

In Table 2, the only two genotypes with tan bodies are ***FFggHH*** and ***ffgghh***. We can infer that the tan bodies are caused by the only thing these two genotypes share: ***gg***.

Table 2

Genotype	Phenotype		
	Wing shape	Body color	Eye color
FFGGHH	long	black	red
FfGGHH	curly	black	red
ffGGHH	short	black	red
FFGgHH	long	striped	red
FFggHH	long	**tan**	red
FFGGHh	long	black	orange
FFGGhh	long	black	white
FfGGHh	curly	black	orange
FfGGhh	curly	black	white
FfGgHh	curly	striped	orange
ffGghh	short	striped	white
ffgghh	short	**tan**	white

C. Allele *g* from its male parent and allele *g* from its female parent.

According to the information given in Table 2, a *D. melanogaster* fly with curly wings, a black body, and white eye color would have which of the following genotypes?

This is a **Get to the Point** question. Using Table 2, we simply need to find the row with the combination of phenotypes listed.

We find our curly-winged, black-bodied, white-eyed friend in the fourth row from the bottom: **FfGGhh**.

G. ***FfGGhh***

Table 2

	Phenotype		
Genotype	Wing shape	Body color	Eye color
FFGGHH	**long**	black	red
FfGGHH	**curly**	black	red
ffGGHH	**short**	black	red
FFGgHH	long	striped	red
FFggHH	long	tan	red
FFGGHh	long	black	orange
FFGGhh	long	black	white
FfGGHh	curly	black	orange
FfGGhh	**curly**	**black**	**white**
FfGgHh	curly	striped	orange
ffGghh	short	striped	white
ffgghh	short	tan	white

Timing Check

It takes practice to get comfortable with the pace of ACT Science.

Don't expect to blaze through error-free on your first try.

Focus on small improvements each passage!

Passage 1 Stats

Time spent: ________

Questions Missed: ________

Passage 2 Goals

Time spent: ________

Questions Missed: ________

PASSAGE II

Passage II

Two studies examined the sizes of the stocks of Pacific Salmon in 3 rivers – the Chum River, the Pink River, and the King River – during a twelve week spawning season. As shown in Figure 1, Stock A must swim through the King River and the Pink River in order to reach the Chum River. Stock B must swim through the King River in order to reach the Pink River. The volume of water in each river is given in megaliters (ML).

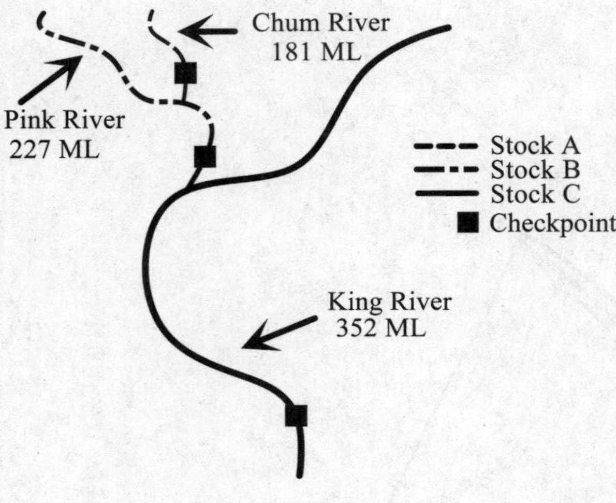

Figure 1

Study 1

Three stocks of Pacific Salmon begin to swim upstream through the inlet on the first day of spawning season. The three stocks are mixed together as they begin their migration, and they begin to separate as they progress North. The maximum number of fish measured in a given place during this migration is called a swarm.

Over the 12 weeks following the start of spawning season, as the Pacific Salmon moved upstream, the number of fish that passed through each checkpoint was continuously measured at the three locations shown in Figure 1. The results are shown in Figure 2. (Note: Once Pacific Salmon begin to swim upstream through a river, they do not return downstream.)

Study 2

The stock concentration over the 12 week spawning season was calculated for each of the three rivers. The stock concentration values allowed the number of Pacific Salmon to be measured as if the 3 rivers had identical volumes of 1 ML. Each stock concentration value was calculated using the following equation:

$$\text{Stock concentration} = \frac{\text{number of fish}}{\text{river volume (ML)}}$$

The results are shown in Figure 3.

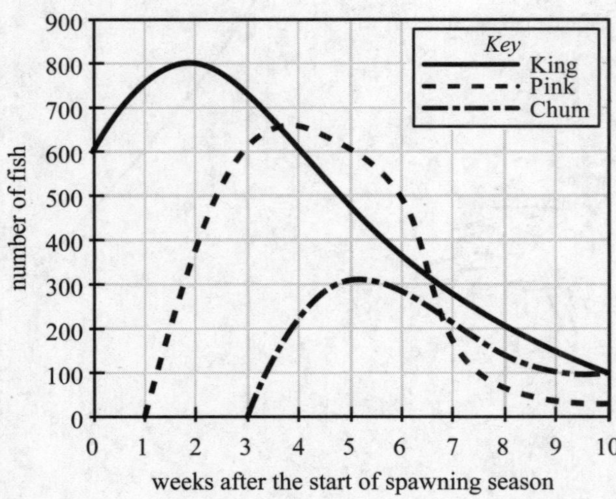

Figure 2

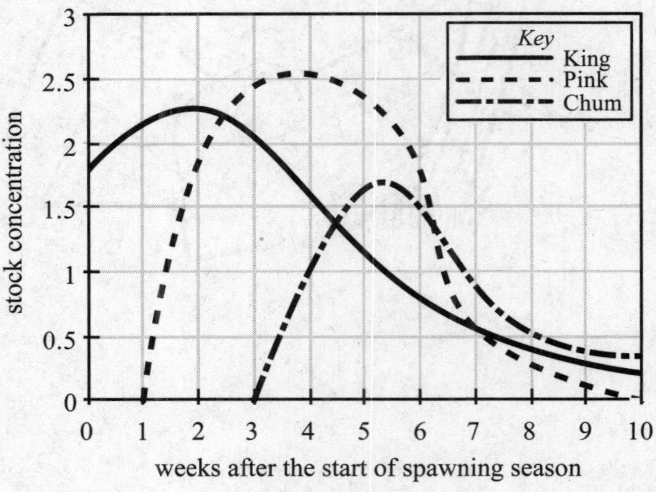

Figure 3

7. According to Figure 2, the maximum number of fish at the Pink River checkpoint after the start of spawning season was closest to which of the following?

A. 450 fish
B. 550 fish
C. 650 fish
D. 750 fish

8. According to Study 1, the King River and the Pink River had close to the same number of fish passing through the checkpoint at which of the following times after the start of spawning season?

F. 0.5 weeks
G. 1 week
H. 4.5 weeks
J. 6.5 weeks

9. An offshoot (a smaller stream flowing into a larger river) of the Chum River shown in Figure 1 would most likely have a water volume:

A. less than 181 ML.
B. between 181 ML and 227 ML.
C. between 227 ML and 352 ML.
D. greater than 352 ML.

10. A student predicted that the same river would contain both the greatest number of fish recorded in any one week and the greatest stock concentration recorded in any one week. Based on Figures 2 and 3, is the student's prediction correct?

F. Yes, because the King River had both the greatest number of fish and the greatest stock concentration.
G. Yes, because the Pink River had both the greatest number of fish and the greatest stock concentration.
H. No, because the King River had the greatest number of fish, but the Pink River had the greatest stock concentration.
J. No, because the Pink River had the greatest number of fish, but the King River had the greatest stock concentration.

11. Based on Figures 1 and 2 and the description of Study 2, the stock concentration of the Chum River 5 weeks after the start of spawning season was most likely calculated using which of the following expressions?

A. 181 ML ÷ 300 fish
B. 181 fish ÷ 300 ML
C. 300 ML ÷ 181 fish
D. 300 fish ÷ 181 ML

GO ON TO THE NEXT PAGE.

7

According to Figure 2, the maximum number of fish at the Pink River checkpoint after the start of spawning season was closest to which of the following?

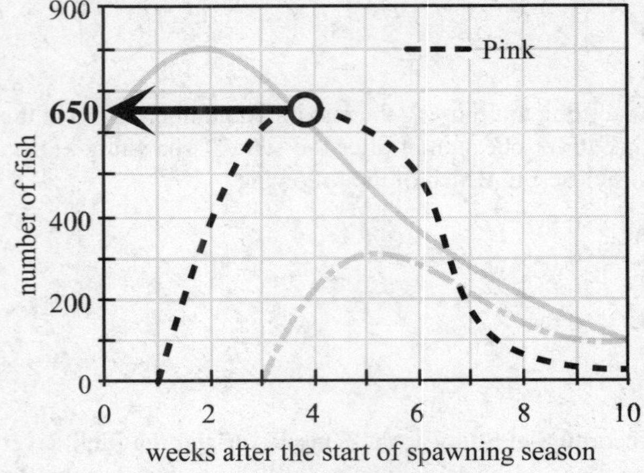

Figure 3

This is a **Get to the Point** question. "Pink River" points us to the **dotted line**, and "number of fish" points to the **y-axis**. "Maximum" tells us to find the **peak**, which looks to occur **between 600 and 700 fish**.

C. 650 fish

8

According to Study 1, the King River and the Pink River had close to the same number of fish passing through the checkpoint at which of the following times after the start of spawning season?

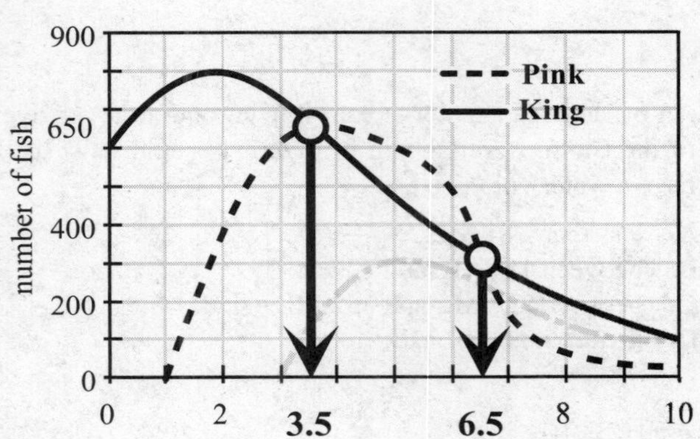

Figure 2

This is a **Get to the Point** question. "Study 1" tells us to go to **Figure 2**, and "King River" and "Pink River" point us to the **solid and dotted lines**.

These rivers have the same number of fish where they **intersect**. We need to grab the x-value for these points of intersection: **3.5 weeks** or **6.5 weeks**.

J. 6.5 weeks

9

An *offshoot* (a smaller stream flowing into a larger river) of the Chum River shown in Figure 1 would most likely have a water volume of:

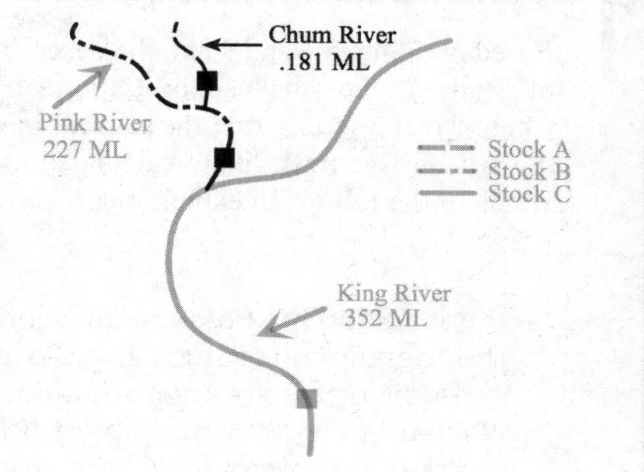

This is an **Inference** question. We're directed to the "Chum River" in Figure 1, and "water volume" tells us to focus on **181 ML**. Since an offshoot is "smaller", our answer must be **smaller than 181 ML**.

A. less than 181 ML.

10

A student predicted that the same river would contain both the greatest number of fish recorded in any one week and the greatest stock concentration recorded in any one week. Based on Figures 2 and 3, is the student's prediction correct?

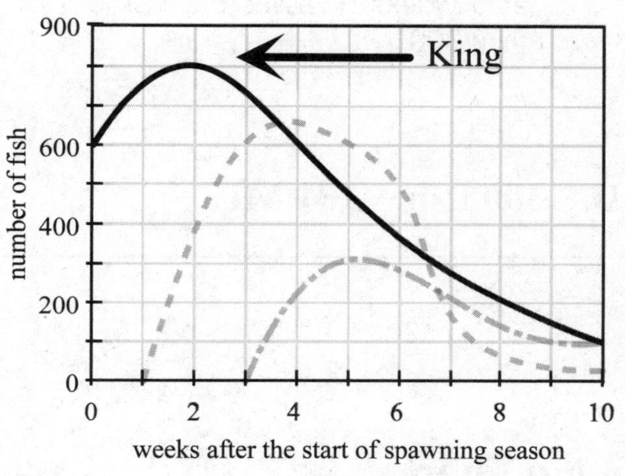

Figure 2

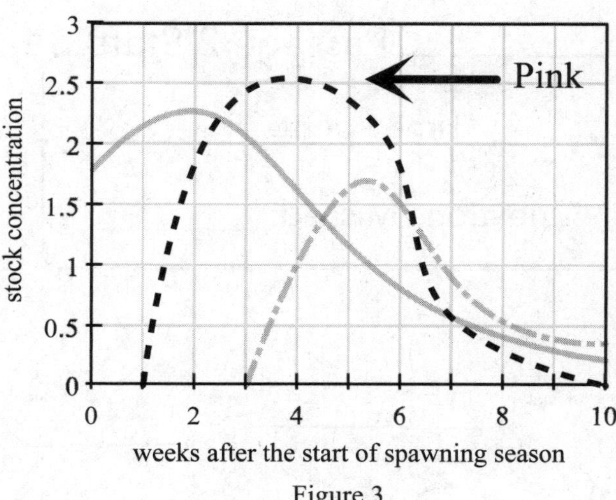

Figure 3

This is a **Compare Two Points** question. "Greatest number of fish" and "greatest stock concentration" tell us to **compare the peaks** of Figures 2 and 3, and "river" tells us we care about the lines rather than any particular value.

Since different lines (rivers) have the highest peaks in the two graphs, we can cross out both "Yes" answers. Since King is king in Figure 2 and Pink is top dog in Figure 3, H is the best answer.

H. No, because the King River had the greatest number of fish, but the Pink River had the greatest stock concentration.

11

Based on <u>Figures 1 and 2</u> and the description of <u>Study 2</u>, the <u>stock concentration</u> of the <u>Chum River</u> <u>5 weeks</u> after the start of spawning season was most likely <u>calculated</u> using which of the following expressions?

$$\textbf{Stock concentration} = \frac{\textbf{number of fish}}{\textbf{river volume (ML)}}$$

Passage

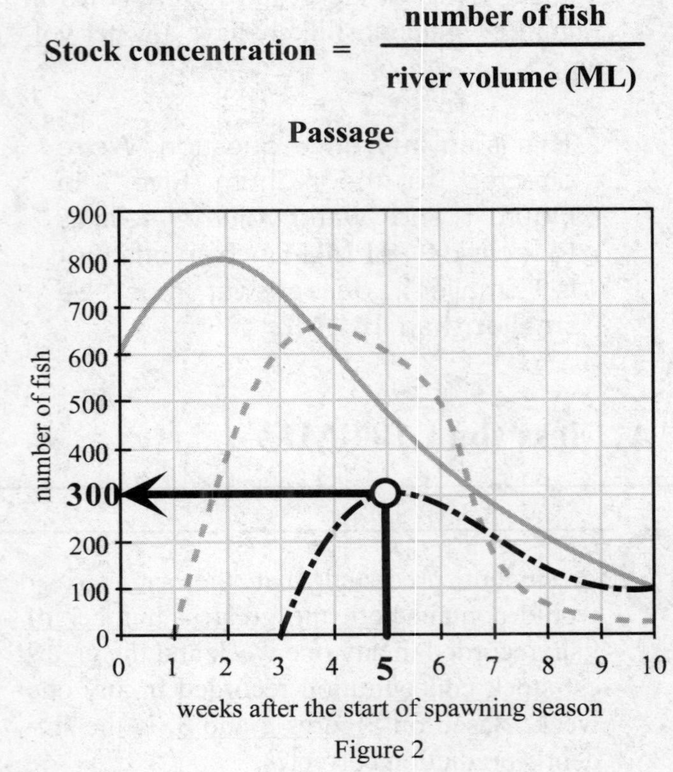

Figure 2

This is a **Read the Passage** question. The "description of Study 2" gives us the equation for stock concentration. We need to find the **number of fish** and **river volume** of the Chum River at 5 weeks.

Figure 1 tells us the river's volume: **181 ML**. In Figure 2, the **dashed line** at 5 weeks gives us our number of fish: 300.

D. 300 fish ÷ 181 ML

Timing Check

Passage 2 Stats	
Time spent:	________
Questions Missed:	________

Passage 3 Goals	
Time spent:	________
Questions Missed:	________

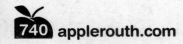

PASSAGE III

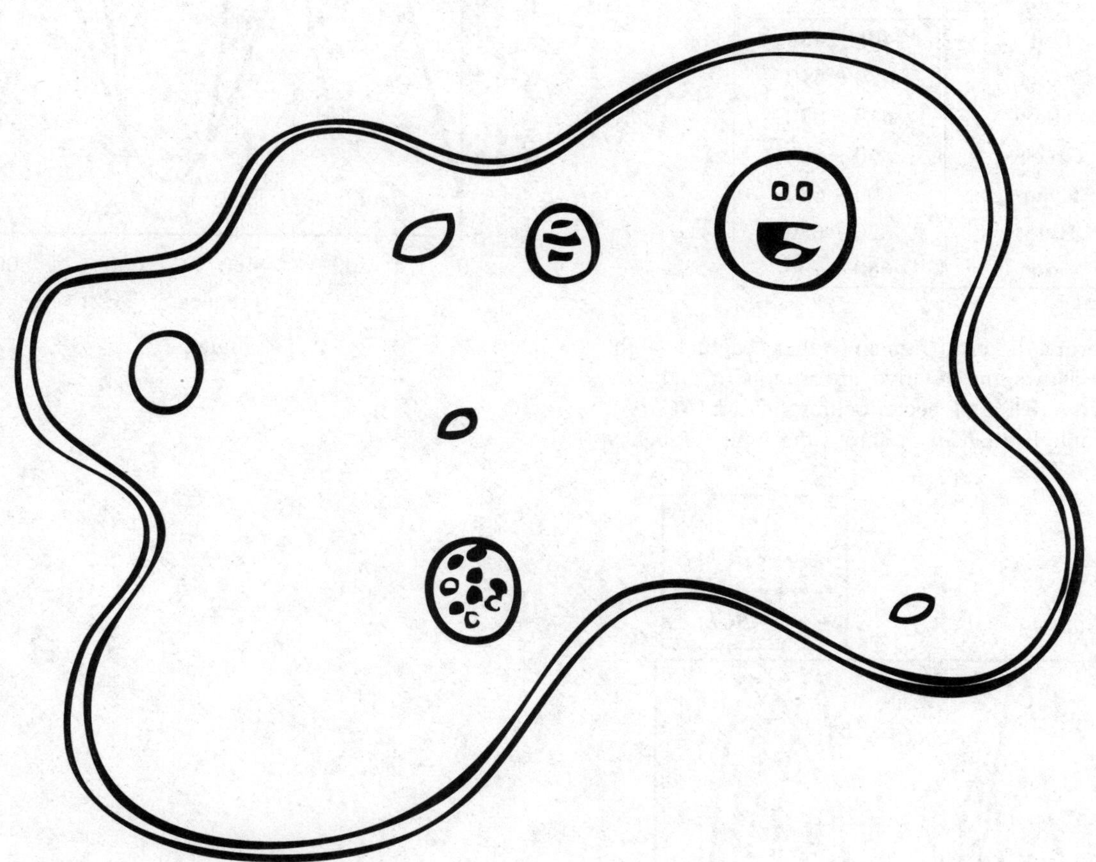

Passage III

Cyanobacteria are a group of aquatic bacteria that capture light from the sun and convert it into chemical energy that can be used as food. This process is summarized by the following equation:

$$6CO_2 + 6H_2O \longrightarrow C_6H_{12}O_6 + 6O_2$$

Table 1 lists frequency ranges for visible light and the color commonly associated with each range.

Table 1

Color	Frequency (THz)
Red	405 – 480
Orange	480 – 510
Yellow	510 – 530
Green	530 – 600
Cyan	600 – 620
Blue	620 – 680
Violet	680 – 790

Bacteriochlorophyll are pigments that capture light energy. Figure 1 shows the relative absorption of light by bacteriochlorophyll *a* (*BChl a*), bacteriochlorophyll *b* (*BChl b*), and bacteriochlorophyll *c* (*BChl c*) across the light frequency from 0 THz to 1000 THz.

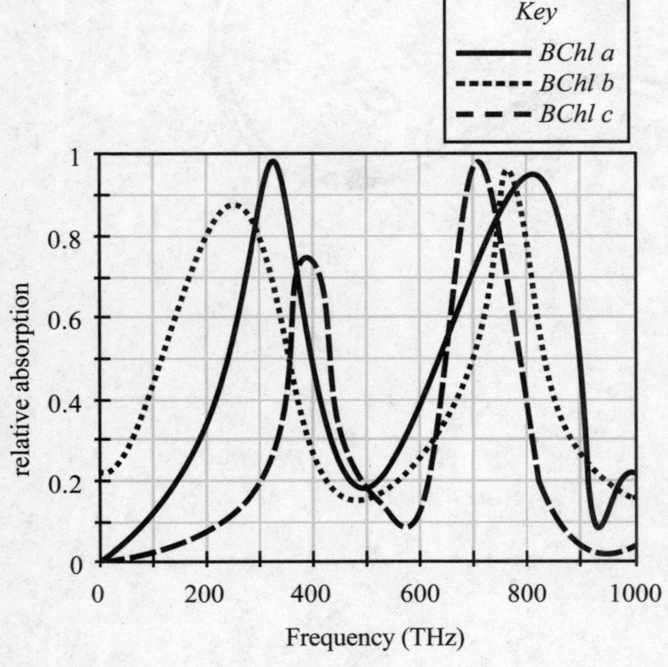

Figure 1

Figure 2 shows two different species of cyanobacteria and the combined relative absorption of their *BChl a, BChl b*, and *BChl c* pigments across various light frequencies.

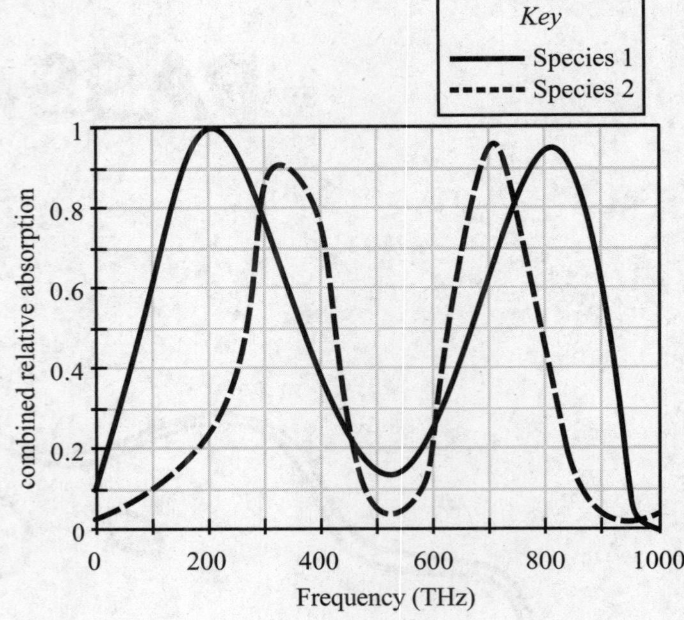

Figure 2

12. Based on Table 1 and Figure 1, which color of light is associated with the frequency of light that results in the greatest absorption by bacteriochlorophyll *c* ?

F. Red
G. Yellow
H. Cyan
J. Violet

13. Which of the following terms best describes the chemical process associated with the chemical equation shown in the passage?

A. Cellular Respiration
B. Fermentation
C. Glycolysis
D. Photosynthesis

14. In Figure 1, at which of the following frequencies does the relative absorption of *BChl a* exceed the relative absorption of *BChl a* at 810 THz?

F. 250 THz
G. 320 THz
H. 680 THz
J. 850 THz

15. A scientist set up an experiment so that red light or green light was transmitted to a sample of Species 2 cyanobacteria. According to the information in the passage, Species 2 would likely convert which color light into a greater amount of chemical energy?

A. Red, since Species 2 absorbs more red than green light.
B. Red, since Species 2 absorbs more green than red light.
C. Green, since Species 2 absorbs more red than green light.
D. Green, since Species 2 absorbs more green than red light.

16. Based on the frequency at which Species 1's combined relative absorption is the highest, it can most reasonably be inferred that Species 1 has:

F. more of pigment *BChl a* than *BChl b*.
G. more of pigment *BChl c* than *BChl a*.
H. more of pigment *BChl b* than *BChl c*.
J. an equal amount of pigments *BChl a, BChl b,* and *BChl c*.

12

Based on <u>Table 1</u> and <u>Figure 1</u>, which <u>color</u> of light is associated with the <u>frequency</u> of light that results in the <u>greatest absorption by bacteriochlorophyll *c*</u>?

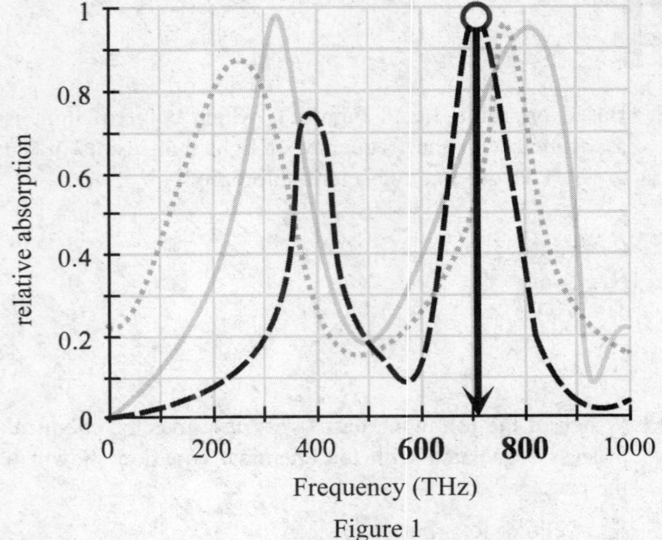

Figure 1

Table 1	
Color	Frequency (THz)
Violet	**680 - 790**

This is a **Get to the Point** question. We're directed to "c," which is the **dashed line** in Figure 1. "Greatest absorption" tells us to find the frequency where this line **peaks**.

It looks like line c peaks around **700** on the x-axis. We can carry this information over to Table 1, which tells us that frequencies between 680 and 790 are **violet**!

J. Violet

13

Which of the following terms best describes the <u>chemical process</u> associated with the <u>chemical equation</u> shown in the <u>passage</u>?

This is a **Read the Passage** question that tests **outside knowledge**. The text accompanying the "chemical equation" reads:

> Cyanobacteria capture **light** from the sun and convert it into chemical energy that can be used as food.

Sound familiar? This is a textbook definition of how plants get energy - **photosynthesis**.

*If you didn't recognize the definition of photosynthesis, you could make an educated guess using **word roots**.*

***Light** is clearly important, and "photo" means light.*

D. Photosynthesis

14

In Figure 1, at which of the following frequencies does the relative absorption of *BChl a* exceed the relative absorption of *BChl a* at 810 THz?

This is a **Compare Two Points** question. Using Figure 1, we need to find a "frequency" on the x-axis where the **solid line** of *BChl a* is higher than it is at 810 THz.

If we **slide up from 810**, we hit the second peak. The only place on the curve higher than this is the first peak, which happens around **320**.

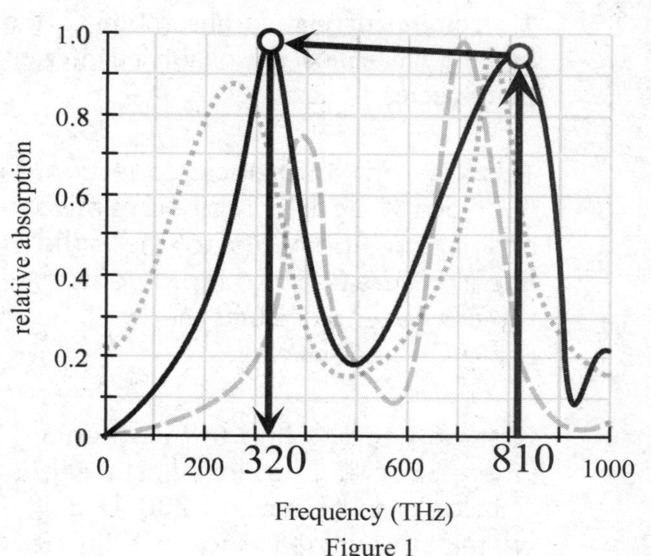

Figure 1

G. 320 THz

15

A scientist set up an experiment so that only red light or only green light was transmitted to a sample of Species 2 cyanobacteria. According to the information provided in the passage, Species 2 would likely convert which color light into a greater amount of chemical energy?

This is an **Inference** question. "Species 2" directs us to the **dashed line** in Figure 2, and "red" and "green" direct us to **Table 1**.

Table 1 tells us that **red** light is associated with **405-480 THz**, and **green** light with **530-600 THz**. Plotting these points along the dashed line in Figure 2, we see that Species 2 has a **higher absorbption of red light**. More absorbed light means more chemical energy!

Table 1

Color	Frequency (THz)
Red	405 - 480
Green	530 - 600

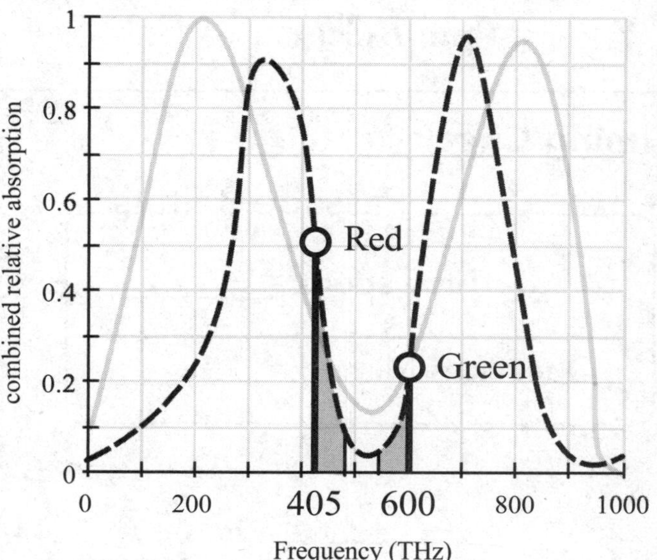

Figure 2

A. Red, since Species 2 absorbs more red than green light.

16

Based on the frequency at which Species 1's combined relative absorption is the highest, it can most reasonably be inferred that Species 1 has:

This is an **Inference** question. "Species 1" and "combined relative absorption" point us to the **solid line** in Figure 2, and the pigments in the answer choices hint that we'll be using Figure 1 as well.

First we need to find the frequency where Species 1 has its tallest **peak**. This looks to be around **200 THz**. If we take this value to Figure 1, find it on the x-axis, and trace a line up, we cross *BChl c*, *BChl a*, and *BChl b*, in that order – with ***BChl b*** having the highest absorption.

We can infer that since Species 1 peaks around 200 THz, it must have ***more BChl b*** than the other pigments.

H. more of pigment *BChl b* than *BChl c*.

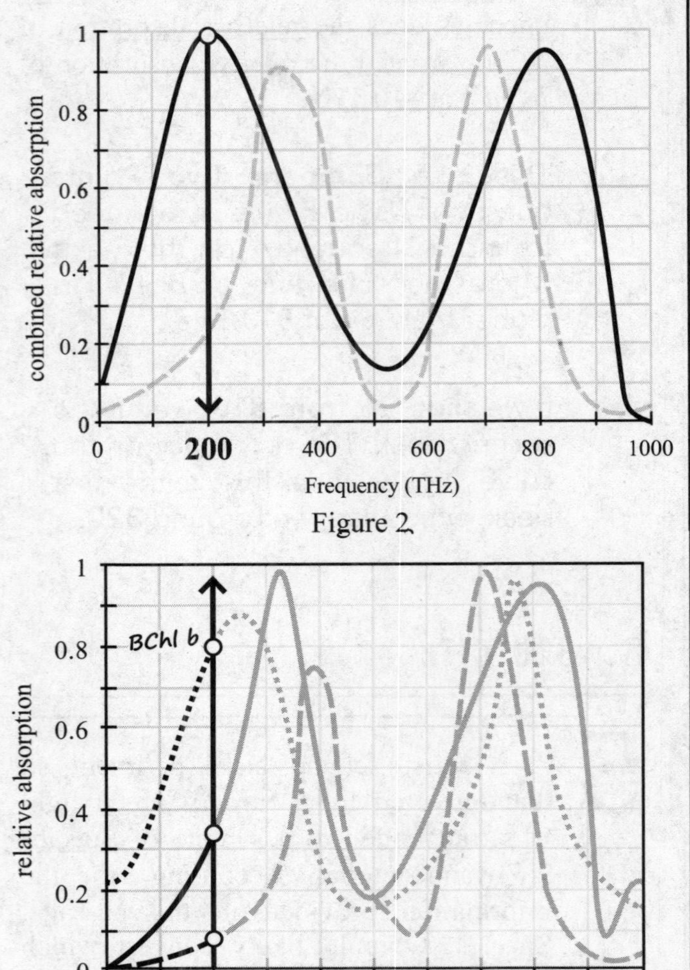

Figure 2

Figure 1

Timing Check

Passage 3 Stats

Time spent: ________

Questions Missed: ________

Passage 4 Goals

Time spent: ________

Questions Missed: ________

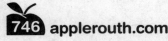

PASSAGE IV

Passage IV

Researchers studied the ability of 4 types of marburgviruses (MARVs) to spread through populations. For each experiment, the researchers prepared four petri dishes of cell colonies. The colonies were exposed to one of 4 types of marburgviruses in a controlled environment.

Experiment 1

Infection saturation measures a virus' ability to infect a population before the rate of infection begins to decline. The lower the infection saturation, the more of the population a virus is able to infect. The mass, in attograms (ag), and infection saturation, in percent of population uninfected, of the 4 marburgviruses were measured. The results are shown in Table 1.

Table 1		
Virus	Mass (ag)	Infection Saturation
MARV-A	12	12%
MARV-B	16	20%
MARV-C	24	53%
MARV-D	27	62%

Experiment 2

Colonies of 30 cells were given a vaccine to each of the MARVs. The petri dishes were then exposed to 1 of the 4 viruses shown in Table 2 for 1 hour at 30° Celsius. Each colony was given an anti-viral drug afterward and cells were allowed to recover for 1 week. During this time, the number of infected cells decreased and the final number of uninfected cells was counted. This process was then repeated with petri dishes that were exposed to the virus a second time before receiving the anti-viral drug. The number of uninfected cells counted is shown in Table 2.

Table 2		
	Number of exposures	
Virus	1	2
MARV-A	14	8
MARV-B	17	12
MARV-C	26	24
MARV-D	28	25

Experiment 3

Petri dishes were handled as described in Experiment 2 with two exceptions: colonies were exposed to the virus only once and the exposure time varied. Table 3 shows the number of uninfected cells counted for Experiment 3.

Table 3			
	Incubation time (hrs)		
Virus	1	3	5
MARV-A	8	6	3
MARV-B	14	9	7
MARV-C	21	16	12
MARV-D	24	19	15
None	30	30	30

17. If Experiment 3 were repeated with MARV-B and an incubation time of 2 hours, the number of cells counted would most likely be:

A. less than 9.
B. between 9 and 14.
C. between 14 and 30.
D. greater than 30.

18. Based on the results of Experiment 1, which virus can infect the most cells in a population?

F. MARV-A
G. MARV-B
H. MARV-C
J. MARV-D

19. In Experiment 2, a result of exposing the colonies to each virus a second time was that the:

A. infection saturation of the viruses increased.
B. mass of the viruses decreased.
C. number of cells counted increased.
D. number of cells counted decreased.

20. Which of the following statements best describes the relationship between mass and infection saturation, as shown in Experiment 1?

F. As mass increases, infection saturation increases.
G. As mass increases, infection saturation decreases.
H. As mass stays constant, infection saturation decreases.
J. As mass decreases, infection saturation stays constant.

21. The procedures used in Experiments 2 and 3 differ because in Experiment 3:

A. Incubation time was held constant, while number of exposures varied.
B. Incubation time was varied, while number of exposures was held constant.
C. Incubation time and number of exposures both varied.
D. Incubation time and number of exposures were both held constant.

22. Based on the results of Experiments 2 and 3, which of the following cell colonies is most likely to contract a virus?

F. A colony with 1 exposure of MARV-D after it has incubated for 3 hours.
G. A colony with 2 exposure of MARV-B after it has incubated for 1 hour.
H. A colony with 1 exposure of MARV-A after it has incubated for 5 hours.
J. A colony with 2 exposure of MARV-C after it has incubated for 1 hour.

GO ON TO THE NEXT PAGE.

17

If Experiment 3 were repeated with MARV-B and an incubation time of 2 hours, the number of cells counted would most likely be:

This is a classic **Expand the Pattern** question. "Experiment 3" directs us to Table 3. We're asked to predict the number of uninfected cells had **MARV-B** incubated for 2 hours. Since there is no "2-hour" column, we'll need to **read between the lines of the 1-hour and 3-hour columns**.

The table tells us there were **14 cells** counted in the 1-hour group, and **9** in the 3-hour group. A **2-hour** group would thus be **between 9 and 14**.

B. Between 9 and 14.

Table 3

Virus	Incubation time (hrs) 1	3	5
MARV-A	8	6	3
MARV-B	14	9	7
MARV-C	21	16	12
MARV-D	24	19	15
None	30	30	30

Table 3

Virus	Incubation time (hrs) 1	2	3	5
MARV-A	8		6	3
MARV-B	14	?	9	7
MARV-C	21		16	12
MARV-D	24		19	15
None	30		30	30

18

Based on the results of Experiment 1, which virus can infect the most cells in a population?

This is a **Read the Passage** question. "Experiment 1" tells us to look at Table 1, but the words "can infect the most cells" don't show up in the table! To get out of this jam, we need to scan the passage for synonyms.

The passage tells us that the virus with the **lowest infection saturation** is able to infect the **most** animals. Taking this information back to Table 1, we find the lowest infection saturation - **12%** - which belongs to **MARV-A**!

F. MARV-A

Experiment 1

Infection saturation measures a virus' ability to infect a population before the rate of infection begins to decline. **The smaller the infection saturation, the more of the population a virus is able to infect.** The mass, in attograms (ag), and infection saturation, in percent of population uninfected, of the 4 marburgviruses on a group of guinea pigs were measured. The results are shown in Table 1.

↓Infection Saturation
↑Population Infected

Table 1

Virus	Mass (ag)	Infection Saturation
MARV-A	12	**12%**
MARV-B	16	20%
MARV-C	24	53%
MARV-D	27	62%

19

In Experiment 2, a result of exposing the colonies to each virus a second time was that the:

This is a **Relationship** question. "Experiment 2" directs us to Table 2. We need to find the **result of moving from column 1 to column 2**. For every virus, the number in column 2 is **smaller**.

Table 2		
	Number of exposures	
Virus	1	2
MARV-A	14 ←	8
MARV-B	17 ←	12
MARV-C	26 ←	24
MARV-D	28 ←	25

Column 2's values are smaller than column 1's.

D. The number of cells counted decreased.

20

Which of the following statements best describes the relationship between mass and the infection saturation, as show in Experiment 1?

This is a standard **Relationship** question. "Experiment 1" tells us to look at Table 1. We simply need to draw trend arrows for "mass" and "infection saturation." The arrows are identical, so our answer should be a direct relationship.

Table 1		
Virus	Mass (ag)	Infection Saturation
MARV-A	12	12%
MARV-B	16	20%
MARV-C	24	53%
MARV-D	27 ↓	↓ 62%

F. As mass increases, infection saturation increases.

21

The procedures used in Experiments 2 and 3 differ because in Experiment 3:

"Procedures" tips us off that this is a **Read the Passage** question. The description of "Experiment 3" gives us the answer in plain English!

Experiment 3

Petri dishes were handled as described in Experiment 2 with **two exceptions**: colonies were **exposed to the virus the same number of times and the exposure time varied.** Table 3 shows the number of uninfected cells counted for Experiment 3.

B. Incubation time was varied, while number of exposures was held constant.

22

Based on the results of Experiments 2 and 3, which of the following cell colonies is most likely to contract a virus?

This is a **Compare Two Points** question. Using Tables 2 and 3, we need to carefully get a point for each of the answer choices.

Remember that if the **exposure time** is greater than 1 hour, then we must look in Table 3. If the **number of exposures** is greater than 1, then we must look in Table 2.

Once we find each point, we need to pick the **lowest number**: since we're counting uninfected cells, a lower number means more infection occurred.

Table 2		
	Number of exposures	
Virus	1	2
MARV-A	14	8
MARV-B	17	**12** ← G
MARV-C	26	**24** ← J
MARV-D	28	25

Table 3			
	Incubation time (hrs)		
Virus	1	3	5
MARV-A	8	6	(3) ← H
MARV-B	14	9	7
MARV-C	21	16	12
MARV-D	24	**19** ← F	15
None	30	30	30

H. A colony with 1 exposure of MARV-A after it has incubated for 5 hours.

Timing Check

Passage 4 Stats

Time spent: ________

Questions Missed: ________

Passage 5 Goals

Time spent: ________

Questions Missed: ________

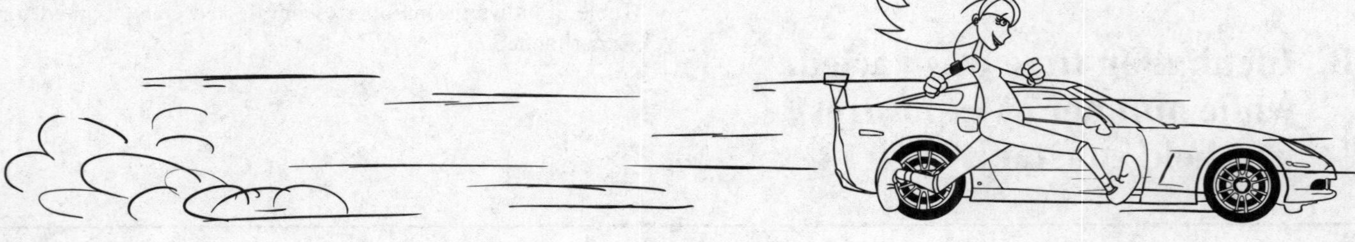

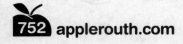

PASSAGE V

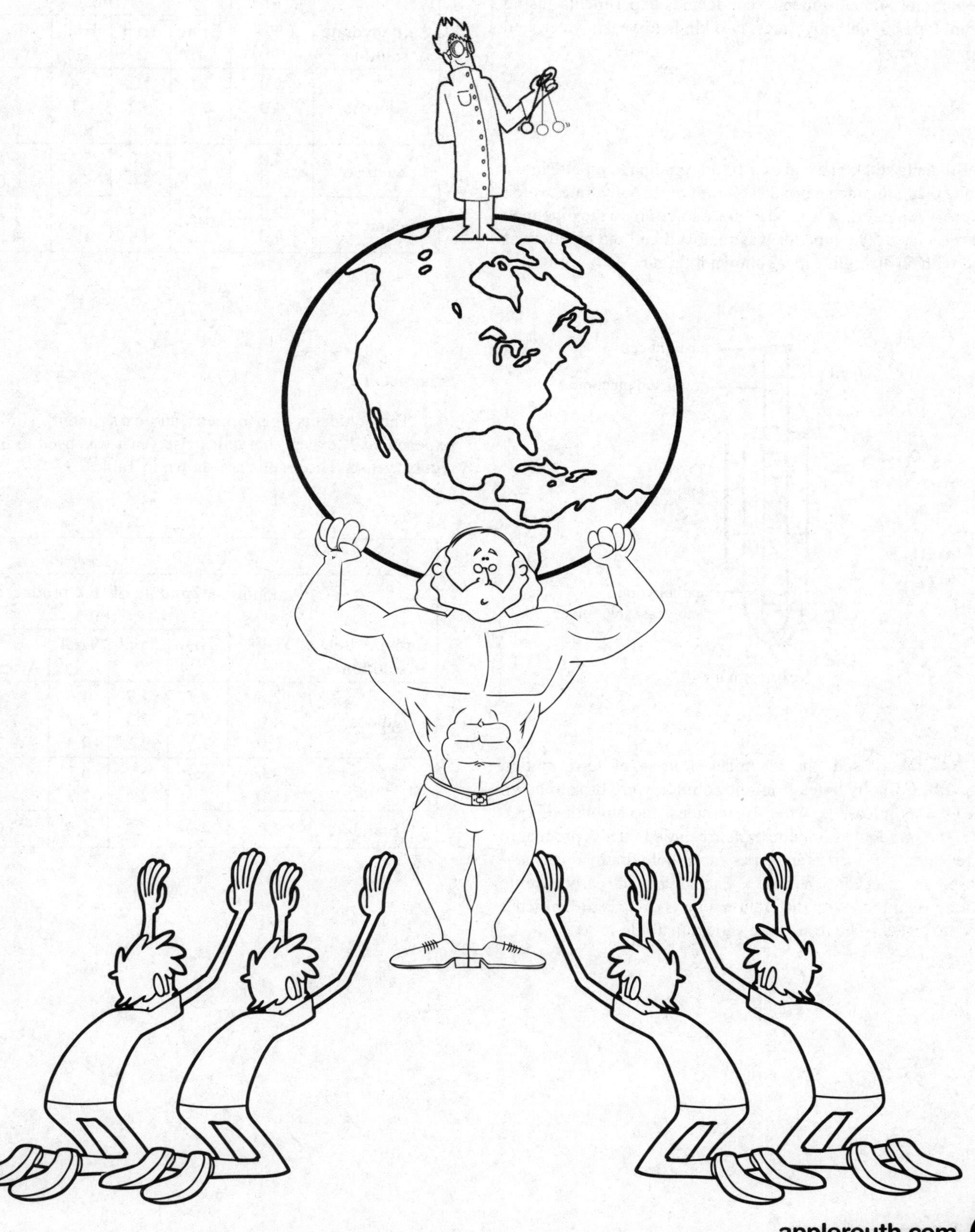

Passage V

In order to explore the factors that affect the rate of fermentation, some students conducted experiments using different types of carbohydrates, two kinds of yeast, water, and a respirometer.

Experiment 1

Students stuck one end of a 10 mL graduated pipette into a test tube that contained a mixed solution of carbohydrate, water, and yeast. A pipettor was used to draw solution up the pipette to the 0 mL mark. The pipettor was removed and the pipette was sealed with an air-tight cap, as shown in Figure 1.

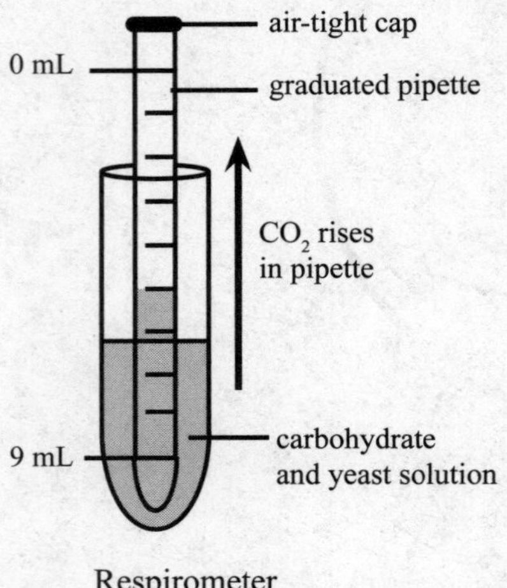

Respirometer

Figure 1

As time passed, the chemical process of fermentation proceeded. Carbohydrates from the solution were broken down and CO_2 was released. After 10 minutes, the amount of CO_2 inside the graduated pipette was recorded. This procedure was repeated for 3 different types of carbohydrate solutions – glucose, sucrose, and starch. Each type of carbohydrate solution was mixed with different amounts of yeast, of which 2 or 3 were tested. The results are shown in Table 1.

Table 1

Carbohydrate solution	Amount of yeast (mL)	Amount of CO_2 produced (mL)			
		Trial 1	Trial 2	Trial 3	Average
Glucose	2.0	3.1	3.3	3.4	3.3
	4.0	6.3	6.2	6.1	6.2
	6.0	9.3	8.8	9.1	9.1
Sucrose	4.0	5.5	5.6	5.3	5.5
	5.0	6.1	6.0	5.8	6.0
Starch	2.0	1.2	0.9	1.3	1.1
	4.0	4.3	4.4	4.3	4.3

Experiment 2

The students performed an experiment similar to Experiment 1, except that quick rise yeast was used in place of regular yeast. The results are shown in Table 2.

Table 2

Carbohydrate solution	Amount of yeast (mL)	Amount of CO_2 produced (mL)			
		Trial 1	Trial 2	Trial 3	Average
Glucose	2.0	4.5	4.7	4.6	4.6
	4.0	7.8	7.3	7.7	7.6
	6.0	9.7	9.8	9.5	9.7
Sucrose	4.0	6.4	6.2	6.1	6.2
	5.0	7.3	7.4	7.7	7.5
Starch	3.0	4.9	5.2	5.0	5.0

23. The results of Experiments 1 and 2 support the conclusion that, for a given carbohydrate solution, as the amount of yeast increases, the amount of CO_2 produced:

A. increases only.
B. decreases only.
C. remains constant.
D. varies, but with no particular trend.

24. In Experiment 2, had glucose solution been tested with 8.0 mL of quick rise yeast, the volume of CO_2 produced would have been closest to:

F. 6.0 mL
G. 9.0 mL
H. 12.0 mL
J. 15.0 mL

25. Based on the average results of Experiments 1 and 2, which of the carbohydrate solutions produced a higher amount of CO_2 with quick rise yeast than with regular yeast?

A. Glucose
B. Glucose and Sucrose
C. Glucose, Sucrose, and Starch
D. None

26. Which types of carbohydrate solutions were tested with only two different amounts of yeast in both experiments?

F. Glucose
G. Sucrose
H. Starch
J. Sucrose and Starch

27. Suppose that the air-tight cap used in Experiments 1 and 2 had an imperfection that caused it to not completely seal. How would this affect the student's measurements? Compared to the actual rate of fermentation for the different solutions, the apparent rate would be:

A. Higher, because there would be more CO_2 inside the graduated pipette than was released by the solution.
B. Higher, because there would be less CO_2 inside the graduated pipette than was released by the solution.
C. Lower, because there would be more CO_2 inside the graduated pipette than was released by the solution.
D. Lower, because there would be less CO_2 inside the graduated pipette than was released by the solution.

28. The students' instructor gave them a carbohydrate solution that contained 5.0 mL of yeast and asked them to identify the carbohydrate. The students repeated the procedures from Experiments 1 and 2 using the solution and obtained average volumes of CO_2 of 7.7 mL for regular yeast and 8.9 mL for quick rise yeast. Which of the following carbohydrate solutions would most likely have produced these results?

F. Glucose only
G. Sucrose only
H. Glucose and Sucrose
J. Sucrose and Starch

GO ON TO THE NEXT PAGE.

23

The results of Experiments 1 and 2 support the conclusion that, for a given carbohydrate solution, as the amount of yeast increases, the amount of CO_2 produced:

Table 1					
Carbohydrate solution	Amount of yeast	Amount of CO_2 produced			
		Trial 1	Trial 2	Trial 3	Average
Glucose	2.0 ↓	3.1	3.3	3.4	↓ 3.3
	4.0	6.3	6.2	6.1	6.2
	6.0	9.3	8.8	9.1	9.1
Sucrose	4.0 ↓	5.5	5.6	5.3	↓ 5.5
	5.0	6.1	6.0	5.8	6.0
Starch	2.0 ↓	1.2	0.9	1.3	↓ 1.1
	4.0	4.3	4.4	4.3	4.3

Table 2					
Carbohydrate solution	Amount of yeast (mL)	Amount of CO_2 produced (mL)			
		Trial 1	Trial 2	Trial 3	Average
Glucose	2.0 ↓	4.5	4.7	4.6	↓ 4.6
	4.0	7.8	7.3	7.7	7.6
	6.0	9.7	9.8	9.5	9.7
Sucrose	4.0 ↓	6.4	6.2	6.1	↓ 6.2
	5.0	7.3	7.4	7.7	7.5
Starch	3.0	4.9	5.2	5.0	5.0

This is a **Relationship** question. "Experiments 1 and 2" directs us to Tables 1 and 2. We need to find the relationship between "amount of yeast" and "amount of CO_2 produced." It's arrow time.

Our arrows for both columns point the same way. There's a **direct, increasing relationship** at work here.

A. increases only.

24

In Experiment 2, had glucose solution been tested with 8.0 mL of quick rise yeast, the volume of CO_2 produced would have been closest to:

Table 2					
Carbohydrate solution	Amount of yeast (mL)	Amount of CO_2 produced (mL)			
		Trial 1	Trial 2	Trial 3	Average
Glucose	2.0	4.5	4.7	4.6	4.6
	4.0 ↓ (+2)	7.8	7.3	7.7 (+2.1)	↓ 7.6
	6.0	9.7	9.8	9.5	9.7
	8.0 ↓ +2			+2.1	↓ 11.8

Expand the pattern!

This is an **Expand the Pattern** question. In Table 2, we can see that increasing the amount of yeast from 4.0 to 6.0 mL increases the average CO_2 from 7.6 to 9.7 mL.

Expanding this pattern, we can predict that increasing yeast by **another 2.0 mL** would increase CO_2 **by about another 2 mL.**

H. 12.0 mL

25

Based on the average results of Experiments 1 and 2, which of the following carbohydrate solutions produced a higher amount of CO_2 with quick rise yeast than with regular yeast?

This is a **Read the Passage** question. It looks like **regular yeast** was used in **Experiment 1**, and **quick rise** in **Experiment 2.**

So we simply need to find a solution that has a **higher average CO_2** in Table 2 than it does in Table 1. As it turns out, they **all** do!

Carbohydrate solution	Table 1: Amount of CO_2 produced (mL) Average	Table 2: Amount of CO_2 produced (mL) Average
Glucose	3.3 →	4.6
	6.2 →	7.6
	9.1 →	9.7
Sucrose	5.5 →	6.2
	6.0 →	7.5
Starch	1.1 4.3 →	5.0

C. Glucose, Sucrose, and Starch

26

Which types of carbohydrate solutions were tested with only two different amounts of yeast in both experiments?

This is a **Get to the Point** question. in both Table 1 and Table 2. By simply counting the number of rows in the "amount of yeast" column for each solution, we can find our answer.

Both sucrose and starch were tested with only two different amounts of yeast in Table 1, but only sucrose was tested with two amounts in Table 2.

G. Sucrose

Table 1

Carbohydrate solution	Amount of yeast	
Glucose	2.0 4.0 6.0	3
Sucrose	4.0 5.0	(2)
Starch	2.0 4.0	(2)

Table 2

Carbohydrate solution	Amount of yeast (mL)	
Glucose	2.0 4.0 6.0	3
Sucrose	4.0 5.0	(2)
Starch	3.0	1

27

Suppose that the <u>air-tight cap</u> used in Experiments 1 and 2 had an imperfection that caused it to <u>not completely seal</u>. How would this <u>affect the student's measurements</u>? Compared to the <u>actual rate</u> of <u>fermentation</u> for the different solutions, the <u>apparent rate would be</u>:

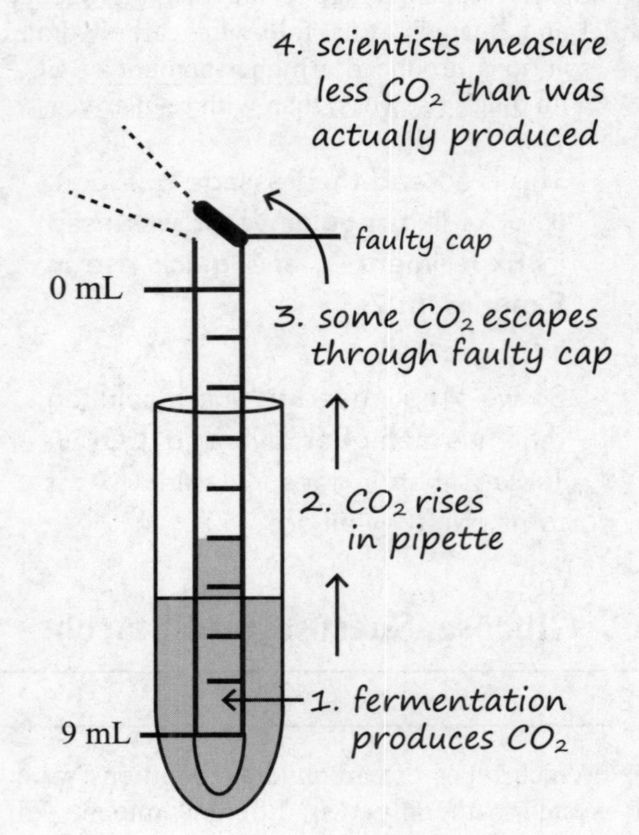

This is a **Measurement Adjustment** question. The passage tells us that "fermentation" is the process that causes CO_2 to be produced. The air-tight cap is **supposed to keep that gas trapped** in the pipette. If the cap isn't doing its job, then the scientists **won't see all the gas** the solution produced.

D. Lower, because there would be less CO_2 inside the graduated pipette than was released by the solution.

28

The students' instructor gave them a carbohydrate solution that contained <u>5.0 mL of yeast</u> and asked them to identify the carbohydrate. The students repeated the procedures from Experiments 1 and 2 using the solution and obtained <u>average volumes</u> of CO_2 of <u>7.7 mL for regular yeast</u> and <u>8.9 mL for quick rise yeast</u>. Which of the following carbohydrate solutions would most likely have produced these results?

<u>5.0 mL of regular yeast = 7.7 mL CO_2</u>

Table 1

Carbohydrate solution	Amount of yeast	Amount of CO_2 produced (Average)	
Glucose	2.0	3.3	
	4.0	6.2	
	5.0 →	*~7.7* ✓	*bingo!*
	6.0	9.1	
Sucrose	4.0	5.5	
	5.0 →	6.0 ✗	*too low!*
Starch	2.0	1.1	
	4.0	4.3	
	5.0 →	*~5.8* ✗	*too low!*

This is an **Inference** question. We should start by finding a solution in Table 1 where 5.0 mL would likely lead to 7.7 mL of CO_2. For **glucose,** 5.0 mL of **regular yeast** should land between 6.2 and 9.1 mL of CO_2. 7.7mL fits that bill! So far so good!

Now let's check Table 2. For glucose, 5.0 mL of quick rise yeast should produce between 7.6 and 9.7 mL of CO_2, and 8.9 mL falls in that range. Glucose is our one and only match!

5.0 mL of quick rise yeast = 8.9 mL CO_2

Table 1

Carbohydrate solution	Amount of yeast	Amount of CO_2 produced (Average)	
Glucose	2.0	4.6	
	4.0	7.6	
	5.0 →	*~8.9*	✓ *bingo!*
	6.0	9.7	
Sucrose	4.0	6.2	
	5.0 →	7.5	X *too low!*
Starch	3.0	5.0	
	5.0 →	*?*	X *who knows?*

F. Glucose only

Timing Check

Passage 5 Stats

Time spent: ________

Questions Missed: ________

Passage 6 Goals

Time spent: ________

Questions Missed: ________

PASSAGE VI

Passage VI

Scientists discuss 3 possible causes of pruning, the temporary formation of wrinkles that occurs when human digits - fingers and toes - are submerged in water.

Scientist 1

Pruning occurs when dead keratin cells in the epidermis, the outermost layer of the skin, absorb water. Once the skin is submerged in liquid, these keratin cells swell. The living tissue stretches in response, and the skin wrinkles. Pruning occurs primarily on the skin of fingers and toes because there is a much denser layer of dead keratin cells in the digits than in any other body part.

Scientist 2

Pruning occurs when blood vessels in the epidermis contract because of a temperature difference between the human body and its environment. When exposed to cold water, the body's thermoreceptors, or nerve cells that sense hot and cold temperatures, react and cause the blood vessels close to the surface to contract. As blood vessels in the digits contract, the surrounding epidermal tissue does not receive the support that it previously did, causing the skin to wrinkle. Pruning occurs primarily on the skin of fingers and toes because there is a higher concentration of thermoreceptors in the digits than in any other body part.

Scientist 3

Pruning occurs when the autonomic nervous system sends an electrical signal to the extremities, causing them to wrinkle. Like treads on tires, pruning creates channels that enable water to escape and, as a result, increases the finger's ability to grip an object in a wet environment. Patients who lack nerve function in their hands have fingers that do not prune when exposed to water. Those patients who regain nerve functioning in their hands also recover the ability to prune in response to water. This demonstrates that pruning is a controlled response of the nervous system.

29. Scientist 1's theory does NOT include the hypothesis that pruning involves:

A. swelling.
B. dead cells.
C. stretching.
D. electrical signals.

30. All 3 scientists would agree with the conclusion that pruning:

F. is the result of fluctuations in temperature.
G. serves a useful purpose.
H. results from submersion in water.
J. is caused by the swelling of keratin cells.

31. Which of the following discoveries, if true, would LEAST support Scientist 2's theory?

A. Pruning occurs more rapidly in colder water than in warmer water.
B. Pruning also occurs in the skin around the ankle, which has a low concentration of thermoreceptors.
C. Pruning does not occur when water is body temperature.
D. Individuals with fewer thermoreceptors experience less pruning.

32. Suppose studies show that pruning can occur in dry, frigid environments. This finding would support the theory of which Scientist(s)?

F. Scientists 1 and 2.
G. Scientists 2 and 3.
H. Scientist 2 only.
J. Scientist 3 only.

33. How does Scientist 3's theory differ from Scientist 2's theory? Scientist 3 claims that pruning is caused by:

A. a nervous system response to moisture, whereas Scientist 2 argues that thermoreceptors cause blood vessels to contract.
B. keratin cells swelling with water, whereas Scientist 2 argues that it is an evolutionary adaption allowing humans to grip wet objects
C. a nervous system response to moisture, whereas Scientist 2 argues that the swelling of keratin cells causes pruning.
D. thermoreceptors causing blood vessels to contract, whereas Scientist 2 argues it is a nervous system response to moisture.

34. Consider the statement "Nerve cells have nothing to do with the process of pruning." This statement is consistent with the theories of which of the scientists?

F. Scientist 1 only.
G. Scientist 3 only.
H. Scientists 1 and 2 only.
J. Scientists 2 and 3 only.

35. Suppose researchers designed an experiment to test the 3 Scientists' theories. One experimental group exfoliated (removed dead skin cells with a rough material) and another did not exfoliate. Both groups were then submerged in either cold water or body temperature water. In which of the following experimental groups would observed pruning support Scientist 3 ONLY?

A. Subjects who exfoliated and were submerged in body temperature water.
B. Subjects who exfoliated and were submerged in cold water.
C. Subjects who did not exfoliate and were submerged in body temperature water.
D. Subjects who did not exfoliate and were submerged in cold water.

Note: Dueling Scientist passages are all about keeping different theories straight. Let's sum up each scientist's theories before looking at the questions.

Pruning occurs when:

Scientist 1: dead keratin **cells swell**, stretching skin

Scientist 2: thermoreceptors detect a **temperature difference**

Scientist 3: **electric signal** comes from nervous system; helps grip

29

Scientist 1's theory does NOT include the hypothesis that pruning involves:

We have "swelling," "dead cells," and "stretching in our notes for Scientist 1. But look at choice D - "electrical signals?" That's Scientist 3's game!

D. Electrical Signals

30

All 3 scientists would agree with the conclusion that pruning:

We're looking for something "all 3 scientists" have in common. Their theories are quite different, so **we must be looking for something pretty basic**. The **introduction** tells us that pruning occurs when "fingers and toes are submerged in water." That's almost choice H verbatim. The other choices simply list the different theories of the individual scientists.

H. results from submersion in water

31

Which of the following discoveries, if true, would LEAST support Scientist 2's theory?

Let's refresh on Scientist 2's theory: thermoreceptors detect a temperature difference and cause pruning. Careful: we're looking for a choice that does **NOT** support this theory.

Choices A, C, and D all give discoveries where thermoreceptors or temperature differences are important. Only the discovery in choice B gives us reason to doubt their role in pruning.

B. Pruning also occurs in the skin around the ankle, which has a low concentration of thermoreceptors.

32

Suppose studies show that pruning can occur in dry, frigid environments. This finding would support the theory of which Scientist(s)?

We have two adjectives here: **dry** and **frigid**.

For Scientist 1, **dry** is a problem: without water, there is nothing to cause keratin cells to swell. Scientist 1 wouldn't like this finding. Neither would Scientist 3: Scientist 3's theory was that the nervous system causes pruning to help wet hands grab objects. A finding that pruning occurs in **dry** environments definitely does not provide any support for this.

Scientist 2, on the other hand, was all about **temperature**, so pruning occurring in a "frigid" environment would seem to help!

H. Scientist 2 only.

33

How does Scientist 3's theory differ from Scientist 2's theory? Scientist 3 claims that pruning is caused by:

Questions like this one are why we made our summary notes. Only one choice describes the theories of Scientist 2 and 3 correctly: choice A.

A. a nervous system response to moisture, whereas Scientist 2 argues that thermoreceptors cause blood vessels to contract.

34

Consider the statement "Nerve cells have nothing to do with the process of pruning." This statement is consistent with the theories of which of the scientists?

We need to pick a scientist who does NOT talk about **nerve cells.** Looking at our notes, we can easily throw out Scientist 3 - he was all about the "nervous system." If we scan Scientist 2's theory, we see:

Thermoreceptors are nerve cells!

> "When exposed to cold water, the body's thermoreceptors, or **nerve cells**..."

Scientist 2 was all about nerve cells as well! That leaves only Scientist 1.

F. Scientist 1 only.

35 Suppose researchers designed an experiment to test the 3 Scientists' theories. One experimental group exfoliated (removed dead skin cells with a rough material) and another did not exfoliate. Both groups were then submerged in either cold water or body temperature water. In which of the following experimental groups would observed pruning support Scientist 3 ONLY?

Those last four words of the question are the key to making this tough-looking question a cinch. We are looking for pruning that does NOT support Scientist 1 OR 2.

Remember that when **Scientist 1** sees pruning, he exclaims **"dead skin cells!"** When **Scientist 2** sees pruning, she shouts **"temperature difference!"** To have a result that would not support either theory, we need to see pruning in subjects with **no dead skin cells** and **no temperature difference.**

A. Subjects who exfoliated and were submerged in body temperature water.

Timing Check

Passage 6 Stats	
Time spent:	________
Questions Missed:	________

Passage 7 Goals	
Time spent:	________
Questions Missed:	________

PASSAGE VII

Passage VII

Figure 1 shows the life cycle of the swarming grasshopper, or locust, *Chortoicetes terminifera.* Egg, nymph, solitary adult, and swarming adult are the primary stages of the locust's life cycle.

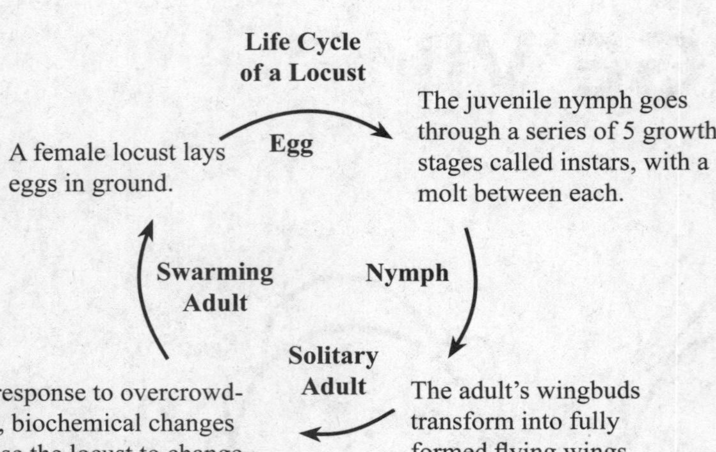

Figure 1

Study 1

In order to determine whether locusts are attracted to a particular food source at each stage of their life cycle, scientists selected three dietary staples of the locust. Table 1 shows the three species selected.

Table 1		
Food source		Species
A	grasses	*Agrostis avenacea*
B	forb leaves	*Bulbine bulbosa*
C	cereal crops	*Triticum monococcum*

In each trial, individual containers with one of the three plant species were placed in separate but identical feeding areas that were attached to the same central compartment (see Figure 2).

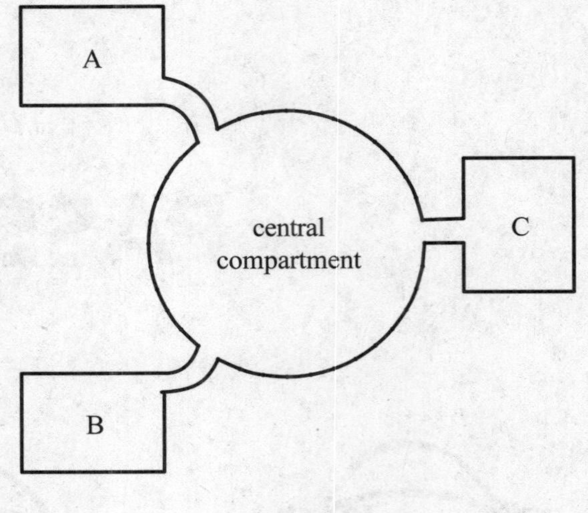

Figure 2

In the first trial, 50 nymphs, 50 solitary adults and 50 swarming adult locusts were simultaneously released in the central compartment. Twenty-four hours later, the insects that had migrated to a particular food source were counted, and the number of insects in each life stage was determined. This procedure was repeated in nine more trials. Figure 3 shows the average number of locusts of each life stage that had migrated to a particular food source.

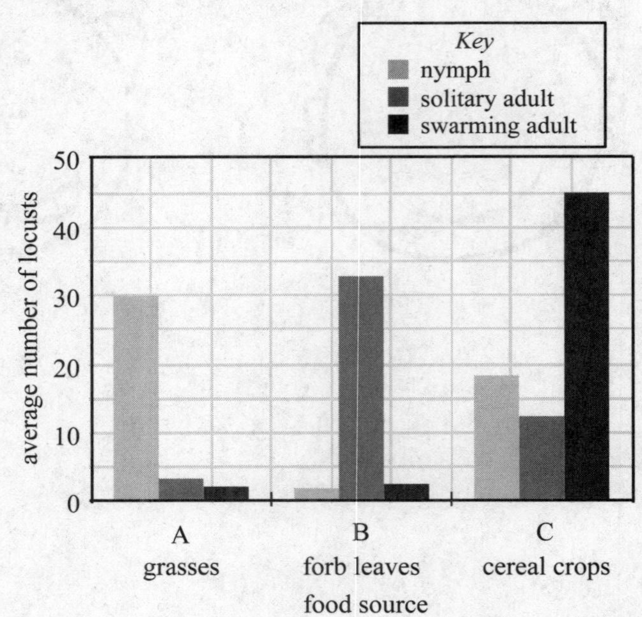

Figure 3

Study 2

Scientists hypothesized that a locust's food preferences depends both on its stage of development as well as environmental conditions. Under stressful conditions, the locusts may shift dietary choices from nitrogen-rich grass, which stimulates growth and aids reproduction, to high-energy carbohydrates, such as cereal crops, to better store energy.

The procedure from Study 1 was modified to test whether locusts in the 5 development phases (instars) of the nymph stage would show different food preferences in a stressed (50° F room) condition versus an unstressed (75° F room) condition. One of the three feeding areas was blocked off, and the food choices were limited to grass, *A. avenacea*, and cereal, *T. monococcum*. In each trial, 50 nymphs from a single instar were released into the central compartment in the stressed condition; the procedure was repeated in the unstressed condition. Figure 4 shows the proportion of nymphs in various stages of development, in the stressed and unstressed conditions, preferring grass (ending up in the grass feeding area) over cereal (ending up in the cereal feeding area).

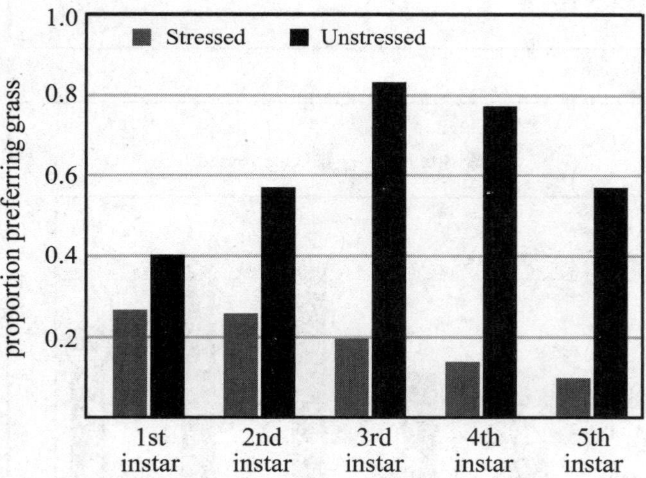

Figure 4

36. Based on Figure 4, *T. monococcum* was least attractive to a nymph in which developmental stage, in which experimental condition?

F. 2nd Instar, stressed condition
G. 3rd Instar, unstressed condition
H. 4th Instar, unstressed condition
J. 5th Instar, stressed condition

37. Based on Figure 4, in how many of the trials did the nymphs prefer grass to cereal in the unstressed condition?

A. 0
B. 1
C. 3
D. 4

38. Do the results of Study 1 support the hypothesis that locusts are attracted to a particular food source at each stage of their life cycle?

F. Yes; on average, more nymphs were attracted to source A, more solitary adults were attracted to source B, and more swarming adults were attracted to source C.
G. Yes; on average, the same number of nymphs, solitary adults, and swarming adults were attracted to source A, source B, and source C.
H. No; on average, more nymphs were attracted to source A, more solitary adults were attracted to source B, and more swarming adults were attracted to source C.
J. No; on average, the same number of nymphs, solitary adults, and swarming adults were attracted to source A, source B, and source C.

39. Which of the following is the most likely reason that forb leaves were not used as a food source in Study 2?

A. Forb leaves are lower in carbohydrates than are the other food sources.
B. Solitary adults are less likely to eat forb leaves than are swarming adults.
C. Nymphs are more likely to eat forb leaves than grasses or cereal crops.
D. Nymphs are less likely to eat forb leaves than grasses or cereal crops.

40. Which of the following procedures was most likely utilized in Study 1 to ensure that the locusts were attracted to a specific food source rather than to a specific feeding area?

F. Releasing all three stages of locusts in each trial.
G. Releasing the same number of locusts into the central compartment for each trial.
H. Assigning the food sources to feeding areas in a random manner in each trial.
J. Assigning the same food source to the same feeding area each trial.

36

Based on <u>Figure 4</u>, <u>*T. monococcum*</u> was <u>least</u> attractive to a nymph in which <u>developmental stage</u>, in which <u>experimental condition</u>?

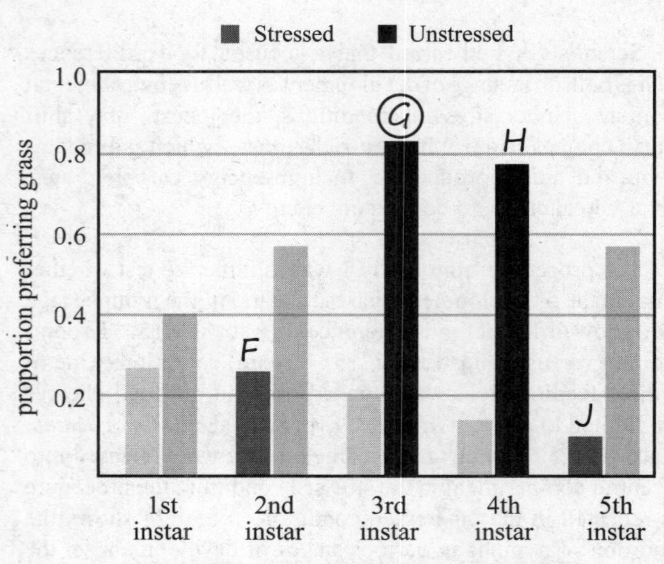

Figure 4

This is a **Compare Two Points** question. We are directed to Figure 4, which shows the proportion of locusts that preferred **grass.** Looking at Table 1, we can see that *T. mono* was the **cereal crop** (NOT the grass).

Since a high bar indicates a love for grass, we want the choice which corresponds with the **tallest bar**. It looks like that's the 3rd instar, unstressed condition.

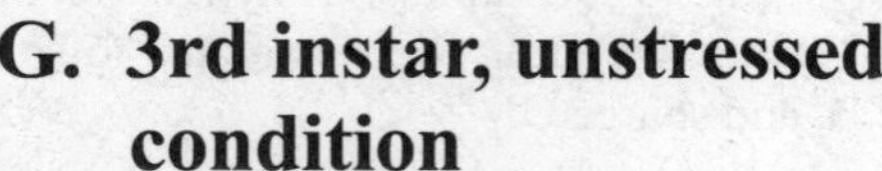

G. 3rd instar, unstressed condition

37

Based on <u>Figure 4</u>, in how many of the trials did a majority of the nymphs <u>prefer grass to cereal</u> in the <u>unstressed condition</u>?

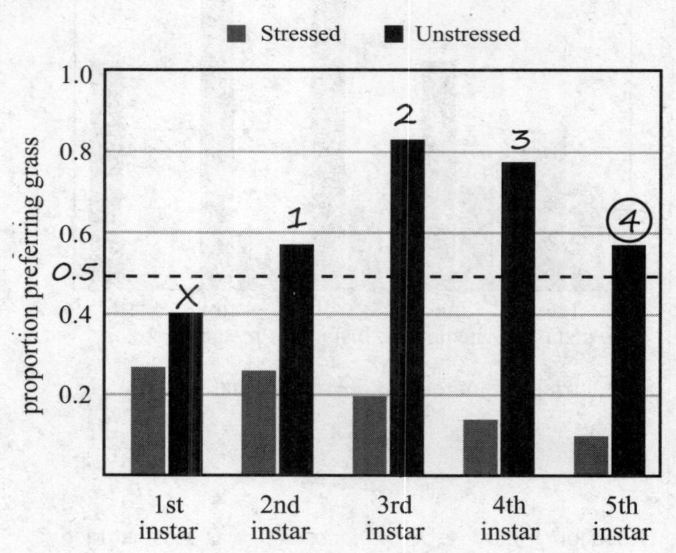

Figure 4

This is a **Get to the Point** question. Figure 4 shows the locusts' love for grass, and **unstressed** points us to the darker bars.

We need to count the number of dark bars that are **taller than 0.5.** This would indicate that over half of the locusts in that trial preferred grass to cereal. Only the dark bar of the 1st instar falls below 0.5.

D. 4

38 Do the results of Study 1 support the hypothesis that locusts are attracted to a particular food source at each stage of their life cycle?

This is a **Relationship** question. We can find the results of Study 1 in Figure 3. We need to identify if there is a relationship between locust stage and attraction to different food sources.

Essentially, we're asked if a different bar is top dog for sources A, B, and C. Looks like this is the case!

F. Yes; on average, more nymphs were attracted to source A, more solitary adults were attracted to source B, and more swarming adults were attracted to source C.

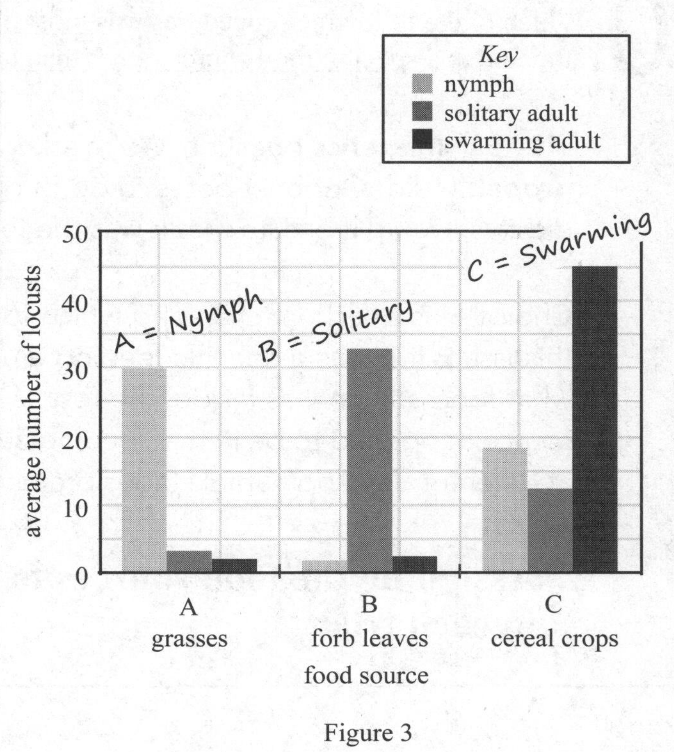

Figure 3

39 Which of the following is the most likely reason that forb leaves were not used as a food source in Study 2?

"Most likely" tips us off that this is a classic **Inference** question. We need to look at the passage and use common sense to explain the absence of forb leaves.

The passage tells us that Study 2 used locusts in the nymph stage. Figure 3 shows that nymphs avoid forb leaves in favor of grass and cereal.

D. Nymphs are less likely to eat forb leaves than grasses or cereal crops.

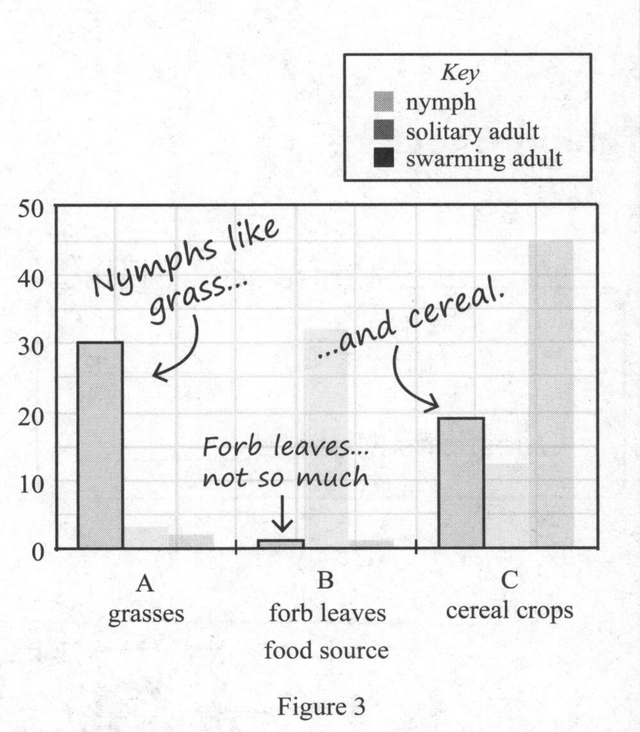

Figure 3

40 Which of the following procedures was most likely utilized in Study 1 to ensure that the locusts were attracted to a specific food source rather than to a specific feeding area?

This is an **Inference** question. We're asked to make an assumption about what the scientists **probably** did. Our best bet is to go through the answer choices asking, "If the scientists did this, would it ensure that it was the food source, not the area, that attracted locusts?"

Choice H is dead on: changing which food source is in which feeding area would settle this issue. If it was a specific feeding area attracting the locusts, then it wouldn't matter what food source was inside; the results would show that locusts went to whatever food source happened to be in that feeding area. Instead, we see a clear pattern where locusts at different developmental stages prefer different foods.

H. Assigning the food sources to feeding areas in a random manner in each trial.

Timing Check

Passage 7 Stats	Practice Test Goals
Time spent: ________	Time spent: ________
Questions Missed: ________	Questions Missed: ________

YOU DID IT!

Science Mantras

Skip the passage!
Get to the point!

Match words from the question with words in the figures.

Use your **pencil** or **finger** to match.

If it's not in the **figures**... it's in the passage.

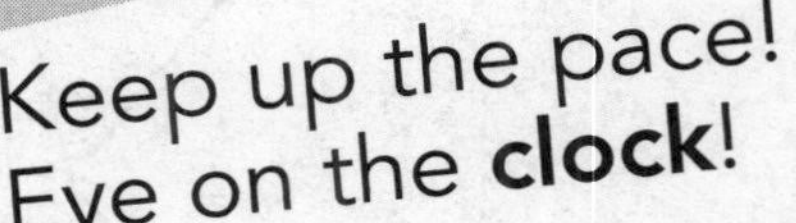

Keep up the pace! Eye on the **clock**!

↑↓ **Draw arrows** when you spot a trend!

Let the **question** guide you to the answer.

Essay

The Essay

Bring on the structure, bring on the flow. Hit that thesis, off you go! To cook up the perfect ACT essay, you just need to follow the recipe.

The ACT graders read your essay in about **2 minutes**! The job of a grader is to tear through his/her pile of essays as expediently as possible and assign each essay a score between 1 and 6. Your job is to give the graders what they want. Let them check the boxes that add up to a score of 5 or 6 and then move on.

Remember, you are not crafting the Great American Novel. It's closer to making a burger at a fast-food chain. Follow the recipe to success.

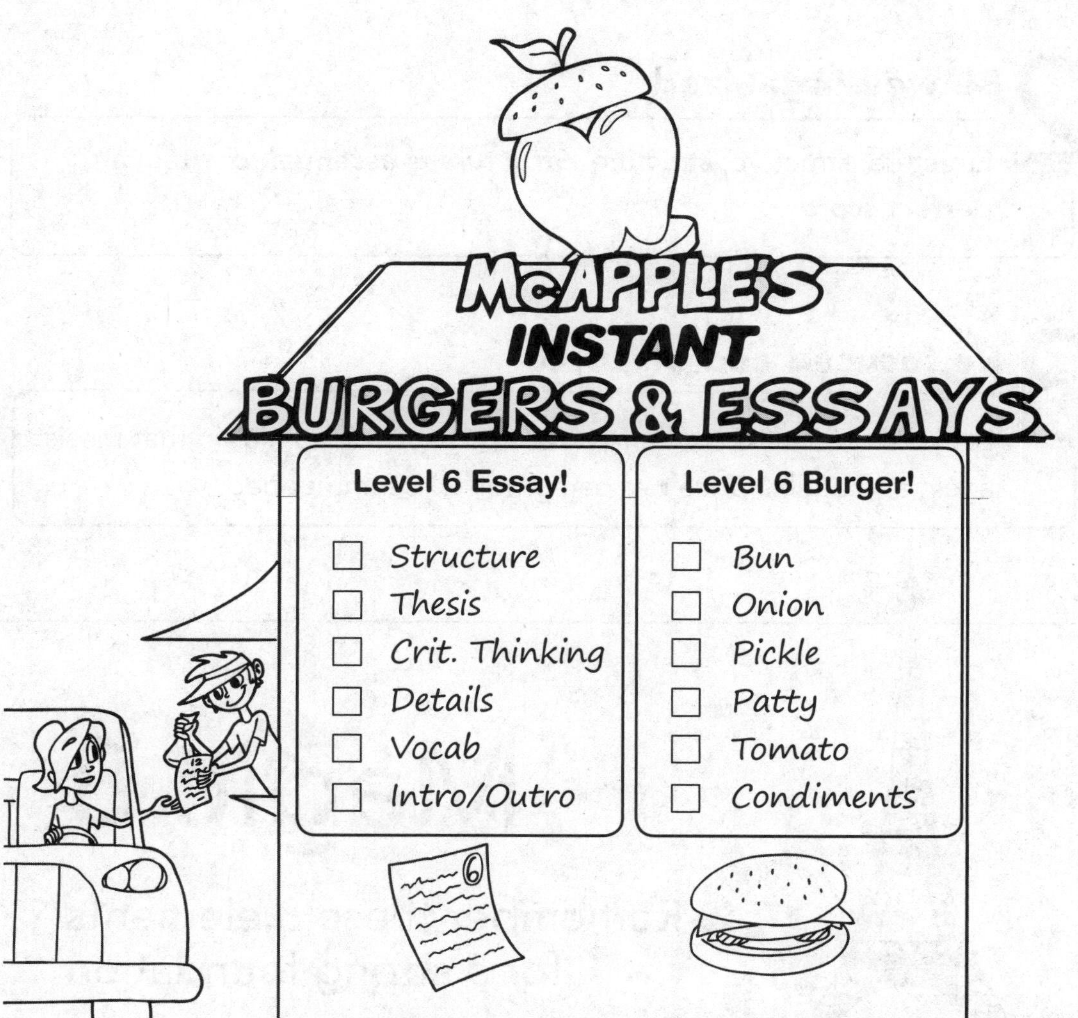

McAPPLE'S
INSTANT
BURGERS & ESSAYS
Level 6 Essay!
Structure
Thesis
Crit. Thinking
Details
Vocab
Intro/Outro
Level 6 Burger!
Bun
Onion
Pickle
Patty
Tomato
Condiments
6

Your essay is scored by two graders on a scale of 1 to 6. Your final score can be anywhere from a 2 to a 12 (a perfect score).

Foundations

Without a proper foundation, the Eiffel Tower would look a lot more like the Leaning Tower of Pisa, and your essay score will lean a lot closer to a 5 than to a 12.

1 Demonstrate mastery of critical thinking

Take a side and, acting like a lawyer in a courtroom, back up your decisive position with solid evidence. You will need to think of counterarguments to your position and attack them without mercy.

2 Be well-organized

Structure, structure, structure. ***Structure is essential to attain a perfect score.***

3 Be focused and on topic

Let your graders know that you are on topic. Keep hitting that thesis again and again. Once per paragraph is recommended.

Magic 8

Remember these 8 elements for a strong foundation

4 Have smooth transitions between paragraphs

The flow of your essay is important; have good segues and transitions that lead from one paragraph or example to the next.

5 Demonstrate skillful use of vocabulary

Instead of writing "this shows that…" break out a more advanced synonym: "this demonstrates/clarifies/delineates/displays..."

6 Use a variety of sentence structures

This is Spot. See Spot run. See Spot get a 2 on his essay. Shake it up: Spot, an aptly name Terrier, may enter your line of vision as he briskly bounds toward a perfect 12 on his ACT essay.

7 Minimize errors

Some errors will certainly occur. Graders expect this. They are more concerned with patterns of errors and consistent lapses in quality.

8 Write as much as you can

Longer essays get higher scores. It is that simple. The ACT graders reward essay length. However, do not sacrifice quality for quantity.

1	Critical Thinking	5	Skillful Vocab
2	Organization	6	Varied Sentences
3	Focus	7	Minimal Errors
4	Smooth Transitions	8	Length

Keep your grader engaged with varied and unique sentence structures. Stand out from the crowd!

- In spite of this...
- Refuting the claim…
- No matter how persistently they tried, the team members were unable to…
- Facing defeat, the coach opted to…
- They gave it all they could; by the third quarter the team…
- It all came down to determination: the desire to win and …

The Pyramid Principle

Without proper structure, even the most critically reasoned argument can lead to a low scoring essay. Good structure enables the graders to easily find the important elements of your essay.

By separating your main points and transitioning smoothly between them, you walk the reader through the development of your argument. If you force the graders to wade through a bog of undifferentiated sentences, struggling to follow your logic, your grade will suffer.

As you expose the weakness of the other argument, you reveal the strength of your own.

Building Critical Thinking into your Essay

Though you will ultimately choose one perspective on an issue to present as the most compelling, you must address **both** sides of an issue to attain a perfect score on the ACT essay.

There are two ways to present your critique of the other side. You can dedicate an **entire paragraph** to exploring and debunking the opposite perspective. Alternately, you can expose the weakness of the other argument piecemeal, **over multiple body paragraphs**.

Single Paragraph Critique

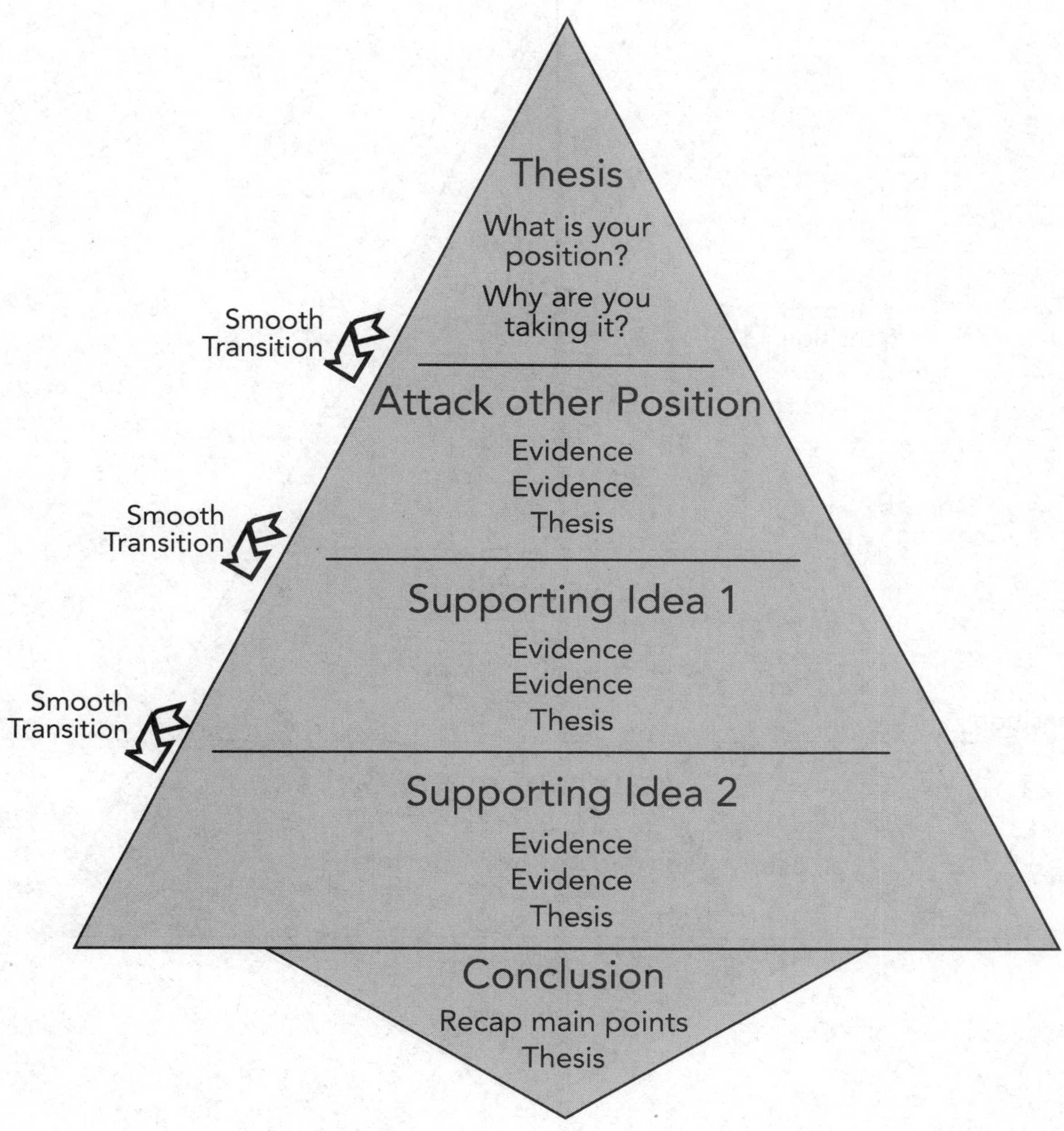

In this format, you utterly dismantle the opposing side in a single paragraph. This paragraph can come after your introduction or just before your conclusion.

Critique in Every Paragraph

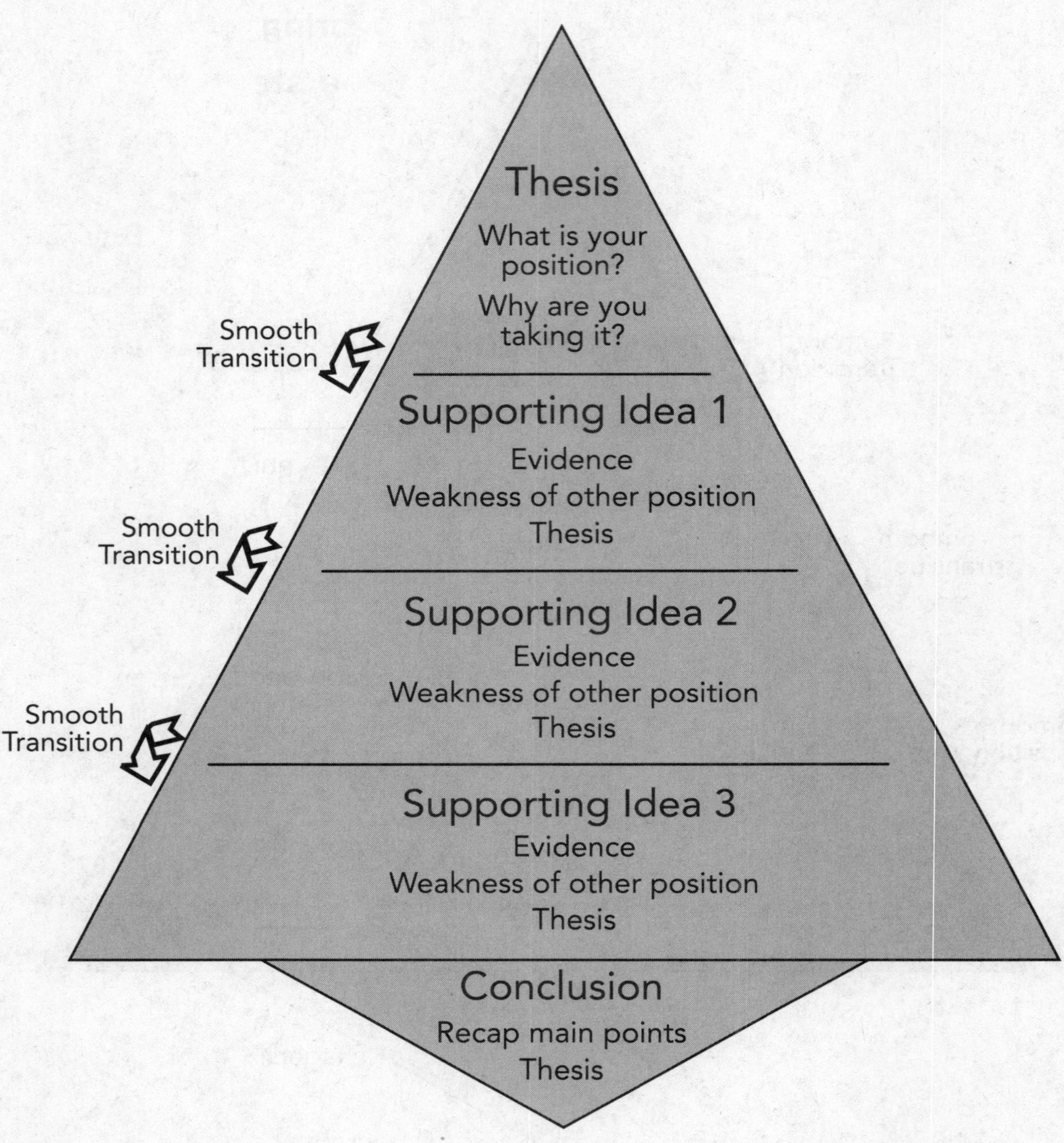

In this format, you divide your critique of the opposing side in every paragraph. You attack the opposing side on a **point-by-point basis**.

Building the Essay

We've discussed the elements of a perfect-scoring essay. But how do you get started? Let's take it one step at a time.

1 Read the prompt

The prompt is a paragraph that provides background on the topic of the essay. Within the prompt, the test writers will actually spell out two sides of an argument, giving a pro and a con on an issue.

> Some administrators have proposed increasing the number of single-gender high schools in the United States. Some educators believe that all-boys and all-girls schools provide a better education because they allow their students to focus on the curriculum, free from distraction. Other educators believe that such schools do not provide a superior education because they hinder their students' ability to develop necessary social and communication skills and work effectively in a mixed-gender environment. **In your opinion, do students receive a better education in a single-gender high school than they do in a traditional high school?**

2 Assume your position

ACT essay topics are always about an issue relevant to teenagers:

- Should parents use GPS to track their children's behavior at all times?
- Should teachers express their political beliefs in the classroom?
- Should high school last five years instead of four?
- Should states require teenagers to maintain a "C" average in school if they want to have a valid driver's license?

You will need to **assume a position** and stick with it!

If you are more passionate about one side, pick it. It will likely be an easier side for you to defend. If you are on the fence, pick the side that seems easier to write about.

Don't forget: there is no right answer. You are being graded on your writing and thinking skills, not your beliefs.

The graders are interested in your writing ability and critical thinking skills, not in the validity of your argument. As long as you take and defend a position with evidence, you are on the right path.

3 Brainstorm your supporting evidence

Once you take your position, it's time to brainstorm for supporting evidence. In this step, you will plan out each paragraph of your essay. The ACT writers have graciously given you **two positions in the prompt,** which can easily become paragraphs in your essay. One perspective you will **support with evidence**; the other you will **attack** with counter-examples and expose its flaws.

To come up with additional examples, simply remember this **acronym**:

Costs/Benefits

Help/Hurt

Over-the-top examples

Practicality

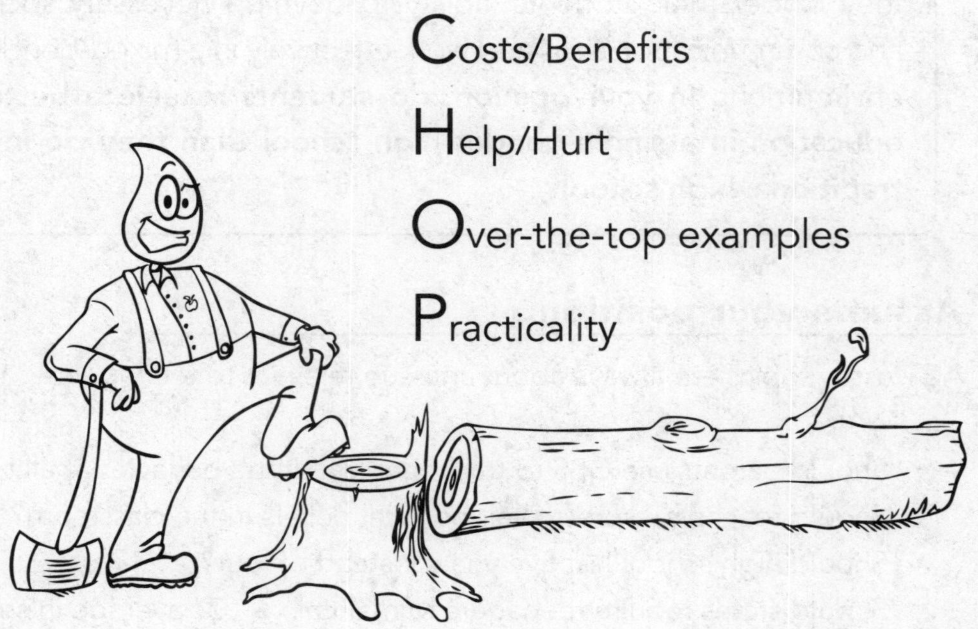

Use CHOP to start asking yourself the right questions:

Costs/Benefits

What are the costs of this position?
What are the benefits?
Do the costs outweigh the benefits?

Help/Hurt

Who would this position help?
Who would it hurt?

Over-the-top Examples

What might happen, in an extreme case?
Could this position lead to an absurd result?

Practicality

Is this position realistic?
Would this likely work, or fall apart, in the real world?

You have creative license here! The graders are not going to fact-check you; they simply do not have time to hit up Google, Wikipedia or Facebook to see if your story checks out. If you can't think of a real example, **make one up!**

4 Order your evidence

Strong examples are those that **directly support your thesis** and that you can support with specific details. You should prioritize by starting with your strongest example and ending with the weakest. This is just in case you run out of time and need to skip one of your weaker points.

The Intro should be short and sweet. This is not the time to flesh things out.

Save evidence for the body!

5 Write Your Essay

Introduction

Your intro must make clear two things:

1. your **thesis**
2. the **rationale** behind your thesis

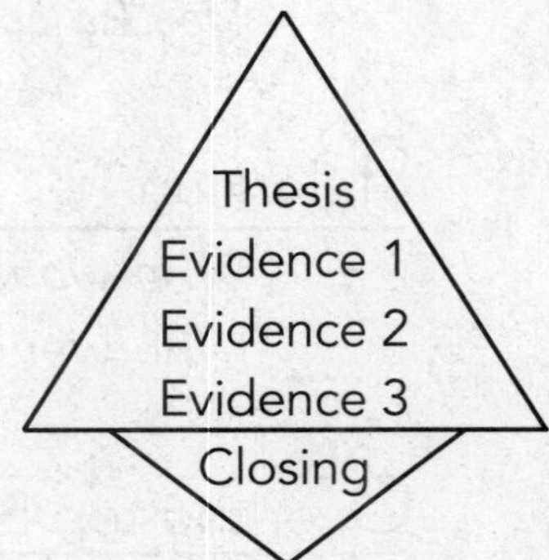

Following the Pyramid principle, it's not a bad idea to hit your grader with your thesis first. However you choose to structure your argument, make sure your thesis is clear!

Body Paragraphs

In each body paragraph, you need three things:

1. A **transition** from the preceding paragraph
2. **Evidence** to support your point
3. A reiteration of your **thesis** statement

Transitions

Every good essay has a logical flow, a natural development from one point to the next. Reiterating early points and incorporating transitional phrases will help you create this effortless progression from one idea to the next.

Evidence

Provide concrete examples supporting your position and specific counterexamples to attack the **other** side of the argument. You can attack in block form, using an entire paragraph, or respond to counter-arguments in each paragraph.

Thesis

You need to reiterate your thesis. Often this is easiest at the beginning or the end of each body paragraph. Restating your thesis is the easiest way to prove to the essay graders that you are on topic!

Closing

You absolutely need a closing. Ending mid-sentence is a no-no. If you only have two minutes left and you are smack in the middle of Supporting Idea 2, end that paragraph, scratch Supporting Idea 3, and immediately write a two-sentence closing.

Short closings are preferable. This is not the time to add new evidence.

6 Review if time permits

If you have a minute left after finishing your conclusion, use that time to review. Check your transitions and look for obvious errors.

Don't carve out 5 minutes of your scarce time to review; if you have that much time left, write another supporting paragraph!

Allocating your Time

You have **30 minutes** to write your essay. Be careful not to spend so much time planning your essay that you never get around to writing it! Remember, longer essays score higher. We recommend the following timetable:

Step 1	Read the prompt	30 seconds
Step 2	Take a position	30 seconds
Step 3	Brainstorm examples	3 minutes
Step 4	Order Evidence	1 minute
Step 5	Write the essay	24 minutes
Step 6	Review if time permits	1 minutes

Essay Grading Process

The diagram below illustrates the essay grading process. Two graders score your essay from 1 to 6, and those scores are then combined into your final score.

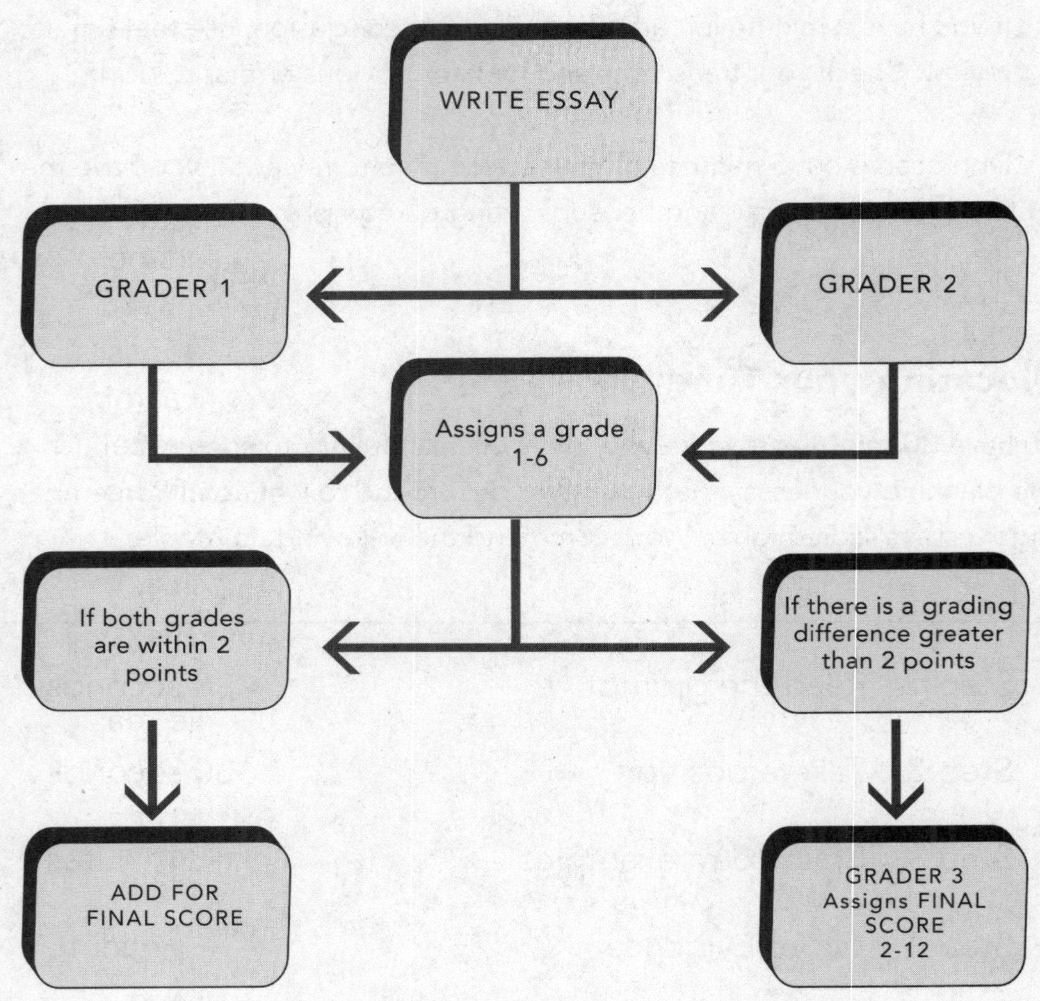

If you receive a score of 8 on your essay, most likely each of your graders scored your essay as a 4. If you receive a 9, one grader probably gave you a 5 and the other gave you a 4. It is unlikely that two graders will differ in their assessment of your essay by more than two points. If this does occur, another grader will be called in to assign a final score between 2 and 12.

Scoring the Essay

To help understand how the ACT scores essays, let's look at 3 essays, in order of descending quality. Each essay was written in response to the following prompt.

Some administrators have proposed increasing the number of single-gender high schools in the United States. Some educators believe that all-boys and all-girls schools provide a better education because they allow their students to focus on the curriculum, free from distraction. Other educators believe that such schools do not provide a superior education because they hinder their students' ability to develop necessary social and communication skills and work effectively in a mixed-gender environment. In your opinion, do students receive a better education in a single-gender high school than they do in a traditional high school?

In your essay, take a position on this issue. You may write about either one of the two points of view given, or you may put forth a different point of view. Provide specific reasons and examples that support your position.

thesis

You will see this symbol over the bolded thesis every time it appears.

detail

You will see this symbol over specific details that have been italicized.

crit.

You will see this symbol over sentences recognizing the other side of the argument.

str.

You will see this symbol over punctuation that signals advanced sentence structure.

trans.

You will see this symbol over every underlined transition.

vocab.

You will see this symbol over skillfully used, advanced vocab.

Level 12 Essay

The ACT describes an essay that receives a score of 12 as one that demonstrates "effective skill in responding to the task." A level 12 essay shows a clear understanding of the assignment, takes a clear position, and examines different views on the issue by providing logical examples. The essay is logically structured, with an effective introduction and conclusion. Sentence structure is varied, and there are few errors to distract the reader.

Do students receive a better education in a single-gender high school than they do in a traditional high school?

When it comes to education, it is entirely natural and desirable for students of both genders to learn, study and grow together. [str.] Although some administrators have [vocab.] posited that single-gender learning is the sure path to optimal student performance and learning outcomes, co-ed learning [vocab.] nurtures the more holistic development of male and female students. [thesis] **Single-gender learning, though useful in some isolated situations, provides an inferior education when compared to mixed-gender education.**

[trans.] Returning to an emphasis on the differences between girls and boys will undo much of the *progress our country has made in education over the past 150 years* [detail]. [str.] Although some [vocab.] pundits yearn for the simpler times when crit.

boys studied with boys, and girls with girls, going back in time is not the

str.

way forward. Does one gender hold the other back? Can students only rise

str.

to their potential in the absence of the other gender? This is nonsense: *old*

detail vocab.

stereotypes that say girls fall behind in math and sciences are antiquated

vocab.

and have shown to be obsolete. *Modern studies reveal that the gender*

detail

gap in math and sciences has been obliterated. This suggests that any

crit.

historic difference in performance between genders was in fact caused by educators expecting girls and boys to perform differently. **Single-gender**

thesis

schools could therefore hurt our nation's teenagers.

trans.

One advantage offered by mixed-gender schools is that they educate boys and girls on how to effectively interact and work with

detail

each other. *The world of work and the world at large are not separated by gender.* To succeed in the *highly competitive global marketplace,*

vocab.

individuals must be able to collaborate skillfully with male and female colleagues. *Males and females have different styles of leading, of*

detail

communicating, and of resolving conflicts. **Spending time together in**

thesis

a co-ed learning environment will afford both males and females the

detail

opportunity to learn from each other and come to *understand and respect the differences that exist between them.* Time together breeds familiarity,

thesis

You will see this symbol over the bolded thesis every time it appears.

detail

You will see this symbol over specific details that have been italicized.

crit.

You will see this symbol over sentences recognizing the other side of the argument

str.

You will see this symbol over punctuation that signals advanced sentence structure.

trans.

You will see this symbol over every underlined transition.

vocab.

You will see this symbol over skillfully used, advanced vocab.

(str.) which leads to increased respect and tolerance. *As males and females will* [detail] *certainly be working together for most of their adult lives,* it's important to set them up with the collaborative skills they will surely need. **Mixed-** [thesis] **gender schools provide this other, equally important type of education.**

(vocab.) (trans.) Proponents of single-gender education argue that the element of distraction is reduced when boys and girls are kept separate, thereby improving education. Although it is true that when you co-mingle the [crit.] (vocab.) sexes some distractions are inevitable, these distractions never go away. *If you don't learn to cope with the distraction of members of the opposite* [detail] *sex, you will struggle in college and in the world of work and beyond!* Furthermore, in all schools, most of the conversations that distract students have *nothing whatsoever to do with gender.* Distractions abound in high (vocab.) [detail] school; learning to overcome such impediments to work is crucial to being [thesis] an effective student. **It is better that students learn this skill early in a** [detail] **mixed-gender school.**

(trans.) (str.) Although some administrators have proposed increasing the number of single-gender high schools, this approach might lower the overall efficacy of education. In a co-ed academic environment, boys and [detail] girls learn a tremendous deal from one another. *Co-ed education builds*

detail

social skills and teaches students how to overcome distractions and focus

thesis

on work. In this way, **mixed-gender schools prepare our young people more effectively** for the future and set them up for success in a *world*

vocab. **detail**

where male-female collaboration is more essential than at any other time in history.

thesis

You will see this symbol over the bolded thesis every time it appears.

detail

You will see this symbol over specific details that have been italicized.

crit.

You will see this symbol over sentences recognizing the other side of the argument

str.

You will see this symbol over punctuation that signals advanced sentence structure.

You will see this symbol over every underlined transition.

vocab.

You will see this symbol over skillfully used, advanced vocab.

Level 10 Essay

The ACT describes an essay that receives a score of 10 as one that demonstrates "competent skill in responding to the task." A level 10 essay shows a clear understanding of the assignment, takes a clear position, and offers a broad context for discussion. Ideas are presented logically, most are elaborated upon, and the introduction and conclusion are generally well developed. Sentence structure is somewhat varied, vocabulary is competent, and errors are rarely distracting.

Do students receive a better education in a single-gender high school than they do in a traditional high school?

When it comes to education, it is entirely natural for students of both genders to learn, study and grow together. **str.** Although some administrators **crit.** have put forth the idea that single-gender learning is the sure path to **vocab.** optimal student performance and learning outcomes, co-ed learning nurtures the complete development of male and female students. **thesis** **Single-gender learning, though useful in some isolated situations, provides an** **vocab.** **inferior education when compared to mixed-gender education.**

trans. <u>Returning to an emphasis on the differences between girls and boys will</u> undo much of the progress our country has made in education. Going back in time is not the way forward. Does one gender hold the str.

other back? This is nonsense. Old stereotypes that say girls fall behind in

vocab.

math and sciences have now been shown to be obsolete. *The gender gap*

detail crit.

in math and sciences is no more. Any historic difference in performance

detail

between genders was in fact caused by *educators expecting girls and boys*

thesis

to perform differently. **Single-gender schools could therefore hurt our nation's teenagers.**

trans. thesis

One advantage offered by mixed-gender schools is that they

detail

educate boys and girls on *how to effectively interact and work with each*

detail

other. To succeed in the highly *competitive global marketplace*, individuals

vocab.

must be able to collaborate skillfully with male and female colleagues.

detail

Males and females have different styles of leading, of communicating,

thesis

and of resolving conflicts. **Spending time together in a co-ed learning environment will give students the opportunity to learn from each other** and come to understand and respect the differences that exist between them. As males and females will certainly be working together for most of their adult lives, it's important to set them up with the

vocab.

collaborative skills they will surely need.

vocab. trans. crit.

Proponents of single-gender education argue that the element of distraction is reduced when boys and girls are kept separate. Although it crit. 

is true that when you co-mingle the sexes some distractions are inevitable, these distractions never go away. If you don't learn to cope with the distraction of members of the opposite sex, *you will struggle in college and in the world of work and beyond!* Learning to overcome such impediments to work is crucial to being an effective student. **It is better that students learn this skill early in a mixed-gender school.**

Although some administrators have proposed increasing the number of single-gender high schools, this approach might negatively impact education. In a co-ed academic environment, boys and girls learn a tremendous deal from one another. *Co-ed education builds social skills and teaches students how to overcome distractions and focus on work.* **In this way, mixed-gender schools prepare our young people more effectively for the future than do single-gender schools.**

thesis

You will see this symbol over the bolded thesis every time it appears.

detail

You will see this symbol over specific details that have been italicized.

crit.

You will see this symbol over sentences recognizing the other side of the argument

You will see this symbol over punctuation that signals advanced sentence structure.

trans.

You will see this symbol over every underlined transition.

vocab.

You will see this symbol over skillfully used, advanced vocab.

Level 8 Essay

The ACT describes an essay that receives a score of 8 as one that demonstrates "adequate skill in responding to the task." A level 8 essay may not demonstrate full understanding of the topic. However, the essay takes a position, and offers some context for discussion by recognizing counterarguments. The thesis is focused, but ideas are organized predictably and transitions are simple. The introduction and conclusion are somewhat well developed. Sentence structure is slightly varied, vocabulary is adequate, and while errors may be distracting, they do not impede understanding.

Do students receive a better education in a single-gender high school than they do in a traditional high school?

Both male and female students enjoy working in a mixed environment. Some people say that separating the genders in high school would provide the best education. I disagree. **Mixed-gender schools allow** [thesis] **students to interact with each other, and this leads to a better overall education.**

[thesis]

A mixed-gender school provides a better education by creating an environment students want to be in. *Teenagers naturally want to* [detail] *interact with peers of the opposite gender.* Students who are not able to do this may become bored or frustrated, and frustration can cause you

thesis

You will see this symbol over the bolded thesis every time it appears.

detail

You will see this symbol over specific details that have been italicized.

crit.

You will see this symbol over sentences recognizing the other side of the argument

You will see this symbol over punctuation that signals advanced sentence structure.

You will see this symbol over every underlined transition.

vocab.

You will see this symbol over skillfully used, advanced vocab.

to lose focus on your studies. detail *Students get more out of their homework and lectures when they want to be there.* Forcing them to wait until after school to interact with teenagers of the opposite gender can lead them to simply watch the clock rather than actively participate in class. **As a result,** thesis **I believe that a mixed-gender school would provide a better education, because the students would be more engaged in the classroom.**

Another reason that mixed-gender schools provide a better education is they teach important social skills. detail *Students need to learn how to work with people of the opposite gender.* This will be important in both detail *college and the workplace.* If a teenage boy doesn't learn how to effectively communicate with girls, he will have trouble in job interviews, in group projects, and on dates. thesis **In a mixed-gender school, students would be able to develop this important social skill every day.** At a single-gender school, this development would be put on hold, and the students will be behind their competitors when they graduate.

str. Although some administrators have proposed increasing the number of single-gender high schools, thesis **this would lead to an overall worse education.** When boys and girls share classrooms, they can learn a vocab. tremendous deal from one another. They can learn important social skills, while developing stronger communication skills as well. This will allow them to be successful in college and in the workplace, where they will have to interact with individuals of the opposite gender. **As a result, I think mixed-gender schools provide a better education than single-gender schools.**

thesis

Level 12 Essays from Opposing Perspectives

Let's look at two essays which argue opposing sides of an argument, but manage to stay at level-12 quality by hitting the Magic 8:

1 Critical Thinking

Address the complexity of the argument. Recognize the other side!

2 Structure

Intro → Thesis → Evidence → Conclusion. Brainstorm first!

3 Focus

Don't wander off-topic. Repeat your thesis every paragraph.

4 Smooth Transitions

Connect your evidence to your thesis with smooth transitions.

5 Strong Vocabulary

Study some strong, flexible words ahead of time and work them in.

6 Varied Sentence Structure

Mix it up with commas, clauses, colons, and semis.

7 Few Distracting Errors

Too many spelling or grammar mistakes will distract the grader.

8 Length

Longer essays score higher. Keep your pencil moving!

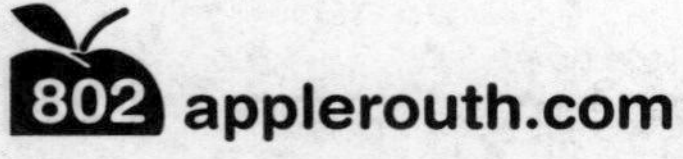

ACT Writing Test
Example Prompt

Some high schools require all students to wear a uniform when on campus. Some educators support such a policy because they think it improves the quality of education by removing distractions from the classroom, allowing students to more effectively focus on their studies. Other educators do not support such a policy because they think it overly restricts students' ability to express themselves as individuals and negatively impacts the friendly atmosphere of the campus. In your opinion, should high schools require students to wear a school uniform?

In your essay, take a position on this issue. You may write about either one of the two points of view given, or you may put forth a different point of view. Provide specific reasons and examples that support your position.

Should high schools require students to wear school uniforms?

The **affirmative** position

A growing number of high schools, both public and private, are opting to require that their students wear uniforms while on campus. Critics of this policy have decried a perceived loss of individuality and freedom of expression that comes with a uniform code. However, these criticisms undervalue the improvement to education brought by uniform policies, as well as underestimate teenagers' ability to express themselves through other means.

CHOP to it!
Cost/Benefit analysis is a great place to start any essay.

In practice, the benefits of a high school uniform policy far outweigh its costs. The predominant benefit of school uniforms is that they remove distractions from the classroom. It is true, as critics point out, that clothing can mean a great deal to many teenagers. In a world where their schedules, meals, and even afterschool activities are planned out by adults, students often latch onto fashion as a last bastion of autonomy. However, the fact that fashion is so important to students is the very reason it becomes so distracting in the classroom. To a student, a jacket isn't just a jacket: it can be a display of wealth, a brand of individuality, or even a weapon with which to compete against fellow students. This connection with the games of affection and competition that all teenagers play is the reason simply banning "inappropriate clothing" fails to keep students focused on their studies. Instituting school uniforms allows students to take a much-needed break from the politics of fashion and focus on their schoolwork.

CHOP to it!
Practicality - what would a normal day be like?

In practice, though students may initially oppose a uniform policy, they invariably come to appreciate the relief and convenience provided by uniforms. First, students no longer need to spend time in front of a mirror or closet planning out their ensemble for the day. These precious minutes are converted into extra sleep, fewer "tardies", and perhaps even a breakfast that would have otherwise gone unconsumed. As a result, students as a whole are better rested, better fed, and on time; this in turn leads to a more energetic and enjoyable classroom experience. Second, students do not need to worry throughout the day if peers are silently rejecting their chosen clothing. Studies have shown that this worry can be a very real stressor for all students, but particularly for students from lower-income families. Students who cannot afford the "cool" clothing are at an unfair disadvantage in the fashion arms race, and this can bring a very complex stress into the classroom. The removal of this stress, at least during school hours, allows all students to take sanctuary within the classroom and focus on receiving a quality education every day.

Address the other side! This shows the grader you see the complexity of the issue.

Finally, critics who say that uniforms inhibit students from expressing individuality simply do not give those students enough credit! High school students are star athletes, gifted artists, burgeoning recording artists, talented actors, political activists, young entrepreneurs, and civil servants. Students who judge peers' clothing in fact do a terrible disservice to the complex individuals beneath the clothing labels; educators serve the very same insult to teenagers when they argue that uniforms somehow stifle self-expression or impose conformity.

In conclusion, high schools would be wise to adopt a uniform policy. Opponents of such policies forget that the primary focus of educators must be the quality of education provided to their students. The stressful obsession students can have with clothing is as real as it is complicated, and it negatively affects some students far more than others. The demands of "fitting in" and "looking cool" distract students while preparing for school in the morning, while walking the halls between classes, and while sitting in class. Uniforms free students from this stressful distraction, and create a more open and energetic learning environment. Once freed, the student who raises her hand to speak is called not by label, but by name.

Should high schools require students to wear a school uniform?

The **negative** position

Although most policy makers and educators are interested in improving the quality of education in our schools, mandating student uniforms is a misguided approach, with negative consequences that far outweigh any potential benefits. Requiring conformity and repressing individual expression is a sure-fire way to stifle the creativity that may have been nurtured in our schools.

The more "sameness" we mandate in our school system, the more we diminish the potential contributions of our students. Do we need to further "process" out any more of the individuality of our students? Have we not done enough to them already by cramming them into a one-size-fits-all box? Have we forced them into a Procrustean bed and insisted that they think, talk and look like everyone else? Must we reduce them to widgets in a system that tolerates no variation? Let our students be free to be themselves!

Mix up your sentence structures! Add some variety with question marks and exclamation points.

Distractions, the critics say. If we let young people dress how they want to dress, we will be unable to handle the distractions. Well. Guess what? The world is one gigantic, enormous, cluster of distractions. We are bombarded by distracting visual and auditory stimuli from the moment we rise to the moment we lay our heads on the pillow. If you cannot filter out the distractions, you will never succeed in the modern world. Variations in clothing, in color, in texture, in fabric, in messaging: these are all fine things to be celebrated - not repressed. If students are unable to focus with a variety of fabrics or colors in their field of vision, a uniform dress code is not going to solve their problems! Variation and variety are everywhere, now more than ever.

Get in the habit of rewording your thesis every paragraph.

When we allow students to express themselves, what do we get? Students with a greater sense of individuality, and a greater understanding of their own preferences. Life is about choices. In the modern era, we must make more and more choices, more quickly, than we have ever had to make at any other time in human history. Mandating a uniform certainly eliminates the choice of what to wear in the morning, but in doing so, it deprives the individual of a chance to listen to oneself and express that self. "Today I feel like wearing black." "I'm in a colorful mood today!" "I'm going to wear my favorite shirt today!" In a land of stifling monotone uniforms, our choices are circumscribed, even negated. We cannot make decisions, as the decisions have been made for us, by adults

Do we not want to mold independent thinkers? Is this not the skill that will be most prized in the 21st century? We need to allow students to constantly think critically. There should be more choices, not fewer. What to wear is the tip of the iceberg. We need choices of what to eat, which classes to take, which books to read, and which activities to pursue. We must prepare young people for the onslaught of choices that will come their way in adulthood. Let us not create a generation of sheep who have no ability to think for themselves. Let's create a generation of adults who have a greater degree of self-awareness and the ability to express themselves.

If a student wants to dress like everyone else- that is that student's right. Let them conform. That's an option too! But it should be a choice to conform, not a command. We must encourage independent thinking and creativity at every turn and minimize forced conformity in all its incarnations. Eradicate the uniform and give our students back their freedom!

End with a BANG!

Brainstorming

It's time to practice the timeless art of brainstorming. Take a look at the essay prompts below and use CHOP to brainstorm. We'll model the first one. The next three are for you.

High school students tend to perform multiple activities while doing homework, often sitting in front of a television or computer. Teachers disagree whether multitasking is too distracting for students. Some teachers believe students should avoid multitasking while doing homework because they think the student's work quality suffers as a result of the distractions. Other teachers think multitasking is an efficient way for students to accomplish multiple goals within the limited time they have available.

In your essay, take a position on this issue. You may write about either one of the two points of view given, or you may put forth a different point of view. Provide specific reasons and examples that support your position.

The Question: *Is Multitasking bad?*

We will flesh out both sides of the argument. But remember: on the test, ***pick a side before brainstorming!***

Position One: *Multitasking is bad*

Support: *It distracts, ↓ HW quality*

Cost/Benefit:

HW takes longer, product is worse.

Helps/Hurts:

Multitasking hurts students and teachers b/c students get less out of the practice. If students don't understand material, the teacher can't cover as much in class.

Over-the-top:

More shallow understanding of the content = less learning is taking place. Grades will drop, college admissions drop, job prospects dip, economy dips.

Practicality:

If MT, students will lose track of time and not finish homework until 3 A.M.; late for school, tired, past curfew... everything falls apart.

Other Side:

It may be distracting at first, but MT is an important skill in the real world. Students need to learn to MT!

Position Two: *Multitasking is OK!*

Support: *Time is tight, MT is efficient!*

Cost/Benefit:

MT makes HW more fun and easier.

Helps/Hurts:

Can use Facebook or computer to get information to help with HW. Being social and getting HW done. Win-Win!

Over-the-top:

If you don't MT, you don't finish HW. Inevitably drop the ball and get stressed. You may become a workaholic machine who never enjoys life.

Practicality:

Work/life balance is very important. MT is the only way to accomplish both social needs and work needs.

Other Side:

Students' lives are busy, but if their grades drop, they'll have even less time for leisure/social activities.

Some school administrators disagree over whether teachers should be allowed to communicate their own social and political views to their students. Some administrators encourage teachers to express their own political and social views in class because they think it sparks conversation and gets students more engaged in critical thinking. Other administrators feel that teachers should withhold their personal views in class because they think it creates an atmosphere in which students who disagree with the teacher's views may be hesitant to participate.

In your opinion, should school administrators allow teachers to communicate their personal views regarding political or social issues to students in the classroom?

The Question: ______

My Position: ______

Cost/Benefit: ______

Helps/Hurts: ______

Over-the-top: ______

Practicality: ______

Other Side: ______

High school administrators and counselors have debated whether teenagers should be encouraged to take a "gap year" before attending college. Supporters of the gap year argue that students who spend a year in the workforce, volunteering, or doing a year of educational enrichment will enter college with a more mature perspective, better prepared to handle the demands and opportunities of college. Others feel that students who step away from the path of education may be less likely to return. They encourage students to continue directly to college once they have attained their high school diploma.

In your opinion, should students be encouraged to take a gap year before attending college?

The Question: ______________________________

____

My Position: ______________________________

____

Cost/Benefit: ______________________________

____

____

Helps/Hurts: ______________________________

____

____

Over-the-top: ______________________________

____

____

Practicality: ______________________________

____

____

Other Side: ______________________________

____

In most states, the minimum age at which a teenager can get a driver's license is sixteen. In response to studies that show that drivers between the ages of sixteen and eighteen are more likely to be involved in traffic accidents than drivers of any other age group, many legislators have promoted increasing the minimum driving age to eighteen. Some legislators support this proposal because they think it will increase safety for both teenagers and older drivers and passengers. Other legislators oppose this proposal because they think it unfairly burdens families that rely upon their teenagers' driving to work or transporting younger siblings to and from school.

In your opinion, should states change the minimum driving age from sixteen to eighteen years of age?

The Question: ______________________________

____

My Position: ______________________________

____

Cost/Benefit: ______________________________

____

____

Helps/Hurts: ______________________________

____

____

Over-the-top: ______________________________

____

____

Practicality: ______________________________

____

____

Other Side: ______________________________

____

Essay Practice

Now that you have learned how to write high-scoring essays, it is time to practice. Remember to write a strong thesis, provide specific examples to support your thesis, address both sides of the argument and include a good conclusion, varied sentence structure, advanced vocabulary and transitions.

> Current GPS technology allows parents to continuously track the whereabouts of high school students' cell-phones. Parents who employ such technology can know exactly where their children are at all times, day and night. Some parents are in favor of using this technology to monitor their children's whereabouts, because they believe the knowledge that they are being "watched" will encourage children to avoid trouble. Other parents are opposed to using this kind of technology because they feel it tells their children they are not trustworthy and also infringes upon basic rights to privacy. In your opinion, should parents use cell phone technology to monitor their children's whereabouts?
>
> In your essay, take a position on this issue. You may write about either one of the two points of view given, or you may put forth a different point of view. Provide specific reasons and examples that support your position.

You have 30 minutes to write an essay, using the space provided in the following pages.

Write your essay in the space provided below.

Essay Mantras

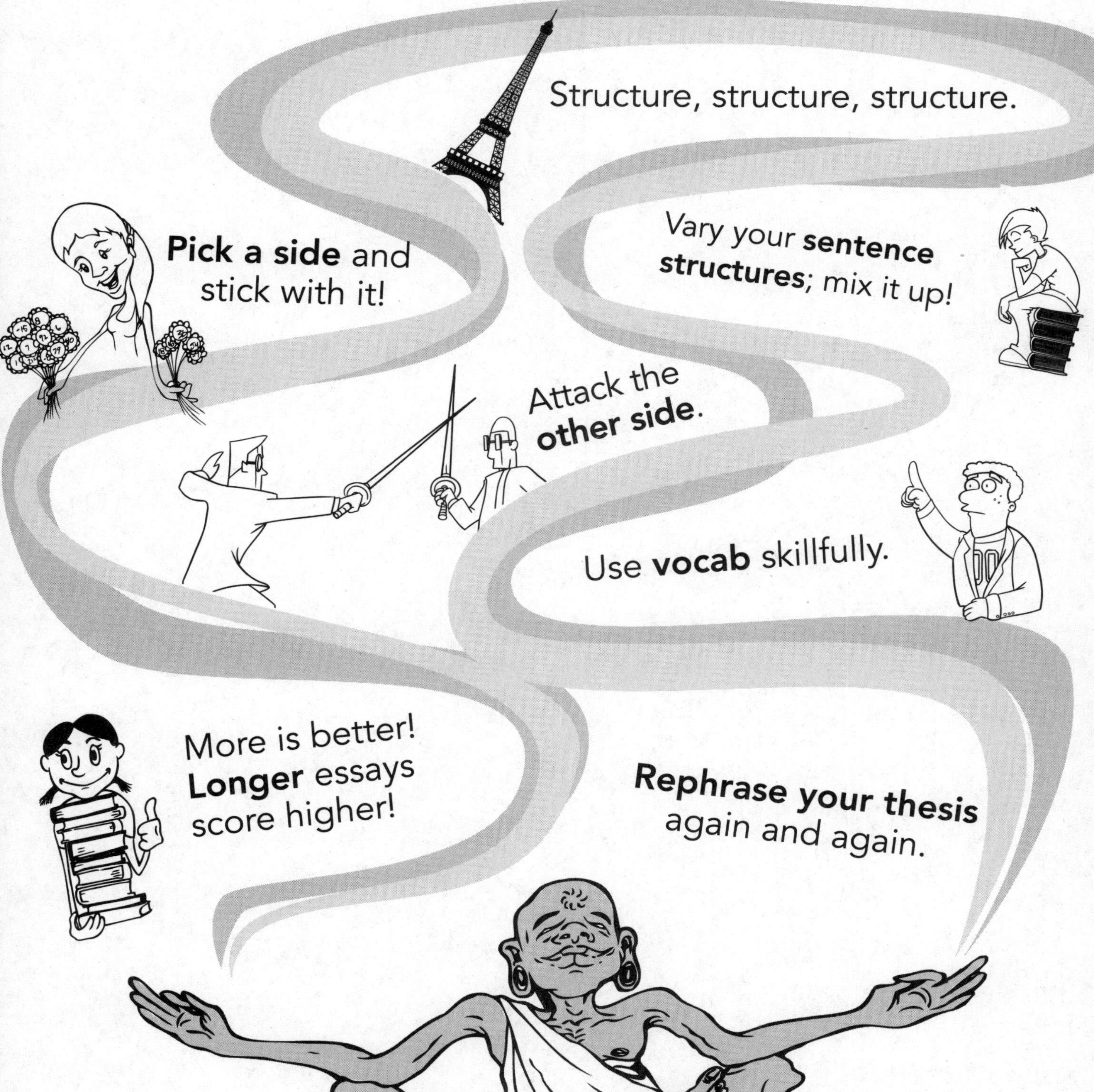

Structure, structure, structure.
Pick a side and stick with it!
Vary your **sentence structures**; mix it up!
Attack the **other side**.
Use **vocab** skillfully.
More is better! **Longer** essays score higher!
Rephrase your thesis again and again.

Beyond the Content

Beyond the Content
The Mental Component of the ACT

To fully prepare for the ACT, you need to accomplish **three goals**:

1. Understand the **structure and format** of the ACT
2. Master the **content** assessed on all sections of the test
3. Master the **test-taking skills** needed to thrive in a 4-hour, pressured testing environment

The final component is generally the most neglected aspect of test preparation, and for many students, it is the most important.

Are you a good test-taker or a bad test-taker?

Whether you believe that you are a good test-taker or a bad test-taker, that belief will impact your score on the ACT. In fact, your self-appraisal of your ability is a better predictor of how you will do on the ACT than your **actual** level of ability!

It doesn't matter how good you are in reality; if you repeatedly tell yourself that you are not going to do well on this test, you can override your actual abilities and sabotage your performance. And conversely, **if you believe you will succeed on the ACT, this belief will improve your performance!** Thoughts are powerful things!

Natural Test Takers

Some of you may fall under the category of natural test takers. You don't mind standardized tests. You actually kind of like them and have found a way to **treat them like a game**. You set challenging goals for yourself and work hard to achieve them. And more than likely, you are actively engaging in a lot of behaviors, both consciously and subconsciously, which are helping you to succeed!

Everybody Else

The majority of people have a different relationship with standardized tests than do the natural test takers. Most students don't love the ACT, though they eventually learn how to work with it and succeed on it. Some students get nervous or a little stressed when they have to sit for an ACT. Other students feel **eternally cursed** when it comes to the ACT or any standardized test. They believe that no matter how much they prepare, they will never do well.

Does bad testing karma really exist? Is there no hope for these students?

Negative Beliefs about Testing

If you feel karmically challenged by the ACT, it's important that you examine the origins of your negative beliefs. When did you start to believe that you were "bad at testing"?

> Are you focusing on a few isolated instances of poor performance and **ignoring instances of strong performance?**
>
> Are you really **always** bad at testing in **every** possible context?
>
> Have you ever had a **single** instance where you did well on a test?

If you can locate a **single** success in your testing past, you can work with it and begin to build from it.

Watch your words: your mind is listening

When it comes to making global statements about your testing abilities, be careful not to sell yourself short. Rather than saying, "I am miserable at testing," shift and rephrase the statement. "I used to struggle with testing, but now I'm open to the **possibility** of doing better." Your mind likes to be consistent, and it tends to back up your words with actions.

Optimists score higher.

Don't close the door on what's possible.

Dealing with Test Anxiety

If you are like most students, you will experience some degree of anxiety around the ACT; this is only natural. For some students, however, this anxiety can stand in the way of improving their ACT score.

Test anxiety stems from a potentially useful thought: "Hey, this test counts. I need to do well." When this thought becomes invested with too much energy, however, it starts to hurt your score.

Fight or Flight

When you are stressed about an upcoming test, your body reacts in the same way it would to an actual physical threat. The thoughts,**"Ahh! A test!"** and **"Ahh! A lion!"** cause the **same** chemicals to surge through your system.

When those stress hormones hit your bloodstream, your muscles begin to tense, your heart rate and respiratory rate change, and your breathing may become increasingly shallow. With less oxygen going to your brain, **you start to lose focus**. Distracted, you no longer think or process information as clearly, and your working memory becomes impaired.

This increases your chances of escaping a lion... but lowers your chances of acing the ACT!

Helpful Anxiety

A **low** level of anxiety is actually **useful** because it drives you to prepare for and stay focused during the ACT. There is a tipping point where things shift from good to bad.

There's a simple graph that illustrates the continuum of anxiety and its impact on performance. As this graph illustrates, some anxiety is good; too much is harmful. We want to reach the optimal point so we have just the right amount of anxiety.

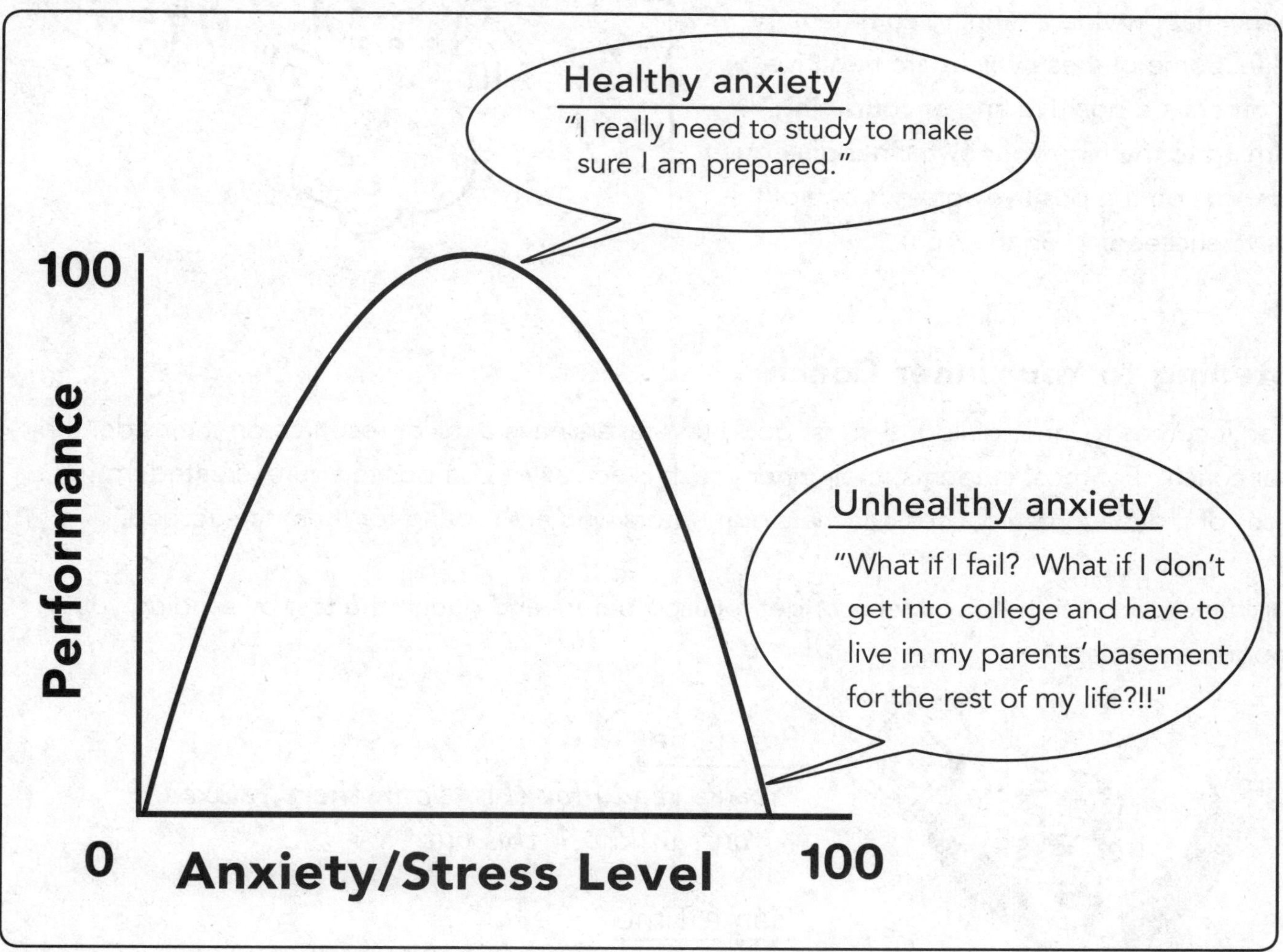

Some stress is helpful.
Too much is harmful.

Mentally Addressing Anxiety

So what can you do about anxiety? There are several strategies to address heightened anxiety.

Inner Dialogue

We each have a number of voices inside of our heads (some of us have more voices than others) that provide a running commentary on life. Some of these voices are negative, but others are **positive** and **encouraging**. Learning to manage your own inner-dialogue and focus on the positive voices is one of the keys to succeeding on the ACT.

Listening to Your Inner Coach

When it comes to inner dialogue, most good test-takers have a major resource on their side: their inner coach. For most students, their inner coach is actually a composite figure, created from pieces of their favorite coaches, teachers or mentors who are rooting for them to succeed.

Your inner coach can help you relax or get focused before and during the test by sending you supportive messages.

Pre-game

"You're ready for this. Go in there relaxed. You can knock this out."

Game Time

"You're doing great." "It's only one question, don't worry about it. Let it go." "Relax...you can do this." "Pace yourself: just two more sections left!"

It's not difficult to imagine how receiving these kinds of positive messages could help you remain focused and centered during the ACT.

Your Inner Anxiety Monster

For other students who have not yet tapped into their inner coach, another creature may appear instead: the anxiety monster. The monster feeds on fear and is continually scanning the environment for potential catastrophes. He frequently appears behind statements such as these:

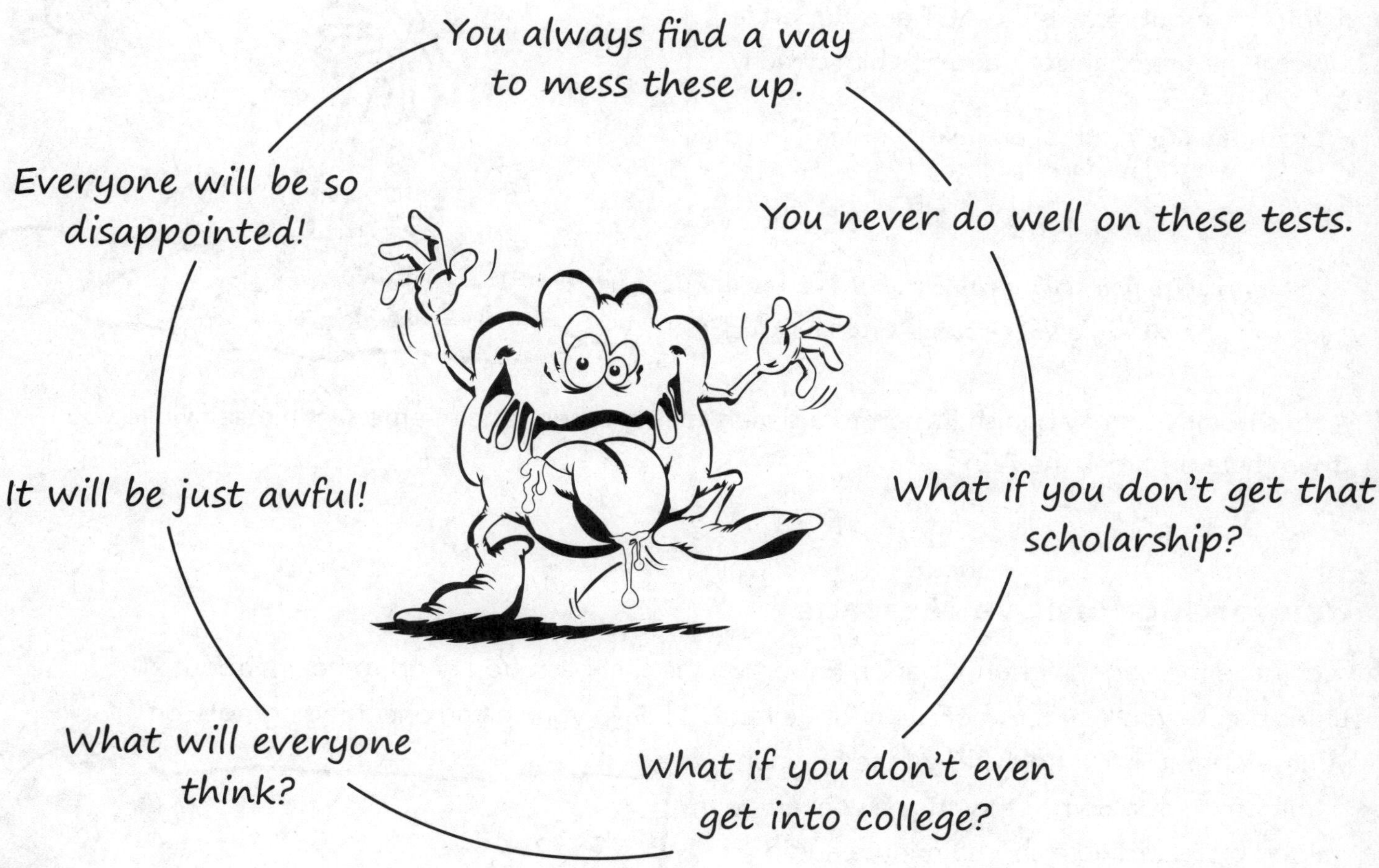
You always find a way to mess these up.
You never do well on these tests.
What if you don't get that scholarship?
What if you don't even get into college?
What will everyone think?
It will be just awful!
Everyone will be so disappointed!

Do not let the monster run rampant in your inner dialogue!

If you don't deal with the monster directly and confront these negative statements, you run the risk of being influenced by them. If you allow yourself to focus your energy on thoughts of failure, your mind may subconsciously begin to turn these thoughts into reality.

Naming and Taming the Monster

If you can give your monster a name, you can deal with him more easily and address him directly. Though you will know the right name for your monster, for now, we'll call him Rupert. It's important to remember that Rupert actually works for you (though he's not the world's best employee), and he is taking up space in your head. If you stop feeding Rupert energy and attention, he will cease to exist.

If you are about to take the ACT and Rupert is stoking the fire of anxiety, address him directly.

*"Listen, buddy. I've had enough. I'm ready for this test. I'm **done** listening to you."*

or

"I appreciate you trying to help, but I've really got this one on my own. Goodbye and good luck."

At this point you may banish Rupert to a deserted island and let him entertain himself while you go in there and rock the ACT.

Reinforcing Positive Messages

A positive message might not banish Rupert on the first pass. You need to hear it about 20 times before you'll start to believe it. So reinforce! Leave yourself an encouraging note on your refrigerator. Put up a sticky note on your bathroom mirror. Some students have even been helped by recording a short 5 minute audio track on their voicemail, iPod, or smart phone reminding themselves to stay positive.

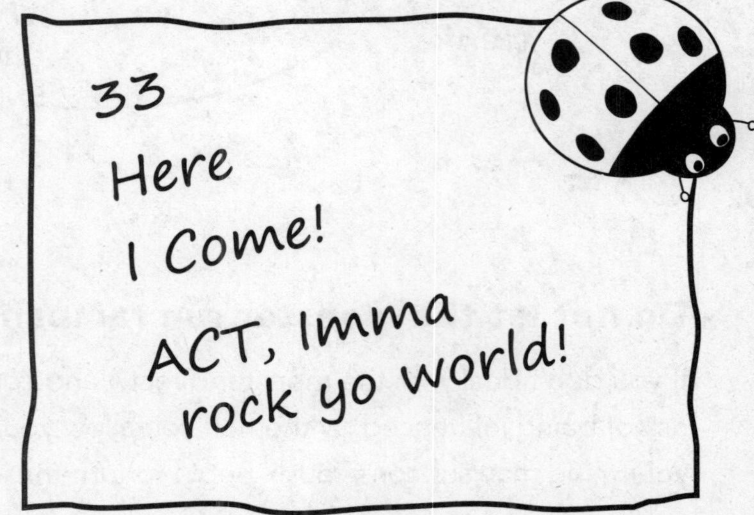

33
Here
I Come!
ACT, Imma
rock yo world!

"You're ready for this. You've worked hard. You are going to rock this."

Mix this message in with your favorite songs and positively rock out on the way to the test. In the right frame of mind, you'll get your best score.

Physically Addressing Anxiety

Just as you can address anxiety by shifting your thoughts and your inner dialogue, you can also address anxiety by making subtle physical adjustments. Below are a few simple physical exercises you can do to regulate anxiety.

Focus on your breath

The quickest way to shift from anxiety to relaxation is through breathing. It is physically impossible to breathe in a deep and relaxed manner and simultaneously feel intense anxiety.

Take deep breaths

Deep breaths come from your diaphragm, not your chest. When you breathe deeply, your stomach should go out (think of the Buddha). If your shoulders rise while you are inhaling, you are breathing from your chest rather than your diaphragm. **Think Buddha.**

Slow things down

Count to 3 during the inhalation, pause at the peak of the breath and then count to 3 during the exhalation: this will begin to automatically relax your entire body.

Practice breathing while counting backwards

Count backwards from 10 to 1, silently in your head, breathing slowly and deeply from your diaphragm with each count. 10....9....8....7.... With each breath, imagine yourself becoming more and more relaxed.

Sigh deeply or make yourself yawn

Yawning is like pressing a reset button in your brain. Yawing has many beneficial effects and can actually help you increase your level of focus and energy.

Use a physical trigger to relax

You can use a physical cue or trigger to bring yourself to a more relaxed state. Create a link between a simple movement and a state of relaxation. Make the movement— start to relax!

1 Choose a cue

Find one that works for you or simply make up your own. Here are a few examples:

- squeezing three fingers together three times
- tapping your knee slowly three times
- putting one hand on top of the other

2 Get relaxed

- Close your eyes
- Take 3 deep breaths
- Feel your body become more relaxed
- Tense your muscles, hold for a full breath, and then release
- Take 3 more deep breaths using the 3 count: Breathe In. Hold. Breathe Out.

3 Link 'em up

Perform your chosen trigger in this relaxed state, and create a mental association between the physical motion and a state of deep relaxation. You will need to do this a few times to create a stronger association.

4 Cue the relaxation during the test

During the test, whenever you feel anxiety coming on, perform your cue to activate your relaxed state. Take several deep breaths, and begin to relax.

Dealing with Anxiety on Test Day

When the Test Begins

Some students become nervous the moment the test begins. They hear the proctor say, "You have 35 minutes... open your test booklet and begin." They hear the sound of turning pages fill the room, and they start to sweat.

When the proctor says "begin," **pause** and **take a moment for yourself**. Once you're centered and calm, turn the page and begin.

At the Five-Minute Warning

Some students lose their cool at the 5-minute warning. They panic and start to rush, even when they are on track to finish in time. In their rush, they are frequently more careless.

When you hear the 5-minute warning, **pause** and **take a moment for yourself**. Once you're centered and calm, make any necessary adjustments, prioritize the remaining questions, and get back to the test.

When You Miss a Problem

Some students start to feel stressed when they just **know** they missed that last problem. They worry so much about that missed point that they have trouble concentrating on the next several questions. They get hung up on one little point, and make that missed question a big deal...

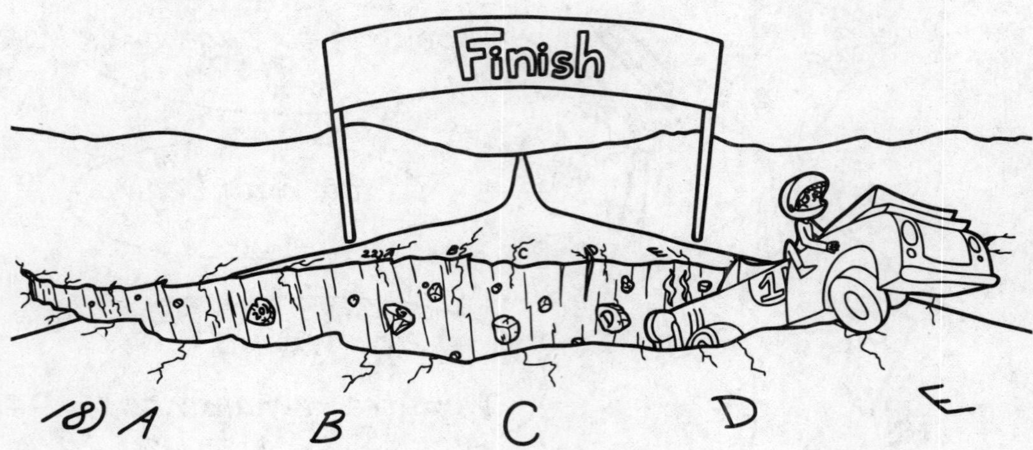

...but it's not! You don't need to get every single question right to get a great score! A missed problem is just a **speedbump** on the way to your best score yet. Remember this if you start to feel worried after a tough problem.

Keep your cool, keep perspective, and keep your eyes on the finish line!

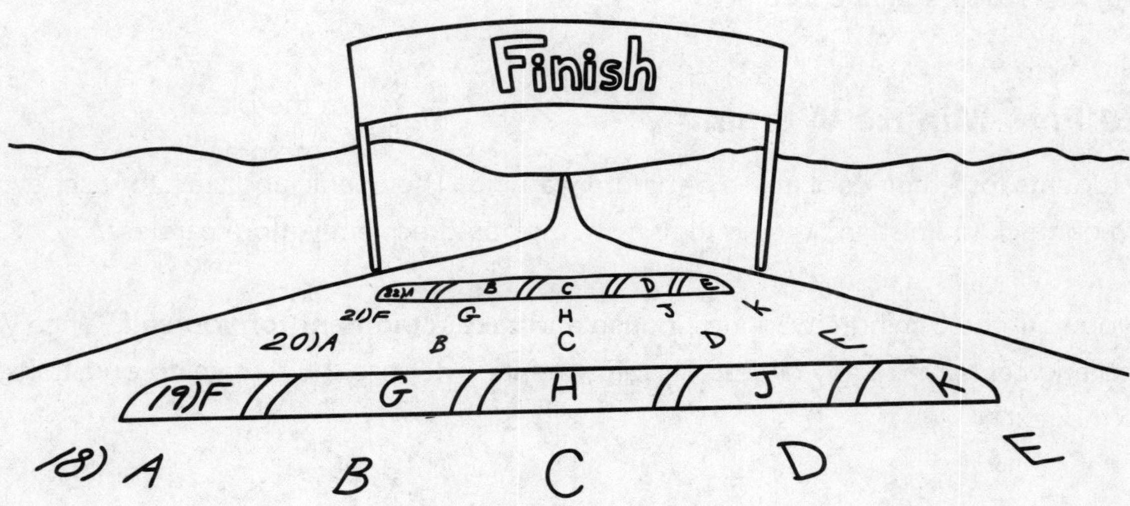

Creative Visualization
Accessing the Power of Your Imagination

Your imagination can be your greatest ally or your greatest obstacle when you are confronted with a high-stakes test such as the ACT. If you are not actively engaging your imagination, you are missing out on a tremendous opportunity.

You can passively allow your imagination to stir up anxiety-inducing scenarios, or you can actively harness the power of your imagination to help you achieve your ACT goals.

Mental Rehearsal

If you want to learn about the power of imagination, you need look no further than to the world's greatest athletes. These individuals must face high stress situations again and again, and to prepare themselves, they tap into the power of **creative visualization**. Just ask Michael Jordan, Michael Phelps, Maria Sharapova, or Tiger Woods. These and many other of the world's greatest athletes practice and rehearse mentally, visualizing their desired outcomes long before they walk onto their respective fields of play.

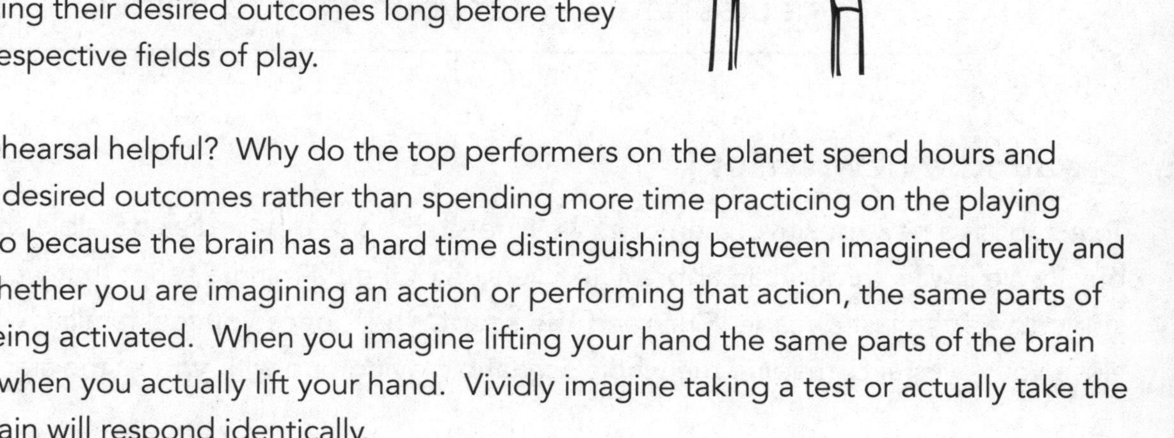

Why is mental rehearsal helpful? Why do the top performers on the planet spend hours and hours imagining desired outcomes rather than spending more time practicing on the playing field? They do so because the brain has a hard time distinguishing between imagined reality and actual reality. Whether you are imagining an action or performing that action, the same parts of your brain are being activated. When you imagine lifting your hand the same parts of the brain are triggered as when you actually lift your hand. Vividly imagine taking a test or actually take the test, and your brain will respond identically.

Rewiring your brain

If you can vividly imagine an event, engage your senses and emotions, and reinforce it through repetition, your brain will begin to treat the event like it is **real** rather than imagined.

THIS IS HUGE!

When you walk into a testing situation, your brain will scan the environment to relate the current situation to past experiences and determine how to respond. If your memory of testing is marked predominantly by anxiety and disappointment, walking into the test room will cause anxiety, again reinforcing this negative cycle!

But with guided imagery and visualization, you can **break that cycle!** You actually have the power to create a new "script" for your brain to follow when you confront new testing situations. Even if you have no positive memories of past testing events, by simply **imagining a positive testing experience** you can override those bad memories.

In effect, you are **rewiring your brain** by creating a new neural pathway for your brain to follow!

Creating a new script

To establish a new, positive"memory," we'll need to be as detailed as possible so your brain will buy it. We'll walk through an abbreviated version of the 20-minute script that we have used with students for the last decade. First **read the script**. Then, once you feel familiar with the content, close your eyes and imagine the whole scenario playing out, with **you** as the star.

Imagine yourself waking up the morning of the ACT. You turn off your alarm and get out of bed. You do your morning routine—breakfast, shower, brush teeth. (Imagine all the specific details of your personal routine in the order you would do them.) You begin to feel more and more awake and alert.

You feel good, relaxed and ready for the task ahead of you. You grab your backpack with your admission ticket, ID, pencils, calculator, water and snacks. As you drive to the test center, you begin to mentally prepare yourself. "I'm ready for this test; I'm going to go in there and knock this out." (Use whatever message feels right for you, in language you would use.) You arrive at the test center.

Before you open the car door, you pause for a moment and take a deep breath as you look in the rearview mirror: "I've worked hard, and I'm ready for this," you tell yourself. And you believe it. You walk into the school and get in the registration line. You show your ID and admission ticket and make your way to your testing room. You see the people in the room. Some are fidgety; others are relaxed; some are totally zoned out. Hear the sound of people rustling around in their seats.

Now find your seat. After you put away your things and get settled in, visualize yourself feeling ready, and relaxed. The proctor asks you to clear your desk and begins to pass out materials. See yourself bubbling-in all the preliminary info: name, date of birth, testing site, etc. Imagine the feel of the pencil in your hand, the motion of marking the bubbles on the Scantron sheet.

The proctor announces the beginning of the first section. "Open your test booklets to Page 1. You have 45 minutes to complete the English section. Begin." Everyone else in the room quickly opens their booklets to begin. You pause for a moment. You take a deep breath. You are feeling ready, so you pick up your pencil and turn to the first page of the test.

You move through the English section, remembering the rules you have practiced so many times before. You use your ear to find commas, you check verb tenses, and you order sentences like a champ. The proctor calls time. Pencils down. You feel confident that you did well on this first section. "Now we are going to open our test booklets to section 2. You will have 60 minutes to complete the Math section. You cannot turn to any other section of the test. You may begin."

You turn the page and approach the first problem. It's easy, as you knew it would be. You've practiced this so many times before and you know what to do. You feel relaxed. You choose your answer and move on to the next one. One by one, you work your way through all the problems on the first section. You arrive at the harder problems; you solve them when you can, and guess and move on if they're too tough. You feel confident and know that you are tracking for your best score ever on this test.

Imagine your ten minute break. You walk outside, feeling good. You're over halfway to the finish line. Just 35 minutes for Reading, and then another 35 for Science. You eat your snack, recenter yourself, and head back in for the last two sections.

You move through the last two sections confidently, watching the clock and skillfully managing the amount of time you spend on each question. You are feeling good and know this is the best test you've ever taken.

Now take a few moments and visualize the score you want to achieve on the ACT. Imagine the number very clearly and hold it in your head. Now move forward in time. Imagine yourself going online or going to the mailbox to find the letter that contains your official score. See your score report, and visualize the goal you set for yourself directly next to your name. Really see it. You've accomplished your goal. All your hard work paid off! Feel the emotions that come with that. It's party time.

Once you have created this vision and filled it with details that work for you, repeat it every few days. Students who have used this technique and tapped into the power of their imaginations have made massive score gains on the ACT! Try this out for yourself and see how it works for you.

Practical Tips
Final Preparation for the ACT

The Final Week Before the ACT

In the last week before the ACT, continue to review your materials. Take a practice test to work on your timing. You cannot cram for the ACT, but you want to keep the momentum going in the final days leading up to the test.

Two Days Before the ACT

The Thursday night before the ACT is a very important night. A good night's sleep **Thursday** will have an enormous impact on your level of energy and ability to focus on **Saturday**. The effects of a poor night's sleep generally hit you the hardest **two days later**. So get to bed early Thursday and give yourself a full 7 to 8 hours of sleep.

The Day Before the ACT

- Light review: walk through a practice test you've completed and go over your notes.
- Mentally walk through the ACT. Rehearse every step of the process and reinforce what you want to happen in the morning.
- Keep your thoughts positive. You're ready. You've worked hard. Tomorrow you are going to do your absolute best.
- Be sure you get 7-8 hours of sleep.
- Set your alarm clock! Use the alarm on your cell phone as a backup.

The Day Before the ACT (continued)

- Pack the following materials in a bag that you can grab in the morning before you go to the test:
    - Your ACT Admission **Ticket**
    - An acceptable (not expired!) **photo ID**
    - Printed directions to the test center
    - 3-4 sharpened No. 2 **pencils** (pens and mechanical pencils are not allowed)

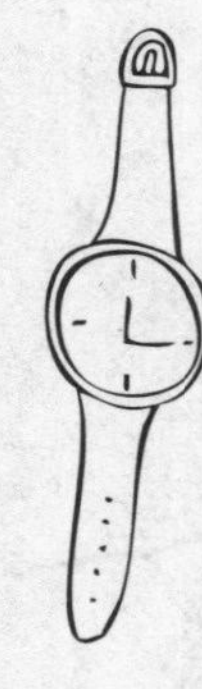

    - A graphing **calculator** with **fresh batteries** (make sure you check, and bring spare batteries if you have them)
    - A **watch** to keep track of time. In some testing centers, the clock will be behind you, or the room will not have a clock. Your proctor may or may not give you 5-minute warnings.
    - Bottle of **water**
    - **Snacks**: fruit and snack bars are great for the short breaks

The Morning of the Test

- Wake up early
- Eat a healthy **breakfast**
- Dress in comfortable clothes and in layers
  Test rooms may be cold or hot; layers give you options.
- **Leave early** for the testing site. Give yourself plenty of time for traffic or other potential delays, especially if you've never been to the testing location before.

Before the Test, Prime your Brain for Success

You really do have a 1-track mind. The 24 hours before your test, **saturate** your brain with thoughts and images of success. Get that mental pathway "primed," or turned on.

Think about Einstein. Think about smart people. Research shows that if you think about great problem solvers and people you admire, you awaken potentials within yourself. By **thinking** about Einstein before the test, you **act** more like Einstein when it counts!

During the Test Administration

- Don't be thrown off by the energy of others. Stay in your zone. You've worked hard; you're prepared. Stay focused on your optimal performance.
- Bubble-in your Scantron sheet carefully. Some students transfer answers one test-page at a time rather than question-by-question. This can save a few minutes, eliminating much of the time spent going back and forth between the test booklet and the answer sheet.
- Pace yourself. Use your watch to regulate your timing.
- Use your break. Drink some water and eat a snack. You will need fluids and some extra fuel to keep you going between 8:00 am and 12:00 pm. Take this time to refocus: "You're doing great...only two more sections left."
- Be your own cheerleader. Be your own coach. Use self-talk to keep yourself engaged and focused. It's a long test. It helps to have some encouragement.

After the Test

Congratulations! Now go out and play! You deserve it!

General Test-taking Mantras

Write **EVERYTHING** down

Stay POSITIVE and **focus on success**

Think for yourself before looking at the answer choices

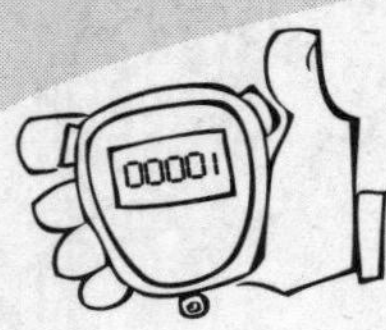

The **clock is your ally**: use the clock to pace yourself

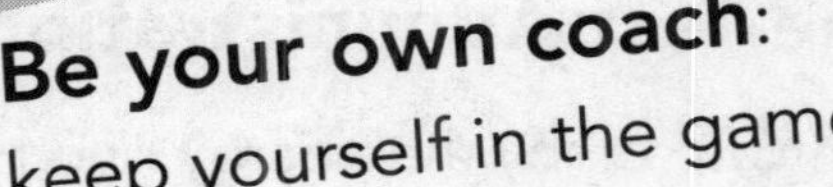

Be your own coach: keep yourself in the game

A **point is a point**: don't get stuck on any one problem

Take deep breaths when you need to **recenter yourself**

Section 1

1 A B C D	20 F G H J	39 A B C D	58 F G H J
2 F G H J	21 A B C D	40 F G H J	59 A B C D
3 A B C D	22 F G H J	41 A B C D	60 F G H J
4 F G H J	23 A B C D	42 F G H J	61 A B C D
5 A B C D	24 F G H J	43 A B C D	62 F G H J
6 F G H J	25 A B C D	44 F G H J	63 A B C D
7 A B C D	26 F G H J	45 A B C D	64 F G H J
8 F G H J	27 A B C D	46 F G H J	65 A B C D
9 A B C D	28 F G H J	47 A B C D	66 F G H J
10 F G H J	29 A B C D	48 F G H J	67 A B C D
11 A B C D	30 F G H J	49 A B C D	68 F G H J
12 F G H J	31 A B C D	50 F G H J	69 A B C D
13 A B C D	32 F G H J	51 A B C D	70 F G H J
14 F G H J	33 A B C D	52 F G H J	71 A B C D
15 A B C D	34 F G H J	53 A B C D	72 F G H J
16 F G H J	35 A B C D	54 F G H J	73 A B C D
17 A B C D	36 F G H J	55 A B C D	74 F G H J
18 F G H J	37 A B C D	56 F G H J	75 A B C D
19 A B C D	38 F G H J	57 A B C D	

Section 2

1 A B C D E	16 F G H J K	31 A B C D E	46 F G H J K
2 F G H J K	17 A B C D E	32 F G H J K	47 A B C D E
3 A B C D E	18 F G H J K	33 A B C D E	48 F G H J K
4 F G H J K	19 A B C D E	34 F G H J K	49 A B C D E
5 A B C D E	20 F G H J K	35 A B C D E	50 F G H J K
6 F G H J K	21 A B C D E	36 F G H J K	51 A B C D E
7 A B C D E	22 F G H J K	37 A B C D E	52 F G H J K
8 F G H J K	23 A B C D E	38 F G H J K	53 A B C D E
9 A B C D E	24 F G H J K	39 A B C D E	54 F G H J K
10 F G H J K	25 A B C D E	40 F G H J K	55 A B C D E
11 A B C D E	26 F G H J K	41 A B C D E	56 F G H J K
12 F G H J K	27 A B C D E	42 F G H J K	57 A B C D E
13 A B C D E	28 F G H J K	43 A B C D E	58 F G H J K
14 F G H J K	29 A B C D E	44 F G H J K	59 A B C D E
15 A B C D E	30 F G H J K	45 A B C D E	60 F G H J K

Section 3

1 A B C D	11 A B C D	21 A B C D	31 A B C D
2 F G H J	12 F G H J	22 F G H J	32 F G H J
3 A B C D	13 A B C D	23 A B C D	33 A B C D
4 F G H J	14 F G H J	24 F G H J	34 F G H J
5 A B C D	15 A B C D	25 A B C D	35 A B C D
6 F G H J	16 F G H J	26 F G H J	36 F G H J
7 A B C D	17 A B C D	27 A B C D	37 A B C D
8 F G H J	18 F G H J	28 F G H J	38 F G H J
9 A B C D	19 A B C D	29 A B C D	39 A B C D
10 F G H J	20 F G H J	30 F G H J	40 F G H J

Section 4

1 A B C D	11 A B C D	21 A B C D	31 A B C D
2 F G H J	12 F G H J	22 F G H J	32 F G H J
3 A B C D	13 A B C D	23 A B C D	33 A B C D
4 F G H J	14 F G H J	24 F G H J	34 F G H J
5 A B C D	15 A B C D	25 A B C D	35 A B C D
6 F G H J	16 F G H J	26 F G H J	36 F G H J
7 A B C D	17 A B C D	27 A B C D	37 A B C D
8 F G H J	18 F G H J	28 F G H J	38 F G H J
9 A B C D	19 A B C D	29 A B C D	39 A B C D
10 F G H J	20 F G H J	30 F G H J	40 F G H J

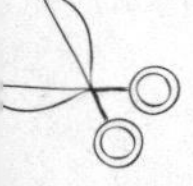

Practice Test 1

There is nothing like good old-fashioned, timed practice to help you get ready for the official ACT.

The two practice tests in this book will allow you to practice your pacing, flex your new skills, and get more comfortable taking a complete ACT. These practice tests simulate the difficulty, language, and timing of the official test. Your raw scores (the number you answered correctly) will help you calibrate how well you have mastered the content in this book.

When you are ready for a highly accurate prediction of your ACT score, your best bet is to take a recently released, nationally standardized, official ACT test. We strongly recommend taking test 4 or 5, the most recently released tests, from *The Real ACT Prep Guide, by ACT, Inc.*

Test Breakdown

Section 1 - English ....75 questions, 45 minutes

Section 2 - Math..................60 questions, 60 minutes

Section 3 - Reading.............40 questions, 35 minutes

Section 4 - Science..............40 questions, 35 minutes

Total Time.................................... 2 hours 50 minutes

To fully mimic the pace of test day, take a **10 minute break** after the Math section. Once you're ready to start your practice test, turn the page and begin!

ENGLISH TEST

45 Minutes—75 Questions

DIRECTIONS: In the five passages that follow, certain words and phrases are underlined and numbered. In the right-hand column, you will find alternatives for the underlined part. In most cases, you are to choose the one that best expresses the idea, makes the statement appropriate for standard written English, or is worded most consistently with the style and tone of the passage as a whole. If you think the original version is best, choose "NO CHANGE." In some cases you will find in the right-hand column a question about the underlined part. You are to choose the best answer to the question.

You will also find questions about a section of the passage, or about the passage as a whole. These questions do not refer to an underlined portion of the passage, but rather are identified by a number or numbers in a box.

For each question, choose the alternative you consider best and fill in the corresponding oval on your answer document. For many of the questions, you must read several sentences beyond the question to determine the answer. Be sure that you have read far enough ahead each time you choose an alternative.

PASSAGE I

Alternate Histories, Parallel Worlds

Joanna Russ was an American author and feminist, whose writings received some of the highest awards in the field. Upon her passing in 2011. Having [1] won the hearts and minds of countless readers, Russ was deeply mourned by the science fiction community she helped shape. But she was not always regarded with such high acclaim.

Raised [2] in New York City in the thirties and forties, Russ grew up in a time when being a female writer was still quite unusual. Despite this obstacle, she pursued her passion with both imagination and determination. As a child and teenager, many notebooks had been filled [3] with handwritten stories and poems. Later, she studied at Cornell University, where she learned from the famous Russian novelist Vladimir Nabokov. She went on to earn an MFA in drama from Yale. In her studies, both personal and academic, she never ceased to maintain a connection to her humble beginnings. [4]

[1] It was not until the late 1960s that her writing attracted notice from the public. [2] In science fiction, her

1. A. NO CHANGE
   B. 2011, having
   C. 2011. She
   D. 2011; having

2. F. NO CHANGE
   G. Her family raising her
   H. Being raised
   J. Having been raised

3. A. NO CHANGE
   B. she filled many notebooks
   C. she fills many notebooks
   D. many notebooks are filled

4. Given that all the choices are true, which one best summarizes this paragraph's description of how Russ "pursued her passion with both imagination and determination"?
   F. NO CHANGE
   G. encounter innumerable barriers to success in science fiction.
   H. explore new creative paths and persist through challenges.
   J. surprise her many acquaintances.

chosen field, most authors and fans were men which were the majority. [3] Additionally, she was an academic and an intellectual; her sharp observations and critical studies inspired a style of fiction that was more serious than her rivals. [4] She often focused on the controversial issue of a woman's right for expressing herself through science fiction. [5] In her 1983 book *How to Suppress Women's Writing,* Russ addresses the controversy head on. [6] Masquerading as a guidebook, the book sarcastically explains how to keep women from publishing creative work, or receiving credit while they had. [7] This attention was not immediately positive, however, since Russ was at first seen as a sort of outcast. [9]

Though her career was always an uphill battle, Russ' talent was inarguable. [A] In time, she earned critical admiration for her many inventive work's; her novel *The Female Man,* which explores different ways that women define their identities in parallel worlds, and her dystopian work, *And Chaos Died,* which examines the suppression of human creativity in a bleak future, were both nominated for a Nebula Award. [12] [B] Initially, her stories were received with negativity and criticism, and regarded as works of propaganda.

5. A. NO CHANGE
   B. men, who were the majority.
   C. men, which were the majority.
   D. men.

6. F. NO CHANGE
   G. when compared to
   H. than that of
   J. in comparison with

7. A. NO CHANGE
   B. expressing
   C. to express
   D. of expressing

8. F. NO CHANGE
   G. if they had
   H. when they do
   J. because they did

9. For the sake of the logic and coherence of this paragraph, Sentence 7 should be placed:
   A. where it is now.
   B. between Sentences 1 and 2.
   C. between Sentences 2 and 3.
   D. between Sentences 3 and 4.

10. F. NO CHANGE
    G. work
    H. works'
    J. works

11. A. NO CHANGE
    B. ways and
    C. way if
    D. ways of

12. Which of the following true statements, if added here, would best develop the point being made in the preceding sentence?
    F. At the time, feminist ideas were still met with hostility within the field.
    G. Russ' sarcasm and sharp wit won her many fans.
    H. In 1983, Russ' novella "Souls" earned her the prestigious Hugo Award.
    J. Despite her talent, Russ had to struggle to make her voice heard.

[C] Yet, as people grew more receptive to feminist thought, and as younger women began entering the field of science fiction, her works came to be praised for their positive influence and are now hailed as classics. [D] Though Russ' climb to prominence was not easy, critics and fans alike will continue to totally be into her work for generations to come. [15]

13. A. NO CHANGE.
B. Therefore
C. Because
D. Comparatively

14. F. NO CHANGE
G. continue to manifest their appreciation for
H. continue to appreciate
J. still study the feminist underpinnings explored in *The Female Man,* using the idea of parallel worlds in

15. The writer wants to divide the preceding paragraph into two, so that the first paragraph discusses Russ' specific works and the recognition they received, while the second focuses on summarizing how critical perception of her works has changed over time. The best place to begin the second paragraph would be at point:
A. A.
B. B.
C. C.
D. D.

PASSAGE II

On Santorini

In the South Aegean sea, among the Greek islands known as the Cyclades, lies a particular place that's called Santorini. On its northern edge is Oia, a village adored by tourists for its gorgeous sunsets and pristine white buildings cascading down scraggy cliffs. As fall sets in, I am lucky to linger here for a few idyllic weeks.

In October, Oia is a strange yet beautiful place. The weather is cool, the rainy season draws near, and most tourists are gone for the season. The locals are left to enjoy the mild weather and astonishing sunsets, along with an unfamiliar peace and quiet. Conversely, it is easy to imagine the

16. F. NO CHANGE
G. Santorini
H. Santorini, a particular location
J. a particular location called Santorini

17. A. NO CHANGE
B. their
C. it's
D. its'

18. F. NO CHANGE
G. Nevertheless
H. Consequently
J. Besides

village as a timeless place. During this season, the contrast
19

between the luxuries of tourism and the joys of a simple life

become most evident.
20

Old people sit on their terraces, play the ancient game
21
of backgammon, and drink Greek coffee, thick and black with

a film of bitter grounds floating at the bottom of the cup. The

bakery at the bottom of the hill offers fresh-baked bread every

morning. [22] The homemade wine flows easily among friends.

At the edge of the village, it is where the road to the beach
23
winds down among the cliffs, sits a little Polish-owned cafe
23
with the best falafel sandwiches and French fries you will

ever taste.

Petros, the fisherman, has already closed his restaurant

for the season. Fishing is a time-honored profession in many
24
parts of the world. Petros satisfies his need to cook by
24

preparing delicious meals for out-of-towners like me and my
25
friends. Late at night, after we dine heartily on traditional
25

19. The writer wishes to add a detail to the preceding sentence that will emphasize the age of the village. Given that all are true, which of the following replacements for *place* would most effectively accomplish this?
   - **A.** place, perched on these cliffs for centuries.
   - **B.** vacation paradise beloved by many.
   - **C.** location, untouched by the outside world.
   - **D.** spot where the cares of the world slip away.

20. **F.** NO CHANGE
   - **G.** is becoming
   - **H.** becomes
   - **J.** was becoming

21. Given that all are true, which of the choices would best help complete an example of the "timeless" quality described in the previous paragraph?
   - **A.** NO CHANGE
   - **B.** watch Greek soaps on television
   - **C.** talk to passing tourists
   - **D.** make crafts for the gift shops

22. The writer wishes to include another example of the simple pleasures of island life enjoyed by locals and remaining visitors. Which of the following true sentences, if inserted here, would best fulfill that goal?
   - **F.** An old yellow chapel with a bright blue bell sits at the edge of a cliff facing the sea.
   - **G.** A car rental agency at the edge of town offers opportunities for trips across the island.
   - **H.** Ferries leave from the port frequently, headed to nearby islands or the port in Athens.
   - **J.** Those who come early can enjoy sweet and savory pastries as they walk along the beach.

23. **A.** NO CHANGE
   - **B.** village that is where the road to the beach winds down among the cliffs. There
   - **C.** village and it is where the road to the beach winds down among the cliffs,
   - **D.** village, where the road to the beach winds down among the cliffs,

24. **F.** NO CHANGE
   - **G.** Many locals still supplement their living with fresh fish from the sea.
   - **H.** Did you know fishermen have been casting off from Santorini's docks for 3,000 years?
   - **J.** DELETE the underlined portion.

25. **A.** NO CHANGE
   - **B.** mine and my friends.
   - **C.** my friends and I.
   - **D.** myself and my friends.

dishes and after having danced to pop hits from his CD collection, he takes his little skiff out on the water and returns with nets full of tiny fish the size of sardines. We help him clean and fry them up for the abundant population of stray cats.

26. F. NO CHANGE
 G. dancing
 H. dance
 J. having danced

27. Given that all of the choices are true, which one is most relevant to the focus of the paragraph?
 A. NO CHANGE
 B. the tourist season.
 C. a delicious late night snack.
 D. tomorrow's lunch at work.

[1] This is a fleeting time, of course. [2] They will engulf the island, bringing cooler weather that slicks the cobblestones and seeps inside the chimneys and flows beneath the cracks under the doors. [3] The last bars will close for the winter, the restaurants will serve their last meal, the gift store's will shut their doors, and everything will be quiet until the tourist season begins again next spring. [4] In a few weeks the great storms will come. [30]

28. F. NO CHANGE
 G. island, therefore,
 H. island, for example,
 J. island, on the other hand,

29. A. NO CHANGE
 B. stores' will
 C. store's shall
 D. stores will

30. Which of the following sequences of sentences makes this paragraph most logical?
 F. NO CHANGE
 G. 1, 4, 2, 3
 H. 2, 3, 4, 1
 J. 4, 1, 2, 3

PASSAGE III

My Big Backyard Chickens

Having recently moved to our first house with a backyard, and knowing we wanted to get chickens. They're not the most cuddly pets, but there is something appealing about gathering eggs from your own backyard. During the winter, we researched coop designs and breeds online. Then spring rolls around. It was time to act.

31. A. NO CHANGE
 B. having known
 C. we knew
 D. knowing

32. F. NO CHANGE
 G. will roll
 H. does roll
 J. rolled

1 ■ ■ ■ ■ ■ ■ ■ ■ ■ 1

[1] One sunny Saturday morning, we drove out to the country. [2] Our destination we were traveling to (33) was an old-fashioned swap meet, where farmers gather to sell and exchange livestock, machinery, housewares and everything else. [3] We walked around appreciatively (34) admiring bunnies, baby goats, and dozens of ducks, geese and chickens. [35]

We particularly wanted (36) some pullets, female chicks that would grow into egg-laying hens. After thirty minutes, we found our birds! The eight chosen chicks, who's (37) tiny bodies were still coated in fluff, were just a few weeks old. Four were yellow, three were dingy white and one was black. We took them home. For the first several weeks, we kept the chicks indoors where they could stay warm. They lived in a large box filled with soft, fragrant pine shavings, which they loved to peck and scratch. [38] As they settled into their home, a bright-shining bulb warmed them nicely (39) hanging in one corner of the box. Not surprisingly, they spent a lot of

33. A. NO CHANGE
B. destination to which were traveling
C. destination to travel to
D. destination

34. F. NO CHANGE
G. approvingly
H. adoringly
J. OMIT the underlined portion.

35. Which of the following sequences of sentences makes this paragraph most logical?
A. NO CHANGE
B. 2, 1, 3
C. 3, 2, 1
D. 3, 1, 2

36. F. NO CHANGE
G. We wanted particular
H. In particularly, we wanted
J. We wanted, in particularly,

37. A. NO CHANGE
B. whose
C. of who's
D. of whose

38. If the writer were to delete the phrase "which they loved to peck and scratch" (ending the sentence with the word *shavings*), the essay would primarily lose a detail that:
F. provides an endearing insight into the chicks' developing personalities.
G. foreshadows the fact that the chicks will soon change in appearance.
H. illustrates how the chicks interact with their new environment.
J. contradicts the assumption that chicks do nothing but sleep.

39. A. NO CHANGE
B. they were kept nice and warm by a bright-shining bulb
C. a bright-shining bulb kept them nice and warm
D. a nicely bright-shining bulb warmed them

time in that corner, asleep in a warm, fluffy heap. But as they grew, they spent more time squabbling. 40

40. Which choice best gives the sense that the chicks are ready to venture outdoors?
 F. NO CHANGE
 G. became eager to explore the world.
 H. began to feel cramped inside their cozy box.
 J. became more independent.

It was time to build them a coop. [41]

41. Assuming that all the choices are true, which one best links the preceding sentence with the rest of the paragraph?
 A. What would the neighbors think about the feathered friends in our backyard?
 B. A chicken coop must provide warmth in the winter and safety from predators.
 C. We carefully worked out a design on graph paper, then started building.
 D. Some coops are big enough for dozens of chickens, but we only needed room for eight.

The chicks new home 42 included an indoor area with three nesting boxes and a tall perch where they could roost. A small ramp led to an outside yard, surrounded by chicken wire. Here, the chicks would have room to grow.

42. F. NO CHANGE
 G. chicks' new home
 H. chick's new home
 J. chicks' new home,

As the summer months passed, the chicks matured into full-grown chickens. They lost their baby fluff and developed glossy feathers. The four yellow ones became a rich, rusty red, flecked with iridescent green; belonging to the breed 43 called Rhode Island Red. The three white ones lost their dingy tint and became pure white, splattered with creamy orange; they were Americanas, also known as Easter Eggers, because of their green and blue eggs. The black one only grew to half the size of the others, but with a sleek shape, glossy color and perky tail, they were 44 the prettiest of the bunch.

43. A. NO CHANGE
 B. the breed to which they belonged
 C. they belonged to the breed
 D. with belonging to the breed

44. F. NO CHANGE
 G. they became
 H. it was
 J. they are

Question 45 asks about the preceding passage as a whole.

45. Suppose the writer had intended to write a comprehensive "how-to" article for people who would like to raise their own backyard chickens. Would this essay successfully fulfill this goal?

A. Yes, because the article describes in detail the necessary steps for the daily care of chickens.
B. Yes, because the article compares and contrasts chickens with other household pets.
C. No, because the author only focuses on a few particular breeds of chickens.
D. No, because the article lacks practical details about the daily care and proper raising of chickens.

PASSAGE IV

The Many Lives of Yogurt

[1]

What comes to mind when you hear the word "yogurt"? You probably think of a sweet dairy product in fruity flavors like strawberry or peach,[46] conveniently packaged for breakfast on-the-go. But while that may be yogurt's most commonly found form in todays[47] American grocery store, many different varieties of yogurt has existed[48] during its 5,000-year history.

[2]

[1] These wandering tribes might have accidentally created yogurt by carrying fresh milk in pouches made from sheep stomachs, a Neolithic substitute for the glass bottle.[49] [2] Some food historians believe that yogurt was discovered as early as the Neolithic era then[50] nomadic herdsmen began domesticating milk-producing animals,

46. F. NO CHANGE
G. flavors like, strawberry or peach,
H. flavors like strawberry, or peach
J. flavors, like strawberry, or peach

47. A. NO CHANGE
B. form, in todays'
C. form, in today's
D. form in today's

48. F. NO CHANGE
G. have existed
H. had existed
J. exist

49. Given that all of the choices are true, which one would provide a potential explanation for how the yogurt was created?

A. NO CHANGE
B. which contain a milk-curdling enzyme.
C. the custom at the time.
D. which were used to transport liquids during travel.

50. F. NO CHANGE
G. era; when
H. era when
J. era: when

the ancestors of today's cows, sheep, and goats. [3] Or perhaps it was in the ancient lands of Mesopotamia that yogurt made its first appearance. [4] <u>Conversely, there is</u> evidence that yogurt played an important role in the diets of people throughout the world, even before recorded history. [52]

51 (underlined: Conversely, there is)

51. **A.** NO CHANGE
B. Either way, there is
C. Because there is
D. There is, therefore,

52. For the sake of the logic and coherence of this paragraph, Sentence 1 should be placed:

F. where it is now.
G. after sentence 2.
H. after sentence 3.
J. after sentence 4.

[3]

The first true description of yogurt was provided around 1000 A.D. by a Turkish author named Mahmud of Kashgar. <u>Not only to include an entry for yogurt, one of the first encyclopedias was written by him</u> firmly establishing its place in Turkish history.

53. **A.** NO CHANGE
B. Not only did he create one of the first encyclopedias, he also included an entry for yogurt,
C. One of the first encyclopedias was created by him, but it included an entry for yogurt
D. Not only did it have an entry for yogurt, but he also wrote one of the first encyclopedias,

[4]

[54] Iranians enjoy sour *kefir* yogurt in dishes such as *ashe-mast*, a warm soup made from yogurt, lentils and spinach. In Eastern European and Balkan countries such as Albania, Bulgaria and Serbia, yogurt is served as a cold soup seasoned with cucumbers and <u>dill – a</u> light and refreshing dish. A similar <u>dish *tzatsiki* is</u> a popular condiment in Greece, served alongside pita sandwiches and grilled meat. In South Asia, a yogurt-based sauce called *raita* – made with cucumbers, onions, mint and cumin – makes a <u>deliciously tasty</u> complement to spicy curries.

54. Which of the following sentences would most effectively introduce the subject of this paragraph and act as a transition from the preceding paragraph?

F. In the ensuing centuries, yogurt's popularity has remained strong in cuisines throughout the world.
G. Americans typically expect yogurt to be served sweet, but this is not the case everywhere.
H. In many recipes, yogurt is accompanied by cucumber.
J. In modern times, refrigeration technology affects the way people consume dairy products.

55. Which of the following alternatives to the underlined portion would NOT be acceptable?

A. dill, a
B. dill, making for a
C. dill: a
D. dill. A

56. **F.** NO CHANGE
G. dish, *tzatsiki* is,
H. dish, *tzatsiki*, is
J. dish *tzatsiki*, is

57. **A.** NO CHANGE
B. tasty delicious
C. delicious amazingly
D. delicious

[5]

To some extent, yogurt's popularity is due in part to its considerable nutritional value; it is full of protein, calcium and vitamins. Surprisingly, even lactose-intolerant people can sometimes eat yogurt, despite the fact that it is made almost completely from milk. This is because much of the lactose in yogurt has already been broken down into lactic acid, the same substance which gives yogurt its trademark sour taste. [60]

58. F. NO CHANGE
G. Yogurt's popularity is due in part
H. To some extent, yogurt's popularity is partly due
J. Yogurt's popularity is somewhat due in part

59. Which of the following alternatives to the underlined portion would be LEAST acceptable?
A. even though
B. although
C. in spite of the fact that
D. in order that

Question 60 asks about the preceding passage as a whole.

60. The writer wishes to add the following sentence in order to show the history associated with yogurt in world cuisines.

These recipes have been perfected over many generations.

This sentence would most logically be placed at the end of Paragraph:
F. 1.
G. 2.
H. 3.
J. 4.

PASSAGE V

Denos' Wheel of Fortune

Coney Island, a beachfront neighborhood at the southern tip of Brooklyn, is a favorite spot for tourists and locals alike. Part amusement park, part beach boardwalk, this recreational spot claims a long yet turbulent history.

61. A. NO CHANGE
B. lays claims for
C. possesses claims upon
D. maintains a claim on

Early in the the twentieth century, Coney Island offered an elegant experience for visitors from all over the world,

62. Which of the following alternatives to the underlined portion would be LEAST acceptable?
F. a luxurious
G. an upscale
H. a costly
J. a refined

they came to stay at fancy hotels and enjoy fabulous rides.

63. A. NO CHANGE
B. whom
C. who
D. which

It was considered, for example, the biggest amusement area in the United States. However, by the sixties, Coney Island was in steep decline; it suffered from the impoverishment and high crime rates of surrounding areas, its attractions were struggling to stay in business at all.

[1] Luckily, a man named Denos wasn't willing to give up on Coney Island. [2] With memory of what it had been in the old days, and he knew it could dazzle visitors once again. [3] Denos was born in Greece in 1920, the eighth of 22 children. [4] At only 14 years old, he struck out on his own, on which he emigrated to the United States. [5] He served a stint in the army, working as a cook, then returned to New York City, where he made a good living for himself and his family as a restaurant operator. [6] Despite his long workdays, Denos still found time to take his family to the boardwalk at Coney Island. [7] Together, they admired the Wonder Wheel – Coney Island's signature attraction. [8] Built in 1920, the Wonder Wheel is a fun ride for families. [9] Denos promised his wife he would buy it for her one day. [70]

Eventually, he opened a little restaurant at Coney Island called the Anchor Bar & Grill. He also opened a food concession stand for the benefit of patrons of the children's amusement park nearby. By this time, it was the 1970's. The park was no longer doing brisk business; times were tough.

64. **F.** NO CHANGE
G. considered, on the other hand
H. considered, therefore
J. considered

65. **A.** NO CHANGE
B. areas, and its attractions struggled
C. areas, then its attractions were struggling
D. areas, suddenly, its attractions were struggling

66. **F.** NO CHANGE
G. He remembered
H. Having memory of
J. Remembering

67. **A.** NO CHANGE
B. own and
C. own, he
D. own, at which he

68. Which of the following alternatives to the underlined portion would be LEAST acceptable?

F. City. There, he
G. City – where he
H. City. Where he
J. City; there, he

69. Given that all the choices are true, which one provides the most specific details about the Wonder Wheel's construction?

A. NO CHANGE
B. treat for young children, who beg to go again and again.
C. unique type of Ferris wheel that measures 150 feet tall.
D. point of pride for residents of south Brooklyn.

70. The writer wants to divide the preceding paragraph into two in order to separate information about Denos' background and early accomplishments from information about his growing interest in Coney Island. The best place to begin the new paragraph would be at the beginning of Sentence:

F. 4.
G. 5.
H. 6.
J. 7.

71. Which of the following alternatives to the underlined portion would NOT be acceptable?

A. this point,
B. now,
C. this,
D. then,

The owners of the children's amusement park and the Wonder Wheel were struggling. Instead, they [72] would be forced to sell. And while they received lucrative offers from interested businessmen, Denos' passion for the park and the Wonder Wheel was evident. He won over the owners and managed to purchase both attractions.

Denos and his children worked hard to rebuild the park and do their part to restore Coney Island to its former glory. They added new rides and games, [73] turning Deno's Wonder Wheel Amusement and Kiddie Park into one of Coney Island's most beloved attractions. [74]

72. **F.** NO CHANGE
G. struggling, but they
H. struggling, conversely they
J. struggling. They

73. Given that all the choices are true, which one most effectively provides new and specific information?
A. NO CHANGE
B. added kids' rides, arcade games and concession stands
C. increased the park's appeal and profitability
D. brought fun and creativity to their work

74. The writer would like to end the essay by offering a sense of how Denos succeeded in securing a lasting legacy for the Wonder Wheel. Given that all the sentences are true, which one best accomplishes the writer's goal?
F. The Wonder Wheel was built the year of Denos' birth; perhaps it was meant to be.
G. Without the Wonder Wheel, Coney Island just wouldn't have held the same allure for Denos.
H. The Wonder Wheel is repainted annually to protect it from weather damage.
J. In 1989, the Wonder Wheel was declared an Official New York City Landmark.

Question 75 asks about the preceding passage as a whole.

75. Suppose the writer's goal had been to write a brief essay describing the role an immigrant played in New York City culture. Would this essay accomplish that goal?
A. Yes, because it discusses how Denos was inspired by his brother to become an American.
B. Yes, because it describes Denos' contributions to reviving Coney Island.
C. No, because it focuses on tourists' experiences at Coney Island.
D. No, because it provides more information about Denos' background than his life in New York.

END OF SECTION 1

MATHEMATICS TEST

60 Minutes—60 Questions

DIRECTIONS: Solve each problem, choose the correct answer, and then fill in the corresponding oval on your answer document.

Do not linger over problems that take too much time. Solve as many as you can; then return to the others in the time you have left for this test.

You are permitted to use a calculator on this test. You may use your calculator for any problems you choose, but some problems may best be done without using a calculator.

Note: Unless otherwise stated, all of the following should be assumed:

1. Illustrative figures are NOT necessarily drawn to scale.
2. Geometric figures lie in a plane.
3. The word line indicates a straight line.
4. The word average indicates arithmetic mean.

DO YOUR FIGURING HERE.

1. The area of a square is 25 square feet. What is the perimeter of the square, in feet?

A. 5
B. 10
C. 20
D. 25
E. 100

2. Anne has 5 shirts, 4 pairs of pants, 4 pairs of socks, and 2 hats. How many different combinations of 1 shirt, 1 pair of pants, 1 pair of socks, and 1 hat can she wear?

F. 2
G. 4
H. 15
J. 80
K. 160

3. For two consecutive integers, the sum of the smaller and quadruple the larger is 79. What are the two integers?

A. 14, 15
B. 15, 16
C. 16, 17
D. 19, 20
E. 39, 40

4. To visit the local aquarium, members pay \$13 per ticket while nonmembers pay \$15 per ticket. What is the total amount, in dollars, from the sale of 55 member tickets and n nonmember tickets?

F. $n + 55$
G. $(15 + 13)n$
H. $15(n + 13)$
J. $15(n + 55)$
K. $15n + 13(55)$

DO YOUR FIGURING HERE.

5. If $13(x - 7) = -11$ then $x = ?$

A. $-\frac{102}{13}$

B. $-\frac{18}{13}$

C. $-\frac{11}{13}$

D. $-\frac{4}{13}$

E. $\frac{80}{13}$

6. Eric's basketball team, the Admirals, has the highest score average in its history after 5 games in which the team scored 66, 85, 73, 81, and 55 points. How many points must the Admirals score in the next game to maintain this average?

F. 60
G. 68
H. 70
J. 72
K. 82

7. $5x^4 \cdot 8x^6$ is equal to:

A. $13x^2$
B. $13x^{10}$
C. $13x^{24}$
D. $40x^{10}$
E. $40x^{24}$

8. On even ground, a basketball goal 15 feet tall casts a 5 foot long shadow. A tree on the same level ground casts a 15 foot long shadow. How many feet tall is the tree?

F. 5
G. 10
H. 15
J. 25
K. 45

9. A school organizes a field trip for a class of 8 students. The school will rent a bus, toward which each student will contribute \$15. On the day of the trip, 2 students cancel, and the others have to pay equally for the bus. How much does each remaining student pay?

A. \$10.00
B. \$13.13
C. \$16.83
D. \$20.00
E. \$30.00

GO ON TO THE NEXT PAGE.

DO YOUR FIGURING HERE.

10. Which of the following expressions is a factor of the expression $x^2 - x - 12$?

F. $x - 1$
G. $x - 3$
H. $x - 4$
J. $x - 6$
K. $x - 12$

11. For the equation $a + 7b = c$, which of the following expressions gives b in terms of a and c ?

A. $\frac{(a - c)}{7}$

B. $\frac{(c - 7)}{a}$

C. $\frac{(c - a)}{7}$

D. $\frac{(c + a)}{7}$

E. $c - a - 7$

12. Manny has calculated that driving at 60 miles per hour is the same as driving at 88 feet per second. Which of the following is the closest to Manny's speed, in feet per second, if he drives at 45 miles per hour?

F. 20
G. 31
H. 66
J. 82
K. 660

13. In the arithmetic sequence given below, how many terms lie between 7 and 43, exclusive of 7 and 43?

3, 7, 11, 15..... 43

A. 4
B. 8
C. 9
D. 35
E. 36

14. The figure below shows Susie's house, her school, and the mall at the 3 vertices of the right triangle formed by 3 roads. Susie takes Inland Road from her house to her school, and then takes Ridge Way to the mall. How much shorter would Susie's trip be, in feet, if she took Peachtree Street directly to the mall?

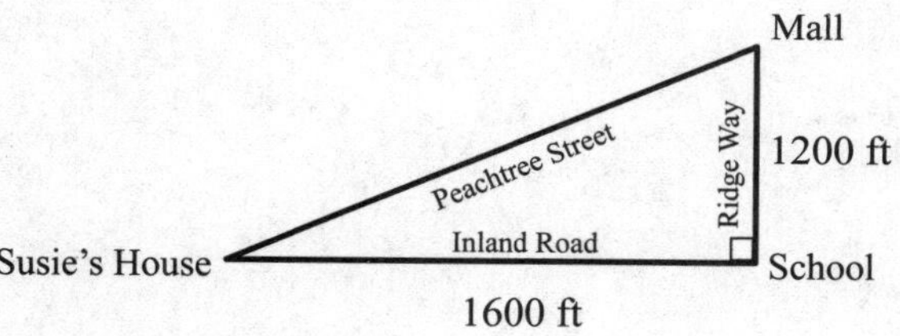

F. 200
G. 800
H. 1,000
J. 1,400
K. 2,000

DO YOUR FIGURING HERE.

15. Leviathan Pool Crafters is building a rectangular reflecting pool for a new customer. The customer wants the pool to be 5 feet deep and 30 feet wide. How long should the pool be, in feet, in order to have a volume of 9,000 cubic feet?

A. 18
B. 27
C. 48
D. 60
E. 75

16. If $f(x) = 7x^2 + 4x - 5$, then $f(-3) =$

F. -80
G. -46
H. 46
J. 63
K. 70

17. A DVD player is regularly priced at \$89.99. It is on sale for 30% off the usual price. How much will the DVD player cost at the sale price, excluding sales tax?

A. \$26.99
B. \$29.99
C. \$59.99
D. \$62.99
E. \$86.66

18. $(2a + 3b + 4c) - (9a + 8b - 7c)$ is equivalent to:

F. $-9a - 11b - 3c$
G. $-9a - 11b + 11c$
H. $-7a + 11b - 3c$
J. $-7a - 5b - 3c$
K. $-7a - 5b + 11c$

GO ON TO THE NEXT PAGE.

DO YOUR FIGURING HERE.

19. A point at $(3, -3)$ in the standard (x, y) coordinate plane is shifted left 7 units and up 3 units. What are the new coordinates of the point?

A. $(-4, 0)$
B. $(0, 4)$
C. $(4, 0)$
D. $(10, -6)$
E. $(10, 0)$

20. A rectangle has an area of 48 square feet and a perimeter of 28 feet. What is the length, in feet, of the longest side?

F. 6
G. 8
H. 10
J. 12
K. 14

21. In ΔDEF, $\overline{DE} = \overline{EF}$ and the measure of $\angle E$ is 106°. What is the measure of $\angle D$?

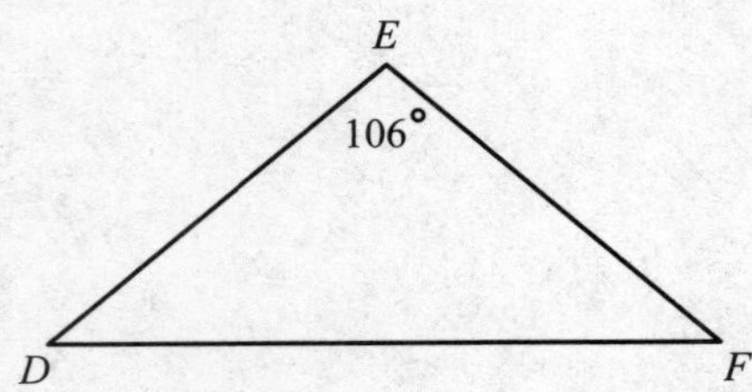

A. 37°
B. 53°
C. 60°
D. 74°
E. 106°

22. The function $y = -8x^2 + 2$ passes through the point $(2, -3a)$ when graphed in the standard (x,y) coordinate plane. What is the value of a?

F. -10
G. 0
H. 2
J. 10
K. 30

23. Jason creates a scaled map of his hometown on a standard (x,y) coordinate plane. Each unit on the map represents 1 mile. He graphs his house at the point $(-4, -5)$ and his school at the point $(-10, -11)$. Which of the following is closest to the distance, in miles, between Jason's school and his house?

A. 3
B. 6
C. 8
D. 12
E. 21

2  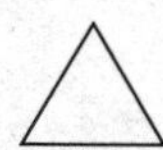      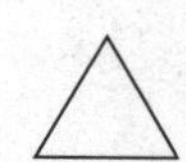 2

DO YOUR FIGURING HERE.

24. For all $x > 20$, $\dfrac{(x^2 + 2x - 8)(x + 5)}{(x^2 + 9x + 20)(x - 2)} =$

F. 1

G. $\dfrac{25}{4}$

H. $(x + 5)(x - 5)$

J. $\dfrac{2(x + 5)}{(x - 2)}$

K. $-\dfrac{3(x + 5)}{(x - 2)}$

25. Lines r and s lie in the standard (x,y) coordinate plane. The equation for line r is $y = 0.45x - 220$. The slope of line s is 0.2 greater than the slope of line r. What is the slope of line s ?

A. −44.0
B. 0.09
C. 0.25
D. 0.65
E. 9.0

26. What is the slope of the line that connects the points (5,7) and (−3,12) in the standard (x,y) coordinate plane?

F. $\dfrac{2}{19}$

G. $\dfrac{15}{2}$

H. $\dfrac{19}{2}$

J. $-\dfrac{5}{8}$

K. $-\dfrac{8}{5}$

DO YOUR FIGURING HERE.

27. The table below shows values of x and y for a certain function. Given that x and y are real numbers, and $y = (x - 2)^2 + 5$, which of the following values of x corresponds to the least value of y ?

x	y
−2	21
0	9
2	5
4	9
6	21
8	41
10	69

A. 1
B. 2
C. 3
D. 4
E. 5

28. In the figure below, what is tan b ?

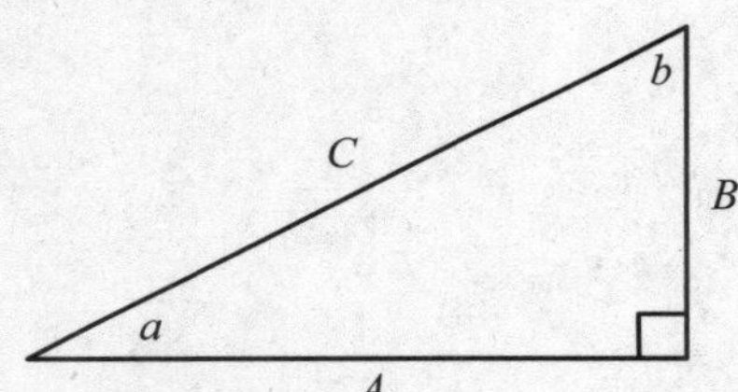

F. $\frac{A}{B}$

G. $\frac{A}{C}$

H. $\frac{B}{C}$

J. $\frac{B}{A}$

K. $\frac{C}{A}$

29. The table below shows the values of two functions, a and b, for given values of x. One of the functions represents a straight line. What is the value of that function when x is 8?

DO YOUR FIGURING HERE.

x	$a(x)$	$b(x)$
−4	3.6	2.1
−2	3.2	2.3
0	2.9	2.5
2	2.7	2.7
4	2.6	2.9
6	2.7	3.1

A. 2.0
B. 2.2
C. 2.8
D. 3.1
E. 3.3

30. Water flows into a rectangular tank at a constant rate. The depth of the water, d feet, is measured every hour, h, and is given in the table below.

h	0	1	2	3	4	5
d	8	11	14	17	20	23

What equation represents this data?

F. $d = h + 8$
G. $d = 3h + 5$
H. $d = 3h + 8$
J. $d = 8h + 3$
K. $d = 11h$

31. Given the equation $a^2 + b^2 = 64$, what is the greatest value of b for which there is a real value of a ?

A. 0
B. 4
C. 8
D. 32
E. 64

DO YOUR FIGURING HERE.

32. The number, N, of birds at Westmeyer Conservatory that will migrate south through Week t of winter is modeled by the function $N(t) = \frac{(600t^2 + 8)}{t^2 + 1}$. According to this model, how many birds will migrate south through Week 6 ?

F. 59
G. 554
H. 584
J. 1736
K. 2124

33. In the standard (x, y) coordinate plane, the graph of which of the following equations is a circle with center $(-3, 7)$ and radius of 5 coordinate units?

A. $(x-3)^2 + (y+7)^2 = 5$
B. $(x+3)^2 + (y-7)^2 = 5$
C. $(x+3)^2 + (y+7)^2 = 25$
D. $(x+3)^2 + (y-7)^2 = 25$
E. $(x-3)^2 + (y+7)^2 = 25$

34. A bag of poker chips contains red, white, and blue chips. Half of the chips are red, one-sixth are white, and the rest are blue. What is the ratio of red chips to white chips to blue chips ?

F. 2:6:3
G. 2:3:6
H. 3:1:2
J. 3:2:1
K. 3:6:2

35. Let x, y, and z be different, positive integers. Given the geometric sequence shown below, what is the 5th term of the sequence?

$$xy,\ x^2yz^2,\ x^3yz^4,\ x^4yz^6 \ldots$$

A. x^5yz^6
B. x^5yz^8
C. $x^5y^2z^8$
D. $x^6y^5z^8$
E. $x^6y^5z^{10}$

DO YOUR FIGURING HERE.

36. A candy jar contains 6 blue gumdrops, 4 purple gumdrops, and 5 yellow gumdrops, all of which are the same size and shape. What is the probability of picking 1 yellow gumdrop from the candy jar?

F. $\frac{1}{15}$

G. $\frac{4}{15}$

H. $\frac{1}{3}$

J. $\frac{2}{5}$

K. $\frac{11}{15}$

37. At Westmore High School, if a student is not more than 5 feet tall, that student cannot participate in the annual three-legged race. If Emily participated in the three-legged race at Westmore High School, then which of the following conclusions can be logically reached?

A. Emily is at least 6 feet tall.
B. Emily is more than 5 feet tall.
C. Emily is exactly 5 feet tall.
D. Emily is less than 5 feet tall.
E. Emily is at most 4 feet tall.

38. What is the area, in square meters, of the figure shown below?

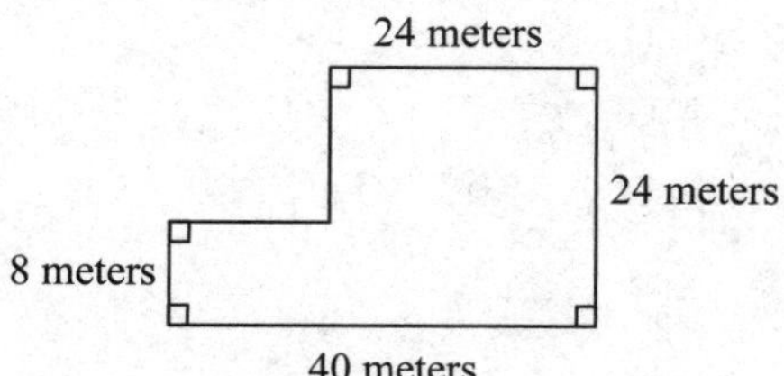

F. 96
G. 128
H. 704
J. 720
K. 960

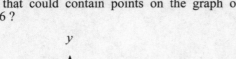

2          2

DO YOUR FIGURING HERE.

39. What are the quadrants of the standard (x, y) coordinate plane below that could contain points on the graph of $2y + 6x = -16$?

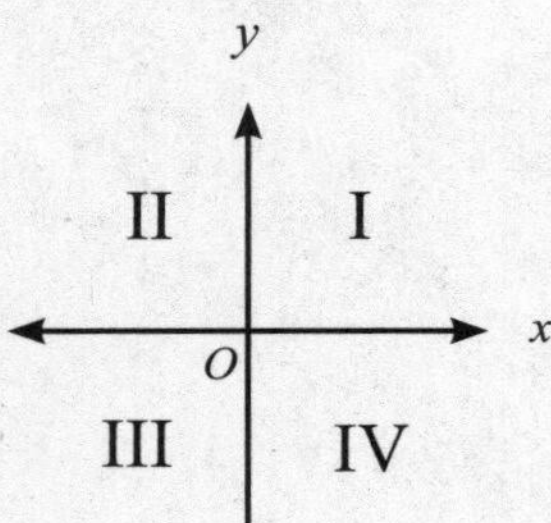

A. II and IV
B. I, II, III
C. I, III, IV
D. I, II, IV
E. II, III, IV

40. Lorraine took 9 days to plant a garden. She planted $\frac{1}{7}$ of the garden each of the first 4 days. For the remaining 5 days, what fraction of the garden, on average, did she plant per day?

F. $\frac{1}{7}$

G. $\frac{1}{9}$

H. $\frac{1}{18}$

J. $\frac{3}{35}$

K. $\frac{6}{35}$

41. If $\log_8(2^{3x-6}) = 3$, what is the value of x ?

A. $\frac{9}{4}$

B. $\frac{262}{3}$

C. 1

D. 5

E. 6

DO YOUR FIGURING HERE.

42. Amy is flying a kite with a taut string length of 65 feet. She wants to determine the vertical distance between the base of the kite and the level ground. She anchors one end of the string to the ground so that the kite's string creates an angle of 25° to the ground, as shown in the figure below. Which of the following expressions could be used to determine the kite's height off the ground?

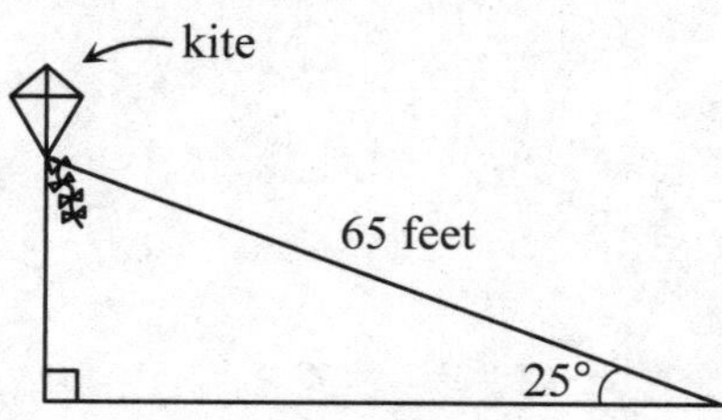

F. $\frac{65}{\cos 25°}$

G. $\frac{65}{\sin 25°}$

H. $65 \tan 25°$

J. $65 \cos 25°$

K. $65 \sin 25°$

43. Four points, W, X, Y, Z, lie on a circle having a circumference of 40 inches. X is 20 inches counterclockwise from W. Y is 15 inches clockwise from W. Z is 15 units clockwise from Y. What is the order of the points, starting with W and going clockwise around the circle?

A. W, X, Y, Z
B. W, Y, Z, X
C. W, Y, X, Z
D. W, Z, X, Y
E. W, Z, Y, X

DO YOUR FIGURING HERE.

44. The distance from Lighthouse C to Ship A is 15 miles, and the distance from Lighthouse C to Ship B is 10 miles. The angle $\angle ACB$ made by the lighthouse and the two ships is 40°. Which of the following gives the distance between ships A and B ?

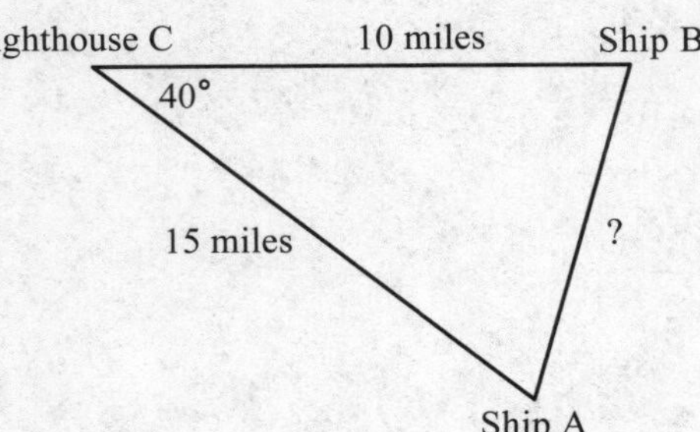

(Note: for a triangle with sides of length a, b, and c, and opposite angles A, B, and C, respectively, the law of sines states $\frac{a}{\sin A} = \frac{b}{\sin B} = \frac{c}{\sin C}$, and the law of cosines states $c^2 = a^2 + b^2 - 2ab(\cos C)$)

F. 10 sin 40
G. 15 sin 40
H. $\sqrt{10^2 - 15^2}$
J. $\sqrt{10^2 + 15^2}$
K. $\sqrt{(10^2) + (15^2) - 300(\cos 40°)}$

45. One of the following equations is graphed in the standard (x, y) coordinate plane below. Which one?

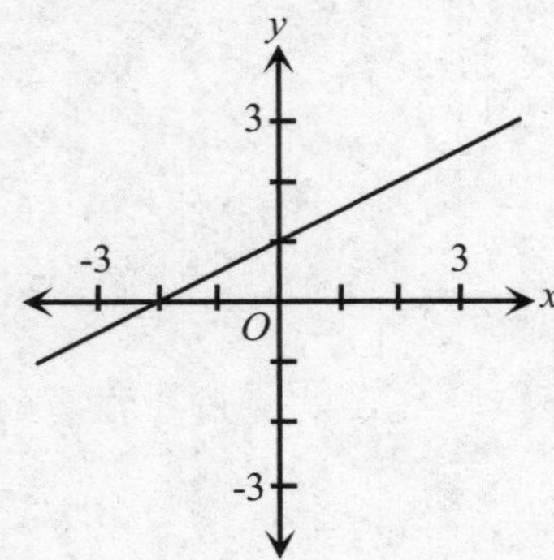

A. $y = -\frac{1}{2}x - 2$
B. $y = -x + 1$
C. $y = \frac{1}{2}x + 1$
D. $y = -2x - 1$
E. $y = 2x + 1$

DO YOUR FIGURING HERE.

46. For a class project, Susie is graphing the money she makes for allowance. She has decided to graph her earnings, E, from working h hours at $5.00 per hour. She also must describe the slope between any 2 points (h, E) on the graph. Her correct answer is that the slope between any 2 points on this graph is always:

F. zero.
G. the same positive value.
H. the same negative value.
J. a positive value, but the value varies.
K. a negative value, but the value varies.

47. A particular cube has a side length of 12 cm. What is the cube's surface area, in square centimeters?

A. 432
B. 576
C. 720
D. 864
E. 1728

48. The 7th term of an arithmetic sequence is 9, and the 11th term is 16. What is the sum of the first four terms of the sequence?

F. 4.5
G. 7.5
H. 10.0
J. 11.75
K. 46.5

49. For the inequality $8(x+3)>2(x-3)$, which of the following is NOT a possible value for x ?

A. -5
B. -3
C. -1
D. 3
E. 5

50. B is an irrational number. If $|B^2-24|-8=0$, what is the value of B ?

F. 4
G. $2\sqrt{2}$
H. $4\sqrt{2}$
J. $2\sqrt{4}$
K. $2\sqrt{6}$

51. Given that $\sin^2 x - 5x + \cos^2 x = 21$, what is the value of x ?

A. -4.4
B. -4.0
C. 4.0
D. 4.4
E. 5.0

GO ON TO THE NEXT PAGE.

2          2

52. Let $f(x) = \sqrt{(x + 1)}$ and $g(x) = 7x - b$. In the standard (x, y) coordinate plane, $y = f(g(x))$ passes through (7, 2). What is the value of b ?

F. −34
G. 28
H. 46
J. 47
K. 48

DO YOUR FIGURING HERE.

53. Parallelogram $ABCD$ is shown below. Segment $\overline{DE}$ bisects $\angle ADC$ and segment $\overline{CE}$ bisects $\angle BCD$. If $\angle ADC$ is 132°, what is the measure of $\angle DEC$, in degrees?

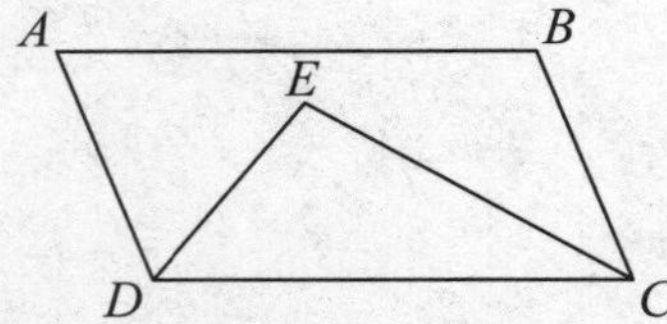

A. 86
B. 88
C. 90
D. 92
E. Cannot be determined from the given information

54. Given that the equation $(4 \# 2)^2 + (1 \# 3)^3 = 91$ is true, which of the following operations could be represented by the symbol # ?

I. Addition
II. Multiplication
III. Subtraction

F. I only
G. II only
H. I and III only
J. II and III only
K. I, II, and III

55. The *determinant* of matrix $\begin{bmatrix} a & c \\ b & d \end{bmatrix}$ is equal to $ad - bc$. For the matrix $\begin{bmatrix} m & m \\ 10 & m \end{bmatrix}$ what must the value of m be to have a determinant of −25 ?

A. −8

B. −5

C. −2

D. $\frac{10}{3}$

E. 5

DO YOUR FIGURING HERE.

56. Triangle *XYZ* is drawn in the standard (x, y) coordinate plane with points at (0,3), (5,0), and (0,–5), as shown below. What is $\tan \angle YXZ$?

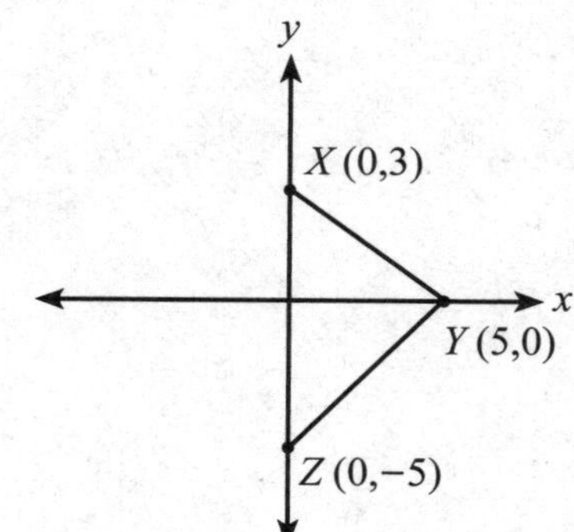

F. $\frac{5}{8}$

G. $\frac{5}{3}$

H. $\frac{8}{5\sqrt{2}}$

J. $\frac{8}{17\sqrt{2}}$

K. $\frac{17\sqrt{2}}{8}$

57. A cube has side lengths of 3 yards each. Another cube has side lengths that are triple the length of the sides of the first cube. The volume of the first cube is how many cubic yards smaller than the volume of the second cube ?

A. 54
B. 216
C. 243
D. 702
E. 729

58. A plane contains 13 horizontal lines and 13 vertical lines. These lines divide the plane into disjoint regions. How many of these disjoint regions have a finite, nonzero area ?

F. 100
G. 144
H. 156
J. 169
K. 196

2         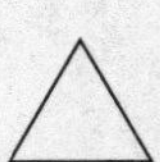 2

DO YOUR FIGURING HERE.

59. In ΔXYZ, the measure of $\angle X$ is 37°, the measure of $\angle Y$ is 53°, and the length of $\overline{YX}$ is 16 inches. Which of the following is an expression for the length, in inches, of $\overline{XZ}$?

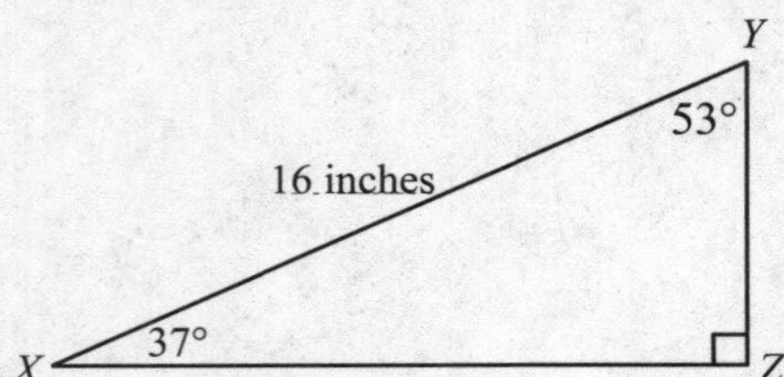

A. $\dfrac{\sin 37°}{16}$

B. $\dfrac{\sin 53°}{16}$

C. $\dfrac{16}{\sin 53°}$

D. $16 \sin 37°$

E. $16 \sin 53°$

60. Which equation below has a solution set consisting of real numbers that are 8 units from −2 ?

F. $|x + 2| = 8$
G. $|x - 2| = 8$
H. $|x + 8| = 2$
J. $|x - 8| = 2$
K. $|x + 8| = -2$

END OF SECTION 2

TURN THE PAGE TO BEGIN SECTION 3

READING TEST

35 Minutes—40 Questions

DIRECTIONS: There are four passages in this test. Each passage is followed by several questions. After reading a passage, choose the best answer to the question and fill in the corresponding oval on your answer document. You may refer to the passages as often as necessary.

Passage I

PROSE FICTION

This year the first real snowfall comes shortly after Christmas, just before New Year's Eve. The hustle and bustle of the holiday season is past, but the lights are still strung across porches up and down the street, and decorated trees glitter in a few of the windows.

Marisa's house is not one of those with lights or a tree. She lives alone, and never feels like taking the time or effort. But she has made a few allowances for the season: a jolly-looking snowman statue positioned on the kitchen table, and a gingerbread-scented candle that she burns in the evenings. There is also a half-eaten box of homemade cookies, which her aunt sent; each cookie is wrapped in plastic wrap, then cradled in crumpled newspaper. This technique actually works, for the most part; the majority of the cookies survived their journey from the West Coast to the Midwest unharmed.

The snow begins falling in late afternoon. Within an hour or so, everything is coated in white, taking on blocky, indistinct shapes. Marisa feels a passive contentment, sitting in the window, reading and watching the snow accumulate in earnest. The neighborhood is full of small rental homes, most of them built in the 1930's and weathering the years with a quiet dignity. Most are inhabited by younger professors and gangs of college roommates. With the snow it has grown very quiet.

When she first moved here from Miami, she imagined that it grew quiet when the snow fell because all activity came to a sudden stop; there were no cars driving through the streets or honking at the intersection two blocks away, no pedestrians with their cheerful conversations ringing out along the sidewalk, no children playing in backyards, no barking dogs… everyone and everything retreated inside to escape the weather and sit by the fire. (Marisa doesn't have a fireplace, but she has a space heater. Her dog, Maisie, an elderly female golden retriever, usually keeps the space heater all to herself, stretched out luxuriously on her big ratty bed. Occasionally she'll get too hot and plod slowly over to the other side of the room to cool off for a few minutes; then pace back over to the bed, stretch out, and get comfortable once more.)

But now Marisa believes that the lack of activity is only one part of it; she's realized that the snow itself acts as a kind of insulation, like a goose-down blanket tacked to the world and muffling any noise. Or perhaps the static white noise of thousands of falling flakes cancels out any other sounds. She likes that. She likes the endless hush, the stillness falling gently across the world. It's like being on the fifth floor of the library with no one else around.

Later, when the snow stops falling, but the silence continues, she'll walk outdoors. If it's evening, the stars overhead will be very clear and very bright in an endless dark sky. If it's tomorrow morning, the sky will be pale white and uniformly overcast. Either way the quiet will remain – nothing but the sound of her feet tramping through the snow, and the snow scuffing away from her toes. Occasionally the hush might be broken by the sound of a child yelling out as he flops into the snow and thrashes his arms and legs in the form of an angel, or lobs a snowball at an unsuspecting sibling who's just walked outside. Or perhaps a pickup truck, ramming its way through the snowy alley, maybe dragging a daring college student behind it, riding a sled, gripping a rope, like a water ski on land. This is very dangerous, and Marisa would never attempt it, but she's theorized that snow makes some people want to do dangerous things, like scale mountain tops, or journey to the poles, or strap skis to their feet and slide down steep hillsides with no good way of stopping.

She's amazed by these adventures; they seem like something from another world. She is fascinated by her colleagues' stories about growing up here, where the snow falls heavy every winter; her friend Sam, a professor of art history, told her about the winter games of his childhood, snowball fights that overtook the neighborhood. Once, one of his friends – not him, of course, another little boy who was much less well-mannered – tossed a snowball at a passing truck. The snowball, packed hard and tight with a core of ice, slammed against the door of the truck with a satisfying clunk. Usually, targeted vehicles only slowed slightly, showing a scowling adult waving their finger for a moment or two before cruising off into the snow. To their shock, this driver was so angry he pulled over and climbed out. They started running; he took up the chase, pursuing them doggedly through knee-deep snow, yelling and shaking his fist. They made it to Sam's front porch just in time.

1. The events in the passage are described primarily from the point of view of a narrator who presents the:
   A. inner thoughts and feelings of Marisa exclusively.
   B. inner thoughts of Marisa and Sam exclusively.
   C. thoughts of different characters in a neighborhood.
   D. inner thoughts and feelings of Marisa, her friends, and her neighbors.

2. Each of the following is referenced in the passage as an "allowance for the season" EXCEPT:
   F. a snowman statue.
   G. a scented candle.
   H. homemade cookies.
   J. a Santa doll.

3. The first three paragraphs (lines 1-24) establish all of the following about Marisa EXCEPT that she:
   A. lives alone.
   B. has no plans for New Year's Eve.
   C. has an aunt who lives on the West Coast.
   D. lives in the Midwest.

4. It can reasonably be inferred from the passage that Marisa enjoys the snowfall because:
   F. the experience is a novelty for her.
   G. it gives her an excuse to get outside.
   H. it means she can take off work.
   J. she enjoys seeing young people playing.

5. Marisa observes each of the following as noises silenced during the snowfall EXCEPT:
   A. cars driving and honking.
   B. pedestrians talking.
   C. bells ringing.
   D. dogs barking.

6. According to the passage, which of the following typically live in Marisa's neighborhood?
   F. Aged professors
   G. College students
   H. Elderly couples
   J. Young families

7. When Marisa refers to "being on the fifth floor of the library with no one else around" (lines 46-47), she is most likely describing:
   A. the amount of time she has available to sit inside and read.
   B. the breathtaking view from her front windows.
   C. the feeling of isolation she experiences over the holidays.
   D. the comforting sense of quiet and stillness.

8. Details in the passage most strongly suggest that Marisa's profession is that of:
   F. writer.
   G. high school teacher.
   H. college professor.
   J. local historian.

9. Marisa's attitude toward the childhood stories of her colleagues can most accurately be described as:
   A. envy.
   B. captivation.
   C. confusion.
   D. indifference.

10. According to the story told by Marisa's friend, he was once chased by:
   F. older children throwing snowballs.
   G. an angry adult who was driving a truck.
   H. a college student riding a sled behind a truck.
   J. another little boy who was "much less well-mannered."

Passage II

SOCIAL SCIENCE

"Cities have the capability of providing something for everybody, only because, and only when, they are created by everybody" – so wrote Jane Jacobs, one of the twentieth century's most influential writers and thinkers on the topic of city planning and urban vitality. Her theories have influenced an entire generation of planners, and have contributed a great deal to the way we think about cities and neighborhoods, streets and parks, economies and communities. Jacobs' story is even more remarkable for the fact that she possessed no formal training in city planning and did not serve as a planning professional. Rather than approaching urban planning from an academic perspective, she based her ideas about cities on her observations of people interacting in her own neighborhood. She was fiercely confident in the strength of her ideas, and challenged several of the most prominent city planners of the day in battles both theoretical and political.

Born Jane Butzner in Scranton, Pennsylvania in 1916, Jacobs moved to New York City's Greenwich Village in 1935. She studied at Columbia University, exploring subjects such as zoology, economics and law, but did not earn a degree. Instead, she accepted a position as associate editor at a magazine called *Architectural Forum*, where she was assigned to covering developments in hospital architecture. Her husband Robert Jacobs was trained as an architect; he helped her learn how to interpret the blueprints and sketches. This private tutoring paid off for both of them: Robert later focused his architectural practice on designing and building hospitals.

Meanwhile, Jacobs got her first moment in the spotlight when an editor at *Architectural Forum* couldn't attend a conference at Harvard – and sent her to deliver a speech in his stead. In the audience was William H. Whyte, Jr., an editor at *Fortune* magazine; impressed by Jacobs' talk, he invited her to contribute an article to the magazine. The resulting article, "Downtown is for People," was instantly controversial. The Rockefeller Foundation offered Jacobs a grant to expand the article into a book, which was eventually titled *The Death and Life of Great American Cities*. To this day, it remains one of the most influential works on cities and urban planning.

In the book, Jacobs attacked many of the major city planning approaches of the day. At the time, city planners assumed an authoritarian approach; they believed the best way to deal with slums, urban blight and deteriorating city centers was to intervene with regulation and planned projects. Some favored a ground-up approach; they wanted to bulldoze declining neighborhoods and build modern high-rises in their place. Others wanted to focus on building suburbs, along with major highways connecting them to the city.

Jacobs argued that it was a mistake to impose these rebuilding projects onto existing neighborhoods; the healthiest neighborhoods were those where the residents were involved in developing their own communities. She proposed the idea of the city as an "ecosystem" – a complex arrangement of organisms growing and developing in response to each other, establishing a kind of synergy. She promoted "mixed-use" developments, with neighborhoods that included a diverse mix of both people and buildings. Most of all, she argued that local members of a community were better suited to understand the needs of their neighborhood than outside government officials or city planners.

She also focused on the importance of sidewalks for maintaining safety and creating a sense of community. She pointed to the "seeming disorder" of a city that nevertheless functions successfully, thanks to the culture of people interacting on the sidewalks and streets. These crowds bring with them "a constant succession of eyes" which ensures safety. She compared this ongoing procession of people to a kind of art form. We might compare it to dance – "not to a simple-minded precision dance with everyone kicking up at the same time, twirling in unison and bowing off en masse, but to an intricate ballet in which the individual dancers and ensembles all have distinctive parts which miraculously reinforce each other and compose an orderly whole. The ballet of the good city sidewalk never repeats itself from place to place, and in any one place is always replete with new improvisations."

Shortly after the book was published, Jacobs became involved as an activist in her own community, fighting a plan to build a proposed Lower Manhattan Expressway that would cut directly through Little Italy and SoHo, two Manhattan neighborhoods. Community members banded together and the plan was eventually defeated. In 1968, Jacobs and her family moved to Canada, in protest of the Vietnam War. Jacobs continued to publish and speak about city planning until her death in 2006.

11. The point of view from which this passage is told is best described as that of:

A. a writer with a historical perspective describing Jacobs' writings and impact.
B. a relative of Jacobs who wants to promote her arguments to other professionals.
C. a city planner who wants to demonstrate how to effectively promote ideas.
D. an opponent of Jacobs' who believes her ideas were given too much credit.

12. It can most reasonably be inferred from the first paragraph that the author believes:

F. formal education hinders innovative thinking in the field of urban planning.
G. Jacobs' love of controversy inspired many of her theoretical and political battles.
H. city planning would be a different field without Jacob's contributions.
J. Jacobs' self-confidence was the primary factor in her success.

13. What does the passage indicate as the main difference between Jacobs' ideas and the prevailing approach?

A. Jacobs believed that cities were best maintained by inhabitants, while leading planners promoted outside intervention.
B. Jacobs wanted to build sidewalks through old neighborhoods, while leading planners wanted to build parks.
C. Jacobs promoted mixed-use developments, while leading planners wanted separate residential and commercial districts.
D. Jacobs argued that a pedestrian city would be safer, while leading planners wanted to build more freeways.

14. According to the passage, what is one reason that Jacobs' career is noteworthy?

F. She was female when most of the professionals in the field were men.
G. She collaborated with her husband, who was a working architect.
H. She did not have a formal education in architecture or city planning.
J. She became even more successful after moving to Canada.

15. The main purpose of the second paragraph (lines 18-29) is to:

A. explain why Jacobs was not able to obtain a degree as a city planner.
B. describe Jacobs' background and experience.
C. detail the relationship between Jacobs and her husband.
D. outline Jacobs' philosophy on urban planning.

16. Which of the following sentences best summarizes Jacob's views as portrayed in paragraph six (lines 64-79)?

F. Despite what seems like chaos, the activity on a sidewalk can provide safety.
G. Part of what makes the city appealing is the presence of street performers.
H. Just as no two dances are alike, no two cities or neighborhoods are alike.
J. However the city evolves, it should be a welcoming space for creative expression.

17. As it is used in line 58, the word *synergy* most nearly means:

A. singular innovation.
B. diverse contribution.
C. architectural mechanism.
D. beneficial cooperation.

18. The passage suggests that Jacobs became personally involved in the politics of city planning because:

F. no other activists agreed with her philosophy of urban development.
G. she felt the need to defend her work amid intense controversy.
H. proposed development threatened her own neighborhood.
J. her husband and many of her friends were involved in political battles.

19. The phrase "favored a ground-up approach" in line 47 most strongly suggests that these planners wanted to:

A. impose rules.
B. build taller buildings.
C. plan better.
D. start over.

20. The passage makes clear that one reason Jacobs moved from her home in Greenwich Village was to:

F. escape construction on a freeway overpass.
G. protest the Vietnam War.
H. avoid the pressures of community activism.
J. pursue a career opportunity in Canada.

Passage III

HUMANITIES

Macondo, the fictional Latin American village whose history comprises the heart of Gabriel García Márquez's acclaimed novel *One Hundred Years of Solitude,* is an imaginary location brought to life by a compelling story and powerful vision. This small town – which is similar in some ways to the Colombian town where Márquez was raised – becomes a microcosm of a larger world. Its history can be understood as an allegorical retelling of the history of Latin-America. (Or even, loosely speaking, the history of the world.) Márquez himself wrote that "Macondo is not so much a place as a state of mind."

The novel chronicles the history of the Buendía family, original founders of the town. It follows them through seven generations, relating their joys and despairs as technology reaches the town, transforming their simple lives. When a foreign banana company sets up shop the town enjoys an economic boom; when it leaves, the town enters a recession. All the turmoil leads to a brutal civil war. Meanwhile, each generation pursues love affairs, raises children, and attempts to better the family's prospects through ambitious business ventures. The fabric of their lives is threaded with uncanny coincidences, implausible twists and miraculous events: an epic rainy spell that lasts for four years, a priest who levitates when he eats chocolate, a woman so beautiful that men devote their lives to her, a rash of amnesia that causes residents to forget the names of simple items, and a few lingering ghosts. The narrative flashes back and flashes forward at will, filling in forgotten details and foreshadowing events to come.

One Hundred Years of Solitude is considered one of the canonical works of the literary subgenre called "magic realism." In magic realist works, fantastical events occur in the course of normal life; surreal elements are seamlessly blended with banal details. The reader must embrace the subjectivity of personal experience, suspending disbelief to a greater extent than usual and allowing herself to be enchanted by the world of the story. In some ways, magic realism is like mythology or folk tales, where universal laws of space and time don't always apply, and miracles can happen every day. Often, magic realist stories carry a deeper meaning. In Latin America, for example, many authors began cloaking subversive political messages in the language of fairytales, in order to escape government censorship.

Gabriel García Márquez won the Nobel Prize for Literature in 1982. The award committee called attention to his skills for combining the fantastic and the realistic "in a richly composed world of imagination, reflecting a continent's life and conflicts." In keeping with this message, Márquez used his acceptance speech to draw attention to Latin American history, which has often been misunderstood by outside observers. He argued that Latin American history is so bold and vibrant – so full of outrageous events and horrible tragedies and fervent desire – that magic realism is the only literary approach that can really make meaning of this history and give its participants a voice. He referenced an explorer who traveled with Magellan and recorded bizarre creatures of all kinds; the mythical city El Dorado that has never been found; the supposed fountain of eternal youth; the crazed dreams of gold that sent so many European explorers and conquerors marching through Latin American jungles. "I dare to think," Márquez states, "that it is this outsized reality, and not just its literary expression, that has deserved the attention of the Swedish Academy of Letters. Poets and beggars, musicians and prophets, warriors and scoundrels, all creatures of that unbridled reality, we have had to ask but little of imagination, for our crucial problem has been a lack of conventional means to render our lives believable. This, my friends, is the crux of our solitude."

In other words: because of their audacious history, the literary challenge for Latin American authors is not a need to imagine vivid adventures, but a need to communicate in a way Western audiences will understand. Later, Márquez seemed to deliver a gentle rebuke to the audience gathered around, saying: "It is understandable that the rational talents on this side of the world, exalted in the contemplation of their own cultures, should have found themselves without valid means to interpret us. It is only natural that they insist on measuring us with the yardstick that they use for themselves, forgetting that the ravages of life are not the same for all…" He asked that they lend support to Latin America in its attempts to define its own history and seek peace and progress on its own terms.

Since its publication in 1967, *One Hundred Years of Solitude* has been published in thirty-seven languages and sold more than 20 million copies, perhaps offering the world a small window into the lives of a people who have previously been condemned to solitude.

21. The passage's author most strongly implies that Gabriel García Márquez's attitude toward the Swedish Academy of Letters was:

A. awestruck and intimidated.
B. respectful yet critical.
C. contemptuous and indifferent.
D. admiring yet restrained.

22. The passage is best described as being told from the point of view of a critic who is:

F. contrasting and comparing various literary subgenres in Latin American literature.
G. advising aspiring Latin American writers on how to establish themselves as celebrated authors.
H. presenting in chronological order the key events of Gabriel García Márquez's literary career.
J. exploring the literary and cultural significance of magic realist elements in Márquez's work.

23. The main purpose of the third paragraph is to:

A. argue that *One Hundred Years of Solitude* is the best known example of magic realism.
B. describe some common elements that characterize magic realist works.
C. explain why Latin American authors adopted a magic realist style.
D. compare magic realism to mythology and folk tales.

24. Lines 74-80 ("It is understandable... same for all.") most nearly mean:

F. The literary establishment's emphasis on logic and rationality kept them from appreciating magic realism for too long.
G. The Swedish Academy of Letters expresses condescension toward writers like Márquez.
H. Outsiders are unable to fully understand Latin American culture.
J. The Nobel prize focuses too much on science and mathematics.

25. It can most reasonably be inferred that Márquez references events of Latin American history in his acceptance speech in order to:

A. demonstrate the depth of his historical knowledge.
B. provide cultural context for his own work.
C. highlight the extensive research he performed.
D. contradict unfounded assertions by opponents.

26. As it is used in line 52, the word *vibrant* most nearly means:

F. showy.
G. brilliant.
H. realistic.
J. dramatic.

27. The passage portrays the fictional Buendía family's history as a:

A. representation of family life during civil war.
B. narrative of domestic relationships in the context of broader events.
C. cautionary tale of the negative effects of globalization on a village.
D. rags-to-riches story of immigrants who better themselves in the New World.

28. It can most reasonably be inferred from the passage that the author views Macondo and its history as all of the following EXCEPT:

F. a symbolic microcosm.
G. an unattainable utopia.
H. an imaginary location.
J. an allegorical narrative.

29. The passage lists all of the following as examples of strange events experienced by the Buendía family EXCEPT a:

A. levitating priest.
B. rash of amnesia.
C. rain of gold.
D. four year rainy spell.

30. It can be reasonably inferred from the final paragraph that one possible result of the novel's success is that:

F. Márquez may lift his relatives out of poverty.
G. readers may better understand the Latin American experience.
H. more Latin American authors may win the Nobel Prize.
J. magic realism may become a more celebrated subgenre.

Passage IV

NATURAL SCIENCE

Now, let us consider the ant; the story of its survival and success is a fascinating tale. By some reckonings, ants are one of the most successful species of all time. They are found on nearly every continent (frozen Antarctica being the one exception). Native ant species have evolved in nearly every location. They dominate their ecological niches, taking advantage of the available resources with a methodical patience that's truly impressive. According to some estimates, ants alone contribute around 20 percent of the terrestrial animal biomass.

Ants are famously hard workers. Foraging varieties can travel up to 700 feet from their nests in search of food. Some are capable of leaping, but most worker ants are wingless and must travel the old-fashioned way: on foot. They can carry a load that's as much as ten to fifty times their own body weight; for a human, that would mean traveling beneath a burden of at least a thousand pounds. Ant society is divided into "castes," in which individuals are born to different roles. The vast majority of ants in the colony are "workers," females that cannot mate but live a life devoted to caring for the colony. Their tasks include caring for the queen; nurturing the next generation of young; maintaining the environment of the nest through tunnel maintenance and digging; and foraging for food and water. Each worker ant will pass through this sequence of roles, moving from career to career as it grows older.

The industrious nature of ants has long been evident, observed by anyone who has ever seen a long trail of ants marching patiently from a picnic table to their nest back home. But the ant's affinity for hard labor is just one part of the story. Their propensity for cooperation also plays a huge role in their ability to thrive. Cooperation enables ants to build grand nests, with separate areas for food storage, waste disposal, and nursing the young. Cooperation enables them to forage effectively, sending the appropriate number of workers in the direction of the best food sources, and abandoning food sources after their resources have been tapped. Cooperation enables ants to divide themselves into specialized groups, each with its own specific task to fulfill.

But how do ants carry out such large schemes? How do they communicate? The answer is pheromones: secreted chemical signals, the ant's form of language. Of course, pheromones are by no means exclusive to the ant kingdom – humans release pheromones, as do other mammals, a variety of insects, and even a few plants – but ants manipulate their chemical language to unique effect.

Each and every ant emits pheromones as it crawls about its business, whether inside the colony or out in the world. An ant that identifies a new source of food will lay down a trail of pheromones with a chemical signature that communicates: "Delicious meal this way." Other ants will use their antennae to explore and interpret this message. Their antennae are thin, long and paired, with articulated elbow-like joints that allow flexibility. By moving their antennae from side to side, ants take in the message through a combination of taste and smell evaporating off the chemical trail. While the specific chemical make-up of the message communicates its content, the intensity of the chemical helps the ant triangulate direction. (Follow the trail that's getting stronger!) And as they follow the trail, they too lay down pheromones.

This mechanism explains ants' ability to always find the shortest path to their destination. Once an ant reaches its destination, it returns home by the same path, applying a second layer of pheromones to the trail. The shortest path therefore receives its second layer first. Other ants, drawn by the stronger chemical traces, will follow the same path, leaving even more pheromones behind. Quickly the rest of the ants adopt this speedy route in favor of other options. Because of this elegant solution, they can adapt quickly and easily to changes in the environment, such as an obstacle that suddenly blocks a previously favored route.

Pheromones are not just used to signal the proximity of food. An ant may also emit pheromones when injured, which can draw other ants to its aid, or warn them to evacuate the area. Pheromones also serve as a kind of identity badge, letting other ants in the colony know to which "work crew" a given ant belongs. Even the queen emits pheromones, which prevent the workers from raising other queens. When her child-bearing years come to an end, this pheromone signature changes, and the workers begin rearing more females capable of mating. In time, these young females will fly from the nest to found their own colonies and take their turn as queens.

31. According to the passage, which of the following is an accurate sequence of the roles performed by a worker ant?

A. Attendant, nurturer, digger, forager
B. Digger, forager, attendant, nurturer
C. Attendant, nurturer, forager, digger
D. Forager, digger, nurturer, attendant

32. The second paragraph indicates that most ants in the colony are:

F. born to do one task alone.
G. soldiers that defend the colony.
H. females who don't reproduce.
J. lifelong caretakers of the queen.

33. According to the passage, ants use their antennae to:

A. dig tunnels.
B. carry food.
C. fight invaders.
D. interpret messages.

34. According to the passage, ant antennae are jointed to improve:

F. flexibility.
G. sense of smell.
H. pheromone production.
J. speed.

35. Which of the following best describes some of the different reasons ants communicate with pheromones, as listed in the passage?

A. Signaling presence of food, warning away intruders, highlighting the shortest path
B. Cooperating on waste disposal, tunnel digging and food storage
C. Signaling presence of food, calling for help, identifying types of workers
D. Determining number of queens, distributing nests, finding a mate

36. According to the passage, ants interpret pheromone messages through all of the following EXCEPT:

F. a manipulation of jointed antennae.
G a combination of taste and smell.
H. a determination of their intensity.
J. a unique visual code.

37. According to the passage, the queen emits pheromones to what purpose?

A. Controlling production of mating females
B. Signaling her location to her attendants
C. Delegating tasks to worker ants
D. Sending a warning to rival queens

38. It can reasonably be inferred from the passage that the author considers which quality to be most significant to the ant's success?

F. Strength
G. Diligence
H. Cooperation
J. Pheromones

39. When the author says that "the industrious nature of ants has long been evident," (line 27) she most likely means that:

A. researchers have conducted studies about ants' "industrious nature."
B. scientists do not fully understand how ants thrive.
C. ants spend most of their lives in the "worker" caste.
D. humans can easily observe ants collecting food.

40. The main purpose of the last paragraph is to:

F. describe different ways that ants use pheromones.
G. indicate what makes ants' use of pheromones unique.
H. explain what keeps workers from becoming queens.
J. explain how new ant colonies begin.

END OF SECTION 3

SCIENCE TEST

35 Minutes—40 Questions

DIRECTIONS: There are seven passages in this test. Each passage is followed by several questions. After reading a passage, choose the best answer to the question and fill in the corresponding oval on your answer document. You may refer to the passages as often as necessary.

You are NOT permitted to use a calculator on this test.

Passage I

When a non-native organism spreads to a new ecosystem, it is called an invasive species. Originally from the rainforest of South America, *Solenopsis invicta,* the red fire ant, is a type of invasive species that builds nests in ecosystems with particular climatic conditions (including temperature and moisture levels), referred to here as Condition Set A. When ants of this species colonize, they form a nest with a diameter that is about 8 times its height. Figure 1 shows the number of ants per colony for a range of ant nest diameters.

Figure 1

Figure 2 shows the average distance between equally-sized ant nests found in the rainforest. Figure 3 shows the percent of the deciduous forest, alpine, and savanna regions that is covered by ant nests of various heights.

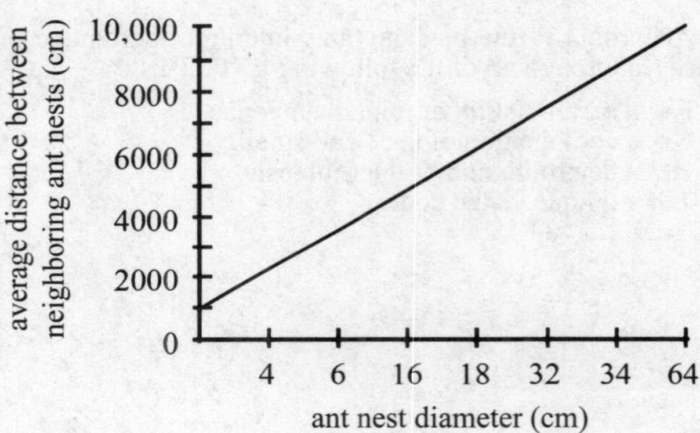

Figure 2

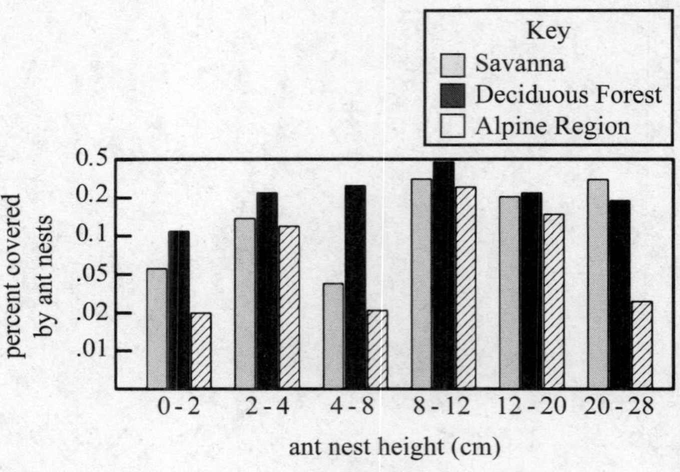

Figure 3

4       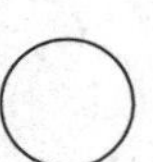 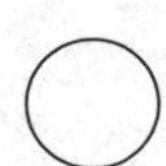  4

1. Suppose that 5,055 ants are found in a particular nest, under climatic Conditions A, in the rainforest. According to Figure 1, the diameter of the ant nest is most likely closest to which of the following?

A. 16 cm
B. 24 cm
C. 32 cm
D. 48 cm

2. According to Figure 2, for progressively larger ant nests, the average distance between neighboring nests:

F. increases only.
G. decreases only.
H. varies, but with no general trend.
J. remains the same.

3. According to Figure 3, for any given range of ant nest heights, the percent of the alpine region that is covered by ant nests is:

A. less than that of deciduous forests and savannas.
B. less than that of deciduous forests but greater than that of savannas.
C. greater than that of deciduous forests and savannas.
D. greater than that of deciduous forests but less than that of savannas.

4. Suppose that under climatic Condition Set A, an ant nest with a height of 4 cm is found in the rainforest. Based on Figure 1 and other information provided, the number of ants in the colony is most likely closest to which of the following?

F. 1,000 ants
G. 2,000 ants
H. 10,000 ants
J. 20,000 ants

5. Assume that an ant nest with a diameter of 64 cm was found in the rainforest 45 meters north of a field station. Also, assume that another 64-cm ant nest is located directly south of the field station. If the distance between these two ant nests is equal to the average distance between neighboring ant nests as given by Figure 2, the southern 64-cm ant nest should be located approximately:

A. 45 meters south of the field station.
B. 55 meters south of the field station.
C. 100 meters south of the field station.
D. 145 meters south of the field station.

Passage II

The sub-order Cryptodira includes freshwater turtles, snapping turtles, tortoises, soft-shelled turtles, and sea turtles. Figure 1 shows the various types of scutes, or bony plates, found on a turtle's shell. Table 1 is a key for identifying some of the Cryptodira that inhabit the oceans of the world. Table 2 describes 4 adult Cryptodira that were found on Sapelo Island, a barrier island off the coast of Georgia.

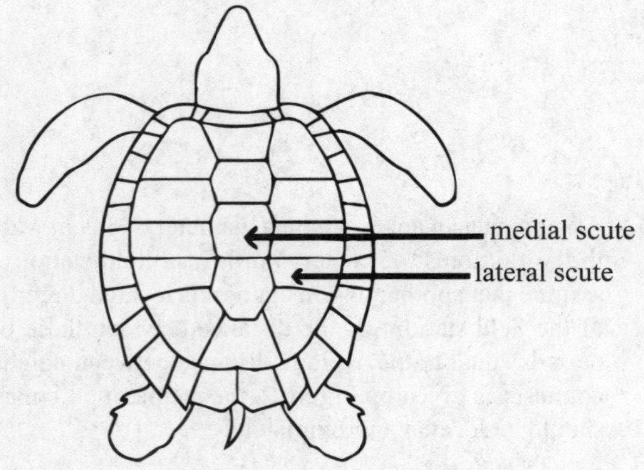

Figure 1

Table 1

Step	Trait	Appearance	Result
1	shell	soft and leathery	*Dermochelys coriacea*
		hard and bony	go to step 2
2	medial scutes	more than five present	*Lepidochelys olivacea*
		five present	go to Step 3
3	lateral scutes	more than four present	go to Step 4
		four present	go to Step 5
4	terminal scute	present at the posterior margin of the plastron*	*Lepidochelys kempii*
		not present at the posterior margin of the plastron*	*Caretta caretta*
5	beak	hooked	*Eretmochelys imbricata*
		not hooked	go to Step 6
6	scute size	lateral scutes larger than medial scutes	*Natator depressus*
		lateral and medial scutes approximately equal in size	*Chelonia mydas*

* A plastron is the bottom side of the shell.

Table 2

Cryptodira	Traits
A	197 pounds Hard reddish brown shell Five lateral scutes Five medial scutes Beak not hooked No terminal scute
B	352 pounds Hard blackish brown shell Four lateral scutes Five medial scutes Beak not hooked No terminal scute
C	589 pounds Leathery black shell with white spots Lateral ridges No scutes Beak not hooked
D	194 pounds Hard yellowish brown shell Four lateral scutes Five medial scutes Beak hooked No terminal scute

6. Table 1 describes which of the following classes of animals?

   F. Amphibians
   G. Insects
   H. Reptiles
   J. Fish

7. Based on the information provided in Tables 1 and 2, Cryptodira B is most likely a member of which of the following species?

   A. *Caretta caretta*
   B. *Lepidochelys olivacea*
   C. *Dermochelys coriacea*
   D. *Chelonia mydas*

8. Based on Table 1, which of the following traits of Cryptodira B indicates it is NOT *Eretmochelys imbricata?*

   F. Five medial scutes present
   G. Four lateral scutes present
   H. Beak not hooked
   J. No terminal scute

9. The results from Table 1 for Cryptodira C and Cryptodira D first diverge at which of the following steps?

   A. Step 1
   B. Step 2
   C. Step 3
   D. Step 4

10. According to Table 1, *Lepidochelys olivacea* and *Lepidochelys kempii* both have which of the following traits?

   F. Leathery shell
   G. Bony shell
   H. Five medial scutes
   J. More than five medial scutes

Passage III

Hemoglobin, a respiratory pigment in red blood cells that transports oxygen and carbon dioxide between lungs and body tissues, has the chemical structure shown below:

Figure 1

Figures 2, 3, and 4 each show how the *partial pressure* of oxygen (PO_2) (a way of measuring the amount of oxygen in the air) affects the percent of hemoglobin (Hb) that is saturated with oxygen. Figure 2 shows this relationship at three pH levels (7.2, 7.4, and 7.6). Figure 3 shows this relationship at a range of temperatures in degrees Celsius. Figure 4 shows the average hemoglobin saturation curve across the four temperatures in relation to the partial pressure of oxygen.

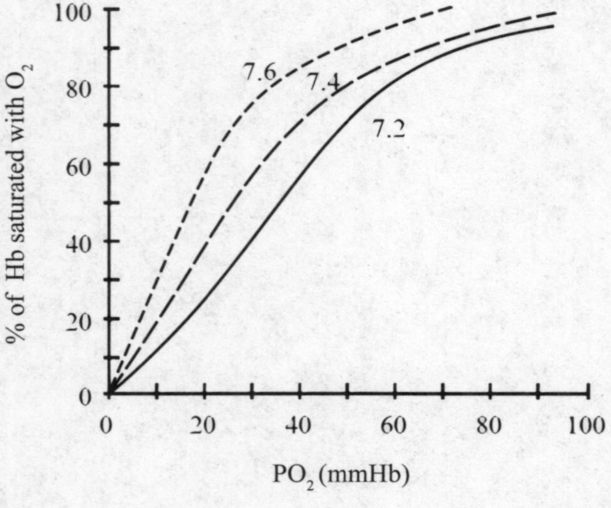

Figure 2

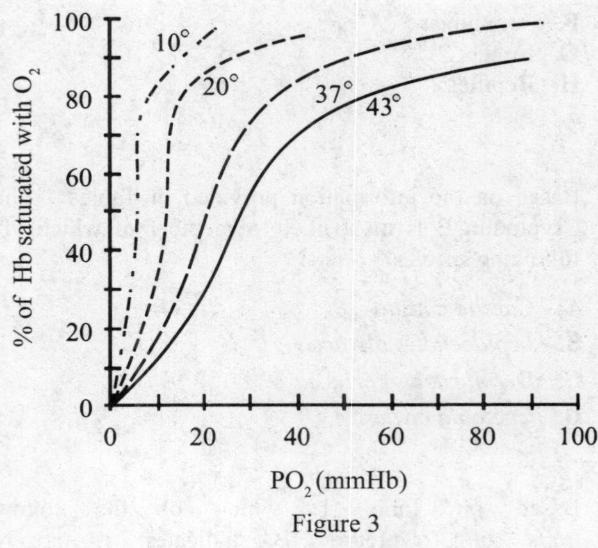

Figure 3

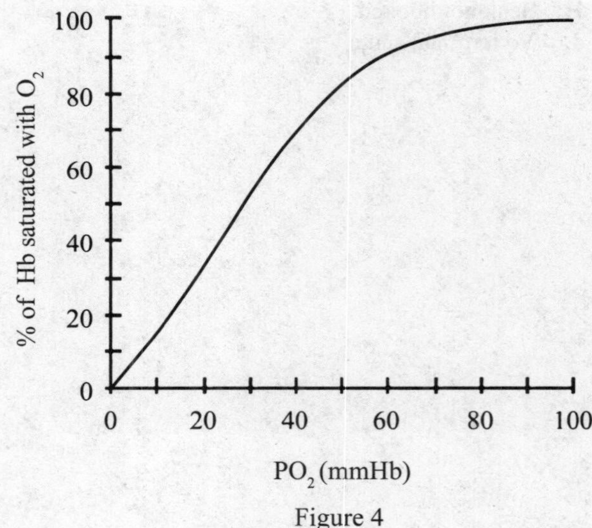

Figure 4

4 ○ ○ ○ ○ ○ ○ ○ ○ ○ 4

11. According to Figure 4, the average hemoglobin saturation when the partial pressure of oxygen is 30 mmHb is closest to which of the following?

A. 18%
B. 50%
C. 72%
D. 89%

12. At 43°C, as the partial pressure of oxygen increases from 0 – 100 mmHb, the percent saturation of hemoglobin with oxygen:

F. increases only.
G. decreases only.
H. increases, then decreases.
J. decreases, then increases.

13. At 60 mmHb, red blood cells with which of the following pH levels will most likely have the highest % of hemoglobin saturated with oxygen?

A. 7.1
B. 7.3
C. 7.5
D. 7.7

14. According to Figures 2 and 3, hemoglobin in an environment with a partial pressure of 40 mmHb and a pH of 7.4 will have a temperature closest to:

F. 10°C.
G. 20°C.
H. 37°C.
J. 43°C.

15. Based on Figure 2, if 50% of the hemoglobin was saturated with oxygen and the pH of the red blood cells was the same as that of pure water, the partial pressure of oxygen would most likely be:

A. less than 15 mmHb.
B. between 15 mmHb and 25 mmHb.
C. between 25 mmHb and 38 mmHb.
D. more than 38 mmHb.

Passage IV

In water, ionic compounds split into anions and cations. Table 1 lists several common ionic compounds and the ions that result when these compounds are dissolved in an aqueous solution.

Table 1		
Ionic Compound	Cation	Anion
HCl	H^+	Cl^-
NaBr	Na^+	Br^-
$AgNO_3$	Ag^+	NO_3^-
$CaSO_4$	Ca^{2+}	SO_4^{2-}
KCl	K^+	Cl^-
H_3PO_4	H^+	PO_4^{3-}
NaOH	Na^+	OH^-
$Pb(NO_3)_2$	Pb^{2+}	NO_3^-

As seen in Figure 1, when two ionic compounds are placed in an aqueous solution, they dissociate into anions (X and Y) and cations (A and B). A double replacement reaction occurs if a *precipitate (s)*, or solid, is formed from these ions.

Double Replacement Reaction Occurs:

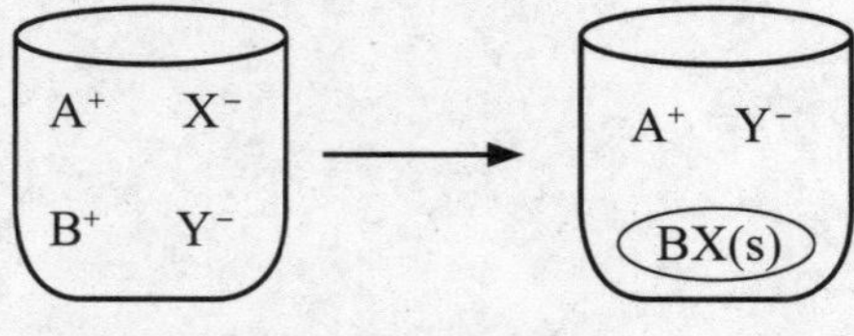

$AX(aq) + BY(aq) \rightarrow AY(aq) + BX(s)$

Double Replacement Reaction Does Not Occur:

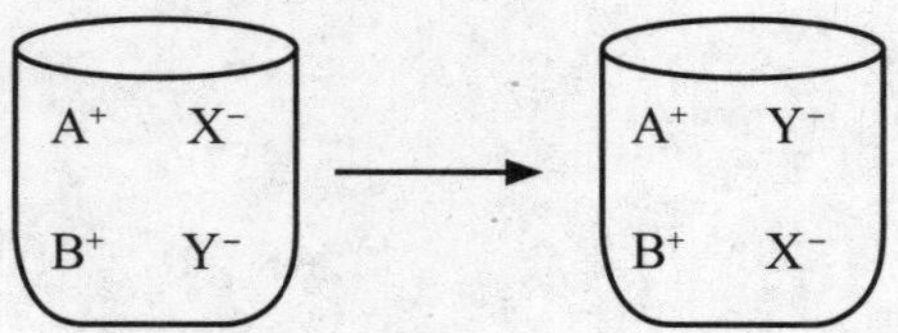

$AX(aq) + BY(aq) \rightarrow AY(aq) + BX(aq)$

Figure 1

Table 2 shows the outcome when various cations and anions are placed in an aqueous solution.

Table 2				
Cations	Anions			
	Cl^-	SO_4^{2-}	NO_3^-	PO_4^{3-}
Pb^{2+}	*s*	*s*	*aq*	*s*
Ca^{2+}	*aq*	*s*	*aq*	*s*
Na^+	*aq*	*aq*	*aq*	*aq*
Ag^+	*s*	*s*	*aq*	*s*

4 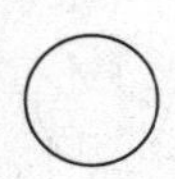 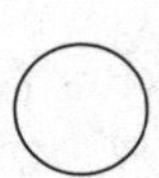 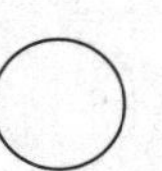 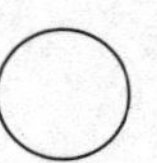  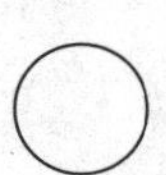 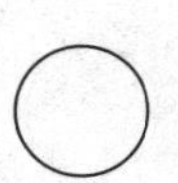 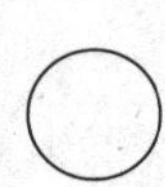 4

16. According to Table 2, which of the following compounds would form a precipitate?

F. Na_2SO_4
G. $Pb(NO_3)_2$
H. $CaCl_2$
J. Ag_3PO_4

17. Based on Figure 1, Table 2, and the information provided, if $AgClO_3$ were mixed with H_2SO_4, would a double-replacement reaction occur?

A. Yes; Ag^+ and SO_4^{2-} form a precipitate.
B. Yes; Ag^+ and SO_4^{2-} do not form a precipitate.
C. No; Ag^+ and SO_4^{2-} form a precipitate.
D. No; Ag^+ and SO_4^{2-} do not form a precipitate.

18. An unknown solution contains either Ag^+ or Ca^{2+}. According to Table 2, which of the following anions should be added to determine the identity of the unknown?

F. Cl^-
G. SO_4^{2-}
H. NO_3^-
J. PO_4^{3-}

19. Based on the information in Tables 1 and 2, the acid that is *least* likely to cause a double replacement reaction to occur is:

A. HCl.
B. H_2SO_4.
C. HNO_3.
D. H_3PO_4.

20. Supposed the following ionic compounds were combined in an aqueous solution and observed for the formation of a precipitate. Which of the following equations indicates that a double-replacement reaction occurred?

F. $2NaBr(aq) + CaCl_2(aq) \rightarrow 2NaCl(aq) + CaBr_2(aq)$
G. $H_2SO_4(aq) + CaCl_2(aq) \rightarrow CaSO_4(s) + 2HCl(aq)$
H. $HOCl_3(aq) + KBr(aq) \rightarrow KOCl_3(aq) + HBr(aq)$
J. $2NH_4I(aq) + Ca(NO_3)_2(aq) \rightarrow 2NH_4NO_3(aq) + CaI_2(aq)$

21. Which of the following graphs best represents the outcomes when Ca^{2+} interacts with the different anions in Table 2 ?

A.

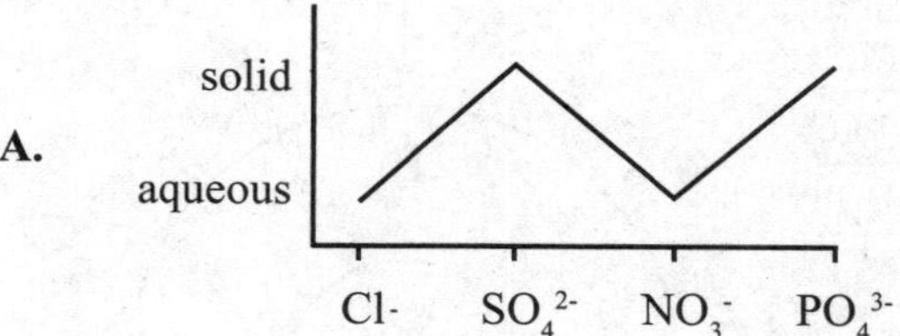

B.

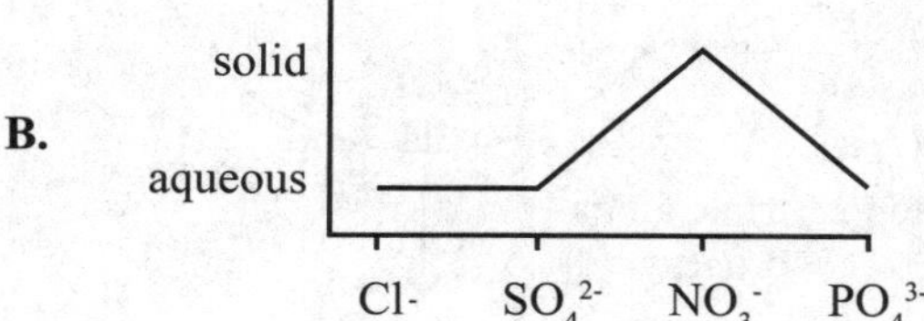

C.

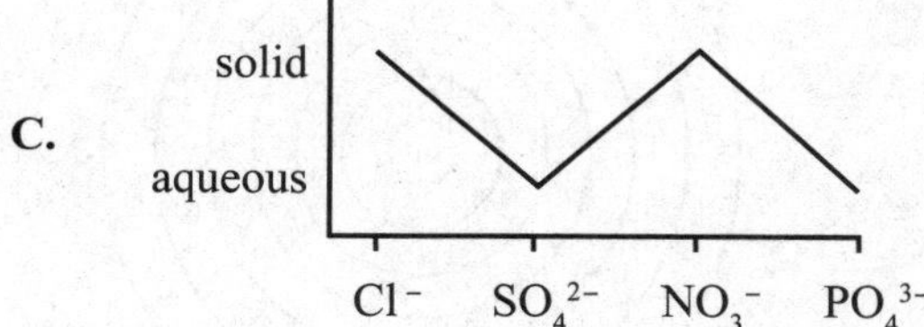

D.

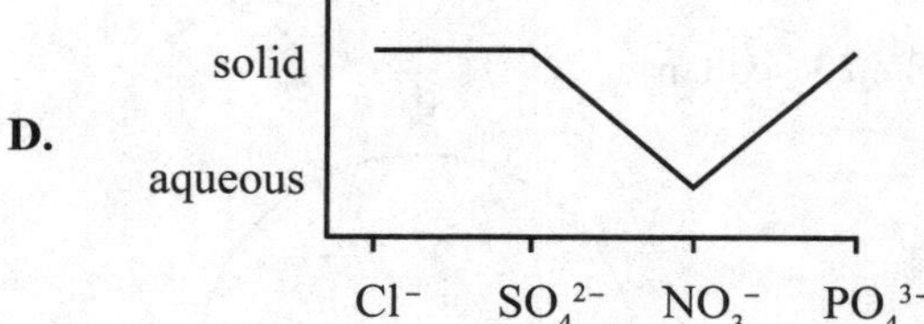

GO ON TO THE NEXT PAGE.

Passage V

Figure 1 depicts some of the steps in the life cycle of a star.

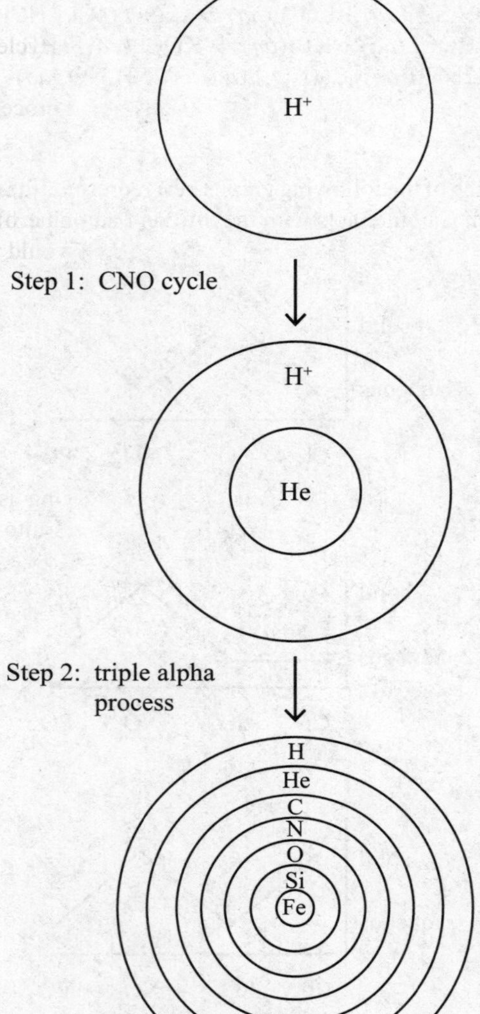

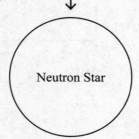

Figure 1

The molecular composition of a star at a given stage depends on various conditions, such as the mass of the star.

A group of galaxies approximately 1000 light years from Earth was observed. The luminosities of all visible stars in 4 galaxies were determined. The relative luminosity (RL) of each star was calculated using the following equation:

$$RL = \frac{\text{Energy emitted by star in one second}}{\text{Energy emitted by the Sun in one second}}$$

The results are recorded in Figure 2.

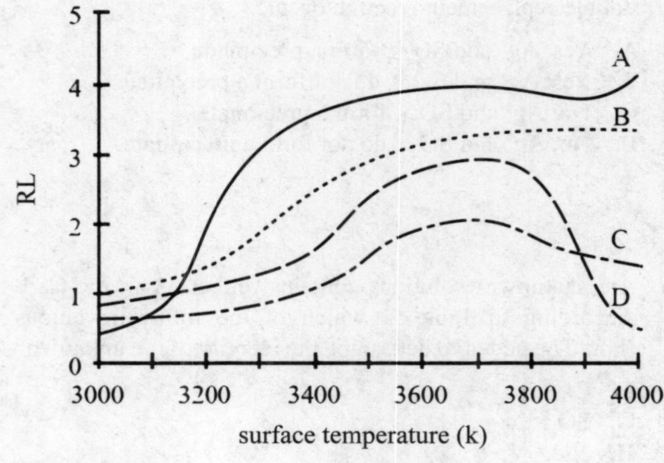

Figure 2

Figure 3 shows the average size of the stars observed during the experiment.

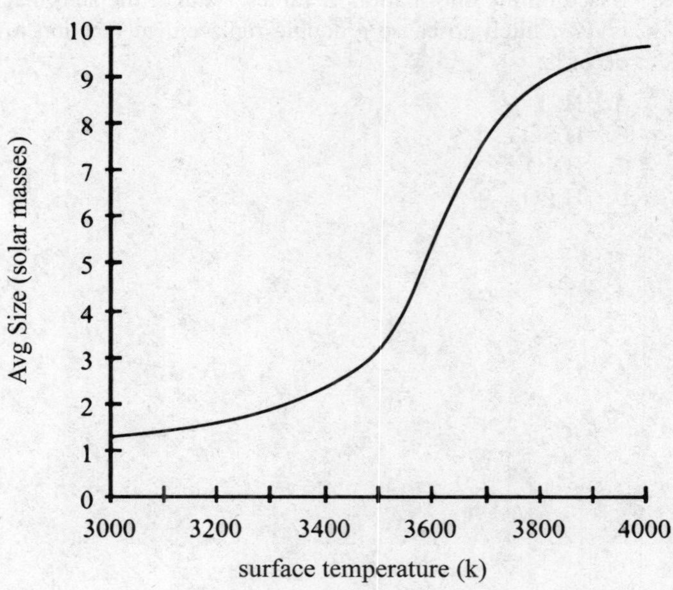

Figure 3

22. At which of the following surface temperatures would the luminosity of a star in Galaxy B be the greatest?

F. 3200K
G. 3400K
H. 3600K
J. 3800K

23. At which of the following surface temperatures would the luminosity of a star in Galaxy B be closest to 2 times the luminosity of a star in Galaxy B with a surface temperature of 3000K?

A. 3100K
B. 3300K
C. 3500K
D. 3800K

24. The data in Figure 3 best support which of the following hypotheses? As the surface temperature of a star increases, the average size:

F. decreases only.
G. increases only.
H. decreases, then increases.
J. increases, then decreases.

25. Based on Figure 1, which statement best describes what happens to Helium in a star?

A. Helium is first formed in the triple alpha process then is released during collapse.
B. Helium is released during collapse then starts the CNO cycle.
C. Helium is first formed from the CNO cycle and then released during collapse.
D. Helium is formed from the triple alpha process, but not the CNO cycle.

26. According to Figures 2 and 3, the RL value of a star in Galaxy D with a mass of 3 solar masses would be closest to which of the following?

F. 1.50
G. 2.50
H. 3.50
J. 4.50

27. Based on Figure 1, which of the following is the final element produced before the star collapses into a neutron star?

A. Helium
B. Hydrogen
C. Iron
D. Oxygen

GO ON TO THE NEXT PAGE.

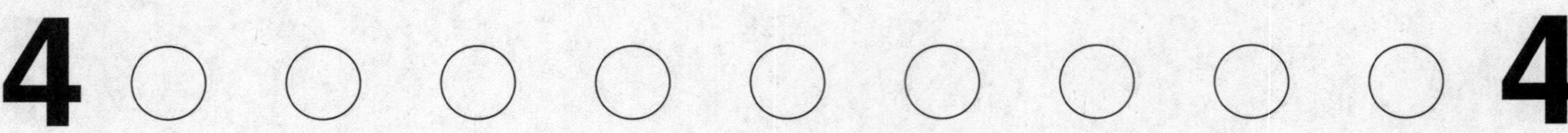

Passage VI

Scientists tested the hypothesis that the resistance of the springs in a spring system will affect its normal modes (the number of collisions the blocks make in the first minute). To measure normal modes, the scientists used a device in which two blocks were placed on a surface and connected by a system of springs (see Figure 1).

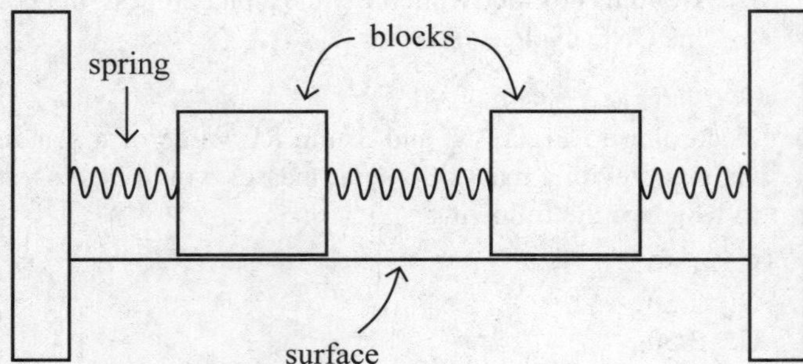

Identical blocks were used in all 3 experiments. In each experiment, the scientists shook the system by striking it with a pneumatic hammer with a discrete force of 800 newtons.

Experiment 1

The spring system, at spring resistance 1, was placed on an ice surface. The scientists activated the pneumatic hammer to shake the system, and measured how many times the blocks collided during the first minute. Next, they shook the system at spring resistance 2 on an ice surface and counted how many times the blocks collided during the first minute. They repeated this procedure on carpet and linoleum. The results are shown in Table 1.

Table 1

		Normal Modes	
Trial	Surface	Spring resistance 1	Spring resistance 2
1	Ice	62	66
2	Carpet	35	39
3	Linoleum	42	51

Experiment 2

The scientists shook the spring system with each spring resistance on a linoleum surface. One minute later, they shook each system again and measured the normal modes for the next minute (Trial 4). The scientists then waited three minutes before shaking each system a final time and measured the normal modes for the next minute (Trial 5). The results are shown in Table 2.

Table 2

	Normal Modes	
Trial	Spring resistance 1	Spring resistance 2
4	45	60
5	42	51

Experiment 3

The scientists shook the spring system with each spring resistance on a linoleum surface. Two minutes later, they shook the system again and measured the number of collisions in each 30-second span over the duration of three minutes. The results are shown in Table 3.

Table 3

	Number of collisions	
Time (sec)	Spring resistance 1	Spring resistance 2
0-30	29	38
30-60	16	22
60-90	11	14
90-120	5	8
120-150	1	4
150-180	0	0

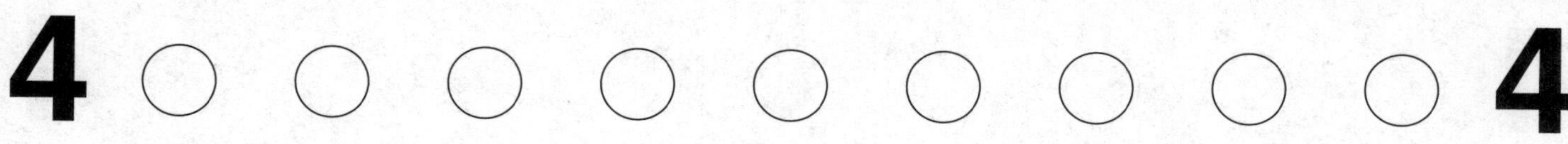

28. In Experiment 3, the most likely reason the scientists shook the spring systems a second time while the blocks were still in motion was that they wanted to:

F. test the results of using the spring systems on multiple surfaces.
G. see how additional shakes would affect the number of collisions.
H. test the strength of the springs in the systems.
J. accommodate for the different spring resistances.

29. Based on Tables 1 and 2, for which of the following trials was the frequency of collisions the same for the spring system at spring resistance 1 ?

A. Trials 1 and 2
B. Trials 1 and 3
C. Trials 3 and 5
D. Trials 3 and 4

30. In Experiment 2, the result of changing from spring resistance 1 to spring resistance 2 was that the:

F. amount of shaking needed was less.
G. force on the surface decreased.
H. normal modes increased.
J. normal modes decreased.

31. For Trial 5, is it likely the blocks were still in motion immediately before the scientists shook the system a third time?

A. Yes; based on Experiment 1, the blocks probably continued moving for less than 1 minutes.
B. Yes; based on Experiment 1, the blocks probably continued moving for more than 3 minutes.
C. No; based on Experiment 3, the blocks probably continued moving for more than 3 minutes.
D. No; based on Experiment 3, the blocks probably continued moving for less than 3 minutes.

32. Suppose that in Experiment 2, 3 minutes after Trial 5 was completed, the scientists measured the normal modes for the spring system at spring resistance 1. Based on the results of Experiment 2, the normal modes would most likely have been:

F. less than 45.
G. between 45 and 50.
H. between 51 and 60.
J. greater than 60.

33. Suppose the scientists conducted a fourth experiment in which they shook the system at spring resistance 1 on varying surfaces. A varying amount of time later, they shook the system again and measured the normal modes for the next minute. Which of the following surfaces and durations between shakes would most likely result in the highest normal modes?

	surface	duration between shakes
A.	linoleum	60 sec
B.	carpet	120 sec
C.	linoleum	180 sec
D.	ice	180 sec

Passage VII

The Earth's crust is broken into tectonic plates (regions of land that sink into and rise from the mantle). Plates can move under each other and rotate around the surface. This process is called continental drift. The relative position of the plates remains the same though they may shrink or grow in size.

During continental drift, one plate's edge enters the mantle and molten rock from the mantle is pushed to the surface. Thus, the order of the plates remains the same as they undergo continental drift.

Four scientists hypothesized about the way 6 adjacent tectonic plates underwent continental drift. They determined that it takes approximately 10 million years for all of the rock material on one plate to sink into the mantle. They also determined that plates are roughly the same size, so it takes 60 million years for all of the plates to each sink once. They disagreed about the order in which the plates sink and rise from the mantle.

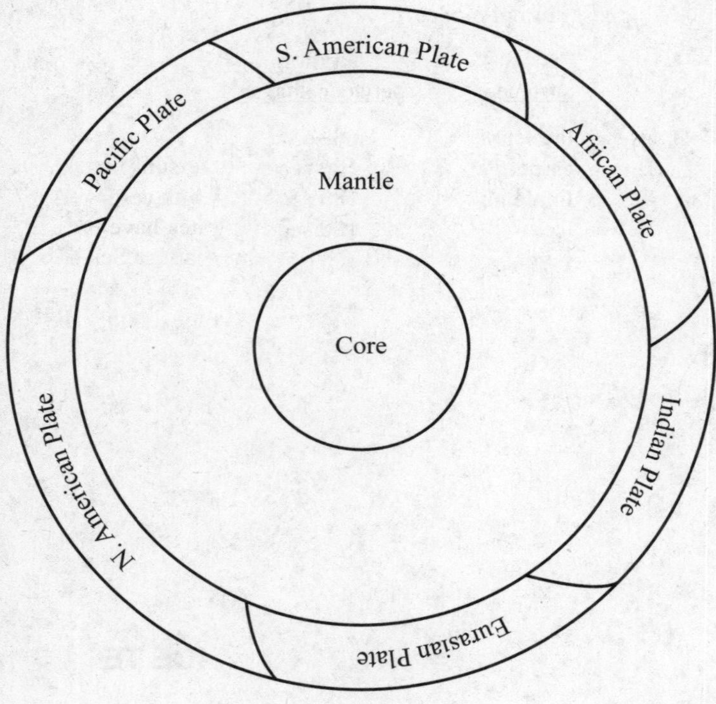

Figure 1

Scientist 1

The African Plate is the oldest plate and was the first to undergo continental drift. Its edge melted under the Indian Plate and the South American Plate began sinking last.

Scientist 2

The African Plate is the oldest plate, but it was the second to undergo continental drift. The African Plate pushed the edge of the South American Plate into the mantle. When the South American Plate began to drift, it pushed the African plate under the Indian Plate. After all of the plates sank once, the direction of drift reversed and the edge of the Pacific Plate sank under the North American Plate.

Scientist 3

It is uncertain which plate is the oldest. Plates drift clockwise relative to the figure. If the Eurasian Plate is the oldest, then it would melt first under the North American Plate, and the Indian Plate would melt last under the Eurasian Plate.

Scientist 4

It is uncertain which plate is the oldest. The plates can melt under adjacent plates and also push them into the mantle. The direction reverses once all of the rock material on the Earth's surface has melted and new molten rock has been ejected from the mantle.

34. Based on the given information, how many tectonic plates would have sunk completely into the mantle 45 million years after the oldest plate started sinking?

F. 2
G. 3
H. 4
J. 5

35. Based on Scientist 3's model, if all of the plates are able to sink once into the mantle and the oldest plate is the Indian Plate, the third plate to sink into the mantle would be the:

A. Eurasian Plate
B. African Plate
C. South American Plate
D. North American Plate

36. Which of the scientists believe that any of the 7 tectonic plates could be the oldest plate?

F. Scientists 2 and 3
G. Scientists 3 and 4
H. Scientists 2 and 4
J. Scientists 2, 3, and 4

37. Suppose that Scientist 1 is correct. Based on the given information, 30 million years after the oldest plate began sinking, which of the following plates would definitely NOT have sunk completely into the mantle?

A. The South American Plate
B. The African Plate
C. The Indian Plate
D. The Eurasian Plate

38. Suppose that Scientist 2 is correct. Based on the given information, 80 million years after the first plate began to drift, which of the following plates could have sunk completely into the mantle a second time?

F. The Pacific Plate and the African Plate
G. The South American Plate and the Indian Plate
H. The North American Plate and the Pacific Plate
J. The Indian Plate and the Eurasian Plate

39. Suppose that all 6 tectonic plates have sunk into the mantle once. Which scientist(s) would argue that the Pacific Plate could have been the last plate to sink into the mantle?

A. Scientist 2 only
B. Scientists 2 and 4 only
C. Scientists 2, 3, and 4 only
D. Scientists 1, 2, 3, and 4

40. Suppose that only some of the plates have sunk into the mantle once, that the most recent plate to sink completely was the Pacific Plate, and that no new plates have begun sinking into the mantle. Given this information, Scientist 1 would most likely conclude that it has been how many millions of years since the oldest plate began sinking?

F. 20
G. 30
H. 40
J. 50

END OF PRACTICE TEST 1

Practice Test 1 Answer Key

Section 1 – English Answers

1. B	11. A	21. A	31. C	41. C	51. B	61. A	71. C
2. F	12. H	22. J	32. J	42. G	52. G	62. H	72. J
3. B	13. A	23. D	33. D	43. C	53. B	63. C	73. B
4. H	14. H	24. J	34. J	44. H	54. F	64. J	74. J
5. D	15. B	25. A	35. A	45. D	55. D	65. B	75. B
6. H	16. G	26. H	36. F	46. F	56. H	66. G	
7. C	17. A	27. C	37. B	47. D	57. D	67. B	
8. H	18. H	28. F	38. H	48. G	58. G	68. H	
9. B	19. A	29. D	39. B	49. B	59. D	69. C	
10. J	20. H	30. G	40. G	50. H	60. J	70. H	

Section 2 – Math Answers

1. C	11. C	21. A	31. C	41. D	51. B
2. K	12. H	22. J	32. H	42. K	52. H
3. B	13. B	23. C	33. D	43. C	53. C
4. K	14. G	24. F	34. H	44. K	54. G
5. E	15. D	25. D	35. B	45. C	55. E
6. J	16. H	26. J	36. H	46. G	56. G
7. D	17. D	27. B	37. B	47. D	57. D
8. K	18. K	28. F	38. H	48. F	58. G
9. D	19. A	29. E	39. E	49. A	59. E
10. H	20. G	30. H	40. J	50. H	60. F

Section 3 – Reading Answers

1. A	11. A	21. B	31. A
2. J	12. H	22. J	32. H
3. B	13. A	23. B	33. D
4. F	14. H	24. H	34. F
5. C	15. B	25. B	35. C
6. G	16. F	26. J	36. J
7. D	17. D	27. B	37. A
8. H	18. H	28. G	38. H
9. B	19. D	29. C	39. D
10. G	20. G	30. G	40. F

Section 4 – Science Answers

1. B	11. B	21. A	31. D
2. F	12. F	22. J	32. F
3. A	13. D	23. B	33. D
4. J	14. J	24. G	34. H
5. B	15. D	25. C	35. D
6. H	16. J	26. G	36. G
7. D	17. A	27. C	37. A
8. H	18. F	28. G	38. H
9. A	19. C	29. C	39. C
10. G	20. G	30. H	40. J

Scoring the Test

Raw Score

To obtain your raw score for each section, subtract the number of **missed** or **omitted** questions from the **total number of questions** in that section.

English	= 75 −	________ # of missed questions	=	________ raw score
Math	= 60 −	________ # of missed questions	=	________ raw score
Reading	= 40 −	________ # of missed questions	=	________ raw score
Science	= 40 −	________ # of missed questions	=	________ raw score

Scaled Score Estimate

To obtain your scaled score estimate for each section, use the tables on the next page. For each section, locate your raw score in the corresponding table. Next to your raw score, you will find the range of scores you would likely receive on the actual ACT.

IMPORTANT: to receive a highly accurate prediction of your performance on test day, you must take an **official, calibrated ACT test.** We recommend test 4 or 5 in *The Real ACT Prep Guide*, by ACT Inc.

Scaled Score Estimates

English

Scale Score	Raw Score
32 — 36	75
31 — 35	74
30 — 34	72 – 73
29 — 33	71
28 — 32	70
27 — 31	69
25 — 29	67 – 68
24 — 28	66
23 — 27	65
22 — 26	63 – 64
21 — 25	61 – 62
20 — 24	58 – 60
19 — 23	55 – 57
18 — 22	53 – 54
17 — 21	50 – 52
16 — 20	47 – 49
15 — 19	44 – 46
14 — 18	42 – 43
13 — 17	40 – 41
12 — 16	38 – 39
11 — 15	34 – 37
10 — 14	32 – 33
9 — 13	30 – 31
8 — 12	28 – 29
7 — 11	26 – 27
6 — 10	23 – 25
5 — 9	21 – 22

Math

Scale Score	Raw Score
32 — 36	59 – 60
31 — 35	58
30 — 34	56 – 57
29 — 33	55
28 — 32	54
27 — 31	53
26 — 30	51 – 52
25 — 29	50
24 — 28	48 – 49
23 — 27	45 – 47
22 — 26	42 – 44
21 — 25	39 – 41
20 — 24	36 – 38
19 — 23	34 – 35
18 — 22	32 – 33
17 — 21	30 – 31
16 — 20	29
15 — 19	27 – 28
14 — 18	24 – 26
13 — 17	20 – 23
12 — 16	16 – 19
11 — 15	12 – 15
10 — 14	9 – 11
9 — 13	7 – 8
8 — 12	6
7 — 11	5
6 — 10	4

Reading

Scale Score	Raw Score
31 — 36	40
30 — 35	39
29 — 34	38
28 — 33	37
27 — 32	36
26 — 31	35
25 — 30	34
24 — 29	33
23 — 28	32
22 — 27	31
21 — 26	30
20 — 25	29
19 — 24	28
18 — 23	27
17 — 22	25 – 26
16 — 21	24
15 — 20	23
14 — 19	21 – 22
13 — 18	20
12 — 17	18 – 19
11 — 16	17
10 — 15	15 – 16
9 — 14	14
8 — 13	12 – 13
7 — 12	10 – 11
6 — 11	8 – 9
5 — 10	6 – 7

Science

Scale Score	Raw Score
31 — 36	40
30 — 35	39
28 — 33	38
26 — 31	37
24 — 29	36
23 — 28	35
22 — 27	33 – 34
21 — 26	32
20 — 25	30 – 31
19 — 24	29
18 — 23	27 – 28
17 — 22	26
16 — 21	24 – 25
15 — 20	22 – 23
14 — 19	21
13 — 18	18 – 20
12 — 17	17
11 — 16	15 – 16
10 — 15	14
9 — 14	12 – 13
8 — 13	11
7 — 12	10
6 — 11	8 – 9
5 — 10	7 – 8

English Score Range

Math Score Range

Reading Score Range

Science Score Range

Section 1

1	A B C D	20	F G H J	39	A B C D	58	F G H J
2	F G H J	21	A B C D	40	F G H J	59	A B C D
3	A B C D	22	F G H J	41	A B C D	60	F G H J
4	F G H J	23	A B C D	42	F G H J	61	A B C D
5	A B C D	24	F G H J	43	A B C D	62	F G H J
6	F G H J	25	A B C D	44	F G H J	63	A B C D
7	A B C D	26	F G H J	45	A B C D	64	F G H J
8	F G H J	27	A B C D	46	F G H J	65	A B C D
9	A B C D	28	F G H J	47	A B C D	66	F G H J
10	F G H J	29	A B C D	48	F G H J	67	A B C D
11	A B C D	30	F G H J	49	A B C D	68	F G H J
12	F G H J	31	A B C D	50	F G H J	69	A B C D
13	A B C D	32	F G H J	51	A B C D	70	F G H J
14	F G H J	33	A B C D	52	F G H J	71	A B C D
15	A B C D	34	F G H J	53	A B C D	72	F G H J
16	F G H J	35	A B C D	54	F G H J	73	A B C D
17	A B C D	36	F G H J	55	A B C D	74	F G H J
18	F G H J	37	A B C D	56	F G H J	75	A B C D
19	A B C D	38	F G H J	57	A B C D		

Section 2

1	A B C D E	16	F G H J K	31	A B C D E	46	F G H J K
2	F G H J K	17	A B C D E	32	F G H J K	47	A B C D E
3	A B C D E	18	F G H J K	33	A B C D E	48	F G H J K
4	F G H J K	19	A B C D E	34	F G H J K	49	A B C D E
5	A B C D E	20	F G H J K	35	A B C D E	50	F G H J K
6	F G H J K	21	A B C D E	36	F G H J K	51	A B C D E
7	A B C D E	22	F G H J K	37	A B C D E	52	F G H J K
8	F G H J K	23	A B C D E	38	F G H J K	53	A B C D E
9	A B C D E	24	F G H J K	39	A B C D E	54	F G H J K
10	F G H J K	25	A B C D E	40	F G H J K	55	A B C D E
11	A B C D E	26	F G H J K	41	A B C D E	56	F G H J K
12	F G H J K	27	A B C D E	42	F G H J K	57	A B C D E
13	A B C D E	28	F G H J K	43	A B C D E	58	F G H J K
14	F G H J K	29	A B C D E	44	F G H J K	59	A B C D E
15	A B C D E	30	F G H J K	45	A B C D E	60	F G H J K

Section 3

1	A B C D	11	A B C D	21	A B C D	31	A B C D
2	F G H J	12	F G H J	22	F G H J	32	F G H J
3	A B C D	13	A B C D	23	A B C D	33	A B C D
4	F G H J	14	F G H J	24	F G H J	34	F G H J
5	A B C D	15	A B C D	25	A B C D	35	A B C D
6	F G H J	16	F G H J	26	F G H J	36	F G H J
7	A B C D	17	A B C D	27	A B C D	37	A B C D
8	F G H J	18	F G H J	28	F G H J	38	F G H J
9	A B C D	19	A B C D	29	A B C D	39	A B C D
10	F G H J	20	F G H J	30	F G H J	40	F G H J

Section 4

1	A B C D	11	A B C D	21	A B C D	31	A B C D
2	F G H J	12	F G H J	22	F G H J	32	F G H J
3	A B C D	13	A B C D	23	A B C D	33	A B C D
4	F G H J	14	F G H J	24	F G H J	34	F G H J
5	A B C D	15	A B C D	25	A B C D	35	A B C D
6	F G H J	16	F G H J	26	F G H J	36	F G H J
7	A B C D	17	A B C D	27	A B C D	37	A B C D
8	F G H J	18	F G H J	28	F G H J	38	F G H J
9	A B C D	19	A B C D	29	A B C D	39	A B C D
10	F G H J	20	F G H J	30	F G H J	40	F G H J

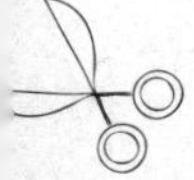

Practice Test 2

There is nothing like good old-fashioned, timed practice to help you get ready for the official ACT.

The two practice tests in this book will allow you to practice your pacing, flex your new skills, and get more comfortable taking a complete ACT. These practice tests simulate the difficulty, language, and timing of the official test. Your raw scores (the number you answered correctly) will help you calibrate how well you have mastered the content in this book.

When you are ready for a highly accurate prediction of your ACT score, your best bet is to take a recently released, nationally standardized, official ACT test. We strongly recommend taking test 4 or 5, the most recently released tests, from *The Real ACT Prep Guide, by ACT, Inc.*

Test Breakdown

Section 1 - English ....75 questions, 45 minutes

Section 2 - Math..................60 questions, 60 minutes

Section 3 - Reading.............40 questions, 35 minutes

Section 4 - Science..............40 questions, 35 minutes

Total Time................................... 2 hours 50 minutes

To fully mimic the pace of test day, take a **10 minute break** after the Math section. Once you're ready to start your practice test, turn the page and begin!

ENGLISH TEST

45 Minutes—75 Questions

DIRECTIONS: In the five passages that follow, certain words and phrases are underlined and numbered. In the right-hand column, you will find alternatives for the underlined part. In most cases, you are to choose the one that best expresses the idea, makes the statement appropriate for standard written English, or is worded most consistently with the style and tone of the passage as a whole. If you think the original version is best, choose "NO CHANGE." In some cases you will find in the right-hand column a question about the underlined part. You are to choose the best answer to the question.

You will also find questions about a section of the passage, or about the passage as a whole. These questions do not refer to an underlined portion of the passage, but rather are identified by a number or numbers in a box.

For each question, choose the alternative you consider best and fill in the corresponding oval on your answer document. For many of the questions, you must read several sentences beyond the question to determine the answer. Be sure that you have read far enough ahead each time you choose an alternative.

PASSAGE I

Grasse

Have you ever walked through the fragrance section of the department store, sniffing perfumes? If so, then you have a connection to Grasse, France: a rural town on the French Riviera, and the perfume capital of the world. Throughout the centuries, Grasse has shaped the history of perfume. Likewise, the perfume industry has shaped the history of Grasse.[1]

The story begins in the 17th century, when perfume came to France. At first, perfume was primarily used to scent the clothing that people would typically wear,[2] particularly leather gloves. Since a great deal of leather was processed in the region, it was the natural location, to[3] begin producing perfume. At the time, the favored scents were floral, made with jasmine grown in India, tuberose grown in Italy, and roses that thrived on Grasse's warm, sunny slopes.

As the years passed, the leather industry, which had spurred perfume's success, becoming[4] less profitable. Perfume, however, grew more fashionable than ever. In the 18th century, the town's business shifted solely to the production of

1. A. NO CHANGE
   B. the history of Grasse has, by the perfume industry, also been shaped.
   C. the perfume industry has shaped also the history of Grasse.
   D. the history of Grasse has been shaped by the perfume industry.

2. F. NO CHANGE
   G. the clothing that people would, typically, wear,
   H. the clothing that was worn
   J. clothing,

3. A. NO CHANGE
   B. location to
   C. location. To
   D. location; to

4. F. NO CHANGE
   G. success and became
   H. success, became
   J. success, with becoming

perfume. By now, Grasse was considered the worldwide leader in perfume. Its surrounding fields were filled with blossoms destined for the fragrance bottle. Inspirational [5] by these blooms, its perfumers concocted fresh floral-infused perfumes. Its signature scents were worn by the most stylish young ladies and gentlemen throughout Europe.

5. A. NO CHANGE
B. Inspired
C. Inspiringly
D. Inspiring

[1] In the 19th century, the Industrial Revolution transformed the way perfume was produced, and change came to Grasse as well. [6] [2] With the Industrial Revolution's developments in machinery and manufacturing, new extraction techniques arose. [3] In 1894, manufacturers in Grasse claimed the first patents on these techniques. [4] These companies expanded their cultivation of aromatic plants, and entrepreneurial types invested in rolling acres of surrounding countryside. [5] Now, aromatic plants could be processed in factories [7]. [6] Floral scents gave way to richer fragrances, incorporating international ingredients like patchouli, cinnamon, musk, lemongrass and vanilla. [7] Grasse began focusing less on crafting perfumes, and instead turned the focus of their attention to [8] producing and extracting raw materials. [9]

6. Given that all of the choices are true, which one would most effectively introduce the main idea of this paragraph?
F. NO CHANGE
G. The 18th century's frenzy for fragrance had spread perfume's popularity far and wide.
H. But perfume lovers were growing tired of the same old fragrances.
J. Europe was not the only place where perfume was enjoyed, either.

7. At this point, the writer is considering adding the following true statement:

> and distributed globally to perfumeries throughout the world.

Should the writer make this addition here?
A. Yes, because it provides useful information about the extraction process in modern factories.
B. Yes, because it helps explain how the Industrial Revolution changed Grasse's perfume trade.
C. No, because it introduces information that is irrelevant to the town of Grasse.
D. No, because it contradicts the idea that Grasse was the perfume capital of the world.

8. F. NO CHANGE
G. turned their attention in
H. turned their focus toward
J. focused on

9. For the sake of the logic and coherence of this essay, Sentence 4 should be placed:
A. where it is now.
B. after Sentence 2.
C. after Sentence 6.
D. after Sentence 7.

In the 20th century, innovations in chemistry introduced a plethora of new fragrance possibilities, as scientists learned how to manipulate scents for the molecular level. [10]

Including the classic perfume Chanel No. 5, some of the most popular fragrances drew on synthetic materials for their startling scent profiles. [11]

Consequently, [12] Grasse's perfumeries continued to focus on natural ingredients. Today, Grasse produces many of the natural scents used in perfumes, alcohol, food and household products. Additionally, many of the world's foremost [13] perfumers are still educated in Grasse, where they learn the tricks of the trade – including the ability to identify thousands of ingredients by scent alone. [14]

10. F. NO CHANGE
    G. at
    H. by
    J. to

11. A. NO CHANGE
    B. Some of the most popular fragrances drew on synthetic materials, including the classic perfume Chanel No. 5, for their startling scent profiles.
    C. Some of the most popular fragrances drew on synthetic materials for their startling scent profiles, including the classic perfume Chanel No. 5.
    D. Some of the most popular fragrances, including the classic perfume Chanel No. 5, drew on synthetic materials for their startling scent profiles.

12. F. NO CHANGE
    G. Indeed,
    H. In fact,
    J. However,

13. Which of the following alternatives to the underlined portion would be LEAST acceptable?
    A. leading
    B. extreme
    C. finest
    D. top

14. Which of the following sentences, if added here, would provide the best conclusion to the essay?
    F. The 27 tons of jasmine produced in Grasse each year lend their fragrance to hundreds of varieties of perfume produced throughout the world.
    G. These trained "noses" become expert perfumers, working for brands such as DKNY, Calvin Klein and Dior.
    H. Isn't it funny that it all began with the French fad for scented leather gloves?
    J. Whatever the 21st century holds for the world of perfume, Grasse will continue to play a part in the story.

Question 15 refers to the functioning of the passage as a whole.

15. Suppose the writer had intended to write an essay focusing on the modern history of perfume. Would this essay successfully fulfill the writer's goal?
    A. Yes, because it describes advances in perfume that were pursued jointly in several great cities throughout France.
    B. Yes, because the essay focuses on global innovations in the perfume industry during the modern era.
    C. No, because it contains no information about advances in perfume over the past century.
    D. No, because the essay limits its focus to Grasse's place in the history of perfume.

PASSAGE II

Ada Lovelace: "Enchantress of Numbers"

Born Ada Augusta Byron in 1815, Ada Lovelace was known in her time as an extraordinary mathematical talent. She is recognized today as a visionary, particularly for her contributions to the machine that would one day become the computer – which, in the nineteenth century, was no more than a fanciful idea. [16] Some consider her the first computer programmer.

[1] Her parents, the famous poet Lord Byron and the Baroness, Annabella Milbanke separated when [17] Lovelace was just a baby. [2] Lord Byron died only nine years later; Lovelace would never know him. [3] Throughout her childhood, she suffered from frequent illness. [4] But despite [18] the severity of these afflictions, she continued with her studies, including private tutoring from some of the foremost thinkers of the day. [19]

Beginning around the point at which [20] Lovelace was 17, her astounding ability with mathematics became evident. One of her tutors introduced her to the inventor and mathematician Charles Babbage, they [21] began a correspondence. It was Babbage who dubbed Lovelace "The Enchantress of Numbers." Impressed by her intelligence, Babbage would later draw on Lovelace's mathematical talents, to [22] flesh out his great concept: the Analytical Engine.

16. If the writer were to delete the underlined portion, the essay would primarily lose:
    - **F.** an explanation of the foundations of Lovelace's success.
    - **G.** a detail indicating why Lovelace might be considered a visionary.
    - **H.** an insight into the reason for Lovelace's interest in math.
    - **J.** interesting but irrelevant information about the time period.

17. - **A.** NO CHANGE
    - **B.** Baroness Annabella Milbanke, separated when
    - **C.** Baroness Annabella Milbanke separated, when
    - **D.** Baroness Annabella Milbanke separated when,

18. Which of the following alternatives to the underlined portion would NOT be acceptable?
    - **F.** Notwithstanding
    - **G.** In spite of
    - **H.** But even with
    - **J.** Moreover with

19. The writer is considering adding the following true statement to Paragraph 2.

    > A serious case of measles and resulting temporary paralysis kept her confined to her bed for nearly a year.

    Should this sentence be added, and if so, where?
    - **A.** It should be added after Sentence 2.
    - **B.** It should be added after Sentence 3.
    - **C.** It should be added after Sentence 4.
    - **D.** It should NOT be added.

20. - **F.** NO CHANGE
    - **G.** By the time in which
    - **H.** By a point occurring around when
    - **J.** By the time

21. - **A.** NO CHANGE
    - **B.** together they
    - **C.** and they
    - **D.** who she

22. - **F.** NO CHANGE
    - **G.** talents to
    - **H.** talents. To
    - **J.** talents – to

GO ON TO THE NEXT PAGE.

The Analytical Engine was a suggested design proposed [23] for a general purpose computer. In 1842, Babbage described this design in a lecture at the University of Turin. Luigi Menabrea, an Italian engineer in the audience who [24] would later become prime minister of Italy, he wrote [25] his own account of Babbage's comment's. [26] Lovelace then translated this paper into English, adding her own notes, diagrams and calculations. In the content of [27] these notes, she described how the Analytical Engine could be used to compute a string of numbers. Her proposed algorithm – a set of instructions encoded for execution by the machine – is considered the earliest computer program. Though Babbage was never able to actually build his hypothetical machine, but [28] in 1991 the London Science Museum constructed a complete working model of the Analytical Engine from Babbage's notes.

Lovelace died when she was only 36 years old. Never in good health, she finally succumbed to cancer. Yet despite her short life, the Enchantress of Numbers made a lasting contribution that is still celebrated today. [29]

23. A. NO CHANGE
B. design proposal that had been put forth
C. design suggested as a possibility
D. proposed design

24. F. NO CHANGE
G. he who
H. whom
J. which

25. A. NO CHANGE
B. Italy and wrote
C. Italy, writing
D. Italy, wrote

26. F. NO CHANGE.
G. Babbage's comments.
H. Babbages comments.
J. Babbages comment's.

27. A. NO CHANGE
B. Within the bounds of
C. Within the space of
D. Within

28. F. NO CHANGE
G. machine and
H. machine that
J. machine,

29. Which of the following true statements, if added here, would best tie the conclusion of the essay to its opening paragraph?
A. Mathematical prodigies like Lovelace don't come along very often, but when they do… they shake up the world.
B. Thanks to her collaboration with Charles Babbage, Lovelace will live forever in the history books.
C. Her life serves as evidence that a person with passion can accomplish great things, whatever the obstacles.
D. Computer science – a field which did not exist in Lovelace's lifetime – now hails her as one of its heroes.

30. Suppose the writer had decided to write an essay that summarizes how mathematical geniuses have influenced the development of modern technology. Would this essay fulfill the writer's goal?

F. Yes, because the essay makes the point that Lovelace's mathematical talents were essential to developing the Analytical Engine.
G. Yes, because the essay indicates that Babbage would never have lectured in Italy if not for Lovelace's encouragement.
H. No, because the essay argues that Babbage did not rely solely on Lovelace's mathematical contributions to create his invention.
J. No, because the essay limits its focus to the particular events surrounding one milestone in the development of modern technology.

PASSAGE III

Kató Lomb

[1]

Conventional wisdom suggests that second language acquisition – the process of learning and assimilating a foreign language – becomes extremely difficult as an adult, making it hard for people to become multilingual after their twenties. But conventional wisdom can be wrong. Consider the case of Kató Lomb, a Hungarian polyglot who studied more than two dozen languages and mastered sixteen.

[2]

Born in Pécs, Hungary in 1909, Lomb did not originally demonstrate an aptitude for foreign languages. Otherwise,[31] her early attempts at learning German in grade school were far from impressive. Instead of languages, she studied science in college and earned a Ph.D. in chemistry. But in 1941, as the nations of Europe was[32] thrust into the tumult of World War II, Lomb decided it would be advantageous to learn Russian. A ragged two-volume Russian dictionary was her first textbook. By 1943, Hungary was involved in the war; as Lomb and her family hid out into[33] their bomb shelter, she read novels in

31. **A.** NO CHANGE
B. Nevertheless,
C. In fact,
D. However,

32. **F.** NO CHANGE
G. was being
H. were
J. was then

33. **A.** NO CHANGE
B. during
C. in
D. OMIT the underlined portion.

Russian. The characters in these stories served as her language instructors, and she soon became fluent by studying <u>its</u> [34] conversations.

[3]

When the war ended, <u>the job of Russian interpreter was applied for soon.</u> [35] She practiced her language skills diligently, and soon <u>after the the relevant appointment, which gave her, through leading the tourism office in Budapest, an</u> [36] opportunity to practice French and English, too.

[4]

[37] In a book called *This is How I Learn Languages,* she laid out the details of her method, <u>first published in Hungarian in 1970,</u> [38] using a made-up language called Azilian <u>as an example</u>. [39] She used a systematic and effective <u>approach: first,</u> [40] she would buy an Azilian dictionary, and review it in detail to get a sense of how the language works.

34. **F.** NO CHANGE
G. it's
H. there
J. their

35. **A.** NO CHANGE
B. the job of Russian interpreter was soon filled by Lomb.
C. she was soon applying for the job of Russian interpreter.
D. Lomb applied for the job of Russian interpreter.

36. **F.** NO CHANGE
G. having also been appointed leading the tourism office in Budapest that would give her
H. appointed to do so, she led the tourism office in Budapest, giving her
J. was appointed to lead the the tourism office in Budapest, giving her

37. Which of the following sentences (assuming all are true), if added here, would best introduce the new subject of Paragraph 4?

A. Lomb also studied East Asian languages such as Chinese and Japanese.
B. Lomb began to develop a reliable strategy for learning a new language.
C. Along with learning languages, Lomb also became an author.
D. Not everyone finds it easy to learn a new language, but for Lomb it was a game.

38. The best placement for the underlined portion would be:

F. where it is now.
G. after the word *Languages*.
H. after the word *example*.
J. after the word *Azilian*.

39. **A.** NO CHANGE
B. as a hypothetical example
C. in an exemplary fashion
D. by way of explanatory example

40. Which of the following alternatives to the underlined portion would NOT be acceptable?

F. approach – first,
G. approach. First,
H. approach; first,
J. approach, first,

1 ■ ■ ■ ■ ■ ■ ■ ■ ■ 1

Then, she would buy a textbook and Azilian novels, completing [41] the exercises and delving into the stories – a good way to learn vocabulary in context. She will also listen [42] to Azilian broadcasts on the radio, gaining a sense of the pronunciation. Finally attempting [43] to find a native speaker of Azilian as a partner in conversation.

[5]

For Lomb, language acquisition was always primarily for her own enjoyment and reward. Even after her career as an interpreter was well established, Lomb still took pleasure in unlocking the secrets of many new languages. [44]

41. Which of the following alternatives to the underlined portion would be LEAST acceptable?
- **A.** doing
- **B.** going through
- **C.** finishing
- **D.** finalizing

42.
- **F.** NO CHANGE
- **G.** She also listens
- **H.** She would also listen
- **J.** She will also be listening

43.
- **A.** NO CHANGE
- **B.** And a final attempt
- **C.** Concluding with a final attempt
- **D.** Finally, she would attempt

44. Which of the following concluding sentences, if added here, is most consistent with the main focus of the essay and provides the most effective link back to the opening paragraph?
- **F.** Her work as an interpreter also enabled her to travel the world, taking her to more than forty countries.
- **G.** Reportedly, she took more pleasure in learning a new language than in having mastered a familiar one.
- **H.** Eventually she acquired fluency in Bulgarian, Danish, Italian, Polish, Romanian, Ukrainian and several others.
- **J.** In fact, she continued to study languages into her eighties, when she began learning Hebrew – demonstrating once and for all that you are never too old to learn a new language.

Question 45 refers to the passage as a whole.

45. Suppose the writer's goal had been to write a how-to article for people who wish to quickly master a foreign language. Would this essay fulfill the writer's goal?
- **A.** Yes, because the essay lays out a method for learning languages in Paragraph 4.
- **B.** Yes, because the article demonstrates that anyone can easily learn a new language.
- **C.** No, because the essay only discusses languages spoken in Europe.
- **D.** No, because the essay focuses mainly on the life of one famous language-learner.

PASSAGE IV

Emmett

Yesterday was a very special day. It was Emmett's three-year-old birthday. Who is Emmett, you ask? He's our French Bulldog, of course. [46] Naturally, we wanted him to have a birthday to remember; a dog only turns three once!

But, for the most part, Emmett's birthday was just like [47] any other day. He spent most of it snoring on the couch– except for meal times, when he gets [48] up to beg for food. (His special technique is waiting patiently, sitting on his haunches and stares [49] up with an expression of reproach.) It works every time. He did his favorite trick and earned his favorite treat, turning in a circle while balancing on his hind legs. [50] He ran around the backyard and sniffed the grass and scratched the fallen leaves that had tumbled from the trees to the ground, [51] before choosing his choice [52] spot to

46. The writer is considering adding the following sentence:

> A relative of the English bulldog, the French Bulldog is a small breed of dog known for their big ears and wrinkly snouts, along with their desire for human companionship.

Would this sentence be a relevant addition at this point in the essay, and why?

F. Yes, because it provides background information that is essential to understanding the essay.
G. Yes, because without this information it would not be clear that Emmett is a dog.
H. No, because it distracts from the essay's focus on one particular dog's birthday.
J. No, because it contradicts the idea that Emmett would enjoy a doggy slumber party.

47. **A.** NO CHANGE
B. birthday, was just
C. birthday was just like,
D. birthday was just, like,

48. **F.** NO CHANGE
G. will get
H. is getting
J. got

49. **A.** NO CHANGE
B. haunches, and staring
C. haunches, and stares
D. haunches, and he will stare

50. **F.** NO CHANGE
G. Turning in a circle while balancing on his hind legs, he earned his favorite treat, and did his favorite trick.
H. He did his favorite trick, turning in a circle while balancing on his hind legs, and earned his favorite treat.
J. Doing his favorite trick, he earned his favorite treat, turning in a circle while balancing on his hind legs.

51. **A.** NO CHANGE
B. leaves, which had fallen from the branches of trees to land on the ground,
C. leaves that had tumbled to the ground from the trees
D. fallen leaves

52. **F.** NO CHANGE
G. favorite
H. darling
J. endorsed

do his business. He was the actual benefiting recipient of [53] lots of attention, with plenty of cuddling and many scratches behind the ears.

If he wondered what his people meant when they said, "It's your birthday! You're three today," he didn't really show it. He just stared [54] at us with his usual big eyes and soulful expression.

We thought about giving him a special celebration for his birthday, and [55] we weren't sure what to do. After all, he already does his favorite things every day when [56] he's stretched out on the couch with his paws in the air, snoring loudly while his people watch TV, he's obviously the happiest dog in the world. Maybe every day when you're a dog is like your birthday. [57] Think about it. You get to relax, you get to eat treats, and you get to do whatever you want, whenever you want. As far as one is [58] concerned, the whole world revolves around you.

[1] He might have enjoyed a doggy slumber party, complete with sleeping bags and pillow fights. [2] He and his doggy friends could have watched *101 Dalmatians*, eaten Pupperoni Pizza, and celebrated his birthday in style. [59] [3] Unfortunately, we just don't know many other dogs. [4] It would have been a great time. [5] And three years old is still pretty young for a slumber party, anyway. [6] Maybe we'll throw him a big party when he's older. [7] Maybe in another year, when he's four. [60]

53. **A.** NO CHANGE
B. was the recipient of
C. did truly get
D. received

54. **F.** NO CHANGE
G. keeps staring
H. would stare
J. stares

55. **A.** NO CHANGE
B. But
C. For
D. So

56. **F.** NO CHANGE
G. day, when
H. day
J. day. When

57. **A.** NO CHANGE
B. every day, when you're a dog, is like your birthday.
C. every day is like your birthday, when you're a dog.
D. when you're a dog, every day is like your birthday.

58. **F.** NO CHANGE
G. one might be
H. you are
J. you were

59. Given that all choices are true, which one provides information that is new and specific?
A. NO CHANGE
B. and done other fun party activities.
C. and enjoyed themselves fully.
D. and played hide-and-seek all night long.

60. For the sake of the logic and coherence of paragraph, Sentence 4 should be placed:
F. where it is now.
G. between Sentences 1 and 2.
H. between Sentences 5 and 6.
J. between Sentences 6 and 7.

PASSAGE V

Superstorm

It was March 12, 1993. Off the coast, in the Western Gulf of Mexico, a storm was brewing. This storm would become known as the "1993 Superstorm," the "White Hurricane," or the "Storm of the Century." It caused damage and loss of life from Cuba to Maine. For quite a few Americans, especially residents of the South, it was the worst storm within memory, and its impact is still recalled [61] by many.

Even before it made landfall, weather experts knew this was not your run-of-the-mill spring storm. Professionals at the National Weather Service issued storm warnings five days in advance and blizzard warnings two days in advance, unusual [62] at the time. In fact, it was the first time it had [63] predicted such a massive storm. Thanks to their warnings, millions of people to take [64] precautions and prepare for the storm.

[65] Hurricane-force winds were accompanied by [66] huge amounts of precipitation, both rain and snow. In Florida, a storm surge flooded the coast line; the storm surge was as high as 12 feet in some places. Tornadoes formed at

61. Which of the following alternatives to the underlined portion would NOT be acceptable?

A. reminisced about
B. remembered
C. recollected
D. returned

62. Which of the following alternatives to the underlined portion would NOT be acceptable?

F. advance – unusual
G. advance, which was unusual
H. advance. Unusual
J. advance. This was unusual

63. A. NO CHANGE
B. it
C. they then
D. they had

64. F. NO CHANGE
G. taking
H. that took
J. could take

65. Given all are true, which of the following sentences, if added here, would best introduce the new subject of the third paragraph?

A. Records for severe weather were shattered in many regions.
B. As the storm moved up the coast, it carried devastation in its wake.
C. There is no doubt that many lives were saved by the emergency preparations.
D. Winds of above 74 miles per hour are classified as being hurricane strength.

66. F. NO CHANGE
G. when
H. along
J. with

the high-pressure edge of the storm front. Snow began to fall [67] heavily as the hurricane moved into colder regions. Even the southeastern states, normal [68] mild and temperate in March, received quantities surpassing the previous record amounts [69] of snowfall. Birmingham, Alabama, received 13 inches of snow, more than a foot. [70] This was more snow than they'd ever received in an entire year!

Unprepared for these wintry conditions, southern cities ground to a halt, as surprised municipal governments such as Chattanooga [71] struggled to remove more than two feet of snow. Many of these towns later established plans for emergency response, making them better prepared to deal with freak weather in the future – one of the few positive outcomes of the storm.

Even in the mid-Atlantic regions and the northeast, which are typically prepared for wintry weather, the snowfall was surprisingly astounding. [72] Furthermore, [73] Syracuse, New York, received 43 inches of snow. Record low temperatures accompanied the storm, and [74] millions of customers lost power for a day or more. By the time the White Hurricane had spent its fury, causing nearly $7 billion in damages, it had impacted a larger area than any other storm recorded in U.S. history of the country. [75]

67. **A.** NO CHANGE
B. falls
C. is falling
D. would fall

68. **F.** NO CHANGE
G. that are normal
H. normally
J. typically normal

69. **A.** NO CHANGE
B. record amounts
C. what can truly be described as record-breaking amounts
D. amounts surpassing previous recorded levels

70. **F.** NO CHANGE
G. snow – more than a foot.
H. snow amounting to greater than a foot.
J. snow.

71. The best placement for the underlined portion would be:
A. where it is now.
B. at the beginning of the sentence.
C. after the word *conditions*.
D. after the word *cities*.

72. **F.** NO CHANGE
G. quite surprising and astounding.
H. astounding.
J. surprisingly, astounding.

73. **A.** NO CHANGE
B. In contrast,
C. Nevertheless,
D. For example,

74. Given that all the choices are true, which one provides information that is new and specific?
F. NO CHANGE
G. left people in the cold as
H. contributed to the wintry weather, and
J. were observed in 68 different cities, and

75. **A.** NO CHANGE
B. impacted a larger area of the country than any other storm recorded in U.S. history.
C. impacted a larger area recorded in U.S. history than any other storm in the country.
D. impacted more than any other storm a larger area of the country recorded in U.S. history.

END OF SECTION 1

2 △ △ △ △ △ △ △ △ 2

MATHEMATICS TEST

60 Minutes—60 Questions

DIRECTIONS: Solve each problem, choose the correct answer, and then fill in the corresponding oval on your answer document.

Do not linger over problems that take too much time. Solve as many as you can; then return to the others in the time you have left for this test.

You are permitted to use a calculator on this test. You may use your calculator for any problems you choose, but some problems may best be done without using a calculator.

Note: Unless otherwise stated, all of the following should be assumed:

1. Illustrative figures are NOT necessarily drawn to scale.
2. Geometric figures lie in a plane.
3. The word *line* indicates a straight line.
4. The word *average* indicates arithmetic mean.

DO YOUR FIGURING HERE.

1. What is the perimeter, in inches, of a rectangle with a width of 4 inches and a length of 9 inches?

A. 13
B. 18
C. 26
D. 36
E. 72

2. To determine a student's overall quiz grade for the quarter, Mr. Lincoln deletes the lowest quiz grade and calculates the average of the remaining quiz grades. Lucy took all 7 quizzes and earned the following grades in Mr. Lincoln's class this quarter: 37, 55, 77, 78, 89, 92, and 95. What overall quiz grade did Lucy earn in Mr. Lincoln's class this quarter?

F. 71.3
G. 74.7
H. 78.0
J. 81.0
K. 81.5

3. If $y = (m - n + p + r)(n - p)$, $m = 2$, $n = -5$, $p = 3$, and $r = 0$, what is the value of y?

A. -80
B. -20
C. 0
D. 2
E. 80

4. At her stand Carla sells lemonade at 25 cents per glass and cookies at 50 cents each. If she sells g glasses of lemonade and c cookies, which expression gives the total sales in cents?

F. $25c + 50g$
G. $25g + 50c$
H. $75(g + c)$
J. $25(g + c)$
K. $50(g + c) + 25g$

2 △ △ △ △ △ △ △ △ △ 2

DO YOUR FIGURING HERE.

5. What is the value of x in the equation $\frac{16}{24} = \frac{20}{x}$?

A. 6
B. 12
C. 28
D. 30
E. 36

6. Rachel is an avid bird watcher, and she keeps track of the number of different bird species that she spots each day. Over the course of 7 consecutive days, she sees the following numbers of species: 1, 10, 9, 0, 9, 6, and 4. What is the median number of species that she has spotted?

F. 5
G. 6
H. 7
J. 8
K. 9

7. Mark is paid \$8.20 per hour for working up to 40 hours each week. He is paid 1.5 times this amount for every hour above 40 that he works in a week. If he works 45 hours in one week, how much does he earn in total?

A. \$266.50
B. \$369.00
C. \$389.50
D. \$451.00
E. \$553.50

8. Which of the following is the lowest common denominator for adding the fractions $\frac{2}{35}$, $\frac{1}{112}$, and $\frac{3}{32}$?

F. 160
G. 1,120
H. 3,920
J. 8,960
K. 125,440

9. Machine A makes 40 widgets per minute. Machine B makes 60 widgets per minute. Machine B turns on 2 minutes after Machine A does, and both turn off at the same time. If Machine A runs for 6 minutes, how many widgets do both machines produce?

A. 240
B. 360
C. 400
D. 480
E. 520

10. The expression $(4x - 5y^2)(4x + 5y^2)$ is equivalent to:

F. $16x^2 + 25y^4$
G. $16x^2 - 25y^4$
H. $16x^2 - 10y^4$
J. $8x^2 - 25y^4$
K. $8x^2 - 10y^4$

2 △ △ △ △ △ △ △ △ △ 2

DO YOUR FIGURING HERE.

11. If $p = -3$, what is the value of $\frac{p^2 - 1}{p - 1}$?

A. −4
B. −2
C. 2
D. 4
E. 5

12. Sophie is running a bake sale to raise money for her school. She sells cookies in small boxes for \$8 per box and in large boxes for \$10 per box. Her goal is to raise at least \$3,000 from the sale. If Sophie sells 139 small boxes of cookies, what is the minimum number of large boxes she will need to sell in order to meet her goal?

F. 188
G. 189
H. 236
J. 300
K. 314

13. An amusement park offers a special group rate on large groups. For groups with 25 or more people, the cost is \$17.00 per person. If a single person wishes to purchase a ticket, the cost is \$18.50 per person. Leila's science class, which has 27 students, is going on a field trip to this amusement park. How much less will the class pay if they purchase their tickets as a group, rather than individually?

A. \$25.00
B. \$26.00
C. \$37.50
D. \$40.50
E. \$50.00

14. The expression $\frac{(6 + \frac{1}{5})}{(1 + \frac{1}{10})}$ is equal to:

F. $\frac{62}{11}$

G. $\frac{341}{5}$

H. 3

J. 4

K. 8

DO YOUR FIGURING HERE.

15. The figure below is divided into 4 congruent squares. The total perimeter of the figure is 40 centimeters. What is the area, in square centimeters, of the figure?

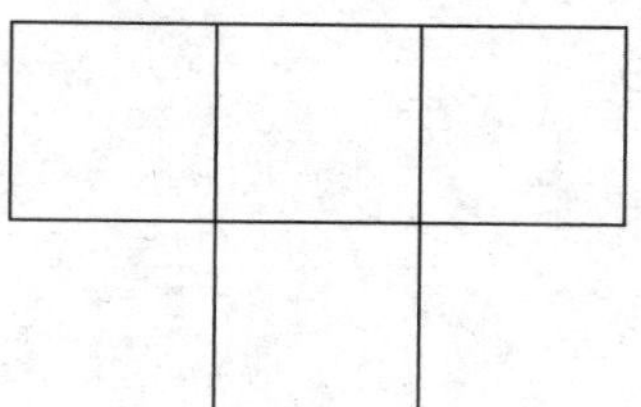

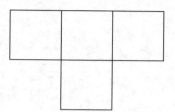

A. 16
B. 25
C. 40
D. 64
E. 100

16. $-5\,(|-4 + 10|\,) = ?$

F. −70
G. −30
H. 1
J. 30
K. 70

17. In January, a TV cost $800. In February the TV is discounted to $600. This discount is what percent of the original price?

A. 13%
B. 20%
C. 25%
D. 30%
E. 33%

18. Two rectangles, R and S, have the same width. The length of rectangle R is 5 times the length of S. If A is the area of rectangle S and kA is the area of rectangle R, what is the value of k ?

F. $\frac{1}{25}$

G. $\frac{1}{5}$

H. 1

J. 5

K. 25

DO YOUR FIGURING HERE.

19. A ladder leans against a wall as shown in the figure below. If the ladder is 26 feet long, and the base of the ladder is 24 feet from the wall, how many feet up the wall does the ladder reach?

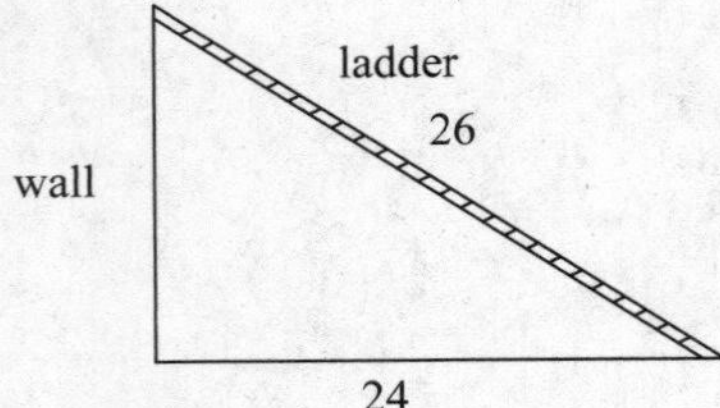

A. 2
B. 4
C. 8
D. 10
E. 12.5

20. A circle with a radius of 2 inches is inscribed in a square as shown below.

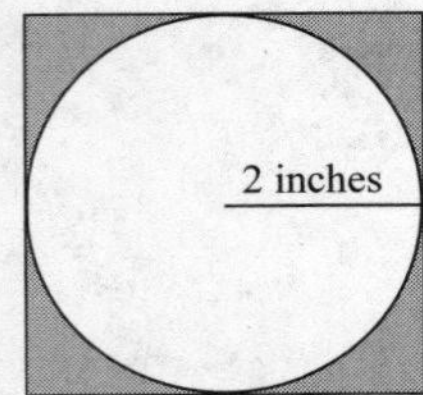

What is the area of the shaded region, in square inches?

F. 4π
G. $16 - 4\pi$
H. $8 - 4\pi$
J. $4 - 4\pi$
K. $2 - 4\pi$

21. In ΔXYZ (not shown), the sum of the measure of $\angle X$ and $\angle Z$ is 68°. What is the measure of $\angle Y$ in degrees?

A. 44
B. 68
C. 112
D. 122
E. 136

22. Line segment $\overline{AB}$ has endpoints $(-3,-3)$ and $(13,3)$ when plotted on a standard (x,y) coordinate plane. What is the x-coordinate of the midpoint of $\overline{AB}$?

F. 0
G. 2
H. 3
J. 5
K. 8

DO YOUR FIGURING HERE.

23. Triangle A has side lengths of 9 inches, 15 inches, and 21 inches, respectively. The ratio of the perimeter of triangle A to the perimeter of triangle B is 3:5. What is the perimeter, in inches, of triangle B ?

A. 45
B. 48
C. 60
D. 75
E. 108

24. The expression $-7x^5(5x^4 - 3x^3)$ is equivalent to:

F. $-14x^7$
G. $-35x^9 - 21x^8$
H. $-35x^9 + 21x^8$
J. $-35x^{20} + 21x^{15}$
K. $-35x - 21x^{15}$

25. Triangles ABC and DEF are similar. ABC has side lengths of 6 centimeters, 8 centimeters, and 10 centimeters. The shortest side length of DEF is 9 centimeters. What is the perimeter of DEF, to the nearest tenth of a centimeter?

A. 12.0
B. 15.0
C. 21.6
D. 24.0
E. 36.0

26. Line segment $\overline{AB}$ lies in the standard (x, y) coordinate plane. Point A is found at $(2, -6)$ and the midpoint of $\overline{AB}$ is $(1, 2)$. What is the y-coordinate of point B?

F. −2
G. 0
H. 4
J. 8
K. 10

27. The acceleration of an object in meters per second per second can be given by the equation $a = \frac{2d}{t^2}$, where the object travels a distance of d meters in t seconds. If a car accelerates from a stop at a rate of 15 meters per second per second for a span of 6 seconds, approximately how many meters did the car travel?

A. Between 100 and 200
B. Between 200 and 300
C. Between 300 and 400
D. Between 400 and 500
E. Between 500 and 600

GO ON TO THE NEXT PAGE.

28. For ΔABC, which expresses y in terms of x ?

DO YOUR FIGURING HERE.

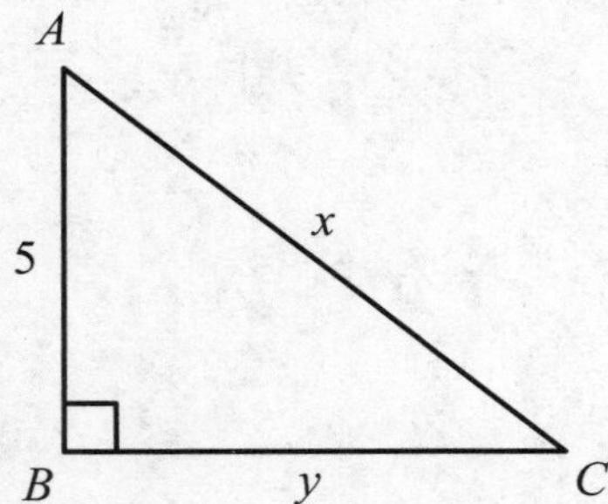

F. $\sqrt{x^2 + 10}$
G. $\sqrt{x^2 + 5}$
H. $\sqrt{x^2 - 25}$
J. $\sqrt{x^2 + 25}$
K. $x - 5$

29. Over the course of five days, a bakery sold 1,245 cupcakes. The graph below shows the number of cupcakes sold on each of the five days. Which of the following is closest to the percent of the total number of cupcakes that were sold on Friday?

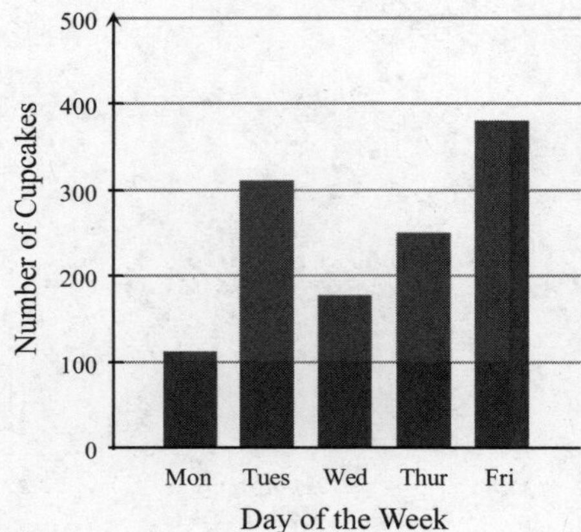

A. 15%
B. 20%
C. 25%
D. 30%
E. 35%

30. When $(3p - 4)^2$ is written in the form of $xp^2 + yp + z$, where x, y, and z are integers, what is the value of $x + y + z$?

F. −31
G. −7
H. 1
J. 25
K. 49

DO YOUR FIGURING HERE.

31. A bag of mixed nuts contains 9 macadamias, 13 cashews, and 18 peanuts. How many additional cashews must be added so that the probability of randomly drawing a cashew is $\frac{2}{5}$?

A. 3
B. 5
C. 7
D. 15
E. 40

32. A racetrack, shown below, encloses a square field with dimensions as shown. What is the length, in meters, of the track?

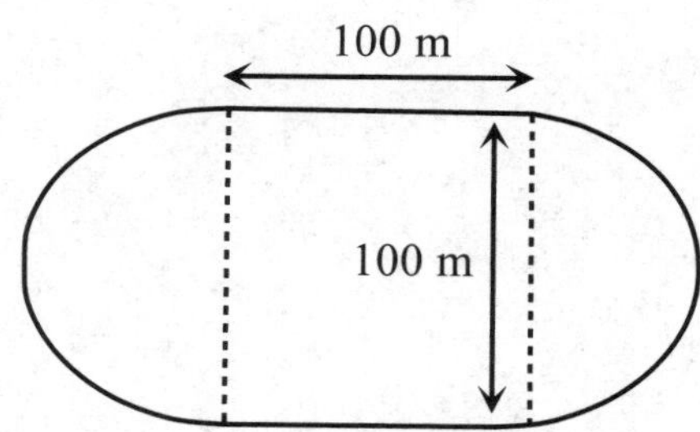

F. $100 + 100\pi$
G. $200 + 100\pi$
H. $200 + 200\pi$
J. $400 + 100\pi$
K. $400 + 200\pi$

33. A certain circle graphed onto the standard (x,y) coordinate plane is defined by the equation $(x - 8)^2 + y^2 = 22$. What are the radius of the circle, in coordinate units, and the coordinates of the center of the circle?

	Radius	Center
A.	22	(8,0)
B.	11	(−8,0)
C.	$\sqrt{22}$	(8,0)
D.	11	(8,0)
E.	$\sqrt{22}$	(−8,0)

DO YOUR FIGURING HERE.

34. The equations below are linear equations of a system where a, b, and c are positive integers.

$$ay - bx = c$$
$$ax + by = c$$

Which of the following describes the graph of at least 1 such system of equations in the standard (x,y) coordinate plane?

I. 2 perpendicular lines
II. 2 parallel lines
III. 2 intersecting lines

F. I only
G. II only
H. III only
J. I, and III only
K. I, II, or III

35. In the geometric sequence shown below, what is the 5th term?

$$2, -3, 4\frac{1}{2}, -6\frac{3}{4}...$$

A. $2\frac{1}{4}$

B. $7\frac{5}{7}$

C. 9

D. $10\frac{1}{8}$

E. $13\frac{1}{2}$

36. The number of bees in a hive is determined each month and follows the formula $N = 24(3)^m$, where N is the number of bees and m is the number of months. How many bees will be in the hive after 5 months?

F. 120
G. 360
H. 5,832
J. 58,290
K. 69,120

37. Taylor is contemplating which local gym to join. One gym charges a monthly membership fee of $75, plus an hourly fee of $10 to use the facility. A nearby competitor charges a monthly fee of $60, plus an hourly fee of $15. If m represents the number of hours Taylor plans to use the gym each month, which of the following equations could be used to determine the number of hours for which the cost of using either gym would be equal?

A. $75 + 10m = 60 + 15m$
B. $75 + 15m = 60 + 10m$
C. $(75 + 15)m = (60 + 10)m$
D. $(15 + 10)m = 75 - 60$
E. $(15 - 10)m = 75 + 60$

38. Karen has a rectangular piece of cloth with corners A, B, C, and D. She marks the midpoint of $\overline{AB}$ as point W and the midpoint of $\overline{CD}$ as point Y. She then cuts away fabric by cutting from Y to A, from Y to B, from W to C, and from W to D. The result is quadrilateral $WXYZ$. What is the ratio of the area of $WXYZ$ to the area of the material that Karen cut away?

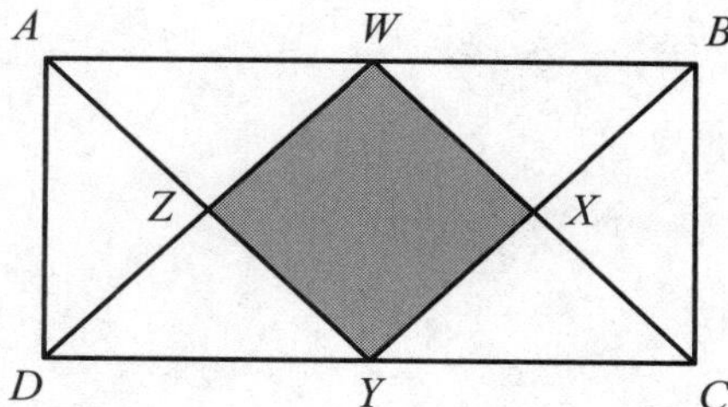

F. 1:2
G. 1:3
H. 1:4
J. 1:6
K. Cannot be determined from the given information

39. A square is graphed on a standard (x, y) coordinate plane with units in centimeters. The sides are 4 cm long, and one vertex is at $(3, 0)$. Which of the following points could be another vertex of the square?

A. $(-5,0)$
B. $(0,1)$
C. $(1,-1)$
D. $(7,0)$
E. $(7,-1)$

40. If x and y are nonzero integers, and $x < y$, which of the following inequalities must be true?

F. $x^2 > y^2$
G. $-x > -y$
H. $x + y < 2x$
J. $x - y > y - x$
K. $x^2 > x + y$

41. For θ with a measure between π and $\frac{3\pi}{2}$ radians, $\sin\theta = -\frac{5}{13}$. What is the value of $\cos\theta$?

A. $-\frac{12}{13}$

B. $-\frac{5}{13}$

C. $\frac{5}{13}$

D. $\frac{5}{12}$

E. $\frac{12}{13}$

DO YOUR FIGURING HERE.

DO YOUR FIGURING HERE.

42. As shown in the figure below, a hot air balloon rose into the air directly upward for 50 feet, then traveled 12 feet at a 45 degree angle from the vertical, and then traveled 18 feet at a 30 degree angle from the vertical. At that point, how many feet above the ground was the hot air balloon?

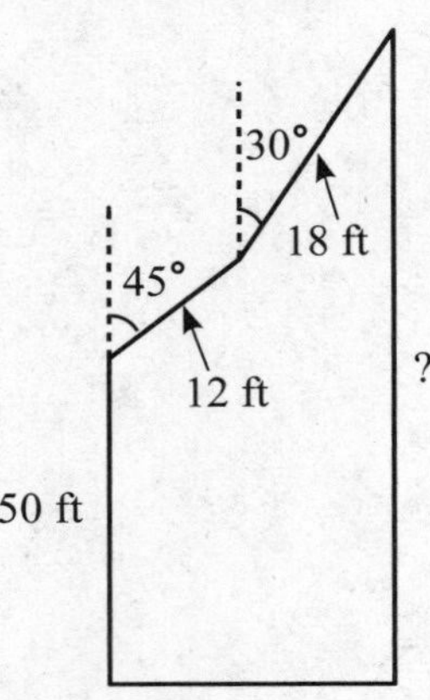

F. 50
G. 80
H. 98
J. $6\sqrt{2} + 9\sqrt{3}$
K. $50 + 6\sqrt{2} + 9\sqrt{3}$

43. The chart below shows a pool of eligible jury participants for a local jurisdiction, grouped by neighborhoods. If a person from the pool is selected at random, what are the odds (from the neighborhood:not from the neighborhood) that he or she is from the Elm neighborhood?

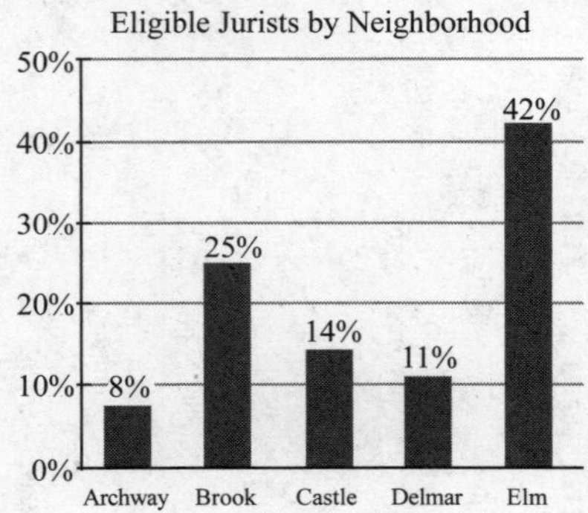

A. 1:3
B. 7:8
C. 7:43
D. 21:29
E. 42:25

44. A straight pole is leaning against a 20ft wall at an angle of 65°, as shown in the figure below. Which of the following expressions gives the length, in feet, of the pole?

DO YOUR FIGURING HERE.

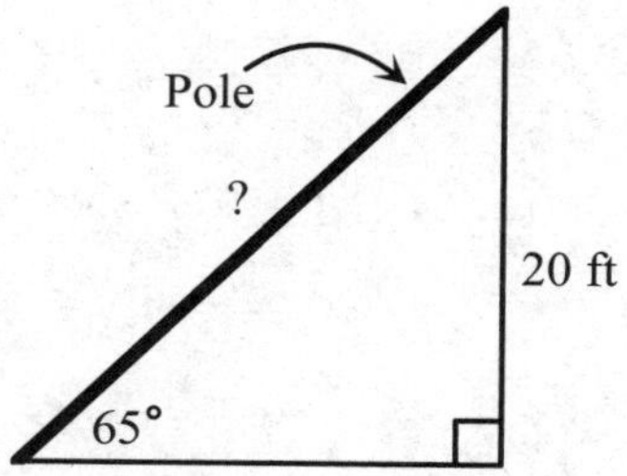

F. $20 \sin 65°$

G. $20 \cos 65°$

H. $20 \tan 65°$

J. $\dfrac{20}{\sin 65°}$

K. $\dfrac{20}{\cos 65°}$

45. Parallelogram *ABCD* is rotated counterclockwise by 90° about the origin. At what ordered pair is the image of *A* located?

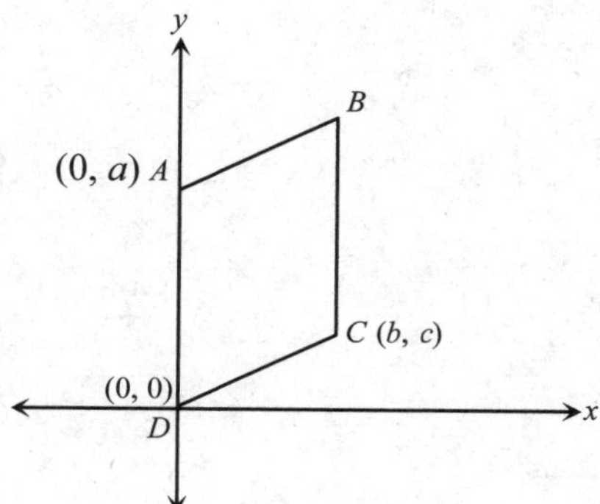

A. $(-a, 0)$
B. $(0, -a)$
C. $(0, 0)$
D. $(a, 0)$
E. (b, c)

DO YOUR FIGURING HERE.

46. In the circle shown below, chords AC and DB intersect at point Q, the center of the circle. $\angle DAC$ is 60°. What is the angle measure of minor arc $\overset{\frown}{DC}$?

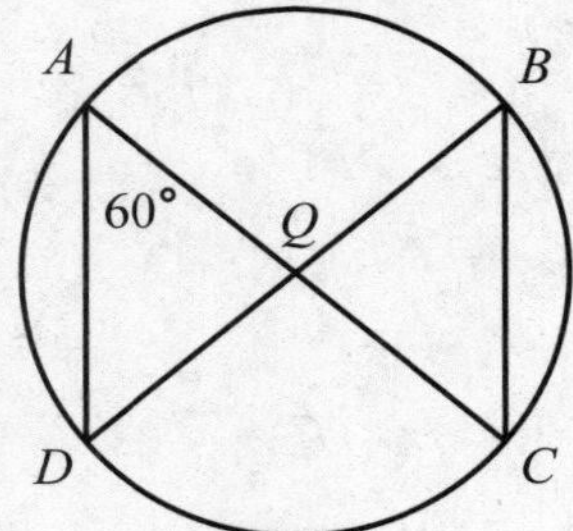

F. 30°
G. 60°
H. 120°
J. 240°
K. Cannot be determined from the given information.

47. If $x > 0$, and $\log_x(\frac{1}{16}) = -4$, then which of the following is equal to x ?

A. 2

B. 4

C. 20

D. $\frac{1}{2}$

E. $\frac{1}{4}$

48. If x and y are real number such that $0 < x < 1$ and $-1 < y < 0$, then which of the following *must* be true?

F. $\frac{x}{y} > 1$

G. $|x|^2 > |y|^2$

H. $x^2 + 1 > y^2 + 1$

J. $\frac{x}{4} - 4 > \frac{y}{4} - 4$

K. $x^{-2} > y^{-2}$

49. If $x \leq 4$, then $|x - 4| = ?$

A. 0
B. $x + 4$
C. $x - 4$
D. $-x - 4$
E. $-x + 4$

DO YOUR FIGURING HERE.

50. Triangle ABC is a right triangle with a hypotenuse of 16 inches, as shown in the figure below. $\angle C$ has a sine of $\frac{3}{5}$. What is the length, in inches, of side $\overline{AB}$?

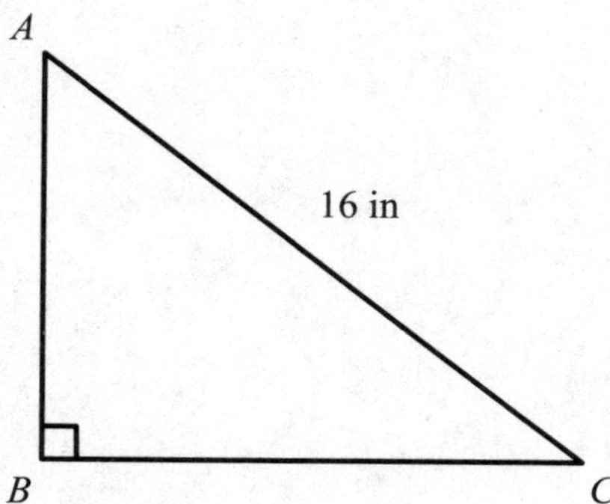

F. 9.6
G. 12.0
H. 12.8
J. 20.0
K. 26.7

51. A man pushes a box to the top of a ramp resting on a 10-foot high wall. If the ramp has an incline of 20°, which of the following expressions gives the horizontal distance, in feet, that the box travels from the base of the ramp to the wall?

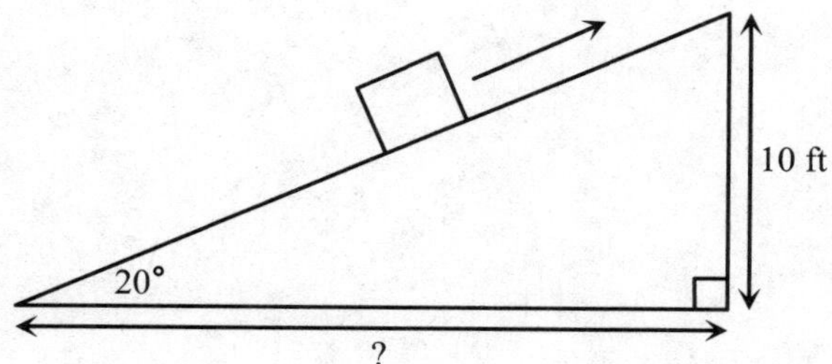

A. $10 \sin 20°$

B. $10 \tan 20°$

C. $\dfrac{10}{\tan 20°}$

D. $10 \cos 20°$

E. $\dfrac{10}{\sin 20°}$

52. In the figure below, a sector is shown shaded in a circle with radius 8. The length of the arc of the unshaded sector is 14π. What is the measure of the central angle of the shaded sector?

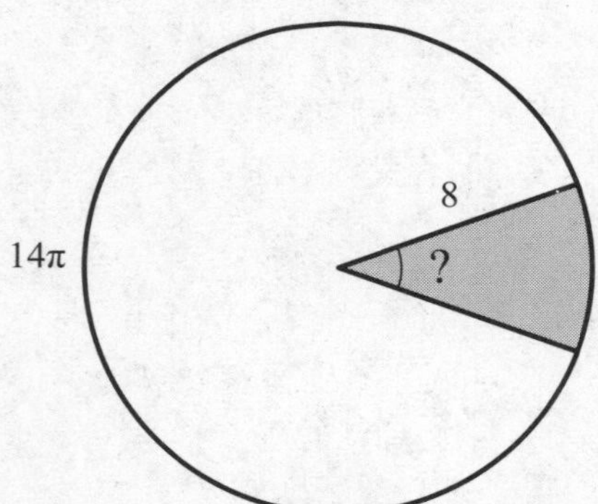

F. 35°
G. 40°
H. 45°
J. 50°
K. 55°

DO YOUR FIGURING HERE.

The following information is required for problems 53 to 55:

A toy manufacturer makes trains and dolls. His weekly profit P is given by the formula $P = 50t + 25d$, where t and d represent the number of trains and dolls sold that week, respectively. The shaded region in the graph shown below represents the constraints of the toys he can make in a given week.

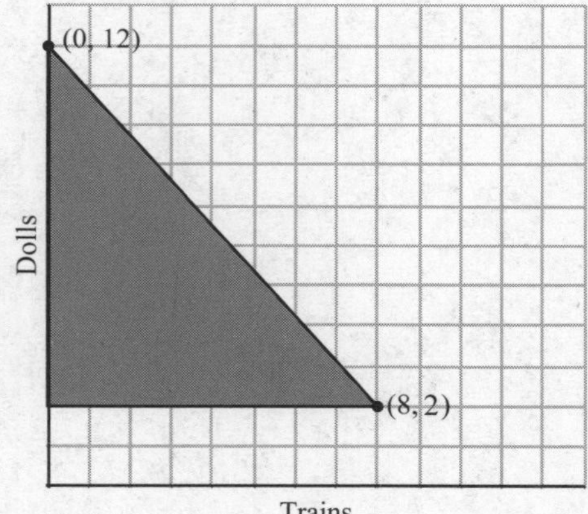

53. The horizontal line segment in the constraint graph above containing the point (8, 2) indicates that, each week, the manufacturer makes a minimum of:

A. 2 trains
B. 8 trains
C. 2 dolls
D. 8 dolls
E. 10 dolls

54. It takes the toy manufacturer 3 hours to make each train and 2 hours to make each doll. For every hour he works, he sets aside \$2 toward retirement. If he sells 7 trains and 3 dolls in one week, what is the approximate percentage of his profit that he contributes toward retirement?

F. 5%
G. 10%
H. 13%
J. 19%
K. 50%

55. What is the maximum profit the toy manufacturer can earn in one week?

A. \$300
B. \$350
C. \$400
D. \$450
E. \$650

---

56. The distance between the points (2,1) and (x,7) as graphed on the standard (x,y) coordinate plane is 10. What is one possible value for x ?

F. −10
G. 5
H. 6
J. 8
K. 10

57. For what value of a would the following system of linear equations have an infinite number of solutions?

$$3x - y = 14$$
$$15x - 5y = 7a$$

A. 2
B. 10
C. 14
D. 70
E. 98

58. If $\cos x = -\frac{1}{4}$, what is the value of $\cos 2x$?
(Note: $(\cos x)^2 = \frac{1 + \cos 2x}{2}$)

F. $-\frac{3}{4}$
G. $-\frac{7}{8}$
H. $-\frac{1}{8}$
J. $\frac{1}{16}$
K. $\frac{3}{4}$

DO YOUR FIGURING HERE.

DO YOUR FIGURING HERE.

59. As shown below, a solid, right circular cylinder is cut through its center, perpendicular to its bases. Which of the following images shows the best representation of the plane section?

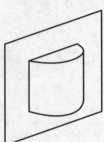

A.

B.

C.

D.

E.

60. What percent of the *even* numbers from 4 to 52, inclusive, have a units digit that is twice the tens digit?

F. 4%
G. 8%
H. 12%
J. 16%
K. 36%

END OF SECTION 2

TURN THE PAGE TO BEGIN SECTION 3

3 3

READING TEST

35 Minutes—40 Questions

DIRECTIONS: There are four passages in this test. Each passage is followed by several questions. After reading a passage, choose the best answer to the question and fill in the corresponding oval on your answer document. You may refer to the passages as often as necessary.

Passage I

PROSE FICTION

When I was just six years old, my parents read a series of novels to me and my sister: *The Chronicles of Narnia* by C. S. Lewis. I can still remember the anticipation we felt each night before bed, as we settled in for our nightly chapter. Sometimes, after a long day, my dad would have trouble staying awake as he read. He would drift off to sleep in the middle of a sentence, leaving a long pause that only increased our desire to find out what happened next. We would slap his arm and say "Daddy, wake up!" He would startle awake and read another couple sentences before drifting off again. Finally, we would admit defeat, resigned to waiting until the next day to hear more. After we finished the series, I was determined to read it for myself, despite the small print and long chapters. The Narnia books helped me learn how to read grown-up books; little did I know they would also influence my life in many other ways in the years to come.

The first book, *The Lion, The Witch and The Wardrobe*, tells the story of the four Pevensie children: Peter, Susan, Edmund and Lucy. Sent off to the English countryside, where they would be safe from the bombings of World War II, they amuse themselves by playing hide-and-seek in the large estate of their eccentric host. Lucy, the youngest, hides in a wardrobe – an old-fashioned stand-alone closet – but to her surprise, the closet goes much deeper than it should, leading her into the magical land of Narnia. Narnia is peopled by talking animals and mythical creatures, and is locked in a battle of good and evil between the cruel White Witch, who wants to keep the word plunged in permanent winter, and the good and mighty lion Aslan, the world's true ruler. Eventually, all of the children find their way into Narnia, where they join together to free its people from the reign of the White Witch.

In future books, the Pevensie children return to Narnia to assist in other times of social crisis and participate in many glorious adventures. When Peter and Susan become too old for Narnia, Edmund and Lucy return a third time, along with their unlikeable cousin, Eustace Scrubb, who is just as nasty as his name makes him sound. They embark on an incredible journey on a beautiful ship called *The Dawn Treader,* steered by King Caspian and his magical crew, including an intrepid and spirited mouse named Reepicheep. In the far East, beyond the edges of their known world, they encounter things so strange and wonderful that they can hardly be described… but I dreamed about them for years.

There were seven books in all. As I grew older, I read them again and again. Each time, I discovered new allusions and jokes that I'd missed before. As I grew older, the books grew older too. Sadly, one of the books – it was *The Dawn Treader*, in fact, my favorite – was lost forever when I left it in the park.

Although I'm embarrassed to admit this, part of me always hoped that the Narnia books might be at least a little bit real. I imagined that one day, I might walk around a corner, or open a door, or come to the end of an empty street, and I too would find myself in the land of talking animals where good always triumphed over evil. But I never found the door to Narnia. Eventually, I stopped reading the books, and I stopped looking for it.

Or so I thought. However, in reality, even though I stopped thinking about Narnia, I was always looking for a door into another world. As I grew older, my love for fantasy gave way to an obsession with other worlds of all kinds: civilizations on other planets, travels through the galaxy, and the high-tech future of the human race. Science fiction seemed more adult. Fantasy seemed like something for children. I thought I'd put it behind me.

But then something changed; I found it again. I started writing stories about the worlds beyond the doors, worlds more or less like our own, except that occasionally the magic is real. A boy falls in love with a mermaid, and follows her into the sea. A girl wizard saves her world from disaster by sacrificing herself. A vial of perfume holds the power to transport whoever smells it to a far away world. When I wrote these stories, it was like I was calling on some deep magic that had remained with me since I'd first imagined the land of Narnia and all the adventures it held.

As I've gotten older, the way I imagine other worlds has changed. The "magical land" beyond the edge of our own is big enough told hold many futures, many fantasies, many tales. But I know that whatever happens, I will never stop looking for that door.

1. Throughout the passage, the image of the door is used primarily as a metaphor for the boundary between:

   A. waking and dreaming.
   B. fantasy and science fiction.
   C. England and Narnia.
   D. reality and imagined worlds.

2. According to the passage, the first of the Pevensie children to discover Narnia was:

   F. Peter.
   G. Susan.
   H. Edmund.
   J. Lucy.

3. According to the narrator's account of the story, what was the significance of World War II in the Pevensie children's lives?

   A. They were forced to escape to Narnia so they could be safe from the war.
   B. They were sent to live with a relative after their father was killed in the war.
   C. They found Narnia while staying in the country to avoid the fighting.
   D. They helped fight a similar version of the war in Narnia.

4. According to the narrator's accounting of the story, Edmund and Lucy take more trips to Narnia than Peter and Susan because:

   F. Edmund and Lucy were the first to discover Narnia.
   G. Peter and Susan become too old.
   H. Edmund and Lucy had to accompany their cousin.
   J. Peter and Susan found their cousin too unpleasant.

5. When the narrator says "but I dreamed about them for years" (line 44), she is most likely referring to the:

   A. crew of The Dawn Treader.
   B. things the ship encountered in the far East.
   C. dangers faced by the Pevensie children.
   D. edges of their known world.

6. According to the passage, one of the books was lost when the narrator:

   F. loaned it to a friend.
   G. left it outside in the rain.
   H. left it at the park.
   J. became too old to read it.

7. The passage indicates that compared to fantasy novels, the narrator considered science fiction stories to be:

   A. more mature.
   B. somewhat boring.
   C. more inspiring.
   D. easier to read.

8. According to the passage, the narrator writes stories containing each of the following elements EXCEPT:

   F. mermaids.
   G. wizards.
   H. perfume.
   J. dragons.

9. The main function of the first paragraph is to:

   A. explain why the narrator found the books so intriguing.
   B. detail the narrator's introduction to the books.
   C. provide evidence of the importance of reading to children.
   D. offer insight into the narrator's relationship with her family.

10. The narrator most likely mentions the "intrepid and spirited mouse Reepicheep" to:

   F. introduce another important villain in the series.
   G. indicate the fantastical nature of the ship's crew.
   H. provide a contrast to the villain Eustace Scrubb.
   J. explain why *The Dawn Treader* was her favorite book in the series.

Passage II

SOCIAL SCIENCE

In the wake of the devastation of World War II, 44 Allied nations joined together to create a new international monetary system, designed to help rebuild shaken economies around the world. At the Bretton Woods conference in 1944, the International Monetary Fund (IMF) and the World Bank were first born. Over the years, their roles have evolved considerably with the changing times.

Originally, the World Bank (which was then referred to as the International Bank for Reconstruction and Development, or IBRD) supplied funds targeted toward specific programs alleviating poverty and social problems. The IMF assisted struggling member nations by loaning them money supplied by wealthier nations in the fund. The IMF also helped maintain consistent standards for currency and stabilized exchange rates, ensuring that member nations could trade effectively. During the Great Depression in the 1930s, countries adopted policies that strongly discouraged foreign trade, in a failing attempt to strengthen their own economies. The IMF worked to counteract this, by encouraging member nations to trade more freely with one another, and creating a stable environment for them to do so. Up until 1971, new member nations pledged to maintain exchange rates that were fixed to the dollar and its value in gold. This system of ensuring market stability was called the Bretton Woods system.

The Bretton Woods era came to an end around 1970, when the United States decided to move away from the gold standard. Up to this point, the number of dollars in circulation in the US was always tied to the amount of gold the nation held in reserve. In the absence of the gold standard, the dollar became what is known as a "fiat" currency: its value is only defined by government regulation or decree, and is not tied to any particular form of measurement. This development also meant that member countries could value their currency however they wished. With this flexibility in the system, it became even more important to have an overseeing body to help avoid major fluctuations, such as hyperinflation (which occurs when a government prints money at such a high rate that it quickly loses its value).

Today, the IMF boasts 187 member countries, and continues to play a major role in the global economy. In 2008, the mortgage lending collapse in the United States led to a financial crisis that spread rapidly throughout the world, wreaking havoc on the economies of many nations. Because of this, many countries have struggled to pay their debts. The IMF called upon its wealthier members, and increased its lending capacity to about $750 billion, which it dispersed to countries in financial crisis.

However, the IMF is not without its critics. One particularly controversial aspect of the IMF's work is the fact that its loans are tied to "conditionalities" – changes the struggling nations must make in order to receive the financial aid. The IMF will often require that a country cut public spending and increase taxes so that it can balance its budget and avoid shortfalls in the future. In these instances, funding for healthcare, education and agricultural subsidies are often the first to go. Reduced access to healthcare, education, and local crops impacts the poorest citizens first, which can make it even harder for a developing nation to pull itself out of poverty. For instance, in one recent study conducted by researchers at Cambridge and Yale, tuberculosis incidence increased by 16 percent in Eastern European countries that received IMF loans following the collapse of the Soviet Union.

The IMF's policies have also been accused of causing negative effects on the environment. In order to generate cash flow and repay loans, critics argue, debtor nations often pursue projects such as strip-mining for coal, drilling for oil, or clear-cutting forests for lumber without instituting safeguards to protect the local environment. Though these projects increase cash flow in the short term, they can have lasting negative effects on the ecology of a country and the lifestyle of the people who live there.

As the world continues to recover from the global financial crisis, international leaders are discussing the role that the IMF will play in the future. Some have called for an overhaul of the IMF, along with the international financial system in general, stating the need for "a new Bretton Woods." The British Prime Minister, French President, Greek Prime Minister, and Italian Economics Minister are among those who've advocated publicly for these reforms. The world has changed dramatically since the original Bretton Woods, and with a new balance of financial power in the world, changes are certainly on the horizon.

11. According to the passage, the World Bank was originally called:

A. International Monetary Fund.
B. International Bank for Reconstruction and Development.
C. Bretton Woods International Bank.
D. International Lending System for Market Stability.

12. The Bretton Woods system was designed to:

F. encourage free trade and market stability among member nations.
G. base financial aid on conditionalities.
H. replace the gold standard with fiat currency.
J. help debtor nations to repay the IMF.

13. According to the passage, the value of a fiat currency is defined by:

A. the amount of currency in circulation.
B. the amount of gold held in reserve.
C. the value assigned to it by government.
D. its value relative to the dollar.

14. The passage uses hyperinflation as an example of:

F. a major fluctuation that could occur in the market.
G. a shortcoming of the Bretton Woods system.
H. a common side effect of fiat currency.
J. when money is valued by government decree.

15. The passage mentions all of the following as either prerequisites or likely consequences of receiving IMF aid EXCEPT:

A. cutting public spending.
B. increasing taxes.
C. utilizing natural resources.
D. increasing educational standards.

16. The author mentions the results of the tuberculosis study in the fifth paragraph (lines 49-64) primarily to:

F. illustrate the potential negative effects of IMF policy.
G. criticize the practices of the Bretton Woods system.
H. demonstrate the high cost of healthcare in industrialized nations.
J. suggest that poorer nations have a higher rate of disease than wealthier nations.

17. The main purpose of the fourth paragraph (lines 40-48) is to:

A. describe the significance of the IMF in contemporary times.
B. compare today's economic challenges to the Great Depression.
C. defend the IMF against the allegations leveled by critics.
D. note how little the IMF has expanded since 1944.

18. The passage lists political leaders who have advocated for reforms of the international financial system from all of the following nations EXCEPT:

F. France.
G. Greece.
H. Italy.
J. Russia.

19. It can most reasonably be inferred from the last paragraph (lines 74-84) that the author believes:

A. the IMF will gradually lose relevance over time.
B. global interconnectivity poses a risk to the stability of world economies.
C. IMF policies will have to adapt to a changing world.
D. the IMF's quick response mitigated the effects of the global financial crisis.

20. In terms of the passage as a whole, one of the main functions of the fifth paragraph (lines 49-64) is to suggest that:

F. the Bretton Woods system may be due for reform.
G. the conditions required by the IMF may actually make it more difficult for nations to reduce poverty.
H. nations should attempt to cut spending and raise taxes on their own before approaching the IMF for a loan.
J. researchers at Cambridge and Yale are alone in studying the effects of IMF loans on debtor nations.

Passage III

HUMANITIES

Born in Greece in 1888 and raised by Italian parents, the artist Giorgio de Chirico lived a strange and complicated life. His artistic output spanned several distinct styles over the years of his career. His early work laid the foundations for a style that would later be known as Surrealism, popularized by the more famous Salvador Dali. But de Chirico himself abandoned Surrealism (which he referred to as *Pittura Metafisica*, or Metaphysical Art); instead of working in the Surrealist style, he began campaigning against modern art, and advocating for a classical style. Throughout his lifetime, and to this day, his earlier pieces remain his most famous works. These pieces, which depict unsettling scenes from uncanny cities, leave a haunting impression with the viewer. However, de Chirico himself practically disowned these early works, and amused himself in later life by creating forgeries of them, leading to confusion and bafflement among art dealers and critics. Is there any explanation for these strange actions, or is the man himself as much of a mystery as the scenes he painted?

Biographers point to his childhood in Greece as an influence on his work in the Metaphysical Art period. He and his brother Andrea, who renamed himself Alberto, grew up among a rich, ancient culture, surrounded by the open spaces and strong lines of classical architecture, and the tragic and heroic themes of Greek mythology. Their father was an engineer who designed railroads, and a railroad bisected the town where they lived; this imagery would later surface in the odd urban scenes of de Chirico's work.

As a young adult, de Chirico traveled Europe, and lived in Munich and Paris. He also studied the work of the philosopher Frederick Nietzsche, fueling his preoccupation with the idea of parallel worlds, alternate realities, and the tension between landscapes and dreams. In 1910, he painted his first significant piece: *Enigma of an Autumn Afternoon.* He also became fascinated by Ariadne, a princess of Greek myth. As the story goes, Ariadne's father built a labyrinth which housed the minotaur. Young men and women from rival nations would be sacrificed regularly to this grotesque creature: a monster with the body of a man and the head of a bull. But then Ariadne fell in love with Theseus, an adventurer sentenced to be delivered to the minotaur. Ariadne helped Theseus navigate the labyrinth and slay the Minotaur. By placing Ariadne in his urban dreamscapes, de Chirico seemed to be implying that they were labyrinths, mazes, perhaps inescapable except through some act of revelation.

From 1910 to 1915, de Chirico continued to produce these landscapes, scenes from cities that seem to exist in some alternate reality; the town squares are deserted, the angles skewed, the lighting harsh, and the clean elegance of classical marble architecture is disrupted by the intrusion of odd objects like a red ball or a yellow glove. Emptied of humans, illuminated by a strange sun, these scenes contain a feeling of anticipation, as if something is just about to happen, but never does. The artistic elite greeted these new paintings with excitement and admiration. In 1915, Giorgio and his brother Alberto were called to join the army. They were stationed in Ferrara, a city in northern Italy. Inspired by this new urban setting, de Chirico continued his work.

But in 1919, the artist underwent a major change. While viewing a painting by an Italian Renaissance painter of the 16th century, de Chirico experienced an epiphany; he wanted to work in that style, depict the human figure, and become a classicist, returning to older, now outmoded traditions of painting. He began criticizing the modern art movement, including his old allies. In an article called "The Return of Craftsmanship" he criticized modern art and argued for more traditional styles.

Unfortunately, his new work was largely ignored by critics; barely mediocre, it certainly did not arouse the same awed respect as his early works. As the artistic community abandoned de Chirico and rejected his new attempts, they continued to praise his Metaphysical Art, which also commanded a high price among dealers and collectors. Perhaps for financial reasons, or perhaps to take revenge upon these dealers, de Chirico continued to make "self-forgeries" of these works, even after he had publicly disavowed their importance to art. When an exhibition of his early metaphysical paintings opened in Paris in 1947, he declared them all fakes -- "faked" by himself. In the 1960s, as an old man, he began working in a style described as "neo-metaphysical," revisiting his own early work as a historical phenomenon in need of modern perspective.

In the end, perhaps we shall never fully understand the motivations and mindset of this powerfully talented artist. In 1911, at the beginning of his career, he inscribed a self-portrait with the caption, "What shall I love if not the enigma?" Perhaps the artist's own understanding of himself —as a mystery to be embraced but never explained—is all we need to know.

21. According to the passage, de Chirico may have been influenced by his father's profession as:

A. a teacher.
B. an artist.
C. an engineer.
D. a Greek historian.

22. De Chirico's later attitude toward his early Surrealist pieces could best be characterized as:

F. embarrassment at their lack of completion.
G. nostalgia for his earlier fame.
H. pride in his unusual success.
J. denial of their importance.

23. According to the passage, De Chirico's use of the mythological figure of Ariadne in his paintings offered a thematic link to:

A. Greek philosophy.
B. the concept of the maze.
C. adventure and tragedy.
D. the power of the feminine.

24. As it is used in line 61, the word *epiphany* most nearly means:

F. a sudden insight.
G. a religious experience.
H. a disclosed secret.
J. a public announcement.

25. Which of the following statements best describes the art world's reaction to de Chirico's new work in the Renaissance style?

A. They reacted with excitement and admiration.
B. At first the work was controversial, but eventually gained acceptance.
C. Prominent critics wrote articles attacking the work.
D. It received very little attention.

26. The passage indicates that one possible reason de Chirico made forgeries of his own early works was:

F. lack of inspiration that led him to plagiarize his own popular pieces.
G. retaliation against art dealers who rejected his current work.
H. mixed feelings on the style in which he'd chosen to work.
J. to mimic the style of an Italian Renaissance painter.

27. The passage describes the minotaur of Ariadne's myth as:

A. the inspiration for *Enigma of an Autumn Afternoon*.
B. a bull with the head of a man.
C. a grotesque creature.
D. Ariadne's deformed brother.

28. According to the passage, de Chirico termed his version of Surrealism:

F. Metaphysical Art.
G. Painting Metafisica.
H. Enigmatic Art.
J. Pittura Surrealism.

29. The main function of the third paragraph (29-45) is to:

A. explain the myth of Ariadne.
B. explore connections between Nietzsche's philosophy and Greek myth.
C. describe de Chirico's travels in Europe.
D. discuss influences on de Chirico's early work.

30. It may be reasonably inferred from the passage that the author believes that the inscription "What shall I love if not the enigma?" on de Chirico's self-portrait:

F. reveals that even de Chirico did not fully understand himself.
G. references a philosophical essay that explains his approach to his work.
H. indicates that this self-portrait was actually one of his self-forgeries.
J. suggests secret information that he chose not to reveal to his supporters.

Passage IV

NATURAL SCIENCE

The developing field of paleoclimatology is sending scientists to some of the harshest environments on the globe to research the climates of past epochs. These research projects have revealed vast variations in Earth's climate, including glacial periods when much of the Earth was covered in ice, and interglacial periods when temperatures warmed up and the polar ice caps shrunk. By gathering and refining data about what Earth's climate was like thousands or even millions of years ago, scientists can make better calculations about what Earth's climate will be like in the future. They can also better understand the complex mechanisms that triggered climate changes in the past, and build better models to understand today's climate trends. Right now, they're working to solve a crucial question: what is the exact relationship between increased greenhouse gases and increased temperatures?

While there are several options for gathering data about past climates, the best method is ice core drilling. At the North and South poles of Earth, in Greenland and Antarctica where the ice never melts, scientists can drill down deep and unearth ice that has been frozen there for nearly half a million years. Once, that ice fell as snow. As more snow fell on top of it, it was compressed into thinner and thinner layers and became ice. Preserved in that ancient ice is valuable information about Earth's changing climate and atmosphere.

The evidence is encoded in many ways: bubbles of gas trapped in the ice, microscopic dust and soot, even the variation of darker and lighter bands. (These striations show the changes throughout the seasons; dark bands correspond to the heavier snow of winter, while light bands correspond to the lighter snow of summer.) The amount of oxygen isotopes in the ice shows the variation in seasonal temperatures. Light carbon isotopes hint at the amount of vegetation present on the globe, and traces of calcium reveal deserts. Methane points to rainfall. From these substances, scientists are able to piece together a story of ancient environmental conditions.

Taking ice core samples isn't easy. Each project requires the large-scale cooperation of dozens of scientists, academic institutions and research laboratories, with millions of dollars worth of equipment. One such endeavor is the WAIS Divide, a United States deep ice coring project on the West Antarctic Ice Sheet. The goal of the project: delving 3,540 meters into the ice (that's more than two miles!), revealing the past 100,000 years of climate history, with year-by-year chronology for the recent 40,000 years. This will also provide the most detailed record currently available of greenhouse gases over the past 100,000 years.

The site, 600 miles from the South Pole, was chosen for its relatively smooth topography (which leads to nice, even layers in the ice core) and its high snowfall rate (which leads to wider annual ice layers, making it easier to identify each year). Every piece of equipment and every item in the camp had to be ferried in from McMurdo Station, the U.S. supply base on the coast of Antarctica, 885 miles away.

The weather conditions are some of the harshest on Earth. The sunlight reflected off the snow is blindingly bright. The average yearly temperature is a cool -24 F. The camp is a small assortment of tents, huddled around a buried lab which houses an 8-million-dollar ice drill. The snow accumulation is so heavy and constant, staff and scientists must dig themselves out of their tents each morning. They string ropes between the structures to navigate blizzard winds. Even so, the camp is only operational from November to February, high summer near the South Pole; the remainder of the year, conditions are simply too brutal.

What is day-to-day work like, out in the snow and ice? At the heart of the project is the Deep Ice Sheet Coring (DISC) Drill, an electromechanical drill designed by a team of engineers and technicians from the University of Wisconsin-Madison. The rotating drill head contains four razor sharp cutters, capable of capturing and removing a cylinder of ice ten feet long. The core is pushed out of the drill into a room where the temperature is always frigid, and is then wrapped in a green plastic net that protects the ice from damage. After it's packaged up, the ice is shipped 8,000 miles, to the National Ice Core Laboratory in Denver. There, it's divided up and sent out to be analyzed. Over the next few years, 27 independent laboratories will get a look at the ice and take measurements; this process ensures accuracy, with plenty of double and triple checking. Every step of the way, the valuable ice cores will be handled with utmost care; they must remain frozen at about -4° F, or some gases may escape, and the quality of the samples will degrade.

31. One of the main ideas established by the passage is that:

A. antarctic ice cores provide a more accurate picture of long-term climate than equivalent samples from Greenland.
B. scientists working with ice cores must maintain exacting technical standards to ensure accuracy.
C. since paleoclimatology is such a rigorous field, the hiring process is extremely challenging and competitive.
D. less and less snow is falling in West Antarctica, so each layer of ice is increasingly thin.

32. According to the passage, scientists can identify annual cycles in the ice because of:

F. the level of nitrogen isotopes.
G. variations in summer and winter snow.
H. textural differences in the layers.
J. the proportion of gases to ice.

33. The main purpose of the first paragraph is to:

A. explain the relevance of paleoclimatology within the broader field of climate research.
B. compare paleoclimatology to other areas of environmental science.
C. argue that paleoclimatology is the most important field of climate research today.
D. discuss the necessity of making paleoclimatologists endure extreme weather conditions.

34. The passage states that the WAIS Divide site is characterized by:

F. smooth topography and high snowfall.
G. high variation in seasonal temperatures.
H. its convenient location near McMurdo Station.
J. pristine wilderness untouched by civilization.

35. According to the passage, why is research only conducted November through February?

A. The research timeline is based on the academic year.
B. The researchers' budget is very limited.
C. The weather is best during these months.
D. The researchers split their time between the North and South Poles.

36. As it is used in line 28, the word *striations* most nearly means:

F. minuscule particles.
G. visual patterns.
H. scientific measurements.
J. textured grooves.

37. According to the passage, after removal the ice cores are:

A. immediately tested for oxygen isotopes, light carbon isotopes, calcium and methane.
B. equally divided and immediately shipped to 27 laboratories throughout the US.
C. sorted by size and age and stored at -4 F to prevent degradation.
D. wrapped in plastic, shipped to Denver, divided into samples and sent to other laboratories.

38. According to the passage, the WAIS Divide project aims to achieve all of the following EXCEPT:

F. Reveal generalized climate data from the past 100,000 years.
G. Measure West Antarctica's susceptibility to climate change.
H. Provide year-by-year climate data for the past 40,000 years.
J. Detail greenhouse gas measurements over the past 100,000 years.

39. As it is used in line 71, the word *capturing* most nearly means:

A. apprehending.
B. captivating.
C. enclosing.
D. amassing.

40. According to the passage, how deeply will researchers drill at the WAIS Divide?

F. About a thousand meters
G. Less than 3,500 feet
H. About 3,500 feet
J. More than two miles

END OF SECTION 3

SCIENCE TEST

35 Minutes—40 Questions

DIRECTIONS: There are seven passages in this test. Each passage is followed by several questions. After reading a passage, choose the best answer to the question and fill in the corresponding oval on your answer document. You may refer to the passages as often as necessary.

You are NOT permitted to use a calculator on this test.

Passage I

The subatomic process of Beta Decay (β-decay), where a neutron decays into a proton and an electron, can be described by the following chemical equation:

$$\text{neutron} \rightarrow p^{+} + e^{-} + \text{energy}$$

Table 1 lists several subatomic particles and the energies they possess in β-decay.

Table 1

Subatomic Particle	Energy (*MeV*)
Neutron	143
Proton	71
Electron	32
Photon	8

Figure 1 shows the velocity (m/s) of 3 subatomic particles at different energy levels (*MeV*).

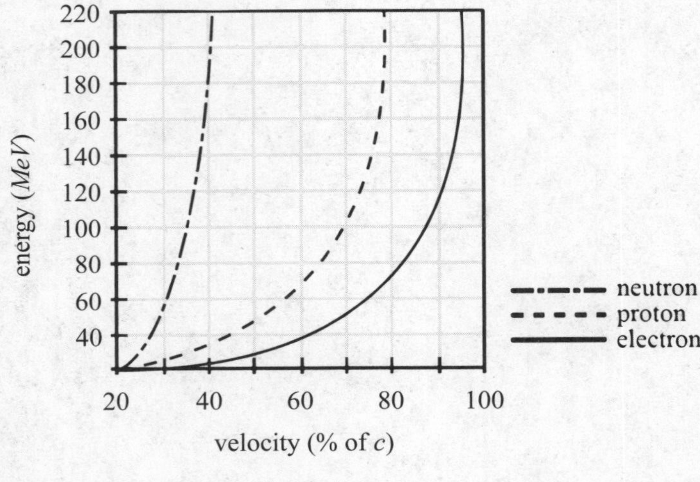

Figure 1

Figure 2 shows the frequency of radiation emitted by an electron at various velocities measured as a percent of the speed of light (*c*).

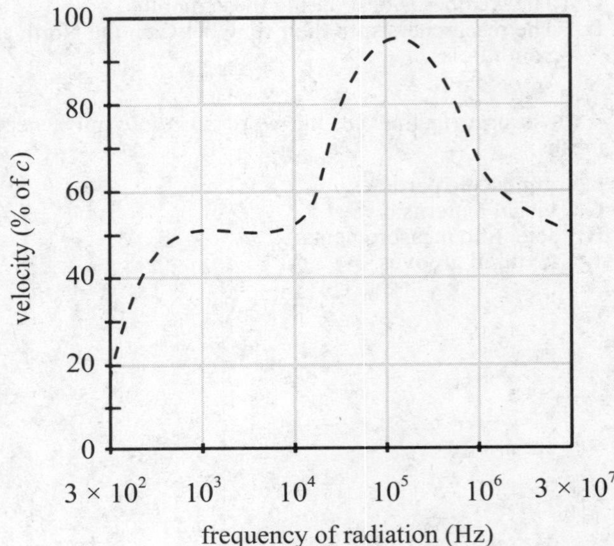

Figure 2

  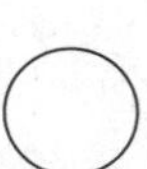 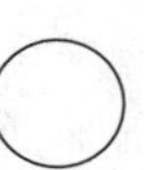   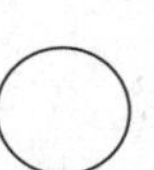 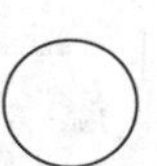  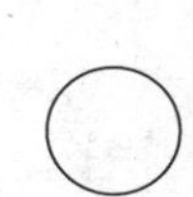

1. Based on Table 1 and Figure 1, the velocity of a proton during β-decay is approximately what percent of the speed of light (*c*)?

A. 40
B. 50
C. 60
D. 70

2. If an atom undergoes β-decay, and the net result is that the atom gains a proton, then the atom:

F. forms a molecule.
G. becomes a different element.
H. becomes negatively charged.
J. loses an electron.

3. According to Figure 2, an electron with a velocity less than 40% of the speed of light (*c*) could emit which of the following frequencies of radiation?

A. 3.0×10^2 Hz
B. 3.0×10^3 Hz
C. 3.0×10^5 Hz
D. 3.0×10^7 Hz

4. According to the information provided, how much energy is emitted when a neutron undergoes β-decay, independent of the proton and electron released?

F. 40 MeV
G. 100 MeV
H. 120 MeV
J. 140 MeV

5. Which of the following conclusions do Figures 1 and 2 best support? The velocity at which an electron emits the highest frequency of radiation is:

A. less than the velocity of an electron at 60 MeV.
B. greater than the velocity of an electron at 60 MeV.
C. less than the velocity of a neutron at 80 MeV.
D. greater than the velocity of a proton at 80 MeV.

6. In an experiment, a proton travels at a velocity equal to the velocity of an electron at a frequency of radiation of 3×10^6 GHz. Based on Figures 1 and 2, what is the difference in energy between these two subatomic particles?

F. 10 MeV
G. 30 MeV
H. 50 MeV
J. 70 MeV

Passage II

A tunneling probability density diagram (TPDD) shows how the probability of an electron to tunnel through a barrier varies with the energy of the electron and the length of the barrier at 20° Celsius. The *critical tunneling point* is the point where the 3 regions of the TPDD with a probability of tunneling greater than 0 meet. It indicates the point where a small change in energy has the greatest effect on the probability of tunneling. Figure 1 is a TPDD for electrons emitted from Iron. Figure 2 is a TPDD for electrons emitted from Gold.

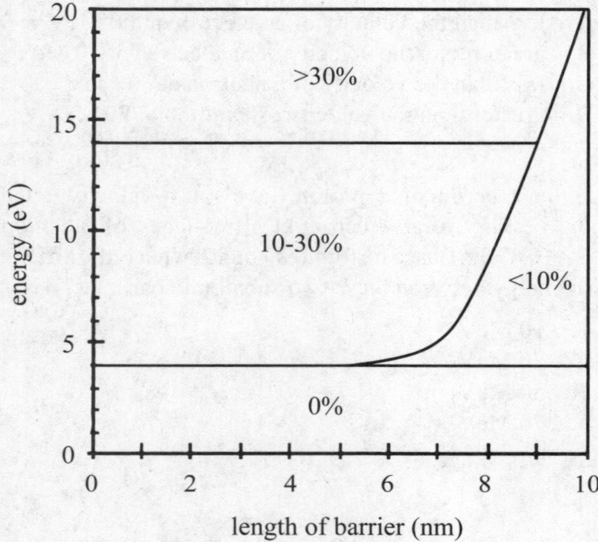

Figure 1

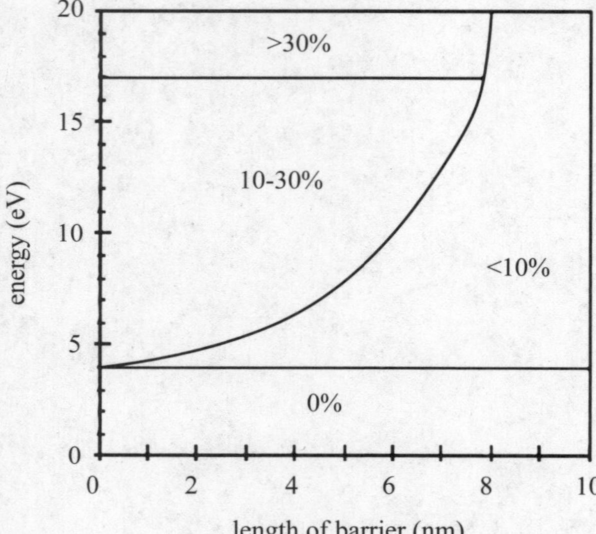

Figure 2

7. According to Figure 2, at 20° Celsius, an electron could have a 15 percent chance of tunneling through a 7 nm barrier at which of the following energies?

A. 8 eV
B. 12 eV
C. 16 eV
D. 20 eV

8. According to Figure 1, at 20° C, an electron emitted from Iron with 15 eV of energy could have which of the following probabilities of tunneling through a 5 nm barrier?

F. 5%
G. 15%
H. 25%
J. 35%

9. Suppose an electron is emitted from Iron at 20° C and attempts to tunnel through a 9 nm barrier. Based on Figure 1, at which of the following energies would a slight change in energy have the greatest impact on tunneling probability?

A. 8 eV
B. 14 eV
C. 16 eV
D. 20 eV

10. Suppose an electron in an Iron atom, at an energy of 18 eV, released energy until it was at 3 eV, and then absorbed light until it had an energy of 15 eV (all at 20° Celsius). It was then emitted to tunnel through a 4 nm barrier. Based on Figure 1, at the end of this procedure the probability of the electron tunneling successfully was:

F. 0%
G. less than 10%
H. between 10% and 30%
J. greater than 30%

11. Based on Figures 1 and 2, the lowest energy at which it is possible to detect an electron before it begins tunneling is closest to which of the following?

A. 2 eV
B. 4 eV
C. 6 eV
D. 8 eV

4 ○ ○ ○ ○ ○ ○ ○ ○ ○ 4

Passage III

Meteorologists use computer models to simulate weather patterns. The symbol w_0 indicates the wind speed on the ground in km/hr and w_t indicates the wind speed t hours later.

w_t is computed by the relationship between w_0, the rate of thermal diffusion (σ) of the wind (the rate at which heat is lost as it moves through the atmosphere), and the thermal absorption (y) of the wind (the number of degrees Celsius that the wind current gains when closest to the Earth's surface).

Table 1 lists the computed values for 8 computer simulations (S).

Table 1

S	w_0	σ	y	w_5	w_{10}	w_{20}
1	5	.6	10	20	−10	110
2	5	.8	15	45	−75	645
3	5	.7	5	5	5	5
4	5	.3	15	20	12.5	20
5	5	.4	25	45	5	85
6	5	.8	5	5	5	5
7	10	.6	20	40	−20	220
8	30	1.0	25	5	105	−695

* A negative sign indicates that the wind current reversed its direction.

12. According to the table, over the 20 hours studied, which of the following simulations had the greatest increase in wind speed?

    F. Simulation 1
    G. Simulation 3
    H. Simulation 5
    J. Simulation 6

13. Based on the table, wind speed remains constant if:

    A. $w_0 > y$
    B. $w_0 = y$
    C. $\sigma = .8$
    D. $\sigma > .8$

14. The thermal absorption of the wind was less than the initial wind speed on the ground in which of the following simulations?

    F. Simulation 1
    G. Simulation 3
    H. Simulation 4
    J. Simulation 8

15. Based on the table, a wind current's speed ($w_0 = 5$) will have the greatest total increase if it has which of the following rates of thermal diffusion and thermal absorption?

    A. A rate of thermal diffusion of .1 and a thermal absorption of 5
    B. A rate of thermal diffusion of .4 and a thermal absorption of 15
    C. A rate of thermal diffusion of .2 and a thermal absorption of 25
    D. A rate of thermal diffusion of .8 and a thermal absorption of 25

16. If an additional simulation were run with $w_0 = 5$, $\sigma = .8$, and $y = 25$, based on the table, the value of w_{20} would be closest to which of the following?

    F. −75
    G. 45
    H. 645
    J. 1,250

17. Suppose that a computer simulation measuring wind speed change over time was run and that the results were plotted in the graph shown below.

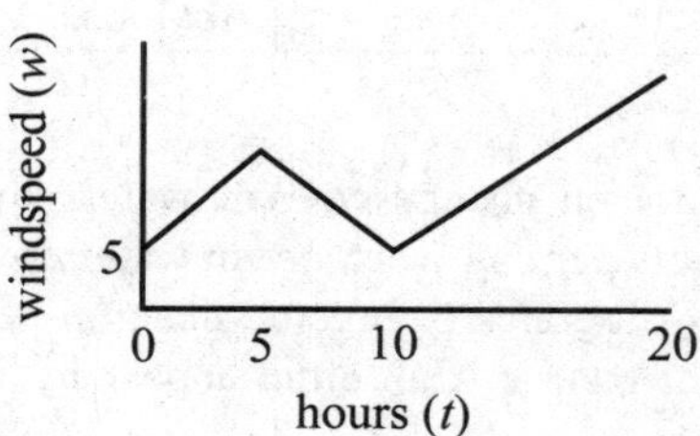

Based on the information provided, it can be inferred that the rate of thermal diffusion and the rate of thermal absorption were most likely closest to:

	σ	y
A.	.3	15
B.	.4	25
C.	.5	10
D.	.6	15

Passage IV

The intertidal zone refers to the part of the coastline where the ocean and the land meet, parts of which are covered with water and parts of which are not covered with water at varying periods throughout the day.

Table 1 shows the vertical zone (area within the intertidal zone) for different distances in meters (m) from the high tide line on a piece of rocky shoreline in California, as well as the dominant species found in each zone.

Table 1

Distance (m)	Vertical Zone	Dominant Species
0-2	Spray	Periwinkle Lice Isopod Whelk Limpet
2-5	High Tide	Barnacle Hermit Crab Anemone Brittle Star Muscle
6-25	Mid Tide	Green Algae Sponge Sea Star Sea Lettuce
26-45	Low Tide	Brown Seaweed Sea Cucumber Tube Worm Abalone

The estimated changes in salt water coverage (average number of hours per day when ocean water covers the ground) and biomass (kilograms of organic material per square meter) in an intertidal zone in California appear in Figures 1 and 2, respectively.

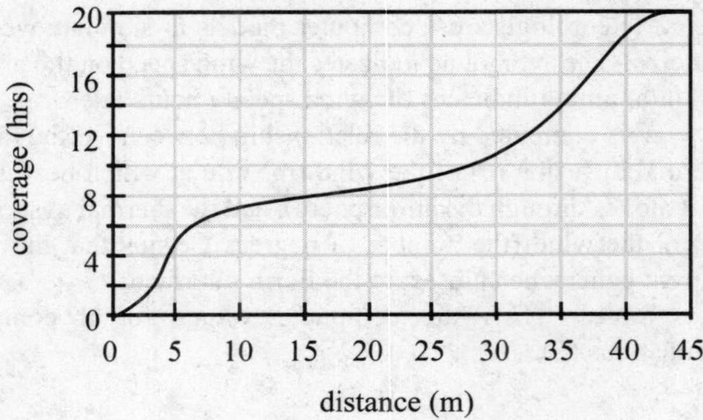

Figure 1

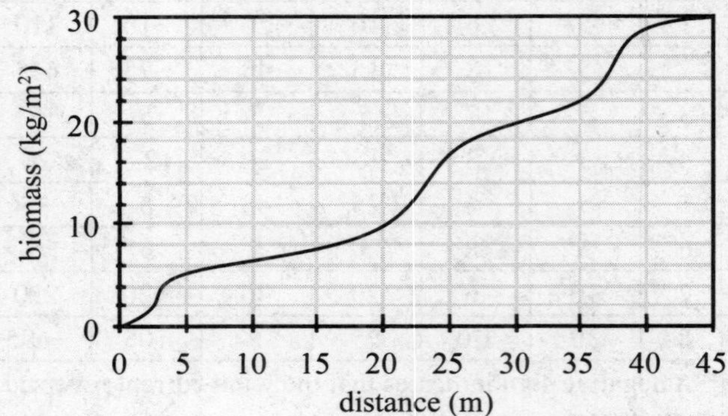

Figure 2

18. According to Figure 1, at a distance of 35 m from the high tide line the salt water coverage of the land was closest to:

F. 8 hrs
G. 12 hrs
H. 14 hrs
J. 16 hrs

19. Based on the data in Figures 1 and 2, the researchers should make which of the following conclusions about the overall change in salt water coverage and biomass over the 45 meters of intertidal zone?

A. Both salt water coverage and biomass increased.
B. Both salt water coverage and biomass decreased.
C. Salt water coverage increased and biomass decreased.
D. Salt water coverage decreased and biomass increased.

20. Which of the following conclusions about salt water coverage is consistent with the results shown in Figure 1?

F. Salt water coverage was lowest in the high tide zone.
G. Salt water coverage was lowest in the low tide zone.
H. Salt water coverage was highest in the spray zone.
J. Salt water coverage was highest in the low tide zone.

21. A student learned that a particular species could only live in areas that were covered by salt water for at least 12 hours of the day. According to the information provided, this species could be which of the following?

A. Sea Star
B. Sea Cucumber
C. Green Algae
D. Brittle Star

22. According to Figure 1, total salt water coverage increased the most within which of the following distances from the high tide line?

F. From 0 meter to 5 meters
G. From 5 meters to 10 meters
H. From 10 meters to 30 meters
J. From 30 meters to 40 meters

Passage V

In an *oscillating chemical reaction,* a catalyst reacts with H_2O_2 liquid and produces a second catalyst. The produced catalyst immediately reacts with the H_2O_2 liquid and produces more of the original catalyst. Iodine (I) and oxygen (O) are emitted as gas over time. This cycle repeats until only water remains in the solution. This process can be seen in the two reactions below.

Reaction 1: $5\,H_2O_2 + I_2 \rightarrow 2\,IO_3 + 2\,H^+ + 4\,H_2O$

Reaction 2: $5\,H_2O_2 + 2\,IO_3 + 2\,H^+ \rightarrow I_2 + 5\,O_2 + 6\,H_2O$

In the first reaction, catalyst I_2 reacts with H_2O_2, and produces IO_3 – also a catalyst. In the second reaction, the produced IO_3 reacts with H_2O_2 and produces more I_2.

Figures 1 and 2 show how the catalyst percent for IO_3 ($\%IO_3$) changed over time for Reactions 1 and 2, respectively, at two temperatures.

$$\%IO_3 = \frac{\text{mol of } IO_3}{\text{mol of solution} \times 100}$$

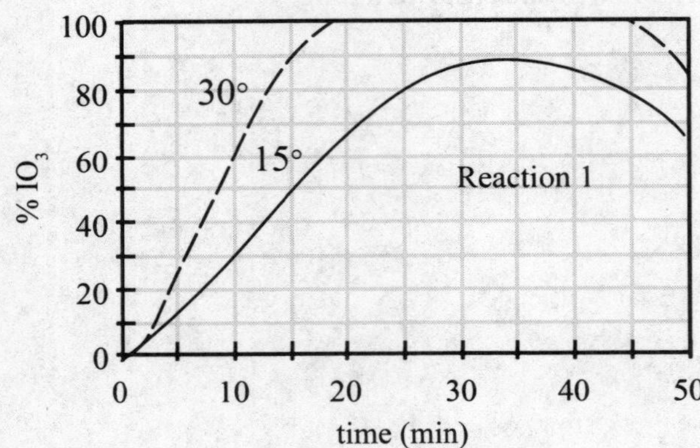

Figure 1

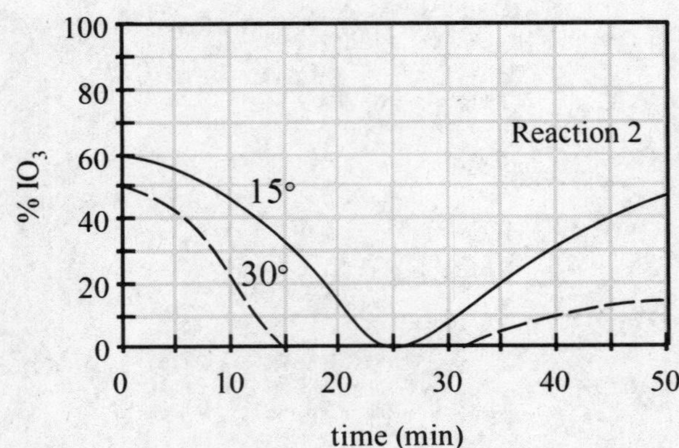

Figure 2

23. According to Figure 1, during the first reaction at 30° C, the $\%IO_3$ at 5 min was closest to which of the following?

A. 15%
B. 25%
C. 35%
D. 45%

24. Suppose that during Reaction 2 at 30° C, the temperature had been lowered to 15° C at time = 35 min. Ten minutes later, at time = 45 min, the $\%IO_3$ would most likely have been:

F. less than 10%.
G. between 10% and 40%.
H. between 40% and 50%.
J. greater than 50%.

25. Based on Figure 1, in Reaction 1, what effect did the lower temperature have on the $\%IO_3$? At 10 min, the $\%IO_3$ of the solution at 15° C was:

A. $\frac{1}{4}$ the $\%IO_3$ of the solution at 30° C.

B. $\frac{1}{2}$ the $\%IO_3$ of the solution at 30° C.

C. The same as the $\%IO_3$ of the solution at 30° C.

D. Twice the $\%IO_3$ of the solution at 30° C.

26. A scientist hypothesized that the $\%IO_3$ will always reach 0% or 100% slower at higher temperatures than lower temperatures. Do Figures 1 and 2 verify this?

F. Yes; the $\%IO_3$ reached 100% in the solution at 30° C before the solution at 15° C in both reactions.
G. Yes; the $\%IO_3$ reached 0% in the solution at 30° C before the solution at 15° C in both reactions.
H. No; the $\%IO_3$ reached 100% in the solution at 30° C before the solution at 15° C in Reaction 2.
J. No; the $\%IO_3$ reached 0% in the solution at 30° C before the solution at 15° C in Reaction 2.

27. Which of the following is the best explanation for what happens to the $2H^+$ produced in Reaction 1 by the conclusion of the oscillating chemical reaction?

A. It served as a catalyst in Reaction 2.
B. It was emitted as hydrogen gas.
C. It was released as H_2O_2 vapor.
D. It bonded with oxygen to form water.

28. Suppose that Figure 2 had been plotted as percent of I_2 ($\% I_2$) versus time:

$$\% I_2 = \frac{\text{mol of } I_2}{\text{mol of solution} \times 100}$$

Which of the following best demonstrates how Figure 2 would have appeared?

F.
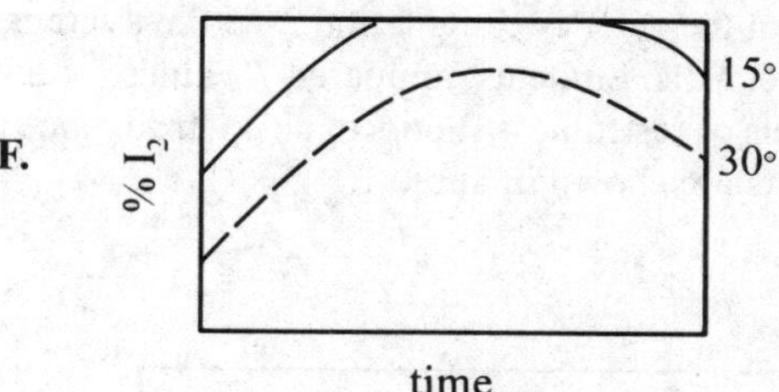

G.
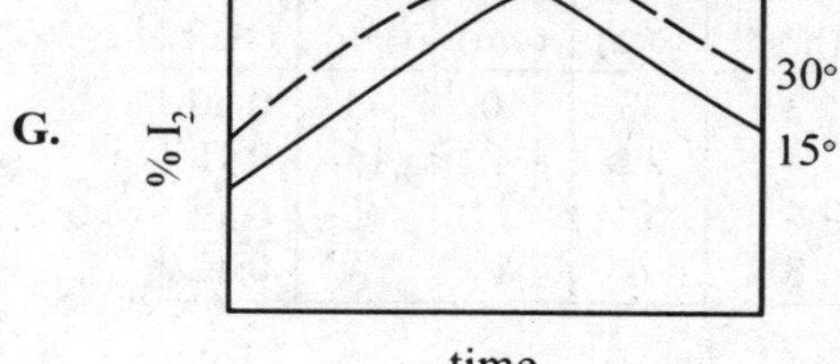

H.
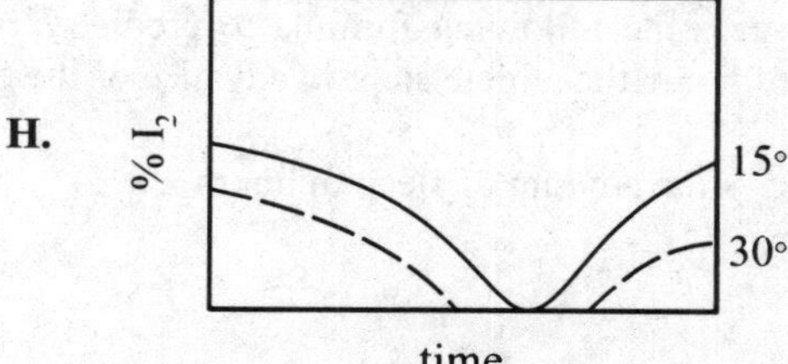

J.
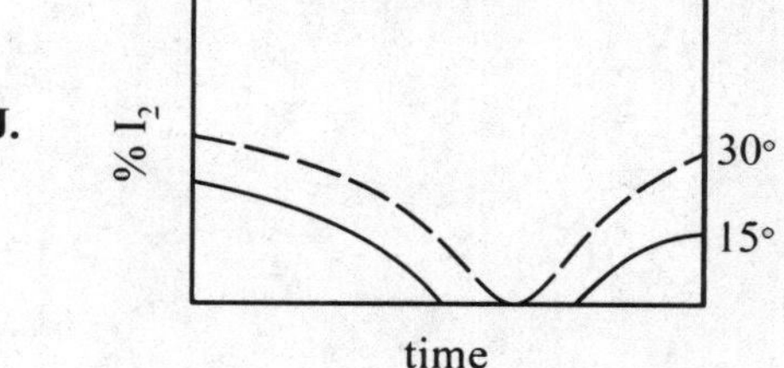

Passage VI

Students used 2 systems of measurement for calculating T, an athlete's reaction time using the *ruler test*. The test measures the lapse of time between stimulus (when the ruler is released by the evaluator) and response (when the ruler is caught by the athlete).

In System 1, M is the average distance the ruler drops before the athlete initiates a physical response, P is the average distance the ruler falls from the athlete's first physical response to the time when the ruler is caught, and D is the average total distance the ruler falls. Students compared T values for athletes at different levels of restfulness (hours of sleep in advance of the trial). The results are shown in Table 1.

Table 1

Sleep (hrs)	M (cm)	P (cm)	D (cm)	T (sec)
2	33	10	43	0.30
4	11	4	15	0.18
6	7	2	9	0.14
8	6	1	7	0.12

System 2 uses the following formula to predict T based on the number of hours the athlete slept in advance of the trial:

$T = -0.015 \times$ the amount of sleep in hours $+ 0.24$

Table 2 lists predicted T values for various amounts of sleep using System 2.

Table 2

Sleep (hrs)	T (sec)
2	0.21
4	0.18
6	0.15
8	0.12

Figure 1 compares T values measured using System 1 to those predicted by System 2.

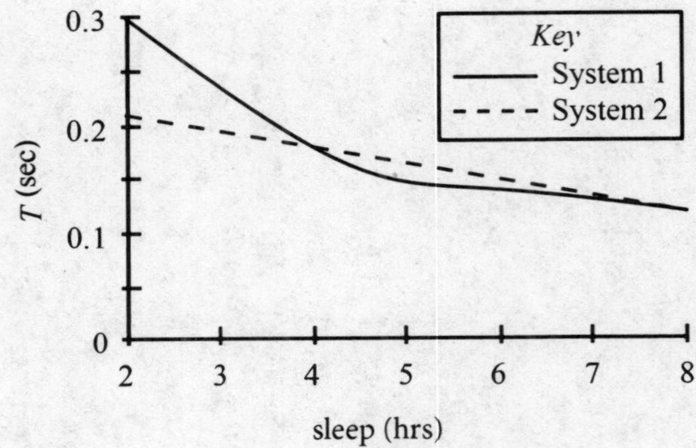

Figure 1

29. Compared to *P* at a sleep amount of 6 hours, *P* at a sleep amount of 2 hours is:

A. 5 times as great.

B. 2 times as great.

C. $\frac{1}{2}$ as great.

D. $\frac{1}{5}$ as great.

30. In System 1, *D* equals:

F. $M + P$
G. $M \div P$
H. $M \times P$
J. $M - P$

31. According to Figure 1, the 2 systems yield the same value for *T* when the amount of sleep is closest to:

A. 3 hours.
B. 4 hours.
C. 5 hours.
D. 6 hours.

32. Suppose an athlete has only slept for 6 hours before being given the ruler test. System 2 would predict the athlete's reaction time, *T*, to be:

F. 0.12 sec.
G. 0.15 sec.
H. 0.18 sec.
J. 0.21 sec.

33. Based on Table 1 or Figure 1, if an athlete has slept for 1 hour, *T*, according to System 2, will be:

A. less than .12 seconds.
B. between .15 and .18 seconds.
C. between .18 and .21 seconds.
D. greater than .21 seconds.

Passage VII

At the turn of the 20th century, scientists were developing the tools and techniques necessary to better understand the most basic unit of matter, the atom.

Three scientists of the day proposed models to explain the structure of an atom and the phenomenon of radiation.

Scientist 1

Atoms contain negatively charged subatomic particles, or electrons, that are one thousand times smaller than the atom itself. These negatively charged particles are not stationary, and they regularly shift within a positively charged sphere. The total positive charge of the sphere is equal to the combined negative charge of the electrons, resulting in an atom that is neutral. As an electron moves closer to the positive shell, it experiences a stronger repulsive force. When an electron absorbs additional energy, it overcomes the repulsive force and collides with the shell. This collision causes the electron to emit radiation and return to its original, unexcited state.

Scientist 2

Atoms are made up of three subatomic particles: protons, which are positively charged; electrons, which are negatively charged; and neutrons, which are not charged. Every atom of a particular element has the same number of protons and electrons. A nucleus is found at the center of each atom and is made up of protons and neutrons. Electrons float freely in a cloud around the nucleus. When two electrons absorb additional energy and collide, they emit radiation and return to their previous, unexcited state.

Scientist 3

Atoms consist of electrons that orbit a nucleus in fixed orbits, just as planets orbit the sun. The net charge of the atom is neutral because the number of protons in the nucleus equals the number of electrons outside of the nucleus. Electrons are not free to travel throughout the atom. Instead, an electron can only exist in a particular energy level, where it contains a set amount of energy. When an electron absorbs additional energy, it "jumps" to a higher energy orbit that is further from the nucleus of the atom. When an energized electron emits energy, it will emit radiation and fall back into its original orbit.

34. Based on the passage, would Scientist 2 or Scientist 3 be more likely to argue that the energetic level of an electron is due to its distance from the center of an atom?

F. Scientist 2, because according to Scientist 2 energetic electrons are able to freely float away from the center of the atom.
G. Scientist 2, because according to Scientist 2 energetic electrons are able to jump to orbits further away from the nucleus.
H. Scientist 3, because according to Scientist 3 energetic electrons are able to freely float away from the center of the atom.
J. Scientist 3, because according to Scientist 3 energetic electrons are able to jump to orbits further away from the nucleus.

35. Which of the following concepts would all 3 scientists agree on?

A. The behavior of an excited electron
B. The number of subatomic particles in an atom
C. The orbital paths of electrons
D. The negative charge of electrons

36. Suppose it was discovered that radiation is occasionally emitted from halfway between the center and the outer edge of the atom. Which scientists' model can account for this discovery?

F. Scientist 1 only
G. Scientist 2 only
H. Scientists 1 and 2 only
J. Scientists 2 and 3 only

37. How does Scientist 2's model differ from Scientist 3's model? Scientist 2 claims that electrons are located:

A. at discrete distances away from the nucleus.
B. in a cluster isolated from the nucleus.
C. in specific orbits around the nucleus.
D. anywhere in the volume around the nucleus.

38. Scientist 1's model would be most weakened by which of the following?

F. Observation of multiple electrons at varying distances from the nucleus
G. Discovery of the proton
H. Evidence of the net neutral charge of the atom
J. Discovery of a positively charged atomic shell

39. Scientist 2's model would be most supported by which of the following observations?

A. A single electron jumping from one energy level to another
B. Electrons following a fixed orbit
C. Emission of radiation from the nucleus of an atom
D. Collision of electrons within the atomic radius

40. The models of which of the scientists describe atoms as having a positively charged center?

F. Scientists 1 and 2 only
G. Scientists 1 and 3 only
H. Scientists 2 and 3 only
J. Scientists 1, 2, and 3

END OF PRACTICE TEST 2

Practice Test 2 Answer Key

Section 1 – English Answers

1. A	11. D	21. C	31. C	41. D	51. D	61. D	71. D
2. J	12. J	22. G	32. H	42. H	52. G	62. H	72. H
3. B	13. B	23. D	33. C	43. D	53. D	63. D	73. D
4. H	14. J	24. F	34. J	44. J	54. F	64. J	74. J
5. B	15. D	25. D	35. D	45. D	55. B	65. A	75. B
6. F	16. G	26. G	36. J	46. H	56. J	66. F	
7. B	17. B	27. D	37. B	47. A	57. D	67. A	
8. J	18. J	28. J	38. G	48. J	58. H	68. H	
9. A	19. B	29. D	39. A	49. B	59. D	69. B	
10. G	20. J	30. J	40. J	50. H	60. G	70. J	

Section 2 – Math Answers

1. C	11. B	21. C	31. B	41. A	51. C
2. J	12. G	22. J	32. G	42. K	52. H
3. A	13. D	23. D	33. C	43. D	53. C
4. G	14. F	24. H	34. J	44. J	54. H
5. D	15. D	25. E	35. D	45. A	55. D
6. G	16. G	26. K	36. H	46. H	56. K
7. C	17. C	27. B	37. A	47. A	57. B
8. G	18. J	28. H	38. H	48. J	58. G
9. D	19. D	29. D	39. D	49. E	59. B
10. G	20. G	30. H	40. G	50. F	60. J

Section 3 – Reading Answers

1. D	11. B	21. C	31. B
2. J	12. F	22. J	32. G
3. C	13. C	23. B	33. A
4. G	14. F	24. F	34. F
5. B	15. D	25. D	35. C
6. H	16. F	26. G	36. G
7. A	17. A	27. C	37. D
8. J	18. J	28. F	38. G
9. B	19. C	29. D	39. C
10. G	20. G	30. F	40. J

Section 4 – Science Answers

1. C	11. B	21. B	31. B
2. G	12. F	22. J	32. G
3. A	13. B	23. B	33. D
4. F	14. J	24. G	34. J
5. A	15. D	25. B	35. D
6. H	16. J	26. J	36. J
7. C	17. B	27. D	37. D
8. J	18. H	28. G	38. G
9. B	19. A	29. A	39. D
10. J	20. J	30. F	40. H

Scoring the Test

Raw Score

To obtain your raw score for each section, subtract the number of **missed** or **omitted** questions from the **total number of questions** in that section.

Section		Total		# of missed questions		raw score
English	=	75	–	______	=	______
Math	=	60	–	______	=	______
Reading	=	40	–	______	=	______
Science	=	40	–	______	=	______

Scaled Score Estimate

To obtain your scaled score estimate for each section, use the tables on the next page. For each section, locate your raw score in the corresponding table. Next to your raw score, you will find the range of scores you would likely receive on the actual ACT.

IMPORTANT: to receive a highly accurate prediction of your performance on test day, you must take an **official, calibrated ACT test.** We recommend test 4 or 5 in *The Real ACT Prep Guide*, by ACT Inc.

Scaled Score Estimates

English

Scale Score	Raw Score
32 — 36	75
31 — 35	74
30 — 34	72 – 73
29 — 33	71
28 — 32	70
27 — 31	69
25 — 29	67 – 68
24 — 28	66
23 — 27	65
22 — 26	63 – 64
21 — 25	61 – 62
20 — 24	58 – 60
19 — 23	55 – 57
18 — 22	53 – 54
17 — 21	50 – 52
16 — 20	47 – 49
15 — 19	44 – 46
14 — 18	42 – 43
13 — 17	40 – 41
12 — 16	38 – 39
11 — 15	34 – 37
10 — 14	32 – 33
9 — 13	30 – 31
8 — 12	28 – 29
7 — 11	26 – 27
6 — 10	23 – 25
5 — 9	21 – 22

Math

Scale Score	Raw Score
32 — 36	59 – 60
31 — 35	58
30 — 34	56 – 57
29 — 33	55
28 — 32	54
27 — 31	53
26 — 30	51 – 52
25 — 29	50
24 — 28	48 – 49
23 — 27	45 – 47
22 — 26	42 – 44
21 — 25	39 – 41
20 — 24	36 – 38
19 — 23	34 – 35
18 — 22	32 – 33
17 — 21	30 – 31
16 — 20	29
15 — 19	27 – 28
14 — 18	24 – 26
13 — 17	20 – 23
12 — 16	16 – 19
11 — 15	12 – 15
10 — 14	9 – 11
9 — 13	7 – 8
8 — 12	6
7 — 11	5
6 — 10	4

Reading

Scale Score	Raw Score
31 — 36	40
30 — 35	39
29 — 34	38
28 — 33	37
27 — 32	36
26 — 31	35
25 — 30	34
24 — 29	33
23 — 28	32
22 — 27	31
21 — 26	30
20 — 25	29
19 — 24	28
18 — 23	27
17 — 22	25 – 26
16 — 21	24
15 — 20	23
14 — 19	21 – 22
13 — 18	20
12 — 17	18 – 19
11 — 16	17
10 — 15	15 – 16
9 — 14	14
8 — 13	12 – 13
7 — 12	10 – 11
6 — 11	8 – 9
5 — 10	6 – 7

Science

Scale Score	Raw Score
31 — 36	40
30 — 35	39
28 — 33	38
26 — 31	37
24 — 29	36
23 — 28	35
22 — 27	33 – 34
21 — 26	32
20 — 25	30 – 31
19 — 24	29
18 — 23	27 – 28
17 — 22	26
16 — 21	24 – 25
15 — 20	22 – 23
14 — 19	21
13 — 18	18 – 20
12 — 17	17
11 — 16	15 – 16
10 — 15	14
9 — 14	12 – 13
8 — 13	11
7 — 12	10
6 — 11	8 – 9
5 — 10	7 – 8

English Score Range ______ *Math Score Range* ______ *Reading Score Range* ______ *Science Score Range* ______

Acknowledgements

Passage, page 99: Young, Emma. "10 Mysteries of you: Superstition." New Scientist 05 Aug. 2009. 09 Sept. 2009 < http://www.newscientist.com/article/mg20327201.400-10-mysteries-of-you-superstition.html> Printed with permission of newscientist.com.

Passage, page 109: Callaway, Ewen. "Orangutans fashion only known animal instrument." New Scientist 05 Aug. 2009. 09 Sept. 2009 < http://www.newscientist.com/article/dn17557-orangutans-fashion-only-known-animal-instrument.html> Printed with permission of newscientist.com.

Passage, page 142: Twain, Mark. *A Dog's Tale.* New York: Harper & Brothers, 1904. 1-6.

Passage, page 155: Bell, Clive. *Art*. London: Chatto and Windus. 1914.

Passage, page 155-156: Reynolds, Sir Joshua. "Discourse I." *Seven Discourse on Art*. 1769.

About the Author

Jed Applerouth, PhD, is a wordsmith, an artist, an educator, a Nationally Certified Counselor, a djembe drummer, a standardized testing enthusiast, and the founder of Applerouth Education.

Jed grew up in Atlanta, Georgia, where he graduated Valedictorian of Pace Academy's 1994 class. In 1998 he graduated with honors from the University of Pennsylvania's Huntsman Program for International Studies and Business. In 2007 Jed received an M.S. in Professional Counseling from Georgia State University. The eternal student, Jed went on to earn his PhD in educational psychology at Georgia State University. With his research, he continues to gain insights into memory and cognition, motivation, test-anxiety, and more.

For 14 years, Jed has helped thousands of students make sense of the college admissions tests. He has found a way to merge his counseling insights, visual talents, whimsical sense of humor, and educational background into one highly effective and original method for teaching the tests. Applerouth Tutoring Services (a branch of Applerouth Education) serves markets in Atlanta, New York, Washington, DC, Seattle, and other cities across the country. Through its cutting-edge online tutoring platform, ATS works with students across the country and around the world.

Notes

Notes

Notes

Notes

Notes

Notes

Notes

Notes